W9-AWT-578

Note to the Student

Dear Student,

If you winced when you learned the price of this textbook, you are experiencing what is known as "sticker shock" in today's economy. Yes, textbooks are expensive, and we don't like it any more than you do. Many of us here at PWS-KENT have sons and daughters of our own attending college, or we are attending school part-time ourselves. However, the prices of our books are dictated by cost factors involved in producing them. The costs of typesetting, paper, printing, and binding have risen significantly each year along with everything else in our economy.

The prices of college textbooks have increased less than most other items over the past fifteen years. Compare your texts sometime to a general trade book, i.e., a novel or nonfiction book, and you will easily see substantial differences in the quality of design, paper, and binding. These quality features of college textbooks cost money.

Textbooks should not be considered only as an expense. Other than your professors, your textbooks are your most important source for what you learn in college. What's more, the textbooks you keep can be valuable resources in your future career and life. They are the foundation of your professional library. Like your education, your textbooks are one of your most important investments.

We are concerned, and we care. We pledge to do everything in our power to keep our textbook prices under control, while maintaining the same high standards of quality you and your professors require.

Wayne A. Barcomb

Wayne A. Barcomb
President
PWS-KENT Publishing Company

KENT SERIES IN BUSINESS LAW

Cihon/Castagnera   *Labor and Employment Law*

Davidson/Jespersen   *The American Legal System*

Davidson/Knowles/Forsythe/Jespersen   *Business Law: Principles and Cases,* Third Edition

Davidson/Knowles/Forsythe/Jespersen   *Comprehensive Business Law: Principles and Cases*

Jennings   *Business and the Legal Environment*

Jennings   *Real Estate Law*, Second Edition

Litka   *International Dimensions of Legal Environment of Business*

Shaw/Wolfe   *The Structure of the Legal Environment: Law, Ethics, and Business*

Thompson/Brady   *Essential CPA Law Review*, Seventh Edition

REAL ESTATE LAW

Second Edition

MARIANNE M. JENNINGS
Arizona State University

PWS-KENT PUBLISHING COMPANY
Boston

For Terry, Sarah, and Claire

PWS–KENT
Publishing Company

Sponsoring Editor: **Rolf Janke**
Production Editor: **Wanda K. Wilking**
Interior Design: **Trisha Hanlon/Wanda K. Wilking**
Cover Design: **Jean Hammond**
Manufacturing Coordinator: **Margaret Sullivan Higgins**
Composition: **Modern Graphics**
Cover Printer: **John P. Pow Company, Inc.**
Text Printer and Binder: **Halliday Lithograph**

PWS-KENT Publishing Company is a division of Wadsworth, Inc.

Printed in the United States of America
1 2 3 4 5 6 7 8 9—93 92 91 90 89

Library of Congress Cataloging-in-Publication Data

Jennings, Marianne.
    Real estate law / Marianne M. Jennings.—2nd ed.
        p.   cm.
    Includes index.
    ISBN 0-534-91639-2
    1. Vendors and purchasers—United States.   2. Real estate business—Law and legislation—United States.   3. Real estate development—Law and legislation—United States.   4. Real property—United States.   I. Title.
KF665.J4   1989
346.7304'3—dc19
[347.30643]   88-21932
                                                                      CIP

PREFACE

STATEMENT OF PURPOSE

Real estate law was once regarded by attorneys and scholars as a lay term for the law of real property. However, with the phenomenal growth of the real estate market in the past twenty years, the term real estate law more accurately reflects and is used more often to describe the legal issues in the ownership, transfers, and development of land or real property. Those involved in the real estate market require a better grasp of the legal issues involved in their day-to-day transactions. Legal issues no longer revolve around how the law of real property developed in England but how real estate law can help to streamline transactions. Real estate professionals need a clear set of rules that will enable them to recognize, solve, and prevent legal problems. These rules and the ability to analyze should be taught in a three-step approach as follows:

1. What law is applicable to this area of real estate and this particular transaction?
2. What issues exist in the circumstances?
3. Can a legal problem be prevented or solved?

In spite of this strong need for clear and quick reviews of legal issues and solutions, the need has not been met by existing books on real estate law. This dynamic field is still treated by many books as a history course, in which the students are required to memorize the structure of feudal land systems in fifteenth-century England. Such learning is of no use to a broker faced with a due-on-sale problem.

Further, many of the new developments in real estate financing and marketing remain untreated by many books. For example, significant issues of taxation in land ownership and transfer are lightly treated or ignored. The complications of real estate development through limited partnerships or syndications are overlooked, even though these entities are today one of the most common sources of funds for development.

In addition to the omission of many topics, most real estate law books have chosen a straight, black-letter law approach. In the text, the rules and terms are given but there are no cases or examples to help students with application.

With these problems and needs in mind, this book was developed. The problems and cases have been used by my students for nine years with remarkable results—the students really understand and learn the material, and they are able to use their knowledge and problem-solving skills in personal and professional real estate transactions. If there were ever a remark that I dreaded to hear from a student it was, "I'll never use this!" Since using this book, the remark has slipped from my students' minds.

Real estate law has too long been labeled a boring subject that was acknowledged as existing but not worth the effort of authors and publishers in the development of a helpful book. This book will put to rest any such labels— real estate law is anything but boring. There are cases on mules attacking neighbors, rats in beach homes on Waikiki, and neighbors shutting off each other's sewer lines. There are problems with high-rise hotels casting shadows in neighboring hotels' swimming areas and eccentric people with eccentric wills. This book shows the life and color of real estate law in day-to-day settings.

This book cannot make real estate lawyers of readers, but it can help them recognize problems related to real estate law. When the reading of this book is complete, the law will stick in the minds of readers because of the mules, the hotels, and the fighting neighbors.

THE REVISED EDITION

As the saying goes, "If it ain't broke, don't fix it." The first edition of *Real Estate Law* was well received by students and instructors. Indeed, many brokers, agents, developers, and lawyers have found *Real Estate Law* to be a useful handbook. *Real Estate Law* has proved to be a successful textbook as well as a practical guide for those who work in the industry.

Nevertheless, the complexion of the real estate industry has changed since the first edition. Therefore, the primary focus of the second edition has been updating the materials in light of the changes in the tax laws, the financial markets, the social environment and the judicial imposition of liability on brokers, agents, and developers. Critical social issues such as all-adult covenants, group homes, and the unavailability of low-cost housing have created new legal issues. The environmental concerns about toxic waste and acid rain have also raised new legal questions and resulted in additional environmental regulation.

The real estate industry has continued its rapid pace of activity and a new body of case law has developed over the past few years. These new cases have been added or substituted in the second edition in order to provide cutting-edge information for the classroom as well as for practical use.

While pedagogically *Real Estate Law*, Second Edition is changed very little, changes made to keep pace with its field have been dramatic. But the color, charm, and interest levels of the first edition have only been increased with the second edition. The real life is still present in *Real Estate Law*.

ORGANIZATION

This book is divided into four parts. The divisions are structured so that the materials build on the prior parts. Part I consists of the basics of real estate law; part II deals with transferring real estate; part III addresses ownership issues, and part IV conquers the complicated aspects of commercial real estate. The coverage by readers can be as extensive or limited as each reader chooses. More depth can be given a subject by covering all related Chapter Problems and Consider questions, and chapters can be expedited simply by highlighting the materials.

Topics that some readers may wish to pass over are separated by chapter so that this is possible. For example, Future Interests in Real Estate (Chapter 3) or Describing Interests in Real Estate (Chapter 8) could be eliminated according to reader preference.

PEDAGOGICAL DEVICES

Cases

Very few real estate law books have the benefit of reported cases. This book includes reported cases to illustrate major points of law. I have rewritten the case facts to help simplify the sometimes complex real estate issues. After the judge's name appears, the remainder of the case is actual case language. I have also edited the language to zero in on the particular point of law. Included in the cases are United States Supreme Court decisions on such controversial topics as redlining, due-on-sale clauses and eminent domain. A case index is provided so that the better-known cases can be easily found by the curious reader. The second edition contains new cases to provide the most recent legal theories and offer insight into social issues affecting the real estate market.

Case Discussion Questions

In spite of fact summaries and careful editing, readers still find it difficult to wade through judicial language and reasoning. Because of the problems with case study that I have experienced, discussion questions follow each of the cases in this book. These questions help readers sort out the facts and reach their conclusions about the court's decision. They can guide a reader through a case. Answers for the case discussion questions are in the teacher's manual.

Consider Questions

Throughout each chapter, numbered Consider questions can be found. These questions appear immediately following the material tested in the problems and were written to help readers grasp the segments of the chapter as they read along. The Consider questions refine reading habits as well as understanding. Answers for these questions are provided in the teacher's manual. The Consider questions have also been updated in the second edition.

Chapter Problems

At the end of each chapter are problems. Most of the problems are actual cases with the case cites and decisions provided in the teacher's manual. The cases are short enough to spark interest and yet detailed enough to allow discussion and testing of chapter concepts and have been revised to include more recent developments.

Charts, Diagrams, and Illustrations

Throughout the book are charts, diagrams, and illustrations to aid readers' understandings of lengthy and complex topics. For example, there are charts depicting the relationships of land interests, sample leases, and easement diagrams.

Glossary

In the back of the text is a glossary of key terms used in the text. The glossary gives a short definition of all key terms.

SUPPLEMENTAL ITEMS

Teacher's Manual

The teacher's manual was designed to help in lecture preparation. Each chapter is outlined in detail with examples and illustrations of each of the chapter points. The cases are briefed within the outline as they appear in the text. All of the Case Discussion questions, Consider questions and Chapter Problems are answered within the manual. When the problems were taken from reported cases, the case citation is given. For the second edition, the manual has been updated to include coverage of the new Cases, Consider problems, Case Discussion questions and the new Chapter Problems.

Each chapter has a list of books and law review articles called Resource Materials. These materials can be used to enhance the instructor's understanding of a topic or as assignments for students to encourage more in-depth coverage of a topic. These Resource Materials were increased substantially for the second edition.

Also included in the manual are sample examination questions. There are true/false, multiple choice, and essay questions in each of the chapters. The true/false questions are easier and can be used for a quick quiz. The multiple choice and essay questions test the ability of students to apply real estate law principles. The second edition offers additional questions to provide a larger menu for the instructor. Those cases that have been eliminated from the first edition to make way for new ones have been added to the teacher's manual to provide supplemental readings for the instructor or for class use.

DEBTS OF GRATITUDE

Although only my name appears on this book, I cannot claim it as *my* book. As with all achievements in my life, my finished work is the result of the cooperation, work, and sacrifice of many. I cannot name everyone who has helped but there are those who labored long hours to bring this book to its present state:

- Dick Crews, my original editor, who had the educational foresight to see the need for this book and who has been proven correct through the success of the first edition.
- Rolf Janke, who inherited me and my projects and provided input and support for the second edition.
- Wanda Wilking, the ever-patient production editor, whose attention to detail helped ensure the quality of the second edition.
- The students of *Real Estate Law*, who provided feedback on the first edition. They have my gratitude for their responsiveness and encouragement.
- The instructors who used *Real Estate Law* and have provided feedback on how to improve the book. Their feedback is a labor of love and evidence of their dedication to seeing higher education at its best.
- All of the realtors, insurers, publishers, lenders, contractors, and real estate professionals who consented to have their forms and works reproduced in this text. Their names cannot be listed here, but their works are acknowledged throughout the book. Their dedication to education is evidenced by their complete cooperation in granting permission for these items to be used.

My thanks to the following reviewers who labored long and hard over the thousand-page manuscript in its typed form to give comments, suggestions, and encouragement: George J. Burak, University of Massachusetts, Amherst; H.M. Bohlman, Arizona State University; Donald W. Cantwell, University of

Texas; Richard C. Coffinberger, George Mason University; Gerard Halpern, University of Arkansas, Fayetteville; Charles J. Hartmann, Wright State University; Kennith King, East Texas State University; Paul M. Lange, California State University, Fresno; Arthur Marinelli, Ohio University; and Dwight D. Murphey, Wichita State University.

Last, but certainly not least, I am grateful to both my immediate and extended family for their support of me, my work and this project. My husband (Terry) and two small daughters (Sarah and Claire) not only provided great mental support but also sacrificed some of their "quality" time to go to the law library and even help with page proofs. While only my name appears as the author, it is truly a team project.

A WORD FOR STUDENTS

In using the book, read the narrative material which describes the law first. Follow that by reading the cases that appear after each section. Be sure to answer the discussion questions after each case to make sure you understood the case and that you grasped the issues and principles of law. Try to solve the Consider questions and Chapter Problems on your own before answers are given by your instructor. If you can solve all of the Consider questions and Chapter Problems, you understand the chapter materials. The figures in chart form are designed to streamline ideas and summarize lengthy topics so that you can commit the concepts to memory. The charts are an excellent form of review for examinations or quizzes.

Finally, be sure to apply what you have learned when your course is over. Application is the true test of learning. Good luck with the book and its application. Enjoy the color and the flavor of real estate law—it is abundant in this book.

MMJ

CONTENTS

|11|

The Purchase Contract   272

Contents

xviii

PART III
Real Estate Ownership—Methods, Problems, and Responsibilities

|15|

|21|

Multiunit Housing   595

|24|
Real Estate Syndication 668

|25|
Subdividing Real Estate for Residential Development 690

Contents

I

THE NATURE OF REAL ESTATE
AND REAL ESTATE INTERESTS

1

INTRODUCTION AND SOURCES OF REAL ESTATE LAW

Possession is nine points of the law.

—Source unknown

The above quote is but one example of a principle of law relating to ownership of property. As indicated, the source of this principle is unknown. However, there are a significant number of sources of real estate law, and this chapter answers the question, Where can real estate law be found? One distinguishing factor of real estate law is that problems are not solved by turning to a single statute or ordinance. A question on a zoning issue cannot be answered by examining only city ordinances, and a question on adverse possession is not always answered by turning to a statute.

Real estate law is not one simple body of law as its name implies. Rather, it is made up of many different types of laws that have been passed by many different bodies at varying levels of government. No single governmental body possesses laws that are complete or exclusive sources of real estate law. To engage in real estate transactions, the parties should at least be familiar with the laws affecting the transactions and the sources from which those laws come. A familiarity with who and what is involved in the making of real estate law is a help to those engaged in the real estate business and to those simply involved in some type of real estate transaction. Knowing which sources to check to determine applicable legal boundaries for a real estate transaction enables parties to the transaction to complete their business in a manner that will avoid major problems, dissatisfaction, and perhaps even litigation.

SOURCES OF REAL ESTATE LAW

If all the sources of real estate law were diagramed in a scheme depicting their relationships in terms of priority, such a scheme would probably take the pyramidal form depicted in Figure 1.1.

The discussion of these sources of law will begin at the bottom of the pyramid with the United States Constitution. This is because all other sources of real estate law must act consistently with the rights set forth in this foundation of the pyramid. Court decisions will be the final topic of discussion, and their

Figure 1.1 *Sources of Real Estate Law*

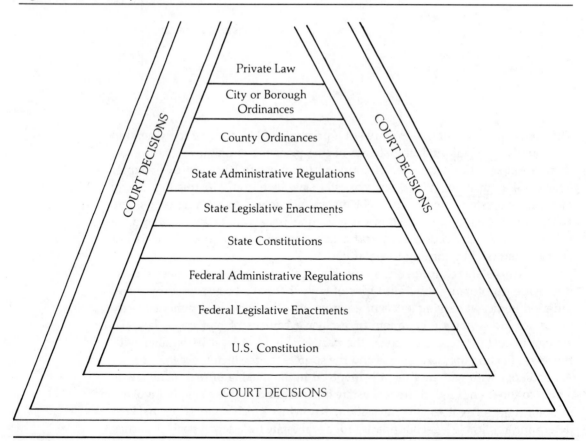

position in the pyramid as well as in the discussion is explained by the fact that court decisions can deal with laws of any of the listed pyramid sources.

The United States Constitution

The *United States Constitution* has several provisions that apply to transfers and ownership of real estate. The Fourth Amendment affords property owners the right to be secure in their "houses," and from this language has sprung a long series of cases providing rights that pertain to searches and seizures and the issuance of search warrants for real property.

The provisions of the Constitution most relevant to real estate law are two similar clauses found in the Fifth and Fourteenth Amendments. The *Fifth Amendment* prohibits the federal government from depriving any person of "property without due process of law" and also prohibits the federal government from taking private property for public use "without just compensation." The due-process-of-law provisions have resulted in many cases that contain legal discussions on obtaining judgments against a person's property and foreclosing on a security interest in real property. (See Chapters 6, 12, and 19.) The just-compensation provision offers protection for landowners when their property is to be taken by the government. This practice, referred to as *eminent domain*, has resulted in a long series of litigated cases (Chapter 19) involving questions such as, When is the government actually taking property? and, What constitutes just compensation? For example, one issue related to the taking of property by the government might be whether landowners are entitled to compensation when noisy air force jets use the air space above their property.

The *Fourteenth Amendment* has wording almost identical to the language of the Fifth Amendment, but it is applicable instead to state governments. The Fourteenth Amendment provides that no state may "deprive any person of . . . property, without due process of law." The amendment puts further restrictions on laws passed by the states in that a state law that denies or interferes with any rights given to citizens in the Constitution will be unconstitutional and invalid. Also, the Fourteenth Amendment requires the states to apply the law equally to all citizens so that all are afforded the same protections, entitled to the same forms of relief, and provided with equal opportunities for land ownership. Many of the racial discrimination cases on land purchases and sales have been based on this part of the Fourteenth Amendment, which is referred to as the *Equal Protection Clause*.

These constitutional provisions set the boundaries or establish the minimum rights that cannot be violated by the other governmental bodies in the pyramid involved in making the laws. Although these constitutional provisions seem very broad and general, such provisions protect fundamental rights that cannot be infringed by the remaining makers of real estate law.

Federal Legislative Enactments

The Constitution establishes a legislative branch of the federal government, which is authorized to enact laws to carry forth the objectives of the Constitution and the operation of the federal government. On the basis of authority given, Congress passes legislation to carry out its responsibilities, and regulation of real estate transactions is one of the responsibilities Congress may properly exercise. All enactments of Congress are printed in a series of volumes called the *United States Code (U.S.C.)*. Each of the major enactments of Congress relating to real estate transactions will be discussed in great detail in subsequent chapters, but the following examples serve to illustrate the types of laws passed by Congress and found in the United States Code:

- *The Interstate Land Sales Full Disclosure Act (ILSFDA)* deals with the sale of undeveloped land to out-of-state residents. 15 U.S.C. §1701 et seq. (discussed in Chapter 11).
- *The Real Estate Settlement Procedures Act (RESPA)* deals with maximum closing costs and good faith estimates of closing costs. 12 U.S.C. §2601 et seq. (discussed in Chapter 13).
- *The Internal Revenue Code (I.R.C.)* deals with the income tax and depreciation aspects of real estate transactions. 26 U.S.C. §1 et seq. (discussed in Chapter 17).

With each of the above-mentioned statutes, there is an abbreviation such as 26 U.S.C. §1 appearing after the name of the statute. This abbreviation is referred to as a *citation* or *cite* and represents the location of the statute in the series of volumes that make up the United States Code. The number preceding U.S.C. is the title or volume number of the United States Code where the statute may be found. The symbol § following U.S.C. means "section"; the following number is the section number, which represents the location of the statute within the particular volume. For example, 26 U.S.C. §305 would be a cite for a statute that could be found in the 26th volume of the United States Code where Section 305 appears. This particular section describes the proper methods for depreciating property for purposes of determining income. When a cite is furnished, the applicable law can be found by looking in the United States Code according to the citation system described.

Federal Administrative Regulations

For each federal legislative enactment passed by Congress, a new agency will be created to enforce the particular enactment or an existing agency will be assigned the task of enforcing it. For example, the Interstate Land Sales Full

Disclosure Act (ILSFDA) is enforced by a federal agency, the Department of Housing and Urban Development (HUD). The Department of Housing and Urban Development has been delegated the responsibility of carrying out the general provisions of the act and will be required to develop procedures for compliance with the law and enforcement of its provisions. Congress passes the general scope and purpose of the law, and it is the responsibility of the agency designated in the act to fill in the details by passing regulations on procedures, compliance, and enforcement.

For example, the ILSFDA was passed by Congress in a general form and was intended to protect those who purchased undeveloped property without first having the opportunity to visually inspect their purchases. The general provision established in the statute was for each buyer to be furnished with a full report disclosing critical information about the property, such as whether there is available water and whether the property is accessible by road.

Given the responsibility of enforcement under the act, HUD was then required to pass regulations establishing the details for disclosing the information Congress had required. The Department of Housing and Urban Development has since passed regulations that establish how such information is to be disclosed, what information must be on file, what form the disclosures are to take, and how disclosures are to be organized. The regulations of an administrative agency fill in the details on the skeletal purpose outline given in the congressional enactment.

Another example of a pertinent federal regulation is the *Truth-in-Lending Regulation* or *Regulation Z* (12 C.F.R. §226 et seq.), which comprises the details passed by the Federal Reserve Board (a federal agency) in carrying out a congressional enactment: the *Consumer Credit Protection Act* (15 U.S.C. §1601 et seq.). The Consumer Credit Protection Act has the general purpose of providing borrowers with full disclosure of the cost of borrowing. The Federal Reserve Board regulations provide the forms and specific items required to be disclosed. (Regulation Z is discussed in detail in Chapter 12.)

All federal regulations appear in a series of volumes referred to as the *Code of Federal Regulations (C.F.R.)*. When an abbreviation, citation, or cite such as 12 C.F.R. §226 appears in a book or a real estate document, it is possible to find the particular regulation referred to from the given cite. In the example, 12 is the volume number within the Code of Federal Regulations and 226 is the section number of the regulation within that particular volume.

The Code of Federal Regulations is a series of paperback volumes that is reprinted every year because of the many changes in administrative agency regulations. In addition, a daily update to the Code of Federal Regulations, called the Federal Register, is published each working day and includes changes and proposed changes in existing regulations.

State Constitutions

In manners similar to the United States Constitution, the state constitutions provide a framework within which state legislative bodies and agencies must act. However, most state constitutions tend to be more detailed than the basic structure and language of the United States Constitution, which emphasizes the preservation of rights. For example, California's state constitution has a provision covering usury or charging in excess of a certain maximum interest rate in a credit transaction (Cal. Const. Art. 15, §1). Two additional examples of provisions from state constitutions are as follows:

– *Nevada*—several sections governing the assessment and taxation of agriculture and open space property (Nev. Const. Art. 15, §1).
– *New York*—several sections creating preserves, recreational areas, reservoirs, and wildlife conservation policies (N.Y. Const. Art. XIV, §§1–3).

These examples illustrate the point that state constitutions tend to be more specific than the United States Constitution and constitute viable sources for relevant real estate law.

State Legislative Enactments

Just as at the federal level, the legislative bodies in each state enact various provisions governing property rights and transactions. In most states, there are statutes that set forth procedures for obtaining licenses for selling real estate, methods of financing real estate purchases, time periods for adverse possession, and provisions for creating a will or probating an estate. A great amount of the detail of real estate law is found within the state legislative enactments.

These state legislative enactments are found in varying volumes and sources. In Texas, the legislative enactments are found in Vernon's Texas Code Annotated (for example, V.T.C.A. Water Code §1.001). In Illinois, the state statutes are found in Smith-Hurd's Annotated Illinois Statutes (S.H.A. Ch. 96 TP4601).

State Administrative Regulations

Just as at the federal level, state legislative bodies also create administrative agencies to enforce their enacted legislation. These state agencies perform the same functions as the federal agencies in that they provide details, forms, and procedures necessary for compliance with state laws. For example, all states have laws regarding the licensing of real estate agents and brokers. In each state an agency is responsible for the collection of licensing fees, administration of any exams, enforcement of state laws, and passage of regulations related to the state statutes.

County, City, and Borough Ordinances

A great amount of real estate law can be found in the smallest and most local entity, such as a county, city, or borough. For example, most of the laws relating to zoning can be found in the laws passed by local entities and are referred to as *ordinances*. Other topics covered by ordinances on a local level include building permits, building inspections, fire codes, building height restrictions, noise regulations, and curfews. All of these topics affect the transfer and use of real estate. (A complete discussion of zoning is found in Chapter 16.)

Private Law

In addition to the law of governmental bodies, one additional type of law comes from individuals and landowners: *private law*. Private law consists of those rules and regulations created by landowners for their protection in the use of their land by others. For example, landlords are permitted to pass and post regulations pertaining to the use of common facilities such as pools, laundry areas, parking lots, and walkways. (A complete discussion of landlord–tenant relationships is found in Chapter 18.) In some instances private developers have placed deed restrictions and covenants on the use of property sold or transferred to others. For example, some residential developments permit only those above the age of eighteen years to live as residents in the area. (See Chapter 19 for a complete discussion.) Many private laws are required to keep townhouses and condominiums operating smoothly. (See Chapter 21.)

Private law also comprises the rights and obligations parties choose to impose on themselves through a contract for the purchase, sale, lease, or pledging of real estate. The parties who validly and voluntarily enter into contractual obligations are bound by the terms of the contract as a form of private law, and such obligations can be enforced through the courts just as public laws can be enforced.

All private law is still subject to the boundaries and rights established in the previously discussed constitutional and statutory sources. A private law related to real estate may not abridge constitutional rights and freedoms. (A complete discussion of constitutional restrictions on real estate law is found in Chapter 19.)

Court Decisions

The prior discussions of the various sources of law seem complete, and it would be difficult to imagine that much more detail could exist in real estate law. However, the constitutions, statutes, and ordinances are only general statements of the law, which leave many terms undefined and also result in questions of application and interpretation. To whom does the law apply? When does the law apply and how is it to be applied? Finding the answers to these questions requires interpretation of law from all levels, which is carried out by the various courts in the state and federal judicial systems. The role of the courts is to answer the questions of application and to clarify ambiguities in statutes, ordinances, and contracts.

Permanent records of the courts' decisions are found in opinions published in books that far exceed in numbers the volumes of statutes. These opinions must be consulted in discerning the complete meaning of a statute or ordinance. Further, an opinion can be used as a precedent when a later, factually similar set of circumstances again results in the need for the court's interpretive function.

In addition to their interpretive function, the courts also have the responsibility of making, applying, and analyzing the *common law*. Common law is law that is recognized as being law but is not in any code or statute. Common law originated in England and continues to exist within case law, changing and growing on a case-by-case basis. Because most American real property concepts can be traced to the English rules on real estate ownership and transfer, common law is a source to be checked regardless of whether a statute is involved.

Reliance on common law or prior court opinions in developing resolutions to factually similar problems is also called following *case precedent*. Precedent can be used as a guideline for contracts and transactions occurring after the judicial decision. Thus once a court has interpreted a particular statute or contract, other parties can use the court's interpretation to assist them in carrying out their transactions and intentions in those transactions.

The following case illustrates how a court plays the interpretive role when an ambiguity arises in a statute. In this case the court is dealing with the interpretation of a zoning statute. Zoning ordinances are laws that regulate how land can be used, the types of buildings that can be placed on the land, and how many buildings can be located on each parcel of land. (Zoning ordinances are discussed in detail in Chapter 16.) Because of variations in use and building structure and the human element involved in land use, there are many zoning ordinance interpretation cases. The following case deals with the application of a zoning ordinance in a particular situation. Notice the details that the court must review in interpreting the ordinance and how the court interprets the spirit of the law in answering the technical question the facts present.

HOPPER v. CLACKAMAS COUNTY
741 P.2d 921 (Oreg. 1987)

Grigory and Anna Anfilofieff reside in an existing dwelling on their property that is located in an exclusive farm use (EFU) zone. They applied for a zoning exception so that they could construct a dwelling for their son, Efrem, who would then serve as a full-time manager of the farm's berry operation. The zoning ordinance on EFU property provides the following:

A dwelling on real property is used for farm use if the dwelling is:

   a. located on the same lot or parcel as the dwelling of the farm operator, and

b. occupied by a relative, which means grandparent, grandchild, parent, child, brother, or sister of the farm operator or the farm operator's spouse, whose assistance in the management of the farm use is or will be required by the farm operator.

The application was approved by the county and also the Land Use Board of Appeals (LUBA). The Hoppers (neighbors/petitioners) appealed.

RICHARDSON, Presiding Judge

Petitioners make two assignments of error. The second is without merit and requires no discussion. The first is that LUBA erred by rejecting their contention:

The occupant of the accessory dwelling will replace, rather than assist, the farm operator in the management of the farm. This result violates CLACKAMAS County Code Section 401.04B(2) and ORS 215.213(1)(e)(B).

Petitioners summarize their argument under the assignment:

LUBA and Clackamas County applied the wrong test to the proposed dwelling and failed to apply tests to the existing dwelling and thereby may have authorized a nonfarm dwelling in violation of ORS 215.283(3).

Petitioners posit that Efrem will not simply assist his parents in operating the farm; he will replace them and "be the farmer." Consequently, petitioners reason, there is no justification to use agricultural land for a second dwelling, because the "son would become the farmer and the father's house would cease to be the farm operator's house."

There is both a factual and a legal aspect to petitioners' argument. We find their factual assertions to be most difficult to reconcile with the record. They represent that "both elder Anfilofieffs are employed full time in jobs off the farm" and that "the father retired from farming to work at another job." The record shows instead that, in addition to his farm work, Grigory is a self-employed tree-thinner and has been for a period of many years preceding the application. His forest work is seasonal, and he is active in farm work when he is at home. Anna has recently become employed in a cannery and is unable to manage the farm in Grigory's absence, as she did before she became so employed. However, she continues to participate in farm operations. At the time of the application, several of the Anfilofieffs' children, apparently including Efrem, were living with them and assisting at the farm. The county found that the parents' "other jobs keep them from active management of the farm" and that it is necessary that Efrem undertake "the day-to-day management." The finding does not say, nor would the record permit a finding, that Grigory no longer participates to a significant extent in farming activities. LUBA did not, and we do not, agree with petitioners' implication that both parents have given up farming, taken other work and essentially installed Efrem in Grigory's stead as the sole real participant in farm operations.

The central point of petitioners' legal argument is that the "county applied the wrong test to the son's house." The tests which the county did apply were those of ORS 215.283 (1)(e) and the ordinance provision relating to "relative dwellings." Petitioners contend that the county should not have applied those tests because, notwithstanding that the application *is* for an accessory dwelling for a relative who assists the farmer, the county should have treated it as an application for a primary farm dwelling because Efrem rather than Grigory is in reality to be the farmer. If the proposed dwelling passed the test, according to petitioners, the application could still not be granted unless the *existing* dwelling qualified as an *accessory* one under ORS 215.283(1)(e), which it could do only if Efrem, "as the new farm operator, required his father's assistance in order to manage the farm." If that standard could not be met, petitioners assert, the new dwelling could not be approved unless it or the existing one qualified as a nonfarm dwelling under the rigorous criteria of ORS 215.283(3).

Petitioners' elaborate approach seems to us to replace the one right question with three wrong ones. The question *is* whether the application for Efrem's dwelling should have been granted under ORS 215.283(1)(e) and the ordinance provision. It is unnecessary to treat the application as being for something other than it is to answer that question *and* to reach

the real point at which petitioners' argument is—or should be—directed. The point of their argument is that the proposed dwelling cannot qualify as an *accessory* dwelling, because Efrem, rather than his father, will be principally responsible for the farm and an accessory dwelling for a relative should not be permitted unless the present farmer rather than the relative is to remain the dominant participant in the farming activity.

LUBA rejected petitioners' point and explained:

The county states that the occupants of both existing and proposed dwellings will be involved with the farm operations; and therefore, the additional residence is not meant as a replacement for the dwelling.

The county concludes that the ordinance and the statute do not require that activities in furtherance of the farm use be broken down 50/50; nor do they require that the occupant of the original farm dwelling spend more time on farming than the occupant of the new dwelling.

The ordinance and ORS 215.283(1)(e), authorizing an accessory dwelling for a specified relative, appear to place the determination of when the accessory dwelling is 'required' on the farm operator. Here, there has been a change in the operator's farm management. Mrs. Anfilofieff is no longer able to provide the management services she provided while Mr. Anfilofieff was away from the farm. The owner is not relinquishing all farm duties, but the management has changed, and nothing in the ordinance [or statute require] a particular breakdown of farm duties between the owner and the relative occupying the accessory dwelling.

We agree generally with that reasoning. The critical criterion in ORS 215.283 (1)(e)(B) is whether the accessory dwelling is sought for a relative "whose assistance in the management of the farm use is or will be required by the farm operator." We do not construe that phrase to mean that the *amount* of the required assistance is the determinant of whether there may be a relative's dwelling, as long as the "farm operator" continues to have some significant involvement in the farm's operations. Nothing in the statutory language suggests that the permissibility of the accessory dwelling is inversely proportional to the level of assistance the relative provides. Indeed, if the level of assistance could be regarded as a determining factor consistently with the statutory language, its relevance would seem to us to cut in the opposite direction from the one petitioners suggest: the more assistance the farmer requires, the greater would be the justification for allowing farm land to be used to house the person whose assistance is required.

Petitioners contend, correctly, that there is an overriding statutory and regulatory policy to prevent agricultural land from being diverted to non-agricultural use. However, they do not persuade us that the policy requires that the statute be construed as precluding the construction of this proposed dwelling; the statute's clear import is that the construction of such dwellings, under circumstances of the precise kind present here, is related to and promotes the agricultural use of farm land. LUBA did not err in any of the respects the petitioners assert.

Affirmed.

Discussion Questions

1. What exception were the Anfilofieffs applying for?
2. What did the applicable ordinance provide?
3. What will Efrem's role be?
4. Why did the outside jobs of Efrem, Anna, and Grigory become issues?
5. What three questions did the Hoppers wish to substitute for what the court views as the one relevant question?
6. What interpretation of the statute did the Hoppers urge the court to adopt?
7. Why does the court state that even with that interpretation the result would be the same?
8. Will Efrem be permitted to have his dwelling on the property?

(1.1) Consider:

Albrecht's Flowers and Greenhouses, Inc. (Albrecht's) has operated a florist shop and nursery business on a tract of land since the early 1900s. Their use of the land predated the enactment of the Lower Merion Zoning Ordinance in 1927 and hence Albrecht's prior use of the land allowed them a legal nonconforming use. Albrecht's property is an irregularly shaped lot, of approximately 2 to 3 acres. The tract is divided among three zoning districts: C-1 commercial; R-4 (single family), and R-5 (townhouses). Just prior to 1985, a flower shop, boiler house, and six greenhouses were located on the property. In 1985, Albrecht's demolished two of its greenhouses to provide room for a fifteen-space employee parking lot.

Merion Park Civic Association filed an appeal to the Zoning Board on the grounds that the parking lot constituted a "change in use" and should be prohibited as not within the scope of Albrecht's nonconforming use.

Has Albrecht's lost its rights to a nonconforming use or is the use as a parking lot part of its business operations? *Merion Park Civ. v. Zon. Hearing Board* 530 A.2d 968 (Pa. 1987) Consider the following relevant ordinances in developing your answer:

> Section 155-99(E) of the Lower Merion Zoning Ordinance provides as follows:
>
>> *Discontinuance.* If a nonconforming use of land or of a building ceases or is discontinued for a continuous period of one (1) year or more, subsequent use of such building or land shall be in conformity with the provisions of this chapter (zoning).
>
> Section 155-4(B) does permit accessory uses of property:
>
>> *Accessory use.* A use subordinate to the principal use of land or of a building on a lot and customarily incidental thereto.

(1.2) Consider:

Louis Scott Holding Co. (Scott) purchased a lot in the city of Hackensack, New Jersey, and filed an application to erect a five-story building. The building would contain 16 one-bedroom condominiums with 703 square feet each. A city zoning ordinance required that each dwelling unit contain a minimum of 725 square feet. However, the method of computing square feet per unit was to take the size of the lot (11,250 square feet) and divide it by 725 square feet, which results in 15.51 units. Scott Holding rounded the figure to 16 and claimed it was in compliance. Several residents filed complaints about the proposed construction.

The Zoning Board can grant a variance for an increase in density, provided "such variance or other relief can be granted without substantial detriment to the public good and will not substantially impair the intent and purpose of the zone plan and zoning ordinance." Is Scott Holding within the spirit of the ordinance? Can an exception be justified? *Trinity Baptist Church of Hackensack v. Louis Scott Holding Co.* 530 A. 2d 828 (N.J. 1987)

On the basis of the *Hopper* case and the discussion problems, it is clear that ambiguities in legal terms and interpretive problems can lead to expensive litigation. The following section discusses other reasons for understanding real estate law.

JUSTIFICATIONS FOR STUDYING
REAL ESTATE LAW

Real estate is an industry in which small investments can yield high returns; property appreciation alone exemplifies this profitability. However, investment profits can be easily absorbed if legal difficulties arise with the property or the transaction providing the return. A piece of property that doubles in value in 2 years is not worth much if there is a defect in the title that prevents the owner from selling the property to realize that profit. A new home purchased at a bargain price is a comfort and achievement for a young couple until the announcement that a feed lot is to be constructed only 200 feet from their front door. The purchase of an apartment complex by an overextended corporation is a good tax write-off and cash producer until the discovery is made that the furniture, refrigerators, and stoves did not transfer with the property.

All of the errors made in these transactions involve legal issues that could have been avoided if the parties had a basic familiarity with some fundamental aspects of real estate law. The remainder of this book is devoted to providing parties with such familiarity. Although many would choose to rely on attorneys to handle transactions in real estate, the following article illustrates that even attorneys are often unfamiliar with the pitfalls of a particular transaction:

Rating Lawyers

Hal Lancaster

When the Supreme Court gave attorneys the right to advertise, the fledgling legal-clinic industry promised a revolution in the legal profession.

When advertising to build high volume for their streamlined operations, the clinics reasoned, they could dispense cut-rate legal services to a middle class that was already being priced out of the market.

When the legal job can't be done by the numbers, legal clinics, which tend to rely on young, inexperienced attorneys, are often the wrong place to go for advice. And for tough jobs they frequently cost as much as their traditional competition. There are some bargains available, however.

That's a personal conclusion born of personal observations during a survey conducted by this newspaper of Southern California legal clinics and traditional law firms.

At each of the eight firms I posed as a man who was selling his home and needed a review of his sales contract. Although I volunteered no information about my marital status, I was prepared to say, if asked, that I was selling my house because of an impending divorce. The contract I showed each firm contained a number of defects. For example, it called for the buyer to assume my mortgage, held by a federal thrift institution. But in California, federally chartered savings and loan associations aren't allowing most assumptions. A common practice that is legal but ethically dubious is for the buyer to make payments to the seller, who continues to pay the thrift without notifying it of the sale. That's the kind of information a layman might expect a lawyer to provide. And a layman might also expect that an attorney would know how to structure the tricky installment sale I was seeking, or, if not, to send me to an accountant.

Six of the eight firms I visited were advertised as, or appeared to be, legal clinics. The others, for comparison, were traditional firms— O'Melveny & Myers, perhaps Los Angeles's most powerful and prestigious firm and Spierer & Woodward, a smaller, neighborhood firm.

With the firms' identities concealed, their efforts were judged by a panel of specialists in real-estate law. The panelists reviewed the contract before any clinics were visited. They agreed that it was a fair test in the context of the limited time the clinics' operating methods would provide.

In an admittedly unscientific survey that in most cases amounted to only an initial consultation, even the panel couldn't agree on everything, but some interesting conclusions emerged:

— A storefront operation that does most of its work by phone, the Law Store, was rated ahead of O'Melveny & Myers by one panelist.
— Visits to two offices of Jacoby & Meyers, the largest of the clinics, yielded markedly different results in both quality and potential cost.
— None of the attorneys caught everything they should have, the panel felt, including the one from O'Melveny & Myers, who had the luxury of an extra office visit, several days for review and a tax department to consult.
— Two of the eight, including one Jacoby & Meyers man, did dangerously bad jobs, the panel said.
— Four of the seven attorneys I met got low marks on one or both of the major points, loan assumption and installment sale.
— Overall, the firms exceeded Mr. Rasch's expectations somewhat, matched Professor Elickson's, but didn't come up to Mr. Seaman's. All three felt a lot of lawyers missed a lot of issues.

KEY TERMS

United States Constitution
Fifth Amendment

eminent domain
Fourteenth Amendment

Equal Protection Clause
United States Code (U.S.C.)
Interstate Land Sales Full Disclosure
    Act (ILSFDA)
Real Estate Settlement Procedures
    Act (RESPA)
Internal Revenue Code (I.R.C.)
citation
cite

Truth-in-Lending Regulation
Regulation Z
Consumer Credit Protection Act
Code of Federal Regulations
    (C.F.R.)
ordinances
private law
common law
case precedent

CHAPTER PROBLEMS

1. A farmer is having the southwest corner acre of his 40-acre parcel taken by the state for the construction of a superhighway. Name at least two sources of real estate law involved in determining the farmer's rights.

2. Mr. and Mrs. Ralph Williams of Montana purchased an acre of land in a new Florida development called Sunnydale. When the Williamses arrived at Sunnydale they did not find the green, lush parcels they were told of, but instead found property resembling the moon's surface. In determining their rights, to which sources of law should Mr. and Mrs. Williams turn?

3. The Internal Revenue Service is challenging Iva Case's depreciation deduction of her law office building. What sources of law will govern the issue?

4. When Tom Buttom purchased his home, he was promised by the builder that the neighborhood would consist of single-family dwellings. Tom has just learned that because of economic conditions, the builder will be constructing duplex houses on Tom's street. What sources of law will be helpful to Tom in determining his rights?

5. Jane Jenkins, a licensed real estate agent in New York, will be moving to California. To what sources of law can Jane turn to find the requirements for becoming licensed in California?

6. A deed restriction requires every house in a subdivision to have a "minimum of 2000 square feet of living space." Although the restriction seems clear, consider the following interpretive problems:
   a. Is a garage part of the 2000 square feet?
   b. Are porches part of the 2000 square feet?

7. A cite of 16 C.F.R. §1 comes from which source of law?

8. Some isolated parcels within national forests are privately owned. Often, the United States Forest Service will try to arrange exchanges with land-owners. With an exchange, the Forest Service will then have a clean parcel and the landowner is given property in an area with development potential near a city or small town. Discuss the types of laws and government agencies that would be involved in such an exchange.

9. Brad and Betty Lemitt have defaulted on their mortgage payments for their home. They have been given a notice of foreclosure but want to know if they will have a chance to appear in court. The Lemitts claim that they stopped making their payments because the builder would not repair a leaky roof. Does the Constitution provide for a "day in court" for the Lemitts?

10. Pamela Walker has just leased an apartment in the Wood Stream complex. Shortly after completing her move, Pamela discovers that the apartment has no hot water and that the sinks back up each time the dishwasher is run. Pamela suffers through a weekend with no hot water and with the stench from the dishwasher back-up. To what sources of law should Pamela turn to discover her rights in this situation?

2

PRESENT LAND INTERESTS AND RIGHTS IN REAL ESTATE

> *Land is, like any other possession, by natural right wholly in the power of its present owner; and may be sold, given or bequeathed, absolutely or conditionally. But natural law would avail little without the protection of the law.*
>
> —Samuel Johnson

The major question answered in this chapter is, How can an owner hold title to property? Additional related questions are, How long can an interest be held? and Can interests be transferred? The degree and extent of ownership are the focus of this chapter's discussion. Figure 2.1 depicts the full extent and the interrelationships of land interests.

Figure 2.1 *Land Interests*

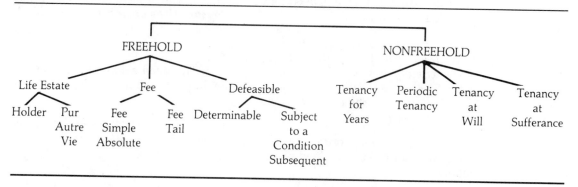

LAND INTERESTS—FREEHOLD ESTATES

Freehold Estates

The terms freehold and fee, adopted from English common law, hold significance for understanding the methods of land ownership. *Freehold* means that
an interest in land is uncertain or unlimited in duration. *Fee* here means that
an interest in land is inheritable. Thus the fee freehold estates are uncertain
or unlimited in duration and can be passed to others upon the death of the
interest holder.

Fee Simple Absolute Ownership

A *fee simple absolute* estate (a form of freehold estate and sometimes referred to
as a fee simple) is an interest in land representing the greatest extent of property
ownership available. In lay terms the fee simple absolute estate would be described as absolute ownership. The owners of fee simple absolute estates are
free to transfer their interest at any time and can pass their interest to others
upon death.

At common law, a fee simple absolute estate was created when the
transfer or grant made by the owner or grantor read: "To A and his heirs," with
"and his heirs" used to indicate the inheritability of the interest. However, in
three-fourths of the states, the language requirement of "and his heirs" has
been eliminated so that a fee simple absolute estate can be created simply by
using "To A" language. The following case involves a fee simple interest and
emphasizes the need for using clear language in any instrument granting an
interest in land.

WAYBURN v. SMITH
239 S.E.2d 890 (S.C. 1977)

W. J. Wooten deeded property to his
daughter, Allie Walker, in a deed that
provided as follows:

*Know All Men by These Presents, That
I, W. J. Wooten of Blythewood, S. C.
desire to convey to Allie Walker this tract
of land (100) acres to have and to hold her
natural life, at her death it is to revert to
heirs of her body.*

The pertinent portion of the
granting clause in the deed is as
follows:

*. . . . I have granted, bargained, sold and
released and by these presents do grant,
bargain, sell and release unto the said Allie Walker. . . .*

The deed also contains the following habendum clause:

*To Have and To Hold all and singular the
premises before mentioned unto the said
Allie Walker her Heirs and Assigns
forever.*

In an attempted transfer by Walker, several relatives contended she did not have fee simple title but rather held only a lesser title of a life interest. The trial court found that Walker held a fee simple absolute title and the relatives appealed.

LITTLEJOHN, Justice

It is the rule in this State that where an incomplete or indefinite estate is conveyed by the granting clause, as for instance where no words of inheritance accompany the grant, or where the granting clause creates a life estate, resort may be had to the habendum for the purpose of ascertaining the intention of the grantor and thus a life estate may be enlarged into a fee simple estate.

The granting clause in the subject deed gave the property "to Allie Walker," and contained no words of inheritance. Thus a life estate by implication was granted to Allie Walker. Since the granting clause did not make a complete disposition of the title to the property, resort must be had to the habendum clause for the purpose of ascertaining the quantity of the estate intended to be conveyed. The habendum contained the traditional words of inheritance, and therefore had the effect of enlarging the life estate conveyed by the granting clause into a fee simple.

The case of *Zobel v. Little*, 113 S.E. 68 (1922) is factually similar to the instant case. There, the granting clause states:

Said property is conveyed to Edna Hyatt Zobel and is her property during her natural life. At her death it is to become the property of her heirs then living.

The deed also contained the following habendum:

To Have and to Hold all and singular the premises before mentioned, unto the said Edna Hyatt Zobel, heirs and assigns forever.

The court construed the habendum as enlarging the life estate conveyed by the granting clause into a fee simple.

While we concede that it appears from a reading of the language in the premises of the deed that the grantor may have intended to convey a life estate to Allie Walker with a remainder to the heirs of her body, it is essential that the long established law affecting title to real estate be maintained.

Affirmed.

Discussion Questions

1. What type of estate was given in the first clause of the deed?
2. What did the granting clause of the deed (the language of conveyance) provide?
3. What did the habendum (the language following the conveyance that restricts or limits the type of estate granted) clause of the deed provide?
4. Under the law of South Carolina, which clause is controlling?
5. What does the court perceive was Wooten's intent?
6. What type of estate does the court hold Allie Walker has?

Fee Simple Defeasible

A *fee simple defeasible* is an interest in land that is uncertain or unlimited in duration and that has the potential of being terminated. There are two types of fee simple defeasible estates—the fee simple determinable and the fee simple subject to a condition subsequent.

Fee Simple Determinable According to Figure 2.1, this land interest is uncertain and inheritable. In *fee simple determinable,* the grantor is giving the grantee full title and right to the property so long as the grantee complies with an attached restriction. An example of language creating a fee simple determinable is "To A so long as the premises are used for school purposes." Thus the one characteristic distinguishing a fee simple determinable from a fee simple absolute is that A's interest will terminate if the property is not used for school purposes. If A does not comply with the restriction, title to the property will revert to the grantor. (The grantor's interest is discussed in Chapter 3.)

In some situations, it is difficult to determine whether the grantee has complied with the grantor's restriction that is part of the fee simple determinable. In the following case, the court deals with a question about whether a grantor's restriction has been violated.

KINNEY v. STATE OF KANSAS AND KANSAS FISH AND GAME COMMISSION
710 P.2d 1290 (Kans. 1985)

On 8 February, 1934 Kinney Land and Cattle Company, by warranty deed, conveyed to the state of Kansas real estate located in Finney County. The property conveyed was 790 acres and is currently known as Finney County State Park. Clauses 5 and 6 of the warranty deed provided as follows:

It is understood by the parties hereto that this conveyance constitutes a donation of the above property for state park purposes.
CLAUSE OF REVERSION
It is further agreed and understood by and between the parties hereto that the premises herein described are to be used by the party of the second part as a public forestry, fish and game preserve and recre-

ational state park, and in so using the said premises a lake of at least 150 acres is to be constructed thereon, and said premises are to be used and maintained for purposes aforesaid, and if party of the second part fails to so use and maintain said premises, then and in that event the title to the said property hereinbefore described shall revert to the party of the first part, its successors or assigns.

Between 1934 and 1970, the park has had a lake intermittently but the lake has never reached the 150-acre minimum. Kinney Land and Cattle Company was dissolved but the heirs of the shareholders (plaintiffs) brought suit seeking to quiet title in the land claiming that the intermittent presence of the lake and its failure to meet minimum size requirements caused title to the park to revert to them. The

trial court granted the State and the Fish and Game Commission (defendants) a summary judgment, and the shareholders' heirs appealed.

PRAGER, Justice

Simply stated, it is the claim of the plaintiffs that the warranty deed of 1934 conveyed to the State a fee simple determinable, sometimes described as a fee simple subject to a condition subsequent, whereby the interest of the State was to be terminated and the title revert to the grantor, its survivors or assigns, if the State, as the grantee, failed to use and maintain the premises for the purposes set forth in the reversion clause. The plaintiffs contend that the State has failed to use and maintain the premises for the stated purposes, and therefore, title to the land has reverted to them as survivors in interest of the Kinney Land and Cattle Company.

The basic issue raised on the appeal is this: Does the fact that the Finney County State Lake located on the land no longer contains a body of water of 150 acres serve as a basis for the activation of the reversion clause so as to terminate the State's title to the real estate and cause title to revert to the plaintiffs? In order to determine this basic issue it would be helpful to consider certain general principles of law which are applicable in cases involving reversion clauses. In this case, the State, as grantee, owns a determinable or qualified fee in real estate which has all the attributes of a fee simple except it is subject to being defeated by the happening of a condition which is to terminate the estate. An estate in fee simple determinable is created by any limitation which: (1) creates an estate in fee simple and (2) provides that the estate shall automatically expire upon the occurrence of the stated event.

In the past, this court has determined issues involving estates in fee simple determinable. In *Curtis v. Board of*

Education, 23 P. 98 (1890), it was stated that the authorities are uniform that an estate upon condition subsequent, which estate after having been fully vested may be defeated by a breach of the condition, is never favored in law, and that no deed will be construed to create such an estate unless the language to that effect is so clear that no room is left for any other construction. In *Ritchie v. K.N. & D. Rly. Co.,* 39 P. 718 (1895), it was held that an instrument containing a condition subsequent, working a forfeiture of an estate, is to be strictly construed and its terms will never be extended by construction. This general rule is based upon the theory that, since the deed is the act of the grantor, it will be construed most strongly against him. Where, however, a deed clearly creates a fee simple determinable and reserves a reversionary interest in the grantor, such provisions will be enforced.

The clause of reversion contained in paragraph six of the warranty deed requires that the premises be used by the State, as grantee, as a "public forestry, fish and game preserve and recreational state park." At the time the deed was executed, the statutes of Kansas provided for the establishment of public forestry, fish and game preserves, and recreational grounds. G.S. 1935, 32-315 authorized the forestry, fish and game commission, among other things, to establish, maintain, and provide for sanctuaries, in which game, game birds, fur-bearing animals or fish may breed or rest; to replenish hunting and trapping grounds and water or fishing waters; and to establish, maintain, and improve recreational grounds for the purpose of affording recreational facilities for the citizens of Kansas. That statute was enacted in

1927 and was in full force and effect the time the warranty deed was executed in the present case.

These same basic powers are given to the fish and game commission today by virtue of our present statutes. [These statutes] gave the forestry, fish and game commission broad power and authority to acquire lands by donation or by purchase for the purpose of establishing and maintaining the same as a public forestry, recreational grounds, and fish and game preserves; to acquire or provide for the building of reservoirs, dams or lakes for impounding water . . . and to do all and anything possible to carry out the intent of the act. Thus, by statute, the fish and game commission, acting on behalf of the State, is obviously vested with great power and discretion in using donated funds for a public forestry, fish and game preserve or a recreational state park.

In the *City of Witchita v. Clapp,* 263 P. 12 (Kan. 1928), it was held that the use of a portion of a public park as an airport came within the proper and legitimate uses for which public parks are created. In the opinion the court discussed the meaning of the term "park purposes." The court stated:

The specific question for consideration is whether park purposes may include an airport or landing field for airplanes. Under various authorities, the expression 'park purposes' has been held to include a race track, a tourist camp, bridle trails, boating, bathing, refreshment and lunch stands, providing bathing suits, towels and rooms for bathers, dressing pavilion, waiting room for street cars, refreshment and shelter room for the public, grandstand, ball games, baseball diamond, race meets, tennis courts, croquet grounds, children's playgrounds, hotels, restaurants, museums, art galleries, zoological and bo-tanical gardens, conservatories, and many other recreational and educational facilities.

A park may be devoted to any use which tends to promote popular enjoyment and recreation.

These various statutes and authorities are cited to show the broad interpretation which has been given to the terms "forestry, fish and game preserve and recreational state park." The trial court in this case granted partial summary judgment in favor of the defendants, holding that the terms of the deed do not support a forfeiture of the State's interest in the property simply because the lake constructed on the premises contained a body of water of less than 150 acres prior to and subsequent to the filing of this action. We agree with the trial court. The deed should be construed to require only that the State in good faith maintain the property as a public forestry, fish and game facility and as a recreational state park. The grantor obviously had in mind an area dedicated to the protection and conservation of natural surroundings, game and fish, and a place where the people could enjoy such natural beauties. The lake is an important factor to be considered in determining whether the State in good faith has maintained the entire property for the intended uses. The maintenance of the lake, however, is not the controlling consideration but is only part of the big picture. Under the circumstances, we hold that the trial court correctly held that the State of Kansas had not forfeited its title to the land simply because the quantity of water contained in the lake has not been sufficient to completely fill an area of 150 acres. The quantity of water contained in the lake is bound to vary from year to year depending upon the amount of rainfall and any other available sources of water in the area.

Affirmed.

Discussion Questions

1. Who made the original land conveyance?
2. What restriction was placed on the conveyance?
3. What was the language in the warranty deed?
4. Who has brought suit? Why?
5. What did the trial court do?
6. What definition is given of the term "park"?
7. Does the interest in the land revert?
8. After reading the following section in the chapter on fee simple subject to a condition subsequent, review the judge's opinion and determine whether there are any inaccuracies or misuses of terms.

Fee Simple Subject to a Condition Subsequent A grantor can accomplish the same purposes of a fee simple determinable grant through the use of a grant of a *fee simple subject to a condition subsequent*. This interest is created with slightly different language such as, "To A on the condition that the land be used for school purposes and if the land is ever not used for school purposes, O (the grantor) may re-enter and repossess the land." (O's interest is also discussed in Chapter 3.) The fee simple subject to a condition subsequent is similar to a fee simple determinable in that A will lose the interest if there is not compliance with the restriction. The difference between the two is that the violation of a fee simple determinable restriction terminates A's interest immediately, whereas violation of a condition subsequent grant requires some action on the part of the grantor (O) before the interest of A terminates.

Without the language of re-entry and repossession in the grant, it is difficult to distinguish between a fee simple determinable and a fee simple subject to a condition subsequent. A general rule is that words and phrases such as "until" or "so long as" create fee simple determinables and phrases such as "on the condition that" and "provided that" create fee simples subject to conditions subsequent. The presence of conditional language is an indicator that a fee simple subject to a condition subsequent exists. Also, some states have statutes that favor a presumption of a condition subsequent interest so that land interests are terminated only upon appropriate action by the grantor. The following case illustrates the difficulties encountered in determining whether a fee simple determinable or a fee simple subject to a condition subsequent exists.

MAHRENHOLZ v. COUNTY BD. OF SCHOOL ETC.

417 N.E.2d 138 (Ill. 1981)

On 18 March 1941 W. E. and Jennie Hutton executed a warranty deed conveying the Hutton School grounds to the Trustees of School District 1 (defendant/appellee). The deed provided "this land to be used for school purpose only; otherwise to revert to Grantors herein." Both Huttons have passed away and left their son, Harry, as their only heir.

The property deeded by the Huttons was used for classroom purposes until 1973, when the property became used by the district for storage purposes.

Harry conveyed his interest in the property in 1977 to Mr. and Mrs. Mahrenholz (plaintiffs/appellants) who brought an action to quiet title to the property in them because the property was being used for storage purposes (in violation of the alleged fee simple determinable language used by the Huttons in the deed to the school). The school board contended they had title since Harry Hutton never brought an action to reenter and reclaim title to the property. The trial court found for the school board and the Mahrenholzes appealed.

JONES, Justice

The basic issue presented is the legal interpretation of the language contained in the March 18, 1941 deed from W. E. and Jennie Hutton to the Trustees of School District No. 1:

this land to be used for school purpose only; otherwise to revert to Grantors herein.

In addition to the legal effect of this language we must consider the alienability of the interest created and the effect of subsequent deeds.

The parties appear to be in agreement that the 1941 deed from the Huttons conveyed a defeasible fee simple estate to the grantee, and gave rise to a future interest in the grantors and that it did not convey a fee simple absolute, subject to a covenant. The fact that provision was made for forfeiture of the estate conveyed should the land cease to be used for school purposes suggests this view is correct.

The future interest remaining in this grantor or his estate can only be a possibility of reverter or right of re-entry for condition broken. Consequently, this court must determine whether the plaintiffs could have acquired an interest in Hutton School from Harry Hutton. The resolution of this issue depends upon the construction of the language of the 1941 deed of the Huttons to the school district. As urged by the defendants and as the trial court found, that deed conveyed a fee simple subject to a condition subsequent followed by a right of re-entry for condition broken. As argued by the plaintiffs, on the other hand, the deed conveyed a fee simple determinable followed by a possibility of reverter. In either case, the grantor and his heirs retain an interest in the property which may become possessory if the condition is broken. If the grantor had a possibility of reverter, he or his heirs become the owner of the property by operation of law as soon as the condition is broken. If he has a right of re-entry for condition broken, he or his heirs become the owner of the property only after they act to re-take the property.

It is alleged and we must accept, that classes were last held in the Hutton School in 1973. Harry Hutton, sole heir of the grantors, did not act to legally retake the premises but instead conveyed his interest in that land to the plaintiffs in 1977. If Harry Hutton had only a naked right of re-entry for condition broken, then he could not be the owner of that property until he had legally re-entered the land. Since he took no steps for legal re-entry, he had only a right of re-entry in 1977, and that right cannot be conveyed inter vivos. On the other hand, if Harry Hutton had a possibility of reverter in the property, then he owned the school property as soon as it ceased to be used for school purposes. Therefore, assuming (1) that cessation of classes constitutes "abandonment of school purposes" on the land, (2) that the conveyance from Harry Hutton to the plaintiffs was legally correct, and (3) that the conveyance was not pre-empted by Hutton's disclaimer in favor of the school district, the plaintiffs could have acquired an interest in the Hutton School grounds if Harry Hutton inherited a possibility of reverter from his parents.

A fee simple determinable may be thought of as a limited grant, while a fee simple subject to a condition subsequent is an absolute grant to which a condition is appended. In other words, a grantor should give a fee simple determinable if he intends to give property for so long as it is needed for the purposes for which it is given and no longer, but he should employ a fee simple subject to a condition subsequent if he intends to compel compliance with a condition by penalty of forfeiture.

. . . [T]he Huttons would have created a fee simple determinable if they had allowed the school district to retain the property so long as or while it was used for school purposes or until it ceased to be so used. Similarly, a fee simple subject to a condition subsequent would have arisen had the Huttons given the land upon the condition that or provided that it be used for school purposes. In the 1941 deed, though the Huttons gave the land "to be used for school purpose only; otherwise to revert to Grantors herein," no words of temporal limitation, or terms of express condition, were used in the grant.

The plaintiffs argue that the word "only" should be construed as a limitation rather than as a condition. The defendants respond that where ambiguous language is used in a deed, the courts of Illinois have expressed a constructional preference for a fee simple subject to a condition subsequent.

We believe that a close analysis of the wording of the original grant shows that the grantors intended to create a fee simple determinable followed by a possibility of reverter. Here, the use of the word "only" immediately following the grant "for school purpose" demonstrates that the Huttons wanted to give the land to the school district only as long as it was needed and no longer. The language "this land to be used for school purpose only" is an example of a grant which contains a limitation within the granting clause. It suggests a limited grant, rather than a full grant subject to a condition, and thus, both theoretically and linguistically, gives rise to a fee simple determinable.

The second relevant clause furnishes plaintiff's position with additional support. It cannot be argued that the phrase "otherwise to revert to grantors herein" is inconsistent with a fee simple subject to a condition subsequent. Nor does the word "revert" automatically create a possibility of reverter. But, in combination with the preceding phrase, the provisions by which possession is returned to the grantors seem to trigger a mandatory return because it is not stated that the grantor "may" re-enter the land.

The terms used in the 1941 deed, although imprecise, were designed to allow the property to be used for a single purpose, namely, for "school purpose." The Huttons intended to have the land back if it were ever used otherwise.

We hold, therefore, that the 1941 deed from W. E. and Jennie Hutton to the Trustees of School District No. 1 created a fee simple determinable in the Trustees followed by a possibility of reverter in the Huttons and their heirs.

Reversed and remanded.

Discussion Questions

1. Who owned the property in issue originally?
2. When the property was transferred, what language was used?
3. How did the Mahrenholzes acquire an interest in the property?
4. When was the property used for a purpose other than the one designated in the original grant?
5. When did the Mahrenholzes acquire their interest?
6. Which of the fee simple defeasibles does the court classify as a limited grant and which is an absolute grant with a restriction?
7. What type of interest was created by the language in the case?
8. Who holds title to the property?

In some cases the language used to create a type of fee simple is more detailed, and it is difficult to determine what type of land interest was created. The following case involves a detailed grant and the court's resolution of the dilemma created by the grantor's use of confusing language.

HIGBEE CORP. v. KENNEDY
428 A.2d 592 (Pa. 1981)

Higbee Corporation (plaintiff/appellee) and Kennedy (defendant/appellant) both claimed title to a narrow strip of property located in Bethel Park, Allegheny County, Pennsylvania. Higbee filed suit to quiet title. The original grant on the property to Kennedy provided as follows:

To have and to hold the said piece of land above-described the hereditaments and premises hereby granted or mentioned and intended so to be with the appurtenance unto the said party of the second part his heirs and assigns to and for the only proper use and behoof of the said party of the second part his heirs and assigns forever provided the party of the second part his heirs and assigns wishes to make use of it for the purpose of a road. THE PARTY OF THE SECOND PART AGREES TO

KEEP A GOOD FENCE AROUND THE ABOVE-MENTIONED LOT, FAILING TO DO SO FORFEITS HIS CLAIM, whenever the party of the second part wishes to give up his claim to said lot he is to have full privilege to remove all fencing materials whenever the party of the second part his heirs and assigns fails to fulfill this agreement the land is to revert to the party of the first part.

The lower court held that the above language created a fee simple determinable, the breach of which would cause the title to revert to the grantor or his successors. On the basis of Kennedy's admission that he did not maintain a fence around the lot, the court held that title had reverted and was vested in Higbee. Kennedy appealed.

PRICE, Judge

The sole issue for our consideration is whether the estate created by the deed was a fee simple determinable or a fee simple subject to a condition subsequent. A fee simple determinable is an estate in fee that automatically reverts to the grantor upon the occurrence of a specified event. The interest held by the grantor is a possibility of reverter. Words of indubitable limitations, such as "so long as," "during," "while" and "until," are generally used to create the fee simple determinable.

If, on the other hand, the deed conveyed a fee simple subject to a condition subsequent, then upon noncompliance with the stated condition the grantor or his successor in interest would have the power to terminate the preceding estate. Thus the grantors would have a right of re-entry. The principal distinction between the two [interests] is that a right of re-entry requires some action to perfect title by the grantor or his successor, while a reverter vests automatically.

Moreover, the policy of the law is to render the alienation and transfer of land as free as possible, and conditions are not favored in law. In accordance with our policy of favoring the free alienability of land, "a deed which would convey an estate in fee simple except for certain words, or for a phrase or clause must be interpreted strictly against any such limitation unless the grantor's intention to so limit the fee is clearly expressed or necessarily implied."

We first examine the effect of the following clause: "forever provided the [grantee] his heirs and assigns wishes to make use of it for the purpose of a road." We concur with the parties' consensus that the portions of the deed preceding this phrase create a fee simple. However, we cannot agree with appellee's contention that this conditional language limits the estate to a fee simple determinable. Words such as "provided," "if," or "upon the condition that" express condition and, therefore, indicate the existence of a fee simple subject to a condition subsequent.

We find the following clause more perplexing:

the [grantee] agrees to keep a good fence around the above-mentioned lot, failing to do so forfeits his claim, whenever the [grantee] wishes to give up his claim to said lot he is to have full privilege to remove all fencing materials whenever the [grantee] his heirs and assigns fails to fulfill this agreement the land is to revert to the [grantor].

The term "forfeits" is conditional language and, coupled with the absence of words of incontestable limitation, indicates the existence of a fee simple subject to a condition subsequent. The provision of reverter to the grantor, on the other hand, infers that the estate is a fee simple determinable. Since a fee simple determinable automatically divests a grantee of his interest in an estate, without regard to the current status of a grantor or his successors in interest, it is more cumbersome upon the alienability of land than a fee simple subject to a condition subsequent. It is our opinion that the grantor, as draftsman of the deed, bears the heavy burden of using clear and unambiguous language to make explicit his intent to create this type of onerous limitation to an estate in land. Therefore, only in the absence of ambiguity will we find in favor of a fee simple determinable. Accordingly, in absence of contrary intent, we view the conflicting terminology herein as creating a fee simple subject to a condition subsequent.

Reversed.

Discussion Questions

1. What type of interest does Higbee claim is created by the language?
2. Has Kennedy violated the restriction imposed in the deed? What is the restriction?

3. What rule does the court establish for ambiguous language in deeds?
4. Which land interest will be favored in the event of an ambiguity in language?

5. What type of interest was created by the language in this case?

Fee Tail Ownership

The position of *fee tail* interest in Figure 2.1 establishes it as an uncertain or unlimited estate that is inheritable. However, the distinction between fee simple and fee tail is that fee tail is inheritable only by lineal descendants or direct descendants of the grantee. Lineal descendants are children, grandchildren, great-grandchildren, and so on. Thus while fee tail grantees are alive, they may transfer only to these individuals. The language used to create a fee tail interest is "To A and the heirs of his body." The language in this fee tail creates a *fee tail general*. A *fee tail special* is created when language such as "To A and the heirs of his body by his wife, B," is used. When language such as "To A and the female heirs of his body" is used, a fee tail female is created.

Fee tail interests present substantial problems because of the transfer restrictions and because finding lineal heirs can be cumbersome and confusing. To alleviate the problems of fee tail, many states have passed statutes that convert fee tail grants into fee simple absolutes. Some states retain the fee tail interest but permit holders of fee tails to eliminate the fee tail restrictions through a series of transfer transactions. Other states permit fee tail grantees to hold a life estate and then pass title to the land to their heirs at death. Finally, there are a few states that still recognize and enforce the fee tail grant.

Life Estate Ownership

Creation Another type of freehold estate is the *life estate*, which is an interest in land valid only for the life of the holder or for some other measured life. A life estate is uncertain in its duration because termination occurs upon the death of the measuring life. A conventional life estate is created with the language, "To A for his life." A's interest will automatically terminate at death. This type of life estate is one measured by the life of the holder of the interest. A second type of life estate, measured by a life other than that of the holder, is created by language such as "To A for the life of B," and is called a *life estate pur autre vie*.

The life estate appears to be an odd method of land ownership, but it is used effectively as an estate planning tool so that estate taxes may be postponed or reduced. For example, a wife who predeceases her husband might have a will granting her husband a life estate in some property with the provision that the property be given to the children at the termination of the husband's life interest. The husband holds a lesser interest only for life, and the distribution will be taxed at the time of the children's receipt.

Also, some states provide for the automatic creation of legal life estates in certain instances. Marital rights such as dower and curtesy are rights afforded surviving spouses to entitle them to some portion of their deceased spouse's property. In some states, these marital rights are given to the surviving spouse in the form of a life estate imposed by statute. (A complete discussion of dower and curtesy rights appears in Chapter 15.)

(2.1) Consider:

Viva Parker Lilliston died in 1969 and in her will provided as follows:

> Item Twelve: I give and devise my farm situated on the Seaside from Locustville, in the county of Accomack, State of Virginia . . . to my daughter, Margaret Lilliston Edwards, upon the conditions, set out in Item Fourteen. . . . Item Fourteen: all gifts made to my daughter, Margaret L. Edwards, individually and personally, under Items Eleven and Twelve of this Will, whether personal estate or real estate, are conditioned upon the said Margaret L. Edwards keeping the gift or devise herein free from encumberances of every description, and in the event the said Margaret L. Edwards shall attempt to encumber same or sell her interest, or in the event any creditor or creditors of Margaret L. Edwards shall attempt to subject her interest in the gift or devise herein made to the payment of the debts of the said Margaret L. Edwards, then and in that event the interest of said Margaret L. Edwards therein shall immediately cease and determine, and the gift or devise shall at once become vested in her children, viz: Betty Belle Branch, Beverly Bradley, John R. Edwards, Bruce C. Edwards, Jill A. Edwards, and Jackie L. Edwards, in equal shares in fee simple . . .

In 1979, Margaret tried to obtain the consent of her children to sell the farm. Beverly Bradley, one of the listed children of Margaret, refused to give such consent. Margaret died in 1980 and left $1.00 to Beverly and directed that the farm be sold and the proceeds distributed among her other children. Beverly challenged the will claiming that her interest had vested and could not be taken away. She claims that Margaret had a life estate and she and the other children had a remainder. Margaret's lawyer claims that Margaret held a fee simple subject to a condition subsequent that she could convey at her death in the manner that she did.

What type of interests did Margaret and her children hold? *Edwards v. Bradley*, 315 S.E.2d 196 (Va. 1984)

Rights of Life Tenants The holders of life estates, referred to as *life tenants*, have certain rights in the use and possession of their property. Holders of life estates have the right of undisturbed possession during the time of their estate. However, life tenants do have the obligation not to waste or destroy the property interest. If life tenants jeopardize holders of future interests (Chapter 3), then such future interest holders may bring action to stop the life tenant from engaging in the wasteful conduct. For example, cutting timber on the life estate property for the purpose of building fences or for fuel is appropriate conduct for a life tenant; however, cutting timber for commercial sale would be inappropriate because there is a dissipation of the value of the property and the interests of the future holders of title. The following case involves the issue of whether a life tenant was committing waste.

MELMS v. PABST BREWING CO.
79 N.W. 738 (Wis. 1899)

In 1864 Charles T. Melms built a large home at a cost of $20,000 on Virginia Street in Milwaukee. At the time of construction Melms owned all of the surrounding real estate and a brewery located on that property. Upon his death Mr. Melms left the home and its quarter-acre location to his wife for her life, with the children of the couple inheriting the property upon her death.

Mrs. Melms transferred her interest to Pabst Brewing Co. (defendant/appellee) to help solve some of her husband's financial difficulties. After this transfer, the character of the real estate on Virginia Street changed substantially. Factories and railway tracks increased in the vicinity, and the balance of the property consisted of brewery buildings. The large home would not rent because it was wholly undesirable as a residence, and the taxes and insurance on the property could not be paid because the property could not produce income.

Pabst sought to level the property and use it as business property so that its value could be enhanced. The Melms children (plaintiffs/appellants) brought an action against Pabst, alleging waste. After a jury finding for Pabst, the Melms children appealed.

WINSLOW, Judge

Our statutes recognize waste, and provide a remedy by action and the recovery of double damages therefore; but they do not define it. The following definition of waste was approved by this court in *Bandlow v. Thieme*, 53 Wis. 57: "It may be defined to be any act or omission of duty by a tenant of land which does a lasting injury to the freehold, tends to the permanent loss of the owner of the fee, or to destroy or lessen the value of the inheritance, or to destroy the identity of the property, or impair the evidence of title." . . . [I]t was also said that "any material change in the nature and character of the buildings made by the tenant is waste, although the value of the property should be enhanced by the alteration."

The defendants are the grantees of a life estate, and their rights may continue for a number of years. The evidence shows that the property became valueless for the purpose of residence property as the result of the growth and development of a great city. Business and manufacturing interests advanced and surrounded the once elegant mansion, until it stood isolated and alone, standing upon just enough ground to support it, and surrounded by factories and railway tracks, absolutely undesirable as a residence and incapable of any use as business property.

Here was a complete change of conditions, not produced by the tenant, but resulting from causes which none could control. Can it be reasonably or logically said that this entire change of condition is to be completely ignored, and the iron-clad rule applied that the tenant can make no change in the uses of the property because he will destroy its identity? Must the tenant stand by and preserve the useless dwelling-house, so that he may at some future time turn it over to the reversioner, equally useless? Certainly, all analogies are to the contrary. As we have before seen, the cutting of timber, which in England was considered waste, has become in this country an act which may be waste or not, according to the surrounding conditions and the rules of good husbandry; and the same rule applies to the change of a meadow to arable land. The changes of conditions which justify these departures from early inflexible rules are no more marked nor complete than is the change of conditions which destroys the value of residence property as such and renders it only useful for business purposes.

Suppose the house in question had been so situated that it could have been remodeled into business property; would any court of equity have enjoined such remodeling under the circumstances here shown, or ought any court to render a judgment for damages for such an act? Clearly, we think not. Again, suppose an orchard to have become permanently unproductive through disease or death of the trees, and the land to have become far more valuable, by reason of the new conditions as a vegetable garden or wheat field, is the life tenant to be compelled to preserve or renew the useless orchard, and forego the advantages to be derived?

This case is not to be construed as justifying a tenant in making substantial changes in the lease-hold property, or the buildings thereon, to suit his own whim or convenience, because, perchance, he may be able to show that the change is in some degree beneficial. Under all ordinary circumstances the landlord or reversioner, even in the absence of contract, is entitled to receive the property at the close of the tenancy substantially in the condition in which it was when the tenant received it; but when, as here, there has occurred a complete and permanent change of surrounding conditions, which has deprived the property of its value and usefulness as previously used, the question whether a life tenant, not bound by contract to restore the property in the same condition in which he received it, has been guilty of waste in making changes necessary to make the property useful, is a question of fact for the jury under proper instructions, or for the court where, as in the present case, the question is tried by the court.

Affirmed.

Discussion Questions

1. Who was the grantor of the life estate?

2. Who was the life tenant?

3. Who currently holds the life interest?

4. Who will receive the property upon Mrs. Melms's death?

5. Why has the value of the property declined?

6. What does Pabst wish to do with the property?
7. On what legal theory is the suit based?
8. Can Pabst legally proceed with its proposed actions?

9. Does the court issue a general rule on the doctrine of waste?
10. Who determines whether waste has been committed?

While alive, life tenants can transfer their interests, but buyers of such interests should be aware of the restricted time of the life estate: a transferee's interest lasts only as long as the tenant/transferor is alive. Any attempt by a life tenant to convey an interest at death is invalid. Similarly, creditors of the life tenant can have security in the property only until the life tenant's death. Issues of the responsibility of payment for taxes between life tenants and reversioners are treated differently among the states.

LAND INTERESTS—NONFREEHOLD ESTATES

The nonfreehold estate is one limited in duration and noninheritable. Four types of nonfreehold estates are examined in the following sections. In lay terms, nonfreehold estate refers to the landlord–tenant relationship.

Tenancy for Years

A *tenancy for years* is created by a lease, which will run for a time period specified in that lease. Other language used to describe the tenancy for years includes "estate for years," "tenancy for a term," or "tenancy for a period." Every tenancy for years has fixed beginning and ending dates and is created by language such as "To A for 7 years;" or "To A from 31 March 1987 until 30 June 1988." When the termination date is reached, this land interest automatically terminates.

In a tenancy for years, the parties involved have a continuing relationship and should have a written agreement setting forth all of their rights and obligations. A tenancy for years that runs for a period longer than 1 year is required to be in writing. (Details on the content of such written agreements are discussed in Chapter 18.)

Periodic Tenancy

A *periodic tenancy* has no definite ending date: It continues until one of the parties takes proper legal steps to terminate the interest. A periodic tenancy can be expressly created, and an example of language used to create such an interest is "To A on a month-to-month basis beginning 30 June 1988."

The periodic tenancy or estate from period to period can also result or be implied from the conduct of the parties as opposed to being created expressly.

A periodic tenancy will result in the following circumstances: One party moves into another's property on an oral lease agreement that is to run for 24 months. In the jurisdiction in which the parties reside, lease agreements running for longer than one year must be in writing to be enforceable. According to the provision of law the parties do not have a valid lease agreement, but once the landowner accepts the tenant's rent, a periodic tenancy results and is terminated only through the proper actions of the parties.

Proper actions required for termination of a tenancy are specified by statute in each of the states, but the key to termination in all of the states is notice. The type or length of notice will vary, but the requirement of notice is universal. At common law, 6-months' notice was required to terminate a year-to-year tenancy and a full period's notice was required to terminate a periodic tenancy with periods running less than a year. For example, on a month-to-month tenancy, a full period's notice would be one month.

Tenancy at Will

A *tenancy at will* can be created expressly and arises when the parties agree to the lease of property but provide no time period for the lease. Language to create a tenancy at will would be, "To A at O's discretion or will."

In a tenancy at will, both parties have the right to terminate the tenancy at any time and are not required to provide advance notice of such termination. In some states, statutory provisions have changed this freedom and require some form of notice to terminate. In such states the tenancy at will is in essence a periodic tenancy by statute.

Tenancies at will can arise in situations with a financed property, where there is a default by the party possessing the property. For example, suppose A leases the land on which her mobile home is located, and her mobile home is financed through a bank. She [A] leaves and the mobile home remains on the leased land. If A defaults on her payments and the bank is forced to repossess the mobile home, then the bank becomes a tenant at will on the land.

Tenancy at Sufferance

This final nonfreehold interest, *tenancy at sufferance*, arises when a tenant from a properly created tenancy holds over on the landlord's property for a period beyond that authorized. For example, suppose a landlord leased a building to a tenant for 2 years with a lease termination date of 31 March 1988. The tenant should vacate the premises by the termination date, but if the tenant remains then he or she is nothing more than a trespasser. A landlord may have such a holdover tenant evicted. However, if the tenant chooses to remain on the property at the landlord's sufferance and if the landlord accepts rent after the termination date, a periodic tenancy can be created.

(2.2) Consider:

Determine what types of estates are created by the following language and examples:

a. "To A for life"

b. "To A and his heirs"

c. "To A"

d. "To A and B"

e. "To A for 10 years if she lives that long"

f. "To A for life, but in no event longer than 10 years"

g. "To A for 10 years, beginning 1 January 1988"

h. "To A and his female bodily heirs"

i. "To A provided the premises are never used for the sale of liquor"

j. "To A on the condition that the premises are never used for a dance hall"

k. "To A so long as the premises are used for church purposes"

l. "To my husband Ralph for life"

m. "To the trustee for First County Church so long as the premises are never used for the playing of bingo"

n. "To my granddaughter, Alfreda, and all of Alfreda's female issue"

o. "To my son John for his use for five years"

p. "To my daughter, Sara, for the life of my brother, Sam"

q. "To my granddaughter so long as the premises are used for a library for Whitman College"

r. "To my son John and his bodily heirs"

s. "To Jess S. Long, and the children of his body begotten, and their heirs and assigns forever"

ECONOMICS OF LAND INTERESTS

To this point, the discussion of land interests has centered around the legal rights and responsibilities provided for each type of interest. These legal protections are a central concept in the law of real property. However, the basis for these protections can be traced to economic factors. The following excerpt explains the economic rationale for real property rights and protections.

An Economic Theory of Property Rights

Richard Posner

Imagine a society in which all property rights have been abolished. A farmer plants corn, fertilizes it, and erects scarecrows, but when the corn is ripe his neighbor reaps it and sells it. The farmer has no legal remedy against his neighbor's conduct since he owns neither the land that he sowed nor the crop. After a few such incidents the cultivation of land will be abandoned and the society will shift to methods of subsistence (such as hunting) that involve less preparatory investment.

This example suggests that the legal protection of property rights has an important economic function: to create incentives to use resources efficiently. Although the value of the crop in our example, as measured by consumer willingness to pay, may have greatly exceeded the cost in labor, materials, and foregone alternative uses of the land, without property rights there is no incentive to incur these costs because there is no reasonably assured reward for incurring them. The proper incentives are created by the parceling out among the members of society of mutually exclusive rights to the use of particular resources. If every piece of land is owned by someone in the sense that there is always an individual who can exclude all others from access to any given area, then individuals will endeavor by cultivation or other improvements to maximize the value of the land.

The creation of exclusive rights is a necessary rather than sufficient condition for the efficient use of resources. The rights must be transferable. Suppose the farmer in our example owns the land that he sows but is a bad farmer; his land would be more productive in someone else's hands. The maximization of value requires a mechanism by which the farmer can be induced to transfer rights in the property to someone who can work it more productively. A transferable right is such a mechanism.

An example will illustrate. Farmer A owns a piece of land that he anticipates will yield him $100 a year, in excess of labor and other costs, indefinitely. The value of the right to a stream of future earnings can be expressed as a present sum. Just as the price of a share of common stock expresses the present value of the anticipated earnings to which the shareholder will be entitled, so the present value of a parcel of land that yields an annual net income of $100 can be calculated and is the minimum price that A will accept in exchange for his property right. Farmer B thinks he could net more than $100 a year from working A's land. The present value of B's higher expected earnings stream will, of course, exceed the present value calculated by A. Assume the present value calculated by A is $1000 and by B $1500. Then the sale of the

Reprinted with permission from Little, Brown and Company: *An Economic Analysis of Law.*

property by A to B will yield benefits to both parties if the price is anywhere between $1000 and $1500. At a price of $1250, for example, A receives $250 more than the land is worth to him and B pays $250 less than the land is worth to him. Thus, there are strong incentives for the parties voluntarily to exchange A's land for B's money, and if B is as he believes a better farmer than A, the transfer will result in an increase in the productivity of the land. Through a succession of such transfers, resources are shifted to their highest valued, most productive uses and efficiency in the use of economic resources is maximized.

The foregoing discussion suggests three criteria of an efficient system of property rights. The first is universality. Ideally, all resources should be owned, or ownable, by someone, except resources so plentiful that everybody can consume as much of them as he wants without reducing consumption by anyone else (sunlight is good, but no perfect example—why?). No issue of efficient use arises in such a case.

The second criterion—is exclusivity. We have assumed so far that either the farmer can exclude no one or he can exclude everyone, but of course there are intermediate stages: the farmer may be entitled to exclude private individuals from reaping his crop, but not the government in time of war. It might appear that the more exclusive the property right, the greater the incentive to invest the right amount of resources in the development of the property.

The third criterion of an efficient system of property rights is transferability. If a property right cannot be transferred, there is no way of shifting a resource from a less productive to a more productive use through voluntary exchange. The costs of transfer may be high to begin with; a legal prohibition against transferring may, depending on the penalties for violation, make the costs utterly prohibitive.

Discussion Questions

1. How do property rights serve to protect landowners?
2. Why is it sometimes more economically efficient for a property owner to transfer property?
3. What are the three criteria for an efficient system of property rights?

Note: For the answer to the question on the exclusivity of sunlight see Chapter 4.

Land Interests—Some Precautions

Knowledge of the information in this chapter will most often be needed in situations where land titles are being transferred. In the case of a transfer, all parties (buyers, sellers, brokers, agents, and financiers) need to analyze the transfer by checking the following issues:

1. What type of interest does the seller hold?
2. If there are restrictions on the transfer, what are they? Is there a risk that land title could be lost?
3. Does the seller have the right and ability to transfer the property? Can the seller transfer full title or simply a lesser interest, such as a life estate?
4. What type of language is being used in the conveyance? Is the buyer getting a fee simple absolute or a life estate? Are restrictions being imposed upon the buyer?

An examination of the land records (discussed in Chapter 12) should provide the parties with answers to most of the above questions. The important point is that the answers be found before the transaction is completed.

KEY TERMS

freehold	fee tail special
fee	life estate
fee simple absolute	life estate pur autre vie
fee simple defeasible	life tenants
fee simple determinable	tenancy for years
fee simple subject to a condition subsequent	periodic tenancy
	tenancy at will
fee tail	tenancy at sufferance
fee tail general	

CHAPTER PROBLEMS

1. Name all of the land interests that are transferable.
2. Name all of the land interests that are inheritable.
3. Define the terms *fee* and *freehold*.
4. Alfreda's commercial unit 2-year lease expired on 31 January 1988. Alfreda continued to use and possess the unit and paid the usual rent for February, March, and April. Applying the common law, discuss the type or types of tenancies involved since 31 January 1988. Discuss Alfreda's landlord's rights in these circumstances.
5. What types of land interests are created by the following examples?
   a. "To A and his heirs, so long as the property is used for nonresidential purposes."
   b. "To my niece Carla Corleone for the time that she uses the property for an olive oil warehouse."

    c. "To the City of Mesa on the condition that the property always be used for a city park."

    d. "To Canyon State University provided a golf course be built on the property."

6. Which of the following are rights of life tenants?

    a. Selling the property

    b. Mortgaging the property

    c. Committing waste

    d. Possession

7. Annie Potts made the following grant in her will: "To my daughter and all of her female issue so long as the property is used for a shelter for abused women." On Annie's death, who holds what interests?

8. Steven Stolarick made the following grant: "To my sons so long as they permit their mother to live on the property and provide her with clothing but if they fail in meeting this condition, this grant shall be null and void." What type of interest was created?

9. What is the difference between a holder life estate and a life estate pur autre vie?

10. Which interest gives the grantor automatic termination, determinable or condition subsequent?

3

FUTURE INTERESTS
IN REAL ESTATE

At the death of my wife, SALLY, all my real property shall vest in my son, FRANK: PROVIDED That he has lawful issue. If he does not have lawful issue then he shall have the said realty for his natural life only.

The above epigraph provides for the creation of land interests in Frank at some future time. The grant language used does not create any of the types of land interests discussed in Chapter 2, which discussed present land interests only. In reality there is a second group of land interests that fits into the organizational scheme of Figure 2.1, which consists of future land interests or interests that will exist or become possessive at some time after the grant is made. Figure 3.1 reflects the full scheme of property ownership.

In this chapter the following questions are answered:

- What types of future interests exist?
- To what present land interests do they correspond? What are the rights of future interest holders?
- What language is necessary to create a valid interest?

Figure 3.2 summarizes the future interests this chapter discusses and their interrelationships with the present interests discussed in Chapter 2.

41

Figure 3.1 *Present and Future Land Interests*

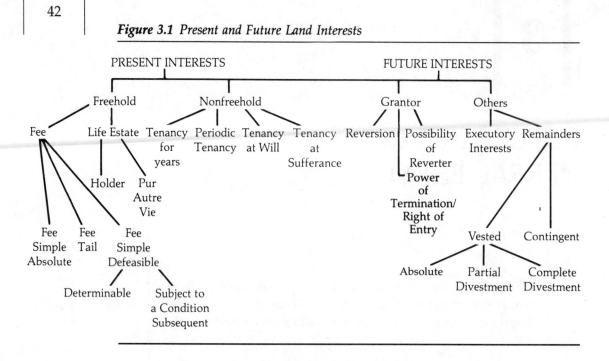

TYPES OF FUTURE INTERESTS

Possibility of Reverter

In the discussion of fee simple determinable it was stated that when the grantor's expressed desire was violated, the grantee's interest terminated. For example, suppose the grant is made, "To A so long as the property is used for residential purposes." The rule for fee simple determinable requires that upon A's violation of the restriction, A's interest terminates and title to the property reverts to the grantor. This potential loss of title is a future interest called the *possibility of reverter*.

At common law, grantors are free to transfer their possibilities of reverter any time while alive (inter vivos), and their reverters pass upon their death (testamentary) to their heirs or devisees. Many states have now passed statutes regulating the possibility of reverter. In some states this future interest cannot be transferred or inherited. In others statutes have been enacted that restrict the possibility of reverter by placing a time limit on validity of the interest—in many states the maximum is 40 years. Still other states require the grantor or holder of the interest to periodically re-record a notice that the interest exists. All of these state-enacted statutes are notice systems, which are tremendous helps in land transactions because the future interests of others can be determined with-

Figure 3.2 *Interrelationships of Present and Future Interests*

PRESENT INTERESTS	CREATION LANGUAGE	GRANTOR OR FUTURE INTERESTS	OTHERS' FUTURE INTERESTS
Fee Simple absolute	"To A" "To A and his heirs"	None	None
Fee tail	"To A and the heirs of his body" "To A and the female heirs of her body" "To A and the heirs of his body and his wife J"	Reversion if no heirs	None
Fee simple determinable	"To A so long as the property is used for church purposes"	Possibility of reverter	Executory interest
Fee simple subject to a condition subsequent	"To A on the condition that the property is used for church purposes"	Right of entry Power of termination	Executory interest
Life estate/holder	"To A for life"	Reversion	Executory interest Remainder
Life estate pur autre vie	"To A for the life of B"	Reversion	Executory interest Remainder

out having to examine the granting language in each deed transferring title to the property.

Right of Entry/Power of Termination

When the present interest of a fee simple subject to a condition subsequent is created, the grantor is permitted to re-enter the property and take possession if the grantee violates the terms of the condition. For example, the following language creates a fee simple subject to a condition subsequent in the grantee, but also reserves an interest for the grantor: "To my niece Sally on the condition that liquor never be served on the premises, and should liquor ever be served,

I reserve the right to re-enter and take possession of and title to the property." Sally holds the present interest of a fee simple subject to a condition subsequent, but the grantor/uncle holds a future interest called a *right of entry* or *power of termination*.

The distinction between right of entry and the possibility of reverter is that right of entry requires some action on the part of the grantor to be effective, whereas the grantor's rights are automatic with a possibility of reverter.

At common law, the right of entry could not be transferred inter vivos (while the grantor is alive) but could be transferred at death. Some states have passed statutes that vary these common law rules. However, at common law and in most states, the grantor is permitted to transfer the right of entry to the present interest holder of the fee simple subject to a condition subsequent. If such a transfer is made, the present and future interests merge, and the present holder of the fee simple subject to a condition subsequent will then hold a fee simple absolute interest. In the example, if Sally's uncle conveyed his interest to her, Sally would then have a fee simple absolute. As with the fee simple determinable, many states have passed time limitations and recording requirements for the continuing validity of the future right of entry interest. The restrictions and recording requirements are similar or identical to those described for possibilities of reverter.

It may be difficult to distinguish between the creation of a possibility of reverter and a right of entry. When re-entry language is used as part of the grant, the task of determining the type of future interest created is easy. However, in the absence of such language the distinction is a fine one, and several judicial rules for interpretation have developed. First the courts will examine the entire document to determine the grantor's intent. They will also look for certain phrases and words that are used as keys in determining the type of interest created. For example, language such as "until," "so long as," or "for so long" indicates a possibility of reverter. Language such as "but," "provided that," or "on the condition that" indicates a right of entry. In many states the issue of which type of interest is created is resolved by a presumption in favor of the right of entry, because this type of future interest requires some action on the part of the parties to affect title to the property and does not have the immediate effect on title that a possibility of reverter would have.

(3.1) Consider:

In 1949, Log Cabin Association, Inc. conveyed to Jackson County Board of Education a parcel of land using the following language:

> TO HAVE AND TO HOLD the above-released premises, subject to the
> right of way reserved therein, unto the party of the second part and its

successors and assigns to it and their only proper use and behoof forever; so that neither the party of the first part nor any other person in its name and behalf shall or will hereafter claim or demand any right or title to said premises or any part thereof by virtue of any claim or right now existing in the party of the first part shall, by these presents, be excluded and forever barred, upon the condition that in the event a new public school building is not erected upon the above described land within a period of two (2) years from the date of this deed or in the event that at any time thereafter the premises hereby dedicated should cease to be used for public school purposes, then and in either of those events, the premises hereby dedicated shall revert to the party of the first part, its successors and assigns.

In 1962, Log Cabin Association conveyed by warranty deed its interest in the school property "subject to the restrictions" noted in the deed to Kelley W. Byars. In 1964, Byars transferred his interest to C. Shelby Dale. Also in 1964, Dale conveyed the interest to Anderson.

In 1963, Log Cabin Association was dissolved and it provided that all assets be distributed to the Samuel H. Kress Foundation. In 1978, the Kress Foundation executed a deed purporting to give its "contingent reversionary interest" originally held by Log Cabin Association to the Jackson County School Board.

Who owns what and could the School Board now sell a clean title to the property? *Anderson v. Jackson County Board of Education,* 333 S.E.2d 533 (N.C. 1985)

(3.2) Consider:

Determine what types of future and present interests are created by the following language:

a. "To A so long as the premises are used for church purposes."

b. "To A and his heirs provided that the premises never be used for commercial purposes."

c. "To Cal Trans so long as the land is used for the construction of an off-ramp for access to Harrah's Club Casino."

Reversions

A *reversion* is a future interest in the grantor arising when the grantor has given someone else a lesser estate, that is, something less than a fee simple absolute. For example, when the grantor makes the grant, "To A for life," the present life estate of A will terminate upon A's death. At that point the land must be transferred to someone, and in this case it will transfer or revert to the grantor.

Thus, all during A's life estate the grantor has a future interest called a reversion. Other types of conveyances that would give the grantor a reversion include fee tails and the nonfreehold estates. For example, at the termination of any type of tenancy the land reverts to the grantor.

Remainders

A *remainder* is a future interest created in one other than the grantor. It is also a future interest that must follow a life estate or a fee tail. An example of language creating a remainder would be, "To A for life, then to B." B holds the remainder interest, which is a future interest, because the interest becomes possessory only upon the death of A. In this example the grantor has given what would have been a reversion to another, thereby creating a remainder. Two types of remainders may be created: vested and contingent.

Vested Remainders A *vested remainder* is one given to persons ascertained and in existence who have the immediate right to the land interest upon termination of the prior freehold estate. In the example "To A for life, then to B," B holds a vested remainder because (1) B is ascertained and in existence at the time of the grant and (2) B will have the immediate right to the estate upon A's death. B's remainder is an example of one that is absolutely vested. Two other types of vested remainders that may be created are *vested remainder subject to partial divestment* and *vested remainder subject to complete divestment*.

To illustrate vested subject to partial divestment, the following grant can be used: "To A for life, then to the children of B." A vested remainder exists if B is alive and has one child. However, the possibility exists that B will have additional children during A's life estate. Thus, B's child holds a vested interest but could be divested of one-half or two-thirds of the interest should B have one or two more children before A's death. Thus if A dies when B has three children, each child would receive a one-third interest. If A dies when B has one child, that child would receive the full interest. The potential for loss of part of the interest is referred to as divestment. Since the child of B who is in existence will never lose the full interest, the divestment can be only partial. The vested remainder created in the example when B is still alive is a vested remainder subject to partial divestment.

Vested remainder subject to complete divestment is illustrated by the language, "To A for life, then to B, but if B is not married, then to C." At the termination of A's life interest, B, ascertained and in existence at the time of the grant, will have a possessory interest. However, B could lose the interest by not marrying prior to A's death. In this instance B not only is divested of a portion of the interest, but loses the entire interest if the marriage requirement is not fulfilled at the time of A's death. This type of remainder in B is a vested remainder subject to complete divestment. In the following case, the court deals with an interesting twist in facts in the eventual disposition of property according to a vested subject to complete divestment grant. Note that the language interpreted is that appearing at the beginning of the chapter.

IN RE ESTATE OF MOSES
300 N.E.2d 473 (Ill. 1973)

Elijah Moses died in 1952 and through his will made the following disposition of his property:

All my real and personal property to my wife, SALLY to have and to hold for her natural life. EXCEPT—That my son FRANK, shall have one room in my house at 1906 Ashbury Avenue as his home during the life time of my wife, SALLY. And that my son, FRANK, shall receive the rents from the WEST room in the basement of said house beginning July 15, 1955.

THIRD—At the death of my wife, SALLY all my real property shall vest in my son, FRANK: PROVIDED That he has lawful issue. If he does not have lawful issue then he shall have the said realty for his natural life only.

FOURTH—If my son FRANK dies without issue all my real property shall vest in my nearest blood relative and the nearest blood relative of my deceased wife, LOUISE BURTON MOSES. One-half share to each of our respective heirs.

In 1954, Frank, the son of Elijah and Louise, murdered his stepmother, Sally. Frank was convicted of the murder and served 13 years of his sentence.

John Burton, the son of Sally by a prior marriage, was the executor of her estate, and his distribution of the property of Sally was challenged by Frank and other heirs of Elijah and Louise.

The trial court agreed with John's distribution, and Frank and other relatives appealed.

SULLIVAN, Justice

Burton contends that the court erred in denying her [Sally's] estate an award from the estate of Elijah Moses of a sum equal to the value of her life estate had she lived her natural life. In support of this contention, he argues that because her successor life tenant, Frank Moses, accelerated his own life estate by murdering her, he would be unjustly enriched if Sally's estate did not receive this award. We believe that there is a public policy in this state that no man should profit by his own wrong or his own crime. It is reflected in Section 15a of the Probate Act which provides that an heir who murders an ancestor may not inherit from that ancestor, and under Section 49a which provides that a legacy or devise to a murderer in a victim's will is void.

Here the interest of Frank Moses was contingent upon his surviving Sally Moses and he might have received nothing except for the murder since there is no way of ascertaining with certainty whether he would have survived Sally.

Although there is apparently no decision in this state which extends the public policy against unjust enrichment to one who accelerates his own life interest by murdering a predecessor life tenant, we hold that the public policy should be so extended to prevent such a murderer from gaining any benefit from his crime and we affirm that part of the order holding Frank Moses had no interest in Elijah's estate and we hold that Frank Moses, by virtue of the murder of Sally Moses, is deprived of his life interest under the will of Elijah Moses.

The will of Elijah Moses provided that Frank Moses was to have a room in Elijah's home during the life time of Sally Moses and was also to receive the rents from a basement room from July 15, 1955. These are benefits he acquired before the murder of Sally and because our holding is limited to acquisition of any benefits resulting from the murder, Frank Moses will not be deprived of them. Therefore, the administrator should be directed also . . . to determine:

1. *the value, if any, of the rental of the west basement room for the number of years of the determined life expectancy of Sally Moses and to pay from the balance the amount of that value to Frank Moses, and*

2. *the value, if any, of the use of a room in the home for the number of years of the determined life expectancy of Sally Moses, excluding the number of years Frank Moses was in the penitentiary for her murder, and to pay from the balance the amount of the value to Frank Moses.*

Affirmed in part and reversed in part.

Discussion Questions

1. Who is the life tenant?
2. Who holds the future interest? What specific grant was made?
3. Who was murdered and who did it?
4. What happens to the murderer's future interest? Why?

Contingent Remainders *Contingent remainder* is the opposite of vested remainder. That is, a contingent remainder is one in which the taker of the interest is unascertained or the interest has a condition precedent to its existence and thus does not pass automatically upon the termination of the prior estate. An example of a contingent remainder that is classified as such because its takers are unascertained would be, "To A for life, remainder to the children of B [a bachelor with no children]." It is possible that B may have children at the time of A's death and the children would be entitled to their interest, but at the time of the grant the takers (nonexistent children) are unascertained.

An example of a contingent remainder that is classified as such because of a condition precedent would be, "To A for life, then if B is married, to B." In this example, B's interest does not automatically follow A's death for B must comply with the condition precedent of marriage to obtain the interest. There is a fine distinction between a condition precedent contingent remainder and a vested remainder subject to a complete divestment. That distinction is that a condition preceding the remainder makes the remainder contingent whereas a condition following the remainder makes the remainder subject to complete divestment.

If a contingent remainder fails (B is not married or has no children), the interest would revert to the grantor. Thus, when a contingent remainder future interest is created, a reversion or interest in the grantor is also created.

All types of remainders are transferable both inter vivos and at death. Obviously a conveyance at death would be invalid if a condition of survival were attached to the remainder.

(3.3) Consider:

Determine what types of present and future interests are involved in the following grants. Be sure to classify remainders according to their type, vested (partial or complete divestment) or contingent:

a. "To A for life, then to B." *absolute vested remainder*

b. "To A for life, then to B and her heirs." — *absolute vested remainder*

c. "To B for life, then if A is married, to A." — *A contingent remainder — grantor. condition precedence — reversion*

d. "To A for life, then to B's heirs." (B is alive.) — *Contingent remainder — unascertained — B heir's*

e. "To A for life, then to B, but if B does not survive A, to C." — *VESTED REMAINDER*   *EXECUTORY INTEREST*

Executory Interests

In the preceding example e, a third party, C, has an interest that cannot be identified from the prior discussions of future interests. In this example, C holds an executory interest. An *executory interest* is a future interest created in one other than the grantor that is not a remainder. An executory interest is not vested at the time the grantor makes the grant and is considered to be vested only when it becomes possessory. An executory interest usually arises in one of three circumstances. The first circumstance is when a fee simple determinable or a fee simple subject to a condition subsequent is given to two parties at the same time. For example, a grant "To A, so long as the premises are never used for commercial purposes and if they are so used, then to B," creates a fee simple defeasible interest in A and an executory interest in B. B's interest does not follow a life estate and is not a remainder. Further, B's interest is similar to a right of reversion or right of entry, but B is not a grantor; hence, B's interest must be an executory interest.

The second circumstance that causes an executory interest occurs when the grantor creates a gap between present and future interests. An example would be: "To A for life, then 1 year after A's death, to B." B has a life estate but does not have a remainder because there is no immediate vesting of B's interest. The gap of 1 year causes B to hold an executory interest.

The third circumstance occurs when the grantor creates some future freehold estate, for example, "To A in 10 years." No present interest is created, and the 10-year future interest cannot be classified as a grantor's interest because A is not the grantor. The interest is not a remainder because it does not follow another estate. Thus, A holds an executory interest.

RULES GOVERNING FUTURE INTERESTS

There are three rules or doctrines relating to future interests that developed as common law in England and still apply to the construction and use of future interests: the Rule in Shelley's Case, the Doctrine of Worthier Title, and the Rule Against Perpetuities.

Rule in Shelley's Case

The *Rule in Shelley's Case* applies to grants made with the language, "To A for life, remainder to the heirs of A." If the rules set forth in the preceding discussion were followed, A would have a life estate and the heirs would have a contingent remainder since heirs are unascertainable until the death of A. The Rule in Shelley's Case requires the merger of the present and future interests, with the result that A will have a fee simple absolute. Some states have passed legislation eliminating the effect of the Rule in Shelley's Case so that the present and future interests are not merged.

Doctrine of Worthier Title

The *Doctrine of Worthier Title* applies to grants with the language, "To A for life, remainder to the heirs of the grantor." Following the future interest rules, A would have a life estate and the heirs would have either a vested remainder or contingent remainder (depending on whether the grant was inter vivos or testamentary). However, under the Doctrine of Worthier Title, A has a life estate, the heirs have no interest, and the grantor holds a reversion. Legislation in some states has eliminated this doctrine or has permitted courts to determine the grantor's true intent in making the grant.

Rule Against Perpetuities

The basic idea of the *Rule Against Perpetuities* is to limit the length of time during which grantors may control the transfer, conveyance, and vesting of land interests. The purpose is to ensure that property is not tied to the grave and its transferability and flexibility in use restricted. However, the rule is arbitrary in application, applying only to contingent remainders and executory interests.

Generally stated the rule provides that an interest is good only if it vests no later than 21 years after the death of the last individual who is part of the group of measuring lives for the grant. A measuring life is defined as the lifetime of individuals named in the grant. Vesting is defined as the absolute right to receive property, not actual possession. If the 21-year vesting rule is violated by a grant, the grant is lost and title reverts to the grantor or the grantor's estate to be distributed according to the grantor's desires or according to state law if no will exists.

To understand the application of the rule, it is best to explain each portion of the rule in the context of an example. Here we will use the grant, made in a will, "To my children for life, remainder to any and all of my grandchildren who reach age 21" as the example for working through the rule's application:

- *Step One—Determine the type of interest involved.* The children have a life estate. The grandchildren are unascertained (more could be born during the children's life estate) and therefore hold a contingent remainder. Furthermore, because there is a potential gap between the life estate of the children and the grandchildren (who must be 21), the grandchildren's interest could be classified as an executory interest.

- *Step Two—Determine whether the Rule Against Perpetuities is applicable.* Because the Rule Against Perpetuities applies to both contingent remainders and executory interests, the rule is applicable to the grandchildren's interests.

- *Step Three—Determine when the interest would vest.* The interest would vest when the last grandchild reached age 21.

- *Step Four—Determine the measuring lives in being.* At the time of the will's grant, the children are alive and thus would be the measuring lives for purposes of the 21-year rule for vesting.

- *Step Five—Determine whether all interests will vest within 21 years after the death of the last measuring life. Consider all possibilities of birth and survival.* Upon the death of the last child, there can be no more grandchildren. Thus, the longest it can take for a grandchild's interest to vest is 21 years after the death of the last child. (Gestation periods are not included in the 21 years.)

- *Step Six—Determine if the Rule Against Perpetuities is violated.* Because all grandchildren will have the interest vested within 21 years after the lives in being of the other children, the Rule Against Perpetuities is not violated and the grant is valid.

(3.4) Consider:

Determine whether the Rule Against Perpetuities is violated by the following grant, made while the grantor is alive, "To my children for life, remainder to any and all of my grandchildren who reach age 21." Be sure to use the six steps in your analysis.

Because this complex rule could present difficulties in wills and other transfers, some states have passed statutes eliminating the rule or restricting its harsh effects. Even in states without such legislation, the effect of the Rule of Perpetuities can be avoided simply by placing a *saving clause* in the will or grant of property. A saving clause either provides an alternative for distribution should the grant violate the rule or provides that the grant is to be interpreted so as to avoid violation of the rule. To make confusion about the rule less embarrassing, consider that violation of the Rule Against Perpetuities in drafting wills and trusts is the largest area of malpractice litigation for estate-planning attorneys.

Figure 3.3 summarizes the future interests, their related present interests, their language of creation, and the rules that govern them.

THE PRESENT VALUE OF FUTURE INTERESTS

One point about future interests should be perfectly clear—they are complicated beasts. However, this brief overview of a complicated field is intended to help the student, broker, agent, or financier to recognize restrictions on property use and transfer. If a property to be sold is being transferred with a condition subsequent, all parties need to be aware of the grantor's restriction and potential interest. Failure to spot such a restriction and inform the parties can result in misunderstandings, complications, and even liability lawsuits. The ability to recognize the complications a future interest can impose on property may help in making the right buying or selling decision, or may provide an opportunity for giving sound advice.

For example, if you buy a possibility of reverter, there is a likelihood that the purchase will never have any value as long as the present owner complies with the restriction or restrictions imposed by the grantor. On the other hand, if a future and present interest can be merged, then the value of the land interest can be increased. If a landowner who is subject to use limitations under a fee simple determinable that he holds acquires the possibility of reverter from the grantor or the grantor's heirs, he has just transformed his fee simple determinable into a fee simple absolute. The knowledge of present and future interests can be used not only to avoid paying too much for an interest that may never

Figure 3.3 Summary of the Creation and Rules of Future Interests

FUTURE INTEREST	RELATED PRESENT INTERESTS	CREATION	APPLICABILITY OF RULES
Possibility of reverter	Fee simple determinable	"To A so long as the property is used for church purposes"	Some state limitations and filing requirements
Right of entry/ power of termination	Fee simple subject to a condition subsequent	"To A on the condition that the property is used for church purposes"	Some state limitations and filing requirements
Reversion	Life estate/fee tail	"To A for life" "To A for the life of B"	Doctrine of Worthier Title
Vested remainder	Life estate	"To A for life, then to B"	Rule in Shelley's Case Doctrine of Worthier Title
Vested subject to partial divestment	Life estate	"To A for life, then to B's children" (B is alive, with two children)	Rule in Shelley's Case Doctrine of Worthier Title
Vested subject to complete divestment	Life estate	"To A for life, then to B, but if B is not married, to C"	
Contingent remainder	Life estate	"To A for life, then to B's children" (B is a bachelor) "To A for life, then if B is married, to B"	Rule Against Perpetuities
Executory interest	Life estate Fee simple defeasible Fee tail	"To A for life, then in 10 years to B" To B in 10 years"	Rule Against Perpetuities

exist but also to maximize the value of land by understanding how to combine present and future interests to create a full land interest—the fee simple absolute.

KEY TERMS

possibility of reverter	vested remainder subject to
right of entry	complete divestment
power of termination	contingent remainder
reversion	executory interest
remainder	Rule in Shelley's Case
vested remainder	Doctrine of Worthier Title
vested remainder subject to partial	Rule Against Perpetuities
divestment	saving clause

CHAPTER PROBLEMS

1. Moise Dreyfus died in 1937, leaving a widow, a daughter, and a son. By his will a separate trust was set up for each child under which income was payable to the widow for life and then to the particular child for life, with the remainder to be distributed as the child should appoint by will. What types of interests were created by the will provisions?

2. Edwin Duncan, Sr., passed away and left a will that provided for the creation of a trust, with the income to go to Edwin Duncan, Jr., for life. Upon the death of Edwin Duncan, Jr., the income was to go to Bessie Lee Duncan (the wife of the younger Edwin) for her life. Upon the death of Bessie Lee, the income was to go to Jane Cannon Duncan for her life, and upon her death the trust was to be terminated and all amounts distributed equally among the then-living grandchildren of Edwin Duncan, Sr. What estates have been created?

3. In each of the following, determine what type of present and future interests are created, and also the applicability of any of the three rules: the Rule in Shelley's Case, the Doctrine of Worthier Title, and the Rule Against Perpetuities. (Key G = grantor; L/E = life estate; rem = remainder.)

   a. G_____ L/E_____→ A

   _____L/E_____→ A's widow

   rem to A's children living at the death of the widow

   b. G_____ L/E_____→ A

   c. G_____→ A and her heirs on the condition that liquor never be sold on the premises

d. G____ L/E_____→ A
                        └____→ rem to B and his heirs if B shall sur-
                              vive A

Suppose A (during her lifetime) gave D the right to use the land for 10 years. What type of estate would be created?

e. G_____→ A so long as liquor is not sold on the premises
Suppose G later left all his interest to A. What type of estate would be created?

f. G_____→ A when A reaches age 25

g. G____ L/E_____→ A (80 years old)
                        └__L/E____→ children for life

                              rem to grandchildren

h. G____ L/E_____→ A
                        └____→ B and his heirs but if B shall
                              predecease A
                                    └____→ C

i. G____ L/E_____→ A_____→ heirs of A

j. G____ L/E_____→ A_____→ B if B lives to attain the age of 30
                                    years (B is 5 years old)

4. Is there any future interest created by the following language? *U.S. Trust Co. of New York v. State,* 529 A.2d 1035 (N.J. 1987)

> And whereas, the said Secretary of the Treasury deems it advisable to acquire, on behalf of the United States, the right to use and occupy the hereinafter-described lot of land as a site for a Life-Saving Station, . . . With full right of egress and ingress thereto in any direction over other lands of the grantor by those in employ of the United States, on foot or with vehicles of any kind, with boats or any articles used for the purpose of carrying out the intentions of Congress in providing for the establishment of Life-Saving Stations, and the right to pass over any lands of the grantor in any manner in the prosecution of said purpose . . .

5. Compute the type of real property interest that results from the following equations involving the addition of estates:

   a. Life estate + vested remainder
   b. Fee simple determinable + possibility of reverter
   c. Life estate + contingent remainder
   d. Fee simple determinable + reversion
   e. Fee simple subject to a condition subsequent + right of entry

4

EXTENT OF REAL ESTATE INTERESTS

The owner of the soil owns also to the sky and to the depths [Cujus est solum ejus est usque ad coelum et ad inferos]

—Blackstone

Fee simple, fee tail, remainder estate, and life estate all indicate types of land interests and their transferability. However, these terms do not indicate what parts of the subject land are actually owned by the holders of the interests. For example, there are issues of whether air and subsurface rights are included. This chapter answers the question, How much do these various interest holders own? The focus, therefore, is the determination of what an interest holder owns in the real estate or real property. As the epigraph indicates, the owners of property own far more than just the ground.

EXTENT OF LAND INTERESTS

Attachments

Landholders generally think of themselves as the owners of the ground or soil and any buildings attached to the land. However, there are many additional items present on land, and it must be determined whether these are part of the real property. For example, many pieces of property contain trees, bushes, and grasses, which are referred to as *fructus naturales* and are considered part of the real property. When the land is sold or mortgaged, these naturally growing elements are simultaneously sold or mortgaged.

On the other hand, growing crops or *fructus industriales (emblements)* are not treated as part of the real property; they are instead classified as personal property. These crops must be raised yearly, and they require human labor for cultivation. In recent years, courts have been clear in their position that few, if any, fructus naturales crops are remaining. In most instances and unless specifically excluded, however, growing crops are included in a sale or mortgage of property. If a tenant grows crops on leased property, the crops belong to the tenant even though they may not be ready for harvesting upon the termination of the tenant's lease. This right of removal of crops by the planting tenant is referred to as the *doctrine of emblements*.

Many times personal property becomes attached to the land, and the question arises whether such property passes with title to the land. When personal property is permanently and intentionally attached, it is called a *fixture* and passes with the land. For example, window screens, storm doors, and windows are generally classified as fixtures and pass with the land. (A complete discussion of fixtures is found in Chapter 6.)

Air Rights

As Blackstone stated, the owners of property do own the skies above their property. The discussion of *air rights* can be divided into two topics: (1) a determination of who can use the air and to what extent, and (2) a determination of what air interests can be transferred.

Who Can Use the Air In dealing with topic 1, it must first be noted that the airspace of all property owners is used by others. In addition to constant air traffic in the airspace above property, manufacturers, processors, and auto drivers use the airspace in that their gases, smokes, and fumes invade the airspace in many pieces of property. Landowners enjoy only limited protections in these types of uses in that environmental legislation offers general controls (see Chapter 22), but specific relief for individual landowners often requires suits in nuisance or trespass to be brought. (The concepts of nuisance and trespass are discussed later in this chapter.) The following case is an example of how much the airspace of another can be used and deals with the rights of landowners in preventing and controlling the use of their airspace.

UNITED STATES v. CAUSBY
328 U.S. 256 (1946)

Mr. and Mrs. Causby (referred to as respondents) owned 2.8 acres of land near an airport outside of Greens-boro, North Carolina. On the property were a house (in which the Causbys resided) and various outbuildings used for raising chickens. The end of the airport's northwest–southwest runway was 2220 feet from the Causbys' barn and 2275 feet from their house. The path of glide to the runway passed directly over their property at 67 feet above the house, 63 feet above the barn, and 18 feet above the highest tree. The United States government leased the airstrip in 1942, with the lease carrying renewal provisions until 1967. Bombers, transports, and fighters all used the airfield. At times the airplanes came close enough to blow old leaves off trees, and the noise of the air-

planes was startling. As result of the noise, six to ten of the Causbys' chickens were killed each day by "flying into the walls from fright." After losing 150 chickens, the Causbys gave up their business. The Causbys could no longer sleep well and became nervous and frightened.

The Causbys sued the United States government on the grounds that the United States was taking their airspace by eminent domain without compensating them. The lower court found for the Causbys, and the United States government appealed.

DOUGLAS, Justice

The United States relies on the Air Commerce Act of 1926. Under those statutes the United States has "complete and exclusive national sovereignty in the air space" over this country. They grant any citizen of the United States "a public right of freedom of transit in air commerce through the navigable air space of the United States."

And "navigable air space" is defined as "airspace above the minimum safe altitudes of flight prescribed by the Civil Aeronautics Authority." And it is provided that "such navigable airspace shall be subject to a public right of freedom of interstate and foreign air navigation." It is, therefore, argued that since these flights were within the minimum safe altitudes of flight which had been prescribed, they were an exercise of the declared right of travel through the airspace. The United States concludes that when flights are made within the navigable airspace without any physical invasion of the property of the landowners, there has been no taking of property. It is ancient doctrine that at common law ownership of the land extended to the periphery of the universe—Cujus est solum ejus est usque ad coelum. But that doctrine has no place in the modern world. The air is a public highway, as Congress

has declared. Were that not true, every transcontinental flight would subject the operator to countless trespass suits. Common sense revolts at the idea. To recognize such private claims to the airspace would clog these highways, seriously interfere with their control and development in the public interest, and transfer into private ownership that to which only the public has a just claim.

But the general principle does not control the present case. For the United States conceded on oral argument that if the flights over respondents' property rendered it uninhabitable, there would be a taking compensable under the Fifth Amendment. It is the owner's loss, not the taker's gain, which is the measure of the value of the property taken. Market value fairly determined is the normal measure of the recovery. And that value may reflect the use to which the land could readily be converted, as well as existing use. If, by reason of the frequency and altitude of the flights, respondents could not use this land for any purpose, their loss would be complete. It would be as complete as if the United States had entered upon the surface of the land and taken exclusive possession of it.

The path of glide for airplanes might

reduce a valuable factory site to grazing land, an orchard to a vegetable patch, a residential section to a wheat field. Some value would remain. But the use of the airspace immediately above the land would limit the utility of the land and cause a diminution in its value.

We have said that the airspace is a public highway. Yet it is obvious that if the landowner is to have full enjoyment of the land, he must have exclusive control of the immediate reaches of the enveloping atmosphere. Otherwise buildings could not be erected, trees could not be planted, and even fences could not be run. The principle is recognized when the law gives a remedy in case overhanging structures are erected on adjoining lands. The landowner owns as least as much of the space above the ground as he can occupy or use in connection with the land. The fact that he does not occupy it in a physical sense—by the erection of buildings and the like—is not material. As we have said, the flight of airplanes, which skim the surface but do not touch it, is as much an appropriation of the use of the land as a more conventional entry upon it. We would not doubt that if the United States erected an elevated railway over respondents' land at the precise altitude where its planes now fly, there would be a partial taking even though none of the supports of the structure rested on the land. The reason is that there would be an intrusion so immediate and direct as to subtract from the owner's full enjoyment of the property and to limit his exploitation of it. While the owner does not in any physical manner occupy that stratum of airspace or make use of it in the conventional sense, he does use it in somewhat the same sense that space left between buildings for the purpose of light and air is used. The superadjacent airspace at this low altitude is so close to the land that continuous invasions of it affect the use of the surface of the land itself. We think that the landowner, as an incident to his ownership, has a claim to it and that invasions of it are in the same category as invasions of the surface.

The airplane is part of the modern environment of life, and the inconveniences which it causes are normally not compensable under the Fifth Amendment. The airspace, apart from the immediate reaches above the land, is part of the public domain. We need not determine at this time what those precise limits are. Flights over private land are not a taking, unless they are so low and so frequent as to be a direct and immediate interference with the enjoyment and use of the land. We need not speculate on that phase of the present case. For the findings of the Court of Claims plainly establish that there was a diminution in value of the property and that the frequent, low-level flights were the direct and immediate cause. We agree with the Court of Claims that a servitude has been imposed upon the land.

Affirmed.

Discussion Questions

1. What type of business did the Causbys operate?
2. How close was the airstrip to the Causbys' home?
3. How close were the airplanes (in altitude) upon their runway approach?
4. What happened to the Causbys' chickens as result of the airplanes?
5. What happened to the Causbys as result of the airplanes?
6. Are the Causbys suing for nuisance?
7. What statute does the government say is controlling?
8. Can the use of airspace diminish the value of the surface of the land?
9. Do the Causbys win?

The *Causby* case illustrates the limitations on the use of airspace. The landowner is subject to use of the airspace by air traffic but is entitled to compensation in the event that the airspace is used in such a manner as to prevent use of the surface property. Other uses of airspace can interfere with the land of another. For example, when the eaves of a building or branches from a tree located on one parcel of land hang over onto another landowner's parcel of land, there is a taking of airspace. In the *Causby* case, the court mentioned that a remedy is available for overhang. The property owner affected by the overhang can bring suit for a court order requiring the removal of the eaves or branches, and in some states is even permitted to unilaterally end the invasion by clipping the tree branches.

Additional rights of property owners are affected by the use of airspace. For example, the Fourth Amendment prohibits searches of private property without a warrant. Does the use of airspace to conduct a search of ground surface require a warrant? The United States Supreme Court provides the answer in the following case.[1]

DOW CHEMICAL COMPANY v. UNITED STATES
471 U.S. 130 (1986)

Dow Chemical (petitioner) operates a 2,000 acre chemical plant at Midland, Michigan. The facility, with numerous buildings, conduits, and pipes, is visible from the air. Dow has maintained ground security on the facility and has investigated low-level flights by aircraft. However, none of the buildings or manufacturing equipment is concealed.

In 1978, the Environmental Protection Agency (EPA) conducted an inspection of Dow. EPA requested a second inspection but Dow denied the request. The EPA then employed a commercial aerial photographer to take photos of the plant from 12,000, 3,000, and 1,200 feet. The EPA had no warrant but the plane was always within navigable air space when the photos were taken.

When Dow became aware of the EPA photographer, it brought suit in Federal District Court and challenged the action as a violation of its Fourth Amendment rights. The District Court found the EPA had violated Dow's rights and issued an injunction prohibiting the further use of the aircraft. The Court of Appeals reversed and Dow appealed.

BURGER, Chief Justice
The photographs at issue in this case are essentially like those used in map-making. Any person with an airplane and an aerial camera could readily duplicate them. In

---

[1] This case is adapted from Marianne Jennings, *Business and the Legal Environment* (Boston: PWS-KENT Publishing Company, 1988), 163–64. Reprinted by permission.

common with much else, the technology of photography has changed in this century. These developments have enhanced industrial processes, and indeed all areas of life; they have also enhanced enforcement techniques. Whether they may be employed by competitors to penetrate trade secrets is not a question presented in this case. Governments do not generally seek to appropriate trade secrets of the private sector, and the right to be free of appropriation of trade secrets is protected by law.

That such photography might be barred by state law with regard to competitors, however, is irrelevant to the questions presented here. State tort law governing unfair competition does not define the limits of the Fourth Amendment. The Government is seeking these photographs in order to regulate, not compete with, Dow.

Dow claims first that EPA has no authority to use aerial photography to implement its statutory authority of "site inspection" under the Clean Air Act.

Congress has vested in EPA certain investigatory and enforcement authority, without spelling out precisely how this authority was to be exercised in all the myriad circumstances that might arise in monitoring matters relating to clean air and water standards.

Regulatory or enforcement authority generally carries with it all the modes of inquiry and investigation traditionally employed or useful to execute the authority granted. Environmental standards cannot be enforced only in libraries and laboratories, helpful as those institutions may be.

The EPA, as a regulatory and enforcement agency, needs no explicit statutory provisions to employ methods of observation commonly available to the public at large; we hold that the use of aerial photography is within the EPA's statutory authority.

Affirmed.

DISSENTING OPINION

POWELL, MARSHALL, BRENNAN, BLACKMUN, Justices

The Fourth Amendment protects private citizens from arbitrary surveillance by their Government. Today, in the context of administrative aerial photography of commercial premises, the Court retreats from that standard. It holds that the photography was not a Fourth Amendment "search" because it was not accompanied by a physical trespass and because the equipment used was not the most highly sophisticated form of technology available to the Government. Under this holding the existence of an asserted privacy interest apparently will be decided solely by reference to the manner of surveillance used to intrude on that interest. Such an inquiry will not protect Fourth Amendment rights, but rather will permit their gradual decay as technology advances.

EPA's aerial photography penetrated into a private commercial enclave, an area in which society has recognized that privacy interests may legitimately be claimed. The photographs captured highly confidential information that Dow had taken reasonable and objective steps to preserve as private.

Discussion Questions

1. What of Dow's plant could be seen from the air?
2. Did Dow take any privacy protection steps?
3. Is the EPA specifically given aerial surveillance authority?
4. Did the EPA need a warrant for its aerial photographs?
5. What objection does the dissent raise to the decision?

(4.1) Consider:

Would the ruling in the *Dow* case apply to a search by an airplane that uncovers growing marijuana plants? Are there differences in the rights of landowners in these two cases?

What Air Rights Can Be Transferred The second aspect of landowners' rights in the air is concerned with the ability of landowners to transfer interests in the air located above their property. The air above property is divided into two areas, the *column lot* and the *air lot*. The column lot comprises everything between the earth's surface and an imaginary plane 23 feet above the surface, and the air lot comprises everything above the 23-foot plane. It is possible for landowners to transfer some interest in their column or air lot.

For example, both the column lot and the air lot could be sold for the construction of a large building. Those constructing the building need only have title to small segments of the land surface for the placement of beams, and may even acquire only an easement for the placement of the steel girder foundations of the building. (Easements are discussed in Chapter 5.) In these types of transfers of column and air lots, landowners retain title to the surface but have conveyed their air rights or a portion thereof.

The construction and sale of condominiums is an example of the use and transfer of airspace. When buyers purchase condominiums, they are actually purchasing the airspace located between the walls of their particular units. Ground or surface ownership is not conveyed as part of the title, but the condominium owners do hold real property interests. (See Chapter 21 for a complete discussion of condominiums.)

There are several examples of large buildings constructed through the use of airspace: In Chicago, The Prudential Mid-America building is built in both the air and column lots above the Illinois Central Terminal. In Boston, the 52-story Prudential Tower is built in the column and air lots above the Massachusetts Turnpike. In New York, the 59-story Pan American building is built in the column and air lots above Grand Central Station. These examples illustrate that dividing air and surface ownership enables maximum use of real property.

Light

Corresponding to the ownership of air as part of a real property interest is the ownership of light. In this period of energy-technology development, the issue of who owns the light is becoming a critical one. Suppose the following hypothetical situation has occurred:

> A and B are neighbors. A has installed a series of solar collectors on the roof of her home. The collectors are positioned so that A obtains maximum efficiency in the use of the sun. However, B has decided to plant several trees for backyard shade and within 3 years of planting, the now tall trees are interfering with the collection of sunlight by A's collectors.

In the absence of any statutory right and under common law, A has no legal rights against B unless A can establish that B's conduct was malicious and done with the intent of obstructing light from the collectors.

Many states have passed some statutory protections for the right to light, and New Mexico and Wyoming both grant a statutory right to sunlight (W.S.A. §34-22-101 et seq.). Under the statutes, the first user of light for solar-energy purposes acquires the right to unobstructed continued use. Other states have passed *solar easement laws* that permit the execution and recognition of easements for the protection of solar access.[1] These easement laws do not, however, create or protect solar rights. Some states have encouraged zoning as a tool to be used to incorporate solar access considerations.[2] Other states have enacted statutes that permit solar energy users to petition administrative review boards when adjoining landowners refuse to negotiate solar access easements.[3] Finally, California has passed a shade control act, which makes it a public-nuisance offense to interfere with solar collectors in certain circumstances (Cal. Civ. Code §714 and 801.5).

The courts have undertaken some protection for solar rights through the use of property theories. In *Prah v. Maretti,* 321 N.W.2d 182 (Wis. 1982), the court held, "The law of private nuisance is better suited to resolve landowners' disputes about property development in the 1980s than is a rigid rule which does not recognize a landowner's interest in access to sunlight."

[1]California, Colorado, Florida, Georgia, Idaho, Illinois, Kansas, Maryland, Minnesota, New Jersey, North Dakota, and Virginia.

[2]California, Connecticut, Minnesota, and Oregon.

[3]Iowa and Wisconsin.

64

At common law, the *doctrine of ancient lights* provided protection for the use of light. Under the doctrine, anyone who used the light for an uninterrupted period of 20 years was entitled to protection for use of that light, and obstruction was prohibited. However, this doctrine has been rejected by the American courts with most courts following the ruling set forth in the following light-obstruction case.

FONTAINEBLEAU HOTEL CORP. v. FORTY-FIVE TWENTY-FIVE, INC.
114 So.2d 357 (Fla. 1959)

The Fontainebleau, a luxury hotel, was constructed in Miami facing the Atlantic Ocean in 1954. In 1955, the Eden Roc, another luxury hotel, was constructed adjoining the Fontainebleau and also facing the Atlantic Ocean. Shortly after the construction of the Eden Roc, in 1955, the Fontainebleau undertook the construction of a 14-story addition to extend 160 feet in height and 416 feet in length running from east to west. During the winter months from about 2:00 in the afternoon and for the remainder of the day, the shadow of the addition would extend over the cabana, swimming pool, and sunbathing areas of the Eden Roc.

The Eden Roc (Forty-Five Twenty-Five Corp., plaintiff/appellee) brought suit against the Fontainebleau Hotel Corp. (defendant/appellant) to stop construction of the addition after eight stories had been constructed. The Eden Roc alleged the construction would interfere with their sunlight, cast a shadow, and interfere with the guests' use and enjoyment of the property. The Eden Roc further alleged the construction of the addition was done with malice. The trial court found for Eden Roc. Fontainebleau appealed.

PER CURIAM

It is well settled that a property owner may put his own property to any reasonable and lawful use, so long as he does not thereby deprive the adjoining landowner of any right of enjoyment of his property which is recognized and protected by law, and so long as his use is not such a one as the law will pronounce a nuisance.

No American decision has been cited, and independent research has revealed none, in which it has been held that—in the absence of some contractual or statutory obligation—a landowner has a legal right to the free flow of light and air across the adjoining land of his neighbor.

Even at common law, the landowner had no legal right, in the absence of an easement or uninterrupted use and enjoyment for a period of 20 years, to unobstructed light and air from the adjoining land.

There being, then, no legal right to the free flow of light and air from the adjoining land, it is universally held that where a structure serves a useful and beneficial purpose, it does not give rise to a cause of action, either for damages or for an injunction even though it causes injury to another by cutting off the light and air and interfering with the view that would otherwise be available over adjoining land in its natural state, regardless of the fact that the structure may have been erected partly for spite.

We see no reason for departing from this universal rule. If, as contended on behalf of plaintiff, public policy demands that a landowner in the Miami Beach area are [*sic*] to refrain from constructing buildings on his premises that will cast a shadow on the adjoining premises, an amendment of its comprehensive planning and zoning ordinance, applicable to the public as a whole, is the means by which such purpose should be achieved.

The record affirmatively shows that no statutory basis for the right sought to be enforced by plaintiff exists. The so-called Shadow Ordinance enacted by the City of Miami Beach at plaintiff's behest was held invalid in *City of Miami Beach v. State* ex rel. *Fontainebleau Hotel Corp.* It also affirmatively appears that there is no possible basis for holding that plaintiff has an easement for light and air, either express or implied, across defendant's property, nor any prescriptive right thereto—even if it be assumed, arguendo, that the common-law right of prescription as to "ancient lights" is in effect in this state. And from what we have said heretofore in this opinion, it is perhaps superfluous to add that we have no desire to dissent from the unanimous holding in this country repudiating the English doctrine of ancient lights.

Reversed.

Discussion Questions

1. Who owns the Eden Roc?
2. Who brought the original suit?
3. Why was the suit brought?
4. Will the court recognize the doctrine of ancient lights?
5. Will the court recognize an easement?
6. What remedy does the court suggest?
7. Who wins on appeal?

Today the *Fontainebleau* case is considered an extreme view in response to the question of whether landowners have a right to light. Many courts have begun to use a theory of prescriptive easements (see Chapter 5) or one of nuisance (discussed later in the chapter) to afford some protection for a landowner's light.

However, there are still only limited statutory and judicial protections afforded for solar access, so it is easy to conclude that parties desiring to maintain rights to light should do so through the execution of private agreements with adjoining landowners that will give them easements for such rights. Some mortgage lenders that are lending for property with solar panels will require such easements to be obtained before the mortgage money will be advanced to the borrower. However, in spite of the need for such easements many parties do not take the time to protect their rights. Recent surveys reveal that 95 percent of all owners of solar-energy systems have not obtained easements for the protection of sunlight.

If an easement for light is executed, the document should carefully specify the extent of the easement. Setting forth the purpose (for solar panels, windows, or a swimming pool) indicates the intent of the parties as to the extent and scope of the easement. Including the times of day when the sun is to be unobstructed will make the rights of the parties clear and can limit the burden on the adjoining land. An easement may be required from more than just the adjoining landowners because light obstructions can come from larger structures located some distance away. Establishing rights and remedies for obstruction in the parties' agreement can prevent litigation later. The agreement should set forth in detail the types of structures (height, width and so on) that cannot be constructed. Finally, every agreement and easement should comply with any statutory restrictions.

Mineral/Subsurface Rights

The preceding discussion centered on ownership of rights above the land. This section deals with the second part of Blackstone's famous quote, which is the ownership of subsurface rights. Ordinarily landowners own to the center of the earth, so that *mineral rights* are included in fee simple absolute ownership. However, landowners are free to convey their subsurface rights as liberally as the air rights can be conveyed.

Oil and Gas Ownership Perhaps the most frequently transferred types of mineral rights are those relating to oil and gas. Although frequently referred to as oil and gas leases, such agreements do not result in a landlord–tenant relationship. Rather, the transfer of these rights is generally classified under one of two categories. In the first category, the *incorporeal hereditament* or *profit a prendre* theory, the right of removal of all of the agreed-on minerals is conveyed to the transferee. In the second category, the transferee is given a fee simple determinable interest in all of the oil and gas. Both categories have similarities in that both recognize the *rule of capture* that permits the owners of tracts or their designees to take all oil and gas drawn from wells on the tract even though the oil and gas may have been drawn from deposits located beneath adjoining tracts. In those states recognizing the rule of capture, there are limitations on the number of wells that can be drilled per tract of land and there may also be limitations on the amount of oil or gas that can be drawn from each drilled well.

A second similarity between the two categories is that leases are treated as real property interests and must be executed according to the requirements for land leases. The distinction between a standard lease and an oil or gas lease must still be made: a lease is a nonfreehold interest, while a profit a prendre is a freehold, transferable interest.

Terms in Oil and Gas Leases There are several items that must be included in oil and gas leases so that both parties are protected. A summary of several basic items is as follows:

1. *Granting clause* This clause will provide the transferee with the mineral rights. Minerals included in the lease should be listed. Many agreements will list "oil and gas and other minerals" as a description of the rights being given. Courts disagree, however, as to what is included with "other minerals." The list should be specific and cover items such as copper, silver, gold, gypsum, limestone, gravel, coal, and iron. Without such a listing, courts will often limit "other minerals" to the types that would cause the same amount of damage to remove as those minerals specifically listed. For example, in *Western Nuclear, Inc. v. Andrus*, 664 F.2d 234 (10th Cir. 1981), the court held that gravel was not included in "other minerals." A granting clause will also set forth how the transferee can use the surface of the land to obtain the minerals: how much equipment can be used, how much land can be used, and whether any damage to the surface must be corrected. Frequently the parties will include a Mother Hubbard clause, which is a clause designed to give the transferee all subsurface rights in the land owned by the transferor.

2. *Consideration clause* This is the portion of the lease in which the parties set forth payment terms. Within the consideration clause there will be a *royalty clause*, which serves to give the lessor a certain percentage of the profits from the mining (usually a one-eighth interest on private lands). Sometimes the lessor will be offered an advance bonus as an inducement for the lease. Many consideration clauses will include a delay rental provision, which allows the lessor to collect rent (usually a dollar amount per acre) when there is no production.

3. *Habendum clause* This clause establishes the length of the lease, the grounds for termination of the lease, and the penalties for delays in drilling.

Geothermal Energy One relatively minor problem in the area of subsurface rights is that of geothermal resources, because of the difficulty of classifying them. Because *geothermal energy* consists of steam in rock-surrounded pockets, some states classify it as a water resource and use their water laws to determine ownership and other rights, while other states classify it as an energy resource similar to oil or coal and treat it as a mineral. However, in *United States v. Union Oil*, 549 F.2d 1271 (1977), the Ninth Circuit Federal Court held that geothermal resources are not minerals. Some states (such as Idaho) have declared that geothermal resources are neither minerals nor a water resource, and have developed a specialized scheme of regulation for this interest in real estate. Parties transferring land with geothermal resources should specify whether title to those areas is conveyed or reserved in the transferor.

The federal government has passed two acts relating to geothermal resources. The Geothermal Steam Act of 1970 (30 U.S.C. §1001 et seq.) and its Geothermal Energy Research and Development Act amendment encourage the development of this resource. Much of this resource is found on federal lands.

Water Rights

Water rights vary according to the type of water body involved. For landowners the water bodies of most concern are natural and artificial lakes, rivers, and streams. Two theories of water rights are applicable to these bodies of waters: the Riparian Doctrine and the Prior Appropriation Doctrine. Most states east of the Mississippi follow the *Riparian Doctrine,* and the arid western states follow the *Prior Appropriation Doctrine.*[4] Some states employ a combination of the two theories.[5]

The Riparian Doctrine is based on sharing, and the Prior Appropriation Doctrine is based on first in time is first in right, or the first to use the water has first claim to it. Figure 4.1 summarizes and compares the two doctrines. (The figure deals only with water use rights and not with the actual ownership of the land [riverbed] beneath the water.)

(4.2) Consider:

A owns a 40-acre tract along a stream. B owns another 40-acre tract farther downstream. There is only enough water provided by the stream for crops to be raised on one of the 40-acre parcels. Each 40 acres requires 3 feet of water for a successful crop, but if the water is divided there will be only 18 inches of water and no crop can be successful. What is the result under the Riparian Doctrine? In contrast, what would be the result under the Prior Appropriation Doctrine?

(4.3) Consider:

Stratton owned a small mill on a small stream. The owner of the Mount Hermon Boys' School, located upstream, diverted 60,000 gallons of water daily from the stream for domestic uses at the boys' school. Stratton brought suit. What is the result under each of the two doctrines?

[4]Alaska, Arizona, Colorado, Idaho, Montana, Nevada, Utah, and Wyoming.

[5]California, Kansas, Mississippi, Nebraska, North Dakota, Oklahoma, Oregon, South Dakota, Texas, and Washington.

Figure 4.1 *Water Rights*

THE COMMON LAW RULES OF RIPARIAN WATER
RIGHTS COMPARED WITH AND DISTINGUISHED
FROM THE DOCTRINE OF PRIOR APPROPRIATION

Common Law Riparian Rules

1. THE DISTINGUISHING FEA-TURES OF THE COMMON LAW RIPARIAN RULES ARE EQUAL-ITY OF RIGHTS AND REASON-ABLE USE—there is no priority of rights, the reasonable or permitted use by each is limited by a similar use in every other riparian.

2. To be a riparian one needs only to be an owner of riparian land. Riparian land is land which abuts or touches the water of a lake or stream.

3. No one can be a riparian who does not own riparian land.

4. Riparian lands are lands bordering the stream and within the watershed. Under the natural flow theory a riparian cannot use water on non-riparian lands. Under the reasonable use theory a riparian may use water on non-riparian lands if such use is reasonable.

5. Under the common law riparian rules the use of water for natural purposes is paramount and takes precedence over the use of water for artificial purposes. Natural uses include domestic purposes for the household and drinking, stock watering and irrigating the garden. Artificial purposes include use for irrigation, power, mining, manufacturing and industry.

Prior Appropriation Doctrine

1. THE DISTINGUISHING FEA-TURE OF THE PRIOR APPRO-PRIATION DOCTRINE IS FIRST IN TIME IS FIRST IN RIGHT—there is no equality of rights and no reasonable use limited by the rights of others.

2. To be a prior appropriator one must do four things, (a) have an intent to appropriate water, (b) divert the water from the source of supply, (c) put such water to a beneficial use, and (d) when applicable follow the necessary administrative procedures.

3. One need not own any land to be a prior appropriator. There is one exception—in some jurisdictions like Arizona if the appropriation is for irrigation purposes then the appropriator must own arable and irrigable land to which that water right is attached.

4. The prior appropriator may use the appropriated water on riparian and on non-riparian lands alike. The character of the land is quite immaterial.

5. The prior appropriation doctrine makes no distinction between uses of water for natural wants and for artificial and industrial purposes.

Figure 4.1 *(continued)*

Common Law Riparian Rules	Prior Appropriation Doctrine
6. The riparian owner, simply because he owns riparian land, has the right to have the stream of water flow to, by, through or over his land, under the riparian rights doctrine.	6. An owner of land, simply as such owner, has no right to have a stream of water flow to, by, through or over his land, under the prior appropriation doctrine.
7. The riparian has the right to have the water in its natural state free from unreasonable diminution in quantity and free from unreasonable pollution in quality.	7. The prior appropriator has the right to the exclusive use of the water free from interference by anyone, reasonable or unreasonable.
8. The rights of the riparians are equal.	8. The rights of the appropriators are never equal.
9. The basis, measure and limit of the riparian's water right is that of reasonable use (unless natural flow states which limit use to not interrupting the natural flow).	9. The basis, measure and limit of the water right of the prior appropriator is the beneficial use to which he has put the water. He has no right to waste water. If his needs are smaller than his means of diversion, usually a ditch, then his needs determine his right. If his ditch is smaller than his needs, then the capacity of his ditch determines his right.
10. The doctrine of riparian rights came to this country from the common law of England although it seems to have had its origin in the French law.	10. The doctrine of prior appropriation is statutory in our western states although its origin seems lost in antiquity.

Source: Reprinted from Boyer's *Real Property* with permission of West Publishing Co.

PROTECTION OF PROPERTY RIGHTS

Trespass

Trespass is defined as the intentional interference with landowners' reasonable use and enjoyment of their property. General examples of trespass include parties' walking across another property owner's land or placing objects on another's land, although trespass can also arise from indirect objects intentionally set in motion by the trespasser. For example, if one landowner were to dam water so that the water flooded an adjoining landowner's property, trespass has occurred. Even the simple act of opening shutters so that they extend across a boundary line to an adjoining property owner's land is an act of trespass. Bullets fired across the land of another also constitute trespass. In one unique trespass case, a child hurled a brick at a neighbor. When the neighbor reached across the boundary line and grabbed the child, he committed not only the torts of assault and battery but also the act of trespass.

Landowners faced with periodic trespassers should take certain precautions in protecting themselves from liability. Signs and barriers should be erected so that trespassers do not gradually become classified as guests because of the owners' implied acquiescence through inaction. Furthermore, if physical action does not stop the trespass, a court injunction or damages may be appropriate so that the landowners have judicial records of their positions on and relationships to trespassers.

(4.4) Consider:

Garrett operated a slaughterhouse on his land. His land is separated from a dirt road by a tract of frontage owned by Jackson. Garrett freely uses the frontage tract as access for cattle coming to the plant. What are Jackson's rights? What action should he take?

Nuisance

"Use your own property in such a manner as not to injure that of another [Sic were tuo et alienum non laedas]." *Nuisance* is the unreasonable interference with others' use and enjoyment of their property. Nuisances are generally thought of as bad odors and excessive noise. Pollutants from a factory causing property damage and medical problems can constitute a nuisance. "A nuisance may be merely a right thing in the wrong place, like a pig in the parlor instead of the barnyard."[6]

Nuisances can be classified as private, public, or frequently a cross between the two. A nuisance affecting an indeterminate number of persons is a public nuisance, while one affecting one property owner or a small group of property owners is a private nuisance. For example, a restaurant's storage of garbage bins behind a store is a private nuisance affecting the immediate neighbors. However, the burning of used car materials to salvage metal can create smoke and smells affecting an entire community and would thus be labeled a public nuisance.

The remedies for nuisance usually fall into one of two categories: mon-

[6]*Village of Euclid, Ohio v. Ambler Realty Co.*, 272 U.S. 365 (1926).

72

etary or equitable relief. Monetary relief is compensation for illness and medical expenses or compensation for the reduction in property values because of the nuisance. For example, destruction of plants or paint caused by pollutants would be compensable. Equitable relief is injunctive relief where the nuisance-creating party is ordered by a court to cease the nuisance-creating activity. This injunctive relief is used sparingly since in some circumstances the result will be the closing of a business. In determining whether injunctive relief will be afforded, courts balance the extent of the property owner's harm against the beneficial aspects of the wrongdoer's conduct. The following case is one in which the court deals with the balancing of landowners' interests against an economically beneficial industry, in a suit where the landowners have requested injunctive relief.

SPUR INDUSTRIES, INC. v. DEL E. WEBB DEVELOPMENT CO.
494 P.2d 700 (Ariz. 1972)

Spur Industries (Spur/defendant/appellant) operates a cattle feedlot near Youngtown and Sun City (communities located 14 to 15 miles west of Phoenix). Spur had been operating the feedlot since 1956 and the area had been agricultural since 1911.

In 1959 Del E. Webb (Webb/plaintiff/appellee) began development of the Sun City area, a retirement community. Webb purchased the 20,000 acres of land for about $750 per acre.

In 1960 Spur began an expansion program in which it grew from an operation of 35 acres to 115 acres. Webb began to experience sales resistance on the lots nearest Spur's business because of strong odors. Nearly 1300 lots could not be sold. Webb then filed suit alleging Spur's operation was a nuisance. Webb maintained that flies and odors were constantly drifting over Sun City.

At the time of the suit, Spur was feeding between 20,000 and 30,000 head of cattle, which produced 35 to 40 pounds of wet manure per head per day, or over one million pounds per day. No citizens were represented in the suit. The trial court permanently enjoined Spur's operations and Spur appealed.

CAMERON, Judge

The difference between a private nuisance and a public nuisance is generally one of degree. A private nuisance is one affecting a single individual or a definite small number of persons in the enjoyment of private rights not common to the public, while a public nuisance is one affecting the rights enjoyed by citizens as a part of the public.

To constitute a public nuisance, the nuisance must affect a considerable number of people or an entire community or neighborhood.

Where the injury is slight, the remedy for minor inconveniences lies in an action for damages rather than in one for injunction. Some courts have held, in the "balancing of conveniences" cases, that damages may be the sole remedy. We have no difficulty, however, in agreeing with the conclusion of the trial court that Spur's operation was an enjoinable public nuisance as far as the people in the southern portion of Del Webb's Sun City were concerned. Before an otherwise lawful (and necessary) business may be declared a public nuisance, there must be a "populous" area in which people are injured.

It is clear that as to the citizens of Sun City, the operation of Spur's feedlot was both a public and private nuisance. They could have successfully maintained an action to abate the nuisance. Del Webb, having shown a special injury in the loss of sales, had standing to bring suit to enjoin the nuisance.

In addition to protecting the public interest, however, courts of equity are concerned with protecting the operator of a lawful, albeit obnoxious, business from the result of a knowing and willful encroachment by others near his business.

In the so-called "coming to the nuisance" cases, the courts have held that the residential landowner may not have relief if he knowingly came into a neighborhood reserved for industrial or agricultural endeavors and has been damaged thereby.

Were Webb the only party injured, we would feel justified in holding that the doctrine of "coming to the nuisance" would have been a bar to the relief asked by Webb, and, on the other hand, had Spur located the feedlot near the outskirts of a city and had the city grown toward the feedlot, Spur would have to suffer the cost of abating the nuisance as to those people locating within the growth pattern of the expanding city.

There was no indication in the instant case at the time Spur and its predecessors located in Western Maricopa County that a new city would spring up, full-blown, alongside the feeding operation and that the developer of that city would ask the court to order Spur to move because of the new city. Spur is required to move not because of any wrongdoing on the part of Spur, but because of a proper and legitimate regard of the courts for the rights and interests of the public.

Del Webb, on the other hand, is entitled to the relief prayed for (a permanent injunction), not because Webb is blameless, but because of the damage to the people who have been encouraged to purchase homes in Sun City. It does not equitably or legally follow, however, that Webb, being entitled to the injunction, is then free of any liability to Spur if Webb has in fact been the cause of the damage Spur has sustained. It does not seem harsh to require a developer, who has taken advantage of the lesser land values in a rural area as well as the availability of large tracts of land on which to build and develop a new town or city in the area, to indemnify those who are forced to leave as a result.

Having brought people to the nuisance to the foreseeable detriment of Spur, Webb must indemnify Spur for a reasonable amount of the cost of moving or shutting down. It should be noted that this relief to Spur is limited to a case wherein a developer has, with foreseeability, brought into a previously agricultural or industrial area the population which makes necessary the granting of an injunction against a lawful business and for which the business has not adequate relief.

It is therefore the decision of this court that the matter be remanded to the trial court for a hearing upon the damages sustained by the defendant Spur as a reasonable and direct result of the granting of the permanent injunction.

Affirmed in part, reversed in part and remanded.

Discussion Questions

1. What is Spur's business?
2. What is Webb's business?
3. Are both industries economically significant?
4. Who brought suit? What was the basis of the suit?
5. Did Webb move to the nuisance?
6. Must Spur cease doing business?
7. What is the "coming to the nuisance" doctrine?
8. Does Webb recover damages?
9. Does Spur recover damages?

(4.5) Consider:

In each of the following circumstances, determine whether a nuisance is involved, whether it is public or private, and what remedy would be appropriate. Apply the *Spur* case and determine any additional facts that would aid in the decision.

a. Noise from a gun club located near a residential mobile-home court.

b. Damage and annoyance caused by blasting in a nearby quarry (the town developed because of the quarry).

c. Operation of a dog kennel.

d. Construction of a proposed nuclear power plant.

(4.6) Consider:

Glenn Prah constructed a residence during 1978 and 1979. He installed solar collectors on the roof for purposes of supplying energy for heat and hot water. Richard Maretti purchased the lot adjacent to Prah's and submitted proposed home plans that would result in a substantial obstruction of Prah's solar collectors and a corresponding reduction in the system's output and efficiency. Prah brought suit claiming that the construction of the home would be a private nuisance. If Maretti simply repositioned the layout of his home, the impact on Prah's system would be reduced, but Maretti has refused because his plans are in compliance with all zoning ordinances and other regulations. What factors should the court examine in balancing the parties' interests? *Prah v. Maretti*, 321 N.W.2d 182 (Wis. 1982)

Duties of Landowners

In addition to avoiding the problems of trespass and nuisance, landowners owe certain responsibilities to those entering their property. Those parties entering property are classified into one of three categories: trespassers, licensees, and invitees. Each category has a different status when on another's property, and landowners owe different degrees of responsibility to those in each category.

Trespassers *Trespassers* are persons on the property of another without permission. Landowners may take the appropriate actions to seek removal of the trespassers, but while trespassers are on their property, landowners have the responsibility of not intentionally injuring them. That is, landowners may not intentionally injure trespassers or erect mantraps to injure or kill trespassers.

Licensees *Licensees* are persons on the property of another who have some form of permission to be there. For example, in most states, fire protectors, police officers, and medical personnel would be classified as licensees. These groups have an implied invitation to a landowner's property so that their services are available to the landowner when needed. It is possible that meter readers would be classified as licensees because the implied invitation arises from the use of the utility or service. In some states, social guests are classified as licensees because although there may not be an express invitation to all social guests, an implied invitation arises from friendship.

To the licensees, landowners owe a greater duty of care. In addition to the duty not to injure intentionally is the responsibility of warning licensees of any defects of which landowners have knowledge. Thus, landowners must warn of broken steps, cracked concrete, or dangerous animals.

Invitees *Invitees* are persons on the property of another by express invitation. Every public place and every store offers an express invitation to all members of the public. A repair person on the premises to fix a washer or refrigerator is there at the landowner's express request. Invitees are afforded the greatest degree of protection by landowners. Landowners must not only warn invitees of any defects of which they have knowledge but must also inspect their property for defects and correct those defects. For example, a leaf of lettuce on the floor in the produce section of a grocery store is a hazard for all invitees. Grocery store owners are required to periodically check and sweep aisle areas to protect invitees.

Breach of Duty

A landowner's breach of any of the above responsibilities can result in the imposition of tremendous liability especially if the trespasser, licensee, or invitee is seriously injured. Landowners must be cautious in exercising their responsibilities and can be further protected through maintenance of adequate insurance.

PRECAUTIONS FOR LANDOWNERS

The discussion in this chapter has centered on ownership of land and what is included as part of that land. To avoid problems in this area, there are several circumstances in which the parties should take precautions. In the first circumstance, a buyer is purchasing property and all parties (seller, buyer, agents, and financiers) should analyze the sale with the following questions:

1. What water is available? Are the water rights protected?
2. Are mineral rights being transferred? What minerals are included? If minerals are not being transferred, who owns them and what do they own? What land use rights do they have? What are the royalties or payments and who is entitled to receive them?
3. Is light available to the buildings, landscaping, and solar panels? If not, is an easement possible? Will future structures block the light?
4. Are the column and air lots included or have they been transferred? Who owns them?
5. Is air traffic unusually burdensome, close, or noisy?
6. Do any nuisances such as pollution, smell, or insects exist? Can they be remedied?
7. Are there any persons using the property? Do they hold any rights or are they trespassers?

Failure to check on these seven factors can result in losses to the buyer and the possible imposition of liability on the seller or the broker or agent for failing to disclose relevant information.

In the second circumstance, a property owner wishes to convey mineral rights and may be faced with a complex and lengthly document. The situation may be clarified by answering the following questions:

1. What interest is being conveyed? What minerals? Subsurface only? Fee simple interest? Lease? Right of removal?
2. What rights are given on surface use? Will the lessee pay for restoration?
3. How much is the royalty? Are there any other fees to be paid? If no minerals are drawn, is there any payment?
4. Can the land be sold to someone else? Who gets the royalties?
5. Can they transfer the mineral rights to someone else? Will the same restrictions apply?

In the third and final circumstance, property owners are responsible for the way they use their property and may want to answer these questions in assessing potential liability:

1. Are there significant noises, smells, or other emissions from the property? Do they interfere with others' use and enjoyment of their own property?
2. Are there individuals using the property in an unauthorized manner? Are there trespassers? Are there any mantraps to injure them? Have steps been taken to prevent trespass?
3. Are there licensees on the property or potentially on the property? Are there appropriate signs and methods of warning them of dangers?
4. Do invitees enter the property? Are there any dangerous conditions? Have they been remedied? Are periodic inspections done to find and eliminate dangerous conditions?
5. Are nuisances from others affecting the property? Can action be taken to stop the conduct or recover damages?

The topics in this chapter have significant impact on landowners in various circumstances. The preceding questions integrate the topics and serve as a checklist to prevent or minimize legal problems.

KEY TERMS

fructus naturales
fructus industriales (emblements)
doctrine of emblements
fixture
air rights
column lot
air lot
solar easement laws
doctrine of ancient lights
mineral rights
incorporeal hereditament
profit a prendre
rule of capture

granting clause
consideration clause
royalty clause
habendum clause
geothermal energy
water rights
Riparian Doctrine
Prior Appropriation Doctrine
trespass
nuisance
trespassers
licensees
invitees

CHAPTER PROBLEMS

1. Barger, the chief of police of the town of West Hickory, had a neighbor Barringer, whose stables were filthy. The chief reported the condition of Barringer's property to the proper authorities. When Barringer dis-

covered that the complaint had been made, he built an unsightly board fence (8 feet high) along the division line of their properties. Barger found that his air, view, and light were so affected that he did not have enough sunlight to shave in the morning. Does Barger have any legal claim against Barringer for removal of the fence?

2. Brian Hunter installed a $14,000 solar energy system at his home and then learned that a 17-story, 310-unit condominium project was to be built on the next block. The high-rise project will shade his solar collectors and rob the system of 30 percent of its capabilities. Does Hunter have any remedies? Any suggestions for helping him?

3. River Raisin Company manufactured cardboard and discharged their waste into the Raisin River. Monroe Carp Pond Company was located downriver and operated an adjacent carp pond to store and feed carp. Monroe began losing carp because of the manufacturing wastes discharged by River Raisin Company. Monroe filed suit as a lower riparian and sought an injunction against the manufacturer. What was the result?

4. Frontier Telephone Company strung telephone wires across Butler's land without Butler's permission. Butler alleges that the action is a trespass. What is the result?

5. Napoli planted an olive tree near the property of his neighbor, W. Douglas Carothers, Jr. Carothers objected to the planting of the tree because its branches hung over his property. Does Carothers have any basis for suit? What steps should be taken?

6. Station WRCPA has a Bell Ranger jet helicopter that lands in a lot next to the station building and across the street from several residences. Mrs. Mildred owns one of the residences and has found that the updraft from the landing helicopter swirls leaves onto her yard and dust into her home. According to Mrs. Mildred, "my yard looks like someone has thrown loose hay all over it and it [the helicopter] is noisy and interferes with television reception and telephone conversations." Discuss any legal theories that might help Mrs. Mildred.

7. McCuistion resided in Huachuca City and owned property next to the city's landfill. On two occasions, the city's landfill washed down to McCuistion's property, depositing offensive and foul-smelling debris and garbage. McCuistion and his wife became so ill that they required medical attention. Furthermore, McCuistion's vegetation was damaged when the city's bulldozers and trucks came to remove the debris. McCuistion alleges the deposits would not have occurred if the city had properly maintained the dump. Discuss whether McCuistion has any legal basis for the suit.

8. A group of residents living near the Los Angeles International Airport filed suit against the city of Los Angeles for the nuisance of airplane noise. The residents stated in their complaints that the jet noise made their homes vibrate, broke windows, blew shingles off roofs, and interfered with sleeping, watching television, and enjoying sexual relations. Discuss whether the residents are entitled to any form of relief. What interests should be balanced?

9. Consider whether the following types of conduct would constitute a nuisance and discuss the type of remedy available. Be sure to use the *Spur* doctrine of balancing interests.

    a. The operation of a dump causing smoke, odors, flies, rodents, and wild dogs to enter neighboring properties.

    b. Stadium lights on at night that disturb a neighbor's sleep.

10. Robert George has maintained, on a year-round basis, his red and white home with snow-covered roof and 300,000 lights as Santa's Dream House. He dresses as Santa and allows disabled and terminally ill children to visit his home. The city of Glendale has brought suit alleging that the house is a public nuisance because the decorations distract motorists and create a safety hazard. Is the house a public nuisance?

11. Classify each of the following parties and state the landowner's responsibilities to each of them:

    a. Paramedic

    b. Customer in a department store

    c. Marketing researcher doing a door-to-door survey

    d. Burglar

12. A burglar slipped and fell on a grape in the grocery store that he was burglarizing. Will the burglar be able to recover costs incurred from his injuries? Would the result be different if a paramedic fell on a grape while making an emergency call for a customer with a heart attack? What questions would you want to ask before you determined liability?

5

NONPOSSESSORY INTERESTS IN REAL ESTATE

Good fences make good neighbors.

–Robert Frost

Nonpossessory land interests are those that give their holders certain definite and clear-cut rights, but the given rights always fall short of possession of the land. These nonpossessory interests might be labeled privileges, liberties, or advantages. Nonpossessory interests give their holders limited use and enjoyment of property. This chapter discusses the creation and extent of those nonpossessory interests. Easements can now be added to the scheme of legal land interests, which appears in its final form in Figure 5.1.

EASEMENTS

An *easement* is a liberty, privilege, or advantage one landowner holds in another's property. It is nonpossessory but may be valid for perpetuity. There are many different types of easements and methods for their creation, and these are discussed in the sections that follow.

Appurtenant v. Easements in Gross

An *easement appurtenant* is one attaching to or benefiting a particular tract of land. The purpose of an easement appurtenant is to benefit a land possessor.

Figure 5.1 *Legal Interests in Land*

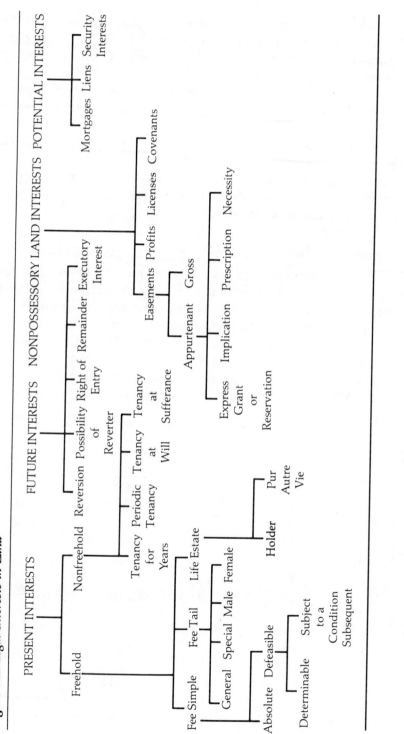

For example, suppose both landowners C and A need access to the highway that runs parallel to B's property (see Figure 5.2). The dark strip represents the appurtenant easement held by C and A to benefit them in the use and possession of their land.

In contrast, an *easement in gross* is not created to benefit any landowner with respect to a particular tract of land; rather, it belongs to the holders regardless of whether any adjacent property is owned. Generally, public utilities hold easements in gross through residential property (in the back 6 or 8 feet of the lots, for example) so that telephone, electrical, and water lines can be connected to all parcels of property. At common law, easements in gross were not transferable, but in most states such easements in gross are now transferable if they are commercial in nature.

Affirmative v. Negative Easements

The situation diagramed in Figure 5.2 is an example of an *affirmative easement*, which means that the owner of the easement right can use another's land (the land subject to the easement). In Figure 5.2, A and C have an affirmative easement in B's property. Likewise, C has an affirmative easement in A's property.

A *negative easement* is one in which the holders of the easements prevent the property owners from using their property in a particular way or prevent particular acts by other landowners; for example, an easement restricting the building heights on adjoining property. These negative easements, often called

Figure 5.2 *Easements Appurtenant*

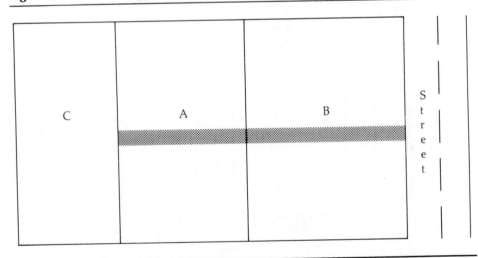

scenic easements, can have a possible twofold tax advantage. First, the taxpayer/ landowner can perhaps take a charitable contribution deduction. For example, a business might grant a neighboring church a negative easement that prevents the blockage of sunlight from the church's stained glass windows. The business can take the value this easement subtracts from its property as a charitable contribution deduction. Second, the taxpayer/landowner's property taxes can be reduced by the decrease in value brought about by the easement restrictions. An easement preventing the casting of shadows on solar panels (as discussed in Chapter 4) is an example of a negative easement.

Dominant v. Servient Estates

In an easement relationship, the property owned by the easement holder is called the *dominant estate* and the property through which the easement runs is called the *servient estate*. Thus in Figure 5.2, B holds the servient estate for dominant tenants A and C. Since C also has an easement through A's property, A is also a servient estate to C's dominant estate.

(5.1) Consider:

For each of the following, determine what type (affirmative, negative, appurtenant, gross) of easement is being created and who will hold the dominant and servient estates:

a. A holds an easement that prevents B from planting willow trees. (A and B are adjoining landowners, and A obtained the easement because she felt the roots of willow trees would harm her in-ground swimming pool.)

b. Community Cable has just placed television wires along the back wall lines of several neighbors' lots in a new subdivision. The landowners object—they allege a trespass has occurred.

Creation of Easements

Easements by Express Grant or Reservation An *easement by express grant* is one in which the parties actually draw up papers as if transferring an interest in land. Since an easement is a land interest, express creation must comply with all requirements in the state for the conveyance of land interests. Most states require the conveyance of a land interest to be in writing. Whether an easement is created by express grant or express reservation depends on the physical circumstances of transfer. The two contrasting physical setups for easements are illustrated in Figure 5.3.

The same easement is involved in both circumstances, but the method

Figure 5.3 *Express Grant and Express Reservation Easements*

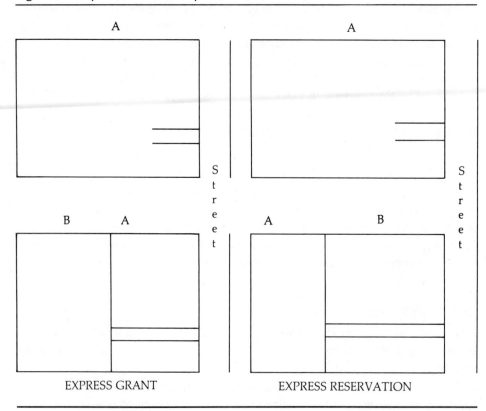

of acquisition is different. In express grant, A as the servient estate holder retains that portion of the land with the access route. In conveying B's interest in the deed transferring title to the property, A would convey that portion of the parcel now labeled for B, but would also grant B a means of egress and ingress by granting an easement to B.

In *easement by express reservation,* A, as dominant estate holder would sell to B that portion of the parcel containing the access route. In conveying B's interest in the deed transferring title to the property, A would convey that portion of the parcel now labeled for B, but would retain or reserve the means of egress and ingress as an easement.

In either circumstance, A should be cautious in wording the easement language. The following suggestions should be kept in mind:

1. Accurately describe the location, length, and width of the easement.
2. Describe the intended use of the easement. Is it for a right of way? Is it for ingress and egress?

3. Are there limitations on the use of the easement? Is it residential or commercial?

4. Who is responsible for maintenance of the easement?

5. Describe any limitations. For example, "Until the construction of the highway along the southern boundary of the property is completed."

An express easement need not arise solely in the circumstances of land partition. It may be executed alone without the division or transfer of title to property. For example, a solar easement may be drafted and executed between two neighbors who already own their adjoining parcels of land.

Easements by Implication An *easement by implication* is one arising from necessity. Suppose, for example, that in the express grant of Figure 5.3, B's property is landlocked and that crossing A's parcel is B's only method of ingress and egress. Suppose further that in the conveyance from A to B no provision or express grant was made to provide B with an easement. To prevent B from having to hold title to a worthless piece of inaccessible property, the doctrine of easement by implication was developed and may be used to assist B in the landlocked predicament.

In order to establish that an easement exists by implication, several factors must be present. First, there must have been unity of ownership between the two tracts prior to the partition and sale. In this case there was unity of ownership, since A owned the entire parcel prior to the division. Second, there must have been a *quasi-easement* at the time of the sole ownership of the parcel. A quasi-easement is an access route used by the landowner when the land was not yet divided. Figure 5.3 indicates that A used the road as a means of access, and so a quasi-easement existed. The term *quasi* is used because landowners cannot hold an easement in their own property. Third, the prior quasi-easement must have been apparent and used continuously. This requirement is satisfied in the figure and is easily satisfied in most access cases because the road or path is visible. However, visibility is not required to meet the apparent standard in most jurisdictions. For example, sewer-line accesses, although not visible, have been held to be apparent because of their need in property use. Although not shown in the figure, continuous use can probably be assumed in most access cases where, as here, the roadway is the only means of access. Continuous use is normal use and does not require use every day.

The final requirement for an easement by implication is to establish that requiring the dominant estate to obtain access any other way would require unreasonable expense. In Figure 5.3, B's landlocked circumstances would indicate that the access through just one parcel is the least expensive and least troublesome method of obtaining access.

Easements by implication can arise in either grant or reservation cases, so that there are both easements by grant implication and easements by reservation implication. The following case involves a factual issue of whether an easement by implication exists.

GRANITE PROPERTIES LIMITED PARTNERSHIP v. MANNS
521 N.E.2d 1230 (Ill. 1987)

Granite Properties Limited Partnership (Granite/plaintiff) owned all of the parcels shown in the following diagram. Between 1963 and 1982, Granite conveyed certain of the parcels, and, in 1982, parcel B was conveyed to Larry Manns and others (defendants). The present status of the parcels is as follows:

- Parcel A contains a shopping center (built in 1967) (currently owned by Granite). To the north of the shopping center is an asphalt parking lot with 191 feet of frontage on Bethalto Drive.
- Parcel B is undeveloped and is owned by the defendants.
- Parcel C contains five 4-family

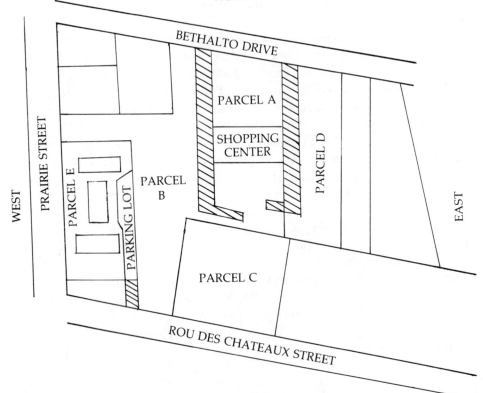

apartment buildings (owned by a third party).
- Parcel D contains a health club (owned by a third party).
- Parcel E contains the Chateau des Fleurs Apartments (owned by Granite).

The rear of the shopping center is used for deliveries, trash storage and removal, and utilities repair. To gain access to the rear of the shopping center for these purposes, trucks use a gravel driveway that runs along the lot line between parcel A and parcel B. A second driveway (noted in diagram), located to the east of the shopping center on parcel D, enables the trucks to circle the shopping center and deliver to the stores, including Sav-a-Lot Grocery, without having to turn around in the limited space behind the stores. The trucks can thus make a convenient entrance, delivery stop, and exit.

The two pictured driveways existed before Manns purchased the property, and he saw them during an inspection of the land prior to his purchase. There are no references to the driveways in any of the deeds relating to the parcels.

The trial court testimony offered extensive information on the driveways and the store deliveries. Robert Mehann, owner of the Save-a-Lot grocery store located in the shopping center, testified on direct examination that groceries, which are delivered to the rear of the store, are loaded by forklift on a concrete pad poured for that purpose. Mehann indicated that there are large, double-steel doors in the back of the store to accommodate items that will not fit through the front door. Mehann testified that semi-trailer trucks make deliveries to the rear of the grocery store four days a week, with as many as two or three such trucks arriving daily. An average of ten to twelve trucks a day, including semitrailer trucks, make deliveries to the grocery store. Mehann further explained on direct examination that because the area behind the Save-a-Lot building extends only 50 feet to the rear property line, it would be difficult, if not impossible, for a semitrailer truck to turn around in the back and exit the same way it came in. In response to a question as to whether it would be feasible to have trucks make front door deliveries, Mehann suggested that such deliveries would be very disruptive; pallets that would not fit through the front door would have to be broken down into parts, requiring extra work, and there would not be adequate space in the front of the store to do such work during business hours. Mehann admitted on cross-examination that he had not investigated the cost of installing a front door that would be big enough for pallets of groceries to be brought in by forklift. Further cross-examination revealed that there would not be enough space to manipulate the forklift around the front of the store, although it could be run between the shelves of food to the back of the store.

Darrell Layman, a partner for Granite, testified that, although it was very difficult, he had seen semitrailer trucks exit the same way they came in. Layman also acknowledged on cross-examination that he had not investigated the cost of expanding the size of the front doors of the building. He also claimed it "would seem impossible" for him to put in any kind of a hallway or passageway that would allow equipment to bring supplies into the store from the front. On redirect examination, Layman explained that the delivery trucks follow no set schedule and, therefore, their presence may overlap at times. He stated that he had seen as many as four or five delivery trucks backed up. Layman opined that there was "no way" the trucks could back up and turn around when there were multiple trucks present.

Granite claimed an easement by implication for the shopping center and the parcel E apartment complex. The trial court found an easement by implication for the apartment complex but denied such for the shopping center. Granite appealed. The appellate court affirmed the apartment complex easement and also reversed the trial court's ruling on the shopping center easement and found that one also existed by implication there. Manns appealed.

RYAN, Justice

The plaintiff contends in this court that it acquired, by implied reservation, easements over the driveways which provide access to the rear of the shopping center located on parcel A and to the parking lot of the apartment complex situated on parcel E. Plaintiff alleges that parcels A, B and E were held in common ownership by the plaintiff and its predecessors in title until 1982, at which time the defendants received a warranty deed to parcel B; that the driveways in question were apparent and obvious, permanent, and subject to continuous, uninterrupted, and actual use by the plaintiff and its predecessors in title until the time of severance of unity of ownership; and that the driveways are highly convenient and reasonably necessary for the beneficial use and enjoyment of the shopping center and the apartment complex. Therefore, the plaintiff maintains that, upon severance of unity of title, the defendants took parcel B subject to the servitudes then existing, as the parties are presumed to convey with reference to the existing conditions of the property.

We note at the outset that the attempt here is to establish easements by implied reservation rather than by implied grant. Illinois may be said to follow the generally accepted view recognizing the implication of easements in favor of a grantor as well as a grantee.

On the merits, the crucial issue is whether, in conveying that portion of its property now owned by the defendants (parcel B), the plaintiff retained easements by implication over the driveways in question.

The easement implied from a prior or existing use, often characterized as a "quasi-easement," arises when an owner of an entire tract of land or two or more adjoining parcels, after employing a part thereof so that one part of the tract or one parcel derives from another a benefit or advantage of an apparent, continuous, and permanent nature, conveys or transfers part of the property without mention being made of these incidental uses. In the absence of an expressed agreement to the contrary, the conveyance or transfer imparts a grant of property with all the benefits and burdens which existed at the time of the conveyance of the transfer, even though such grant is not reserved or specified in the deed.

The Restatement describes a doctrine creating easements "by implication from the circumstances under which the conveyance was made." This implication "arises as an inference of the intention of those making a conveyance." The Restatement operates on the basis of eight "important circumstances" from which the inference of intention can be drawn:

whether the claimant is the conveyor or the conveyee; the terms of the conveyance; the consideration given for it; whether the claim is made against a simultaneous conveyee; the extent of necessity of the easement to the claimant; whether reciprocal benefits result to the conveyor and the conveyee; the manner in which the land was used prior to its conveyance; and the extent to which the manner of prior use was or might have been known to the parties. These eight factors vary in their importance and relevance according to whether the claimed easement originates out of necessity or for another reason.

In applying the Restatement's eight important circumstances to the present case, the fact that the driveways in question had been used by the plaintiff or its predecessors in title since the 1960s, when the respective properties were developed; that the driveways were permanent in character, being either rock or gravel covered; and that the defendants were aware of the driveways' prior uses before they purchased parcel B would tend to support an inference that the parties intended easements upon severance of the parcels in question.

. . . [T]he defendants, nevertheless, argue that there are two factors which overwhelmingly detract from the implication of an easement: That the claimant is the conveyor and that the claimed easement can hardly be described as "necessary" to the beneficial use of the plaintiff's properties. Relying on the principle that a grantor should not be permitted to derogate from his own grant, the defendants urge this court to refuse to imply an easement in favor of a grantor unless the claimed easement is absolutely necessary to the beneficial use and enjoyment of the land retained by the grantor. The defendants further urge this court not to cast an unreasonable burden over their land through imposition of easements by implication where, as here, available alternatives affording reasonable means of ingress to and egress from the shopping center and apartment complex allegedly exist.

While the degree of necessity required to reserve an easement by implication in favor of the conveyor is greater than that required in the case of a conveyee, even in the case of the conveyor, the implication from necessity will be aided by a previous use made apparent by the physical adaptation of the premises to it.

The requirement that the quasi-easement must have been "important for the enjoyment of the conveyed quasi-dominant [or quasi-servient] parcel" is highly elastic. Some courts say that the use must be one which is "reasonably necessary to the enjoyment of the [conveyed or retained] land." Others demand a use which is necessary for the beneficial, convenient, comfortable or reasonable enjoyment of such land.

Notwithstanding their difference in use of terminology, the authorities agree that the degree or extent of necessity required to create an easement by implication differs in both meaning and significance depending upon the existence of proof of prior use. Hence, given the strong evidence of the plaintiff's prior use of the driveways in question and the defendants' knowledge thereof, we must agree with the appellate court majority that the evidence in this case was sufficient to fulfill the elastic necessity requirement.

The evidence, moreover, regarding the difficulty of making deliveries to the front of the shopping center was sufficient to demonstrate the unreasonableness of such an alternative measure.

Affirmed.

Discussion Questions

1. Who originally owned all the parcels of land?
2. How was each parcel used?
3. Could delivery trucks find an alternate means of access to the shopping center?
4. Did the buyers know of the use of the driveways by the trucks?
5. Were the driveways mentioned in any of the deeds?
6. What eight factors does the court examine as "important circumstances" in deciding the case?
7. Does the standard of proof differ if there is a claim for an easement by implied reservation as opposed to one implied by grant?
8. Does the court use a standard of absolute necessity?

Easements by Necessity An *easement by necessity* is one that can arise solely on the basis of necessity, and the requirements of prior use need not be established. However, this type of easement lasts only so long as the necessity continues whereas an easement by implication may go on in perpetuity. In some states, condemnation procedures are available to assist landowners who need to obtain access to their property.

In Figure 5.2, B's circumstances could be changed to require an easement by necessity if the properties were surrounded by water. Then B's only method of access would be through A's land, unless and until a bridge or causeway to B's land was constructed. The following case deals with the issue of whether an easement by necessity exists.

MARSHALL v. SPANGLER
686 S.W.2d 8 (Mo. 1984)

Mr. and Mrs. Ament originally owned a tract of ground along Highway 291 at Harrisonville with "Don's Texaco Truck Stop" and the "Dinner Bell Restaurant" located on it. The Aments operated the service station until 1973 when they leased it to the Marshalls (plaintiffs) who purchased the service station in 1980. Spangler (defendant) leased the restaurant from 1966 to 1973 and then purchased it.

During the whole history of the restaurant and the service station they have operated side by side, except for an interval of unspecified length before the Marshalls' purchase of the service station property in 1980. During that period the service station was closed.

Until the events that precipitated this lawsuit in 1982, the service station and the restaurant, although under different management, had always operated in tandem as a "truck stop" (except for a brief time at the beginning when the operator of the restaurant undertook to operate a gourmet restaurant). It was attractive to truckers because they could get fuel at the service station and eat at the restaurant. There was a good deal of space around both establishments to accommodate large trucks. Sometimes the two establishments sponsored joint advertising.

There were seven wide driveways from Highway 291 for ingress and egress to the service station and restaurant. There was no barrier between the two facilities, and the customers of both used a common parking lot.

When the land was divided, Spangler built a concrete barrier parallel to the boundary between his restaurant property and Marshalls' service station property and 50 feet south thereof. Spangler explained that the barrier was installed to prevent trucks from rolling across the prem-

ises and to prevent oil spills from flowing onto his paved parking lot. After the erection of the barrier, the trucks could no longer pass from the service station property to the restaurant without driving onto the highway. The barrier also blocked several of the seven driveways.

The Marshalls claim that they have an implied easement for their customers to park on and drive over the restaurant lot. There is no reference in the deeds to any easements. The Marshalls brought suit seeking their implied easement, which was denied by the trial court. The Marshalls appealed.

KENNEDY, Presiding Judge

The evidence in this case shows that the availability of the restaurant parking area and driveways for parking and for ingress and egress would be an advantage, a benefit, a convenience to Marshalls' service station property. That is not enough; there must be a reasonable necessity therefor. The emphasis is more on the word "necessity" than on the word "reasonable."

The principle of the law of implied easements is applicable when the easement is necessary; the rule is not one of absolute or strict necessity, but of reasonable necessity—the benefit must be reasonably necessary to the enjoyment and use of the dominant estate—but the rule is nevertheless one of necessity, not of convenience.

At the outset it may be stated that the tendency of the courts, as a general rule, is to discourage implied grants of easements, since the obvious result, especially in urban communities, is to fetter estates, retard buildings and improvements, and violate the policy of recording acts.

Have the Marshalls shown such a

degree of necessity for the claimed easement that it must be implied as a matter of law? We hold that, under the evidence in this case, the trial court may not be held in error in rejecting the Marshalls' claim of implied easement.

It would appear from the pictures that it would be difficult for a 50- to 65-foot 'railer truck which had parked parallel to the diesel pumps to turn out of the southernmost service station driveway. It would have to turn almost at a right angle. Mr. Marshall testified, "It would take some maneuvering." This makes it much more convenient and inviting for them to drive forward and go out on one of the restaurant driveways.

Mr. Marshall also testified to limited parking on his property because of congestion caused by his own and customers' vehicles.

There seems to be several alternative arrangements which could be made. The trucks could drive into the diesel fuels pumps going east and west—at right angles with the highway—and could enter or depart by a driveway along the south part of the service station property, exiting on a road which runs along the north side of the service station property and which connects with the highway. A second alternative would be to move the diesel pumps toward the north, which would al-low trucks to enter and depart from the southernmost service station driveway. There is no evidence of the expense involved in either of these alternative arrangements, but they would not be prohibitive.

Affirmed.

Discussion Questions

1. Was the property once under single ownership?
2. How was the property used?
3. When was ownership divided?
4. What caused the lawsuit?
5. Who is asserting an easement by necessity?
6. Will there be additional costs without the easement?
7. Does the court imply an easement?
8. What could the parties have done to prevent the suit?

(5.2) Consider:

At one time, the parcels shown in the following diagram were owned by Harry Borst, who built the garage and used it for his car.

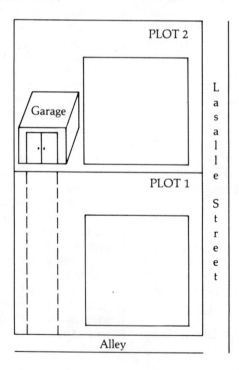

In 1947, Hunt purchased plot 1 and in 1951, the Zimmermans purchased plot 2. Hunt had leased the garage from Borst until the sale to the Zimmermans in 1951. Hunt tried to rent the garage from the Zimmermans but was refused. The Zimmermans used the driveway on the Hunts' land to gain access to the garage. After numerous disputes and gates, the Zimmermans brought suit to stop the Hunts from blocking the driveway. The Zimmermans claim that they have an easement because there is no other way to use the garage. There is no mention in the deeds of any driveway or easement. Do the Zimmermans have an easement? *Hunt v. Zimmerman*, 216 N.E.2d 854 (Ind. 1966)

Easements by Prescription Obtaining an easement by *prescription* is somewhat similar to obtaining title to property through adverse possession. However, the term adverse possession (discussed in Chapter 9) is inappropriate for easements because easements are nonpossessory land interests. Several elements must be established before an easement by prescription is created:

1. *The easement must be used for the appropriate prescriptive period.* The prescriptive period will vary from state to state but generally corresponds to the state's adverse possession period, which ranges from 5 to 20 years throughout the United States.
2. *The use of the easement must be adverse (not permissive).* If the landowner has given the prescriptive taker an oral license of passage, such use is permissive and will not qualify for prescription. The permissive use must be mutually agreed upon—a landowner's posting of a permission sign will not prevent prescriptive rights.
3. *The use of the easement must be open and notorious.* In most states this requirement means that the prescriptive taker must use the property in such a way that a landowner would, under ordinary circumstances, be aware of the use. Because actual knowledge of use is not required, landowners not periodically inspecting their property run the risk of having a prescriptive use accumulate.
4. *The use of the easement must be continuous and exclusive.* This requirement forces the prescriptive user to confine use to a particular area. Thus the user is required to use the same strip of land or access route consistently. A prescriptive claim can be based only on the user's use and not on use by others. An exception is the rule of tacking, which permits those in privity of contract (buyers and sellers) and those who inherit title to land to add their use to that of the seller or deceased in making up the prescriptive period. For example, a father using an easement for 5 years and then passing his property to his son also passes his 5 years of prescriptive use of the easement.

To prevent a prescriptive taking, the landowner may take several steps, most of which are recognized by the majority of states. Written protest is one method of interrupting the prescriptive period as is physical interruption (for example, the use of a gate). Perhaps court-obtained injunctive relief is the best alternative because such action provides the landowners with full records for establishing a cutoff of the prescriptive period.

(5.3) Consider:

Garrett operated a slaughterhouse on land used for that purpose since 1895. Garrett's land is separated from a county road by a frontage tract owned by Jackson. The slaughterhouse owners had freely crossed the frontage tract for years. In 1958 Jackson built a fence across the passageway. Garrett cut the wire fence, built a gate, and notified Jackson. In 1976 Jackson padlocked the gate and sent a letter to Garrett accusing him of trespass. What rights does Garrett have?

(5.4) Consider:

Jerry Branch owned property adjacent to the Shors. The Shors and their predecessors had gained access to their property by a road on Branch's property (from 1972 to 1976). In 1976, Branch installed a locking gate but the Shors continued to use the road by going around the gate on foot, snowmobile, and motorcycle. Branch also put up "no trespassing" signs. Has Branch halted an easement by prescription? *Shors v. Branch*, 720 P.2d 239 (Mont. 1986)

Scope and Extent of Easements

The extent of permissive use of an easement is determined according to the type of easement. If an express easement has been created, determining the extent of the easement is simply a task of interpretation of the deed or contract granting the easement. A court must undertake this task of interpretation and will employ the *rule of reason* in executing its task. The rule of reason prohibits a court from imposing unreasonable burdens when the parties have expressed their desires and intentions in general terms. Thus the rule of reason prohibits a court from imposing a strained construction on the language used by the parties.

For example, if the parties expressly provide for an easement across servient land in a definite location, then the court may not impose a different route for the easement upon the parties. On the other hand, an express easement for a pipeline that does not specify depth can be interpreted to permit the dominant estate holder to move the pipe to a greater depth because of technological changes and necessities. Likewise, the grant of an easement to use a beach "for the purpose of boating, bathing, fishing, or other recreation" does not include the right to use the beach for the purpose of commercial boat rental. An easement for "foot passage" will not be expanded to permit vehicles, but an easement for "the right to pass" may be properly interpreted to permit vehicular traffic.

The extent, location, and use of a prescriptive easement is determined according to the type of use made during the prescriptive period. For example, a prescriptive right acquired through foot use does not include the right of vehicular use, and a vehicular private prescriptive use does not include an expansion to commercial use.

The task of determining the extent, use, and location of easements is perhaps the most difficult in easements by implication. With this type of easement, an assumption is made that the parties would recognize the normal development of the dominant estate. Normal development is defined according to the initial use of the property. For example, if the dominant estate is used for residential purposes, it is within the normal development that such land may be subdivided for numerous residences. However, it is not within the normal development for the property to be used as a commercial rock bed with the accompanying use of large trucks.

The use of an easement by implication cannot be expanded to benefit properties other than the dominant estate. For example, the dominant estate holder may not permit adjacent landowners to use the easement acquired only by the dominant estate holder's reasonable necessity.

However, all types of easements may be enlarged in their scope through prescription. For example, an easement "for the purpose of transporting milk to a factory" may be used for all purposes for a prescriptive period and thus expand to a general easement. All elements of prescription must be present for the prescriptive period.

The following case illustrates some of the difficulties encountered in determining the scope and extent of an easement.

WETMORE v. LADIES OF LORRETTO, WHEATON
220 N.E.2d 491 (Ill. 1966)

Since 1928 Wetmore (plaintiff/appellee) and his family have owned an 80-acre parcel of land near Wheaton, Illinois. In 1946 Wetmore sold 10 acres of the land to the Ladies of Lorretto (Ladies/defendants/appellants), a non-profit corporation. The diagram depicts the location of the parcels of property involved.

The Ladies improved the parcel with a large mansion house, swimming pool, sunken gardens, and var-

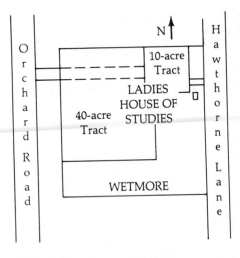

ious outbuildings. Because the 10-acre parcel was landlocked, Wetmore granted to the Ladies an express easement across the remainder of the tract to the east. The easement was an existing driveway that ran in front of Wetmore's house.

Wetmore negotiated the sale of the 40-acre tract (as shown) to the Ladies in 1957. The Ladies had originally wished to purchase a 33-foot strip for a road but Wetmore would agree only to the sale of the entire tract. Wetmore asked the Ladies to give up a small strip near Hawthorne Lane and they declined; however, they stated that when their new 33-foot road was built, they would direct their traffic to that road.

Prior to the road's completion in 1960, relations between Wetmore and the Ladies deteriorated substantially.

Throughout the 1950s the Ladies conducted kindergarten and mu-

sic classes on the 10-acre tract. The result was that 40 to 50 vehicles and pedestrian traffic passed by Wetmore's house daily. Occasionally the Ladies had picnics, parties, and garden parties, which resulted in hundreds of cars passing by Wetmore's house in a single day.

After their road was completed in 1960, the Ladies made verbal requests and sent out maps and directions asking that Wetmore's driveway not be used. Traffic on the driveway was reduced to five vehicles per day.

Still unsatisfied, Wetmore hired a deputy to turn back vehicles, and at times Wetmore had confrontations with the sisters and visitors, which frightened these parties. On one of Wetmore's complaining visits to the convent, the sheriff had to be called to have him removed.

Wetmore installed a gate with a bell and alarm on the driveway to alert him to those using it.

In 1962 the Ladies built a House of Studies partially on the 10-acre tract and partially on the 40-acre tract (see diagram). This new building and its purpose of holding classes caused an increase in traffic.

Wetmore objected to use of the driveway for the House of Studies on the grounds that it was an unintended expansion of the easement for use by the 40-acre tract. The Ladies alleged they had an implied easement for both tracts. The trial court found for Wetmore and issued an injunction against the Ladies, and the Ladies appealed.

DAVIS, Justice

The essential elements of an easement by implication are: (1) The existence of a single tract of land so arranged that one portion of it derives a benefit from the other, the division thereof by a single owner into two or more parcels, and the separation of title; (2) before the separation occurs the use must have been long, continued, obvious or manifest, to a degree which shows permanency; and (3) the use of the claimed easement must be essential to the beneficial enjoyment of the parcel to be benefited.

We believe that the first two requirements are clearly present in this case. The plaintiff owned the entire 80 acre tract in 1946, and after the conveyance to the defendant of the 10 acre tract, still owned the 70 acre tract, which he severed in 1957. At the time of the conveyance of the 10 acre tract to the defendant in 1946, there was a well-defined roadway—extending from the north where the driveway was located—over which an express easement had been granted, within and along the east side of the 10 acre tract to its south edge, where a corner of the 40 acre tract adjoined.

The roadway was surfaced with some semi-permanent material, was clearly visible, and had been long and continuously used.

We do not believe, however, that the third requirement—that the easement be essential to the beneficial enjoyment of the land is present.

Where alternative means of access to property are available without passing over the lands of another and the use of such means does not result in an unreasonable burden, courts should exercise due continence in implying and imposing a burden over the lands of another. The land conveyed to the defendant gave it direct access to a public road. Under such circumstances an easement by implication was not sanctioned.

The plaintiff obtained an injunction preventing the continued use of the express easement appurtenant to the 10 acre tract by reason of its use for the benefit of the nondominant 40 acre tract. The defendant contends that not every extension of the use of an easement to an additional tract is a misuse; and that it is only where the extension materially changes the burden on the servient estate, either as to the type of use or the amount, that there is a misuse.

We do not understand that to be the law. If an easement is appurtenant to one tract of land, any extension thereof to another tract of land is a misuse.

While the erection of the House of Studies building on part of the 40 acre tract results in a technical misuse of the easement granted appurtenant to the 10 acre tract, such trivial and inconsequential misuse neither justifies the issuance of an injunction restraining defendant's right to use the easement expressly granted, nor warrants the authorization granted to plaintiff to close Hawthorne Lane as a means of access to defendant's property.

Defendant is entitled, however, in view of plaintiff's past conduct, to an injunction restraining the plaintiff and his agents from wrongful entry upon defendant's property and from interfering with defendant's proper use of the express easement.

Reversed.

Discussion Questions

1. Who originally owned all of the land in question?
2. Had the Hawthorne driveway been in use at that time?
3. What types of activities were conducted by the Ladies of Lorretto on their property?
4. How much traffic was there on the Hawthorne driveway prior to the construction of the 33-foot road? How

much traffic was there after the road construction?

5. What actions did Wetmore take to inhibit the use of the Hawthorne driveway?

6. Where was the House of Studies built? Why is its location critical?

7. Who won at the trial court level? What relief was awarded the prevailing party?

8. What type of easement exists according to the appellate court?

9. Did access for the House of Studies constitute an impermissible use of the easement?

10. Who wins at the appellate level? What did the court give as a remedy?

Rights and Obligations of Estate Holders in an Easement

Each of the parties in an easement relationship has certain legal responsibilities and rights. It is the responsibility of the easement owner (dominant estate) to keep the easement on the servient estate in repair. This responsibility of repair exists even though the servient estate owner is responsible for damages or the state of disrepair in the easement. The easement owner has the right to enter the servient land for purposes of repair. Furthermore, the easement owner may improve the easement with pavement or gravel when the easement is a right of passage.

The owners of servient estates have the right to use their property in any way not interfering with the dominant holder's use of the easement. For example, the servient owner may grant more than one easement to more than one party.

Servient estate owners may also construct fences along the easement and install gates so long as there is no interference with the easement owner's use of the easement.

The dominant estate has the right to transfer an easement. An easement is transferred along with the dominant estate even though it is not specifically mentioned in the deed. An "all other appurtenances" clause serves to transfer an easement. Likewise, a servient estate is sold subject to any prior-acquired easements.

Termination of Easements

The termination or extinguishment of an easement may be accomplished in several different ways depending on the type of easement involved. An easement is terminated when there is one owner for the dominant and servient estates or when the nonpossessory and possessory interests become united in one owner.

As discussed earlier, an easement by necessity is terminated when the necessity terminates.

All easements can be terminated through abandonment. Abandonment occurs through prescriptive nonuse. Two elements are required to establish abandonment: (1) The easement owner must possess the intent to abandon; and (2) the intent to abandon must be accompanied by conduct indicating the intent to terminate. For example, the owner of a railroad easement who removes the tracks and destroys the shipping factory using the railway has manifested the intent to abandon through conduct. Permitting an easement to fall into a state of disrepair may constitute sufficient conduct manifesting an intent to abandon. For example, allowing an irrigation ditch to become inoperable is an example of disrepair indicating intent to abandon.

All easements may be terminated if the servient owner successfully prevents the dominant holder's use of the easement for the required prescriptive period. Thus an easement may be created and terminated through prescription.

Some easements are created for a specific time or purpose and are terminated upon the expiration of time or elimination of purpose. For example, a right-of-way given so long as the dominant land is used for a stable would terminate if the land becomes used for other purposes.

An easement may be terminated through estoppel. This occurs when the servient owner, believing there has been abandonment, constructs improvements over the easement in reliance upon the abandonment. The idea supporting this theory of termination is that the easement owner should notify the servient landowner that such improvements interfere with the easement. If the easement owner were not required to object, then the servient landowner would make costly changes only to have them eliminated after completion. Estoppel requires prompt action to minimize expense.

PROFITS

A *profit* (or *profit a prendre*) is an easement plus the right of removal. A profit gives the holder the right not only of access to another's land, but also to remove oil, minerals, water, or some other part of the real property.

A profit is not the same as the ownership of subsurface rights because such ownership is exclusive and unlimited. More than one party can hold a profit in a piece of property, and a profit can be limited by the types of minerals that may be taken, the quantity that may be taken, or the time allowed for taking.

A profit is not the sale of personal property because the landowner does not sever the mineral or soil—the profit owner does. For example, the right to remove coal is a profit whereas the right to buy coal after removal is the sale of personal property.

A profit can be appurtenant, as in the right to remove water for use on an adjoining tract; or it can be in gross, as in the example of an oil company that owns no property in the area which is given the right to remove oil from a particular parcel.

Apart from these definitional differences, the creation, rights, and obligations of the parties in a profit a prendre relationship are governed by the same principles of law discussed in the easement portion of this chapter.

LICENSES

A *license* is a right to use land in the possession of another, but it passes no land interest and does not alter or transfer property. A license only makes certain conduct on another's land lawful, such as hunting, fishing, or simply being on the property.

A licensee holds a privilege, and that privilege may be revoked at any time by the landowner. A license may be created by an oral agreement, since it is not an interest in land. If the parties attempt to create an easement by oral agreement, a license results.

The following case deals with the distinction between a license and an easement.

BUNN v. OFFUTT

222 S.E.2d 522 (Va. 1976)

In 1962, Temco sold property located at 900 South Wakefield Street to Harvey and Rosabelle Wynn. In the purchase contract the following provision was found: "use of apartment swimming pool to be available to purchaser and his family." The Wynns were told that subsequent purchasers of their property would also have use of the swimming pool, which is located in an apartment complex next to the Wynns' home. No reference to use of the swimming pool was made in the Wynns' deed.

In 1969 the Bunns (plaintiffs/appellants) purchased the Wynns' home. The Bunns were told of their right to use the pool but upon moving in were denied access. The Bunns insisted on access but were still denied. They filed suit against the owner of Temco, Offutt (defendant/appellee), seeking a declaration of their easement rights. The trial court found for Offutt and the Bunns appealed.

HARRISON, Justice

The testimony of Offutt, owner of appellee corporations, is unequivocal that at no time did he ever intend to extend the privilege of using the swimming pool beyond the original purchasers of certain houses which were located adjacent to his apartment development. He said that at one time he thought he would experience difficulty in selling the houses without an added inducement, and therefore included in his sales contract a clause to the effect that the use of the apartment swimming pool would be available to the purchaser and his family. Offutt further testified he never intended the right to run with the land and inure to successors in interest and in fact had never extended pool privileges to anyone beyond the first purchasers.

The dispositive issue in this case is whether the language in the contract, "use of apartment swimming pool to be available to purchaser and his family," amounted to a grant of a mere license to the Wynns and their family; or whether the Wynns acquired thereby a private easement across the land of appellees to the swimming pool and to the use of the pool, which easement was thereafter transferred to the Bunns.

A license is personal between the licensor and the licensee and cannot be assigned. . . .

[T]he deed is silent as to the pool, and the contract made the use of the pool available only to "purchaser and his family." The trial court found this language consistent with appellees' theory that a mere license and not an interest in land was created. . . .

The trial court further found that no easement had been created by implication for there was neither a showing of preexisting use of the easement prior to the conveyance by Temco to the Wynns, nor any showing that the use of the swimming pool was essential to the beneficial enjoyment of the land conveyed.

The Wynns and their family were given a mere license to use the swimming pool.

Affirmed.

Discussion Questions

1. Who sold the property to the Wynns?
2. What did the swimming pool clause provide?
3. Where was the clause found?
4. From whom did the Bunns purchase their home?
5. What happened when the Bunns tried to use the swimming pool?
6. Did the Bunns have an easement?
7. Did the Wynns have an easement?

COVENANTS

A *covenant* is a restriction placed in a deed that is, in effect, a nonpossessory interest in land. Covenants serve to restrict or control some aspect of the use of the land. The common law rule with respect to such covenants is that they are enforceable against the grantor and grantee but not against any subsequent transferees. For example, a covenant in a grant of land for a railway requiring the construction of a depot and station would be enforceable against the grantee but not against subsequent transferees. For this reason, covenants are not effective in enforcing residential use restrictions. However, equitable servitudes may provide a solution. Equitable servitudes are restrictions on building and the use of land. These restrictions are enforceable against subsequent transferees in the restricted areas.

The recognition of equitable servitudes results from the need of residential home buyers for assurance that areas will remain residential and at a certain quality and level. Zoning laws are also helpful in restricting land use. Zoning laws are discussed at length in Chapter 16, and covenants and equitable servitudes are discussed in Chapter 25.

CONCLUSIONS AND RECOMMENDATIONS

If all persons involved in real estate transactions were knowledgeable and cautious enough to provide for easements, much of the discussion and quoted cases in this chapter would be unnecessary. In applying the tools and risks discussed in this chapter, those involved in a sale transaction should answer the following questions:

1. Is the property accessible or is it landlocked?
2. If the property is accessible, where is the access and who owns it?
3. If the property is landlocked, how can access be obtained?
4. Where is the access route (or where should it be) located?
5. How large an access route is necessary?
6. What types of uses can be made of the access route?
7. Is the access route recorded in any of the land records?
8. Will the deed in the transaction provide for an easement?
9. What parties are using the property, why, when, and for how long?
10. Who will be responsible for maintenance?

If buyers, sellers, agents, brokers, and financiers would take the time to check land records and physically inspect the property involved, many of the expensive easement litigations noted in this chapter could be avoided. The cases used in this chapter demonstrate the types of strong feelings and reactions that can result from misunderstandings on property use. This expensive hostility might be avoided by determining answers to the previous ten questions.

KEY TERMS

easement
easement appurtenant
easement in gross
affirmative easement

negative easement
dominant estate
servient estate
easement by express grant

easement by express reservation
easement by implication
quasi-easement
easement by necessity
prescription

rule of reason
profit
profit a prendre
license
covenant

CHAPTER PROBLEMS

1. Oscar told Bert that he (Bert) could walk his dog (Ernie) on Oscar's property any time. After 20 years of dog walking, Oscar sold his property to Mr. G. After moving in, Mr. G told Bert and Ernie to stay off his land. Bert and Ernie protest. What is the result?

2. Salt Agua Project had been granted the right to lay a pipeline across the rear 8 feet of a piece of land 6 miles long. Since the grant was written the land had been subdivided many times, and many landowners have pipeline in the rear of their yards. Salt Agua lost its license to operate and sold all of its assets (property included) to Consolidated Phoenix, Inc. Salt Agua deeded the pipeline to Consolidated. The landowners claim that the pipeline was not transferrable. Who is correct? Why?

3. Alfonso owned a tract of land depicted in the diagram. Alfonso could

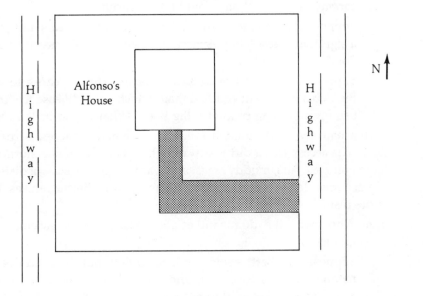

no longer afford the property taxes and decided to sell the western half of the property to Billy. In the deed no mention was made of the access road on Alfonso's eastern half. Billy wishes to use the access road, but Alfonso refuses. The highway on the eastern side goes directly to town (3 miles). The highway on the western side is a major travel route with the nearest two exits 25 miles away.

    a. What is the result?

    b. Suppose Alfonso had told Billy he could use the access road. Would the result be different?

    c. Suppose Alfonso had told Billy he could use the access road; then Alfonso transferred the property to Sam; and Sam refused Billy's request to continue using the access road. What would be the result?

4. Rachael owns a small tract of land in Idaho but lives in Boston. Rachael's Idahoan neighbor, Big Bob, has been using a path on Rachael's tract of land to transport his potatoes for 15 years. Rachael has not visited the property for 16 years but has paid taxes on it. Everyone in the area knows of Big Bob's use of Rachael's land. Upon discovery of Big Bob's use, Rachael wishes to know her rights.

    a. What are Rachael's rights?

    b. Suppose Rachael discovered the problem after 3 years and put up a fence with a locking gate, which Big Bob then kicked down to continue his use. What would be the result?

    c. Suppose Rachael discovered the problem after 3 years and put up a sign that read: "No trespassing. Keep out. This means you, Big Bob." What would be the result?

    d. Suppose Rachael discovered the problem after 3 years and wrote Big Bob a note (sent certified mail) which read, "Please feel free to use my adjoining property, Big Bob." What would be the result?

5. Bertha had, by deed, granted Linda an easement of access across her land. The access was a dirt roadway, which because of bad storms had large potholes, ruts, muddy areas, and was in a general state of disrepair. Linda demanded that Bertha repair the access way. Bertha refuses. What is the result?

    a. Who owns the dominant estate? What type of easement was granted?

    b. Suppose that Bertha sold her land to Bob, but the deed does not mention Linda's easement, and Bob refuses to let Linda use the access way. What are Linda's rights?

6. Ted has just sold a portion of his ranch to Ned. Geographically the land is located as pictured at the top of page 105. No mention of any right-

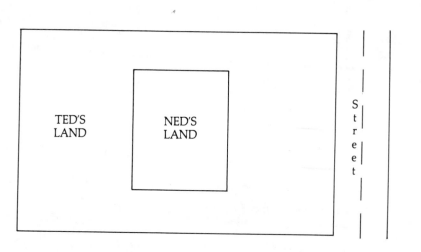

of-way is made in the deed. Is the transaction proper? Is there anything Ned can do?

7. Rob has just given Public Industries, Inc., the right to release their waste products into the air above Rob's land. (Rob's land adjoins Public's plant.) Is this a legal conveyance? Explain.

8. What type of easement is necessary to protect solar panels from shade?

9. Squaw Peak Community Church has an access easement across lands owned by Anozira Development. Anozira wishes to subdivide the property and will need to pave streets and put in sidewalks. Curbs will be put in across the Church's easement. Although the Church will still have access, the curbs will have to be negotiated. Can the Church stop the placement of the curbs? *Squaw Peak Community Covenant Church of Phoenix v. Anozira Dev., Inc.,* 719 P.2d 295 (Ariz. 1986)

10. Sylvia Tenn owns a six-story building that has air conditioners in the windows. 889 Associates, Ltd., is planning to construct a twelve-story building next to Tenn's building. The result will be that Tenn's window air conditioners will no longer be effective. Tenn claims that she has had the air conditioners for more than 20 years and that she has acquired a prescriptive easement for the air conditioners. Is she correct? *Tenn v. 889 Associates, Ltd.,* 500 A.2d 366 (N.H. 1985)

6

FIXTURES

Is the refrigerator included with the house?

—The American Home Buyer

Every lawyer knows that cases can be found in this field that will support any proposition.

—Powell, Real Property

In Chapter 4, the possibility was discussed that personal property could become attached to real property in such a manner as to change the character of the real property and hence become part of it. A *fixture* is real property that was once personal property. This chapter answers the questions, What is a fixture and when does personal property become a fixture? How is the title to a fixture transferred? What rights do creditors have in fixtures?

DEFINITION OF A FIXTURE

Whether a particular item of personal property will become real property depends on several factors discussed in the following sections. No single factor controls; rather, the different factors must be considered together in their entirety in order to determine whether an item is real or personal property. The distinction between real and personal property is critical in two primary areas: First, it will control whether an item passes with the real property or if it may be removed prior to the title transfer. Second, it will affect the determination of the creditor's rights, that is, how much the mortgage holder is entitled to and how much belongs to the personal property creditors.

Degree of Annexation Test

The degree of annexation test is the first factor to be considered in determining the status of an item of property, and its purpose is to examine the fixture's degree of attachment. Under the English rule for fixtures, annexation was the controlling factor and anything attached by mortar, nail, screw, or bolt was classified as a fixture.

Currently, annexation is defined as attachment to the reality with a use or purpose related to the realty. A furnace in a home is an example that meets the degree of annexation necessary for a fixture because the home cannot function without the presence of the furnace (which was once personal property). On the other hand, a ship or boat does not become part of the real property of a dock simply because an anchor is dropped because its attachment to the realty is unrelated. A painting on a wall can be hung on any wall but the sculptures within building columns are a part of the building and hence meet this annexation test.

The degree of annexation test applies to personal property attached to realty but not to accessions. Accessions are those items of personal property that are used in the construction of a building and become so integrated into the building that their identity is lost. Examples of accessions are lumber, bricks, and beams.

(6.1) Consider:

Applying the degree of annexation test to each of the following, determine the likelihood of having the item treated as a fixture.

a. Wall-to-wall carpeting
b. Draperies and curtain rods
c. Underground gas tanks for a gas station
d. Above-ground swimming pool

Nature and Use of the Property

The unique nature of the property attached is also examined to determine its necessity in relation to the effective functioning of the building. For example, storm windows are especially built and installed for a particular home and work to help control heat in the home. Likewise, a pipe organ in a church with the pipes serving as decoration for the building has an intricate relation to the building. In a garage, an air compressor that is used to hoist cars for repair is central and necessary to the function of that building.

Relationship Between the Annexor and the Premises

Another factor to be examined is what type of land interest the party attaching the personal property (the annexor) owns. In brief, the higher the degree of interest in the land, the more likely it is that the item or property will be treated as a fixture. For example, a small cottage or bungalow placed on cement blocks on the land by a fee simple owner is a fixture. That same bungalow placed on leased land by a tenant will probably retain its characteristics of personal property.

A tenant does not hold as great an interest in the land as a life estate holder or a fee simple holder. Therefore, annexations by tenants are less likely to be treated as fixtures. Two additional questions to examine in analyzing this factor are: (1) Did the tenant intend the item to be a gift to the landlord (that is, Did the tenant intend to leave the property at the termination of the lease?), and (2) Will removal of the property cause substantial damage? For example, a floor replaced with a new covering by a tenant will be substantially damaged if the covering is removed upon termination of the tenancy. On the other hand, temporary wall bookshelves may not cause irreparable damage when removed and would be classified as a tenant's personal property.

Intent

This factor can be the controlling factor in cases where the issue of fixture versus personal property is a close decision, as well as in cases where the parties have reached an agreement (or have placed a provision in their contract or lease) covering the issue of whether an item will be real or personal property. For example, the refrigerators may be included in the sale of residences or apartments, and according to the parties involved may be considered a fixture. Likewise, washers and dryers may be part of the real estate according to the terms of the parties' agreement.

Trade Fixtures

The term *trade fixture* is a misnomer. This term covers a special rule for machines and equipment used in a trade or business. Under the rule, those items used in a trade or business are treated as personal property, in spite of their degree of annexation. In the absence of an agreement between the parties, title to the equipment or machinery does not pass with the sale of the factory, business, or other real property. For example, a large printing press bolted to the floor is a trade fixture and thus personal property. Likewise, display counters in stores are attached but are classified as trade fixtures.

Who Wants to Know?

Although the treatises on real property do not list this factor as one to be used in the determination of real versus personal property, the question of who wants to know has affected judicial decisions in this area. This factor permits differing results depending on what party is seeking to determine the classification for an item of property.

For example, in litigation between a buyer and seller, the buyer is favored because the seller usually presents the form contract and has failed to make all intentions clear in that contract. In an eminent domain valuation procedure, the landowner is favored with a liberal finding of fixtures because just and fair compensation is the court's concern in these circumstances. If a question arises on the application of real property insurance for certain items, the insured will be favored with liberal fixture treatment because of the insurer's failure to clarify coverage provisions. In taxation valuations, fixtures are more liberally found because of the increased value of the property when the fixtures are included in the valuation determination.

The following cases are examples of courts applying the various factors used in the determination of whether an item is real or personal property.

MICHIGAN NATIONAL BANK, LANSING v. CITY OF LANSING
293 N.W.2d 626 (Mich. 1980)

The Michigan Tax Tribunal held that Michigan National Bank's (petitioner) night depository equipment, drive-up window equipment, vault doors, and remote transactions units, which were physically integrated with the bank's land and buildings, were fixtures and subject to taxation as realty by the city of Lansing (respondent). The bank appealed.

GILLS, Presiding Judge

This is an appeal from a Michigan Tax Tribunal order affirming six real property assessments made by the respondent on certain items of petitioner's property. Five of the assessments concern properties owned by the petitioner and one of the assessments involves property leased by the petitioner. The matter in dispute is whether certain items of bank equipment, specifically, bank vault doors, night depository equipment, drive-up teller window equipment and remote transaction systems, are subject to assessment and taxation as real property or whether they are items of personal property and are exempt from taxation.

The test to be applied in order to ascertain whether or not an item is a fixture summarizes three factors:

1. Annexation to the realty, either actual or constructive;

2. Adaptation or application to the use or purpose of that part of the realty to which it is connected or appropriated; and

3. Intention to make the article a permanent accession to the realty. The intention which controls is that manifested by the objective, visible facts. It is sufficient if the item is intended to remain where affixed until worn out, until the purpose to which the realty is devoted is accomplished or until the item is superseded by another item more suitable for the purpose.

Applying these factors to the present case necessitates the conclusion that the Tribunal properly found the items in question to be fixtures. All four items are physically annexed to the realty. The night depository equipment, drive-up window equipment and the vault doors are all cemented into place. Once installed, they are integrated with and become part of the wall in which they are mounted. The remote transaction units are also physically integrated with the land and the buildings. Such a unit consists of a roof-type canopy supported by pillars which extends from the building wall or roof over the customer unit. The customer unit is mounted with steel bolts to a specially constructed concrete island. A pneumatic tube system runs either up into the canopy or down into the ground and then into the building.

Furthermore, each item is adapted to the use of the realty. In fact, not only is the present use of these buildings dependent on the presence of these items, none of these items can be used unless they are affixed to a building or land.

Taken together, these factors establish the petitioner's intent to permanently affix these items to the realty.

The petitioner further contends that, even if these items are found to be fixtures, they are trade fixtures and as such are classified as personal property which is exempt from taxation.

A trade fixture is merely a fixture which has been annexed to leased realty by a lessee for the purpose of enabling him to engage in a business. The trade fixture doctrine permits the lessee, upon the termination of the lease, to remove such a fixture from the lessor's real property. With respect to the lessee's right of removal, a trade fixture is characterized as personalty. The doctrine by its terms applies only in leasehold situations.

The rule regarding trade fixtures which arose out of commercial necessity for the limited purpose of protecting tenants in the ownership of certain kinds of property has no application between other parties in other relationships. Although as between lessor and lessee trade fixtures might be personal property, as to third parties they are properly considered as a part of the realty.

Affirmed.

Discussion Questions

1. Describe the property in question.
2. Why was a determination of real versus personal property necessary?
3. What factors did the court of appeals examine in determining whether a fixture was involved?
4. Did the rule for trade fixtures apply?
5. Were the items real or personal property?

CONSIGLIO v. CAREY
421 N.E.2d 1256 (Mass. 1981)

During the summer seasons, Carey (defendant/appellant) operated a restaurant called Dorsie's Steak House in a wood-frame building in West Yarmouth from 1975 to 1978. He paid rent ranging from $4,500 to $8,500 per month in 1978. In 1979, Carey and Consiglio (plaintiff/appellee) discussed the possibility of Carey's purchasing the restaurant and 1 acre of land for $195,000. Carey took no action and Consiglio then notified Carey of the 1979 rent, which would be $35,000 per month. Consiglio hoped to induce Carey's purchase with the rent increase. Instead, Carey prepared to move his operation to another building roughly 1 mile away. Consiglio brought suit to enjoin Carey from removing the restaurant equipment. The trial court held that Carey could remove all but six items from the building, and Carey appealed.

ARMSTRONG, Justice

The six items of equipment are a walk-in freezer, a compressor which supplies the cold air to the freezer, two air conditioners, a dishwasher, and a bar. The judge made no findings concerning the circumstances in which these items came to be on the premises, apparently because of his opinion, which is made explicit in his findings, that the decisive question was the manner in which the equipment items were attached to the building. The testimony at the trial was specific. Only one of the six contested items was on the premises when the defendant began his tenancy; namely, the dishwasher, which the defendant purchased from the prior occupant, Carl's Restaurant, Inc., along with many of the other items which the judge ruled the defendant had properly removed from the premises. The defendant purchased the two air conditioners and installed them in two of the three window casings on the street side of the building. The units were large; their installation necessitated removal of the sash from each casing. The walk-in freezer and the compressor were purchased by the defendant from a restaurant supply company. The freezer was twelve feet high—too high to be brought into the building. It was installed at the back wall of the building on an insulated concrete slab. A hole was cut in the rear wall of the building to provide access to the freezer door. A plywood shell was erected around the freezer to protect it from the sun and weather. The freezer itself is "portable" in the sense that a person using only an "Allen set wrench" can break it down into panels for easy transportation and reassembly. The compressor, bought at the same time, is also located outside the building and is attached only to the freezer. The defendant built the bar in 1979, shortly before the dispute which led to his departure. The nature of its attachment to the building does not appear in the recorded evidence, but the judge made a general finding that each of the items in question is attached to the realty.

A determination that the items are affixed to the realty does not, however, dispose of the case, as it might, for example, if the items had been installed by the owner of the realty, and the dispute was with a purchaser of the realty, or between the owner as mortgagor and mortgagee. . . .

Many articles annexed by a tenant can be removed by him which, if annexed by the owner, become part of the realty and pass under a deed or mortgage. . . .

[T]he things which the tenant has at his own expense affixed to the freehold for purposes of ornament or domestic convenience, or for purposes of trade, business or manufactures, may be removed by him before the expiration of his term. The right of removal depends upon the mode in which the thing to be removed is annexed to the freehold, and the effect which its removal would have upon the premises.

Applying these principles to the present case, we think it is clear that the items in dispute, except the dishwasher, are tenant's fixtures, having been installed by the defendant during his tenancy for the purpose to which he was putting the rented premises, and that they can be re-moved without damage to the items themselves and with only minor damage to the premises.

As to that damage, the defendant has an obligation to restore the premises to the condition they were in before the tenancy, reasonable wear and tear excepted.

The record does not enable us to determine whether the dishwasher is a tenant's fixture. It is unnecessarily speculative to attempt to infer that the dishwasher was installed by Carl's Restaurant, Inc. solely from the fact that it treated the dishwasher as its personal property by selling it to the defendant, when the matter may be made certain by direct evidence. If, on a rehearing . . . it should be shown that the dishwasher was installed by Carl's Restaurant, Inc., and was thus removable during its tenancy, it would retain its character as a tenant's fixture.

The judgment is reversed.

Discussion Questions

1. What type of property did Carey lease? What type of business was operated?
2. Why was Carey removing the six items of property?
3. What were the six items?
4. Who added the six items to the property?
5. Why is Carl's Restaurant involved?
6. Are any of the items trade fixtures?
7. Is any damage caused by removal? Who is responsible for repair of that damage?
8. What evidence about the dishwasher does the appellate court need?
9. Who wins at the court of appeals level?

(6.2) Consider:

Applying the factors for determining what constitutes a fixture and the preceding cases, determine the status of each of the following:

a. Floor-to-ceiling bookcases installed in an apartment by a tenant
b. Automatic garage door opener control
c. Landscaping
d. Electric ceiling fans
e. Partitions nailed to the floor in an office building

f. Paneled refrigerator (paneled to match kitchen cabinets)

g. Bank vault door

h. Murphy bed (bed that folds into wall)

i. Seats and screens in a theatre

j. Ski lifts at a ski resort

k. Storage bins on a farm

A Word on Precautions

Once again the cases in this chapter have demonstrated that emotions and litigation can arise very easily over what appear to be insignificant items. Also, most of the confusion, emotion, and litigation could again be avoided if parties would clearly determine their positions at the outset through written agreements. Figure 6.1 summarizes the questions that should be addressed in various types of land transactions to cover the issue of fixtures.

***Figure 6.1** Fixture Analysis*

PARTIES	QUESTIONS TO BE ANSWERED
Landlord/Tenant	1. Does the lease contain a provision on what types of attachments the tenant may make and remove? 2. Does the lease contain a provision on payment for damages for removal? 3. Does the lease require prior notification before a tenant attaches property?
Buyer/Seller	1. What items are included with the real property? 2. Are any items specifically excluded? 3. Does the contract list questionable items, such as drapes? 4. Does the contract prevent substitution or removal of fixtures before closing? 5. Is a bill of sale drawn up for questionable items such as washers, dryers, and refrigerators?
Creditor/Attacher	1. Who owns the land where the property is being attached? 2. How permanent will the attachment be? 3. Can removal occur without damage to the property? 4. Are there other creditors with protected interests in the real property?

TRANSFER OF TITLE TO FIXTURES AND PERSONAL PROPERTY

If property is classified as a fixture and part of the real property, title to it will pass with the deed transferring title to the property. However, for items not classified as fixtures, some method of transferring title is necessary. Whenever a question exists as to whether an item is real or personal property, a bill of sale should be used to assure complete transfer of title.

CREDITORS' RIGHTS IN FIXTURES

One of the reasons given for the determination of whether an item is personal property or a fixture was that creditors' rights are affected by the determination. There are provisions in each state to protect creditors' interests in personal property that becomes attached to real estate and is then classified as a fixture.

This protection is afforded under *Article 9* of the *Uniform Commercial Code (UCC)*. The UCC is a set of laws drafted by a group of scholars, attorneys, and business people with the idea of having state-to-state uniformity in commercial transactions.

Article 9 is concerned with creditors' rights and responsibilities in collateral pledged by debtors for loans. Forty-nine states have adopted some version of Article 9. Article 9 has had several different versions since 1972 and some states have a mixture of versions. In passing Article 9, each state has made some variations in the sections adopted and in the language of each section. Thus the actual Article 9 language discussed in this portion of the chapter will vary from state to state.

Scope of Article 9

Article 9 of the UCC governs the use of personal property or the use of fixtures as collateral (9-101). The concern in this book will be fixtures because of their relationship to real estate law.

Article 9 permits the creditor to obtain an interest in the collateral called a *security interest*, which provides the creditor with certain rights, opportunities, and priorities.

Creation of the Security Interest

There are three requirements for creating a valid security interest: a security agreement, a debtor with rights in collateral, and value given by the creditor.

The Security Agreement A security interest begins with the execution of a *security agreement* by the creditor and debtor (9-201). A security agreement has several requirements: (1) It must be in writing; (2) it must be signed by the debtor; (3) it must contain language indicating a security interest is being created; and (4) it must contain a description of the collateral that reasonably identifies it. Since fixtures will be attached to real property, a description of the real property involved is helpful in clarifying the identity and location of the property (although such a description is not technically necessary under the UCC).

Form security agreements, available in each state, generally meet all of the requirements for a valid security agreement.

Debtor's Rights in the Collateral (9-203) In some cases the debtor may already own the collateral and is simply pledging such property as security for a debt. In most fixture cases, however, the creditor is selling goods to the buyer and the buyer is pledging the purchased goods as collateral. In these cases, the debtor has rights in the collateral at the time of delivery so that the pledge can be properly made. For example, a seller of air conditioners who has the buyer execute a security agreement will have a valid security interest when the buyer takes possession of the air conditioner. Thus the security agreement can still be validly executed in advance and become effective upon the buyer's possession.

Value Given by the Creditor (9-203) In the preceding example the creditor gives value through the binding commitment to extend credit. A creditor may give value in any way that would constitute consideration in a simple contract. In the case of fixtures the promise to extend credit is most frequently given as value by the creditor.

Once all three requirements are met (written agreement, collateral interest, and value), the security interest attaches. Just having a security interest gives the creditor certain rights to a superior position over that of other creditors. A secured creditor is always given priority over unsecured creditors. Also, the creation of a security interest entitles the creditor to repossession of the secured property in the event the debtor defaults on payments for the collateral.

However, for the creditor to enjoy the most complete protection available under Article 9, perfection must be reached.

The Purchase Money Security Interest in Fixtures (9-107)

One way for a creditor to obtain more complete protection is to hold a *purchase money security interest (PMSI)*. A PMSI is given to secure all or part of the purchase price of the item purchased. For example, when a home owner or a business purchases an air conditioner on credit from a seller or manufacturer of such units and the seller or manufacturer takes a security interest, a PMSI exists. The distinction between a PMSI and a security interest is important because the PMSI creditor is entitled to certain priorities in the event the debtor (buyer) defaults on payments for the fixture.

Perfection of the Security Interest

The Financing Statement (9-402) *Perfection* (when fixtures are involved) is obtained through the filing of a *financing statement*. A financing statement is a written form that will vary from state to state but must include the following items:

1. Names of the debtors and the secured party
2. Signature of the debtor
3. Address of the secured party from which information can be obtained
4. Mailing address of the debtor
5. A statement describing the items of collateral

Also required on a fixture financing statement is a statement that the financing statement will be filed in the real estate records. Most of the information required on the financing statement is self-explanatory, but the description item is critical. (Here, for fixtures, a description of the real estate involved is necessary.) The following discussion of filing will also explain why this description of the land is of critical importance.

Filing the Financing Statement Once a valid financing statement has been executed, perfection for fixture security interests is obtained by filing the financial statement under Article 9. Filing is done either centrally, locally, or both. Central filing is generally done with the secretary of state of the particular state where the property is located, and local filing is generally done at the county level where land records are kept.

Article 9 fixture filings are done locally because fixtures are land interests and all records of creditors' interests in land should be reflected in the same series of records. An accurate land description is needed to make clear where the fixture is located and for proper notification of all parties interested in the land.

Upon filing of the financing statement in the proper office, the creditor's interest is perfected. This perfection entitles creditors to priority over subsequent creditors and even priority over some prior creditors. These priorities are discussed in the next section.

Length of Perfection A filing under the UCC is good for a period of 5 years (this time may vary from state to state). However, if the debt is paid prior to that time, the financing statement and security interest can be terminated. If necessary, the creditor may renew the financing statement any time during the final 6 months of the 5-year term and will thus receive the protection for another 5 years.

The General Rules of Priority Among Secured Creditors (9-313)

To determine priorities among creditors in the event of the debtor's default, certain rules and exceptions will be applied. These general rules are the starting point for determining the priorities in payment rights when a debtor is in default on loans secured by mortgages and security interests in fixtures:

1. A secured creditor has priority over an unsecured creditor.
2. A perfected secured creditor has priority over an unperfected secured creditor.
3. A perfected secured creditor has priority over subsequent real estate interests. (For example, a filing on 3 January gives the secured party priority over filings occurring later in that month or simply later in time.)
4. A prior real estate interest (mortgage, deed of trust, lien, or judgment) has priority over a subsequently filed security interest.
5. Between perfected secured creditors the date of filing is controlling, with the first creditor to file having priority.

Exceptions to the General Rules

PMSI Exception A PMSI creditor may take priority over prior real estate encumbrances if the financing statement is filed before the goods become fixtures or within 10 days after they become fixtures. This priority applies even though language in the mortgage provides that all after-attached property and fixtures are subject to the mortgage. To illustrate, suppose that a home owner has a mortgage on property, which was filed in August 1979. The home owner is in need of a solar water-heating system. The system is purchased from Solar Systems Company on credit, and a security agreement is executed and a financing statement filed on 3 June 1986. The solar system is then attached and installed. Solar Systems Company (as a PMSI) would have priority over the 1979 mortgage holder.

The reason for the PMSI exception is that without some form of special priority for the secured party, creditors would be hesitant to finance improvements and added fixtures to existing structures still subject to a mortgage. The following case illustrates the effect of the PMSI exception.

HARTFORD NATIONAL BANK & TRUST CO. v. GODIN
398 A.2d 286 (Vt. 1979)

The Godins (defendants) owned land in Halifax, Vermont, and gave a mortgage on that land to Greenfield Savings Bank (appellant) on 27 October 1972. Greenfield recorded the mortgage on 28 October 1972. The Godins purchased a mobile home in New Hampshire for the lot on 10 May 1973. Hartford National Bank & Trust (plaintiff/appellee) financed the purchase. The Godins then moved the mobile home to Halifax, Vermont, and Hartford filed a UCC financing statement with the Halifax town clerk on 1 July 1975.

Next the Godins installed the mobile home on their lot. A concrete-block foundation supported the mobile home, and there were attached steps, a connected septic system, and encasement of the foundation in aluminum foundation siding.

The Godins defaulted on their payments to Hartford, and Hartford brought suit to repossess the mobile home. Greenfield objected on the grounds that the home was a fixture, part of the realty, and subject to their prior mortgage. The trial court ruled for Hartford, and Greenfield appealed.

LARROW, Justice

The trial court concluded, we think correctly, that the mobile home became a fixture with its installation on the mortgaged premises.

There is annexation to the realty, adaptation to the use of the realty, and an intent to make the property a part of the real estate. The mobile home became . . . a fixed residence. The only consequence flowing from this, however, is that it is subject to the Greenfield mortgage. Whether that mortgage lien has priority over the security interest of the plaintiff Hartford is governed by the applicable statutes.

9A V.S.A. Section 9-313 is our enactment of the applicable section of the Uniform Commercial Code. It relates to the priority of security interests in fixtures, excluding building materials from the definition but leaving state law other than Title 9A to determine when other goods become fixtures. Under our statutes (enacted prior to the Final Report of the Review Committee for Article 9 of the Uniform Commercial Code), a security interest which attaches to goods before they become fixtures takes priority, as to the goods, over real estate interests, with certain exceptions.

There can be no doubt in the instant case that the security interest here asserted by Hartford attached at the time the mobile home was purchased. The Uniform Act draws a clear distinction between when a security interest attaches and when it is perfected. The security interest attaches when there is an agreement that it attach, value is given, and the debtor has rights in the collateral. 9A V.S.A. Section 9-204(1). For a fixture, it is perfected by the filing of a financing statement with the appropriate office. In the instant case, because the security interest now asserted by Hartford attached to the collateral before it became a fixture, the time of perfecting becomes immaterial. The security interest has priority, under the statute, over a mortgage which existed prior to affixation.

Affirmed.

Discussion Questions

1. Who owned the land?
2. Who held the mortgage?
3. When was the mortgage filed or recorded?
4. Where was the mobile home purchased?
5. Who was the secured party?
6. When did the security interest attach?
7. When was the security interest perfected?
8. Who has priority?

There is one exclusion to the PMSI exception that deals with mortgages. If a lender makes an advance on an existing loan (with a recorded mortgage) without knowledge of the PMSI and before perfection of the PMSI, the lender will have priority for at least that advance. For example, Thrift records a mortgage on Eaton Inc.'s property on 1 July 1986. The mortgage amount is to be given to Eaton in $50,000 advances with one advance scheduled for 15 June 1988. On 10 June 1988, Eaton enters into a PMSI with Window Fashions for blinds. Window Fashions has 10 days from the 10 June to file, and during this 10-day period, the advance could be made without recorded notice of this new security interest. Thrift is given priority if the $50,000 advance is made during that 10-day period and no financing statement has been filed.

Construction Mortgage Exception A construction mortgage is a mortgage used for the construction on and improvement of land. It has priority over fixture security interests for fixtures installed during construction.

Readily Movable Exception Secured creditors with perfected interests in readily removable office or factory machines or in replaced consumer goods and appliances have priority over conflicting real estate interests. Readily removable office equipment includes items such as typewriters, photocopy machines, and small computers. Consumer appliances include items such as stoves, dishwashers, and garbage disposals. Creditors for consumer appliances obtain automatic perfection in these items when the security interests are executed. For example, homeowner A has a 1980 mortgage on the property and in 1988 purchases a dishwasher from Ace Appliance on credit as a replacement for the original dishwasher built into the kitchen. Since Ace has an automatically perfected security interest in a consumer good, it will have priority over any other real estate interests, including the 1980 mortgage.

Consent Exception Subsequent perfected secured parties may obtain priority by obtaining the consent of others holding encumbrances against the subject property. The reason for this exception is to allow parties involved to reach an agreement on priorities if they are able.

Tenant Exception Creditors of tenants who have attached fixtures to leased property have priority over other prior and subsequent real estate encumbrances so long as the tenant has the right to remove such items upon termination of the lease. For example, a secured creditor of a tenant who attaches the financed, movable air conditioner to the landlord's property has priority over a mortgage on the property executed by the landlord.

Good Faith Purchaser Exception Good faith purchasers (9-307) who purchase realty or fixtures without notice of a perfected interest (either actual knowledge or a filed financing statement) will have priority over secured parties so long as they purchase for value. Purchasers are thus protected when the creditor or secured party does not file the required financing statement.

Figure 6.2 summarizes the Article 9 priorities and exceptions. Several issues of priorities among secured creditors are also highlighted by the following case.

UNITED STATES v. BALLARD
645 F. Supp. 788 (Mont. 1986)

On 28 April 1980, First Citizens Bank of Butte (the Bank/defendant) began lending money to John and Patsy Ballard (the Ballards/also defendants). The loans were used to establish and operate Ballard Dairy. On 18 June 1980, the Ballards borrowed additional funds from the Bank and gave the Bank a security interest in all their equipment and livestock (what was owned then and thereafter acquired). The Bank filed a financing statement in the county recorder's office on 25 June 1980.

The United States, acting through the Farmers Home Administration (FmHA) (plaintiff), had made the following loans to the Ballards:

1. A farm ownership loan of $197,660
2. An operating loan of $97,750
3. An economic emergency loan of $150,000

In return for the farm ownership loan, the Ballards executed and de-livered to the FmHA a real estate mortgage covering land situated in Jefferson County. The FmHA filed that mortgage with the Jefferson County Clerk and Recorder on 3 September 1980. To secure the other two loans, the Ballards gave FmHA a security interest in all their livestock, farm machinery, and equipment. The FmHA perfected its security interest by filing a financing statement with the Jefferson County Clerk and Recorder on 24 September 1980.

On 21 June 1982, the Ballards declared bankruptcy. The Bank took possession of certain farm items and sold them. FmHA claimed a PMSI in the milk tank and in certain livestock. The Bank said its after-acquired clause in its agreement covered those items and gave it priority. The present litigation resulted because of this dispute.

Figure 6.2 Priorities in Fixtures Under Article 9-313

TYPE OF PARTY	PRIORITY OVER	EXCEPTIONS TO GENERAL PRIORITY RULES
Secured party	Unsecured party, secured party whose interest attached after	Good faith purchasers
Perfected secured party	Secured party, unsecured party, subsequently filed real estate encumbrances (mortgages, deeds of trust, liens, judgments, security interests)	Good faith purchasers
PMSI perfected secured party	Secured party, unsecured party, subsequently filed real estate encumbrances	Construction
		Mortgages with advancements yet to be made
	Prior perfected security interests and real estate encumbrances if financing statement filed before attachment or within 10 days of attachment	Good faith purchasers
Construction mortgage	All subsequent encumbrances and security interests	
Secured party for: readily removable office or factory machines	No fixture filing required/perfection required	Construction
	Priority over all real estate encumbrances (prior and subsequent)	
readily removable replacement of a domestic appliance	Automatic perfection on consumer goods	
Secured party for a tenant	Priority over all real estate encumbrances regardless of perfection so long as tenant holds the right to remove property	
Good faith purchaser	Prior security interests if purchase is made without knowledge of the security interest and before perfection	

HATFIELD, District Judge

ISSUES

1. Did the Bank have a valid perfected security interest in the Ballards' livestock and equipment?

2. If so, does the FmHA have a purchase money security interest in some of the Ballards' livestock that takes priority over the Bank's security interest?

3. Did the Bank's security interest in

equipment, specifically the milk tank, continue even though the tank was subsequently affixed to real property?

When all the evidence is considered, it is clear that the Bank has a valid perfected security interest creating a superior first lien on all equipment and livestock owned and thereafter acquired by the Ballards. This is especially true in light of the letter from Lyle Seaman, the FmHA's former County Supervisor. In that letter, Seaman admits it was the FmHA's intention that the Bank have a first security interest in all the Ballards' livestock and equipment then owned or thereafter acquired. The Bank's security agreement of 19 June 1980 gave it a valid first lien on the Ballards' livestock and equipment then owned or thereafter acquired.

The question then becomes whether the FmHA can successfully assert a purchase money security interest in certain livestock and thereby take priority over the Bank's security interest. A purchase money security interest, as defined in 9-107(b), includes an interest "taken by a person who by making advances or incurring an obligation gives value to enable the debtor to acquire rights in or the use of collateral if such value is in fact so used." A purchase money security interest in collateral other than inventory takes priority over a conflicting security interest in the same collateral provided it is perfected at the time the debtor receives possession of the collateral or within 20 days thereafter.

In the instant case, the FmHA perfected a security interest in livestock and farm equipment by filing a financing statement on 24 September 1980. Therefore, in order for the FmHA to attain purchase money secured status and take priority over the Bank's security interest, it must show that the money lent was in fact used to acquire an interest in the collateral in question, namely the livestock.

[T]he Minnesota Supreme Court [has] addressed the issue of whether a creditor's secured interest was a purchase money security interest. According to the Minnesota Supreme Court,

the definition of purchase money security interest . . . contemplates that the loaned funds be intended, and actually used, for the purchase of an identifiable asset which stands as the secured party's collateral.

This court agrees with the Minnesota Supreme Court's interpretation of the requirements to attain purchase money secured status as set forth. In the instant case, the FmHA has failed to prove that the funds it loaned to the Ballards were intended, and actually used, for the purchase of identifiable livestock.

As discussed earlier, the statement of Lyle Seaman, FmHA's former County Supervisor, clearly shows it was the FmHA's intention that the Bank have a first security interest in all the Ballards' collateral. Regardless of the Bank's first lien, the FmHA could have established a purchase money interest by documenting which livestock the Ballards purchased with FmHA loan funds. However, it seems clear that the FmHA failed to maintain any record of what was purchased with its loan funds.

The only evidence the FmHA produced to establish its purchase money status were copies of checks drawn from their controlled checking account with the Ballards. The dates on those checks range from 18 September 1980 to 20 July 1981. However, no copies of any bills of sale have been introduced to show when John Ballard took possession of the livestock in which the FmHA is claiming a purchase money security interest.

The third issue before the court is a priority dispute over the milk tank. The FmHA contends the tank became a fixture when it was bolted to the milk barn's floor and, therefore, was covered by its real estate mortgage of 29 August 1980. On the other hand, the Bank asserts the tank was initially "equipment" and that it had a perfected security interest in all the Ballards' present and future acquired equipment on 25 June 1980. Therefore, the Bank claims its security interest attached before the tank became a fixture which gives it priority under 9-313(2).

As set forth in the final pretrial order, the Ballards purchased the milk tank with Bank funds. Furthermore, as discussed above, the Bank had a valid first lien on all the Ballards' present and future acquired livestock and equipment from and after 25 June 1980. The milk tank was clearly equipment, at least until it was bolted to the floor of the milk barn.

Section 9-313 governs the priority of security interests in fixtures. Subsection (2) of that statute provides:

A security interest which attaches to goods before they become fixtures takes priority as to the goods over the claims of all per-

sons who have an interest in the real estate except as stated in subsection (4).

None of the exceptions in subsection (4) apply to the facts in the instant case. Therefore, the sole remaining question is whether the Bank's security interest attached to the milk tank before it became a fixture.

Section 9-204 governs the attachment of a security interest. A security interest attaches when: (1) the debtor signs a security agreement, (2) value is given, and (3) the debtor has rights in the collateral. In the instant case, it is clear that the above requirements were met and the Bank security interest attached before the tank was bolted to the milk barn's floor. Therefore, since the Bank's security interest attached before the tank became a fixture, the Bank has priority under 9-313(2). Furthermore, based on its prior interest, the Bank was justified in repossessing the tank from the Ballards' property.

Judgment is hereby entered for the defendant, First Citizens Bank of Butte.

Discussion Questions

1. What was the security for the Bank's loan?
2. When was the Bank's interest perfected?
3. What loans did FmHA make?
4. What was the security for the loans?
5. When did FmHA perfect their security?
6. Whose security interest in the milk tank has priority?
7. How could FmHA have enjoyed priority over the Bank?
8. What proof was FmHA missing?

(6.3) Consider:

Mrs. Kellerman remodeled her kitchen. Since her built-in oven needed to be replaced, she purchased an oven from Al's Appliance and TV. Mrs. Kellerman financed the purchase, and she and Al executed a security agreement on 30 June 1988. Mrs. Kellerman's property has a mortgage on it that was filed in 1980 to secure the financing of her home.

1. Is Al's interest perfected?

2. Can Al obtain priority over the 1975 mortgage?

3. Is Al required to file a financing statement to obtain priority over the mortgage?

4. Is the oven readily removable? Does the answer make a difference in the outcome of priorities?

5. Would the result be different if the mortgage covered all after-attached property and fixtures?

Default by the Debtor and Rights of the Secured Party (9-501)

If a secured party has priority and the debtor has defaulted, the secured party has the right to remove the collateral from the real estate but must reimburse the owner or other encumbrancers for the cost of repairing any injury to the property. However, the security agreement may provide that the debtor is responsible for paying the cost of repair. Neither the debtor nor the secured party is responsible for paying any decrease in value caused by the removal of the fixture. For example, if mirrors are removed from a wall, the cost of repair may be $30 for restoring the wall surface. However, the $1,000 decrease in value of the property need not be paid. Another example would be the removal of a roof-top air conditioner: the hole in the roof is easily repaired but the decrease in value, which may be substantial, need not be remedied.

Precaution on Security Interests

Article 9 affords creditors tremendous protection in collateral rights and priorities. However, creditors need to be certain of their positions, and the following questions should help them to insure that they will have the best position and best available protection for their secured debt:

1. Is there a written security agreement with all of the necessary information?
2. Has the value been given?
3. Has the security interest attached?
4. To whose property is the item being attached?
5. What other creditors have interests in that property? Is there a construction mortgage? Have the land records been checked?
6. Is the financing statement complete? Is the legal description included and accurate? Is the collateral sufficiently identified?
7. Has the financing statement been filed, and filed in the correct place?
8. Has the financing statement been filed within the appropriate time limits (10 days on a PMSI)?

9. Is renewal necessary? When?

10. Can removal damage be minimized?

By answering these questions and following through on tasks at the outset, creditors can avoid the problems of forgotten filings, incomplete documents, and the resulting lack of protection.

For those involved in a real property transfer, the presence of Article 9 interests is to be checked and provided for in the parties' contract. If an Article 9 interest is not disclosed or is overlooked, the door for litigation and liability is immediately opened. The following checklist is suggested for buyers, sellers, brokers, agents, and others involved in real estate transactions:

1. Have the records been checked to determine if a perfected security interest exists?

2. If a perfected interest does exist, who is the creditor? What property is covered? How much is owed? What payments are made? Is all of the paperwork proper? Does this creditor have priority?

3. Does an unperfected security interest exist on any items on the property? Who is the creditor? How much is owed? What payments are made? Is all of the paperwork proper?

4. Who will pay the balance due? Will it be paid from sale proceeds? Is the buyer to assume responsibility for payment?

5. Is there a provision in the contract for the disposition of debts and collateral pledges?

KEY TERMS

fixture

trade fixture

Article 9

Uniform Commercial Code (UCC)

security interest

security agreement

purchase money security interest (PMSI)

perfection

financing statement

CHAPTER PROBLEMS

1. Determine whether each of the following would constitute a fixture. Discuss any further information that would be helpful in making the determination.

   a. A marble monument with a cement foundation in a cemetery

   b. Bookshelves in a library

    c. Wall mirrors installed by a tenant

    d. A furnace that is bolted to the floor in a factory

    e. A hog house (with a cement foundation) on a farm

    f. Ceiling fans in a home

2. Thrifty is the construction mortgagee for a large motel. According to the terms of the recorded mortgage, the construction money is to be used for the construction, the acquisition of a central air-conditioning unit, and the furnishings for each unit. A small loan company has also loaned the builder money for the purchase of the central air-conditioning unit and the furnishings. The loan company has a valid security agreement and files a financing statement before the items are placed on the property.

    a. Who has priority in the air conditioning unit?

    b. Who has priority in the furnishings?

    c. What would be the rights of a buyer purchasing the motel after installation of the furnishings and the central air-conditioning unit?

3. Bill leased an apartment from Windmere Apartments, Inc. Under the lease agreement, Bill is permitted to remove all fixtures installed on the property. Bill arranged to have some custom bookshelves placed along one wall (the shelves are attached to the wall). Bill financed the shelves with Carl's Cabinetry, and Carl's filed a valid financing statement for the fixtures on 1 December 1988. Windmere has had a mortgage on the property since 1980.

    a. If Bill defaults, may Carl's remove the cabinets?

    b. What obligations does Carl's have?

    c. If Windmere defaults, does their mortgagee get the shelves?

    d. What would the position of Carl's be if no filing was made?

4. First Western Mortgage is the construction mortgagee for a series of tract houses being developed by Cross Continental. The mortgage is recorded and covers built-in appliances such as stoves, ovens, and dishwashers. Cross Continental purchases the stoves, ovens, and dishwashers from Builders' Wholesale, Inc. Builders' Wholesale files a valid financing statement. Upon Cross Continental's default, who has priority on the stoves, ovens, and dishwashers?

5. Office Equipment, Inc., sold several small computers and photocopy machines to Data Processing, Inc. Data Processing is in a building that is mortgaged to U.S. West Savings and Loan for 30 years. The mortgage was filed in 1977. Office Equipment took a security interest in the equipment in 1982 but did not file a financing statement. Both types of equip-

ment must be attached to the floor in some way to prevent movement. Data Processing defaults on the payments to Office Equipment and Office Equipment seeks to repossess. U.S. West claims that its mortgage, with its after-acquired fixtures clause, has priority. Who has priority in the equipment?

6. Homeowner Y is remodeling her home. She purchased the tile for the floor from Tile World on credit. Tile World has a security agreement executed 3 June 1988. Y also purchased a ceiling fan from Light World on credit. Light World has a security agreement executed 5 June 1988. Neither Tile World nor Light World filed a financing statement.
   a. Who has priority?
   b. Is a filing necessary in both cases?
   c. If Light World had no security agreement, who would have priority?
   d. To obtain priority over Y's existing mortgage, what action is necessary?

7. Harry owns Harry's Discount Clothiers, Inc. Harry has a 5-year lease on the building in which his store is located. The building had concrete flooring, which was not appropriate for a clothing store, so Harry had parquet flooring installed. The flooring was installed in the same fashion as tile flooring. Determine whether the flooring will be treated as a fixture, trade fixture, or as personal property in the following situations:
   a. When the lease terminates, Harry wants to take the flooring with him. What is the result?
   b. Harry purchases the building and then sells it to Bob who claims that the flooring goes with the building. What is the result?
   c. Harry's fire insurance policy covers personal property but no real property. What is the result?
   d. The county tax assessor wishes to increase the value of the property on the basis of the value added by the floor. What is the result?

8. On 20 January, Tom purchased a new hot water tank for his home from Tanks, Inc. Tanks agreed to carry Tom on part of the price of the tank and took a security interest in the tank. The tank was then installed. On 1 February, Tom borrowed money from First Federal, and First Federal took a second mortgage on the house. On 1 March, Fiesta Fun-time Pools obtained a judgment against Tom and his house for the unpaid balance due on Tom's pool.
   a. Who has priority?
   b. What would be the result if Tanks had filed a financing statement on 31 January?

c. What relation would a first mortgage have in the situation?

d. If Tom defaults to Tanks, what can be done under Article 9?

9. X builds an addition to his home for a recreation room. The room will include a built-in bar with a refrigerator and a new television. Without X's consent and knowledge, the contractor X has hired purchases the refrigerator and television from Seller under a security agreement. Seller files a financing statement. The contractor installs the refrigerator and television but fails to pay Seller. Is Seller's security interest in the refrigerator and television good against X?

10. On 3 March, 1982, Wesley Brandt purchased a Harvestore farm silo from Minnesota Valley Breeders Association. Minnesota Valley had a security agreement that provided as follows:

> 17(b) The Harvestore equipment is and shall remain personal property, and shall not constitute fixtures or real estate for any purpose irrespective of the use or manner of attachment to any premises.

The Harvestore, a large metal structure, was bolted to a concrete foundation on Brandt's farm. It was designed to be taken apart or added to in sections. Brandt defaulted on his payments to Minnesota Valley. Minnesota Valley sought to repossess the Harvestore but the mortgagee on Brandt's land claimed priority. Can Minnesota Valley repossess the silo? *Minnesota Valley Breeders Association v. Brandt*, 348 N.W.2d 115 (Minn. 1984)

7

LIENS

I thought I dealt with the general and now I find three subs have liens on my property.

A *lien* is a special encumbrance that makes real property the security for the payment of a debt or obligation. In this chapter several questions about liens are answered. What types of liens exist? How are liens created and enforced? How can liens on real property be satisfied and removed from the property? By the end of the chapter, you will understand the predicament of the party in the epigraph.

TYPES OF LIENS

Statutory Liens

A *statutory lien* is a lien that may exist because of some enabling statute. For example, a mechanic's lien is a statutory lien. *Mechanic's lien* statutes enable those furnishing labor and materials for construction and improvement of real property to file a lien against that property for debt or payment security. Mechanic's lien statutes are found in most states. There are also state statutes that permit the attachment of a lien on real property when taxes are not paid.

Equitable Liens

An *equitable lien* is created pursuant to a mortgage arrangement. Sometimes referred to as a *contractual lien,* these liens are created as a method for securing repayment of money borrowed to purchase the property or borrowed against the property.

Judicial Liens

A *judicial lien* arises from some action taken by a court. For example, there are many cases that a plaintiff wins, but winning and collecting the judgment are two separate issues. To collect the judgment, the plaintiff must attach the defendant's property. Plaintiffs can attach wages, bank accounts, equipment, inventory, and, more relevantly here, real property. A judicial lien is the means by which the defendant's property is sold to satisfy or secure the plaintiff's judgment.

Once a judgment is recorded against real property, it becomes a creditor's lien. If the property is sold, then the plaintiff has the priority of a secured creditor in the proceeds from the sale. The priority of the judgment or judicial lien is determined on the basis of first in time is first in right. If the property is already subject to a mortgage, then the plaintiff is a secured creditor with priority after the mortgagee. In some cases, the plaintiff can initiate sale action by foreclosing on the judicial lien. Even without foreclosure, the plaintiff's lien is recorded against the property and the title will not be passed or insured until the judgment has been paid or otherwise resolved between the parties.

Most states permit either the judgment that awards damages or an abstract of that judgment to be recorded in the land records, so that the lien is effective against any property owned by the judgment debtor.

Voluntary v. Involuntary Liens

A *voluntary lien* is agreed to in advance by both parties; a mortgage is an example. Both parties agree to the placement of the lien on the property as security for the advance of money to purchase the property or simply as security for a loan of money.

An *involuntary lien* is attached to the property not done pursuant to any contractual arrangement. Involuntary liens are placed on property for satisfaction of property, state, or federal taxes (see Chapter 17).

Mechanic's and Materials Liens

Mechanic's and *materials liens* arise because persons have supplied labor, material, or both for the construction, improvement, alteration, or repair of real property or real property structures. This type of lien is the focus of the remainder of this chapter.

CREATION OF MECHANIC'S LIENS

Who Is Subject to a Lien?

Any property owner who contracts expressly or by implication with another person for the improvement of land or furnishing of materials is subject to the provisions of that particular state's mechanic's lien provisions. However, it is important to note that such a party must be the property owner or must be acting as an agent or representative of the owner. For example, a lessee having improvements made on the leased premises does not have the authority for the imposition of a lien unless the landlord consents or the lessee is acting as an agent for the landlord.

Any person who may validly contract may be subject to the imposition of a lien (the party subject to the lien is called the *lienee*). Corporations owning property are subject to the mechanic's liens on contractually improved corporate property. In the absence of a specific statutory provision, a lien may not be imposed against the United States government or any of the state governments. The idea behind this governmental exemption is to prevent the taking of state land for the satisfaction of a mechanic's lien. Thus, construction of schools and public buildings such as courthouses and office complexes would be exempt from the attachment of mechanic's liens. For quasi-public entities, such as utilities, some states recognize an exemption while others do not.

Most state lien statutes require that the *lienor* have an underlying contractual arrangement to enforce a lien. However, the degree and type of contractual arrangement varies significantly from state to state: Some states require only an express or implied agreement before a lien may be attached (*consent statutes*). Others require the owner of the property to sign a contract for the work or materials (*contract statutes*). The difference between these contract and consent statutes is that under the contract statutes, the lienor must establish the existence of a contract to attach a lien. Under the consent statutes, the lienor need only establish that the owner consented through circumstances such as an owner permitting work to continue after witnessing the work being initiated or continued.

The formalities required in the contract vary significantly in the states but the following items should be included. Compliance with this list will satisfy the requirements of any of the states following the contract requirements.

1. Amount due under the contract (for labor, materials, and so on).
2. Amount of time within which work is to be completed.
3. Amount of time permitted for payments and any schedule of payments.
4. Description of the real property involved.

5. Description of the work to be completed.

6. Signature of the parties. (If the property is community or held in tenancy by the entirety, then both spouses' signatures are required.)

7. If the property being repaired or improved is consumer property, Regulation Z (12 C.F.R §226) requires the following disclosure to be made:

> The buyer may cancel this transaction at any time prior to midnight of the third business day after the date of this transaction.

Under Regulation Z, the contract must also include cancellation information such as how and to whom cancellation notice must be given.

8. Provisions for breach of the agreement (i.e. nonpayment or nonperformance) such as withholding payment or obtaining another contractor.

It is possible, particularly in construction contracts, to have an open-end agreement so that supplies are purchased as necessary. It is also possible for a contract executed by an agent of the owner to be valid against the owner, so long as the agent held proper authority to enter into the contract. Care should be taken when lienors are dealing with unincorporated associations such as churches and foundations to make sure that the person signing holds proper authority for the transaction of the business. Without such proper authority, the property of the church or foundation is not subject to a lien. Trustees and executors of estates may also have authority to make improvements on real property that is part of the trust or estate, but such authority should be verified by the lienor so that the property may be properly liened. The following case deals with the issue of whether a tenant may subject a landlord's property to a lien.

DUNLAP v. HINKLE

317 S.E.2d 508 (W.Va. 1984)

In October 1981, Robert E. Hinkle (appellee) leased to Raymond Arington the Raina or Dixie Plaza in Upshur County, West Virginia. The lease agreement contained the following clause:

Any improvements made to the leased premises shall, upon termination of this lease or the termination of any extension thereof, become the property of the lessor.

Arington hired Dunlap and others (appellants) to do electrical and carpentry work to a building located on the premises. Arington went out of business shortly thereafter owing Dunlap money for wages and materials.

On 3 March 1982, Dunlap filed a mechanic's lien against the property. That same day he filed a suit to enforce the lien against Arington and

Hinkle. The trial court dismissed the suit on the grounds that there was no express or implied contract between Hinkle and Dunlap and that the lack

of privity prevented the attachment and foreclosure of a lien on his property. Dunlap appealed.

McHUGH, Chief Justice

The issue in the case before us revolves around the interpretation of W.Va. Code, 38-2-1 (1931). That statute provides as follows:

Every person, firm or corporation, which shall erect, build, construct, alter, remove or repair any building or other structure, or other improvement appurtenant to any such building or other structure, under and by virtue of a contract with the owner for such erection, building, construction, alteration, removal or repair, either for an agreed lump sum or upon any other basis of settlement and payment, shall have a lien upon such building or other structure or improvement appurtenant thereto, and upon the interest of the owner thereof in the lot of land whereon the same stands, or to which it may have been removed, to secure the payment of such contract price or other compensation therefor.

Lilly v. Munsey involved a lease wherein the owners of a certain parcel of real estate leased such real estate to the lessee for the purpose of constructing and operating a race track, "and it was provided that the said lessee was authorized to erect all buildings necessary to the operation of the said race track, or for any other lawful purpose, on the land owned by . . . [one of the lessors] . . . and included in said leased premises" (63 S.E.2d at 520). The lessee hired the plaintiff to construct the racetrack which included grading work. The plaintiff was not paid for the grading work and he filed a mechanic's lien against the property interest of the lessors and sought to enforce it in the circuit court.

This Court reversed the circuit court's judgment in favor of the plaintiff and held as follows:

A mechanic's lien for supplies and labor used and employed in the improvement of real estate, to bind the interest of the owner of such real estate, or any interest therein, must be based on contract for such improvement with such owner, of said real estate or interest therein, or his duly authorized agent.

This Court's holding in *Lilly v. Munsey* is in accord with the general view that:

In the absence of some special provision creating a lessee as an agent for the lessor, the mere relation of lessor and lessee does not make the lessee the agent of the lessor to contract for work on leased premises, although the interest of the lessee in the land, created by the lease, may be made the subject of a mechanic's lien.

Where the terms of a lease simply authorize a lessee to make improvements to the leased premises, although the improvements become the property of the lessor upon termination of the lease, a party with whom the lessee has contracted to make the improvements may not assert a mechanic's lien against the property interest of the lessor in the leased premises.

There must be some other evidence that the lessee was acting as the agent of the lessor in making improvements to the leased premises; however, mere acquiescence or inactive consent by the lessor of the leased premises to the improvements by the lessee is not sufficient to con-

stitute a finding of agency between the lessor and lessee for the purpose of asserting a mechanic's lien against the property interest of the lessor.

Usually, a mechanic's lien will arise against the property interest of the lessor if the improvements made to the property by the lessee are performed pursuant to an express agreement between the lessor and lessee or where the terms of the lease impliedly obligate the lessee to make the improvements. See generally 57 C.J.S. Mechanic's Liens 65(c) (Supp. 1983). However, when such conditions do not exist, as in the case before us, it has been noted that "[I]n determining whether an agency should be implied the courts have often, perhaps of necessity, gone beyond the agreement and into the whole circumstances of the letting in order to find the answer."

This Court has held in numerous cases that "[t]he trial court, in appraising the sufficiency of a complaint, should not dismiss the complaint unless it appears beyond doubt that the plaintiff can prove no set of facts in support of his claim which would entitle him to relief."

The complaint in the case before us alleges that "Defendants [appellee and Arington] caused plaintiffs to enter upon the hereinabove described premises during the months of October, November and December, 1981, to perform labor and supply materials in and for the remodeling, rewiring, reconstruction and alterations of said premises" and demands judgment therefor. Although the appellants rigidly assert that they should be afforded relief under W.Va. Code, 38-2-31 (1939), the appellants should not be precluded from asserting a mechanic's lien theory under W.Va. Code, 38-2-1 (1931). Based upon the principles set forth above, the complaint is sufficient to allege that a contract, express or implied, existed between the appellants and the appellee which caused the appellants to perform the labor in question. For the sole purpose of asserting a mechanic's lien against the lessor's property interest in the leased premises pursuant to W.Va. Code, 38-2-1 (1931), the appellants should be afforded the opportunity, if they so desire, to present evidence, as contained in the lease and surrounding its execution, that Arington was acting as the agent of the appellee when he contracted with the appellants to perform work on the leased premises.

Reversed and remanded.

Discussion Questions

1. Who owned the property?
2. Who contracted for the improvements?
3. Is there privity of contract between Hinkle and Dunlap?
4. Why did the trial court dismiss the action for lien foreclosure?
5. What provision in the lease is relevant?
6. Will Dunlap be able to foreclose on the lien?
7. Is there an issue of unjust enrichment involved?

(7.1) Consider:

Suppose that a state statute permits tenants in residential property to contract for repairs for malfunctioning heaters once they have made demands on the

landlord but the landlord does not make repairs. Could the repair companies hired by the tenants lien the landlord's property?

Who Is Entitled to a Lien?

The classes of persons entitled to place liens on real property will vary from state to state but will be set forth in the applicable mechanic's lien statutes. Ordinarily the right is given to mechanics and laborers, but state statutes have extended the availability of the right to others. In some states the right of lien is given to contractors, subcontractors, those furnishing materials, those acting in a supervisory capacity, and in some cases to architects. In each of these instances the coverage may be limited, or it may require that special notice be given to the landowner or that the landowner be aware of the work of all of those claiming a lien. In some states, only those in the groups that are properly licensed (if licensing is required) are entitled to levy liens on property.

The question of who is entitled to a mechanic's lien is in large part controlled by whether the state is a contract state or a consent state, or whether specific provisions have been made for those other than lienors in direct contract with the landowner. For example, a property owner who has construction done hires and has a direct contractual relationship with the contractor—there is privity of contract between them. On the other hand, the owner does not have a direct contractual relationship or privity with others involved in the construction project such as subcontractors, suppliers, and laborers. Thus, in the absence of some specific provisions in the applicable state statutes, the ability to lien stops at the direct contractual relationship.

To provide payment assurances for subcontractors, suppliers, and laborers not in privity with the landowner, state statutes usually permit them to place a lien on property provided they meet some notice and other preliminary requirements prior to the time the lien is filed. Basically the statutes permit them to lien if the property owner is aware of their work.

In some states, it is possible that if all claims (of subcontractors, suppliers, and so on) are pursued and made into liens, the landowner could have liens in excess of the contract price. Other states follow the New York rule and limit the amount of the liens to the contract price less any amounts paid to the general contractor.

What Property Is Subject to a Lien?

Once a lien is obtained, it applies to the whole of the real property and not simply the portion of the structure that was the subject of the lienor's work, labor, or materials. The lien attaches to both the building and the lot on which the building is located.

Procedural Aspects of Obtaining a Lien

The procedures for obtaining a lien vary from state to state, but the general idea behind the procedures remains the same despite different forms and language. Many states follow a prenotification procedure, especially for those performing work who do not have a direct contractual relationship with the property owner. Those not having such a contract who desire lien protection must file a preliminary notice within a certain period of time after their work has begun or their supplies have been delivered. Such notice is served on the owner of the property, the contractor (who has a contractual agreement with the property owner), and the construction lender. Basically, the notice serves to alert all concerned to the possibility of a lien. Because this notice gives a right to an eventual lien, the party giving the notice should be able to prove that such notice was sent, to whom it was sent, and when it was sent. In some states the notice must be served personally or sent certified mail. This notice is not a lien; it simply makes all three parties aware of those working on the project, what they are doing, and the supplies and costs involved. The preliminary notice gives only the right to execute a lien in the future. In those states requiring the preliminary notice, failure to give the notice may cost the lienor the right of the lien. In the following case, the court deals with the problem of a lienor attempting to enforce a lien when a project becomes complex in its starting and finishing dates.

FLORIDA STEEL CORPORATION v. ADAPTABLE DEVELOPMENTS, INC.

503 So.2d 1232 (Fla. 1986)

Logan and Clark, general contractors, were hired by a group of developers known as Adaptable Developments to construct a high-rise condominium. Logan and Clark hired Florida Steel in October 1980 to supply the reinforcing steel needed for the building. Florida Steel had no contract with Adaptable but Adaptable knew of their work because Logan and Clark submitted monthly bills to Adaptable that showed the cost of work and who was performing it. Also, Adaptable issued joint checks to Logan and Clark and Florida Steel.

In April 1981, because of financial difficulties, Logan and Clark abandoned the project while still owing money to Florida Steel. In June 1981, Florida Steel properly filed a mechanic's lien in accordance with Florida statutes.

Construction was halted for 8 months until Adaptable hired Rogers and Ford to complete the building. The cost of Rogers and Ford's completion was much higher than the original contract price. Adaptable filed a new notice of commencement and work resumed in January 1982.

In May 1982, Florida Steel brought suit to foreclose its lien. The trial court entered a default judgment against Logan and Clark and found Adaptable liable. The appellate court reversed and Florida Steel appealed.

PER CURIAM

In the present case the owner, Adaptable Developments, did not comply with all the requirements of chapter 713. The statute meticulously lays out the procedures which must be followed. Section 713.07(4) requires that an owner who recommences construction on an abandoned job must, if he has not paid the lienors in full or pro rata, file an affidavit of intention to recommence and a new notice of commencement or he cannot subtract the cost of completing the project from the contract price. It is a rule of statutory construction that any statute in derogation of the common law requires strict compliance with its provisions by one seeking to avail himself of its benefits.

Adaptable argues that the purpose of chapter 713 is to protect owners by placing limits on their liability to lienors. This is indeed one of the purposes of the Mechanics' Lien Act, but the legislature had another purpose in enacting mechanics' lien legislation, i.e., preventing unjust enrichment of owners at the expense of lienors. Florida's Mechanics' Lien Act is an attempt to reconcile these conflicting purposes. Underlying the concept of a mechanics' lien is the premise that the construction industry needs more protection for extensions of credit than contract remedies provide. This is necessary because, as a rule, those in the construction industry require large amounts of credit for long periods of time and often commit all of their capital to ongoing construction projects.

Florida first enacted mechanics' lien legislation in 1887 to give materialmen and mechanics, among others, a lien right superior to the rights of others. A provision in the 1885 constitution directing the legislature to draft laws giving mechanics and laborers liens on property which they had improved through supplying materials or services further strengthened this statutory right to a lien. In 1935 Florida became the only state to adopt the Uniform Mechanics' Lien Act. One of the primary purposes in adopting the act was to protect lienors by ensuring that all funds possible were made available to pay off liens. The legislature repealed the act in 1963, but preserved its approach in the revised Mechanics' Lien Act of 1963.

The history of Florida's mechanics' lien statute demonstrates that an important basic purpose of the act is to protect the materialman who uses his material to add value to the property of another and who is not paid for his contribution. This right to a lien is predicted upon performance, not upon contract. To deny Florida Steel recovery would thwart one of the fundamental purposes underlying the statute. During February, March, and April of 1981, Florida Steel delivered steel to the job site pursuant to its contract with Logan and Clark. At the time that Florida Steel was faithfully delivering the steel, Adaptable had decided that Logan and Clark had breached its contract, mainly because of its failure to provide a performance bond. In March Adaptable stopped making payments to Logan and Clark and began looking for a replacement contractor. Neither Adaptable nor Logan and Clark informed Florida Steel of these developments although both knew that Florida Steel was still making deliveries to the job site.

Subsections 713.06(d)(3)6 and 713.06(3)(e) provide that upon abandonment of a project before completion the owner should determine the amount due each lienor who has given notice and pay or prorate that amount. The section does not define what constitutes abandonment. It does not state any time period from which abandonment can be inferred nor does it state whether or not the owner-contractor must communicate his plans for the project to any interested party.

We cannot make a rule which would allow an owner to take advantage of an abandonment which he has permitted to extend for such a lengthy period of time.

Under such a rule an owner could, for example, close down when condominium sales were slow and start up again when sales improved, thereby forcing the lienor to bear the burden of the shutdown because the owner would not have to concern himself with any fluctuations in the cost of labor or materials. Innocent lienors who have faithfully performed and then properly perfected their liens should not be subjected to such risks.

As a practical matter, owners are generally better able to protect themselves than materialmen. They can distribute risks by requiring a bond from the contractor conditioned on the full faith and performance of all lien claims. It is not possible for subcontractors and materialmen to spread risks the way an ordinary merchant does. As we have noted, in the building trades considerable labor and material go into a single operation, generally for an extended period of time. As a result, materialmen and subcontractors cannot take on numerous projects because of the amount of capital tied up in each project. Because of the vulnerable position materialmen are in and because of the importance of their survival to the construction industry, we cannot make a rule which would allow them to be taken advantage of by irresponsible owners or contractors.

Reversed.

Discussion Questions

1. Who is the owner?
2. Who is the general contractor?
3. Did the subcontractor perform the necessary work?
4. What happened to the general contractor and the project?
5. What Florida statute is at issue?
6. Why does the court say it is important to protect subcontractors and suppliers?
7. What steps will general contractors and owners have to take to avoid such litigation in the future?

Because mechanic's liens are statutory, the aspects of creating and enforcing a lien will vary from state to state, but the fundamentals are the same. Time for filing, perfection, and period of effectiveness of liens are areas of difference among the states. Since the lien is a land interest, it will be recorded in the appropriate governmental land-record office. In most states, liens are probably filed in the same office as fixtures or financing statements. Figure 7.1 is a sample lien form. Note that a place is provided in the form for a real property description.

The length of time allowed for filing a lien also varies as does the date that the allowed time period begins. Some statutes begin the 60- or 90-days' period for filing the lien on the date the work is completed or on the date the supplies are delivered. Even completion of work is defined differently from state to state: it may mean the end of work or the completion of the project with the issuance of an architect's certificate.

The time period for which the lien, once filed, is effective also varies. In some states the period of effectiveness is 6 months (measured from the date

Figure 7.1 Sample Lien Form

This instrument was recorded at request of:

The recording official is directed to return this instrument or a copy to the above person.

Space Reserved For Recording Information

NOTICE OF CLAIM OF MECHANIC'S PROFESSIONAL SERVICES', MATERIALMAN'S LIEN
M 1 © LawForms 10-85, 10-87

CLAIMANT (Name, Mailing Address and Zip Code)

OWNER OR REPUTED OWNER
(Name, Mailing Address and Zip Code)

Nature of Improvements to be Charged with a Lien

Amount of Claim After Deducting Just Credits and Offsets
$

Subject Real Property (Address or Location, City and County)

Legal Description Proofed by Person Whose Initials Appear to the Right | 1. | 2. | 3.

Subject Real Property (Legal Description)

1. I am the Claimant or have knowledge of the facts of this claim and make this affidavit in compliance with ARS § 33-993.

2. Claimant has furnished labor, professional services, materials, machinery, fixtures or tools in the construction, alteration or repair of the buildings, other structures or above described improvements on Subject Real Property. This was done at the request of Owner or Reputed Owner, or the request of a person whom Claimant reasonable believed to be the lawful agent of Owner or Reputed Owner.

3. The person by whom Claimant was employed or to whom Claimant furnished materials, if not the Owner or Reputed Owner, was _____ .

4. The labor, professional services, materials, machinery, fixtures or tools were furnished ☐ pursuant to a written contract, a copy of which is attached; ☐ pursuant to an oral contract, the terms, time given and conditions of which are attached.

5. Labor, professional services, materials, machinery, fixtures or tools were first furnished to the jobsite on _____ .

6. The building, structure or improvement or the alteration or repair of such building, structure or improvement was completed on _____ .

7. The Preliminary Twenty Day Notice required by ARS § 33-992.01 was served on _____ . A copy of this notice and proof of service as required by ARS § 33-992.01 are attached.

8. If the lien is against the dwelling of a person who became an owner-occupant prior to the construction, alteration, repair or improvement, the Claimant has executed a written contract directly with the owner-occupant. ARS § 33-1002.

WHEREFORE Claimant demands a lien on Subject Real Property and all improvements thereon in the amount set forth above, and in order to fix this lien has made this Notice and Claim in two or more original copies, causing one to be filed in the Office of the County Recorder of this County and causing others to be served upon Owners or Reputed Owners.

SIGNED THIS DATE: _____

Signature of Claimant

STATE OF
COUNTY OF
ss.

Date of Acknowledgment

Verification. On this date, before me, a Notary Public, personally appeared

who, being duly sworn upon oath, stated that he had read this document and knows of his own knowledledge that the facts stated within are true and correct, except for those matters based on information which he believes to be true.

ss.

Signature of Notary Public

Notary Expiration Date

Source: Reprinted with permission of Law Forms.

of filing). If payment is not made by the owner or other assigned party during the time the lien is effective, then the lienor will bring suit (a form of foreclosure suit) to execute upon the lien to satisfy the payment due. If suit is not brought within the statutory period of effectiveness, the lien is lost.

PRIORITY OF LIEN INTERESTS

Attachment of the Lien

In the prior discussion, the method of perfecting a mechanic's lien was established, but the times and dates of perfection may also be important in terms of the priority of the recorded lien. In the majority of states, a lien for the construction of a building ordinarily dates back to the commencement of construction. Thus, if construction begins on 1 January 1988 and is completed on 1 June 1988 and a lien is filed on 1 July 1988 (assuming a proper filing time), the priority of the lien dates back to 1 January 1988 when construction began. If new financing were obtained for the building in June, the new lender's mortgage would be second in priority to the contractor's lien, because the contractor's lien has a priority date of the start of construction, or 1 January 1988. This principle is critically important for construction lenders, who must be certain construction has not begun prior to the recording of their mortgage in order not to lose priority. For permanent lenders, this means that all construction costs and subcontractors must be paid and all liens must be satisfied before the lenders record their mortgage or lend the money (so that they are not last in priority behind all those who have worked on the project and who have not yet been paid).

In another group of states the priority date for liens is the date the particular lienor began work, not the date overall construction was begun.

In the final group of states the lien is effective from the date of filing. For example, if the lender records the mortgage before the liens are filed, the lender would have priority because the liens would not date back to the time the construction was begun.

Rights of Purchasers

Whether a bona fide purchaser of property is subject to a preexisting lien or free from that lien will depend on the state's rule regarding attachment. For states that have a rule on attachments dating back to the time construction was commenced, a purchaser would be subject to the lien. In other states the purchaser would be subject to the lien only if the lien were filed and recorded prior to the time of the purchase and the recording of the deed transferring title. In some states there is a residential property exemption that prevents the placement of liens on newly constructed residences when the home has been purchased in good faith from a contractor for use as a residence. This exemption protects the buyers even if the priority of liens dates back to the start of the home's construction.

Priority Among Mechanic's Liens

The statutes on the priority among mechanic's liens are widely varied but can be grouped as follows:

1. Statutes in which all liens are treated equally: as if all began work at the start of the project
2. Statutes in which liens are given priority according to the time the liens were perfected
3. Statutes in which liens are given priority according to the time individual work began
4. Statutes in which liens are given priority on the basis of the lienor's status

The common law rule, which more than half the states follow, is that all mechanics are on equal footing and there is no priority among them. Thus, under common law all liens go back to the time when construction of the project first began. The reason for this rule under common law was to protect those furnishing labor and materials at the last from always being left without payment or recourse. For example, if first workers or suppliers were given priority, the foundation workers would always be paid but the carpet layers would not.

This method of dating all liens back to the time construction was begun puts all on an equal basis with an equal opportunity for recovery. The criteria for determining when construction began varies from state to state, but at common law the construction began with "the first stroke of the ax or spade." Many construction lenders will have the property inspected before a mortgage is recorded, so that they can be assured that no work has begun and that they will have priority over all other lienors who will enjoy equal footing from the time construction begins.

If there are insufficient funds available to pay lienors on an equal footing, a mathematical formula is used. Suppose that there is $15,000 left to be distributed, and the following amounts are due to lienors A, B, and C:

$$A = \$15,000$$
$$B = \$10,000$$
$$C = \$\ 5,000$$
$$\text{Total liens} = \$30,000$$

The method of distribution is based on proportions. Since the total amount of liens is $30,000, the proportions for the parties are as follows:

A = 15,000/30,000, or 1/2

B = 10,000/30,000, or 1/3

C = 5,000/30,000, or 1/6

Therefore, the $15,000 would be distributed as follows:

A = 1/2 × 15,000 = $7,500

B = 1/3 × 15,000 = 5,000

C = 1/6 × 15,000 = 2,500

In the second group of states, priority of lienors is determined by the times each lienor's project or portion of the work began. Again, this gives lienors involved with the initial stages of construction a greater chance of payment.

In the remaining two groups of states, claims are paid according to the time the lien is filed. Laborers may be given special priority over other lienors, or subcontractors may obtain relief after general contractors have been satisfied. The following case deals with a priority question.

UNITED PARCEL SERVICE, INC. v. WEBEN INDUSTRIES

610 F. Supp. 13 (D.C. Tex. 1985)

On 26 April 1982, United Parcel Service (UPS) and Weben Industries (Weben) entered into a written contract for the construction and installation of a conveyor system for a UPS facility in Atlanta, Georgia. On 10 May 1982, Weben subcontracted (written contract) with CoMaster to install the system. CoMaster began work on 9 July 1982.

On 10 September 1982, Weben filed for bankruptcy under Chapter 11. UPS owed money to Weben and Weben had not yet paid CoMaster.

On 17 September 1982, CoMaster recorded a materialmen's lien against the property for $131,886.15.

Weben had assigned its accounts receivable to MNB, a national banking association over a period of time between 6 December 1977 and 8 June 1982. MNB had filed a financing statement on the assignment of accounts on 7 April 1981.

UPS deposited $1,190,089.64 with the court, and the parties raised the issue of who was entitled to priority in the funds.

FISH, District Judge

The court must still determine which party has the superior right to the contract fund. MNB argues that CoMaster does not have a valid lien on any portion of the contract fund under Georgia law for the reasons that: (1) CoMaster expressly waived any lien rights it may have had to UPS property; (2) CoMaster failed to perfect any possible lien as required by Georgia law; and (3) even if CoMaster has a valid lien, that lien attached only to real estate and not to the contract fund. These arguments need not be decided, however, because the court has concluded that even if CoMaster has a valid mechanic's lien, MNB's previously perfected security interest in Weben's accounts receivable takes priority over CoMaster's lien.

Georgia Code Annotated §109A-9-310 provides in part that:

Except as is expressly provided to the contrary elsewhere in this Article, a perfected security interest in collateral takes priority over each and all of the liens, claims and rights described in section 67-1701, relating to the establishment of certain liens, as now or hereafter amended. . . .

The "collateral" provided as security for the loans by MNB to Weben is an interest in Weben's accounts receivable. Texas law governs the contractual relationship between Weben and MNB in this case because both entities have their principal places of business in Texas, and because Weben executed and delivered the promissory notes to MNB in Dallas. Thus Texas Business and Commerce Code Ann. 9.106 (Vernon Supp. 1985) governs the definition of accounts receivable here. In any event, the definition is identical under Ga. Code Ann. §109A-9-106 (1972).

Section 9.106 provides in part that:

"Account" means any right to payment for goods sold or leased or for services rendered which is not evidenced by an instrument or chattel paper, whether or not it has been earned by performance.

When UPS deposited the contract fund in the registry of this court, UPS allocated $358,449.33 as the amount it owed to Weben under the UPS-Weben contract for construction at the Atlanta facility. Under the definition in §9.106, this amount constitutes accounts receivable of Weben. The fact that the money is now in the registry of this court does not change its essential character.

Thus, that portion of the contract fund allocated to construction of the Atlanta facility constitutes accounts receivable of Weben in which MNB undisputedly has a perfected security interest.

It is a fundamental principle in adjudicating the right to priority of competing lien claimants that "the first in time is the first in right." MNB's security interest in Weben's accounts was perfected no later than 7 April 1981. CoMaster's lien, on the other hand, dates back at the earliest to 9 July 1982, the date upon which CoMaster first performed work at the Atlanta facility. Consequently, MNB's claim is prior in time to CoMaster's. Under Georgia law, therefore, MNB's perfected security interest undoubtedly takes priority over CoMaster's mechanics' lien.

Judgment for MNB (as Weben's assignee).

Discussion Questions

1. Who is the landowner?
2. Who is the contractor?
3. Who is the subcontractor?
4. What is MNB's involvement?
5. When was MNB perfected?
6. When did Weben's lien arise?
7. Why did UPS just deposit the money?
8. Who has priority?
9. What conflicting perfecting interests existed?

Mechanic's Liens and Fixture Filings

It is possible for an Article 9 UCC fixture filing to have priority over a mechanic's lien. When the security interest is a purchase money security interest (see Chapter 6) and the filing was completed before the item became a fixture or within 10 days after its attachment as a fixture, then the Article 9 interest takes priority, even over previously filed mortgages and (in this case) previously filed or attached mechanic's liens.

Mechanic's Liens and the Homestead Exemption

Some states provide for property protection for residential dwellers, called a *homestead exemption*. This exemption provides protection from the attachment of mechanic's liens or at least from the forced sale of property for the satisfaction of a mechanic's lien. Likewise, in those states with dower protection a mechanic's lien may not attach to a dower or curtesy interest (see Chapter 15), or cause the sale of that interest. The homestead exemption can also preclude foreclosure on a judicial lien.

Mechanic's Liens and Mortgages

As mentioned in the discussion of attachment, whether or not a mortgage (construction or permanent) will have priority over a mechanic's lien depends on the state's law regarding the time of attachment. If the priority of liens dates back to the time construction was commenced, then the mortgage must have been recorded prior to that time in order to enjoy priority. If the time of attachment is determined from the date of filing, then the mortgage must have been recorded prior to the time the lien was filed in order to enjoy priority. This priority also applies to mortgages in which the funds are to be advanced in a series of construction draws over a period of time.

TERMINATION OF MECHANIC'S LIENS

Waiver or Release by Agreement

A mechanic's lien may be eliminated by agreement of the parties. The first type of agreement is called a *waiver agreement*, in which a party waives the right (either before, during, or after construction) to file a lien for work on materials furnished. A sample waiver agreement is found in Figure 7.2. Some states recognize waivers in original contracts, which makes the waiver automatic and enforceable, while other states require the execution of a separate waiver agreement. Waivers executed during and after construction are recognized as valid in all states.

Figure 7.2 *Sample Waiver Agreement*

This instrument was recorded at request of:

The recording official is directed to return this instrument or a copy to the above person.

Space Reserved For Recording Information

WAIVER OF MECHANIC'S AND MATERIALMAN'S LIEN
M-2 © LawForms 10-71, 10-85

Effective Date:	County and State where property is located:		
CLAIMANT (Name, Address and Zip Code)	OWNER OR AGENT OF OWNER (Name, Address and Zip Code)		

| SUBJECT REAL PROPERTY (Address or Location) | Legal Description Proofed by Persons Whose Initials Appear to the Right | 1. | 2. | 3. |

SUBJECT REAL PROPERTY (Legal Description)

| Nature of Improvements: | Amount of Claim After Deducting Just Credits and Offsets: $ |

Claimant having performed labor or furnished materials, machinery, fixtures or tools in the construction, alteration or repair of the buildings, structure, or other improvements upon the subject Real Property in the amount of claim stated above, acknowledges receipt of full payment of the amount of claim, and waives all rights to any liens whatever against subject Real Property, which liens may have accrued or vested in favor of Claimant prior to this effective date. **ARS §33-981 to 33-1006.**

This lien was dated: _____, and recorded in the Office of the County Recorder of the above mentioned County and State in Docket _____, at Page _____.

Signature of Claimant

STATE OF	Acknowledgement. On this date, before me, a Notary	Signature of Notary Public
COUNTY OF	ss. Public, personally appeared: ss.	
Date of Acknowledgement	known to me or satisfactorily proven to be the person whose name is subscribed to this instrument and acknowledged that he executed the same. If this person's name is subscribed in a representative capacity, it is for the principal named and in the capacity indicated.	Notary Expiration Date

Source: Reprinted with permission of Law Forms.

Waiver or Release by Breach

A contractor who has breached the construction agreement and has not completed the agreed-upon work may validly execute a lien against property. If such an attempt to execute a lien is made, the owner of the property may offset the amount of the lien by any damages caused by the contractor's nonperformance. In some states the failure of the contractor to perform is also a defense for liens brought against the owner's property by subcontractors.

Transfer of Property

The sale or transfer of property or any interest therein does not terminate a validly executed and attached lien. The sale will be subject to the lien, and in many cases the buyer will require the seller to remove the lien to deliver good title. (See Chapter 11 for a discussion of adequate title.)

THE CONSTITUTIONALITY OF MECHANIC'S LIENS

Several state and federal courts have examined the issue of whether mechanic's lien statutes are constitutional. Most have found them to be constitutional so long as adequate notice is given to the landowner of the lien or potential lien. In recent years, challenges have been brought to lien statutes on a due-process theory that the landowner is being deprived of a land interest. The basis for these challenges is that a lien may be filed without prior judicial action, thereby affecting the title of the land without a chance for the owner to rebut the lien. However, most courts faced with this due-process issue have held that no significant property interest is taken because although the lien decreases the property value there is a corresponding increase in value for the improvements made. The liens are also upheld because the owner is given a chance to be heard before the amount of the lien is paid or the property is subjected to foreclosure.

FINAL PRECAUTIONS

The discussions in this chapter affect three parties: property owners, lienors, and lenders. Each group should take appropriate precautions to insure that liens affect them in only a positive manner.

For property owners, the following questions should be answered:

1. Are licensed, reputable contractors being used?
2. If a general contractor is involved, what guarantees exist for payment

of subcontractors and material suppliers? Is there adequate payment supervision?

3. Are there preliminary notice requirements for liens other than that by the general contractor?

For lienors, the following questions should be answered:

1. Who owns the property?
2. Is there a prior mortgage? Is there a construction mortgage?
3. If a general contractor is involved, how is payment set up?
4. Is preliminary notice of a lien required? If so, how is it properly given?
5. Are there time limits for filing a lien?
6. How long is the lien effective?
7. How long may a lienor wait before foreclosing on a lien?
8. What priorities exist among lienholders?

For lenders, the following questions should be answered:

1. Who owns the property?
2. Is there a prior mortgage? Are there current liens?
3. Has construction or work already begun?
4. Are preliminary notices required?
5. Was the mortgage filed prior to the beginning of the work?
6. Who is the general contractor? What payment supervision is provided?

By assessing their positions and determining their rights and obligations at the outset, property owners, lienors, and lenders can often avoid the pitfalls of liens and enjoy the protections and benefits offered by them.

KEY TERMS

lien
statutory lien
mechanic's lien
equitable lien
contractual lien
judicial lien
voluntary lien
involuntary lien

materials lien
lienee
lienor
consent statutes
contract statutes
homestead exemption
waiver agreement

CHAPTER PROBLEMS

1. Building A was completed on 1 June 1988. Plumber X filed his notice and claim of lien on 1 July 1988. Drywall man Y filed his notice and claim of lien on 25 July 1988. Who (assuming proper paperwork and service) has priority?

2. After proper action on a lien, $30,000 is available for distribution among lienors. There are three lienors (A, B, and C), who have liens for the following amounts: A (cement company), $20,000; B (carpeting company), $10,000; and C (cabinet company), $10,000. How will the $30,000 be distributed?

3. E and R sign a mortgage whereby E agrees to advance $45,000 to R in three installments according to R's needs. E records the mortgage on 1 June 1988 and makes the first advance of $15,000 on 1 August. R has failed to pay a lienor who filed on 27 July. What is the result?

4. A is a bricklayer and has completed the framing of eight homes for G, the general (prime) contractor. Prior to A's work, B had leveled and graded the property; C had put in the foundation; D had staked out the driveways and homes; and E had partially installed the plumbing fixtures. The tasks were completed on the following dates:

   A, 22 November 1988

   B, 1 August 1988

   C, 15 September 1988

   D, 15 August 1988

   E, 30 August 1988

   All parties properly served a preliminary notice. A construction mortgage was filed 1 August 1988. No one has been paid, and A, B, C, D, and E have all filed liens by 1 December 1988. Who has priority, the mortgage company or the lienors? What order of priority exists among the lienors? What happens if there is not enough money to pay the lienors?

5. Fifteen couples purchased homes in the Green Meadows subdivision, and they had all moved in by August 1988. Two days before Christmas, workman's liens were filed against the homeowners' properties. The filing of the liens dated back to the time construction began, May 1988. The homeowners wish to know their rights. What is the result?

6. The following is a timetable of construction events for a home:

   1 July, construction on new dwelling begins

   1 August, mortgage recorded by builder

1 September, work completed

25 October, general contractor not paid and liens are filed

Who has priority?

7. What types of liens are the following?

    a. A lien for plumbing work

    b. A judgment for $350 in back child-support

    c. A federal income tax penalty

    d. A lien by a contractor for remodeling a home

8. A contractor's lien covers which of the following?

    a. The constructed building

    b. The lot on which the building is located

    c. An existing parking garage on the lot

    d. A PMSI in the blinds hanging on the windows of an office building

9. Contractor A has contracted to build a recreational building for the First Avenue Baptist Church, an unincorporated association. The church moderator signs the contract. When the church refuses to pay because the moderator acted without authority, Contractor A attempts to place a lien on the property but the church officers object. Who is right and why?

10. A concrete subcontractor has just completed work on a project and is notified by the owner's attorney that the general contractor will no longer be working on the project. What steps should the subcontractor take to ensure payment?

8

DESCRIBING INTERESTS
IN REAL ESTATE

*I hereby transfer 32 acres more or less in the southwest of lot no. 105
in the 13th District and 2nd section of my county.*

—*Matthews v. Logan*, 247 S.E.2d 865 (Ga. 1978)

An accurate, legally sufficient description of a land interest being transferred is
as important as the proper language to create the desired type of land interest.
Certain minimum standards are set by statute and judicial precedent, and only
those descriptions complying with the standards will be legally sufficient to pass
title to property.

In this chapter the following questions are answered: What are the methods used to describe land? What precautions should be taken in drafting and
checking land descriptions?

METHODS OF DESCRIBING LAND INTERESTS

Government Survey

History The first method of describing a land interest is by the *United States
government survey*. This survey was done in 1785 because there was such a vast
section of land west of the original thirteen colonies and so many claims were
being made for it. The purpose of the survey was to provide a uniform system

for describing property, which is based on dividing the vast lands into rectangular segments.

Principal Meridians and Baselines The geographer for the United States who was assigned the survey task had to develop a system for the survey that would compensate for the Earth's curved surface.

The survey began with the establishment of *prime* or *principal meridians* and *baselines*. These first guidelines serve as the solution for the curvature of the Earth's surface. The lines were positioned at uniform distances apart so that the curve would not affect the accuracy of the survey. There are thirty-five prime or principal meridian lines, which run north to south, and there are 32 baselines, which run east to west. The meridians are named according to their locations: Chickasaw, Michigan, Willamette, and Tallahassee are examples of principal meridians.

Guide Meridians and Parallels Between each of the baselines and principal meridians, the surveyors placed correction lines to further compensate for the Earth's curved surface. *Guide meridians* were placed between principal meridians, and *parallels* were placed between baselines. These supplementary lines were placed every 24 miles. The result is that the surveyed land is divided into a *grid* of 24-mile squares.

Townships and Ranges This grid of 24 miles is broken down even further with *township* lines placed every 6 miles between the parallels and *range* lines placed every 6 miles between the guide meridians. The divisions are illustrated by Figure 8.1. In the figure, the 6-mile squares (townships) are identified by their distances (in the number of squares) from the principal meridian. This distance is labeled as either east or west of the principal meridian. For example, in Figure 8.1 the upper right-hand square is one square west of the principal meridian, or R1W. However, because all squares adjacent to the meridian will have that same label, the townships are further identified according to their distance from the baseline. The upper right-hand square is the fourth square north of the baseline, or T4N.

(8.1) Consider:

Label each of the sixteen squares in Figure 8.1 according to their location with respect to the Salt Lake Meridian and the baseline.

Each 6-mile square or township in Figure 8.1 is further broken down into thirty-six 1-mile squares. Each of these 1-mile squares is called a *section*.

Figure 8.1 *24-Mile Grid of U.S. Government Survey*

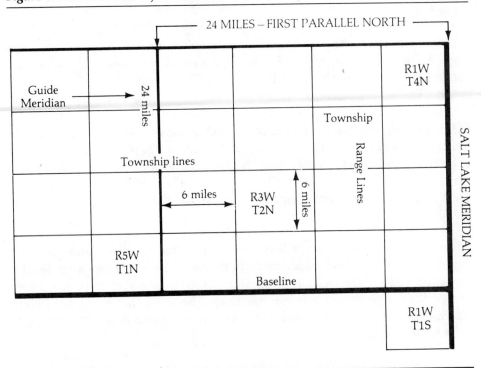

Sections are numbered in a serpentine fashion starting at the upper right corner and proceeding left (see Figure 8.2).

Each section is 1-mile square or a total of 640 acres, and each section can be broken down into fractional portions to more precisely describe the land involved. These fractional portions are described according to directional locations. Figure 8.3 is an example of a section with fractional portions labeled. To start, each section can be divided into quarters. The upper right-hand corner is the northeast quarter and the lower left-hand corner is the southwest quarter. In the same manner, each of the quarters can be broken into quarters and labeled.

(8.2) Consider:

In Figure 8.3, finish filling in the descriptive names of the unmarked portions (A, B, C, D, and E) of each section.

Figure 8.2 *Sample Township*

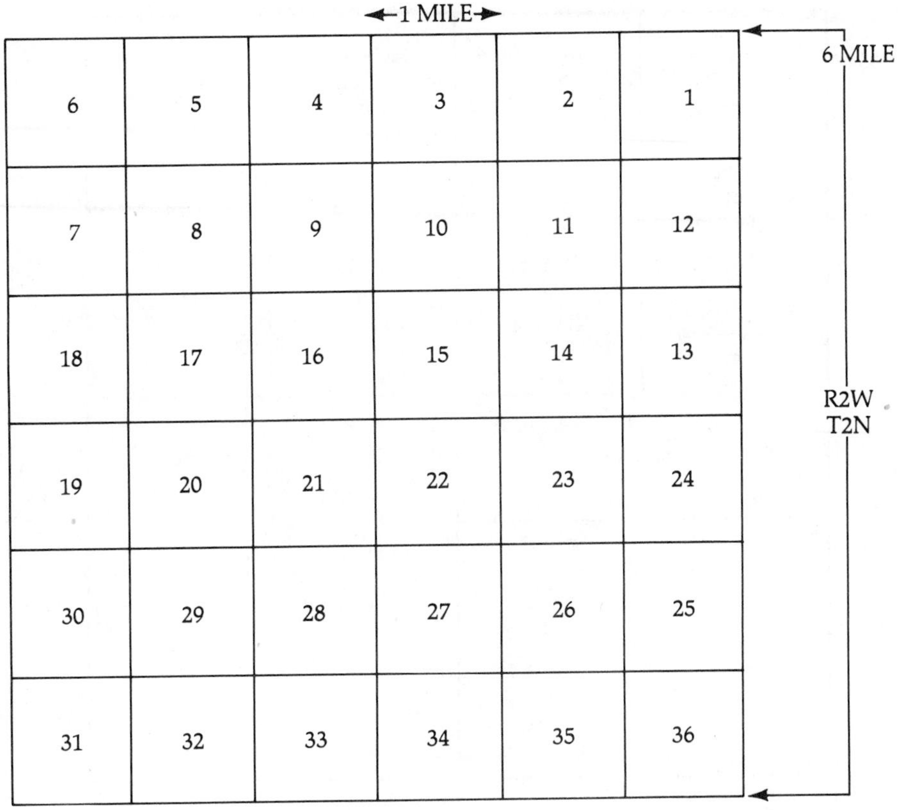

Description and Size Pulling together all divisions of the government survey, a sample land description would be "SE 1/4 of Section 12, Township 3 North, Range 2 East of the Salt Lake Meridian, Iron County, State of Utah." The addition of the county and state helps in determining which baseline is involved.

Because the government survey is uniform, it is possible to determine the size of a described parcel of land once the exact description is known. For example, if the land described is the NE 1/4 of a section, then the size of the parcel is 1/4 of 640 acres (the size of a section), or 160 acres. If the land described were the NE 1/4 of the NE 1/4, then the parcel would be 1/4 of 160, or 1/16 of 640, or 40 acres.

Figure 8.3 *Sample Section*

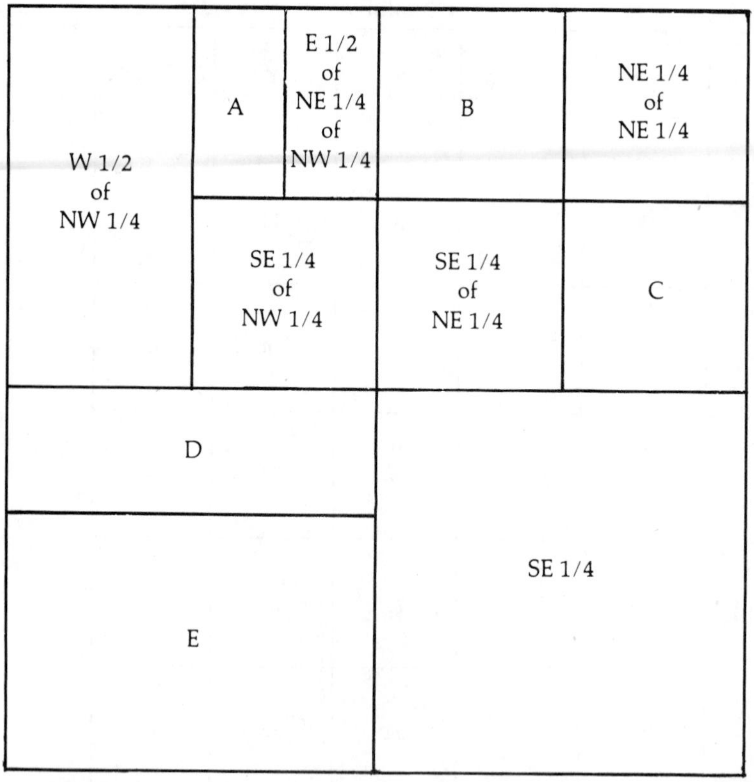

Metes and Bounds

The metes and bounds method is a technique of describing the boundary lines of a particular parcel. *Metes* refers to distance while *bounds* refers to the direction of the distance to be taken.

A *metes and bounds description* consists of a series of instructions that could be followed to walk-out the boundary lines of the land parcel. A permanent beginning point must be used since the entire description is based on that point. The beginning point can be natural (such as a stream or river) or artificial (such as a bridge). Monuments are frequently used as starting points for metes and bounds descriptions.

For example, a metes and bounds description of the shaded portion in Figure 8.4 would be as follows:

Figure 8.4 Sample Land Parcel for Metes and Bounds Description

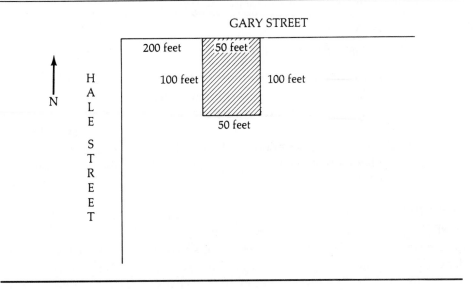

Beginning at a point on the south side of Gary Street, 200 feet east from the corner formed by the intersection of the south side of Gary Street and the east side of Hale Street, then proceeding south parallel to the east side of Hale Street 100 feet; then proceeding east parallel to the south side of Gary Street 50 feet; then proceeding north parallel to the east side of Hale Street 100 feet to the south side of Gary Street; and then proceeding west on the south side of Gary Street, 50 feet or to the beginning point.

Metes and bounds descriptions, because of their dependency on starting points (which can be moved) and because of the potential for inaccurate measurement, may result in problems when land is transferred.

Plat Map

Probably the most frequently used method for describing property in residential areas is the *plat map*. In this form of description, a map of a subdivision is recorded at some state or local agency responsible for property records. Each plat map contains the size and shape of each lot, the numbers of blocks and lots, the names of all streets, indications of alleys and easements, and a list of covenants and restrictions. A sample plat description would be, "Lot 27 of

Candlelight Estates IV, as per plat recorded in Book of Maps 30, page 80, in the Office of the County Recorder of Holim County, Utah."

ADEQUACY OF DESCRIPTIONS

When properly followed, the three methods of description just discussed provide legally sufficient descriptions. However, many other different methods of description are used, some of which are legally sufficient and others that only create confusion and cause litigation. The most important criterion in evaluating the legal sufficiency of a description is whether the land is described in such a manner that only one possible tract can be identified from the description.

Description by Popular Name

Often a popular name such as "my ranch, the Double T" is used as a description for conveying land. This type of description may or may not be sufficient, depending on whether the landowner holds one or several tracts of land.

In the following case, the issue of the legal sufficiency of a description by popular name is addressed.

WADSWORTH v. MOE
193 N.W.2d 645 (Wis. 1972)

L. W. Anacker owned two parcels of land in the town of Stanton, Dunn County. One parcel consisted of a 130-acre farm with a dwelling and a number of other buildings. The other parcel was a 1-acre piece of land with a remodeled schoolhouse in which Anacker lived. The schoolhouse was enclosed by a fence and was located 1/8 mile from the other buildings.

After his wife's death in 1962, Anacker became depressed and stopped farming. He lived in the schoolhouse near his daughter, Mabel Moe (appellant).

Anacker decided to sell the farm without the schoolhouse and the farm was listed for $18,000. Wadsworth (respondent) learned of the listing, and he and Anacker went to a bank and had a real estate option document drawn up. (A standard legal form was used.)

In the blanks provided, the real estate was described as "The L. W. Anacker farm in the town of Stanton." Wadsworth paid Anacker $1,500 for the option and could buy the property by paying an additional $14,000 by 4 January 1968. The contract also provided:

Party of the second part may occupy the land and other buildings from this date forward. Party of the first part may occupy the dwelling and keep possession of the same up to November 1, 1968. Present insurance to be assigned to party of the second part free. The electric stove in the kitchen to remain for party of the second part.

On 18 December 1968, Wadsworth informed Anacker of his intention to exercise the option.

When Mabel Moe learned of the option she refused to let her father convey title, claiming that the legal description in the option was inadequate.

The trial court entered a judgment for Wadsworth and granted him specific performance. Mrs. Moe appealed.

WILKIE, Justice

An option to purchase real estate which does not conform to the statute of frauds is void and a nullity. To comply with the statute, the contract or memorandum must be reasonably definite as to the property conveyed. Here the trial court determined that the description of the real estate as "the L. W. Anacker farm in the town of Stanton" was not sufficiently definite but that the entire document, considered as a whole together with the stipulation of facts by the parties, did comply with the statute of frauds and was, therefore, valid.

The trial court was entirely correct in deciding that the bare description on the option did not comply with the statute of frauds. When an individual owns more than one parcel of land in the same general locality, the description in the document must be sufficiently definite so that a person might know to a reasonable certainty to which parcel or parcels the document relates.

The trial court did find, however, that although the option description was not sufficient, the whole option when taken together with information in the stipulation of facts was sufficient to meet the statute of frauds. All the terms of a contract may be considered when deciding whether the document conforms to the statute of frauds.

The land description in the option document was admittedly vague as to what constituted the "L. W. Anacker farm." The extent of the land is not shown. The other terms of the option contract do not clear up this ambiguity, neither does the stipulation. The extrinsic evidence shows either that both the farm and all of the schoolhouse land were conveyed, that only the schoolhouse land was conveyed; or that the farm, but not the schoolhouse was conveyed. In short, the contract, even when considered together with this extrinsic evidence, continues to be vague about the extent of the land sold.

In the end, the option contract here does not sufficiently show the extent of the land conveyed and for that reason must be held null and void.

Reversed and remanded for dismissal of the complaint.

Discussion Questions

1. Describe the size, nature, amenities, and locations of Anacker's land.
2. Where did Anacker reside?
3. Did Anacker farm the land?
4. Who is Mabel Moe?
5. What type of agreement did Anacker and Wadsworth execute?
6. How was the land described?
7. What is the significance of the stove clause?
8. Did Wadsworth exercise the option to purchase?
9. What were Mrs. Moe's objections to the agreement?
10. Who won at the trial court level?
11. Is the description legally sufficient?
12. Did the court examine extrinsic evidence?
13. What is the appellate court's decision?

(8.3) Consider:

On 13 December 1945, Percy C. Harris conveyed by warranty deed to P. H. Coleman some land described as "twenty (20) acres out of the southwest quarter of Section 7 . . . containing one hundred sixty acres."

Harris actually owned the west half of the northeast quarter and the west half of the southeast quarter of Section 7.

Coleman claims that he now owns the full 160 acres because Harris was conveying the full parcel and the 20-acre reference was because he thought that he owned segments of various quarters. How much does Coleman own? *Mounce v. Coleman*, 650 P.2d 1233 (Ariz. 1982)

Description by Street Number

Many times in residential sales, the description used for the property being conveyed is the street address. Although this type of description may be used as a supplement, it should not be used as the sole description. One reason is that street numbers and names may change. Also, the use of the street address alone does not describe the exact segment of land being transferred.

General Conveyances

Sometimes a legal description such as "all my real estate" is used. Such a description is inadequate because it does not provide the location, extent, and boundaries of the interest being conveyed.

Impermanent Descriptions

Often metes and bounds descriptions use a starting point that is impermanent in its character such a "pile of rocks" or "fences." These types of descriptions create problems because there can be movement or even destruction of the beginning point, thus rendering the description invalid.

Interpretation of Descriptions

In determining the adequacy or meaning of a description, courts follow certain rules that are uniformly applied:

- *Rule 1.* The language of the description is construed against the grantor (seller) of the property and in favor of the grantee. This rule is based on the idea that the grantor drafted the deed and had the opportunity to check it for accuracy.

- *Rule 2.* If there are two descriptions, one ambiguous and one nonambiguous, the nonambiguous description prevails so that a legally sufficient description is found.

- *Rule 3.* Ambiguities may be clarified by reference to other portions of the document and to oral testimony. This clarification by outside evidence is permissible only if there is a latent as opposed to a patent ambiguity in the deed. A latent ambiguity is one that is not apparent to the parties when the deed is written. Examples of latent ambiguities are typing errors or the simple carryover of an erroneous legal description of which the parties are unaware. A patent ambiguity (as in the *Wadsworth* case) can be clarified only by reference to other parts of the deed or document and not by reference to extrinsic evidence.

The following case deals with the adequacy and interpretation of descriptions.

AMOS v. COFFEY
320 S.E.2d 335 (Va. 1984)

R. L. Shelton, by will probated in 1952, devised all his real estate to his wife for life or during widowhood, with remainder in fee to his twelve children. Included in his estate was a farm located in Pittsylvania County southwest of Gretna. In 1957, Lottie Shelton Amos, one of Shelton's children, and her husband executed a deed conveying to B. E. Coffey "all of those certain tracts or parcels of land . . . in or near the town of Gretna." Following the metes and bounds description of the parcels in Gretna (the residue of property Mrs. Amos had acquired from her husband), the deed provided:

*It is the intention of the parties of the first part to convey to the party of the second part all the real estate which they now own in Pittsylvania County, Virginia, includ-*ing but not restricted to the lands described above.*

The interest Shelton's widow held in the farm expired with her death in 1979, and the Shelton children had the farm sold at auction. When the purchaser learned about the 1957 deed, he questioned title and refused to close.

Mrs. Amos filed a quiet title action asking the court to construe the 1957 deed as conveying only the real estate located in Gretna and to declare that she is the owner of a one-twelfth interest in the farm.

At trial, it was established that in 1957, Mr. and Mrs. Amos were in Florida and had trouble managing the Gretna property. Mr. Coffey, who bought the land from Mr. and Mrs. Amos while vacationing in Florida, said, "I've bought something, I don't know what I bought, I don't know where it is, I'll probably never see it, it'll probably never amount to anything." Mr. Coffey also argued about the price but was told by Mr. Amos that the transaction included an interest which Mrs. Amos had inherited from her father.

The trial court ruled that Mrs. Amos had conveyed to Mr. Coffey her one-twelfth interest in her father's farm.

POFF, Justice

Asserting that she did not intend to sell Coffey her interest in her father's farm, Mrs. Amos argues that the testimony in question should have been admitted "to ascertain and carry out the intentions of the parties who executed the document." But most of the cases she cites involve exceptions to the parol evidence rule not relevant to the issue on appeal.

The only exception pertinent to this appeal is that the rule, by definition, does not apply if the language of the written instrument is ambiguous. "An ambiguity exists when language admits of being understood in more than one way or refers to two or more things at the same time."

However, a document is not ambiguous "merely because the parties disagree as to the meaning of the language employed by them in expressing their agreement."

"[W]hen the parties set out the terms of their agreement in a clear and explicit writing then such writing is the sole memorial of the contract and . . . the sole evidence of the agreement."

Mrs. Amos insists that "the deed . . . is ambiguous . . . when examined on its face." She says that it is unclear whether the Coffey deed was "intended to include only property which the Amoses 'owned' in fee simple or . . . to include property in which Mrs. Amos had inherited a one-twelfth remainder interest." But the distinction she draws to support her claim of ambiguity does not exist; the remainder interest was an ownership interest which vested in Mrs. Amos when her father's will was probated in 1952 and, thus, was part of the real estate she owned at the time she executed the 1957 deed.

Suggesting another ambiguity, Mrs. Amos says on brief that, prior to the execution of the Coffey deed, she and her husband had sold portions of the Gretna tract to third parties. Consequently, she argues, the "broad conveyancing language" inserted in the deed to Coffey could be construed to have been employed only "to insure that the Amoses conveyed all of the Gretna property which they had retained from the original tract."

We believe that language is simply too broad to lend itself rationally to such a narrow construction. The deed conveyed not only the parcels "in" Gretna, that is, those particularly described by metes and bounds, but also land "near" the town. Moreover, in explication of the habendum clause, the deed recited that "[i]t is the intention of the parties of the first part to convey . . . all the real estate which they now own in Pittsylvania County, Virginia, including but not restricted to the lands described above."

We conclude that the metes and bounds description of the property "in" Gretna exhausted that particular class, and that the general words can only be construed to convey all the real estate the Amoses owned "near" the town in Pittsylvania County.

Affirmed.

Discussion Questions

1. What interest did Mrs. Amos hold at the time of the 1957 conveyance?
2. What interests did her mother and brothers and sisters hold? Refer to Chapters 2 and 3 for help.
3. What did Mr. Coffey buy in 1957?
4. What was ambiguous about the description?
5. How did the problem in the title become evident?
6. Was the language in the deed ambiguous?
7. Was the description a metes and bounds description?
8. What could have been done to clarify the description in the deed?
9. Does the court allow parol evidence (evidence outside the contract) regarding the deed?

FINAL CAUTION

In preparing or proofreading a land description, too much caution is never a problem. A sale of land may have been negotiated to the final detail, but if the deed description is inaccurate, litigation, liability, and other difficulties will result. The following questions are suggested for consideration by anyone involved in a land transaction and should help avoid the difficulties of mistakes, inadequacies, or inaccuracies:

1. Is a legal description used? Is there more than a street address or common description?
2. If a metes and bounds description is used, is a better description available? If not, are permanent beginning points used?
3. If a government survey description is used, are all portions present? Is the prime meridian included?
4. If a plat map is used, is the location of the plat map in the land records accurately identified?
5. If two or more parcels are being conveyed, are they described separately? Are the descriptions distinct and not run together?
6. Have two or more persons proofread the description?

KEY TERMS

United States government survey
prime meridians
principal meridians
baselines
guide meridians
parallels
grid

township
range
section
metes
bounds
metes and bounds description
plat map

CHAPTER PROBLEMS

1. Diagram each level of the following descriptions:
   a. SW 1/4 of the SW 1/4 of Section 27, T2N, R3E of the Gila Salt River Meridian.
   b. N 1/2 of the E 1/2 of the E 1/2 of the SW 1/4 of Section 12. How many acres of land does this describe?
   c. NE 1/4 of the NW 1/4 of Section 14, T3N, R4W, Gila Salt River Meridian.

2. Using metes and bounds, describe the property at the junction of Ash and Elm Streets as shown below.

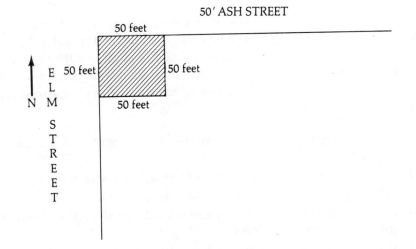

3. The Smiths have just purchased a home, and the description of the residence on the deed is, "Lot 14 of Hohokam Estates II, Book of Maps 31, page 445, Clark County, Nevada, and also known as 2322 Seville Street." Is the description sufficient?

4. Determine and discuss the legal sufficiency of each of the following descriptions. In the applicable instances, determine if there is a patent or a latent ambiguity.
   a. "The real estate owned by the sellers and located in the town of Oak Grove, now known as the 'Dobie Inn,' and used in the business of sellers."
   b. "My house at Little Chicago."
   c. A metes and bounds description beginning with, "to an iron pipe and a line sighted with a gate marker."

   d. "All my property in Monroe County, Indiana."

   e. "All my real estate wherever situated."

   f. "My farm, Willamena Estates."

   g. "Two acres in SE corner of SE 1/4 of SW 1/4 of Section 12."

5. Property is selling for $1,200 per acre in an area of upstate New York. What would be the price of the following described lot (located in that area)? SW 1/4 of the NE 1/4.

6. Diagram the following:

   a. T3N, R4E

   b. T3N, R7W

   c. T1S, R6E

7. Diagram the following: Commencing at a point on the south side of Hale Street, 200 feet from the intersection of the south side of Hale Street and the east side of Gary Street; from thence south 10 feet parallel to the easterly side of Gary Street; from thence east 5 feet parallel to the southerly side of Hale Street; from thence north 10 feet parallel to the easterly side of Gary Street; from thence 5 feet west on the south side of Hale Street to the beginning point.

8. Diagram a township and identify sections 3, 9, and 36.

9. The following description appears in a deed: "Fairbrother farm recorded at West Fairlee Land Records Book 16, page 107." Is the description sufficient?

10. The language in a deed conveying property reads, "I hereby transfer my home on Elm Street." Is the description sufficient?

II

TRANSFERRING TITLE
TO REAL ESTATE

9

METHODS OF TRANSFER AND CONVEYANCE IN REAL ESTATE

With this clod of earth, I hereby transfer Blackacre.

Traditionally, the transfer of title to real property is thought of as occurring when a buyer and seller reach an agreement and then close the transaction through the appropriate paperwork. However, title to property may be transferred in many ways other than through a sales transaction. Furthermore, whether the property is transferred through a sales transaction or any other means, there must always be compliance with rules of transfer and minimum legal requirements for the transfer to be effective. Also, certain precautions may be taken in any transfer to assure the transferee that the title obtained is good and will remain protected. In this chapter the following questions are answered: What methods exist for transferring property? What rules and requirements are applicable to the methods of transfer? What protections for transfer of title exist?

TRANSFER OF PROPERTY BY ADVERSE POSSESSION

Acquiring title to real property through *adverse possession* (often called *squatter's rights*) can be traced to the Middle Ages. It arose during that time because there was no proper system for keeping records of land titles, and property owners

167

inevitably lost important documents establishing ownership rights. Transfers thus could not be accomplished through paperwork. Adverse possession helped establish title by allowing owners to prove title through possession for a certain period of time. The doctrine arose for a very practical reason.

Even when the American colonies were first settled, the use of the doctrine continued because recording systems were nonexistent or unsophisticated and important documents were still being lost by landowners. Also, the doctrine was important in establishing boundary lines for those who owned large tracts and were seldom sure of the exact boundaries of their properties. When boundary disputes arose, the doctrine of adverse possession was used to help settle them.

Currently, the lack of wide-open-space property, the availability of records, and the high value of property make adverse possession an infrequent method of acquiring title. However, it still has application in cases where title and boundary disputes arise and building encroachments are discovered.

The process of obtaining title to property through adverse possession is similar to the process of obtaining an easement by prescription (discussed in Chapter 5). In acquiring title to real property through adverse possession, there is no exchange of a document of title and no closing or deed conveyance. Instead, the acquirer gains title through certain types of conduct toward and possession of the physical property. The conduct and possession required varies from state to state because adverse possession is a statutory doctrine. However, if the prerequisites of conduct and possession are met, the acquirer will hold title as though there had been a conveyance through the traditional methods of paper or deed transfers. The requirements for conduct and possession are:

- Actual and exclusive possession
- Open, visible, and notorious possession
- Continuous and peaceable possession
- Hostile and adverse possession
- Possession for the required statutory period

The adverse possessor has the burden of proving the co-existence of each of the requirements, which are discussed individually in the following sections.

Actual and Exclusive Possession

Actual and exclusive possession means that the acquirer must have sole physical occupancy of the property. The extent of physical occupancy required is controlled by the nature of the land being possessed. Generally, the extent of physical occupancy must correspond with the customary and appropriate uses made on land of that nature and size. The issue of what constitutes possession is a question of fact and within the province of the jury, but several common case factors in this area help to illustrate the standards for customary and appropriate uses.

For residential property, the adverse possessor is required to take up residence in the appropriate structure on the premises; for farmland, the adverse possessor is required to farm the acres sought to be acquired; and for ranch or grazing property, the adverse possessor is required to use the land for the grazing of livestock. In possession of open acreage, such as farm or ranch land, the fencing in of the possessor's acreage is a commonly recognized method of establishing a customary and appropriate use of the property. The following case illustrates how the requirement of actual and exclusive possession may be met.

KARELL v. WEST
616 S.W.2d 692 (Tx. 1981)

In 1958 Dorothea Karell (defendant/appellant) purchased 18.917 acres of land in Tarrant County. Immediately to the west of this tract is a 3.783-acre tract which in 1967 was purchased by a corporation wholly owned by Rena West and Bob Shobert (plaintiffs/appellees) from Charles Lott and Mary Lott Reese. West and Shobert then purchased the 3.783 acres from the corporation.

When Mrs. Karell purchased the property a fence enclosed the 18.917 acres and most of the 3.783 acres, leaving only a small portion of the 3.783 acres unenclosed. The Karells rented out the property from 1958 to 1972. In 1970 the Karells contracted with Wayne (Curly) Howe to remove topsoil from the land, and in the contract they indicated that they owned the 3.783 acres. In 1972 West and Shobert noticed the removal of soil and asked Howe to halt. Upon refusal, West and Shobert filed suit to recover title and $14,400 in damages for top soil removal. The jury found for West and Shobert and the Karells appealed.

PER CURIAM

It is undisputed that the property in issue was enclosed by a fence. Such enclosure gives rise to a rebuttable presumption that an adverse claim is being made by the party in possession. This presumption is somewhat diluted here, however, due to the fact that the fence was standing at the time the Karells purchased the 18.917 acre tract of land and was not designedly erected by them. In any event, in order for the Karells to establish a title they are required to prove continuous cultivation, use, or enjoyment of the land as well as possession and adverse claim. It is uncontroverted that the Karells never lived on the disputed acreage nor did they personally use or cultivate it. Any claim of title made by them is through the tenants by whom the property was supposedly occupied. Both Mr. and Mrs. Karell testified as to a succession of tenants from 1958 through 1972. (The tenants actually occupied a house located on the 18.917 acre tract.) Neither could testify that for a continuous ten year period each tenant used the disputed tract by cultivating crops, grazing livestock or by using the land in any manner so as to put the true owners on notice that an adverse claim of ownership of the property in issue was being made. Their testimony also shows that periods of non-occupancy would sometimes last as long as two months. The plaintiffs produced witnesses who testified that not all of the tenants had livestock or crops. In fact, one witness testified that other than one tenant named Davis, who occupied the premises for 2 or 3 years, no other tenant had livestock. (Mr. Karell himself testified that the disputed acreage was suitable for cows.) Other than one witness' testimony that one tenant grew a garden near the house located on the 18.917 acre tract there is no evidence that the disputed tract was used to raise crops. Several witnesses testified that at many times the property appeared to be vacant.

The use to which the Karells put the land did not constitute an actual and visible appropriation of the land which was continuous and unbroken.

Affirmed.

Discussion Questions

1. Who is claiming title by adverse possession?
2. How were the 18.917-acre tract and the 3.783-acre tract connected?
3. Did the Karells ever use or cultivate the land?
4. What use did the tenants make of the property?
5. Did the Karells have sufficient use for adverse possession?

(9.1) Consider:

The Kapinskis owned and occupied lot 18 from 1935 to 1950. In 1950 the lot was conveyed to the Wyroskis. The Laurens purchased lot 19 in 1954. The lots were the sites of summer homes. A row of lilac bushes marked the boundary between lots 18 and 19, and the Kapinskis and Wyroskis put in and maintained a lawn and flower bed that bordered the lilacs. A boat house for lot 18 was also located next to the lilac bushes. Lauren claimed the boundary line was too far on his property and in 1960 brought an action to clear title. The Wyroskis claimed they had obtained title by adverse possession. What is the result? Is there sufficient actual possession?

Open, Visible, and Notorious Possession

Under this requirement, the adverse possessor must use the property in a manner that is open to the public and sufficient to put those who would pass the property on notice that there is occupation. This possession must not be secret or clandestine; it must be obvious to those who customarily see or pass the property. Open and visible possession is "calculated to apprise the world that the land is occupied and who the occupant is; and such an appropriation of the land by claimant as to apprise, or convey visible notice to the community or neighborhood in which it is situated that it is in his exclusive use" (*Marengo Cave Co. v. Ross*, 10 N.E.2d 917 [Ind. 1937]). Courts have labeled this element as one of the disseisor (adverse possessor) unfurling a flag over the land and keeping it flying so the owner can see the enemy and the planned conquest.

Continuous and Peaceable Possession

To show continuous and peaceful possession, the adverse claimant must be in possession for the requisite statutory period without being evicted either physically or through court action. The requisite statutory period varies from state to state and is discussed on page 000. This continuity of possession may be established even if the property is used only for certain periods during the year, so long as those periods are consistent and regular.

The adverse possessor may employ the doctrine of tacking to establish continuous possession. This doctrine allows a purchaser or someone inheriting a land interest to incorporate the adverse use of the predecessor into meeting the required statutory period. Tacking may be used between predecessor and adverse possessor where there is privity. Privity requires the parties to have a reasonable connection such as a contract, will transfer, or intestate distribution of the predecessor's interest. Thus if A is adversely possessing tract 1 and dies leaving all property to B after having completed 5 years on tract 1, B could incorporate those 5 years in meeting the statutory period of continuous possession.

Hostile and Adverse Possession

This element of adverse possession requires that the adverse possessor establish that the property possession was against the rights of the property's true owner and such action is inconsistent with the title of the true owner. However, this does not require the adverse possessor (disseisor) to establish ill will, bad feelings, or hatred toward the true owner.

The state of mind of the possessor is the issue in establishing this requirement. The appropriate state of mind may be drawn from the concept of either claim of right or color of title. Under claim of right, the possessor claims to be the owner of the property whether or not such claim has any justification. Under color of title, the possessor has an instrument that is believed to convey title, when in reality such instrument is ineffective or inoperative. Unless specified differently by statute, the claimant may establish hostile and adverse possession under either one of these mental intents. In some states, adverse possession may be established regardless of the presence of either of these two mental states.

Often, factual circumstances arise in which an adverse claim is maintained because there has been a mistake in the placement of a boundary line, and the parties wish to base their claim on that mistaken boundary for the requisite statutory period. Most states find that a mistaken belief about a boundary line is enough to meet the intent requirements for adverse possession. The following case involves an issue of mistaken belief claim.

JOINER v. JANSSEN

421 N.E.2d 170 (Ill. 1981)

The diagram illustrates the land locations involved in the case.

The 14-foot strip of land is the portion at issue. Alfred and Blanche Janssen (defendants/appellants) live on lot 11 and claim title to the 14-foot strip by warranty deed. Hobart and Catherine Joiner (plaintiffs/appellees) purchased lots 205 and 206 in 1951 and reside there. The Joiners believed the 14-foot strip to be part of their property, and there was a tree and

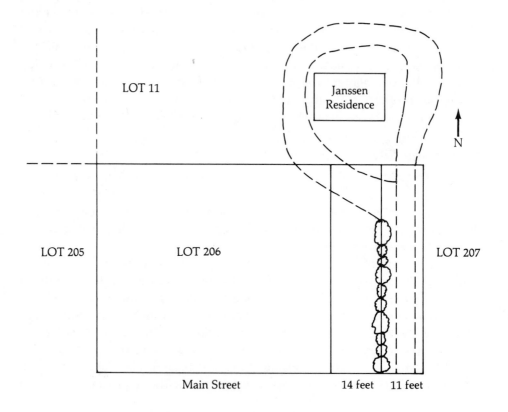

bush line dividing the Janssen driveway from the 14-foot strip. The Joiners mowed the grass on the 14-foot strip in question; they raked leaves; they planted and removed trees, bushes, and flowers; they gave away trees, bushes, and flowers from the land as gifts; they buried their pet dog on the strip when it died; they shoveled snow from the walk in front of the strip; and they generally maintained the property, thus indicating to the neighbors and members of the community that they were in possession of and claiming ownership to the ground west of the line of trees and bushes.

In 1977 a survey revealed the 14-foot strip was part of the Janssen's property. The Joiners filed suit, claiming title. The trial court found for the Joiners, and the Janssens appealed.

UNDERWOOD, Justice

The essence of the doctrine of adverse possession is the holding of the land adversely to the true titleholder. "A party, claiming title by adverse possession, always claims in derogation of the right of the real owner. He admits that the legal title is in another. He rests his claim not upon a title in himself, as the true owner, but upon holding adversely to the true owner for the period prescribed by the Statute of Limitations."

To hold that because the possessor knows or should know that record title is in another precludes any possibility of the possessor's title being adverse is the antithesis of the doctrine of adverse possession as it has existed in this State.

What is essential in order to establish title under the 20-year adverse-possession doctrine incorporated in Section 1 of the Limitations Act is that there must be 20 years' concurrent existence of the five elements: (1) continuous, (2) hostile or adverse, (3) actual, (4) open, notorious, and exclusive possession of the premises, (5) under claim of title inconsistent with that of the true owner.

Using and controlling property as owner is the ordinary mode of asserting claim of title, and, indeed, is the only proof of which a claim of title to a very large proportion of property is susceptible. Such improvements or acts of dominion over the land as will indicate to persons residing in the immediate neighborhood who has the exclusive management and control of the land are sufficient to constitute possession.

Since the claim to ownership need not be spoken or supported by title documents, and one's actions can adequately convey the intent to claim title adversely to all the world including the titleholder, it is apparent that what the property description in a deed held by the adverse possessor excludes or includes is irrelevant to the adverse-possession issues.

As we earlier noted, the possession forming the claimed ownership in the present case was based upon the mistaken belief of the parties that the boundary was the tree and bush line. . . . "[I]n a growing number of jurisdictions occupancy to a visible and ascertained boundary for the statutory period is deemed the controlling feature in determining hostility in mistaken boundary-line cases."

In a case where an adverse possessor is claiming title of land to a mistaken or disputed boundary he bears the burden of establishing by clear and convincing proof the location of the boundary. While it is not necessary that the land should be enclosed by a fence, the boundaries must be susceptible of specific and definite locations. Plaintiffs here have proved the existence of their claimed boundary line, supporting the survey by testimony and documentary evidence. Defendants argue that plaintiffs have not met the 20 year test since plaintiffs' deed to their property was not recorded until 1958 and they brought suit in 1977. As we have noted, however, possession is the important feature in adverse possession, not the date of a deed or other monument of title. It is clear that the plaintiffs went into possession of their property, including the strip west of the tree and bush line, in 1951, when they acquired equitable title under the contract of purchase.

Affirmed.

Discussion Questions

1. Who had title to the 14-foot strip by deed?
2. Who used the strip and how?
3. How long had the Joiners owned lots 205 and 206?
4. What problem does the court have with the suggested test for hostile possession?
5. Who will have title to the 14-foot strip?

If a party is given permission by the true title holder to use the property, such permission prevents the user from asserting an adverse claim because permissive use is not hostile and adverse. Thus, where the true owner grants a license or easement or gives permission for some other use of property, the user or possessor's use or possession may not ripen into an adverse claim.

It is possible for co-owners of property to make adverse claims against one another. Thus a cotenant may oust others of their possession and gain title by possessing the entire interest for the requisite statutory period (see Chapter 15).

Possession for the Required Statutory Period

The possession of the property with the requisite characteristics previously listed must occur for a certain statutory period of time. Although times vary from state to state, the typical adverse period is 20 years. In some states, such as Arizona, the period is as short as 10 years. The adverse claimant must maintain possession continuously for the period of time specified by state statute.

Observations About Adverse Possession

One question often brought out in adverse possession cases is, Who was paying the taxes during the alleged period of adverse possession? Unless a state's statute specifies, the adverse possessor is not required to pay taxes to be allowed to claim title. California's statute, for example, does require the payment of taxes for an adverse claim to be successful. In some states, the failure to pay taxes weakens but does not destroy a claim for adverse possession.

When a title holder is faced with an adverse claimant, the proper method for halting such a claim is to bring a legal action in trespass to have the claimant removed by court order or injunction. This removal serves to interrupt the claimant's continuous possession and thus ends the adverse period. Once judicial action is brought, the claimant's right to possession stops. The filing of the suit stops the adverse period. Such a proceeding may be brought by seeking an injunction or in the form of a *quiet title action* in which the court will determine the parties' rights and interests in the property. A quiet title action requires that notice be given to all interested in the property in advance of a hearing on the property. Once title is quieted in the record holder of title, the adverse claimant would have to begin anew to establish the requisite statutory period.

TRANSFER OF PROPERTY BY INTER VIVOS GIFTS

Title to property may be transferred through an *inter vivos gift* from *donor* (grantor) to *donee* (grantee), that is, the gift is made while the donor is alive. A gift is defined as a voluntary transfer of property by donor to donee where there is no consideration or compensation for the transfer. For title to transfer by gift, three elements must be present: (1) There must be donative intent by the donor or grantor; (2) there must be delivery of the gift; and (3) there must be acceptance by the donee or grantee.

Donative Intent

To establish donative intent, it must be shown that the donor intended to pass title absolutely and irrevocably and to relinquish all rights in the property. The following case deals with the issue of whether the donor had the requisite donative intent for making a gift.

PESOVIC v. PESOVIC
295 N.E.2d 261 (Ill. 1973)

Milic Pesovic (appellee/plaintiff) came to the United States from Yugoslavia in 1950. He left his family behind including a son, Svetozar (defendant/appellant). In 1957 Milic purchased a home in Chicago for $7,500. In 1957 Svetozar was incarcerated in Yugoslavia for his political views. He escaped to Greece, with his wife and family joining him later. Milic, through correspondence, began urging Svetozar to come to the United

States. In one letter Milic wrote the following (in Serbian):

[W]hen you come to me I will dress up and shoe you and your family. I promise you that I will buy everything you and your family need. When you arrive here to me I will need a lot of money to shelter you and your family.

In the closing sentence, Milic asked Svetozar to tell his wife and children that ". . . they will have their own home."

In sponsoring Svetozar's immigration, Milic promised in an affidavit to obtain employment for Svetozar and to provide housing and accommodations. In 1959 Svetozar and his family came to the United States, and Milic gave them possession of the Chicago house. One year later, Milic demanded rent. In 1961 Svetozar had a severe industrial accident and demanded Milic's promised assistance. Milic refused. In 1964 Svetozar sued Milic for not complying with the inducements that brought them to the United States. The court found for Milic and evicted Svetozar. Later Milic took pity on Svetozar and his family, and he allowed them to move back into the house. Svetozar did not pay rent but made $800 in improvements. In 1970 Milic filed the present ejectment action against Svetozar, who alleged Milic had made an oral gift of the property to him. The trial court found Milic to be the owner and that no gift had been made.

LEIGHTEN, Justice

The evidence does not prove that Milic gave Svetozar the house in Chicago as an oral gift of land. One who claims to be a donee has the burden of proving all the facts essential to a valid gift. To prove a valid gift, the evidence must show delivery to the donee with intent of the donor to pass title absolutely and irrevocably and relinquish all present and future dominion over the gift. A gift that is capable of legal conveyance but is not made the subject of a conveyance is revocable.

An oral gift of land does not pass title to the donee. This is true even where the gift is accompanied by possession, unless the possession is continuously adverse to the donor for the statutory period, or after taking possession the donee with his own means makes permanent and valuable improvements, or there are such facts as would make it a fraud on the donee not to enforce the gift. In other words, there must be some equitable circumstance that will require enforcement of the alleged gift.

The only evidence in this record which bears on Svetozar's claim that Milic gave him the house in Chicago as an oral gift is the testimony of Branka, his wife. She testified that in May 1966, Milic came to their home and gave them the house so that she, Svetozar and the children would not go back to Yugoslavia, a communist country. Milic, however, denied the substance of Branka's testimony. He explained that in May 1966 he visited Svetozar's children and found them sick and without food. He felt sorry for them and, because of this, he allowed Svetozar to move back into the house in Chicago. The house cost Milic $7,500. In the affidavit he furnished for Svetozar's immigration proceedings, Milic gave the house a value of $10,000. The improvements that Svetozar made on the property totalled a little more than $800. But there is evidence in this record which shows that after May 1966 Svetozar received from Milic, as unsecured loans, $4,000 or $4,500. Moreover, Milic retained title to the house, paid the insurance premiums and the real estate taxes. A strong presumption exists that the party who pays taxes on the land is its owner. Therefore, in our judgment, the evidence in this record did not prove that the house in question had been the subject of an oral gift of land by Milic Pesovic to his son Svetozar.

Svetozar Pesovic was born in Yugoslavia. During World War II, at the age of 12, he was injured by a land mine that cost him his right eye and his left hand. His formal education took him to the third grade of a Yugoslavian elementary school.

Yet, when this case was heard in the trial court, and because of circumstances not entirely his doing, Svetozar had to represent himself. With credible aptitude, he conducted cross-examination and presented evidence to support his contention that he had been the victim of an injustice at the hands of his father, Milic. When judgment was entered against him, he filed a post-trial motion and later a notice of appeal that bear the imprint of a layman. In his appeal, first before the Supreme Court and now before us, Svetozar has represented himself. Understandably, his brief and abstract do not conform with the requirements of rules that govern the form and content. Because of these shortcomings, we have examined the record on appeal in order to see if, perchance, it supports Svetozar's allegations, but finding no such evidence the decision of the trial court is affirmed.

Affirmed.

Discussion Questions

1. What was the relationship between Milic and Svetozar?
2. What did Milic say and do to bring Svetozar to the United States?
3. How long did Svetozar live on the property?
4. Did Milic make a gift of the property to Svetozar? Why or why not?
5. Who was Svetozar's attorney?

In establishing donative intent, the party seeking to prove that a gift was made is best able to do so through the production of a written instrument conveying title. Occasionally because of the equities of the situation, the courts will enforce an oral gift of land, but for the most part a written conveyance is required.

Delivery

The question of *delivery* of a deed to the donee does not necessarily require a manual transaction, but this requirement is met by proving that the donor intended to part with possession, control, and ownership. In most cases, delivery is accomplished by the simple transfer of possession of the written instrument (the deed) from the donor to the donee.

The delivery of the deed can be actual or constructive delivery. Actual delivery occurs when the donee is given the deed. *Constructive delivery* occurs when the deed is available for the donee and the circumstances are such that only the donee would have access to it. For example, if the donor locks the deed in a desk and gives the donee the only key, there has been constructive delivery.

Constructive delivery can also occur when an instrument or document is transferred to a third person on behalf of the donee. However, in such cases the delivery must be unconditional, and any attempt by the donor to maintain control over the property will cause the gift to fail. In some instances, a donor will deliver the deed to a third party with instructions that the deed be delivered to a designated donee upon the donor's death. Such a delivery is ineffective because the donor retains control while living. If, however, the donor no longer retains control over the deed, then such a delivery is an effective gift.

In other cases, the donor will deliver a document to an attorney or another third party, indicating the desire that a particular donee have the property described in the document but that the instrument not be recorded for a period of time. Again, an effective gift results if control is relinquished, and an invalid gift results if the donor maintains control.

In yet other cases, the donor will place a document in a safe-deposit box specially obtained for housing the document and jointly held with the donee. In most circumstances, the placement of a deed in a joint facility is not delivery.

(9.2) Consider:

Holstein wanted his niece to have a parcel of land upon which she could build a home after her completion of law school. Holstein signed and executed a deed for a small parcel that he owned and turned it over to his attorney with instructions that the deed be recorded upon the niece's graduation. Holstein told his niece of the pending gift to inspire her in her last year of law school but he died before the niece graduated. Both the niece and other heirs claim the parcel. Who wins?

Acceptance

The final requirement for a valid gift of realty is acceptance by the donee. For the most part this element of a gift is presumed unless the donee makes a clear refusal, as by tearing up the deed or refusing to accept the appropriate paperwork.

Gifts may be set aside on some of the same grounds used to set aside apparently valid contracts. For example, a donor (grantor) who executed a deed under duress (force or threat of force or wrongful act) or undue influence may have the gift set aside. Or in the event of the donor's death, heirs or devisees may petition to have the gift deed set aside on these bases. *Undue influence* exists when a party in a confidential relationship is able to exert great influence over the donor for the party's own benefit.

TRANSFER OF PROPERTY BY WILL
OR INTESTATE SUCCESSION

Title to property may be transferred upon the death of the title holder by the provisions in the title holder's will; or if no will was executed, it may be transferred pursuant to a state statutory scheme of distribution for those dying intestate. The passage of title by will and intestate succession are covered in detail in Chapter 14.

TRANSFER OF PROPERTY BY EMINENT DOMAIN

Eminent domain is the taking of private property by a governmental entity for use for the general public good. Such a taking is permissible and serves to transfer full and complete title to the state if the state provides the existing owners with appropriate compensation. The issues of the taking of property and appropriate compensation are discussed in detail in Chapter 19.

TRANSFER OF PROPERTY BY DEED

In England, the transfer of title was accomplished by a ceremony of symbolism, which was called the *livery of seisin*. In the ceremony, the grantor and grantee stood with witnesses on the property to be transferred, and the grantor gave the grantee some portion of the property such as a clump of dirt or a twig to symbolize the conveyance of the land. The grantor also spoke certain words at the time of this physical transfer to indicate what land and what type of interest (such as simple or fee tail) was being conveyed. As noted in the discussion of adverse possession in this chapter, this method of conveyance created difficulties in establishing who owned what parcels and where the boundaries were located.

With the passage of the Statute of Frauds in 1677, England required that a written instrument be used to convey title to property. This written instrument of conveyance is the *deed*. The Statute of Frauds in each state requires that a writing be used to effect the transfer of real property interests. Furthermore, the writing or the deed must meet certain requirements to be valid. There are also variations in the types of deeds that may be used and the promises or warranties of the grantor associated with each.

Requirements for a Valid Deed

The general requirements of all types of deeds are: (a) grantor with legal capacity, (b) signature of the grantor, (c) grantee named with reasonable certainty, (d) recital of consideration, (e) words of conveyance (items d and e are referred to as the *premises*), (f) habendum or type of interest conveyed, (g) description of land conveyed, (h) acknowledgment, (i) delivery, and (j) acceptance.

Grantor with Legal Capacity: Age and Mental Capacity The States have varying rules as to what is required to establish capacity on the part of the grantor. For grantors who are natural persons, there is a minimum age requirement (the age of majority) and a requirement of a sound mind. For purposes of the deed a sound mind generally means that grantors understand the legal significance of a deed conveyance, that they understand to whom the property is being conveyed, and also that they understand the nature and value of the property being conveyed. Legal capacity may still be found to exist in spite of old age and eccentric habits.

When the competency of the grantor is at issue, the issue of undue influence in a confidential relationship also arises; and the two issues generally go hand in hand in court proceedings on the validity of deeds. A confidential relationship exists where one party places continuous trust in another party and relies on that party for his/her skill, judgment, integrity, and assistance in carrying out business transactions or day-to-day activities. If mental weakness is accompanied by a factual situation in which the grantor has a confidential relationship with the grantee, most courts place a presumption of undue influence on the conveyance and require the grantee to overcome that presumption.

Typically, a confidential relationship arises between parent and child when the parent is elderly; and it arises between others, such as client and attorney, when the party who is afflicted or weak is being cared for by a younger, stronger, and capable party. Undue influence exists when the stronger party uses the trust to obtain transfer of property. The following case illustrates a factual situation where the issues of competency, confidential relationships, and undue influence arise.

QUEATHEM v. QUEATHEM
712 S.W.2d 703 (Mo. 1986)

Victor and Irene Queathem were married for more than 50 years and had no children. In 1977, they executed identical wills in which they left all property to their nieces and nephews. Irene died on 26 March 1978. Within a few days, Victor leased their farm to John Pellet, a neighbor. Under the verbal agreement, Pellet made lease payments to Victor through Victor's nephew, Cordell Queathem (respondent). From 1980 to 1984, Pellet made $18,444.48 in lease payments for the farm.

Also after Irene's death, Victor added Cordell's name to his bank accounts and later added Cordell's wife's name, Betty, to his checking account. Between 1979 and 1984, Cordell handled Victor's finances, writing checks and using some funds from the savings accounts to pay off his own personal loans.

After Irene's death, Victor became increasingly withdrawn, pale, and physically weak. He had diabetes and prostate cancer and was hospitalized on 14 June 1980. One week later, he was transferred to a nursing home where he resided until his death, in October of 1981, at the age of 81.

On 2 September 1980, Victor quitclaimed his interest in the farm to Cordell and Betty. The land totaled 43.06 acres and was valued at $278,000.

On Victor's death, the remaining nieces and nephews (appellants) brought suit seeking the return of the bank accounts and land to the estate on the grounds that Victor was mentally incompetent and that Cordell and

Betty had used undue influence. The trial court found that Victor was competent and that there had not been undue influence. The remaining nieces and nephews appealed.

KELLY, Judge

Appellants contend the trial court erred in refusing to set aside and cancel the deed of September 2, 1980 because there was clear, cogent and convincing evidence: (1) that Victor Queathem was mentally incompetent when he executed the deed; and (2) that the deed was executed as a result of undue influence exerted by respondents. Appellants also contend that the trial court erred in refusing to impose a constructive trust on certain assets held in the names of Victor Queathem and respondents as joint tenants with the right of survivorship.

We affirm the judgment of the trial court.

We deal first with appellants' argument that the trial court erred by refusing to set aside and cancel the deed executed on September 2, 1980, due to the lack of mental capacity of the grantor. Appellants argue that lack of mental capacity, coupled with the undue influence exerted by the respondents in a confidential relationship, are grounds for cancelling and setting aside the deed. We disagree.

"The cancellation of a deed is an extraordinary proceeding in equity and in order to justify such cancellation, the evidence in support thereof must be clear, cogent and convincing."

In the instant case, there are a number of facts and circumstances which tend to support a finding that the grantor possessed the mental capacity on September 2, 1980, to understand the nature and effect of the legal transaction of executing a deed. The medical records in the nursing home indicate on September 2, 1980, that Victor was pleasant and cooperative. Dr. Robben, Victor Queathem's family physi-

cian, testified that he interpreted "cooperative" as meaning that Victor Queathem was following normal instruction and the normal routine of the nursing home. Most importantly, on the day that the deed was executed, there is no entry of mental confusion.

Appellants cite several entries in the hospital record from June, 1980 through September, 1980 when Victor Queathem was disoriented, forgetful and depressed. However, in *Flynn v. Union National Bank of Springfield*, 378 S.W.2d 1, 8 [5] (Mo. App. 1964), the court held that "spotty occasions of mental incapacity occurring at intervals do not necessarily prove incapacity at the time the act was done."

Further evidence adduced at trial supports the conclusion that Victor Queathem was not mentally confused at the time of the execution of the deed. Appellant Donald Boenker testified that Victor responded properly to questions. Other appellants testified that Victor recognized them at the nursing home and that Victor would respond during conversations with correct yes or no answers.

Counsel for appellant stresses in her brief that several appellants testified that after the death of Victor Queathem's wife, Victor became physically weak and depressed. However, physical abnormalities and depression do not constitute insufficient mental capabilities. One can be depressed and ill and still retain the ability to execute a deed to real estate.

Appellants contend that in the case at bar, the testimony from Victor Queathem's family and friends indicate that he lacked the mental capacity to execute a deed on September 2, 1980.

However, testimony from Dr. Robben and Victor Queathem's friends, indicates that he was mentally competent. An appellant, Mary Ellen Seeger, testified in her deposition that Victor "seemed in sound mind, seemed natural." Another witness testified that Victor Queathem was active in church activities both before and after his wife died.

In reviewing all of the evidence adduced at trial, appellants have failed to meet their burden of producing clear, cogent and convincing evidence that Victor Queathem was mentally incompetent on September 2, 1980.

Appellants next contend that the trial court erred in refusing to set aside the deed of September 2, 1980, because the deed was executed as a result of undue influence exerted by respondents while in a confidential relationship with the grantor. We find that the evidence does not support a finding of undue influence.

"Undue influence" is that influence which, by force, coercion, or overpersuasion, destroys free agency of grantor to act.

Mere opportunity alone or mere suspicion of undue influence unsupported by evidence showing its actual existence is not sufficient to invalidate a deed. Furthermore, natural influence of affection, attachment or desire to gratify wishes of one beloved and trusted does not constitute "undue influence" invalidating a deed.

Appellants cite the following facts to justify a finding of undue influence: (1) the lack of consideration for the deed; (2) the fact that respondents concealed the existence of the deed from all the relatives; (3) the grantor's reduced mental capacity and physical disabilities; (4) the respondents' use of Victor Queathem's funds; and (5) the fact that respondents were in a confidential relationship with grantor.

The case law is well-settled that lack of consideration in and of itself will not support a finding of undue influence.

Secondly, respondents did not conceal the existence of the deed as it was properly recorded on September 8, 1980 in the County Recorder's office.

We have already discussed at length our finding that Victor Queathem did not lack the mental capacity to execute the deed on September 2, 1980. Therefore, appellants' evidence of reduced mental capacity and physical disabilities to show undue influence is not supported by the record.

Fourthly, bank records were offered at trial to show that respondents paid Victor Queathem's nursing home bills. There is no other evidence in the record before us to show the purposes for which the other funds were used.

Finally, appellants contend that once a confidential relationship has been established, undue influence can be inferred from all the facts detailed in evidence. Even if a confidential relationship has been proved, standing alone it would not have entitled appellants to relief. The mere existence of a confidential relationship does not give rise to a presumption of undue influence. In addition to the confidential relationship, there must be some evidence from which the court can infer undue influence. Under the circumstances presented here, appellants have failed to demonstrate such evidence.

Victor Queathem added Cordell Queathem's name to several bank accounts totalling approximately $45,000.00. Appellants argue that the joint accounts were created as a result of undue influence.

In the instant case, the accounts were originally titled in the name of Victor Queathem, as the survivor of Irene Queathem. There is no evidence that these accounts were intended for use by the plaintiffs, nor had the plaintiffs been wrongfully deprived of the use of Victor Queathem's bank accounts.

The record supports a contention that Victor Queathem was of sound mind when he transferred Cordell's name to the bank accounts. There is evidence that at the time the accounts were created, Victor Queathem wrote the majority of checks. Thus, Victor Queathem had sufficient mental capacity to handle his financial affairs.

There is also evidence that Victor entered into a legal agreement in 1978. Victor Queathem's neighbor, John Pellet, testified that immediately following Victor's wife's death, Victor was of sufficient mental capacity to enter into an agreement, whereby Mr. Pellet would farm Victor's property and receive two-thirds of the profits and give the other third to Victor. Victor Queathem was competent to enter into such an agreement with Mr. Pellet during the same time period that he created the joint accounts.

There is no evidence on record as to the exertion of undue influence on the part of respondent in creation of the accounts. We find no error. We hold there is no merit to this point.

Affirmed.

Discussion Questions

1. What was the relationship between Victor and Cordell?
2. Who is challenging the distribution of Victor's property?
3. What did Victor give to Cordell and Betty?
4. What evidence is offered of lack of mental capacity?
5. What issues were raised with regard to undue influence?
6. Is the deed conveying the farm valid?

Grantor with Legal Capacity: Identification of Grantor Individual grantors should be sufficiently identified in the deed so that their identity is clear. The spelling of the grantor's names should be accurate. In addition, care should be taken to have the grantor's name appear in the deed of conveyance in the same way as the name of the grantee appears in the instrument conveying title. For example, "John Edward Doe" is not the same as "J. E. Doe" and can create later problems in tracing title claims. Titles such as "Mrs. James Doe" should not be substituted for the grantor's name.

In many states the status of the grantor is important because married grantors may not legally convey title to real property unless joined in the conveyance by their spouses. Thus, in addition to correctly stating the name of the grantor, the deed should also delineate the status of the grantor, such as, "unmarried male," "single female," "widow," "spinster," or "divorced and not remarried." These status clauses serve to assure that the deed is executed with proper authority. If the grantor is acting on another's behalf, that also should be indicated. For example, an executor for an estate would have a status description clause as follows: "Paul H. Ramsay as executor for the Last Will and Testament of Mary R. Ramsay whose will was admitted on ___date___ in ___court___ in case # _____."

In many cases the grantor is not an individual but some form of business organization. Business organizations may possess the legal capacity necessary to hold title to property and may be grantors with proper capacity. For example, a corporation may hold and convey title in the corporate name. In this instance the corporation is the actual grantor, but an agent of the corporation will perform the physical act of executing the deed. It is important to make sure that the corporation may properly transfer title to the property and that the conveyance is not an extraordinary corporate transaction requiring shareholder approval.

Under the Uniform Partnership Act and in many states, partnerships may hold legal title to property and are thus grantors with legal capacity. In some states, title to partnership real property may be held only in the individual partner or partners' names. Again, it is important that the conveyance be made with authority, whether the title is in the partnership or individual partner's name. Proof of such authority should be demanded. In the case of a limited partnership, the general partner or partners must be the grantor.

An example of a grantor without legal capacity is a charitable organization that is an unincorporated association. In most states, associations such as these have no legal existence and hence may not hold or convey title to property. In these associations, title must be held and conveyed through the association officers or trustees, unless there is a specific state statute authorizing the holding of legal title by unincorporated associations.

Governmental bodies have no inherent authority to convey title; thus, they must be authorized by statute to do so and must strictly adhere to the guidelines and restrictions set up in their statutory authorizations.

Executors, guardians, trustees, and administrators have legal authority to convey title on behalf of their estates or protected persons but must do so according to the terms of the will or trust and possible only with court approval. Their authority to convey title should always be verified.

Grantor's Signature A grantor with proper capacity must sign the deed, and if the grantor is not signing as an individual there must be an indication of any representative or agent capacity. If two persons hold title, both signatures are required. Again, in most states the signatures of both spouses are required to convey title even in cases where only one holds such title. Verification of authority to sign should always be obtained, particularly for those who sign for business organizations, estates, minors, and so on.

If a party is signing on behalf of an individual grantor, a power of attorney should be furnished. In some states that power of attorney must be recorded along with the actual deed. The power of attorney should be either a general one, conveying upon the signer all authority, or one specifically authorizing the transfer of real estate or the transfer of the particular parcel.

If the party is incapable of signing, an "X" may be placed along with a verification clause to indicate who placed the "X." The name may be typed in for the grantor.

In the case of a corporate agent signing for a corporation, many states require that the corporate seal also be placed on the deed. The signature must indicate that the deed is being executed on behalf of the corporation.

Figure 9.1 summarizes the types of grantors and the identification and signatures necessary for meeting the requirements for a valid deed.

Figure 9.1 *Grantor Capacity, Identification, and Signatures*

GRANTOR	SAMPLE IDENTIFICATION OF GRANTOR	SIGNATURE REQUIRED
Individual	"John Edward Doe, a single man"	"John Edward Doe"
	"John Edward Doe, and Mary Frances Doe, his wife"	"John Edward Doe/Mary Frances Doe"
	"Eileen Jones Doe, a widow"	"Eileen Jones Doe"
Incompetent	"John Edward Doe, as conservator for the estate of Eileen Jones Doe, an adult protected person" (an incompetent)	"Eileen Jones Doe by John Edward Doe, conservator for the estate of Eileen Jones Doe"[a]
Partnership	"ABC Partnership, a partnership organized and authorized to do business under the laws of the State of Arizona"	"ABC Partnership by John Edward Doe, general partner"[b]
Corporation	"LMN Company, Inc.,[c] a corporation incorporated and authorized to do business under the laws of the State of Arizona with its principal place of business in Phoenix"	"LMN Company, Inc., by John Edward Doe, president[d] (corporate seal)"[e]
Executor	"John Edward Doe, as executor of the last will and testament of Eileen Jones Doe, deceased at Mesa, County of Maricopa, State of Arizona"	"John Edward Doe as executor of the last will and testament of Eileen Jones Doe"[a]
Minor	"John Edward Doe, a minor under the age of 18 years"[f]	"John Edward Doe by Willard Scott Doe, as legal guardian of John Edward Doe, a minor"

Figure 9.1 *(continued)*

GRANTOR	SAMPLE IDENTIFICATION OF GRANTOR	SIGNATURE REQUIRED
Individual with power of attorney (attorney in fact)	"John Edward Doe, a single man"	"John Edward Doe by Willard Scott Doe, his attorney in fact"[g]
Illiterate	"John Edward Doe, a widower"	"X," with verification clause to indicate who made the X. Name of grantor should be typed below the X.

[a]Court approval may be required for transfer.

[b]Authority of partner to convey as general partner should be confirmed.

[c]Use name under which it was incorporated.

[d]Authority to transfer should be verified; check to see if it is an extraordinary corporate transaction; board resolution required.

[e]Should be attested to or verified by corporation's secretary.

[f]Or whatever age of majority happens to be.

[g]Power of attorney must authorize real property transfers.

(9.3) Consider:

The following language appears in a deed:

> THIS DEED OF CONVEYANCE, made and entered into this 8th day of April, 1975, between LOGAN MIDDLETON, President of the V. T. C. Lines Incorporated, Harlan, Harlan County, Kentucky, party of the first part, and JOHN CHRISTIAN, Evarts, Harlan County, Kentucky, party of the second part.

The signatory portion of the document in its entirety appears thusly:

> */s/ Logan Middleton*
> Logan Middleton, President
> V. T. C. Lines, Incorporated

The only other reference to the corporate entity is contained in the attestation clause:

Subscribed, sworn to, and acknowledged before me by Logan Middle-
ton, President, V. T. C. Lines, Incorporated, to be his own free act and
deed, and the act and deed of said corporation on this the 8th day of
April 1975.
                      /s/ Mary Alice Hutbank
                          Notary Public
My Commission Expires: 2/27/79

Christian is now attempting to convey the property to Johnny Pace. The Johnsons
have levied the property as creditors of V. T. C. Lines. Christian claims he is the
property owner and that the levy is improper. Using Figure 9.1 and the chapter
discussion, determine if title was conveyed to Christian.

Grantee Named with Reasonable Certainty Identifying the grantees with reasonable certainty is required because the validity of public records on land transfers
depends on the accuracy of the spelling and identity of the parties involved in
the transaction. Accurate spelling will control how effective the indexing system
for land transactions will be. If there are any aliases or AKAs (also known as),
they should be noted on the deed.

    The status of the grantee should also be included in the deed. For ex-
ample, individuals should be identified as single or married, and corporations
should be identified as to their location and place of incorporation. Again, the
grantee must have legal capacity for title to pass effectively.

    The interests and forms of ownership being conveyed to the grantees
should also be noted. For example, the proper language should be used if the
grantees wish to be joint tenants (see Chapter 15). If the grantees are taking
unequal shares the shares should be specified, for example, "one-third to John
Edward Doe, a single man, and two-thirds to Jane Elizabeth Doe, a single
woman, as tenants in common."

    Some states have statutory presumptions for how title will be taken in
the event no form of ownership is specified for the grantees. For example, in
many states, grantees who are married will take the property as tenants by the
entireties unless the deed specifies otherwise.

(9.4) Consider:

In 1921, a grantor conveyed a tract of land to the "Colored Library and Civic
Improvement Association." The purpose of the grant was to provide a place for
a library for the black community of Ormond Beach, Florida. When "white-only"
rules were lifted from other libraries in the community, the building was no longer

used and fell into disrepair. Officers of the Association sought to clear title to make better use of the land. Heirs of the grantor maintained that the Association never existed and that there was never a grantee named so that the title belonged to them. Who is correct? *Daniels v. Berry*, 513 So.2d 250 (Fla. 1987)

Recital of Consideration The requirement for a recital of consideration in a valid deed does not require the parties to actually include the price paid for the land in the deed. In fact, deeds that convey title to real property as gifts really have no consideration present. Generally, there is simply a recital of consideration, such as, "For the consideration of ten dollars, and other valuable considerations," (see Figure 9.2 for placement of the recital clause). The use of a nominal sum presents no problems for the deed's validity. So long as the consideration or some consideration was actually paid, the deed's transfer of title may be enforced.

Words of Conveyance The recital of consideration and words of conveyance portions of the deed are referred to as the premises of the deed. The purpose of requiring words of conveyance is to ensure that the grantor clearly expresses the intent to transfer some title or interest in the property. The words of conveyance also serve to establish any limitations the grantor is imposing in passing title to the property (see discussion of warranties later in this chapter). Standard form deeds use language such as "do hereby grant and convey," "do hereby grant," "do hereby convey and specially warrant," or "do hereby quitclaim." These words effect the transfer and also control the warranties or promises made by the grantor to the grantee in the transferring of the property.

Habendum or Type of Interest Conveyed This requirement for a deed relates to the Part I discussion of land interests as fee simple, fee tail, fee simple defeasible, and so on. In this part of the deed the grantor indicates which land interest is being conveyed. The language used in the *habendum clause* of the deed is discussed in Chapters 1 and 2:

- *Fee simple.* "To A," "To A and her heirs"
- *Fee simple determinable.* "To A so long as the premises are used for a school"
- *Fee tail.* "To A and the heirs of her body"

Any restrictions or encumbrances such as easements or liens should be noted following the habendum clause, and these restrictions generally begin, "subject to."

Figure 9.2 *Sample Warranty Deed*

This instrument was recorded at request of:

The recording official is directed to return this
instrument or a copy to the above person.

Space Reserved For Recording Information

WARRANTY DEED
R-4 © LawForms 10-71, 2-79

Effective Date	County and State where Real Property is located
GRANTOR (Name, Address and Zip Code)	GRANTEE (Name, Address and Zip Code)

Subject Real Property (Address or Location)

Legal Description Proofed by Persons Whose Initials Appear to the Right	1.	2.	3.

Subject Real Property (Legal Description)

For valuable consideration, Grantor conveys to Grantee all right, title and interest of Grantor in Subject Real Property together with all rights and privileges appurtenant or to become appurtenant to Subject Real Property on the effective date, and warrants the title against all persons whomsoever, subject to the matters above set forth.

Signatures of Grantor

STATE OF COUNTY OF ss.	Acknowledgement. On this date, before me, a Notary Public, personally appeared: ss.	Signature of Notary Public
Date of Acknowledgement	known to me or satisfactorily proven to be the person whose name is subscribed to this instrument and acknowledged that he executed the same. If this person's name is subscribed in a representative capacity, it is for the principal named and in the capacity indicated.	Notary Expiration Date
STATE OF COUNTY OF ss.	Acknowledgement. On this date, before me, a Notary Public, personally appeared: ss.	Signature of Notary Public
Date of Acknowledgement	known to me or satisfactorily proven to be the person whose name is subscribed to this instrument and acknowledged that he executed the same. If this person's name is subscribed in a representative capacity, it is for the principal named and in the capacity indicated.	Notary Expiration Date

Source: Reprinted with permission of Law Forms.

Description of Land Conveyed The requirement for a land description in the deed relates to the Chapter 8 discussion of what constitutes an adequate legal description of property. The grantee's protection of title for the property rests upon this description, which for this purpose appears in the public records.

Acknowledgment The purpose of the *acknowledgment clause* of the deed is to establish that the act of conveying was indeed the act of the grantor. Actually, in most states the deed need not be acknowledged to be valid between the parties to the deed, but acknowledgment is required before the deed may be recorded in the public land records.

An acknowledgment occurs when the parties to a deed appear before a notary (or otherwise authorized state official) in order to sign their names and to indicate that such signatures are made willingly and that the parties signing are, in fact, the parties to the deed.

The acknowledgment should appear immediately after the signature. Venue (the county and state) should also be stated. Most states require the following information in an acknowledgment: (1) the date, (2) the name of the notary or other official, and (3) that the person (grantor) signing is identified as the same described in the deed. In most states, a notarial seal is also required. (See Figure 9.2 for a sample acknowledgment.)

For acknowledgment by corporation grantors, the signature of an officer who executes the deed for the corporation will be in the acknowledgment. The form for corporate acknowledgments is generally longer and may require additional information about the officer. The notary may also be required to acknowledge the affixing of the corporate seal.

In some states the form for acknowledgment differs according to the status of the parties to the deed. Thus, in the case of a married grantor executing a deed unilaterally, the notary or other official may be required to question the grantor about the marital status and make a finding before acknowledging the signature. As mentioned earlier, grantors signing with an "X" will generally have a special verification or acknowledgment form for their signatures.

The requirement of witnesses varies from state to state, with some states requiring witnesses in addition to the acknowledgment and others requiring only acknowledgment. In some states, deeds that lack acknowledgment may be established as authentic through use of the testimony of witnesses who were present at the time of the deed's execution.

Delivery Delivery is required to complete the transfer of title by deed. In the majority of transactions, this step is a simple one in which the deed is given in exchange for a purchase price. As noted earlier, the delivery can be actual or constructive. In determining whether delivery has been accomplished, the intent of the grantor is critical. If the deed is delivered to a third party, delivery to the grantee is complete only if the grantor has relinquished all control. If the deed is placed in escrow with instructions to convey it to the grantee upon receipt of funds, there again is no delivery because a condition is attached. Often deeds are executed and placed in a safe-deposit box, with instructions given to relatives for removal of the deed after the grantor's death. Such a transfer is ineffective for delivery. The standards for delivery of deeds are the same as the standards for delivery of deeds as gifts discussed earlier in the chapter.

Most states provide that if a deed has been executed, acknowledged, and recorded (discussed later in this chapter), there is a presumption that the deed was delivered. However, it is possible to rebut the presumption through the production of evidence in a legal proceeding.

Once delivery is accomplished, the grantor's destruction of the deed, change of mind, or conveyance to another is of no legal significance.

(9.5) Consider:

Lillian Cheney signed a deed conveying her real property in Ogden, Utah, to Flora Cheney. Lillian then placed the deed in a sealed envelope and put it in a safe-deposit box held in her name and in the name of Francis Wiggill. Lillian instructed Wiggill that upon her death, he was to go to the bank where he would be granted access to the safe-deposit box and its contents. Lillian Cheney further instructed, "in that box is an envelope addressed to all those concerned. All you have to do is give them that envelope and that's all." At all times prior to her death, Lillian was in possession of a key to the safety deposit box and had sole and complete control over it. Wiggill was never given the key to the safe-deposit box.

Upon Lillian's death, Francis gave the deed to Flora. The heirs now seek to have the transfer set aside for lack of delivery. What is the result?

Acceptance Title to property cannot be thrust upon grantees, but acceptance is presumed if the transfer of property is beneficial to the grantee. This presumption works even when the grantee has no knowledge of the conveyance. If the grantee has possession of the deed, acceptance is again presumed.

TYPES OF DEEDS

The type of deed used by the grantor controls the number and the significance of promises about the title made by the grantor. The types of deeds that may be used are: (1) quitclaim deed, (2) warranty deed, (3) special warranty deed, (4) deed of bargain and sale, and (5) judicial deed.

Quitclaim Deed

A *quitclaim deed* is a deed of no promises. It does not purport to transfer or convey title to the property therein described. What is conveyed by a quitclaim deed is any right, title, and interest the grantor may have in the described property, although there is no promise by the grantor that any right, title, or interest exists. A quitclaim deed is often referred to or used as a release for purposes of clearing a cloud on a title or correcting title defects. This form of deed is also used to convey lesser land interests such as life estates. The language of conveyance used in a quitclaim is "I (grantor) hereby quitclaim to . . ." or "I (grantor) hereby remise, release, and quitclaim unto. . . ."

Warranty Deed

Most land transactions require the grantor to transfer title by warranty deed. The *warranty deed* is so named because it contains several warranties that the grantor makes to the grantee in the transfer. In most states these warranties arise because of the language used by the grantor in the words of conveyance, which usually includes "warrant" but according to state statute may instead include "grant" or "convey." Other states may require that the warranties given be set forth in definite language in the deed.

At common law, there were six warranties given by the grantor in the warranty deed: seisin, right to convey, freedom from encumbrances, covenant of warranty, quiet enjoyment, and further assurances. In most states the warranty or covenant of seisin is a promise that the grantor has title to the property. In other states it is currently a warranty that the grantor is in possession of the property. This warranty is not breached by the presence of easements or encroachments.

The right to convey is simply a warranty that the grantor has the authority to pass title to the property. In states where seisin means only possession, this warranty is important in that the right to transfer is guaranteed.

Freedom from encumbrances is a warranty that assures the title is free from defects. Under this provision, the grantor warrants that the property is free from encumbrances upon the title and free from physical encumbrances upon the property. However, the deed may include a list of any encumbrances that the grantor is passing along, such as an outstanding mortgage or an easement. The types of title defects warranted against (unless specifically mentioned) are: mortgages, unpaid taxes, assessments, leases, judgment liens, right of redemption, and dower rights. Physical defects warranted against (unless specifically mentioned) are: building restrictions, encroachments, easements, profits, party wall agreements, fences, and mineral rights.

The covenant of warranty requires the grantor to compensate the grantee for any loss experienced because of the grantor's failure to convey title to the property described in the deed. Thus, if a grantee is dispossessed of the conveyed property or required to pay an amount to retain title, the grantor agrees to indemnify the grantee for such loss, costs, and expenses.

Under the warranty of quiet enjoyment, the grantor is making the same promise as under the covenant of warranty. That is, the grantor will reimburse the grantee for expenses and losses incurred if a problem with title arises.

The warranty of further assurances requires the grantor "to do, execute, or cause to be executed or done all such further acts, deeds, and things, for the better, more perfectly and absolutely conveying and assuring the lands and the premises conveyed unto the grantee as the grantee may reasonably request." In other words, this warranty requires the grantor to execute documents or institute suits to protect any defects in title that might exist and which the grantee desires corrected.

In the majority of states these common law warranties have been combined into three basic warranties, which are:

1. The grantor possesses an indefeasible fee simple estate.
2. There are no encumbrances against the property except those specifically noted.
3. The grantee shall have quiet enjoyment of the property, and the grantor will warrant and defend title against all claims.

If there is an unbroken chain of warranty deeds conveying title to the property, each grantor is liable to all subsequent grantees on the warranties provided (see Figure 9.2 for a sample warranty deed.)

Special Warranty Deed

A *special warranty deed* offers the same warranties as a warranty deed but limits the time of application. Under a special warranty deed, a grantor's warranties apply only for the period of that grantor's ownership. Thus, a grantor owning property from 1 June 1980 to 1 June 1988 with a special warranty deed would warrant only for the same period of time and would provide no warranties for defects and encumbrances created or arising prior to that period of ownership. In a special warranty deed the covenants are not listed, and the language used is similar to the following: "Grantor hereby covenants that he has not done anything whereby the above described property has been encumbered in any way whatsoever." In some states shortened language in the granting clause, such as "do hereby specially warrant and convey," will have the same effect.

Deed of Bargain and Sale

This form of deed transfers a land interest without providing any warranty to title. A *deed of bargain and sale* does not list any convenants.

Judicial Deed

A *judicial deed* is a deed executed pursuant to court orders. Examples include the deeds of the following: executors and administrators of estates, conservators of estates, guardians of minors or incompetents, and sheriffs. Sheriffs' deeds are issued to parties who have purchased properties at foreclosure sales and are issued after the period of the debtor's right of redemption. (See Chapter 12.) Assuming all legal procedures are followed, these deeds serve to convey good title.

(9.6) Consider:

A deed contained the language, "I, Jacob Smith, of Washington County, warrant and defend unto Christena Smith . . . the following real estate. . . ." Although the deed included all the necessary requirements, the parties are now unclear as to the type of deed given and what warranties, if any, were given. Discuss.

PROTECTION OF TITLE

Having the deed executed, delivered, and accepted serves to transfer title to the property; however, that transfer is known only to the grantor and grantees. Furthermore, there is still the possibility that problems with the title will arise. It is recording the deed that serves to give public notice of the transaction and to protect the grantee against fraudulent transfers of the same property by the grantor. Title insurance can serve to indemnify for losses caused by problems with title that arise after the conveyance has been made.

RECORDING

The process of *recording* as a method of title protection has been practiced in the United States since the days of the colonies. Indeed, the Massachusetts Bay Act of 1634 required records of land transfer to be filed with the court so that an accurate record of land ownership could be maintained. These early acts required the extra work of copying every instrument of conveyance. Every state now has some form of recording act. Although the acts differ, the same topics are covered in each: (1) the documents required to be recorded, (2) the mechanics of recording, (3) a system for maintaining and organizing records, and (4) a method for determining priorities of interests.

Documents Required to Be Recorded

All of the recording acts basically provide that all instruments affecting title to land are to be recorded. These instruments include deeds, mortgages, liens, judgments, and as discussed in Chapter 6, Article 9 financing statements. Many of the acts require these instruments to be in a particular form before they will be accepted for recording. New York's statute requires the following instruments to be recorded (Real Property Law, Sec. 290):

> . . . every written instrument, by which any estate or interest in real property is created, transferred, mortgaged or assigned, or by which the title to any real property may be affected, including an instrument in execution of a power, although the power be one of revocation only, and an instrument postponing or subordinating a mortgage lien; except a will, a lease for a term not exceeding three years, an executory contract for the sale or purchase of lands, and an instrument containing a power to convey real property as the agent or attorney of the owner of such property.

It should be realized that the recording of a land-related document affords both protection and public notice, so that when in doubt the parties should opt for recording. Not everyone could be expected to have actual knowledge or notice about every land transaction. Recording serves to give everyone the chance to verify transactions and thus offers constructive notice to everyone.

Mechanics of Recording

Recording is accomplished at statutorily designated offices. Offices may be local, such as a county recorder office, or may be a state agency or a town clerk. As discussed in Chapters 5, 6, and 7, other documents such as easements, liens, and fixture filings are recorded in the same place. In most states, recording is accomplished at a county office for the location of the property. Some states may have a separate land records office in counties where the population is high.

The difference between filing and recording is that in filing, the document is retained by the governmental agency. In recording, the document is copied and the copy is retained by the governmental agency in an appropriate organizational system (discussed later).

Every state requires the party desiring the instrument to be recorded to pay a fee before the instrument is entered on the records. The fees are set according to the type of document and the number of pages in the document.

When the fee is paid, the party seeking to record the instrument is given a receipt with the date and time stamped on it. The document being recorded will also have a stamp of date and time. Since many documents are accepted at the same time, each document will also be numbered (the number is sometimes called a *fee number*) to indicate the exact order of filing. Each document also indicates where in the agency's records it will be filed, such as "Book 425 of Deeds, p. 585" or "Docket 300 of Book of Maps, p. 700."

System for Maintaining and Organizing Records

With the great number of documents filed annually, every state must have some system for organizing the records so that information about title to a piece of property can be readily obtained. The purposes of such systems or organization are to provide a method whereby the chain of title for a particular piece of property can be effectively traced and to provide title protection. Chain of title simply means that a piece of real estate has been transferred over the years between successive owners. To establish ownership of property today, the current owner must establish that the chain of title passage is unbroken; in other words, that title has been conveyed without any breaks in successive owners.

To be able to effectively establish this chain of title, the records must follow an index system that enables the tracing of successive owners. States have either a grantor/grantee system of indexing, a tract system, or both. Most states have a grantor/grantee system, which is easy to understand but is more difficult to use when establishing the chain of title. In a *grantor/grantee index system*, the agency responsible for recording maintains a running index of transactions alphabetized by the grantor's and grantee's names.

Figures 9.3 and 9.4 are sample grantor and grantee index entries. Supposing the Joneses were purchasing Lot 388 from the Jennings, the Joneses could establish the chain of title by first looking for the Jennings in the grantee index (Figure 9.4) and then verifying the transfer by looking at American Continental in the grantor index (Figure 9.3). To trace further back, they would check American Continental in the grantee index to find its grantor and so on. The presence of the docket or volume number and the page number in the index permits the tracing party to turn to the records and actually examine the joint tenancy deed of conveyance.

Although the tracing of the chain of title is uncomplicated here, many titles require more thorough searches. Also, the grantor/grantee system of indexing has inherent problems: The use of different names, initials, or married

Figure 9.3 *Sample Grantor Index*

DATE OF RECORD-ING	GRANTOR	GRANTEE	TYPE OF DOCU-MENT	BRIEF LAND DE-SCRIP-TION	DOCKET OR VOL-UME	PAGE
4/9/88	American Continental Corporation	Terry H. and Marianne Moody Jennings	Joint Tenancy Deed	Lot 388 of Hohokam Village, Unit Two	14342	913

Figure 9.4 *Sample Grantee Index*

DATE OF RECORD-ING	GRANTEE	GRANTOR	TYPE OF DOCU-MENT	BRIEF LAND DE-SCRIP-TION	DOCKET OR VOL-UME	PAGE
4/9/88	Terry H. and Marianne Moody Jennings	American Continental Corporation	Joint Tenancy Deed	Lot 388 of Hohokam Village, Unit Two	14342	913

names can cause confusion and an apparent break in the chain of title. (See earlier discussion of grantor and grantee.) Title obtained in other ways such as by will may not appear in the land records. Also, not all title defects such as judgments and tax liens will appear in the grantor/grantee index.

The second system of indexing, called the *tract system* (also known as block indexing or numerical indexing), avoids some of the inherent problems of the grantor/grantee system. Many states have both systems, but title companies, which are required to insure the chain of title, use the tract system to avoid the problems in the grantor/grantee system. Furthermore, tracing of the chain of title under the tract system is much faster than under the grantor/grantee system. Under the tract system, the entire county is divided into tracts and the chain of title for each tract is traced back to the time when the land was given in a government grant. Each piece of land is then indexed to a tract, so that every piece of property can have its origins traced to the origination of title. Such a search can be done quickly without reference to grantor/grantee indexes.

Method for Determining Priorities of Interests

One of the major purposes of every state recording act is to provide a method whereby land transfers and interests can be made public. Recording serves as constructive notice of land interests. Once a document is recorded, everyone has notice of the recorded interest. That is, even though a party may not have seen the recorded document, they have constructive notice when it is publicly filed. Actual knowledge of filing is not required.

It is possible that a grantor could convey the same land interests to different parties. When this occurs, the decision must be made as to who is entitled to the property and who is left to collect damages from the fraudulent grantor on the basis of breach of warranty. The state statutes employ three different methods for determining priority: (a) pure race, (b) notice, and (c) race/notice.

Pure Race North Carolina's statute is a pure race statute and provides as follows:

§47-18. Conveyances, contracts to convey, options and leases of land.
(a) No (i) conveyance of land, or (ii) contract to convey, or (iii) option to convey, or (iv) lease of land for more than three years shall be valid to pass any property interest as against lien creditors or purchasers for a valuable consideration from the donor, bargainor or lessor but from the time of registration thereof in the county where the land lies, or if the land is located in more than one county, then in each county where any portion of the land lies to be effective as to the land in that county.

A *pure race statute*[1] means first to record is first in right, or the first party to record the instrument in the proper place will hold title to the property. This rule applies even though deeds may have been executed to the parties prior to the time the recording party received the same interests. An example is as follows:

- *Day 1.* Grantor conveys Blackacre to A.
- *Day 2.* Grantor conveys Blackacre to B.
- *Day 3.* B records interest.
- *Day 4.* A records interest.

[1]Pure race states are Louisiana and North Carolina.

In a pure race jurisdiction B takes title as the first to record even though the interest in Blackacre was conveyed first to A.

Notice Arizona's statute [ARS §33-412, (A)] is an example of a notice statute:

> All bargains, sales and other conveyances whatever of lands, tenements and hereditaments, whether made for passing an estate of freehold or an estate for a term of years, and deeds of settlement upon marriage, whether of land, money or other personal property, and deeds of trust and mortgages of whatever kind, shall be void as to creditors and subsequent purchasers for valuable consideration without notice, unless they are acknowledged and recorded in the office of the county recorder as required by law, or where record is not required, deposited and filed with the recorder.

The key to understanding the system of priorities in notice states[2] is the term *good faith purchaser* or *bona fide purchaser (bfp)*. The *notice statutes* entitle the last good faith purchaser to keep the land interest. However, if a deed is not recorded in a notice state, the purchaser may lose title to a subsequent bona fide purchaser. A good faith purchaser is defined as one who has no knowledge of a prior conveyance either constructive (no prior recorded interest) or actual (no knowledge of a transfer or sale). Thus, a notice example is as follows:

- *Day 1.* Grantor conveys to A (a bfp).
- *Day 2.* Grantor conveys to B (a bfp).
- *Day 3.* Grantor conveys to C (a bfp).

In this case, since A and B did not record C takes title. This would be true even if A and B recorded their interests on day 4 before C recorded on day 5. In a notice jurisdiction the failure to record may cost the parties their interests.

Race/Notice New York is a jurisdiction following the race/notice system of priorities (Real Property 291):

> (1) A conveyance of real property . . . may be recorded. . . . Every such conveyance not so recorded is void,

[2]Notice states are Alabama, Arizona and Colorado (race/notice by judicial decision), Arkansas (except mortgages), Connecticut, Delaware, Florida, Illinois, Iowa, Kansas, Kentucky, Maine, Massachusetts, Missouri, New Hampshire, New Mexico, Ohio (except mortgages), Oklahoma, Rhode Island, South Carolina, Tennessee, Texas, Vermont, Virginia, and West Virginia.

(2) as against any person who subsequently purchases or acquires by exchange or contracts to purchase or acquire by exchange, the same real property or any portion thereof . . .

(3) in good faith and for a valuable consideration, from the same vendor or assignor, his distributees, or devisees

(4) and whose conveyance, contract, or assignment is first duly recorded. . . .

Race/notice statutes entitle the property to go to a good faith purchaser, but it will go to the good faith purchaser who is the first to record. An example would be as follows:

- *Day 1.* Grantor conveys property to A (bfp).
- *Day 2.* Grantor conveys property to B (bfp).
- *Day 3.* Grantor conveys property to C (bfp).
- *Day 4.* B records.
- *Day 5.* A records.
- *Day 6.* C records.

In a race/notice jurisdiction[3] B would take title to the property because B was the first bfp to record the interest; in a notice system C would take title; and in a pure race system, B would take title. However, if B were not a bfp, in a race/notice jurisdiction A would take title; in a notice jurisdiction B's status is irrelevant and C would still take title; and in a pure race jurisdiction B would still take title.

The following case provides a dicussion of the distinction between notice and race/notice statutes.

FEES-KREY, INC. v. PAGE
591 P.2d 1339 (Colo. 1979)

This case arises because of a complex series of transfers summarized as follows:

- *1951.* United States gives oil and gas lease to Marie Maroney for

property in Rio Blanco County, Colorado.

- *1955.* Phillips Petroleum acquires all the lease interests.
- *March 1960.* Phillips conveys to Page (defendant/appellee) one-half

[3]Race/notice states are Alaska, California, Georgia, Hawaii, Idaho, Indiana, Maryland, Michigan, Minnesota, Mississippi, Montana, Nebraska, Nevada, New Jersey, New York, North Dakota, Oregon, Pennsylvania (except mortgages), South Carolina, South Dakota, Utah, Washington, Wisconsin, Wyoming, and the District of Columbia.

of the working rights under the lease.

- *April 1960.* Page transfers his interest to Page Sr. but reserves a 2 percent interest for himself.
- *April 1960.* Page Sr. transfers one fourth of his interest to Beardmore subject to Page's 2 percent interest.
- *July 1966.* Phillips assigns its interest to Shawnee Oil Development Co.
- *August 1966.* Page Sr. and Beardmore assign their interests to Shawnee.
- *August 1966.* Shawnee assigns all of its interest to Fees-Krey (plaintiff/appellant).
- *1972.* Page demands his 2 percent interest from Fees-Krey.

Colorado classifies mineral leases as land interests and requires them to be recorded. All instruments from Page Jr.'s conveyance to Page Sr. were recorded with the Bureau of Land Management but were not recorded in the county land records where the land was located. Only Phillips' conveyance to Page and the conveyances to Fees-Krey were recorded as land interests.

On Page's demand for the 2 percent royalty, Fees-Krey brought a quiet title action. The trial court found that Page Jr. held a 2 percent interest, and Fees-Krey appealed.

ENOCH, Judge

The issue whether §38-35-109, C.R.S. 1973, is a pure notice or a race-notice type of statute is critical in this case because the characterization will determine the priority between the competing interests. An overriding royalty carved out of the working interest in an oil and gas lease is an interest in real property, and is therefore subject to the rules of priority of the Recording Act. If the statute is a race-notice type, a subsequent purchaser will prevail over a prior unrecorded interest only if he purchases without notice and records his interest before the prior interest is recorded. Even if the prior interest is never recorded, the subsequent purchaser must record his own interest before he can assert priority. Thus defendant would have priority here because plaintiffs, though subsequent purchasers without notice, failed to record. If, on the other hand, the statute is a pure notice statute, a subsequent purchaser who purchases without notice of a prior interest prevails over a prior unrecorded interest even though the subsequent purchaser does not record. Thus, plaintiffs, having purchased without

notice of defendant's overriding royalty, would prevail under a notice type statute.

To support his argument that the statute is a race-notice type, and that plaintiffs cannot prevail without having first recorded their interest, defendant cites *Eastwood v. Shedd,* 166 Colo. 136, 442 P.2d 423 (1968), and *Plew v. Colorado Lumber Products,* 28 Colo. App. 557, 481 P.2d 127 (1970), wherein the courts either characterized or implicitly treated the statute as a race-notice statute. In neither case, however, was the characterization of the statute directly in issue. In *Eastwood* the issue was whether a donee was protected by the statute; in *Plew* the question was whether the statute protected a subsequent purchaser who had not yet paid full value, but who had recorded his contract of purchase. In neither case had the prior purchaser recorded before the subsequent purchaser recorded his interest. In both cases the subsequent party in interest would have had priority under either a notice or a race-notice type statute.

Because the characterization of the statute was dictum in *Eastwood* and was not directly addressed in *Plew*, we do not feel constrained to adopt the race-notice label without close analysis of the statute. After careful consideration of the language and purpose of the statute, we are convinced that the better construction is as a pure notice statute.

Section 38-35-109, C.R.S. 1973, reads as follows:

All deeds, powers of attorney, agreements, or other instruments in writing conveying, encumbering, or affecting the title to real property . . . may be recorded in the office of the county clerk and recorder of the county where such real property is situated and no such instrument or document shall be valid as against any class of persons with any kind of rights, except between the parties thereto and such as have notice thereof, until the same is deposited with such county clerk and recorder. In all cases where by law an instrument may be filed, the filing thereof with such county clerk and recorder shall be equivalent to the recording thereof.

The purpose of the statute is to "render titles to real property and every interest therein more secure and marketable" (§38-34-101, C.R.S. 1973). Thus we must liberally construe the statute

with the end in view of rendering such titles absolute and free from technical defects so that subsequent purchasers and encumbrancers by way of mortgage, judgment, or otherwise, may rely on the record title and so that the record title of the party in possession is sustained and not defeated by technical or strict constructions (§38-34-101, C.R.S. 1973).

The statute reads like a pure notice statute, and the language is similar to pure notice statutes in other jurisdictions. Illinois' recording act, which is generally considered as a notice statute, provides that:

All deeds, mortgages and other instruments of writing which are authorized to be recorded, shall take effect and be in force from and after the time of filing the same for record, and not before, as to all creditors and subsequent purchasers, without notice; and all such deeds and title papers shall be adjudged void as to all such creditors and subsequent purchasers, without notice, until the same shall be filed for record (Ill. Rev. Stat. ch. 30, 29 [Smith-Hurd, 1969]).

By contrast, language in race-notice statutes, such as Michigan's, specifies that the subsequent purchaser must first record before he can have priority:

Every conveyance of real estate within this state hereafter made, which shall not be recorded as provided in this chapter, shall be void as against any subsequent purchaser in good faith, and for a valuable consideration, of the same real estate, or any portion thereof, whose conveyance shall be first duly recorded (Mich. Stat. Ann. §26.547 [1970] [M.C.L.A. §565.29]).

Because §38-35-109, C.R.S. 1973, does not specifically state that to assert priority a subsequent purchaser must record his interest, as well as acquire it without notice, we construe the statute liberally to protect those who take without notice of a prior unrecorded interest.

Our decision is buttressed by the fact that a pure notice statute serves to protect subsequent purchasers, allowing them to rely on the record title as it exists at the time of their purchase. The danger of race-notice statute is that a prior interest holder who has failed to record may cut off the claim of a subsequent purchaser who relied on the record at the time of his closing but has not yet had time to record his own instrument. Characterizing the statute as a pure notice rather than race-notice statute will encourage purchasers to record their interests as soon as acquired. Although a subsequent purchaser need not record to protect his interest against prior unrecorded interests, unless he does record, his interest may be cut off by a purchaser subsequent to him.

Defendant contends that even if the statute is a pure notice statute, plaintiffs had constructive notice of the overriding royalty because it was recorded in the office of the Bureau of Land Management. We disagree.

Recording in the office of the Bureau of Land Management is constructive notice only if so recognized by state law. There is nothing in the Colorado statutes which indicates any intent of the General Assembly that such federal records constitute constructive notice to a person acquiring an interest in property in Colorado.

Because the purpose of §38-35-109, C.R.S. 1973, is to strengthen record title by the recording in the County Clerk and Recorder's office, and because recording of a royalty interest with the Bureau of Land Management is only for the purpose of verifying the holdings of the assignee (43 C.F.R. §3106.4 [1977]), we hold that recording with the Bureau of Land Management is not sufficient to constitute constructive notice of an interest in real property.

Having determined that §38-35-109, C.R.S. 1973, is a pure notice statute and that recording with the Bureau of Land Management is not constructive notice of an interest in real property, we find that plaintiffs acquired their interest in the oil and gas lease free of the unrecorded overriding royalty reserved by defendant.

Reversed.

Discussion Questions

1. Describe the series of conveyances that resulted in the dispute.
2. Were any of the interests recorded?
3. What conveyances were part of the land records?
4. Why is the distinction between notice and race/notice important?
5. Which type of state is Colorado?
6. What other states are mentioned and compared?
7. Does Page hold his 2 percent interest?

(9.7) Consider:

Day 1. O conveys to A (bfp).
Day 2. O conveys to B (bfp).
Day 3. A records.
Day 4. B records.

In the above example, who takes title under all three types of recording statutes?

TORRENS SYSTEM

Another method of title protection used instead of a recording system is the *Torrens system*—named after Sir Robert Torrens who introduced the system in

Australia in 1858. The system is one of land title registration; that is, documents of transfer are not recorded, but title to land is registered once by making an entry reflecting the owner. That owner is then given an official certificate of title. If the owner wishes to transfer title to the land, the certificate and a deed are given to the purchaser. The purchaser then takes these documents to the land registration office where the old certificate is surrendered, a change of ownership is entered, and a new certificate is issued to the purchaser. This system eliminates the need for establishing the chain of title.

Initial registration under the Torrens system requires a form of quiet title action, so that all parties with interests or potential interests may be heard before title is registered.

TITLE ABSTRACTS

In many states, parties transferring property interests will hire attorneys to trace the chain of title on a piece of property and then issue an opinion on that chain. That opinion, in written form, is called an *abstract of title* and is defined as a concise statement of the substance of documents or facts appearing on the public records that affect the title. Generally, the abstract will be organized in chronological order of events. The abstract will include summaries of items such as deeds, mortgages, deeds of trusts, *lis pendens* (pending legal action on the property), sheriffs' sales certificates, liens, taxes, assessments, judgments, and bankruptcy petitions.

TITLE INSURANCE

Recording and title abstracts still do not provide protection if a title defect arises. Neither system of title protection offers a guarantee that no problems will arise. In most parts of the United States today, *title insurance* affords the property purchaser financial protection in the event certain types of defects arise in the property.

A title insurer may operate in one of two ways: First, it may hire an attorney to do an abstract and then issue insurance on the basis of that opinion. Or the title insurer may be a complete operation by actually doing the search and abstract and then issuing insurance. Those insurers operating the second type of business maintain a title plant for conducting their operations. A title plant consists of copies of documents taken from the public records. Generally, title companies will organize their records pursuant to a tract index system.

Types of Policies

Title insurers issue different policies according to the type of applicant for insurance and the use to be made of the property. For example, there are different forms for commercial and residential property. Also, different policies are issued for owners of property and for those who wish insurance as mortgage lenders. Neither policy is issued until the insurance company has had an opportunity to examine the records and establish the chain of title.

Process of Issuing a Policy

In many contracts for the sale of real estate today, the condition of delivery of marketable title through the purchase and issuance of a title insurance policy is a prerequisite to closure of the transaction. *Marketable title* is one free of objections or problems that cast doubt upon the chain of title and the seller's right to convey the property. Although the definition of marketable title may vary, adding a requirement that a title insurer issue a policy gives the buyer assurance and financial backing in the event of a problem. A policy will not be issued unless the insurer is reasonably sure no loss will be incurred. A sample contract clause would be: "The seller agrees to deliver and the buyer agrees to accept marketable title as evidenced by a title policy issued by a reputable title insurance company on title to the premises described in this contract."

Upon agreement the seller then applies for a policy with a title insurance company. The company prepares an abstract, and any defects are considered by the title examiner, who decides whether the defects are a risk or whether the property is insurable. If there is a favorable decision, the title insurer issues a preliminary binder that is not a policy but a commitment to insure contingent upon the transaction's closing and the title's being delivered to the buyer.

If the company finds defects that make the property uninsurable, the seller may be given the opportunity to correct those defects and thus make the title insurable. For example, the title abstract will provide a list of all judgments against persons having the same name as the seller. The seller may by affidavit establish that he or she is not the same person as named in those judgments. Tax liens may be removed through payment. When such corrections are made, the insurer will then issue the preliminary binder.

A fee may be charged for the preparation of the abstract and also for the issuance of the policy. In many states the fee charged will be based on an escalating scale set by a state regulatory body, which allows the fee charged to increase with the value of the property. The reason for the escalating scale is that a title problem on a more expensive piece of property will cost the insurer more in terms of correction or compensation.

Many companies will physically inspect the property to be insured in order to determine any adverse possession or occupancy not reflected in the public records. Also, when insuring a construction lender, the title insurer must be certain that construction or work has not begun prior to the recordation of the mortgage. As noted in Chapter 7, any start of construction from the presence of equipment to the digging of one shovelful of dirt will place the mechanics in first priority if those acts are done prior to recording.

Coverage Afforded by the Title Policy

Title insurance differs significantly from ordinary fire or auto insurance in that title insurance covers only defects in title in existence at the time of the transfer. Title insurance does not afford protection for new problems developing after the closing of the transaction and the transfer of title to the buyer. The following case illustrates this retroactive as opposed to prospective coverage.

FIRSTLAND VILLAGE ASSOC. v. LAWYER'S TITLE INSURANCE CO.
284 S.E.2d 582 (S.C. 1981)

Firstland (a developer, plaintiff/appellant) purchased a tract of land designated "Future Development" on a plot of Dorchester Estates Subdivision in Dorchester County. Prior to the purchase, the existing restrictive covenants on the property were amended (first amendment) to permit construction of a planned unit development. The title policy (issued by Lawyer's, defendant/appellee) excepted the original restrictions and first amendment from coverage. After closing, the group of lot owners filed a document to clarify the first amendment. This second amendment further restricted the developer's tract and placed units both under construction and planned in violation of the restrictive covenants. Firstland brought suit asserting a breach of covenants by the title company. The trial court granted summary judgment for Lawyer's, and Firstland appealed.

PER CURIAM

Generally, title insurance operates to protect a purchaser or mortgagee against defects in or encumbrances on title which are in existence at the time the insured takes title. Title insurance is unique in that it is retrospective, not prospective.

The risks of title insurance end where the risks of other kinds begin. Title insurance, instead of protecting the insured against matters that may arise during a stated period after the issuance of the policy, is designed to save him harmless from any loss through defects, liens, or encumbrances that may affect or burden his title when he takes it.

The effective date of the policy (January 7, 1976) preceded the date (March 26, 1976) and recording date (May 12, 1976) of the second amendment. Without admitting the validity of the second amendment, the developer acknowledges in its brief that the filing of the second amendment created a defect in its title. Consequently, the filing of the second amendment, being a defect attaching after the effective date of the policy, does not fall within the purview of title insurance coverage. Moreover, the policy in question specifically excludes "[d]efects, liens, encumbrances, adverse claims, or other matters . . . attaching or created subsequent to Date of Policy. . . . "

The developer argues the filing of the second amendment was not a sub- sequent event since the second amendment arose from and exists by virtue of the original covenants. This theory, if adopted, would not bring the second amendment within policy coverage. The policy expressly excludes coverage for loss or damage by reason of the original restrictions and first amendment under its schedule of exceptions.

We hold the policy does not insure against the defect in question. Accordingly, the title company has not breached covenants under the policy as asserted by the developer.

The order of the trial judge is affirmed.

Discussion Questions

1. Were the restrictive covenants in effect at the time of the developer's purchase?
2. Did the title policy cover the restrictive covenants?
3. When was the lot owner amendment filed?
4. Is the developer covered under the title policy?

The title policy does afford protection for land and buildings up to the date of the transaction closing. However, exceptions for coverage may also be set forth in the policy. Those exceptions are listed in what is called schedule B of the policy. It is important to remember that title insurance insures only the accuracy of the recording system, but the liability is greater. If an unrecorded claim exists or if there is a recorded document that even the most diligent examiner could not find, most title insurers will provide protection against such claims or documents.

Most matters that would be discoverable by survey, such as inaccurate boundary lines, are not covered by title policies. Furthermore, any facts, rights, or claims that are not noted in the public records but are ascertainable by inspection are not covered in the policy. Zoning restrictions are not covered nor is eminent domain (unless proceedings are noted in the records). Unpatented mining claims and defects not in the public records but known to the insured are likewise excluded.

Additional coverage to limit exclusions may be purchased. For example, mechanic's lien protections may be added to a policy. Encroachment protection may be purchased as a rider, so that if a building on the insured's property encroaches on another's property the policy will cover the damages.

The protection afforded under a policy is afforded to the insured (or insureds) named in the policy (a mortgagee or buyer). If the mortgagee is protected and a loss of property results from a title defect, the insurer will pay the balance due on the mortgage, thereby relieving the owner of liability to the mortgage. However, the owner will lose the property and any existing investment or equity. Title policies are not transferable, and the protection afforded a buyer in one transaction may not be passed along to the next buyer.

The seller of the property is afforded no protection by the purchaser's title insurance policy. The seller remains liable to the buyer for breach of any warranties if defects in title arise. In fact it is not unusual for a title insurer to pay the buyer the loss resulting from the title defect and then through subrogation to proceed against the seller for the seller's breach of warranty to the buyer.

Damages

All title policies will have a section dealing with the determination and payment of losses. Under the standard policy, the loss is defined as the least of:

1. The actual loss of the insured claimed; or
2. The amount of the insurance set forth in the policy; or
3. If the policy is for a mortgagee, the amount necessary to pay off the mortgage debt.

In addition to actual loss the title insurer will pay the costs, attorneys' fees, and expenses imposed upon an insured in litigation carried out by the insurer for the insured.

KEY TERMS

adverse possession	acknowledgement clause
squatter's rights	quitclaim deed
quiet title action	warranty deed
inter vivos gift	special warranty deed
donor	deed of bargain and sale
donee	judicial deed
delivery	recording
constructive delivery	grantor/grantee index system
undue influence	tract system
livery of seisin	pure race statute
deed	good faith purchaser
premises	bona fide purchaser (bfp)
habendum clause	notice statutes

race/notice statutes
Torrens system
abstract of title

title insurance
marketable title

CHAPTER PROBLEMS

1. Viola Cain, a widow, decided she needed help in managing her property, so she had a niece, Zaida Mae Morrison, and her husband come to live with her. Zaida Mae conducted all of Viola's business and paperwork. Zaida Mae had a daughter, Marva, of whom Viola was extremely fond. At Viola's direction, Zaida Mae drew up a deed conveying a parcel of land to Marva. The deed was executed but again at Viola's direction, Zaida Mae placed the deed in Viola's safe-deposit box. Viola instructed Zaida Mae to record the deed upon her (Viola's) death. When Viola died, the deed was recorded. Relatives and heirs of Viola objected to the transfer as invalid. Who is entitled to the property?

2. Barnhart told his attorney to draw up a deed transfering title to a 60-acre parcel to his two daughters as tenants in common. After execution, Barnhart told his attorney to record the deed. The daughters were not told of the conveyance. Upon Barnhart's death, his wife sought to have the transaction set aside since there was no delivery or acceptance. Who is entitled to the 60 acres?

3. Dan and Ruth Guilford, husband and wife, lived on a 79-acre farm for 40 years. They had five children: Elmo, Mary Sybert, Ruth Reeves, Lois Boone, and Kenneth. All the children married except Kenneth, who continued to reside at the farm. Dan Guilford died in 1973 when Ruth was 74, and Ruth went to live with Lois. Ruth suffered a stroke and agreed to stay with Lois until Kenneth could put an indoor bathroom in the farmhouse. Kenneth and Lois had their mother sign blank checks and handled all business for her. Lois took her mother to the office of an attorney and had the attorney draw up a deed conveying the farm to Ruth, Lois, and Kenneth as joint tenants with right of survivorship. The deed was recorded 4 years later—1 day before Ruth Guilford died. The other children filed suit to have the deed set aside on grounds of undue influence. After Ruth died, a letter from her was found under the bathroom rug, which stated she wanted Kenneth to have the farm. Should the deed be set aside?

4. Perley Swett was an elderly gentleman who lived alone and was assisted by two friends and two relatives with his meals, mail, and other needs. He executed a deed that conveyed title to his property to the four individuals. He never informed them of the deed but placed it among his

personal papers. White, one of the friends, asked Swett if he could examine Swett's personal papers as research for a book White was writing about Swett. Swett agreed. Swett suffered a stroke, and when White visited him Swett asked him to find the deed in the papers. White could not find the deed. After Swett passed away, White found the deed among the papers in his possession. White and the three others claim title, while Swett's other relatives maintain there was no delivery or acceptance. What is the result?

5. The following is an actual deed recorded on page 215 of volume 40, Cass County, Illinois, deed records.

> I, J. Henry Shaw, the grantor, herein
>   Who lives at Beardstown the county within,
> For seven hundred dollars to me paid today
>   By Charles E. Wyman, do sell and convey
> Lot two (2) in Block Forty (40), said county and town,
>   Where Illinois River flows placidly down,
> And warrant the title forever and aye,
>   Waiving homestead and mansion to both a goodbye,
> And pledging this deed is valid in law
>   I add here my signature, J. Henry Shaw
> [Seal]   Dated July 25, 1881

The acknowledgment on the deed is as follows:

> I, Sylvester Emmons, who lives at Beardstown,
>   A Justice of Peace of fame and renown,
> Of the county of Cass in Illinois state,
>   Do certify here that on the same date
> One J. Henry Shaw to me did make known
>   That the deed above and name were his own,
> And he stated he sealed and delivered the same
>   Voluntarily, freely, and never would claim
> His homestead therein, but left all alone,
>   Turned his face to the street and his back to his home.
> [Seal]   S. Emmons J. P.
> Dated August 1, 1881

Is this a valid deed? What type of deed is it?

6. *Day 1.* O conveys to A (bfp).
   Day 2. A conveys to B (bfp).
         B records.

Day 3. O conveys to C (bfp).

    C records.

Under each of the three types of recording systems, who takes title?

7. San Jacinto Title Guaranty Company issued a standard policy to Lemmon covering Lemmon's property "as shown by the map or plat thereof now of record in the office of the County Clerk of Nueces County, Texas, to which reference is here made for all pertinent purposes." The recorded map referred to an easement across Lemmon's land for a waterline. The title policy did not specifically exclude the easement. The Lemmons brought suit for breach against San Jacinto because of the easement. The trial court found for the Lemmons. San Jacinto has appealed. What is the result?

8. An undeveloped beach front lot has the following history:

    1935. Purchased by Gulf Beach Land and Development Corporation.

    1957. County tax assessor assessed the lot as "owner unknown." Sold for taxes to McDonald.

    1960. McDonald received tax deed.

    1969. Gulf contracted to sell the lots to Perry and Joan Hand for $4,500 with a warranty deed to be delivered upon payment in full.

    September 1974. Gulf sold lot to Boykin Investments subject to Gulf's obligation under "various sale contracts."

    October 1974. Boykin conveyed to Marilyn Stanard.

    1976. Hands paid in full and requested the warranty deed from Stanard. Stanard refused to convey the deed because she had discovered the tax sale to McDonald. The Hands brought a quiet title action against Stanard and McDonald. The trial court found McDonald had title by adverse possession.

The Hands and Stanard have appealed. What is the result?

9. Prepare a deed on the basis of the following information. Be sure to attach to it any comments on missing information or information that is not necessary.

    A. *Land to be conveyed.*

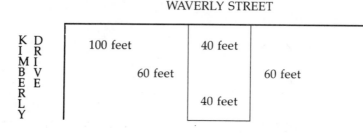

B. *Grantors.* Mr. and Mrs. Paul S. Smith living in a home on the pictured lot, 4141 Waverly Street, Phoenix, Arizona 85003. They own the property as joint tenants. Mrs. Smith's name is Helen.

C. *Grantees.* Mr. and Mrs. Samuel P. Polk, 3232 Holly Drive, Phoenix, Arizona 85204. They wish to own the property as joint tenants. Mrs. Polk's name is Janice.

D. *Date of transaction.* 12 September 1988.

E. *Amount Polks will pay to Smiths.* $152,500.00.

F. A neighbor of the Smiths, Thomas Jones, is a notary public who will furnish his services for free. His commission expires 15 September 1992.

G. The Smiths wish to warrant title only for the time they have held the property.

H. The Smiths have lined up their neighbors Brad Georges and Bill Daves to witness the transaction.

I. There is a school water pipeline through the back 2 feet of the property. There are no other easements, encumbrances, unpaid taxes, or liens on the property.

J. The Polks are paying cash.

10. Determine who gets title to the property under each of the three types of jurisdictions in the following circumstances:

   Day 1. O conveys to A (bfp).

   Day 2. O conveys to B (not bfp).

   Day 3. O conveys to C (bfp).

   Day 4. B records.

   Day 5. A records.

10

THE BROKER'S ROLE IN THE TRANSFER OF REAL ESTATE

HAVE A THIRST FOR LUXURY? Truly a spacious home of superb design and quality. You will love it because it's so versatile, so comfortable and roomy with 3 bedrooms plus den with fireplace. Living room with beautiful burnt orange carpet and glass sliding doors to a covered porch that overlooks your own swimming pool. Kitchen with wood cabinets, built in range, oven, dishwasher and refrigerator, double sinks and breakfast booth. Huge dining room. Two full baths one with corner tub. Beautiful entrance foyer with skylights. Two car attached garage, circuler [sic] driveway entrance leading to this 95' × 35' Cedar siding ranch of 4 yrs. on one acre. $59,900 No. 303

—Ad describing a mobile home
(Lengyel v. Lint, 280 S.E.2d 66 [W. Va. 1981])

Brokers are persons hired to help property owners sell their property. They are employed to help sellers obtain advertising and exposure, and can also be of assistance in explaining the complexities of real property transfers and financing. The purpose of this chapter is to explain the legal role and responsibilities of the broker in the real estate transaction.

THE NATURE OF THE BROKER'S ROLE

A *broker* is an agent hired either by the owner of property to aid in the sale of that property or by the potential owner of property to find property suitable for specified needs. A broker is the middle person acting to bring buyer and seller together. Generally, a broker works on a commission basis rather than on salary. That commission is generally specified as some percentage of the sales price and will probably not be paid until the actual sales transaction is complete (see consideration discussion in this chapter).

Usually the broker is not authorized to enter into land transactions for buyers and sellers but is hired to bring appropriate offers from buyers to sellers and appropriate land parcels for sale to potential buyers.

Brokers are the individuals attuned to opportunities in the real estate market and aware of the needs of buyers in the market for property. Their success comes from matching buyers with the appropriate property. Such success cannot be achieved without legal protections on all sides of the transaction. Brokers, buyers, and sellers must be familiar with their rights and liabilities for the transaction to reach fruition and bring appropriate rewards to all involved.

THE LICENSING REQUIREMENT

In all states and the District of Columbia, some requirements must be met and a license obtained before a person may act as a broker. Such licensing requirements serve to protect two groups: First, licensing affords protection to the public by requiring real estate practitioners to meet certain uniform standards of competency and practice. Second, such requirements afford protections to existing licensees from unscrupulous or illegal conduct by new entrants into the field.

Every state has a statute that sets forth the licensing requirements for those seeking status as real estate practitioners. The power for such a statute stems from the constitutional police powers afforded each state. Licensing, as mentioned previously, is created for the protection of the public.

In each state statute, some type of administrative agency is created to be responsible for the issuing of licenses to real estate practitioners and will have a title such as the real estate board, board of real estate, real estate commission, or department of real estate. These administrative agencies are responsible for establishing licensing procedures and qualifications or for enforcing statutorily imposed licensing procedures and qualifications. Agencies also serve to clarify and interpret applicable legislative provisions. In addition they are usually responsible for the supervision of licenses, investigations of alleged misconduct, and appropriate disciplinary measures such as license revocation or referrals for criminal prosecution.

Requirements for Obtaining Licenses

There are two types of agents who may work for the principal buyer or seller in the real estate transaction. Brokers are licensed to operate their own real estate brokerage businesses. A *salesperson* (sometimes called an *agent*) is licensed only to work for a broker with the broker assuming responsibility for his or her actions. Licensing requirements for brokers are more stringent than those for salespersons, and a salesperson's license is almost universally a prerequisite for a broker's license.

Most state license laws follow the model license law written by the National Association of Real Estate License Law Officials (NARELLO). Each state will have its own variations, but the following list of requirements is part of the NARELLO model. Each requirement is followed by a statement on its status among adopting states.

a. *Educational requirements.* State educational prerequisites for licensing vary from none to an accredited college or university degree. Most states impose a requirement of a high school diploma and a minimum number of classroom hours in real estate education.

b. *Experience.* This requirement is limited to broker licenses. Most states require 2 years experience as a salesperson or 2 years experience in the real estate field as a prerequisite for licensing as a broker. The requirement of experience is coupled, in many states, with classes taken at an accredited college or university in real estate topics (finance, law, appraisal, and so on).

c. *Examination.* All states require both salespersons and brokers to pass examinations to obtain licensing. More than half of the states use a standardized test accompanied by an additional section that covers laws and practices of the particular state. Examinations for brokers cover significantly more material than examinations for salespersons.

d. *Sponsorship.* About half of the states require candidates for salespersons licenses to be sponsored by a licensed broker who will be responsible for the salesperson when the license is awarded.

e. *Minimum age.* In most states the minimum age for licensure is the age of majority in the state (about half of the states list 18 years of age). In some states the minimum age for brokers may be higher than the minimum age for salespersons.

f. *Citizenship.* Some states still require United States citizenship status as a prerequisite for licensing; however, this requirement with respect to other forms of licensing has been struck down on constitutional grounds.

g. *Residency.* Some states require that license applicants be residents of the state for 30 to 90 days before application may be made. Again, such requirements for other license cases have been subject to constitutional challenges.

h. *Criminal record.* Nearly all of the states have provisions prohibiting licensing if the applicant has been convicted of a felony. However, these states usually restrict the length of time for which a license may be denied on this basis.

i. *Application.* All states require potential licensees to submit a completed form provided and developed by the regulating agency. Completion and delivery of the form to the agency is required 30 to 60 days prior to examination. Commonly, the application will require the applicant to give character references from persons in the community or from persons already established in the real estate business.

j. *Payment of fees.* All states require the payment of a licensing fee upon original application. Furthermore, a renewal fee is required to be paid at intervals established by the states.

Issuance of Licenses

Once applicants have satisfied the requirements, their state license will be issued. In all states, all licenses must be displayed in the agent or broker's place of business. Some states also have a requirement whereby licensees must carry pocket cards indicating their licensed status. Some states require the return of the salesperson's license to the state agency upon the termination of that salesperson's employment with a particular broker. When the salesperson is hired by another broker, that broker may request the salesperson's license from the agency.

Doing Business Without a License

The conduct of an individual attempting to act as a salesperson or broker without proper licensing is illegal. The licensing of brokers and salespersons is a regulatory scheme, and any contract for commission between an unlicensed salesperson or broker and a seller would also be void. Hence, court enforcement of such a contract is not available. However, a fee paid to an unlicensed salesperson or broker may be recovered.

Exemptions from Licensing

All states have some exemptions from the licensing requirement. For example, individuals selling real estate for themselves need not be licensed. In all states, attorneys acting for clients in real estate transactions are not required to be licensed as brokers. Those acting as personal representatives, executors, administrators, or trustees for estates need not be licensed to sell or offer to sell property of the estate. All states also have exemptions for public officials dealing with land and its purchase and sale as part of their official duties and responsibilities.

Professional Organizations

Although state licensing is a prerequisite for brokers and salespersons to conduct real estate transactions, membership in professional organizations of real estate practitioners is not required. However, many such organizations have codes of ethics and responsibility, so that membership is indicative of a willingness to subscribe to those standards.

The largest professional association in the real estate industry is the *National Association of Realtors (NAR)*. Only those who are members may use the designation *realtor*, which is a registered trade name of the association. When used by real estate practitioners, this term indicates that they subscribe to the code of ethics of NAR. NAR also promotes and provides educational opportunities for realtors, and local and state chapters often have publications mailed to members that provide updates and information on changes in the field of real estate.

There are also affiliates of NAR for specific real estate professions. The following list is not comprehensive but indicative of the various specialized affiliates of NAR:

1. American Institute of Real Estate Appraisers (AIREA)
2. Institute of Real Estate Management (IREM)
3. Realtors National Marketing Institute (RNMI)
4. Society of Industrial Realtors (SIR)
5. Women's Council of Realtors

In most of these affiliate organizations, substantial educational and experience prerequisites for membership exist.

Other professional and national organizations include the Society of Real Estate Appraisers (SREA), the American Society of Appraisers (ASA), and the National Association of Home Builders (NAHB).

THE LISTING AGREEMENT

The first step taken to assure success in real estate transactions is for the parties to execute a contract of agency (a contract for hiring an agent) appropriately specifying their rights, duties, and responsibilities. This agency arrangement between broker and seller is called a *listing agreement* (see Figure 10.1). State

Figure 10.1 Sample Listing Agreement

Approved by Wisconsin Department of Regulation and Licensing
10-26-87 (optional use date)   3-1-88 (mandatory use date)

Wisconsin Legal Blank Co., Inc.
Milwaukee, Wis.

WB-1 RESIDENTIAL LISTING CONTRACT - EXCLUSIVE RIGHT TO SELL

1 AGREEMENT made between the undersigned real estate Broker and the undersigned Seller.
2 Seller gives Broker the sole and exclusive right to procure a purchaser for the property described below at the price and upon the terms set forth in this contract.
3 If a purchaser is procured for the property by Broker, by Seller, or by any other person, at the price and upon the terms set forth in this contract, or at any other
4 price or upon any other terms accepted by Seller during the term of this contract, or if a binding exchange agreement is entered into or an option which is
5 subsequently exercised is granted during the term of this contract, Seller agrees to pay Broker a commission as set forth in this contract regardless when the
6 transaction closes.
7 If, as to the property or any part of it, a purchaser is procured, a binding exchange agreement is entered into, or an option which is subsequently exercised is
8 granted, within six months after the expiration of this contract to any person or to anyone acting for any person with whom Seller, Broker or any of Broker's agents
9 negotiated or personally exhibited by showing the property prior to the expiration of this contract and in either case whose name Broker has submitted to Seller in
10 writing by personal delivery or by depositing, postage or fees prepaid, in the United States mail or a commercial delivery system, not later than 24 hours after the
11 expiration of this contract, Seller agrees to pay Broker the commission set forth in this contract. A written offer to purchase submitted to Seller or direct negotiation
12 between Seller and purchaser during the term of this listing shall constitute the notice required on lines 7 to 11 without further notice to Seller.
13 (Seller warrants) (Map dated . . . . indicates) the property (is) (is not) located in a flood plain (Strike as applicable).
14 Seller warrants and represents to Broker and Buyer that Seller has no notice or knowledge of any:
15 (a) planned or commenced public improvements which may result in special assessments or otherwise materially affect the property.
16 (b) government agency or court order requiring repair, alteration, or correction of any existing condition.
17 (c) underground storage tanks or any structural, mechanical, or other defects of material significance affecting the property, including but not limited to
18 inadequacy for normal residential use of mechanical systems, waste disposal systems and well, unsafe well water according to state standards, and the
19 presence of any dangerous or toxic materials or conditions affecting the property.
20 (d) wetland and shoreland regulations affecting the property (Caution: see maps).
21 EXCEPTIONS TO WARRANTIES AND REPRESENTATIONS STATED IN LINES 13 TO 20: . . . .
22 . . . .
23 . . . .
24 WARNING: IF SELLER WARRANTIES AND REPRESENTATIONS ARE NOT CORRECT, SELLER MAY BE LIABLE FOR DAMAGES AND
25 COSTS.
26 Seller shall promptly disclose to Broker any facts or circumstances that would modify the above representations and warranties. Seller is aware that Broker is
27 required by state law to disclose material factors affecting the property to all interested parties.
28 Any offer submitted shall be deemed to comply with the terms of this agreement if it includes, in addition to the terms herein contained, in substance, any of the
29 provisions set forth on lines 96 to 133 of this agreement.
30 In consideration for Seller's agreements herein Broker agrees to list and use reasonable efforts to procure a purchaser for the property, including but not limited
31 to the following: . . . .
32 . . . .
33 Seller authorizes Broker and Broker agrees to cooperate with other Brokers, including allowing other Brokers to act as Seller's subagents, except:
34 . . . .
35 Seller agrees to include in the listing price such of the following items as may be on the property which will be delivered free and clear of encumbrances: all
36 fixtures; all garden bulbs, plants, shrubs and trees; screen and storm doors and windows; electric lighting fixtures; window shades; curtain
37 and traverse rods; blinds and shutters; central heating and cooling units and attached equipment; water heaters and softener; sump pump; attached or
38 fitted floor coverings; awnings; exterior attached antennas and component parts; garage door opener and remote control; installed security systems.
39 ADDITIONAL ITEMS INCLUDED IN THE SALE: . . . .
40 . . . .
41 . . . .
42 ITEMS NOT INCLUDED IN THE SALE: . . . .
43 . . . .
44 . . . .
45 The street address of the property is: . . . .
46 in the . . . . of . . . . , County of . . . . Wisconsin, more particularly described as
47 . . . .
48 LISTED PRICE: . . . . Dollars ($ . . . .).
49 MINIMUM EARNEST MONEY $ . . . . WITHIN . . . . DAYS OF ACCEPTANCE WHICH WILL
50 BE RETAINED BY BROKER IN BROKER'S TRUST ACCOUNT, UNLESS OTHERWISE AGREED BY SELLER AND BUYER.
51 TERMS: Cash at closing or . . . .
52 OCCUPANCY DATE: . . . . OCCUPANCY CHARGE if Seller occupies after closing $ . . . . per day.
53 ESCROW TO GUARANTEE OCCUPANCY TO BUYER (AND FOR NO OTHER PURPOSE) $ . . . .
54 CONVEYANCE OTHER THAN WARRANTY DEED, IF ANY: . . . .
55 Seller shall, upon payment of the purchase price, convey the property by warranty deed, or other conveyance provided herein, free and clear of all liens and
56 encumbrances, excepting: municipal and zoning ordinances, recorded easements for public utilities serving the property, recorded building and use restrictions and
57 covenants, general taxes levied in the year of closing and . . . .
58 . . . .
59 provided none of the foregoing prohibit present use, and Seller shall complete and execute the documents necessary to permit recording the conveyance.
60 (WARNING: Recorded building and use restrictions and covenants can have material impact on the use of or improvements to the property. Consideration should
61 be given to the requirements of DILHR's rental weatherization program if the property will not be occupied by Buyer.)
62 BROKER'S COMMISSION, PAYABLE IN FULL WHEN EARNED, BUT NO LATER THAN AT CLOSING, SHALL BE . . . . %
63 OF THE FOLLOWING OR . . . . , whichever is greater:
64 (a) The listed price:
65 (1) if a purchaser is procured in accordance with the terms of this agreement, or,
66 (2) if the property is exchanged.
67 (b) The sales price if an offer is accepted which creates an enforceable contract for the sale of all or any part of the property.
68 (c) The sales price set forth in an option if the option granted is exercised.
69 Within one week from the date of this agreement Seller will provide Broker a written list of all persons whose procurement as purchaser would earn another
70 broker a commission under a prior listing contract. Broker is not entitled to a commission if the property is sold, exchanged, or optioned to any person on such list,
71 to the extent of the prior broker's rights, or to any of the following persons designated by Seller: . . . .
72 . . . .
73 SPECIAL PROVISIONS: . . . .
74 . . . .
75 TERM OF CONTRACT: FROM THE . . . . DAY OF . . . . , 19 . . . .
76 UP TO AND INCLUDING MIDNIGHT OF THE . . . . DAY OF . . . . , 19 . . . .
77 except this Contract is extended through the closing or other termination of any transaction under which Broker earns a commission under lines 3 to 12 hereof for
78 the purpose of that transaction only.   THIS CONTRACT INCLUDES LINES 85 TO 95 ON THE REVERSE SIDE.
79
80 Dated this . . . . day of . . . . , 19 . . . .
81 Broker/Firm . . . .   Seller . . . .
82 Licensee . . . .   Seller . . . .
83
84 Broker's Address and Phone Number   Seller's Address and Phone Number

Figure 10.1 *(continued)*

85   THE FOLLOWING TERMS ARE PART OF THE CONTRACT ON THE REVERSE SIDE.

86   SELLER AND BROKER AGREE THAT THEY WILL NOT DISCRIMINATE AGAINST ANY PROSPECTIVE PURCHASER ON ACCOUNT OF
87 RACE, COLOR, SEX, HANDICAP, RELIGION, NATIONAL ORIGIN, SEX OR MARITAL STATUS OF THE PERSON MAINTAINING A
88 HOUSEHOLD, LAWFUL SOURCE OF INCOME, AGE, ANCESTRY, OR IN ANY OTHER UNLAWFUL MANNER.

89   All funds delivered to Broker shall be retained by Broker in Broker's authorized trust account unless otherwise agreed by Seller and Buyer.

90   Seller agrees to cooperate with Broker in Broker's sales efforts. Seller authorizes Broker to do those acts reasonably necessary for that purpose and to obtain
91 any financial or other information related to the transaction which Broker deems appropriate. Seller shall notify Broker of any potential purchasers with whom
92 Seller negotiates during the term of this Contract and refer all persons making inquiries concerning the property to Broker for further negotiation.

93   If Buyer fails to carry out Buyer's agreement, and Seller elects to take as liquidated damages all earnest money paid by Buyer, then such money shall be applied
94 first to reimburse Broker for cash advances made by Broker and one half of the balance, but not in excess of the agreed commission, shall be paid to Broker as
95 Broker's full commission in connection with said transaction and the balance shall belong to Seller; this payment to Broker shall not terminate this listing contract.

96   **Provisions which may be added in substance to any offer to purchase submitted by or through Broker in performance by Broker with the terms of**
97 **this listing contract.**

98   (General Provisions of Standard Offer to Purchase Form)
99   Buyer agrees that unless otherwise specified, Buyer will, in good faith, pay all costs of securing any financing to the extent permitted by law, and will perform
100 all acts necessary to expedite such financing.
101   The following items shall be prorated as of the day of closing: general taxes, rents, water and sewer use charges, homeowners' association assessments,
102 fuel and ....
103 Any income, taxes, or expenses through the day of closing accrue to Seller.
104   General taxes shall be prorated at the time of closing based on the net general taxes for the current year, if known, otherwise on the net general taxes for the
105 preceding year.
106 CAUTION: If property has not been fully assessed for tax purposes, or reassessment is completed or pending, tax proration shall be on the basis of $ ....
107 estimated annual tax.
108   Special assessments, if any, for work on site actually commenced or levied prior to date of this offer shall be paid by Seller. All other special assessments shall
109 be paid by Buyer. (Caution: Consider a special agreement if area assessments or homeowners' association assessments are contemplated.)
110   Seller shall provide to Buyer at Seller's expense at least three (3) business days before closing, Seller's choice of:
111   **1. An abstract of title prepared by an attorney or abstract company; or**
112   **2. A commitment from a title insurance company licensed in Wisconsin to issue title insurance in the amount of the purchase price upon**
113   **recording of proper documents;**
114 showing title to the property as of a date no more than 15 days before such title proof is provided to Buyer to be in the condition called for in this offer, and further
115 subject only to liens which will be paid out of the proceeds of the closing and standard title insurance exceptions or abstract certificate limitations, as appropriate.
116 Buyer shall notify Seller of any valid objection to title in writing by closing. Seller shall have a reasonable time, but not exceeding 15 days, to remove the objections,
117 and closing shall be extended as necessary for this purpose.
118   If this offer provides for a land contract, prior to execution of the land contract Seller shall provide the same evidence of title as required above and written
119 proof, at or before execution, that the total underlying indebtedness, if any, is not in excess of the proposed balance of the land contract, and that the payments on
120 this land contract are sufficient to meet all of the obligations of Seller on the underlying indebtedness.
121   If the transaction fails to close and the parties fail to agree on the disposition of earnest money, any earnest money held by broker shall be disbursed as follows:
122   1. To Buyer, unless Seller notifies Buyer and broker in writing no later than 15 days after the earlier of the Buyer's written demand for return of the earnest
123   money or the date set for closing, that Seller elects to consider the earnest money as liquidated damages or partial payment for specific performance.
124   2. To Seller, subject to amounts payable to broker, provided the above notice is given and neither party commences a lawsuit on this matter within 30 days
125   after receipt of the notice.
126 In making the disbursement, the Broker shall follow procedures in Section RL 18.09(4), Wis. Adm. Code.
127   Disbursement of earnest money does not determine the legal rights of the parties in relation to this agreement.
128   Both parties agree to hold the broker harmless from any liability for good faith disbursement of earnest money in accordance with this agreement or present
129 Department of Regulation and Licensing regulations concerning earnest money.
130   If the property is damaged by fire or elements prior to time of closing in an amount of not more than five per cent of the selling price, Seller shall be obligated to
131 repair the property and restore it to the same condition that it was on the date of this offer. If such damage shall exceed such sum, this contract may be cancelled at
132 option of Buyer. Should Buyer elect to carry out this agreement despite such damage, Buyer shall be entitled to the insurance proceeds relating to damage to
133 property; however, if this sale is by land contract or a mortgage to Seller, the insurance proceeds shall be held in trust for the sole purpose of restoring the property.

Source: Used with permission of Wisconsin Legal Blank Co.

requirements for valid listing agreements vary, but the parties should be cautious about including certain fundamental topics so that their positions are made absolutely clear.

Agreements in Writing

Nearly all states require that the listing agreement be in writing. In fact, in most states the failure to have listing agreements in writing will cost the broker or salesperson the commission for the listing agreement. This is because if the agreement is oral it is unenforceable, and the aid of the judiciary is not available to those who should be most familiar with the legal requirements for transacting real estate business. The following case illustrates the reluctance of courts to imply the existence of a listing agreement based on conduct or oral communication.

Kohn v. Cohn
567 S.W. 2d 441 (Mo. 1978)

Kohn (plaintiff/appellant) is a licensed real estate broker associated with his father's firm, Louis T. Kohn Realty. As managing agent for the Levee Building at the Laclede's Landing area of St. Louis, one of Kohn's responsibilities was to seek tenants for the building. One of the building owners suggested Kohn look into the possibility of Spaghetti Factory locating a restaurant in the building. The following sequence of events took place.

April 1975
Kohn visited Denver's Spaghetti Factory and presented the idea to the executives.

1 May 1975
Kohn presented the idea to the Spaghetti Factory home office in Portland.

22 May 1975
Kohn met with three representatives of the Spaghetti Factory at the Levee Building.
The Levee Building was determined to be unacceptable in size.
Kohn took the three to Cohn's (defendant/appellee) office to examine his building.

Spaghetti Factory executives asked for floor plan. Kohn, in the presence of Cohn, said he would take care of the details.

26 June 1975
Kohn and Cohn met, and Kohn indicated he was seeking a tenant for Cohn's building. Cohn said he would go to Portland, but did not go.

October 1975
Kohn and Spaghetti Factory executives met.

23 October 1975
Cohn and Spaghetti Factory executives met.

29 October 1975
Spaghetti Factory executives wrote Kohn and declined to lease the Cohn building.

16 September 1976
Cohn and Spaghetti Factory reached a 5-year lease agreement.

Kohn filed suit seeking a commission. The trial court granted summary judgment for Cohn. Kohn appealed.

GUNN, Presiding Judge

Count one of plaintiff's petition charges that on May 22, 1975, defendant "orally employed and retained plaintiff as the agent of . . . [defendant] to procure and negotiate on its behalf, a lease of its aforesaid land and improvements." Plaintiff sought commissions under the alleged agreement. But in his deposition, plaintiff patently conveys that he never discussed any commission at any time with anyone. Plaintiff bases his claim on his past experiences with property he has managed.

Plaintiff's primary argument on appeal is that when the evidence is viewed in the light most favorable to his position, there exists sufficient evidence to create a genuine issue as to whether he and defendant entered into an implied contract of agency. We hold that as a matter of law there was no evidence of an agreement by defendant to employ plaintiff as his agent.

The law in this state regarding the liability of an owner of real estate to pay commission to a real estate broker for services rendered in connection with the sale or lease of his property is well established. The broker has the burden to prove that an employment relationship existed between the owner and himself and that he was the efficient or procuring cause of the sale. In the absence of a contract of employment between the broker and the owner, the owner is not obligated to pay a commission even if the broker was the efficient cause of a sale which is later consummated. A broker who is a mere volunteer is entitled to no compensation for services gratuitously rendered. The mere fact that a broker without request, but of his own volition, brings a customer to a vendor, will not of itself imply an agreement on the part of the vendor to pay for services thus thrust upon him. Officious intermeddling in the business affairs of others, though it may produce valuable results to the interested parties, should go unrewarded.

To establish the agency contract, it must appear that the owner authorized the broker to produce a buyer or lessee and that the broker agreed to do so under such circumstances that the owner had reason to know that the broker's services were not offered gratuitously but were undertaken with an expectation of compensation. It is essential that there be an actual meeting of the minds of the parties involved and that they knowingly and understandingly enter into mutually enforceable obligation. Where the direct words of the parties— either oral or written—acknowledge their agreement, the contract is express. Where, however, the contract is inferred from the acts and conduct of the parties, in light of the subject matter and surrounding circumstances, it is implied.

Although plaintiff has pleaded an express contract the record is destitute of evidence of an oral or written agency agreement between him and defendant. Nor is there evidence of an implied agency contract—the theory plaintiff adopts in his brief on appeal. In order to raise an implied contract, the services rendered by the broker must have been performed under such circumstances that the recipient had reason to know that they were not offered gratuitously nor performed for some other person but with the expectation of compensation from the recipient. Further, the services rendered must have been beneficial to the person sought to be held liable. Where a broker approaches an owner and negotiates for the sale or lease of his property, no promise to pay for the broker's voluntary services will be implied if the owner is justified under the circumstances in presuming that the broker represents the prospective purchaser or lessee.

Plaintiff's theory of recovery based on the affidavits of his fellow real estate brokers—to the effect that the custom in the real estate industry in the St. Louis area is that when a real estate broker is "involved" in the sale or lease of property, the vendor is the party responsible for all real estate commission—is unavailing to him and is dissonant with the prevailing law. A custom which is contrary to established principles of law will not be given recognition. A custom is not a substitute for a contract. Unless a valid contract is first shown, any evidence relating to custom or usage is immaterial and irrelevant to establish contract liability. We have previously held that no contract of agency existed between plaintiff and defendant. The evidence of custom cannot counteract this fatal defect.

The judgment is affirmed.

Discussion Questions

1. Who employed Kohn as an agent?
2. What was his job?
3. What tenant was Kohn trying to obtain?
4. Was the Levee Building appropriate for the Spaghetti Factory restaurant?
5. Who is Cohn?
6. Did Cohn authorize Kohn to act as his agent?
7. Was Cohn's building eventually leased to the Spaghetti Factory?
8. Does Kohn get a commission?

Signature by the Owner

The listing agreement must be signed by the owner of the property. Caution should be used to make sure the true owner has signed the agreement and that if there is more than one owner, all owners have signed. In the case of land owned by a corporation or partnership, it should be verified that the officer, director, or partner signing the listing agreement has authority to do so. The authority of a trustee, executor, administrator, or personal representative who holds land should also be verified, along with any restrictions that may exist on that person's authority to transfer title to the property. For example, such persons may have authority to list the property but not to sell it without prior court approval. This type of restriction should be noted in the listing agreement.

Types of Listing Agreements

Various types of agency relationships that may be created by the listing agreement are discussed in the following sections. The basic difference among all of them is the determination of who is entitled to the commission upon sale of the property.

Open Listing The *open listing* agreement is used when an owner lists the property to be sold with more than one firm. Under this form of listing the seller owes only one commission to the broker who actually sells the property. Furthermore, the seller retains the right to sell the property personally; and if the seller does produce the buyer, no commission is owed to any broker.

The language used to create an open listing agreement will include paragraphs such as the following to specify the characteristics of the open listing:

> Seller agrees to pay broker a commission of _____ percent (_____%) of the selling price should the broker find a purchaser ready, willing, and able to buy at the above agreed upon price and terms, or if the broker sells the property at another price or other terms approved of and agreed to by the seller.
>
> This listing agreement in no way prohibits the seller from selling

the property directly. The seller retains the right to sell property to any person(s) or party(ies) not first contacted by the broker. The seller retains the right to list the above described property with any other broker(s).

Brokers are free to solicit listings from sellers who have listed with other brokers, and the only commission paid will be the one to the broker who actually produces the buyer. The following case illustrates the effect of an open listing agreement.

Lord v. Melton
400 N.E.2d 547 (Ill. 1980)

The Meltons owned a residence and 40 acres of land near Galva and sought to sell the property for $140,000. Because of their friendships with several brokers in town, the Meltons wished to give all of them an opportunity to earn a commission for selling the property. Richard Carlson, an agent for Nancy Lord Realty (plaintiff/appellee), and Mike Clucas, an agent for Colony Realty (defendant/appellant), were invited to the Meltons. The Meltons refused to sign either agent's exclusive listing agreement but orally consented to an open listing. Carlson then went to the home of the Moriaritys and told them of the Melton property. The next day Carlson spent 45 minutes showing the Moriaritys the property. Later that week John Moriarity went to Colony Realty in response to an ad on the Melton property placed in the paper by Colony Realty. Moriarity indicated he did not want to deal with Nancy Lord Realty and that he had a tax problem. Clucas, with two accountants, solved the tax problem, and ultimately Clucas obtained an offer and contract for the $140,000 price for the Meltons. The customary 3 percent sales commission of $4,200 was paid to Colony Realty. Nancy Lord Realty brought suit seeking half or $2,100 of the commission. The trial court awarded $2,100 to Nancy Lord Realty and Colony Realty appealed.

ALLOY, Justice

The basis for the claim asserted by Nancy Lord Realty as against Colony Realty is that Colony tortiously interfered with a contractual relationship between Nancy Lord Realty and the Meltons. The tort of inducing the breach of a contract has long been recognized in Illinois. Intentional and unjustified inducement of breach of another's contract could result in liability. The elements of the cause of action involved a valid contract, defendant's knowledge of the existence of the contract, defendant's intentional and malicious inducement of the breach of contract, and an actual breach of such contract caused by defendant's wrongful conduct with resultant damage to the plaintiff.

To support the claim asserted in this action, Nancy Lord Realty argues that there existed a contract between Nancy Lord Realty and the Meltons. Their brief implies that this was a bilateral contract: that the Meltons had promised to pay a commission upon the sale of the property and that

Nancy Lord Realty promised to make an effort to find a buyer. The facts in the instant case, however, show that the Meltons agreed only to pay the broker who brought them a buyer who was ready, willing and able to buy the premises at the price desired by the Meltons. Nancy Lord Realty did not bring the Meltons a buyer. Colony Realty actually brought the buyer who was ready, willing and able to pay $140,000 to the Meltons.

Under the open listing, no contract actually would exist between the Meltons and Nancy Lord Realty or between the Meltons and Colony Realty, until a buyer was actually obtained by Colony Realty in the instant case. The evidence in the case indicated clearly that the Meltons offered to pay a commission to a broker who actually brought the Meltons a buyer at the price the Meltons desired. The type of arrangement involved was one which the broker could only accept and which would become a binding contract through performance by the broker. There was no failure on the part of Nancy Lord Realty to fulfill or perform under the contract by reason of meddling of Colony, since Moriarity at no time was ready, willing or able to proceed with the purchase of the premises through Nancy Lord Realty, under the facts in the instant case.

Clearly, on the basis of the record, no binding contract was ever formed between the Meltons and the Nancy Lord partnership nor was any such contract interfered with by Colony Realty. In the instant case, it is not the Meltons who failed to perform, but the Nancy Lord partners themselves who were unable to find a customer ready, willing and able to purchase the Melton property.

Brokers are not entitled to commissions for unsuccessful efforts. With the type of open listing involved in the instant case, Nancy Lord Realty did not bring about the sale or procure a purchaser who was ready, willing and able to purchase at the stipulated terms.

Unless an owner of property particularly agrees not to do so, the owner may employ two or more brokers, and in such case, it is the broker, who is the efficient cause of the sale, who is entitled to the commission. This right is not affected by the circumstance that such broker sells to one whose attention to the property had been originally directed by another broker. With an open listing, commission is payable not to the broker who first speaks of the property to a prospect, but to the broker who is the procuring cause of the sale, whether he is the first or second to engage the attention of a purchaser.

As the agency which brought together the parties upon terms which all parties agreed upon, Colony Realty clearly earned the commission for this sale.

For the reasons stated, therefore, the portion of the judgment appealed from, granting $2,100 in damages and costs to the plaintiff is reversed.

Discussion Questions

1. Who owned the property at issue?

2. What type of property was it?

3. What two realty companies were contacted about the property?

4. What agents represented which realty companies?

5. Who first told the Moriaritys of the Melton property?

6. Were any written listing agreements signed?

7. What type of listing existed?

8. Who obtained the offer for sale and eventual contract?

9. How much was the commission?
10. Is Nancy Lord Realty entitled to a commission or any portion thereof?

11. Why did Moriarity not want to deal with Nancy Lord Realty?

Exclusive Agency An *exclusive agency* listing arrangement is one in which the seller is required to pay a commission to the listing broker if that broker sells the property. However, the seller still retains the right to sell the property independently; and if the seller does sell the listed property, no commission is required to be paid to the listing broker. If the seller hires another broker, the original broker retains the right to commission and the seller will be obligated for two commissions. The language used to create this type of listing agreement should be made perfectly clear. A sample of the clauses needed to create such an agreement follows:

> Seller agrees to pay broker a commission of _____ percent (_____%) of the selling price should the broker find a purchaser ready, willing and able to buy at the above agreed upon price and terms, or if the broker sells the property at another price or other terms approved of and agreed to by the seller.
>
> This listing agreement in no way prohibits the seller from selling the property directly. The seller shall have and retain the right to sell the above described property any person(s) or party(ies) not first contacted by the broker.

The major distinction between the open listing agreement and the exclusive agency is that the open listing permits the seller to list the property with other brokers. Under the exclusive agency, sellers should not list with other brokers for they will still be responsible to the exclusive broker for the commission and may pay more than one commission. The open listing and exclusive agency are similar in that the seller may still sell the property independently without being required to pay the commission.

Exclusive Right to Sell or Exclusive Listing to Sell Under the *exclusive right to sell* or *exclusive listing to sell* arrangement, the seller agrees to pay a commission to the broker regardless of who produces a buyer. The seller is required to pay the commission even if the seller produces a buyer independently of the broker. This type of listing agreement, which is beneficial to the broker, is the form of listing agreement used most frequently in the real estate industry. The language required for such a listing is as follows:

> In consideration for the terms of this listing and the promise of the broker to work to effect a sale of the above described property, the seller(s) appoints the broker, the sole and exclusive agent, and gives the broker sole and exclusive right to offer to sell and present any offers received.
>
> In the event the broker produces a buyer in accordance with the above terms and conditions or any other terms and conditions accepted by seller, seller agrees to pay the broker _____ percent (_____%) of the selling price. If such a buyer is produced by the seller or any other person, the same fee shall prevail.

Another type of clause used in exclusive right to sell arrangements indicating the commission arrangement is as follows:

> Should I or anyone acting for me, including my peers, sell, lease, transfer, or otherwise dispose of said property within the time herein fixed for the continuance of the agency, you shall be entitled nevertheless to your commission as herein set out.

Multiple Listing The *multiple listing* agreement is really not a form of agency between seller and broker. Instead, the multiple listing is a service available to brokers who are members of some of the multiple listing services. An example of a *multiple list service* is the *MLS,* a network of exclusive right to sell listings that affords brokers and sellers a larger market for their properties. Through MLS, broker members are able to show the listed properties of other brokers. The listing broker then shares in the commission if a nonlisting broker obtains a buyer for the broker's listed property. The split commission is prenegotiated and determined by the MLS members. Since there is still only one listing agreement, the seller is liable for only one commission. The MLS is a marketing tool enabling brokers to assist each other in finding buyers and to split fees accordingly.

Net Listing In the *net listing* agreement, the seller and broker may have any of the previous types of listing arrangements for determining who is entitled to the commission. This arrangement merely provides a different method for determining the amount of commission the broker is entitled to receive. Generally, the commission is some percentage of the selling price. However, in net listings, the sellers set forth a predetermined amount that they must receive from the sale of the property after expenses, insurance, and so on. The broker's commission is anything received above that predetermined amount. For example, if the seller sets the net figure for receipt at $40,000 and $41,500 remains after expenses, the broker is entitled to receive $1,500 as commission. Again, this form of commission determination may be coupled with an open listing, exclusive agency, or exclusive right-to-sell format.

Importance of Careful Drafting

Regardless of the type of listing agreement chosen, both brokers and sellers should be cautious in drafting the listing agreement so that the type of listing is clear and the commission issue is not clouded with ambiguities. Generally, with greater prices in real estate, brokers stand to receive substantial sums as commissions when buyers are found. With so much money involved, it is only natural that many legal battles have been fought and are pending in the courts over the issue of who is entitled to receive a commission. The best way to avoid such litigation is to make sure the listing agreement is carefully and unambiguously drafted. The following case illustrates the difficulties of a poorly drafted listing agreement.

Insurance Agencies Co. v. Weaver
604 P.2d 258 (Ariz. 1979)

On 15 September 1976 the Weavers (defendants/appellees) signed a written listing agreement for the sale of their home with Insurance Agencies Company (plaintiff/appellant). Some time between 15 September and 30 September 1976 the Weavers sold their home through another broker. Insurance Agencies brought suit for their commission, alleging the Weavers had signed an "agency listing." Insurance Agencies maintained that under an "agency listing" the "custom and practice of the real estate profession" is to entitle the broker to half the stated commission in the written agreement if the property is sold through another broker during the term of the listing.

The listing agreement was a printed form supplied by Insurance Agencies, which, in its unaltered state, would create what it called an exclusive listing. By its terms, the bro-

ker would earn the stated commission if he produced a purchaser himself, if the property were sold through any other broker, or if the owner sold the property directly without any broker. This form was altered by the parties.

In the title, which had read "Exclusive Authorization to Sell," the word "Exclusive" was crossed out and the word "Agency" was substituted for it. In the section of the contract labeled "remarks," the following statement appears: "This is an agency listing till September 30, 1976. Beginning October 1, 1976 (90 days) to December 30, 1976, Exclusive." However, the language in the contract stating that the broker would earn his commission no matter who sold the property was left unaltered.

The trial court granted summary judgment for the Weavers and Insurance Agencies appealed.

GORDON, Justice

It is not clear whether plaintiff's theory is that an agency listing is synonymous with an exclusive agency listing or that it is a separate type of listing. The complaint, read in its best light, does state that an agency listing creates a right to recover a commission for the sale of defendant's property. Defendants, in their unverified amended answer, deny that an agency listing entitles the broker to receive any commission in this situation. Moreover, defendants asserted in their answer that plaintiff made representations to them that an agency listing was the same as an open listing, allowing defendants to sell their property through other brokers without paying plaintiff any commission.

The only pertinent document before the court was a copy of the listing agreement. The question is whether the pleadings and the listing agreement reveal that there is no genuine issue of material fact and that defendants are entitled to judgment as a matter of law, 16 A.R.S., Rules of Civil Procedure, Rule 56(C). We believe that question should be answered in the negative.

The meaning of "Agency Listing," certainly a material fact in this case, cannot be discerned from the contract itself. It is clear that from September 15 to September 30, 1976, the parties contemplated something other than an exclusive listing. Plaintiff claims that "agency listing" means an exclusive agency listing or at least that it is a type of listing entitling it to a commission if the property were sold by another broker. Defendants contend that "agency listing" means an open listing. The intent of the parties must be determined at trial.

Defendants also argue that since the agreement was not an exclusive listing agreement it must be non-exclusive. Defendants then cite cases explaining the rights of brokers under non-exclusive agreements. The problem with this contention is that the parties did more than state that the listing was not exclusive. They said it was an "agency" listing. We cannot, as a matter of law, say what this term means.

Finally, defendants state the rule of interpretation that an ambiguous contract should be construed against the party who drafted it. However, this rule "is a secondary rule of construction to be applied only if the meaning remains uncertain after the application of . . . primary standards. . . ." One primary standard is the surrounding circumstances at the time the contract was made. This is a factual matter and requires a trial.

The judgment of the trial court is reversed, the order granting summary judgment is vacated, and the case is remanded for further proceedings consistent with this opinion.

Discussion Questions

1. Who is the plaintiff in the action?
2. What type of property was listed?
3. Who were the sellers?
4. What type of printed form was used for the listing?
5. What was crossed out on the form?
6. What additional terms were written on the form?
7. What type of commission clause appeared in the agreement? Was it altered?
8. What was the trial court's decision?
9. What was the appellate court's decision?
10. What should have been examined in interpreting the contract?

(10.1) Consider:

Elizabeth Clutter put her 175-acre farm in Knox County, Ohio on the market through Central Realty Company. An exclusive listing with the following language was used:

> If you secure a purchaser for my property, or if the same is sold or exchanged during the term of this listing, or is sold within three months after the period of this listing to anyone with whom you have negotiated with respect to a sale during the period of this listing and of whom I have notice, I agree to pay you a commission of 5 percent upon the price at which same may be sold or exchanged.

During the period of the listing, Central produced an offer from the Merillats, which was too low and not acceptable to Ms. Clutter. After the expiration of the exclusive listing period, Ms. Clutter executed a second exclusive listing with Jim Owen. Jim Owen presented a second offer from the Merillats, which Ms. Clutter accepted. Central now claims a commission. What is the result?

Expiration Date

Most states have some type of law or regulation requiring a definite expiration date to be set forth in the listing agreement. In those states where such a limitation is required, listing agreements not meeting the requirement are treated as unenforceable contracts and may cost the broker the commission in spite of the sale and in spite of the existence of a written listing agreement. A typical termination clause would have the following language:

> This listing agreement and its provisions are to remain in full force and effect and be irrevocable by me or us from this date, for a period which will terminate as of the ____ day of _____, 19____.

The following case illustrates the necessity for a definite expiration date in a contract and discusses the implications of the statute of frauds on renewals.

EVERETT v. BROWN
321 S.E.2d 685 (W.Va. 1984)

Larry and Linda Brown decided to sell their home and in March 1980 contacted Mrs. Delores Wilson of Griffin Real Estate to discuss a listing agreement. On 10 March 1980, the Browns signed an exclusive listing agreement with Griffin for a period of 30 days. The selling price of their home was $106,000 without appliances and $111,000 with appliances.

The listing agreement ended on 10 April 1980 but the Browns continued to allow Griffin and its agents to bring prospective buyers to their home. On 30 August 1980, Dean Everett, an agent with Griffin, brought the Keeneys through the Browns' home with their approval. The Keeneys offered to buy the home for $106,000 without the appliances.

On 8 September 1980, the Keeneys signed a Griffin purchase contract that Everett had prepared and gave him an earnest money deposit of $1,000. Mr. Everett had a number of discussions with the Browns about getting a second deed of trust released from their property. The Browns did not sign the purchase contract because of the uncertainty on the second deed of trust. However, Everett continued to work with the Browns to get the release. In November, the Browns informed Everett they had obtained the release but that he was not entitled to a commission because the listing agreement had expired. The Browns then transferred the home to the Keeneys, and Everett brought suit for his 5 percent commission of $5,300.

The trial court found that there was only an oral listing agreement, which was invalid, and dismissed Everett's claim. Everett appealed.

NEELY, Justice

Part of this case consists of a swearing contest between the parties: The real estate broker and his agent, Mrs. Wilson, testified that upon the expiration of the written agreement the Browns orally agreed that the listing should continue. Larry Brown, on the other hand, testified that there was no agreement to extend the listing and that when Mr. Everett called him for permission to show his house to the Keeneys, Mr. Everett explained that the Keeneys wanted only to see the floor plan for a house they wanted to build.

However, there is other, undisputed, circumstantial evidence that leads us to conclude that Griffin Real Estate proved its case. It is agreed by everyone, for example, that Griffin showed the Brown house three times during the listing agreement and either three or four times after the expiration of that agreement. Furthermore, the Keeneys came to the Brown house in the evening accompanied by Mr. Everett, inspected the house, and almost immediately made an oral offer to purchase at the Browns' asking price. Subsequently, Mr. Everett tendered the Keeneys a written contract, which they signed, and Mr. Everett accepted a $1,000 deposit as evidence of their good faith.

These actions on the part of Mr. Everett corroborate his version of the facts—namely, that after the expiration of the written listing agreement the Browns encouraged him to sell the property on the same terms set forth in the written agreement. It is hardly credible to us that a real estate broker would invest valuable time in showing property that he did not have good reason to believe was listed. And, it is also incredible to us that a married couple who did not want their property sold by a real estate broker would allow that broker to show their property time and time again unless they intended to perpetrate a fraud.

Consequently, we find overwhelming evidence that the Browns actively encouraged Griffin Real Estate to believe that the written listing agreement was extended. Notwithstanding any conflicting testimony about what the parties or their agents said to one another, the actions of the parties themselves—Mr. Everett and his agents in showing the property and Mr. and Mrs. Brown in allowing the property to be shown—speak loudly and convincingly that there was an oral extension of the written listing.

In the trial court the Browns relied upon W. Va. Code, 47-12-17(c) (1959) which says:

A broker or salesman who obtains a listing shall, at the time of securing such listing, give the person or persons signing such listing a true, legible copy thereof. Every listing agreement, exclusive or nonexclusive, shall have set forth in its terms a definite expiration date; it shall contain no provision requiring the party signing such listing to notify the broker of his intention to cancel such listing after such definite expiration date; however, an exclusive listing agreement may provide that upon the expiration of the exclusive feature the listing shall continue to a definite expiration date as a nonexclusive listing only.

Code 47-12-17(c) (1959) is merely one of many statutes of frauds in West Virginia law.

In the case before us the controlling law in this State may be found in *Ross v. Midelburg*, 129 W. Va. 851, 42 S.E.2d 185 (1947) where we said:

Though an oral contract for the sale of land is within the statute of frauds and is for that reason unenforceable, such an agreement may be removed from the operation of the statute by the conduct of the party who would, because of the statute, deny the binding effect of the agreement. "One may become estopped to set up the statute by conduct sufficient to constitute an estoppel in accordance with the usual rules as to estoppel generally." An equitable estoppel may be invoked to preclude a party to a contract from setting up the defense of the statute. This doctrine operates to prevent the perpetration of fraud by one party to the contract upon the other party. "It is a most important principle, thoroughly established in equity, and applying in every transaction where the statute is invoked, that the statute of frauds having been enacted for the purpose of preventing fraud, shall not be made the instrument of shielding, protecting, or aiding the party who relies upon it in the perpetration of a fraud, or in the consummation of a fraudulent scheme. . . . It is a broad general rule that a court of equity will not permit a party to take shelter under the defense of the statute and by so doing commit a fraud on the other party.

Applying Ross' principles, Mr. and Mrs. Brown are estopped by their conduct to assert the statute of frauds because they deliberately misled the plaintiffs. The plaintiffs worked to sell the Brown house and the Browns then took full and complete advantage of the plaintiffs' work. The hornbook law on estoppel in this regard may be found in Restatement (Second) of Contracts §139 where the text provides:

A promise which the promisor should reasonably expect to induce action or forbearance on the part of the promisee or a third person and which does induce the action or forbearance is enforceable notwithstanding the Statute of Frauds if injustice can be avoided only by enforcement of the promise. The remedy granted for breach is to be limited as justice requires.

In determining whether injustice can be avoided only by enforcement of the promise, the following circumstances are significant: (a) the availability and adequacy of other remedies, particularly cancellation and restitution; (b) the definite and substantial character of the action or forbearance in relation to the remedy sought; (c) the extent to which the action or forbearance corroborates evidence of the making and terms of the promise, or the

making and terms are otherwise estab-
lished by clear and convincing evidence;
(d) the reasonableness of the action or for-
bearance; (e) the extent to which the ac-
tion or forbearance was foreseeable by the
promisor.

All of the requirements for the application of estoppel have been met in this
case.

The Browns entered into a definite
and specific written contract for the sale
of their house that expired in April, 1980.
Thereafter, by allowing the plaintiffs to
continue to show their house to prospective purchasers—which everyone agrees
happened either three or four times—they

deliberately misled the plaintiffs into believing that the terms of the original written
agreement would continue to be binding.
When, in August 1980, the plaintiffs presented a couple who were willing to buy
the defendants' house, the defendants took
full advantage of that opportunity and sold
the house to the couple presented. Certainly Griffin Real Estate changed its position and was injured; Griffin incurred
expense and performed valuable work; and
the ultimate purchasers were in the market
for a house in the Buckhannon area and
would probably have bought another of
the plaintiffs' listed houses had they not
been shown the Brown house first.

Reversed and remanded.

Discussion Questions

1. What were the terms of the original listing agreement?
2. When did it expire?
3. What happened when the agreement expired?
4. When did the Keeneys make their offer?
5. What work did Everett do on the sale?
6. Why does the court discuss the concept of estoppel?
7. Will Everett get the commission?
8. How could the litigation have been avoided?

(10.2) Consider:

An extension clause in a listing agreement provides that for 90 days after expiration of the agreement, the broker is still entitled to the commission if the property
is sold to someone who had seen the property prior to the expiration of the listing
agreement. Is such an agreement practical? Does it give a definite termination
date? *Burland, Reiss, Murphy & Mosher v. Schmidt,* 261 N.W. 2d 540 (Mich. 1977)

Brokers may put a clause in the listing agreement that entitles them to
a commission for a certain period of time after the expiration of the listing
agreement for sale to prospective buyers originally introduced to the property
by the broker during the listing period.

The language used for such clauses is as follows:

> If within ninety (90) days after the expiration of this _____ listing agreement, a sale is made directly by the broker to any person to whom this property has been shown by you or the broker or an agent of the broker, the same fee shall prevail, unless this listing is renewed or the property is relisted on the same basis with another broker, and in that case, this stipulation shall be void.

or:

> We agree that if the above described property is sold or exchanged by any person during the term of this listing, or within sixty (60) days thereafter to any person with whom any negotiations were held during the listing term, to pay the broker _____ percent (____%) commission of the sales price or exchange value of the consummated sale.

One additional danger in having a listing agreement without an expiration date and extension clause even in those states recognizing the validity of such listings, is that the seller may cancel the agreement at any time. Such a right of cancellation is often used when a sale is desired but the payment of the commission is sought to be avoided. The courts have implied a duty of good faith on the part of the parties to an indefinite duration listing agreement to preclude commission avoidance.

Clauses covering the expiration date and extension clauses should also cover the rights of termination under the listing agreements. Issues that should be covered in the clauses include whether the listing may be terminated; how termination occurs; what type of notice of termination is required; and what damages will be due and owing, if any.

When the Commission Is Due and Owing

Most form listing agreements provide, and the majority of courts hold (in the absence of an agreement to the contrary), that the broker is entitled to the commission when a purchaser who is ready, willing, and able to meet the terms of the listing agreement has been brought to the seller. Actual closing of the deal is not necessary for the broker to collect the commission.

There are several legal issues arising from this time framework for the awarding of commissions. The listing agreement must make clear that the commission is due and payable when a purchaser's offer that complies with the listing agreement terms is presented by the broker and that the commission is not payable from sales proceeds or escrow funds only.

Also, the listing agreement must contain and clearly set forth all of the material terms and conditions for sale of the property, since the broker's entitlement to commission is tied to those terms. And since the seller becomes liable if all terms are met, the seller must be certain that all necessary provisions desired for the sale of the property are established in the listing agreement.

Producing a buyer who is ready and willing simply means that a buyer is ready to purchase according to the seller's listing terms and has made necessary deposits on the property. The *able* portion of the test for commission entitlement requires the broker to establish that the buyer had the financial ability, credit, or resources necessary to go through with the transaction.

Once such a buyer is produced and the seller chooses to back out of the transaction, the commission is still due and owing. Furthermore, if the seller contacts the buyer directly and gets the buyer to cancel, this attempt to thwart the transaction will be ineffective and the broker's commission will still have to be paid.

The most important factor to remember about the ready, willing, and able standard for the broker's commission is that it is not contingent on the sale's actually closing and the buyer's actually paying the funds. The following case illustrates circumstances in which the brokers obtained their commissions even when the sales did not go through.

WELEK REALTY, INC. v. JUNEAU
596 S.W.2d 495 (Mo. 1980)

The Juneaus (defendants/appellants) signed a 3-month exclusive-right-to-sell listing agreement with Welek (plaintiff/appellee) for the sale of their home in the Lake of the Ozarks area of Missouri. Welek showed the property to Joe Lawrence, who made an offer of $49,500 (the listing price) with a $500 earnest money deposit. Welek talked with Mr. Juneau, who orally assented to the contract but asked for $1,500 additional earnest money. Lawrence complied. The Juneaus received the contract but never signed it and withdrew the property from the market. Lawrence bought another home in the area and Welek brought suit for the commission. The trial court entered judgment for Welek and the Juneaus appealed.

HOUSER, Senior Judge

On appeal defendants make two points: first, that plaintiff produced no evidence that the buyer, Mr. Lawrence, possessed the financial ability to buy on the terms set out in the listing contract; second, that no consideration was given defendants for the listing, because defendants cancelled the listing contract before plaintiff had expended any time or money in its performance, and therefore incurred no liability to plaintiff. Neither point has merit.

On the question of ability of Mr. Lawrence to complete the purchase: it is fundamental that in order for a real estate agent to earn a commission for the sale of property he must produce a buyer ready, *able* and willing to buy on the terms agreed to by the owner.

That Mr. Lawrence was ready and willing to buy the property was established without preadventure of doubt. He inspected the property, agreed to buy, signed a contract of purchase on the terms of the listing agreement, put up $500 earnest money, deposited an additional $1,500 earnest money upon request, threatened to sue defendants for specific performance when they refused to sign the purchase agreement, and shortly thereafter purchased other property in the area.

In a contested case of this nature the agent ordinarily must also prove the prospective buyer's financial ability to consummate the transaction. The word "able" in this context refers to financial ability.

There is the following record evidence of Mr. Lawrence's financial ability: he paid a total of $2,000 as earnest money. He consulted an attorney and threatened defendants with a suit for specific performance if they refused to convey the property (which Mr. Lawrence could not have maintained without the financial ability to perform his obligations under the contract). He purchased another home in the area shortly after defendants refused to perform.

On the question of consideration: defendants claim they revoked plaintiff's agency and cancelled the listing contract before plaintiff expended any time or money in an attempt to produce a buyer; that until such time as a real estate agent has expended time and money in an effort to find a buyer the owner can terminate a listing agreement (even an exclusive three-month listing) without incurring liability, because until that time there has been no consideration to support the owner's agreement not to revoke the agent's authority; that mere permission for the agent to sell property within a specified time, without any consideration or expenditure of time or money on his part is "nudum pactum which may be revoked at any time."

Mr. Welek, testified that the property was shown to prospective buyers on July 23, and again on the morning and in the afternoon of July 24; that defendants did not advise him on July 23 or July 24 that they were not going to sell the house and were cancelling the listing contract, and did not so advise him until "at least July 28."

Additional evidence of consideration is found in the fact, which we find, that in order to get the listing, Mr. Welek gave up a $200 appraisal fee; made four long distance telephone calls to defendants, prepared the purchase contract, obtained the $500 down payment as earnest money, and at the request of Mr. Juneau obtained from Mr. Lawrence an additional $1,500 earnest money.

There is substantial evidence to support the judgment of the circuit court that plaintiff earned its commission by producing a buyer ready, able and willing to purchase on the terms of the listing agreement, and by offering defendants a contract of purchase executed by the prospective purchaser.

The judgment is affirmed.

Discussion Questions

1. What type of listing agreement was signed?
2. Who is the broker? Who is the seller?
3. Who is Lawrence?
4. What additional demands did the Juneaus make after learning of the offer?
5. Did the sale close?
6. Was Lawrence ready, willing and able?
7. Will the broker collect the commission?

(10.3) Consider:

Claude Lemon hired Dade Realty to sell real property that belonged to minors, of whom Lemon was the court-appointed guardian. Dade brought an offer to Lemon and Lemon accepted. However, the agreement was subject to court approval, which required an appraisal. Lemon asked James and Edna Anderson to be appointed appraisers. Lemon then asked the Andersons, who were not qualified appraisers, to overvalue the property so the sale would not be approved and the $6,000 commission to Dade would be avoided. After court rejection of the agreement, Dade filed suit for their commission. Is Dade entitled to its commission?

In some states, courts have rendered decisions that eliminate the ready, willing, and able standards and require the actual closing of a deal before the broker is entitled to a commission. These states are limited, and again if the parties desire such an effect, a *no deal, no commission clause* may be put in the listing agreement.

Description of the Property and Sale Terms

Since the listing agreement will be the basis for advertising the property and a representation of its quality, size, location, and so on, it is important that the broker obtain accurate information about the property to be sold. Raw land parcels should be carefully described so that there is no error about size or which parcels are actually being conveyed.

Furthermore, the broker's right to commission is tied to presenting an offer from a ready, willing, and able buyer that meets the seller's terms set forth in the listing agreement. This turning point of the transaction should therefore be accurately and fully set forth. Obvious terms to be included are price, method of financing, date property may be transferred, fixtures included and not included, seller's agreement to furnish good title, any conditions for rental or occupancy of the property, any easements or other use restrictions, and any required court approval if the property is part of an estate. A provision should also be included on what becomes of the earnest money in the event of a buyer's default. The fewer details left undiscussed at the time of the listing, the easier it will be for the broker to obtain an appropriate offer and the less confusion will arise at the time an offer is presented. Careful attention to details at the time of the listing may save the broker time and earn a commission more easily at a later date.

Conditions Precedent

A *condition precedent* is a happening or event that must occur before the party or parties to a contract are required to perform their obligations under that contract. Conditions precedent may be inserted in the listing agreement as prerequisites for the broker earning the commission. For example, court approval of a sale of estate property may be inserted as a condition precedent to sale, to payment of the commission, or to both. Financing being obtained by the buyer may also be used as a condition precedent to the seller's performance under the listing agreement.

Liability Limitations

Many brokers insert clauses in their listing agreement limiting their liability to the seller to the amount of commissions paid under the listing agreement. In some cases such limitations are effective, but when the seller has suffered tremendously because of the broker's negligence, such a clause may be ineffective. (Brokers' duties of care are discussed later in this chapter.) Furthermore, with new theories that third parties should recover damages directly from brokers, these liability limitations are often irrelevant (also discussed later in the chapter).

A checklist for preparing an effective listing agreement is presented in Figure 10.2.

RESPONSIBILITIES OF BROKERS

Brokers and salespersons may be hired by one principal (seller or buyer) to assist in selling or finding a piece of property, but they owe duties and responsibilities to four parties in carrying out their real estate business and transactions. Brokers owe certain duties and responsibilities to their principals and to the third party buyers who become involved in the real estate transactions. In addition, brokers have certain duties and responsibilities to other brokers who may become involved in the transactions and to the other brokers and salespersons who work in the same business office. Finally, as licensees of the state, brokers owe certain duties and responsibilities to the state in carrying out their real estate transactions. The specific rights and responsibilities of brokers with regard to each group are discussed in detail in the following sections.

It is important to note that the duties of an agent are limited to those situations in which the broker is truly employed by the principal. In recent cases, third parties not truly employing the broker have attempted to impose these

Figure 10.2 Checklist for an Effective Listing Agreement[a]

1. Name of owner
   a. Are they authorized?
   b. Who holds title?
   c. Is there more than one owner?
   d. Signatures

2. Type of listing agreement
   a. Open
   b. Agency
   c. Exclusive right to sell
   d. Net
   e. Multiple listing

3. Duration of the listing
   a. Length
   b. Extension clause for buyers introduced to the property by the broker
   c. Termination: reasons, methods, notice, damages

4. Entitlement to commission
   a. Ready, willing, and able
   b. No sale, no commission
   c. Fraud or bad faith by seller

5. Description of the property
   a. Accurate legal description
   b. Correct parcels

6. Selling Terms
   a. Price
   b. Financing
   c. Date of transfer
   d. Good title
   e. Rental or occupancy
   f. Easements

7. Conditions precedent
   a. Court approval
   b. Buyer financing
   c. Sale of other property

8. Marketing rights
   a. Advertise
   b. Place sign on property
   c. Showings
   d. Multiple listing

9. Rights upon buyer's default
   a. Earnest money
   b. Effect on listing

10. Liability limitations

[a]Should be written.

duties through the creation of an implied agency. As the following case illustrates, courts have been unwilling to extend the doctrine.

HALDIMAN v. GOSNELL

748 P.2d 1209 (Ariz. 1987)

On 5 August 1982, Meredith Haldiman (appellant) entered into a contract to purchase a townhome, which was to be constructed by Gosnell Development Corporation (Gosnell/appellee). The agreement to purchase was prepared by Gael Boden, an employee of Gosnell and a licensed real estate salesman. Haldiman was not represented by a real estate agent nor did she seek outside advice. Boden used a form supplied by Gosnell and simply filled in the blanks.

One portion of the purchase

agreement provided that if the purchaser failed to perform, Gosnell could keep the earnest money as damages. Haldiman paid $2,000 in earnest money and also a $1,300 deposit for options she had selected for her townhome. Boden signed the agreement as a "marketing representative" for Gosnell.

The townhome was completed but Haldiman did not yet have financing because she had not sold her other home. Gosnell extended the time for closing 4½ months. At the end of that time, Gosnell terminated the contract, notified Haldiman, and kept the $3,300 in deposits.

Haldiman filed suit to seek the return of her $3,300, and she also alleged that Gael Boden had breached his duty as an agent to give her full and frank advice. The trial court granted Gosnell's motion for summary judgment and Haldiman appealed.

GREER, Judge

Real estate salesmen and brokers owe a duty of good faith and loyalty to their principal. They must exercise reasonable due care and diligence to effect a sale to the principal's best advantage. They must also disclose to their clients information they possess pertaining to the transaction involved.

In *Morley v. J. Pagel Realty & Insurance*, 27 Ariz. App. 62, 550 P.2d 1104 (1976), Division Two of this court extended this duty one step further. The question before the court was the extent of a real estate broker's duty to his client and specifically, whether the broker should have advised his clients, the sellers, to require security for the buyer's performance. The court stated:

In the case at bench, appellants (the sellers) seek to hold appellees (the real estate broker) liable for failing to inform them that the Haydens' offer contemplated no security and that a mortgage should be required. Although this information might be beyond the average person, it is common knowledge in the real estate business. We think that as part of appellees' duty to effect a sale for appellants on the best terms possible and to disclose to them all the information they possess that pertained to the prospective transaction, appellees were bound to inform appellants that they should require security for the Haydens' performance.

The court specifically stated, however, that its holding was a narrow one and should not be extended beyond the facts before it. The court then stated:

It (the holding) is reinforced by Art. 26, §1 of the Arizona Constitution. Having achieved, by virtue of this provision, the right to prepare any and all instruments incidental to the sale of real property, including promissory notes, real estate brokers and salesmen also bear the responsibility and duty of explaining to the persons involved the implications of these documents.

Haldiman argues that this last phrase suggests that the court was opening the door to an increased duty of salesmen to persons other than their principal or client. She urges this court to adopt a broad interpretation of *Morley*. For the reasons stated below, however, we decline to do so.

We first point out that the *Morley* court specifically stated that its holding was narrow and should not be extended beyond the facts before it. From this very clear statement, we can only conclude that the court meant just that. Its subsequent statement is dicta at best, and therefore not controlling as precedent. The Arizona Supreme Court, when subsequently presented with a similar question to that in *Morley*, refused to impose a duty of disclosure on a real estate agent who was not working for the seller *Buffington v. Haas*, 124 Ariz. 36, 601 P.2d 1320 [1979]. That court concluded:

[T]here was not an agency relationship between appellant Haas (the real estate salesman) and appellee Buffington. Haas had no obligation to inform the appellee that under the contract she did not retain a security interest in her property.

Haldiman nevertheless suggests that this court should impose a duty on real estate agents to explain the implication of real estate documents even in the absence of an agency relationship. She suggests that this duty would be in the public's best interest, and that the court could ensure that all parties to a real estate transaction were informed, thereby reducing litigation involving mistake, misrepresentation and misunderstanding in real estate transactions. Although certainly a laudable goal, this court cannot simply create a legal duty because it might reduce litigation in the future. Haldiman does not expressly argue that Boden was her agent, although she does state in her affidavit that Boden represented her in connection with the real estate transaction and gave her

real estate advice. As a matter of law, however, Boden could not have been Haldiman's agent.

Part of Boden's job was to write purchase contracts for potential Gosnell home purchasers, which is exactly what he did for Haldiman. This brief relationship now forms the basis of Haldiman's claim that he represented her and gave her real estate advice in the transaction. Haldiman's brief that Boden represented her, or was in essence her agent, does not, however, make him her agent.

Haldiman has not presented any evidence, or even alleged, that Gosnell gave Boden permission to represent Haldiman in the transaction. Boden, on the other hand, claims he worked exclusively for Gosnell and at no time represented or worked for Haldiman. Accordingly, Boden only represented Gosnell and could not have been Haldiman's agent.

Haldiman also argues that Boden is liable because he was negligent for failing to adhere to the standards of his profession.

In light of the foregoing, Boden did not have a broker/client relationship with Haldiman, and thus did not breach a duty to uphold real estate professional standards. Haldiman has no cause of action for Boden's failure to suggest that the purchase contract be conditioned upon financing and selling her home, or his failure to explain that she could not recover her deposits if she failed to close escrow for any reason.

Affirmed. Partial reversal on procedural grounds.

Discussion Questions

1. Who is the buyer? The seller?
2. Who is Boden? Who employed him?
3. What were the terms of the agreement regarding nonperformance?
4. How much had been paid in deposits?
5. Why did the transaction not close?
6. Is Boden an agent for Haldiman?
7. What could Boden have done to help avoid the litigation?

(10.4) Consider:

Dortha Walter entered into a contract to sell her mobile home and the land on which it was located to Mr. and Mrs. Moore. Dortha's daughter, Carol, was a real estate agent and agreed to help with the details of the transaction. Mr. Moore talked with Carol and they discussed financing, interest rates, and loans. Carol told Mr. Moore that although she was a licensed real estate agent she was not taking a commission; she was only helping her mother out. She prepared the paperwork and discussed with Mr. Moore the fact that the mobile home was in a flood-prone area. Zoning regulations were pending on the area and Carol was aware of such but did not know the outcome.

Six months after closing, Mr. Moore sought a permit to install a septic tank but was denied such because the final regulation prohibited septic tanks in the flood-prone area. The Moores have brought suit against Carol for breach of her duty of disclosure as an agent. Can they recover? *Walter v. Moore*, 700 P.2d 1219 (Wyo. 1985)

Legal Duties and Responsibilities to the Principal

Since a seller–broker relationship is created by the listing agreement, all of the common law rules of agency are applicable to the parties' relationship.

Authority Through the listing agreement, the broker is given only the authority to market the listed property and bring prospective buyers to the seller, unless additional authority is specified. Extent, restrictions, and limitations of the broker's authority are set forth in the listing agreement. Brokers engaging in conduct beyond the scope of their authority will be held liable for any damages or obligations incurred in excess of that authority. Thus, a broker who reduces the listing price without the seller's consent, or who accepts an offer on behalf of the seller, or who acts in excess of the broker's authority, would be liable for the price difference in the first instance and for the obligation itself in the second and third instances.

(10.5) Consider:

A purchaser contracted with Avegno for the sale of four parcels of land and deposited with Avegno's broker (Byrd) a $10,400 demand note (about 10 percent of the purchase price) as earnest money. Problems resulted with the sale, and the contract was repudiated by the purchaser. Byrd endorsed the note back to the purchaser and told Avegno. Avegno was unable to collect the earnest money deposit as the damages provided for in the contract. What is the result?

Duty of Care A broker is required to exercise care in listing the seller's property, presenting offers, and handling the details of closing.

This duty of care requires the broker to list the property at a reasonable fair market value figure. There is much temptation to underappraise properties and list them accordingly so that a rapid, easy sale and commission can be obtained. But the listing price must be accurately set to assist the seller in the sale and also to ensure a fair return. The broker must be cautious in making overzealous statements about sales potential and abilities because inflated expectations of the seller can cause problems for the broker later.

If the seller needs to net a certain minimum from the transaction, the broker must be cautious in computing the corresponding sales price. Care must be taken to add contingencies such as payment of points and the costs of the transaction such as escrow fees, title insurance, and termite inspection. The broker also must check the terms of the seller's loan to verify assumability and any transfer fees or prepayment penalties that might affect the seller's net.

Once the listing agreement is executed, the broker's duty of care to the seller continues. The broker should evaluate the soundness of all offers and inform the seller (particularly the unsophisticated seller) of the hazards or pitfalls involved in each offer. All implications should be explained, including the form and adequacy of the down payment, the security or need for security in the financing, the advantages and disadvantages of financing alternatives, and any contingencies involved in the sale. Although the broker must never advise which offer to take, weaknesses and strengths should be explained.

In explaining offers the broker must be cautious not to cross the fine line between exercising care and practicing law. A broker may explain to a seller the customs and practices of the real estate industry but should limit remarks to that sphere. Since offering opinions on legal rights and responsibilities could prove costly to the broker, legal details should be referred to an attorney.

The broker should also assume the responsibility of proofreading documents such as the listing agreement, the offer, and the eventual contract for errors in figures, descriptions, and dates. Closing papers should also be carefully scrutinized to assure that the correct terms appear. In states in which brokers may fill out contracts, brokers must exercise care to make sure all the terms are present, carefully drafted, and accurately stated. Forms should be scrutinized to make sure they comply with the parties' intentions.

Brokers can maintain better client relationships by prequalifying prospective buyers. Presenting an offer from a financially unable buyer or even taking the time to show property to financially unable buyers is a waste of time on all sides. Furthermore, the presentation of an offer from an unqualified buyer spells liability for the broker.

In exercising their duties of care, brokers should answer these questions as a self-check:

- Is the property properly priced?
- Is the net accurate and does the seller understand it?
- Is the listing agreement accurate?
- Are potential buyers qualified? Do they have adequate savings and income?
- Are the offers sound? What are the pitfalls?
- Has there been adequate communication with the seller?
- Are escrow papers being drawn? Are they accurate?
- Are clients being kept informed of the progress of escrow?
- Are deadlines being met?

(10.6) Consider:

The Ameses signed an exclusive right to sell listing agreement with a broker, Lucas. Lucas understood the Ameses needed a certain net on the sale of their home in order to have a sufficient down payment for their next home. When pricing the home, Lucas forgot to tell the Ameses of the points loan provision that they might be required to pay if the buyer required new financing. As a result the Ameses' home was underpriced and the Ameses were $3,000 short of their own down payment when a refinancing buyer closed. The Ameses sued Lucas. What is the result?

Often, clauses will be used in listing agreements to try to avoid liability for breach of the duty of care. These clauses are invalid for brokers, as they are for accountants, lawyers, engineers, and other professionals. No professional may be exculpated by a clause for failure to exercise the standards of care established in that profession.

Fiduciary Duty Once a broker is employed by a principal, that broker is expected to act only in the best interests of the principal, regardless of the negative effects and consequences that may result for the broker.

Thus, a broker may not lead the seller into an unsound transaction for the sake of a commission and should inform the seller when problems arise in the negotiation or closing of a transaction. All aspects of the transaction should

244

be represented accurately and disclosed in a timely manner. Any changes affecting the principal's rights or interests must be revealed immediately.

Most states impose a separate fiduciary duty upon brokers with respect to earnest money deposits. Money belonging to the seller should not be commingled with the broker's own funds. Most states require that deposits be placed in trust accounts or escrow accounts, or else require the establishment of escrow funds within a short time after receipt. Brokers in these states who retain deposits for unreasonable lengths of time may be held liable for this loss and may face license revocation or suspension.

In the following case, the broker had successfully brought buyers to the seller, but problems and the issues of breach of fiduciary duty arose afterward.

VICKI BAGLEY REALTY, INC. v. LAUFER
482 A.2d 359 (D.C. App. 1984)

Steven and Daniella Laufer owned a townhouse on Waterside Drive in Northwest Washington. They decided to sell the property, and Dr. Laufer, described as an educated and experienced businessperson with knowledge of the real estate business, listed the property with D'Amecourt. He asked a price greater than its apparent market value.

Vicki Bagley Realty, Inc., was a cooperating broker and submitted an offer for John T. Laye for purchase. The contract provided that Laye would buy the property after renting it for three months at $1,000 per month. Laufer added a clause allowing him to provide financing for the purchase in the event Laye did not qualify for financing. Laye would make a $10,000 deposit and on closing a $50,000 down payment.

On 23 January 1979, the parties signed the purchase agreement and the lease. The Layes tendered three checks. One check was for $3,000 for rent and was paid to the Laufers. A second check was payable to Bagley for $1,000 and apparently was a security deposit for the lease. The third check was for the deposit of $10,000 and was also made payable to Bagley. The $10,000 check was dated 22 January 1979 but the dates on the other two checks were whited out and 1 February had been typed in.

All three checks bounced. Bagley had knowledge that the checks would not clear for 10 days and held on to them but did not tell the Laufers. The Layes had to be evicted. The Laufers filed suit alleging that Bagley had engaged in misrepresentation and had failed to properly account for money. The trial court found for the Laufers, and Bagley appealed.

TERRY, Associate Judge

A real estate broker, like any other agent, owes a fiduciary duty to his principal.

The trial court found that both

D'Amecourt, as the listing broker, and Bagley, as the cooperating broker, owed a fiduciary duty to the Laufers. Cognizant of our limited scope of review, we conclude that this finding is neither plainly wrong nor without evidentiary support.

The record is replete with evidence of the agency relationship that existed between the Laufers and both D'Amecourt and Bagley. For example, Plaintiff's Exhibit 1, which is a "Listing Contract for Residential Multiple Listing," clearly establishes that D'Amecourt was the Laufers' broker. Bagley also had a responsibility toward the Laufers that was very similar, if not identical, to D'Amecourt's. First, Bagley admitted in its answer to the complaint that, like D'Amecourt, it was authorized to solicit offers for the purchase of the property. In addition, Plaintiff's Exhibit 4-A, the contract for the sale of the house, states that D'Amecourt and Bagley were to split the brokerage fee "50/50." Bagley's acceptance of all three checks, on two of which it was named as payee, further attests to Bagley's role as the Laufers' agent.

The fiduciary duty owed by a real estate agent or subagent requires the exercise of the highest fidelity toward the principal. It encompasses an obligation to inform the principal of every development affecting his interest, which would obviously include any facts known to the agent concerning a prospective purchaser's financial difficulties.

In the case at bar, D'Amecourt and Bagley had knowledge of Laye's finances that clearly was significant to their principals, the Laufers. The trial court found, for example, that Bagley "knew or should have known that the $10,000 deposit check [drawn by Laye] could not be cashed until February 1, 1979." This finding is supported by Laye's testimony that he told Deborah Doyle, a Bagley employee, that the check would not clear until February 1, and by the fact that Bagley did not deposit the check until February 1, even though it was dated ten days earlier and had been in Bagley's possession since January 23. The Laufers also introduced into evidence a letter from a "processing officer" with the Bagley firm, stating that she had deposited Laye's $10,000 and $1,000 checks, and that she had "double checked" with the bank and "found these checks to be good." This was not true; Laye's bank dishonored both checks.

As for D'Amecourt, the court found that it "had reason to know that there were suspicious circumstances that had not been fully disclosed such as to make a credit report on the Purchaser desirable." These circumstances included D'Amecourt's receipt of the $3,000 check payable to the Laufers, on which the original date was whited out, as well as other indications that the D'Amecourt staff, at least, lacked pertinent information about Laye's finances. Nicole D'Amecourt, the listing agent for the sale and former officer in the D'Amecourt firm, admitted in her testimony that when she presented the contract to Dr. Laufer, she knew nothing about Laye or his creditworthiness. In addition, D'Amecourt breached its duty to the Laufers by failing to make sure that the $10,000 deposit check had cleared before relinquishing possession of the property.

We are satisfied that the evidence was sufficient to support both the finding that appellants owed a fiduciary duty to the Laufers and the finding that each of them breached that duty.

Affirmed.

Discussion Questions

1. Was Bagley the broker hired by the Laufers?

2. Is the duty any different for a "corresponding" broker?

3. What happened with the property purchase?
4. What should Bagley have disclosed?

5. Was the transaction pushed through?
6. What could have been done to prevent the incident?

(10.7) Consider:

Fornes obtained a listing for Cowie's property. Fornes presented to Cowie an offer from Sutton under the following circumstances:

a. Fornes knew Sutton could not (financially) swing the deal but was hoping other property of his would sell so he could.

b. Sutton did not pay the deposit.

c. The closing was to be 29 March but was repeatedly postponed until mid-August.

d. Cowie lost rental income from 29 March on, since he did not lease because of closing.

The deal did not close because of Sutton's financial position. Cowie brings suit for damages. What is the result?

Duty of Loyalty A broker may not work both ends of the transaction by representing both parties unless there has been full disclosure and both parties consent to such dual representation.

A broker may not profit secretly from a transaction involving the principal. Brokers must disclose to their clients all they know about all parties involved in the transaction. If a broker chooses to deal in listed property, a full and complete disclosure of the interests must be made to the client. If a broker is a partner, shareholder, or relative of a party to the transaction, such a relationship must be disclosed. If a broker does not make the appropriate disclosure and hence realizes a secret profit, that profit must be returned to the principal.

The following case illustrates the types of disclosures brokers must make to fully apprise clients of their interests in the transactions.

SPRAGINS v. LOUISE PLANTATION, INC.
391 So. 2d 97 (Miss. 1980)

C. Allen Spragins, Jr. (defendant/appellant) signed a listing agreement with Kay Taylor for the sale of four Arkansas farms (Veal, Caney, Edith, and Cranston). An offer was submitted to Spragins from Huber Farm Services (plaintiff/appellee). Taylor was vice president and one-third owner of Huber Farms but did not disclose that fact to Spragins. The contract was executed on 24 October 1978. When Spragins refused to perform, Huber and Taylor brought suit

for specific performance. The trial court found for Huber and Taylor, and Spragins appealed.

BROOM, Justice

The facts in this case reveal that Taylor failed to disclose material information to the Spragins. On June 20, 1978, C. Allen Spragins, Jr. and Taylor signed brokerage agreements and option contracts for the sale of four Arkansas farms. Although the option contracts expired on August 10, 1978, no buyers were secured; consequently, Taylor obtained several extensions and on October 24 the sale contracts were executed.

In August, 1978, Taylor contacted E. L. Hutton, a Memphis attorney, to see if he had any client interested in the Arkansas property. In order to exercise the option contract, a deposit was required for each farm. Taylor arranged by telephone with Hutton for him to wire $100,000 in down payment money. The $30,000 September 6, 1978 down payment check on "Emenheiser" was signed by Kay Taylor and made payable to C. A. Spragins, Jr. and/or Ruth Cranston. Hutton had wired the money to the Bank of Cleveland, Cleveland, Mississippi, on behalf of Huber Farm Services of Greenville. Although Taylor had difficulty recalling on whose behalf Hutton acted, she did acknowledge that she was vice-president and owned one-third of the stock of Huber Farms.

Prior to signing the October 24 sales contracts and Dough Boy letters, Taylor's attorney, James W. Haddock of Lake Village, Arkansas, advised her to associate with an Arkansas broker in order to comply with Ark. Stat. Ann. §71-1309 (Repl. 1979). Taylor, however, with the approval of Mr. Spragins, elected to purchase the property in her own name.

We note that neither prior to nor on October 24, 1978, did Taylor make any disclosure to appellants that she was a stockholder, director, and officer in Huber

Farm Services or that the corporation might acquire the four farms. Appellants' testimony, if admitted, indicates that no such disclosure was ever made. Additionally, Taylor failed to inform appellants that Huber Farm Services planned to sell the properties for a profit.

While taking the Huber Farms deposition, appellants' attorney, Mr. Terney, discovered a document that set out anticipated profits that Huber Farms would make from the sale of each piece of property. The list indicated that Huber Farm Services of Greenville, Inc. made or would make profits of: $24,000.00 on the Veal property (Indian Plantation), $98,122.30 on the Caney Bayou property, $108,375.00 on the Edith Farm property, and $112,576.00 was contemplated on the Cranston land (Emenheiser Farm).

Clear from the record is the fact that, according to her own testimony, up and until the time of lapsing of the June 20, 1978, option contracts, Taylor's status was that of a broker which she attempted to change to "purchaser" by the October 24 sales contracts. As a broker she was obligated to reveal to her principals (appellants) all information possessed by the broker concerning the value of the property. The broker must obtain for the principal the best available deal without withholding any information the broker has which is adverse to the principal. The broker must reveal the source and amount of any profit she may make from the transaction, including any relationship she has with any other party to the transaction.

Secret profits are not allowable to the broker. The appellees argue and the chancellor so found, that when Taylor became "purchaser" under the October 24, 1978, contract, all prior negotiations and the earlier June 20, 1978, contracts, whether expired or not, were merged or superseded by the October purchase contract.

The trial court concluded there was no principal and agent relationship between the parties; Taylor was not a fidu-

ciary. We think his ruling in this regard is contrary to the overwhelming weight of the evidence and manifestly in error.

Regardless of what did or did not occur prior to October 24, 1978, when the last sales contract was executed, we think it clear that Taylor was acting as a broker.

Reversed.

Discussion Questions

1. Whose property was listed?
2. What property was listed?
3. Who was the broker?
4. Who was the buyer?
5. What was the relationship between broker and buyer?

6. Was this relationship revealed to the seller?
7. Did the broker breach the duty of loyalty?

(10.8) Consider:

The Taylors listed their property with ARE Realty, with Jensen Timber as the broker and Pamela Creighton as the agent salesperson. The listing was unsuccessful, and 7 days prior to its expiration, Pamela submitted an offer to the Taylors naming herself or her nominee as the buyer. The Taylors accepted the offer. When the final papers were presented for closing, the Taylors noted that Pamela was not buying the property; instead a Walter Wake and wife were the buyers. Walter Wake was also listed as a broker for ARE Realty. The Taylors discovered the Wakes were Pamela's parents and that the down payment of $5,000 was being made with Walter and Pamela's commission. The Taylors refused to go through with the transaction, and the Wakes brought suit for specific performance. What is the result?

Legal Duties and Responsibilities to Third Parties

The broker is hired by the seller to represent the seller in the marketing of the property and to present offers from buyers to that seller. Between the broker and the seller there is a direct contractual relationship. As just discussed, the law of agency applies, and the broker has imposed duties of loyalty, care, and disclosure.

However, the broker and the buyer from whom offers are obtained do not have a direct contractual relationship, so that there is no agency relationship between them. The broker may still have liability to the buyer for misrepresentations as to the condition of and defects in the real property being sold. This liability is based on the common law tort of misrepresentation. This liability has also been expanded dramatically in the last 5 years.

Misrepresentation Misrepresentations about the subject property generally fall into two categories: (1) those made intentionally, and (2) those made negligently. Intentional misrepresentation occurs when the broker knows of a fact and then either misstates it to the purchaser or simply fails to disclose it to the purchaser. Negligent misrepresentation is established by showing (1) that the broker failed to make a reasonable effort to determine whether the fact represented was true or false, and (2) that the purchaser justifiably relied on that misrepresentation in purchasing the property.

Thus, under the theory of negligent misrepresentation a broker making statements without a sufficient knowledge base may be held liable. An example of negligent misrepresentation is when the broker makes statements about the cost of heating, air conditioning, or electricity, and does so without a statement of cost from the seller or without an actual investigation or verification of the cost.

In negligent misrepresentation, ignorance of whether a statement is true or false is no excuse for escaping liability; for it is the broker's responsibility to determine the truth or falsity of statements. When the prospective buyer asks if city sewer, water, and gas are available for the property, the appropriate response for a broker without such knowledge is, "I don't know, but I can check."

Nondisclosure Misrepresentation occurs when the broker is aware of the problems or defects in property but fails to disclose such material information to prospective buyers. Cosmetically covered wall cracks and foundation cracks of which the broker is aware should be disclosed. The traditional water-in-the-basement problem should also be disclosed. The fact that an existing property use violates the city code is another example of a fact requiring disclosure.

Sales Puffing Misrepresentation is even found to exist in the sales puffing techniques often used by brokers and salespersons. The classic line given to induce a purchase is, "If you are going to do anything, you had better do it quickly because I have another buyer on the line for this property." The statement is innocent enough so long as there is, in fact, another buyer. If no other buyer exists, it has been held that such statements serve to inflate the value and desirability of the property, and constitute misrepresentation to the buyer rushed into a purchase by such statements.

Safety Standards A broker may be held liable for conditions on a property that violate codes or are unsafe if the conditions are not disclosed to prospective buyers or remedied prior to the closing of a deal. It is also a good idea for the broker to check for hazards while showing the property, so that new developments or hazards are noted and disclosed.

"As Is" Clauses Often property will be sold with a provision in the contract that says it is sold *as is*, meaning that the buyer is taking the property as it stands with all existing defects and no promises of repair. Such a clause would appear to relieve the broker of liability for latent defects and the failure to disclose material information. However, the courts have held that the use of the as is clause is not a blanket of immunity for the broker from allegations of fraud. Thus, if a broker actively misrepresents the condition of the property or fails to disclose true facts, the as is clause will have no effect and the broker will still be held liable for the silent or affirmative misrepresentation. Thus a delapidated building sold as is will not provide immunity from liability for the broker who failed to disclose that the building had been condemned.

The following is a landmark case in which liability was imposed on a broker for misrepresentation.

EASTON v. STRASSBURGER
199 Cal. Rptr. 383 (1984)

Leticia Easton (plaintiff/respondent) purchased a 1-acre parcel of land in the city of Diablo, California, with a 3000-square-foot home, swimming pool, and a large guest house for $170,000 in May 1976 from the Strassburgers through Valley Realty (defendants/appellants).

Shortly after Easton purchased the property, there was a massive earth movement and, in 1977 and 1978, subsequent slides that destroyed a portion of the driveway. Experts testified that the slides occurred because a portion of the property was fill that had not been properly engineered and compacted. The slides caused the foundation of the house to settle, which in turn caused cracks in the walls and warped doorways. After the damage, the value of the property was set at $20,000. Cost estimates for repairs were $213,000.

Agents Simkin and Mourning represented Valley Realty and inspected the property several times prior to sale. "Red flags" indicated problems but the agents did not have soil tests done and did not mention to Easton any potential soil problems.

Easton filed suit against the Strassburgers and Valley Realty. The trial court found all defendants guilty of misrepresentation. Valley Realty appealed.

KLINE, Presiding Judge

To establish liability for such negligence, respondent was not required to show that appellant had actual knowledge of the soils problems (as would have been required to prove intentional misrepresentation or fraudulent concealment) or that a misrepresentation had been made as to the soils condition of the property (as is required to establish negligent misrepresentation).

We are concerned here only with the elements of a simple negligence action; that is, whether appellant owed a legal duty to respondent to use due care, whether this legal duty was breached, and finally whether the breach was a proximate cause of appellant's injury.

Whether a defendant owes a duty of due care to a particular plaintiff is a question of law. Appellant does not contend that it was under no duty to exercise due care to prevent injury to respondent. Rather, appellant objects to the manner in which this duty was characterized by the trial court. More particularly, appellant challenges the following instruction: "A real estate broker is a licensed person or entity who holds himself out to the public as having particular skills and knowledge in the real estate field. He is under a duty to disclose facts materially affecting the value or desirability of the property that are known to him or which through reasonable diligence should be known to him."

Appellant argues that this instruction elevates a broker's duty beyond the level established by the case law, contending that a broker is only obliged to disclose known facts and has no duty to disclose facts which "should" be known to him "through reasonable diligence." In effect, appellant maintains that a broker has no legal duty to carry out a reasonable investigation of property he undertakes to sell in order to discover defects for the benefit of the buyer. Appellant further argues that since this instruction indicated to the jury that a broker is under such a duty as a matter of law, the giving of the instruction constitutes reversible error.

It is not disputed that current law requires a broker to disclose to a buyer material defects known to the broker but unknown to and unobservable by the buyer. "It is the law of this state that where a real estate broker or agent, representing the seller, knows facts materially affecting the value or the desirability of property offered for sale and these facts are known or accessible only to him and his principal, and the broker or agent also knows that these facts are not known to or within the reach of the diligent attention and observation of the buyer, the broker or agent is under a duty to disclose these facts to the buyer."

If a broker fails to disclose material facts that are known to him he is liable for the intentional tort of "fraudulent concealment" or "negative fraud." As noted, however, appellant's liability was here grounded on negligence rather than fraud. The issue, then, is whether a broker is negligent if he fails to disclose defects which he should have discovered through reasonable diligence. Stated another way, we must determine whether the broker's duty of due care in a residential real estate transaction includes a duty to conduct a reasonably competent and diligent inspection of property he has listed for sale in order to discover defects for the benefit of the buyer.

Admittedly, no appellate decision has explicitly declared that a broker is under a duty to disclose material facts which he should have known. We conclude, however, that such a duty is implicit.

The primary purposes of the rule are to protect the buyer from the unethical broker and seller and to insure that the buyer is provided sufficient accurate information to make an informed decision whether to purchase. These purposes would be seriously undermined if the rule were not seen to include a duty to disclose reasonably discoverable defects. If a broker were required to disclose only known defects, but not also those that are reasonably discoverable, he would be shielded by his ignorance of that which he holds himself out to know. The rule thus narrowly construed would have results inimical to the policy upon which it is based. Such a construction would not only reward the unskilled broker for his own incompetence, but might provide the unscrupulous broker the unilateral ability to protect himself at the expense of the inexperienced and unwary who rely upon him. In any case, if given legal force, the theory that a seller's broker cannot be held accountable for what he does not know but could discover without great difficulty would inevitably produce a disincentive for a seller's broker to make a diligent inspection. Such a disincentive would be most unfortunate, since in residential sales transactions the seller's broker is most frequently the best situated to obtain and provide the most reliable information on the property and is ordinarily counted on to do so.

As one commentator has observed: "Real estate brokers are often in a very commanding position with respect to both sellers and buyers of residential property. The real estate broker's relationship to the buyer is such that the buyer usually expects the broker to protect his interests. This trust and confidence derives from the potential value of the broker's service; houses are infrequently purchased and require a trained eye to determine value and fitness. In addition, financing is often complex. Unlike other commodities, houses are rarely purchased new and there are virtually no remedies for deficiencies in fitness. In some respects the broker-buyer relationship is akin to the attorney-client relationship; the buyer, like the client, relies heavily on another's acquired skill and knowledge, first because of the complexity of the transaction and second because of his own dearth of experience."

Not only do many buyers in fact justifiably believe the seller's broker is also protecting their interest in securing and acting upon accurate information and rely upon him, but the injury occasioned by such reliance, if it be misplaced, may well be substantial. However, the broad definition of the duty we adopt is supported not simply by the magnitude of the benefit thus conferred on buyers but also by the relative ease with which the burden can be sustained by brokers. It seems relevant to us, in this regard, that the duty to disclose that which should be known is a formally acknowledged professional obligation that it appears many brokers customarily impose upon themselves as an ethical matter. Thus, The Code of Ethics of the National Association of Realtors includes, inter alia, the provision that a broker must not only "avoid . . . concealment of pertinent facts," but "has an affirmative obligation to discover adverse factors that a reasonably competent and diligent investigation would disclose."

In sum, we hold that the duty of a real estate broker, representing the seller, to disclose facts, includes the affirmative duty to conduct a reasonably competent and diligent inspection of the residential property listed for sale and to disclose to prospective purchasers all facts materially affecting the value or desirability of the property that such an investigation would reveal.

Accordingly, we find that the instruction at issue in this case was legally correct, for, as the trial judge stated to the jury, a seller's broker in a residential real estate transaction is "under a duty to disclose facts materially affecting the value or desirability of the property . . . which through reasonable diligence should be known to him."

Appellant next contends that the

judgment must be reversed because the verdict was not supported by substantial evidence. Again, we cannot agree. The evidence indicates that appellant's agents had conducted a limited investigation of the property and that they were aware of "red flags" indicating erosion or settlement problems. There was evidence indicating that one or both of the agents knew that the residence was built on fill and that settlement and erosion problems are commonly associated with such soil. It was additionally established that the agents had seen netting on a slope of the property which had been placed there to repair the slide which occurred most recently prior to the sale.

Furthermore, one of the agents tes-tified that he had observed that the floor of a guest house on the property was not level, while the other agent testified that uneven floors were "red flag" indications of soils problems. Although the foregoing does not exhaust the evidence in the record that appellant's agents were on notice of potential soils problems, it is sufficient to establish that there was substantial evidence on the point. Other evidence also established that, despite this notice, the agents did not request that a soils report be prepared, nor take any other significant steps to determine whether there had been slides or other soils problems.

The judgment for negligence against appellant was amply supported by the evidence.

Affirmed.

Discussion Questions

1. What was the problem with the property?
2. How did the problem affect the value of the property?
3. What "red flags" did the court say existed?
4. Was there fraud in the case?
5. Does the court impose liability on the broker?
6. What justifications are given for placing liability on the broker?

(10.9) Consider:

Suppose a broker misrepresented the length of time that a piece of property had been listed. Would such a misrepresentation be a basis for liability? Does the broker harm a seller by such a disclosure? *Beard v. Gress*, 413 N.E.2d 448 (Ill. 1980)

Insurance Protection The number of suits against brokers by third parties for misrepresentation is skyrocketing. Liability, in the form of actual and punitive damages, which may be imposed upon brokers for either intentional or negligent misrepresentation, is tremendous. As noted earlier, a broker may be held liable under a pretense of knowledge even when the broker has no actual knowledge.

As a result of these cases, insurers now offer errors and omissions insurance coverage, which is a form of malpractice insurance for brokers and salespersons in the real estate industry. Such coverage is essential for brokers and salespersons when it is considered that most commercial transactions involve seven-digit figures and hence seven-digit liability.

The coverage may be purchased for an individual or for a real estate company, its broker, and its salespersons. The amount of coverage available usually begins at $100,000 with a deductible of $1,000 for small claims. In choosing coverage, brokers and salespersons should check the policy provisions on legal defense (Will local or company attorneys be used?), including how legal defense costs are treated in terms of policy coverage; what activities are covered (sales, management, and so on); and whether acts committed prior to the policy validity date will be covered.

Self-Protection Perhaps the best protection a broker may obtain against a suit for misrepresentation is preventive protection. Preventive protection includes understanding the property to be sold and all of its defects, restrictions, and limitations. The following is a checklist for brokers undertaking a new listing and handling prospective buyers of that property:

- Ask about the property repair record.
- Ask about the utilities.
- Ask about the condition of appliances, roof, walls, and basement.
- Include pertinent information about physical condition in the listing agreement.
- Make an independent investigation of the property, carefully looking for recent cover-ups, redecorating, and hidden defects.
- Consider a warranty policy for the home.
- Make no statement that is not based on your first-hand information or knowledge.
- Have available a list of addresses and phone numbers for municipal, state, and county offices, so that the prospective buyer may make independent checks on information.
- Do not fail to disclose pertinent information, and do not participate with the seller in a nondisclosure scheme.
- Take measurements to verify room sizes and square footage.
- Follow up on the buyer's questions for which you have no answer or knowledge.

(10.10) Consider:

Guido Langley was the listing broker for the Hopkinses' residence. Guido brought in an offer from Justin McCarthy, which the Hopkinses accepted. Justin would finance the purchase through a VA loan and sold his current home on the basis of the new contract. The Veterans Administration notified Justin that the loan would not be issued because the Hopkinses' property was subject to an adults-only deed restriction. Justin has no home, no financing, and sues Guido. Guido maintains it was not his responsibility to tell Justin of the VA policy on adult restrictions. What is the result?

Fiduciary Duties In addition to the misrepresentation liability, some courts have imposed on the broker a duty of fairness and honesty to the buyer. This duty comes into play when the buyer has made an offer to the seller of property through the broker. The broker has an imposed duty to refrain from secretly competing with the buyer and attempting to outbid the buyer on that property. If the broker does purchase the land directly and secretly from the seller, some courts will impose a constructive trust on the property and will hold that the property is held by the broker for the benefit of the buyer.

Legal Duties and Responsibilities to the State

To this point, the penalties discussed have been private penalties imposed by the courts when those harmed by the conduct of brokers have brought suit for damages. However, because they are licensed by the state, brokers also owe compliance to state laws and regulations. Failure to comply results in the state-imposed penalties of revocation or suspension of license and the possible imposition of fines or penalties.

Suspension or Revocation of the Real Estate License Each state has its own requirements and penalties for forms of illegal conduct, but certain types of conduct are universally prohibited by the states and usually result in suspension or revocation of license.

1. *Commingling of funds.* All states have some provision prohibiting brokers from commingling clients' funds with their own funds and require the maintenance of separate escrow or trust funds.
2. *Discriminating practices.* Refusing to show property on the basis of a prospect's race, color, sex, or national origin not only may bring about a loss of license; it may result in the imposition of federal penalties and

other state penalties for violations of the fair housing laws. Discriminatory practices include steering (where brokers direct certain races to certain areas and away from other areas) and redlining (where sales or listings are agreed to on the basis of the neighborhood racial composition). (See Chapter 19 for a full discussion of these issues.)

3. *Conviction of a felony.* Just as a felony conviction may preclude initial licensing, it may also result in the loss of license.

4. *Advertising.* Placing media advertising that contains misrepresentations will result in disciplinary action in all states. Some states require the written consent of the owner for advertising. (As noted earlier, provision for this may be in the listing agreement.)

5. *Splitting commissions with an unlicensed party.* This conduct is prohibited. Only licensed individuals may split commissions.

6. *Failure to deliver required documents.* Those who fail to deliver required copies of documents to clients, such as purchase contracts and listing agreements, are subject to the suspension or revocation of their licenses.

7. *Failure to submit all offers.* All offers received prior to written acceptance must be submitted to the seller.

8. *Breach of duties to seller and unethical conduct.* Although private action is available to those harmed, the state also may discipline violating parties.

9. *The unauthorized practice of law.* Some states permit brokers to fill in purchase contract forms and closing documents, while other states require attorneys. Brokers exceeding the type of work permitted in their state are subject to disciplinary action by both the agency administering licensing and the state bar.

(10.11) Consider:

Ronald Felecitti was a broker with a listing on the home belonging to the Grants. Felecitti presented an offer to the Grants. The Grants accepted the offer, which included a contingency on Felecitti obtaining financing. In applying for a Federal Housing Administration (FHA) loan and three other loans, Felecitti submitted false information, knowing he would not qualify otherwise. The information overstated his income and assets. The Grant property closed, but Felecitti defaulted on all four loans. The Federal Housing Administration, upon foreclosure, discovered the false application information. Felecitti was sentenced to 5-years imprisonment and was fined $25,000. What further action may be taken?

The following case illustrates the type of disciplinary action that can be taken against brokers violating state laws.

IN RE BASSETTE

518 A.2d 15 (Vt. 1986)

In March 1981, Robert Engler, a principal in Stockard and Engler, Inc. (S&E), approached real estate agent John Bassette and explained his need to acquire exclusive options in the Hartford area so that he could prepare a bid for a HUD "turnkey" project. In a turnkey project, a municipality applies to HUD for a grant to construct federally financed housing for low income and elderly tenants. With HUD approval, the municipality advertises for proposals from developers. An approved builder gets the project and turns it over to the municipality after construction for a fixed price.

It was clear from HUD that the builder with the best sites would be awarded the project. Bassette met several times with S&E agents during April 1981. Bassette understood that he would earn his commission from the seller.

In July 1981, Bassette became a principal in the Hartford Development Company whose activities competed directly with S&E in the bid for the turnkey project. Bassette said that he told Nick Elton, a local architect, of his involvement. Elton worked with S&E, but he did not inform other principals in S&E with whom he had worked of Bassette's involvement.

Both firms were unsuccessful in their turnkey bids but S&E filed a complaint with the Vermont Real Estate Commission on the basis of Bassette's lack of diligence, his failure to disclose his conflict of interest, and his failure to adhere to standards of trustworthiness. Bassette was suspended for 15 days and appealed.

HAYES, Justice

The principal substantive issue in the instant case is appellant's assertion that the Commission and S&E failed to establish that his conduct amounted to bad faith or untrustworthiness within the meaning of 26 V.S.A. §2296(a)(3) or (a)(8). Those sections state as follows:

A licensee commits unprofessional conduct if the licensee . . .

(3) demonstrates incompetency to act as a real estate broker or salesperson . . .

(8) is found by the Commission to have engaged in any act or conduct, whether of the same or different character as that described above, which contributes to or demonstrates incompetency or dishonest fraudulent dealings. . . .

Appellant argues that S&E was simply a prospective buyer of real estate whose contacts with appellant amounted to no more than a casual inquiry which did not give rise to contractual or fiduciary obligations. The Commission, however, concluded that the relationship between appellant and S&E went much further and created fiduciary duties. At the heart of this responsibility, according to the Commission, was the undertaking by Bassette to assist S&E in obtaining exclusive options on properties suitable for the HUD application. While the undertaking by appellant on behalf of S&E was narrow and specific, it fell well within the definition of activities performed by brokers under 26 V.S.A. §2211. See specifically 26 V.S.A. §2211 (a)(4)(E). Obtaining options that would be beneficial to S&E in its HUD project required the exercise of considerable skill. Because of appellant's undertakings, the Commission found that S&E refrained "from using other brokers and more of their own efforts to diligently seek exclusive options on suitable properties." The Commission concluded that such an undertaking implied the duty to perform both skillfully and loyally. We agree. Based on the evidence and findings, it was abundantly clear to appellant that S&E's objective was to write a successful HUD proposal, not simply to purchase a house. The evidence supported the Commission's conclusions that appellant should have known the relationship with S&E was an exclusive one.

The Commission specifically found that appellant violated the applicable standard of trustworthiness under 26 V.S.A. §2296(a) when he entered into competition with S&E for the turnkey proposal without first fully disclosing this fact. Bassette made no disclosure of the extent of his competing interest until the last day of the competition for the HUD turnkey project. In addition to competing with S&E, appellant compounded the breach of trust by using information which he acquired from Engler in preparing his competing proposal. Appellant was under an affirmative duty to give S&E notice of all information of which he was aware relevant to S&E's business, including his own involvement with a competing company. Appellant failed in this duty.

In summary, appellant voluntarily undertook a commitment requiring skill and loyalty to assist S&E in the pursuit of a specific business project. It is unreasonable for appellant to argue, after undertaking complex and specific duties in support of a unique business project, that he owed no greater duties than he was bound to provide to casual home buyers.

Appellant makes much of the point that S&E was not obligated to compensate him, and that at all times they knew that he would remain a broker acting on behalf of sellers with respect to any property put under option. That argument is without avail. Although appellant's ultimate source of remuneration would have been the sellers of any property put under option, his inducement to work with S&E was clear. To the extent that he furthered S&E's HUD application, he enhanced the possibility of earning a brokerage fee on the several properties involved in any successful project application. The relationship was not gratuitous. Even if it had been, however, appellant's undertaking to act on behalf of S&E clearly gave rise to a fiduciary obligation.

Affirmed.

Discussion Questions

1. How did the broker and interested party get involved?
2. What was the nature of the project?
3. What did Bassette later become involved in?
4. Did he tell anyone?
5. Is the penalty imposed appropriate?

Rights upon Suspension or Revocation Since the suspension or revocation of a license, or the imposition of other fines and penalties, adversely affect income, brokers have constitutionally afforded rights in proceedings to impose such penalties. However, the constitutional standards of due process are satisfied with administrative proceedings. That is, the agency responsible for licensee supervision may conduct appropriate hearings and impose penalties even though such an agency is not part of the judiciary.

Although suspension and revocation proceedings are not criminal prosecutions, the alleged violator does have the right to be informed of the charges and to appear and defend the charges and present witnesses. The alleged violator is also entitled to advance notice of the hearing date so that adequate preparation time is available. Additionally, the alleged violator is entitled to advance notice of those witnesses who will be called to testify against him or her in the hearing, so that preparation may be directed toward the specific evidence.

Legal Duties and Responsibilities Among Brokers

In this final category of duties and responsibilities, the concern focuses upon the interrelationships of those acting within the industry.

Broker–Salesperson Relationship A broker will probably have salespersons working in a common office. With such an arrangement, care should be taken to make clear the rights of principals and also the rights among salespersons. First, there should be a contract between broker and salesperson that establishes their rights and obligations. A salesperson is generally classified as an independent contractor, and the agreement should confirm that relationship. The topics that should be covered in such an agreement are included in the following list:

- Broker will maintain a properly equipped office.
- Salesperson is licensed and will maintain licensing status (including the payment of fees).
- Broker will make available to salesperson all listings.
- Broker may supply information to salesperson for prospective listings.
- Broker may not dictate which parties salesperson will solicit.
- Salesperson will work diligently for sales and listings.
- Salesperson and broker will abide by the Code of Ethics of the National Association of Realtors, as well as state, national, and local laws.
- The commission splitting arrangement will be set and followed.
- Termination of agreements will be limited to certain circumstances.
- Arbitration procedures (if arbitration is agreed upon) are set.

Salesperson–Salesperson Relationship Because there is generally more than one salesperson per office, the broker should establish rules and regulations governing their interrelationships. For example, provision should be made for handling a commission split when more than one salesperson is involved in the sale. Also, a policy should be established for distributing information on prospective listings so that prospects are evenly divided. A policy on who will handle office business or walk-ins should also be formulated.

Broker–Broker Relationship Often in open listing agreements, the issue of who actually obtained a buyer for a sale becomes critical and, hence, so does the issue of who is entitled to a commission. The standard used for determining who obtained the buyer and who is entitled to the commission is the *procuring cause of the sale standard.* To be entitled to commission under this standard the broker need not be the one to obtain the actual sale terms, but needs only to establish that seller and the buyer were brought together by the broker.

Bringing seller and buyer together can result from direct contact or newspaper advertisement. If the broker finds and introduces to the principal a person who is ready, willing, and able to purchase or exchange the property according to the principal's terms, the commission is earned. It is immaterial if the final contract is made without the presence or knowledge of the procuring broker.

ANTITRUST IMPLICATIONS OF THE BROKERAGE INDUSTRY

In recent years, real estate transactions have been particularly vulnerable to the long and, at times, all-encompassing arms of the federal antitrust laws. Challenges to real estate procedures have come in the form of charges of price-fixing, restraint of trade, or refusals to deal through multilisting services or local board organizations. These general violations are discussed in the following sections.

Price Fixing

It is not unusual for commission rates to be uniform in a particular area. However, this uniformity often creates a suspicion of *price-fixing* and a resulting violation of the Sherman Act (15 U.S.C. §1). This uniformity in commission rates has caused the Justice Department to bring suit alleging a conspiracy to fix prices. In an effort to countermand these suits, a clause containing language similar to the following frequently appears in form listing agreements: "The commissions payable for the sale, lease, or management of property are not set by any board of realtors, multiple listing service, or in any manner other than between the broker and the client."

Such a clause does not create immunity from Sherman Act proceedings; but for any violation of the Sherman Act to be substantively established, the government must first prove that the broker, brokers, or association engaged in activity affecting interstate commerce. As illustrated by the *McClain* case, interstate commerce is easily established even in local transactions.

McCLAIN et al. v.
REAL ESTATE BOARD OF NEW ORLEANS, INC. et al.
441 U.S. 942 (1980)

McClain (petitioner) asserts a claim individually and on behalf of that class of persons who employed the services of a respondent real estate broker in the purchase or sale of residential property in the Louisiana parishes of Jefferson or Orleans (the greater New Orleans area) during the 4 years preceding the filing of the complaint. The respondents are two real estate trade associations, six named real estate firms, and that class of realtors who at some time during the period covered by the complaint transacted realty brokerage business in the greater New Orleans area and charged a brokerage fee for their services. The unlawful conduct alleged is a continuing combination and conspiracy among the respondents to fix, control, raise, and stabilize prices for the purchase and sale of residential real estate by the systematic use of fixed commission rates, widespread fee splitting, suppression of market interaction useful to buyers and sellers, and other allegedly anticompetitive practices. The complaint seeks treble damages and injunctive relief as authorized by §§4 and 16 of the Clayton Act, 15 U.S.C. §15, 26.

The complaint further alleges that real estate brokers in the greater New Orleans area have engaged in a price-fixing conspiracy in violation of Sec. 1 of the Sherman Act, 15 U.S.C. §1. No trial has as yet taken place on the merits of the claims, since the complaint was dismissed for failure to establish the interstate commerce component of Sherman Act jurisdiction.

The allegations of the complaint pertinent to establishing federal jurisdiction through use of interstate commerce are:

1. That the activities of the respondents "are within the flow of interstate commerce and have an effect upon that commerce."
2. That the services of respondents were employed in connection with the purchase and sale of real estate by "persons moving into and out of the greater New Orleans area."
3. That respondents "assist their clients in servicing financing and insurance involved with the purchase of real estate in the Greater New Orleans area," and "financing and insurance are obtained from outside the State of Louisiana and move in interstate commerce into the State of Louisiana through the activities of the respondents."
4. That respondents have engaged in the unlawful restraint of "interstate trade and commerce in the offering for sale and sale of real estate brokering services."

Respondents moved in the district court to dismiss the complaint for failure to state a claim within Section 1 of the Sherman Act. This motion was supported by a memorandum and by the affidavits of two officers of respondent Real Estate Board of New Orleans. The affiants testified that real estate brokers in Louisiana were licensed to perform their function in that state only; that there was no legal or other requirement that real estate brokers must be employed in connection with the purchase or sale of real estate within Louisiana; and that the affiants had personal knowledge of such transactions occurring without the assistance of brokers. The function of real estate brokers was described as essentially completed when buyer and seller had been brought together on agreeable terms. The affiants also stated that real estate brokers did not obtain and were not instrumental in obtaining financing of credit sales, save in a few special cases; nor were they involved with examination of titles in connection with the sale of real estate or the financing of such sales.

The memorandum in support of the motion to dismiss sought to distinguish this case from *Goldfarb v. Virginia State Bar*, 421 U.S. 773 (1975), in which we held that §1 of the Sherman Act had been violated by conformance with a bar association's minimum fee schedule that establishes fees for title examination services performed by attorneys in connection with the financing of real estate purchases. The respondent construed the applicability of the *Goldfarb* case as limited by certain language in the opinion that described the activities of lawyers in the examination of titles as an inseparable and integral part of the interstate commerce in real estate financing. In contrast, with respect to this case, respondents asserted on the basis of the affidavit that "the role of real estate brokers in financing such purchases is neither integral nor inseparable." Respondents contended:

1. The activities of respondent real estate brokers were purely local in nature.
2. The allegation that respondents assisted in securing financing or insurance in connection with the purchase of real estate had been controverted by the affidavits.
3. The assertion in the complaint that respondents' activities "are within the flow of interstate commerce and have an effect upon that commerce" was insufficient by itself to establish federal jurisdiction.

The deposition testimony of the president of Security Homestead Association, one of the nearly forty savings and loan institutions in the greater New Orleans area, revealed that during the period covered by the complaint the Association lent in excess of $100 million for local purchases of residential property. The Association obtained loan capital from deposits by investors, some of whom lived out of state, and from borrowings from the Federal Home Loan Bank of Little Rock, Arkansas. Toward the close of the relevant period, the Association entered the interstate secondary mortgage market, in which existing mortgages were sold to raise new capital for future loans.

Another deponent was the president of Caruth Mortgage Corporation, an Arkansas corporation doing business in Louisiana, Mississippi, and Texas. Caruth's business was to originate home loans, then to sell the financial paper in the secondary mortgage market. The testimony showed that during the relevant period Caruth made in excess of $100 million in loans on residential real estate in the greater New Orleans area. The overwhelming proportion of these home loans was guaranteed by either the Federal Housing Administration (FHA) or the Veterans Administration (VA). With respect to the FHA-guaranteed loans, Caruth collected and remitted premiums for the guarantee to the FHA in Washington, D.C., on a periodic basis for each account.

Both deponents testified that real estate brokers often played a role in securing financing information on behalf of a borrower and in bringing borrower and lender together, but that after the introductory phases the substance of the mortgage transaction progressed without the involvement of a real estate broker. The president of Caruth testified that his company required title insurance on all the home loans it made. This testimony was accompanied by the deposition of the president of Lawyers Title Insurance Company of Louisiana, which revealed that each of the nearly thirty title insurance companies then writing coverage in the greater New Orleans area was a subsidiary branch of a corporation in another state.

The district court held the interstate activity was incidental and dismissed the complaint. The U.S. Court of Appeals affirmed the dismissal.

BURGER, Chief Justice

The broad authority of Congress under the Commerce Clause has, of course, long been interpreted to extend beyond activities actually *in* interstate commerce to reach other activities that, while wholly local in nature, nevertheless substantially *affect* interstate commerce.

On the record thus far made, it cannot be said that there is an insufficient basis for petitioners to proceed at trial to establish Sherman Act jurisdiction. It is clear that an appreciable amount of commerce is involved in the financing of residential property in the Greater New Orleans area and in the insuring of titles to such property. The presidents of two of the many lending institutions in the area stated in their deposition testimony that those institutions committed hundreds of millions of dollars to residential financing during the period covered by the complaint. The testimony further demonstrated that this appreciable commercial activity has occurred in interstate commerce. Funds were raised from out-of-state investors and from interbank loans obtained from interstate financial institutions. Multi-state lending institutions took mortgages insured under federal programs which entailed interstate transfers of premiums and settlements. Mortgage obligations physically and constructively were traded as financial instruments in the interstate secondary mortgage market. Before making a mortgage loan in the Greater New Orleans area, lending institutions usually, if not always, required title insurance, which was furnished by interstate corporations.

To establish federal jurisdiction in this case, there remains only the requirement that respondents' activities which allegedly have been infected by a price-fixing conspiracy be shown "as a matter of practical economics" to have a not insubstantial effect on the interstate commerce involved. It is clear, as the record shows, that the function of respondent real estate brokers is to bring the buyer and seller together on agreeable terms. For this service the broker charges a fee generally calculated as a percentage of the sale price. Brokerage activities necessarily affect both the frequency and the terms of residential sales transactions. Ultimately, whatever stimulates or retards the volume of residential sales or has an impact on the purchase price, affects the demand for financing and title insurance, those two commercial activities that on this record are said to have occurred in interstate commerce.

It is axiomatic that a complaint should not be dismissed unless "it appears beyond doubt that the plaintiff can prove no set of facts in support of his claim which would entitle him to relief." This rule applies with no less force to a Sherman Act claim where one of the requisites of a cause of action is the existence of a demonstrable nexus between the defendants' activity and interstate commerce. Here, what was submitted to the District Court shows a sufficient basis for satisfying the Act's jurisdictional requirement under the effect on commerce theory so as to entitle the petitioners to go forward. We therefore conclude that it was error to dismiss the complaint at this stage of the proceedings. The judgment of the Court of Appeals is reversed and the case is remanded for further proceedings consistent with this opinion.

Remanded.

Discussion Questions

1. Who are the members of the class represented by McClain?
2. Who offered deposition testimony for the plaintiffs?
3. What defense is alleged by the Real Estate Board of New Orleans?
4. Of what relevance is title insurance?
5. Is there sufficient basis for interstate commerce?
6. Is a violation of the Sherman Act found?

(10.12) Consider:

The newly elected president of a professional organization of real estate agents held a dinner at an exclusive country club. He invited his colleagues who would help him manage the organization during his tenure of office. Their discussion at dinner centered around a new membership drive and the organization of committees. The new president then stood at the meeting and said the following:

My business is dying fast. I have already borrowed $75,000 to keep afloat.

If I am going bankrupt at 6 percent, I might as well go bankrupt at 7 percent.

I don't care what the rest of you do, that is what I am going to do.

Has there been an antitrust violation?

Restraint of Trade—Membership in Local Boards or Multiple Listing Service

Membership in local boards or the Multiple Listing Service (MLS) is an important affiliation for a broker. Sales statistics indicate that 80 percent of all residential purchases involve a multiple listing service broker. However, in recent years these organizations have, like other trade and professional associations, faced review of their anticompetitive effects. Membership restrictions for such boards are particularly suspect when the result is that those denied memberships, on the basis of unjustified criteria, are effectively precluded from the business benefits and activities afforded members. The following case indicates the standards of review courts employ in determining the legality of membership restrictions in trade or professional associations in the real estate industry.

UNITED STATES v. REALTY MULTI-LIST, INC.

629 F.2d 1351 (5th Cir. 1980)

Formed in 1967 by eight real estate brokers in Muscogee County, Georgia, Realty Multi-List (RLM/defendant/appellee) had by the time of the suit grown to be a "significant force" in the county. Although RML provided a number of services, its basic function was to prepare and distribute a monthly listing book, using listing data received from members, and to supplement the book with daily updates. RML, like many other multiples (multiple listing services), operated to overcome market imperfections by reducing information barriers and easing geographical barriers between buyers and sellers. The transactional benefits resulting from multiple listing services are considered to be divided evenly among buyer, seller, and broker.

However, the benefits were not generally available to nonmembers, and to gain membership an applicant was required to meet certain criteria. The most important of the membership criteria still in effect at the time of the suit required applicants to: (1) "have a favorable credit report and business reputation," and (2) have an office "open during customary business hours."

In 1976 the United States (plaintiff/appellant) brought suit under the Sherman Act (15 U.S.C. §1) against the Georgia corporation, RML, which was formed to operate a multiple listing service. The basic issue in the case was whether RML's membership criteria were illegal in that "they authorize RML to establish a group boycott of those real estate brokers who fail to qualify under them."

The United States filed suit in August 1976, alleging that through the membership criteria and other restrictive practices, RML and its members had conspired to restrain interstate commerce unreasonably in violation of the Sherman Act. The federal government sought a declaration that the practices were unlawful and an injunction against their enforcement.

In the district court, both RML and the United States moved for summary judgment and the court entered judgment for RML. The lower court decided that issues relating to RML's past practices were moot and that the present membership criteria in dispute were not unreasonably restrictive. The federal government appealed.

GOLDBERG, Circuit Judge

We begin with RML's membership criteria, the principal issue in this suit. From the formation until settlement renegotiations on this suit began, its by-laws required an applicant for admission to hold a real estate broker's license in the state of Georgia and to agree to abide by all RML's internal rules.

In October 1975, RML instituted its current requirements that an applicant, to be eligible for membership, must:

(b) Have an active real estate office in Muscogee County.
(c) Have a favorable credit report and business reputation.

By-laws of Realty Multi-List, Article V, Section 5, R.683a. It is undisputed that, to meet the first of these requirements, an applicant must have "an office kept open during customary business hours." RML relies, in its application of the second requirement, on a "special character-financial" report supplied by Equifax Credit Bureau, which report includes personal as well as business and financial information. If any question regarding an applicant's qualifications is raised by the Equifax report, RML's Board of Directors then votes on the applicant's fitness to be an RML member. Thus it contends that RML's present membership criteria—the requirements that a prospective member be found by RML to have a "favorable credit report and business reputation," that he or she maintain an "active real estate office" which is "open during customary business hours"—are violations of Section 1 of the Sherman Act.

Specifically, asserting that RML is so powerful a force in the Muscogee County market that a broker who is denied access to its listing pool cannot compete effectively with RML members, the Government argues that RML's criteria either do not have legitimate procompetitive justifications or are overbroad to accomplish any legitimate goals of the association, so that their anticompetitive effects must necessarily outweigh any benefit to competition they may produce. Finally, the Government argues that, even if RML's criteria do not

warrant outright condemnation, their actual anticompetitive effects should have been found to outweigh their benefits to competition under full rule of reason analysis.

We must therefore determine whether this group's boycott offends Section 1 of the Sherman Act.

"There is good in the multiple listing system." In a perfectly competitive market, "[t]ime lags, immobility of capital and labor, ignorance on the part of producer and consumer, . . . [and] irrational decisions by buyers and sellers" are assumed not to exist. Perfect competition is a theoretical concept; all markets are subject to varying degrees of imperfections. . . . In the real estate industry, imperfections constitute a serious handicap to the seller, the purchaser, and the industry. A critical imperfection arises from the immobility of the product—real property is, of course, immovable. This insurmountable geographical imperfection magnifies the importance of communicating useful sales data. Moreover, most homeowners do not possess the necessary experience in the specialized field of effectively presenting to the public essential and enlightening information about property offered for sale. Operating as a knowledgeable middleman, the real estate broker can reduce the level and impact of these imperfections. He cannot, however, completely eliminate them; even with the facilities he has, the broker is still confronted with a sizeable communication imperfection. One method of achieving a further reduction of imperfections is by resort to the trade exchange format of the multiple listing service.

Certainly the antitrust laws must allow reasonably ancillary restraints necessary to accomplish these enormously procompetitive objectives. And restraints of the general types imposed by RML are not subject to out-of-hand condemnation. First, the operation of a multiple listing service is not cost free. While a fee structure could be abused to effectively deter all newcomers from entrance, the service must be allowed to recoup its costs of operation. Further, it may well be necessary to the success of a multiple listing service to establish some standards of competence, professionalism and mode of operation for admission to membership. Without some insurance that the brokers who act as subagents to the listing broker through the listing service are responsible and competent, it is possible that neither brokers nor the public will utilize the service, thus forfeiting the benefits it may yield to all.

While some restraints may in fact be basically internal, membership criteria have both internal and external significance. While they limit a member's freedom to deal with nonmembers, and thus deny to the member potential sellers of his listings, they also are designed to exclude from membership those who do not meet them.

When the association possesses the requisite market power, membership in the listing service becomes essential to a broker's ability to compete effectively, and the unreasonable (in competitive terms) exclusion of a broker may create unjustified harm to the broker and the public. The harm to the excluded broker is the mirror image of the benefits to its members. Whereas members gain wide exposure of their listings, with numerous potential sellers, the nonmember remains dependent upon his individual efforts to find a buyer. Similarly, the nonmember will have only those listings which he has personally procured to sell. "He has only a limited supply of 'shoes on the shelves.' "

Buyers and sellers are also harmed by unjustified exclusions. Even though member brokers still compete with each other to procure listings and to sell any listing in the pool, the public is denied the incentive to competition that new entry may bring. A new entrant into the market might,

for example, be more aggressive and willing to accept a lower commission rate. Exclusion of such a broker would tend to reduce the amount of commission.

Thus, where a broker is excluded from a multiple listing service with the requisite market power without an adequate justification in the competitive needs of the service, both the broker and the public are clearly harmed.

Proceeding from the premise, then, that RML has the requisite power in the market, we turn to the standards for the evaluation of its membership criteria. First, the rules must be shown to be justified by the legitimate competitive needs of the association. Our analysis must focus "directly on the challenged restraint's impact on competitive conditions."

An association's enforcement of membership criteria founded upon professional and ethical norms has sometimes been justified as necessary to induce individuals in a given business to join the association, and thus necessary to make the association's procompetitive goals a realistic possibility. This rationale, however, is only partially applicable to a multiple listing service. The service produces its own incentives to membership by presenting the possibility of significant market efficiencies through its pooling of listings and consequent reduction of market imperfections.

Because RML's "favorable credit report and business reputation" criteria give it the power to exclude brokers from membership on grounds not justified by its competitive needs, the district court erred in upholding them.

The Government also argues that the district court erred in holding facially valid RML's requirement that an applicant must have an office "open during customary hours of business."

RML's defense takes three lines. First, it argues that its "customary hours" rule serves to insure that the applicant will be in a likely position to contribute listings to RML and, since the sharing of listings is the essence of RML's operation, the requirement is justified by its operational needs. Second, RML argues that its "customary hours" rule insures that members will be available to conduct negotiations and to service the listings they do furnish and hence is justified. Finally, RML contends that the "customary hours" rule has never been applied to exclude brokers of the two classes the Government has identified and that therefore it should not be voided. We consider each of the contentions in turn.

It may well be justified for RML to require that a prospective member be actively engaged in the business of being a real estate broker in order that he may contribute to RML's functioning. But a rule requiring that a broker be actively engaged in the business of brokering is a far cry from one requiring that he maintain an office open during customary hours of business. If, for example, a broker holds another job during regular working hours and works in his brokering business on nights and weekends, he may still be very actively engaged as a broker. Indeed, he may find that his hours as a broker mesh well with those of many clients who also hold down jobs during normal working hours and transact their real estate business in their off-hours. In this manner, the off-hours broker may fulfill a genuine market demand. To exclude all brokers who function primarily in this off-hours market on the ground that some may not be "actively engaged" as brokers is clearly a response in excess of need. In such a case as this one, it is incumbent on RML to regulate those *practices* of its members which are necessary to its functioning, instead of needlessly excluding an entire class of brokers from membership.

Similarly, the "customary hours" rule is drawn too broadly to be justified by RML's need to insure that its members be available to service listings and conduct negotiations. As RML asserts, the concept of shared listings, which forms the basis of a multiple listing service, requires that the listing broker be available for negotiations and to close the deal since the listing broker retains the primary responsibility to the seller of the property. This need, however, will not support the total exclusion from membership of all brokers who do not maintain customary office hours. Considering again the example of the broker who conducts his real estate business during his "off hours," one cannot conclude that such a broker will not be reasonably available to carry out the duties relevant to his listings. He may for example, be able to conduct many of his servicing and negotiating duties during his off hours and may be able to absent himself from his other job for those duties which cannot be postponed. In fact, it is in the self-interest of a listing broker to make sure that he is available to supply essential services for his listings. One cannot lightly presume that a broker who supplies a listing will forfeit the commission to which he is entitled by failing to service it. Again, to the extent that there exists a danger that brokers will not be reasonably available to service their listings, it is incumbent upon RML to establish rules governing the troublesome practices of its members and not to exclude from membership an entire class of brokers on the basis of an overly broad generalization.

We thus find RML's "customary hours" rule to be overly broad to accomplish any legitimate goals of the association. RML's final contention is that, since it has never applied this rule to exclude any part-time brokers (even though it concedes none have applied) and does not intend to so apply it, the rule should not be found unreasonable. We cannot accept this contention. In the first place, the requirement by its own terms allows the results about which the Government complains. Moreover, there is record evidence to indicate that RML members believe part-time brokers should be excluded and that this rule allows such exclusion. Finally, as we have already pointed out, the antitrust laws do not require that we wait until the restraint is accomplished before we hold invalid a rule which gives an association power to produce unjustified anticompetitive effects; the Sherman Act is offended by the power as well as the deed.

The district court erred in approving the rule.

Discussion Questions

1. What membership standards are being challenged?
2. What services did RML provide?
3. Does RML have market power?
4. Is the credit report a reasonable standard?
5. Is the "customary hours" a reasonable standard?

KEY TERMS

broker
salesperson
agent
National Association of Realtors (NAR)
realtor
listing agreement
open listing
exclusive agency
exclusive right to sell

exclusive listing to sell
multiple listing
multiple list service (MLS)
net listing
no deal, no commission clause
condition precedent
as is
procuring cause of the sale standard
price fixing

CHAPTER PROBLEMS

1. Hecht, the listing broker on the Mellers' home, found a buyer and the Mellers accepted the offer. Just before closing was to take place, the property was destroyed by fire. Hecht still wants his commission. Must the Mellers pay?

2. Gibson Bowles, Incorporated, was the listing broker on the Montgomerys' property. A buyer's offer obtained by Gibson Bowles was accepted by the Montgomerys. The buyer had to qualify for Veterans Administration (VA) financing, but Montgomery told him to delay so that the sale would fall through. After several postponements, Gibson Bowles sued for the commission. What is the result?

3. Renfro had an exclusive listing on some acreage owned by Meacham. The listing provided that the sales price was $1,250,000 for the entire property (1638 acres), or $687,500 for the open land (550 acres) and $562,000 for the woodland (1088 acres). Renfro brought in an offer from Cane Industries of $1,100,000 for the entire tract, which Meacham refused to accept. Renfro sued for her commission. What is the result?

4. Guaranty Investment Company had the listing on a home that was eventually sold to Pinger. Guaranty represented that the foundation on the house was solid and that it would not settle. After moving in, Pinger discovered the foundation had settled and that the basement walls were cracked and had been filled and painted over. Guaranty claims no knowledge of the problem. Pinger files suit for misrepresentation. What is the result?

5. Ballard signed an open listing agreement with Barrett for the sale of real property. Barrett ran an advertisement in the local newspaper. In response to the advertisement, Scilley visited the property and talked directly with Ballard. The two were able to reach an agreement. When Ballard refused to pay the commission, Barrett brought suit. Barrett maintains she was the procuring cause of the sale. What is the result?

6. Buffington signed an exclusive listing agreement with Clements Realty. Mosier and Westby were the agents handling the listing for broker Eugene Clements. Haas, another broker, brought in an offer on the Buffington property from State Investment Corporation. Buffington accepted the offer and the transaction closed. State Investment was to make monthly installment payments on the property, but Buffington had no security in the property for the payments. When State Investment defaulted, Buffington sued Mosier, Westby, Clements, and Haas for failing to tell her of the need for security. Who is liable and on what basis?

7. Rosen, a broker selling desert land in Nevada, advertised that the area's population would be 50,000 in 10 years. The state predicted a population increase of 4000 for the area. The state licensing agency sought to suspend Rosen's license. What is the result?

8. Brandt was convicted of a felonious federal offense—distribution of a controlled substance—for introducing federal narcotics officers to a cocaine dealer while working as a bartender. When Brandt applied for his real estate license, he was denied because of this conviction. Brandt objected because the conviction had taken place 5 years earlier and he had otherwise led an exemplary life: wife, son, Green Beret in Vietnam, honorable discharge, and full compliance with his probation terms and officer. If Brandt appeals the denial, what will be the result?

9. Tom has listed his house with Ace of Ace Realty, Incorporated. The listing agreement notes that the dining room chandelier and living room drapes are not to be included in the sale. Joan and Bob (a lovely couple and potential buyers) see Tom's home with Ace and are quite impressed. As a matter of fact, Joan and Bob are so impressed that they make Tom an offer that he cannot and does not refuse. No mention is made in the contract of the dining room chandelier or the living room drapes. The house is transferred through a proper closing, but when Joan and Bob take possession they discover the two missing items. Joan and Bob turn to Tom for the items.

   a. Must Tom return the items?
   b. Suppose Tom took the money from the sale, left the country, and cannot be found. Joan and Bob now turn to Ace. What is the liability on Ace's part?

10. Tom listed his property with Ace Realty, Incorporated, on a 90-day listing agreement. The listing agent (Bob) was interested in Tom's property and contacted Bill (Bob's cousin) to act as a purchaser. Bill offered Tom much less than the list price. Bob told Tom, "You better take it—you won't get anything better." Bill agreed to pay Tom for the land in installments. Bob told Tom, "Bill is good for the money. A mortgage will only complicate the transaction and, legally, it is unnecessary." Bob never told Tom of his relationship to Bill. Bill conveyed the land to Bob, and then Bob sold the land for $45,000 more than Tom's list price. Discuss any legal problems in this situation.

11

THE PURCHASE CONTRACT

May 10, 1947. Received from Lucky Hertel $80.00 (eighty dollars) earnest money on lot and house number 960 Union Street. Price $5,000 (five thousand dollars) and balance of $4,920.00 to be paid when papers and title insurance are completed. It is understood this deal would be closed and house vacated on or before June the 10th. All furniture except personal belongings included in this transaction.

It would be interesting to discover whether Lucky Hertel had an enforceable contract for the purchase of real property on the basis of the above simple memorandum. The purpose of this chapter is to discuss the formation of contracts for the sale of real estate, the required and suggested content of such contracts, and the remedies for nonperformance of valid contracts. The discussion will center on contracts for the sale of real estate because a discussion of all contract principles would require the reproduction of an entire business law text.

COMMON LAW PRINCIPLES AS APPLIED TO REAL ESTATE CONTRACTS

Although contracts for the purchase and sale of real estate have certain specific needs and requirements, they are still subject to the minimum requirements for formation of all contracts. That is, a contract does not exist until there has been an offer, acceptance, and consideration; and these prerequisites do not change because real estate is involved.

The Offer

The making of an *offer* is the first step in the real estate transaction. Generally, the offer is made by the buyer. Listing agreements, advertisements, auction flyers, and notices of public sales are treated as invitations for offers. These marketing tools are employed to make the buyer aware of the property offering and catch the buyer's attention.

Elements To be valid an offer must indicate a present intent to contract, it must be certain and definite in its terms, and it must be communicated to the offeree (the party receiving the offer). Present intent to contract is indicated by the language used in the offer. Most offers for real estate purchase are made when the buyer actually fills out, signs, and presents to the seller a form or contract of purchase. The language in such forms contains definite evidence of intent to contract: " ＿＿＿＿＿ as seller, agrees to sell to ＿＿＿＿＿ as buyer, and buyer agrees to purchase from seller the following described property. . . ."

The intent to contract is obvious when form contracts are used, but often contracts are negotiated and entered into through very informal procedures. For example, the buyer's offer may come in the form of a letter or memorandum, and so long as the language used evidences present intent to contract, a valid offer exists. However, language such as, "I'm considering buying," "Would you consider selling?" or "What would your asking price be?" is not indicative of present intent to contract and could only be construed as inquiries or invitations for offers.

Likewise, memorandums or correspondence from seller to buyer must also indicate present intent to contract to be considered offers. Language such as "I might sell," "I'd consider selling," "I'm thinking of offering," or "In December, I'll offer" is too conditional and not indicative of a present desire to enter into a binding sales contract.

Not only must the offer have the proper intent language in order to become the basis of the contract, but it must also contain sufficient information and details: the identity of the parties, the description of the property, the price, and the terms (to be discussed in detail). This criterion is easily satisfied when a form purchase contract is used because the form lists all required information. (See Figure 11.1). If one of the basic requirements for formation is missing, then the offer will not be treated as an offer; instead, it will be treated as an invitation for an offer or simply as a step in the negotiation process. A contract may not be formed on the basis of indefinite terms.

The final element for a valid offer is that it must be communicated to the offeree. In usual cases this is accomplished by delivering the purchase contract form with the buyer's signature to the seller or an agent of the seller. Thus,

Figure 11.1 *Sample Purchase Contract and Receipt*

REALTOR®

RESIDENTIAL
REAL ESTATE PURCHASE CONTRACT AND RECEIPT FOR DEPOSIT

EQUAL HOUSING OPPORTUNITY

THE PRINTED PORTION OF THIS CONTRACT HAS BEEN APPROVED BY THE ARIZONA ASSOCIATION OF REALTORS®. THIS IS INTENDED TO BE A BINDING CONTRACT. NO REPRESENTATION IS MADE AS TO THE LEGAL VALIDITY OR ADEQUACY OF ANY PROVISION OR THE TAX CONSEQUENCES THEREOF. IF YOU DESIRE LEGAL OR TAX ADVICE, CONSULT YOUR ATTORNEY OR TAX ADVISOR.

RECEIPT

1. RECEIVED FROM _____ ("Buyer"),
2. who will take title as (check one) ☐ Joint Tenants with Right of Survivorship, ☐ Community Property, ☐ Tenants in Common, ☐ Sole and Separate Property,
3. or ☐ as determined before close of escrow, the sum of $ _____ evidenced by ☐ cash, ☐ personal check, or ☐ _____ with duly licensed
4. (subject to collection), to be deposited promptly after Seller's acceptance of this Contract ☐ in trust account of Selling Broker named in line 9 ☐ with duly licensed
5. escrow company _____ as earnest deposit and part purchase price for the Premises described below.
6. Any earnest money check shall be held by Selling Broker until Seller's acceptance of Buyer's offer. Upon acceptance, Broker is authorized to deposit the check
7. with the escrow company to which the check is payable, or, if the check is payable to Broker, to endorse the check to and deposit it with a duly licensed
8. escrow company.
9. SELLING BROKER _____

| Firm Name | Agent's Signature | Date |

OFFER

10. Buyer agrees to purchase the real property in _____ County, Arizona, and all fixtures and improvements thereon and
11. appurtenances incident thereto, as follows: _____
12. _____ plus personal property described below (collectively the "Premises") for:
13. $ _____ Full purchase price, payable as follows:
14. $ _____ Earnest deposit as indicated above.
15. $ _____ _____
16. $ _____ _____
17. _____
18. _____
19. _____
20. _____
21. _____
22. _____
23. _____
24. _____
25. _____
26. _____
27. _____
28. _____
29. _____
30. _____
31. _____
32. _____
33. ☐ **Addendum.** An addendum is attached, which is incorporated herein by reference.
34. **Escrow Instructions.** ☐ Separate escrow instructions will be executed.
35. ☐ This Contract will be used as escrow instructions, and the escrow company and title insurer shall be _____
36. NOTE: The Federal Real Estate Settlement Procedures Act (RESPA) often prohibits a Seller from requiring use of a particular title insurance company.
37. **Fire and Extended Coverage Insurance.** ☐ A new policy shall be issued; ☐ premiums for existing insurance shall be prorated; ☐ to be determined on above.
38. **Prorations and Costs.** Insurance premiums and interest on assessments and encumbrances, if assumed, taxes, homeowners association fees and irrigation fees
39. shall be prorated as of ☐ close of escrow ☐ _____
40. **Encumbrances and Impounds.** The balance of any encumbrances being assumed is approximate. Any difference shall be reflected in the ☐ cash payment
41. due at close of escrow ☐ deferred balance due Seller. Buyer shall reimburse Seller for any impounds transferred to Buyer.
42. **Assessments.** The amount of any assessment which is a lien as of the close of escrow shall be ☐ paid in full by Seller ☐ assumed by Buyer. Any assessment that
43. becomes a lien after close of escrow is Buyer's responsibility.
44. **Closing Date.** Seller and Buyer will comply with all terms and conditions of this Contract and close escrow on or before _____
45. _____ If escrow does not close by such date, this Contract is subject to cancellation as provided herein.
46. **Possession.** Possession shall be delivered to Buyer _____
47. **Home Protection Plan.** A home protection plan will be obtained for the Premises by close of escrow ☐ Yes ☐ No. The plan will be obtained at the expense of
48. ☐ Seller ☐ Buyer. Name of plan: _____ Type of plan: _____
49. **Fixtures and Personal Property.** All existing storage sheds, heating and cooling equipment, built-in appliances, light fixtures, window and door screens, sun screens,
50. storm windows and doors, towel, curtain and drapery rods, attached carpeting, draperies and other window coverings, fireplace, pool and spa equipment (including
51. any mechanical or other cleaning system), garage door openers and controls and attached antennas shall be left upon and included with the Premises, except:
52. _____
53. The following additional personal property is included with the Premises: _____
54. _____
55. The following leased equipment is excluded: _____
56. **Time for Acceptance.** This offer must be accepted by Seller on or before _____
57. Written acceptance of this Contract given to the Selling Broker named on line 9 of this Contract shall be notice to Buyer.
58. COMMISSIONS PAYABLE FOR THE SALE, LEASING OR MANAGEMENT OF PROPERTY ARE NOT SET BY ANY BOARD OF REALTORS® OR MULTIPLE
59. LISTING SERVICE IN ANY MANNER OTHER THAN BETWEEN THE BROKER AND THE CLIENT.
60. **Terms on Reverse.** THE TERMS AND CONDITIONS ON THE REVERSE SIDE HEREOF ARE INCORPORATED HEREIN BY REFERENCE.
61. The undersigned agree to purchase the Premises on the terms and conditions herein stated and acknowledge receipt of a copy hereof.

62. _____   _____   _____   _____
    Buyer   Date   Buyer   Date
63. Social Security or Tax I.D. No.: _____   Social Security or Tax I.D. No.: _____
64. _____
    Street   City   State   Zip

ACCEPTANCE

65. Seller agrees to sell the Premises as stated herein. Seller has employed Brokers and for services rendered, agrees to pay a brokerage fee as follows:
66. _____ to _____ ("Selling Broker")
67. _____ to _____ ("Listing Broker")
68. Seller instructs escrow company to pay such fee to Brokers in cash as a condition to closing and, to the extent necessary therefor (or necessary to pay one-half of
69. the earnest deposit as provided below), irrevocably assigns to Brokers Seller's proceeds at close of escrow (or share of the earnest deposit if Buyer defaults).
70. If completion of the sale is prevented by default of Seller, or with the consent of Seller, the entire fee shall be paid directly by Seller. If the earnest deposit is forfeited
71. for any other reason, Seller shall pay a brokerage fee equal to one-half of the deposit, provided such payment shall not exceed the full amount of the fee. Nothing
72. in this paragraph shall be construed as limiting applicable provisions of law or any listing agreement relating to when commissions are earned or payable.
73. Seller hereby waives his right to receive any subsequent offer to purchase the Premises until after forfeiture by Buyer or other nullification hereof.
74. ☐ Counter Offer is attached, which is incorporated herein by reference.
75. **Seller Receipt of Copy.** The undersigned acknowledge receipt of a copy hereof and authorize Broker to deliver a signed copy to Buyer.

76. _____   _____   _____   _____
    Seller   Date   Seller   Date
77. Social Security or Tax I.D. No.: _____   Social Security or Tax I.D. No.: _____
78. _____
    Street   City   State   Zip
79. **Broker Review:** Selling Broker acknowledges by initialing below, that he or his representative has notified Buyer of Seller's acceptance of this offer.

80. Broker's File/Log No. _____   Manager's Initials _____   Broker's Initials _____   Date _____

©Arizona Association of REALTORS® 1987   **This Form Available Through Your Local Board of REALTORS®**   Form No. 1 — RREPCRD 7/87

Figure 11.1 (continued)

81. **Time of Essence.** Time is of the essence of this Contract.

82. **Permission.** Buyer and Seller grant Broker permission to advise the public of the sale, price and terms herein after close of escrow.

83. **Entire Agreement.** This Contract, any attached exhibits and any addenda or supplements signed by the parties, shall constitute the entire agreement between
84. Seller and Buyer, and supersede any other written or oral agreements between Seller and Buyer. This Contract can be modified only by a writing signed by
85. Seller and Buyer.

86. **Title and Title Insurance.** Promptly after the execution of this Contract, Seller shall instruct a title insurance company to furnish to Buyer as soon as practicable a
87. preliminary title report together with complete and legible copies of all documents which will remain as exceptions to Buyer's policy of title insurance. Title to the real
88. property described in lines 10 through 12 of this Contract shall be conveyed by a warranty deed. Title to the personal property described in lines 49 through 54 of this
89. Contract shall be transferred free and clear of any liens or encumbrances. Seller shall furnish to Buyer, at Seller's expense, a Standard Owner's Title Insurance Policy in
90. the full amount of the purchase price issued by a title insurance company, showing good and marketable title to the real property in Buyer, free from defects and
91. encumbrances except as follows: (1) liens and other matters described in this Contract; (2) building, use and other restrictive covenants of record; (3) claims, title
92. or rights to water; (4) zoning regulations; (5) easements and rights-of-way for roadways, canals, laterals, ditches and public utilities; (6) taxes, paving, irrigation
93. and other assessments, not delinquent as of the close of escrow; (7) rights of tenants in possession, if any; (8) rights and minerals reserved in patents or otherwise
94. by any government entity; and (9) printed exceptions contained in the Owner's Title Insurance Policy. If title to the Premises otherwise is defective at the time set
95. for close of escrow. Buyer may elect as Buyer's sole option, either to accept title subject to defects which are not cured or to cancel this Contract whereupon all
96. money paid by Buyer pursuant to this Contract shall be returned to Buyer. Buyer shall furnish to Seller, at Buyer's expense, a Standard Loan Policy, in the full amount of
97. any loan, secured by the real property described in lines 10 through 12 of this Contract, carried back by the Seller. Such Standard Loan Policy shall show that Seller's
98. lien has the priority agreed to by the parties.

99. **Insurance After Closing.** Buyer agrees to maintain fire and extended coverage insurance on the Premises in an amount at least equal to the total unpaid balance
100. of all secured loans encumbering the property as of close of escrow, and provide proof of the fact and the amount of such coverage, until all such loans have been
101. repaid in full.

102. **Documents and Escrow.**
103. A. If Seller and Buyer elect to execute escrow instructions to fulfill the terms hereof, they shall deliver the same to escrow company within 15 days of the
104. acceptance of this offer.
105. B. All documents, including but not limited to, agreements for sale, notes, mortgages, deeds of trust and deeds, necessary to close this transaction, shall
106. be executed promptly by Seller and Buyer in the standard form used by escrow company and deposited in escrow, provided that Seller and Buyer hereby instruct
107. escrow company to modify such documents to the extent necessary to be consistent with this Contract.
108. C. In any conflict between this Contract and any escrow instructions executed pursuant hereto, the provisions of this Contract shall be controlling.
109. D. All closing and escrow costs shall be prorated between Seller and Buyer in accordance with local custom and applicable laws and regulations.
110. E. Escrow company is hereby instructed to send to both Selling and Listing Broker copies of all notices and communications directed to Seller or Buyer and
111. shall provide to such Brokers access to escrowed materials and information about the escrow upon request.

112. **Default and Remedies.** If Buyer defaults in any respect on any material obligations under this Contract, Seller may elect to be released from the obligation to sell
113. the Premises to Buyer. Seller may proceed against Buyer upon any claim or remedy which he may have, in law or equity, or because it would be difficult to fix actual
114. damages, in case of Buyer's default, the amount of the earnest deposit may be deemed a reasonable estimate of the damages, and Seller may, at his option,
115. retain the earnest deposit, subject to the brokerage fee as provided herein, as his sole right to damages. If Buyer or Seller files suit against the other to enforce
116. any provision of this Contract or for damages sustained by reason of its breach, all parties prevailing in such action, on trial and appeal, shall receive their
117. reasonable attorneys' fees and costs as awarded by the court. In addition, both Seller and Buyer agree to indemnify and hold harmless all Brokers and escrow company
118. against all costs and expenses, including without limitation attorneys' fees, expert witness fees, fees paid to investigators and court costs which any Broker or escrow
119. company may incur or sustain in connection with any lawsuit arising from this Contract and will pay the same on demand unless the court shall grant judgment in such
120. action against the party to be indemnified.

121. **Warranties.** Except as otherwise provided in this Contract, Seller shall maintain and repair the Premises so that, at the earlier of possession or the close of escrow,
122. the Premises shall be in substantially the same condition as on the effective date of this Contract. Seller warrants that the roof will be water-tight and all heating,
123. cooling, plumbing and electrical systems and built-in appliances will be in working condition at the earlier of possession or the close of escrow. If the
124. Premises has a swimming pool and/or spa. Seller warrants that the motors, filter systems (and heaters, if so equipped) will be in working condition at close of
125. escrow or upon possession, whichever is sooner. Seller warrants that prior to the close of escrow payment in full will have been made for all labor, materials,
126. machinery, fixtures or tools furnished within the 120 days immediately preceding the close of escrow in connection with the construction, alteration or repair of
127. any structure on or improvement to the Premises. Prior to close of escrow, Seller shall grant Buyer or Buyer's representatives reasonable access to enter and
128. inspect the Premises. By closing hereunder. Buyer acknowledges that all warranties concerning the Premises have been satisfied or extinguished. Brokers are
129. hereby relieved of any and all liability and responsibility from everything stated in this paragraph and the following paragraph.

130. **Sanitation.** Seller warrants that the information in the current listing agreement, if any, regarding connection to a public sewer system, septic tank or other sanita-
131. tion system is correct to the best of his knowledge. Any provision of this Contract to the contrary notwithstanding, this warranty shall survive the closing.

132. **Termite Report and Repairs.** Seller agrees that at his expense he will place in escrow a termite inspection report by a licensed pest control contractor which, when
133. considered in its entirety, indicates that all residences and buildings attached to the Premises are free from evidence of current termite infestation and termite
134. damage. Seller agrees to pay up to one percent of the full purchase price for the repair of damage caused by termites. If the cost of repairing such damage would
135. exceed one percent of the purchase price, (a) Buyer may elect to cancel this Contract unless Seller agrees in writing to pay the cost of repairing all such loss or
136. damage and, (b) Seller may elect to cancel this Contract unless Buyer agrees in writing either to accept the Premises without offset or additional consideration
137. or to pay the cost of repairing such loss or damage to the extent such cost would exceed one percent of the purchase price.

138. **Status of Warranties and Representations.** Any representations or information concerning, without limitation, the Premises, or title, physical condition, value,
139. rent rolls, notice of violations, or other material matters relating to the Premises, given to Buyer, Seller or any Broker are believed to be reliable but were provided
140. by others, and therefore, no Broker is making any warranty, express or implied, as to the accuracy of such information. Neither any Broker nor the Seller is making
141. any representations or warranties concerning rights to, adequacy of or quality of the water supply or water rights with respect to the Premises. Seller warrants
142. that he has disclosed to Buyer all material latent defects concerning the Premises that are known to Seller. Buyer represents by signing this Contract that he has
143. (or will have prior to the closing hereunder) conducted all independent investigations desired by Buyer of any and all matters concerning this purchase, and by
144. closing hereunder accepts the Premises, its fixtures and improvements, the personal property transferred in this transaction and any rentals or business conducted
145. thereon AS IS, AND NO SELLER WARRANTY of any kind, express or implied (including, without limitation, WARRANTY OF MERCHANTABILITY or habitability)
146. shall survive the closing. Seller and Buyer hereby release all Brokers from all responsibility and liability regarding the condition, square footage or valuation of the
147. Premises and neither Seller. Buyer, nor any Broker shall be bound by any understanding, agreement, promise or representation, express or implied, not
148. specified herein.

149. **Recommendations.** If any improvements are to be constructed on the property by a builder or contractor recommended by any Broker, Buyer understands that
150. such Broker may receive a commission from the builder or contractor. If any Broker recommends a builder or contractor or any other person or entity to Seller or
151. Buyer for any purpose, such recommendation will be independently investigated and evaluated by Seller or Buyer, who hereby acknowledge that any decision to
152. enter into any contractual arrangements with any such person or entity recommended by any Broker will be based solely upon such independent investigation and
153. evaluation.

154. **Risk of Loss.** If there is any loss or damage to the Premises between the date hereof and the date of closing, by reason of fire, vandalism, flood, earthquake or act of
155. God, the risk of loss shall be on the Seller, provided, however, that if the cost of repairing such loss or damage would exceed 10 percent of the purchase price,
156. (a) Buyer may elect to cancel this Contract unless Seller agrees in writing to pay the cost of repairing all such loss or damage, and, (b) Seller may elect to cancel this
157. Contract unless Buyer agrees in writing either to accept the Premises without offset or additional consideration or to pay the cost of repairing such loss or damage
158. to the extent such cost would exceed 10 percent of the purchase price.

159. **Deposit Acceptance.** The deposit described in line 3 of this Contract is accepted by Broker subject to prior sale and subject to acceptance by Seller.

160. **Cancellation.** Any party who wishes to cancel this Contract because of any breach by another party or because escrow fails to close by the agreed date and who is
161. not himself in breach of this Contract except as occasioned by a breach by the other party, may cancel this Contract by delivering to escrow company a
162. notice containing the address of the party in breach and stating that this Contract shall be cancelled unless the breach is cured within the 13 days following the
163. delivery of the notice to the escrow company. Within three days after receipt of such notice, the escrow company shall send it by United States Mail to the party in
164. breach at the address contained in the notice and no further notice shall be required. If the breach is not cured within the 13 days following the delivery of the notice
165. to the escrow company, this Contract shall be cancelled.

166. **Broker's Attorneys' Fees.** If any Broker reasonably hires an attorney to enforce the collection of the commission payable pursuant to this Contract, and is success-
167. ful in collecting some or all of such commission, Seller agrees to pay such Broker's reasonable attorneys' fees and costs as set by the court and not by a jury.

168. **FHA or VA.** If applicable, the current language prescribed by FHA or VA pertaining to the value of the Premises and forfeiture of earnest money deposits shall be
169. incorporated in this Contract by reference as if set forth in full herein and Seller and Buyer agree to execute any appropriate FHA or VA supplements to this
170. Contract.

171. **Buyer's Loan.** If Buyer is seeking a new loan or an assumption that requires qualification in connection with this transaction, Buyer agrees to file a substantially
172. complete loan application within five business days after the acceptance of this offer and to supply promptly all appropriate documentation required by the lender.

173. **Severability.** If a court of competent jurisdiction makes a final determination that any term or provision of this Contract is invalid or unenforceable, all other terms and
174. provisions shall remain in full force and effect, and the invalid or unenforceable term or provision shall be deemed replaced by a term or provision that is valid and
175. enforceable and comes closest to expressing the intention of the invalid term or provision.

176. **Construction of Language.** The language of this Contract shall be construed according to its fair meaning and not strictly for or against either party. Words used
177. in the masculine, feminine or neuter shall apply to either gender or the neuter, as appropriate. All singular and plural words shall be interpreted to refer to the
178. number consistent with circumstances and context.

Form No. 1 — RREPCRD 7/87

Source: Arizona Association of Realtors

delivery of the offer to the seller's broker or salesperson is sufficient communication, as these parties are the seller's agents.

(11.1) Consider:

Determine if the following language from a letter by Thompson to Hale (the lot owner) meets the requirements for a valid offer:

> I am very much interested in your lot, zoned C-2, which is located at the southeastern corner of Gilbert and Southern Roads. If the price is $475,000 or less, I can pay cash. I will need it for construction by 6/1/88.
> /s/ Waller Thompson

Termination Since an offer is but one part of the contract formation process, it is not legally binding and may be revoked or withdrawn at any time prior to acceptance by the offeree. When an offer is voluntarily withdrawn prior to acceptance, the offeror has no liability for any damages others may have incurred in relying on the offer.

It is possible to limit an offer so that it terminates upon the expiration of its time of validity. For example, a valid offer may include as one of its terms, "This offer good only until noon on April 5, 1988." Thus, the offer would automatically terminate at that time and date unless there is acceptance by the offeree prior to that time. By law, even offers without specific time limits terminate after the passage of a reasonable amount of time, although it is probably best for the offerors to withdraw or revoke any long-outstanding offers. The determination of reasonable time varies according to the nature and location of the property and the terms of the offer.

The death of either an offeror or the offeree serves to terminate the offer (with an exception noted in the next section: Options). At the moment of death the offer is automatically terminated or withdrawn.

Rejection of the offer by the offeree terminates the original offer. A rejection is generally in the form of a negative response, such as, "No, I'm not interested." But in real estate transactions, a rejection may be given indirectly. If an offeree makes the acceptance of an offer conditional on certain additional terms and requirements, the acceptance is in reality both a rejection of the original offer and a *counteroffer*, placing the original offeree in an offeror position. The following sequence of excerpts from correspondence illustrates this point:

a. *Offeror.* "I will buy Blackacre (legal description) from you for $10,000 cash, to close 6/1/88."

b. *Offeree (counteroffer)*. ''I accept your offer but must have cash in hand by 5/1/88.''

c. *Offeree (original offeror)*. ''That is agreeable.''

When the offeree conditioned acceptance on a change in closing date (b) the acceptance was in reality a counteroffer that the original offeror, now an offeree, was free to accept or reject.

In practice, when brokers and salespersons run between buyer and seller with changes in terms and addenda to the purchase contract, they are engaging in a series of events where the parties are constantly changing roles as offerors and offerees. It is important to note that the offeree must accept all of the offeror's terms without change or qualification for the contract to exist. Any material change results in a rejection and a counteroffer, which must be accepted by the other party.

(11.2) Consider:

On 17 December 1987 Daniel Swenson submitted an offer to purchase "Lot 104, Village Park Four, Unit Two, Mesa, Arizona (also known as 700 North Cholla)." The offer (submitted on a standard purchase contract and receipt) had a $14,500 down payment, with an assumption of $30,000, and with Henry Wilson (the seller) carrying $19,000. Wilson put an addendum to the contract, which required a $17,000 down and a carrying of $16,500. Swenson told the salesperson upon presentment of the addendum, "I simply can't afford it." The salesperson told Wilson, who said "OK, I'll sign the original form." Does a contract exist between the parties?

Options

1. Requirements Often a buyer is unsure of making a purchase of property and requires further time for investigation. However, since an offer may be revoked by the offeror any time prior to acceptance, the opportunity to purchase may not be available when the eventual decision is made. The buyer requires some type of guarantee that the offer will remain open for a stated period of time. However, simply having the seller include a time provision in the offer ("This offer to remain open until June 15, 1988") is insufficient because the seller is still able to revoke the offer provided there is proper notice to the offeree.

However, if the buyer obtains an option from the seller, this problem is alleviated. An *option* is a contract for time whereby the seller agrees to hold an offer open for a specified period in exchange for pay (consideration passes).

Either a buyer or seller can turn an offer into an option with proper consideration (payment) from the offeree.

The important aspect of the option, which distinguishes it from the ordinary offer, is that the offeror is paid consideration to keep the offer open. If payment is not made, the offeror is free to revoke the offer at any time. However, if an offeror has been paid for an option on property and sells the property to another party, the offeror is in breach of contract and will be required to pay damages to the option holder. The amount of consideration is not important so long as it is actually paid. The following case deals with the issue of consideration in options.

BOARD OF CONTROL OF
EASTERN MICHIGAN UNIVERSITY v. BURGESS
206 N.W.2d 256 (Mich. 1973)

On 15 February 1966 Burgess (defendant/appellant) signed a document that provided Eastern Michigan University (EMU/plaintiff/appellee) a 60-day option for the purchase of Burgess's home. The document, drafted by an agent of Burgess, indicated receipt of "one and no/100 Dollar ($1.00) and other valuable consideration." The dollar was never paid. On 14 April 1966 EMU notified Burgess of its acceptance, but Burgess refused to close and deliver title. EMU brought suit for delivery of the property or specific performance. The trial court found for EMU, and Burgess appealed.

BURNS, Judge

Options for the purchase of land, if based on valid consideration, are contracts which may be specifically enforced. Conversely, that which purports to be an option, but which is not based on valid consideration, is not a contract and will not be enforced. In the instant case defendant received no consideration for the purported option of February 15, 1966.

A written acknowledgment of receipt of consideration merely creates a rebuttable presumption that consideration has, in fact, passed. Neither the parol evidence rule nor the doctrine of estoppel bars the presentation of evidence to contradict any such acknowledgment.

It is our opinion that the document signed by Burgess on February 15, 1966, is not an enforceable option, and that Burgess is not barred from so asserting. In the instant case Burgess claims that she never received any of the consideration promised here.

That which purports to be an option for the purchase of land, but which is not based on valid consideration, is a simple offer to sell the same land. An option is a contract collateral to an offer to sell whereby the offer is made irrevocable for a specified period. Ordinarily, an offer is revocable at the will of the offeror. Accordingly, a failure of consideration affects only the collateral contract to keep the offer open, not the underlying offer.

A simple offer may be revoked for any reason or for no reason by the offeror at any time prior to its acceptance by the offeree. Thus, the question in this case becomes, "Did defendant effectively revoke her offer to sell before plaintiff accepted that offer?"

Defendant testified that within hours of signing the purported option she telephoned plaintiff's agent and informed him that she would not abide by the option unless the purchase price was increased. Defendant also testified that when plaintiff's agent delivered to her on April 14, 1966, plaintiff's notice of its intention to exercise the purported option, she told him that "the option was off."

Plaintiff's agent testified that defendant did not communicate to him any dissatisfaction until sometime in July 1966.

If defendant is telling the truth, she effectively revoked her offer several weeks before plaintiff accepted that offer, and no contract of sale was created. If plaintiff's agent is telling the truth, defendant's offer was still open when plaintiff accepted that offer, and an enforceable contract was created. The trial judge thought it unnecessary to resolve this particular dispute. In light of our holding the dispute must be resolved.

An appellate court cannot assess the credibility of witnesses. We have neither seen nor heard them testify.

Accordingly, we remand this case to the trial court for additional findings of fact based on the record already before the court.

Discussion Questions

1. How long was the option?
2. What property was involved?
3. How much was the consideration?
4. Was the consideration paid?
5. Was there a valid option?
6. What issue remains to be determined?

2. Termination Another distinguishing feature about the option provision is that, unlike an ordinary offer, it does not terminate with the death of the offeror or the option holder. In other words, the estate of an option holder could elect to exercise the option for the estate. Likewise, the estate of the offeror is required to honor the option if the option holder decides to exercise the right after the death of the offeror.

Another circumstance that arises in option cases is when the option holder rejects the option prior to the time the option is scheduled to terminate. For example, A gives B an option on some property to run from 1 February 1988 to 2 March 1988, and B pays A $30 for the option. On 16 February 1988, B notifies A of rejection of the offer. The following questions arise: (1) Must A still hold the offer open until 2 March 1988? (2) Is B entitled to a refund of a portion of the option payment? (3) Must A refund a portion of the option payment in order to sell the property prior to 2 March 1988?

The rejection or termination of the offer must be clear, and it is probably best for the offeror not to rely on an oral statement, as the following case illustrates.

HAYES v. GRIFFIN

186 S.E.2d 649 (N.C. 1972)

On 25 July 1969 Mr. and Mrs. Hayes (plaintiffs/appellees) obtained a written option agreement from Mr. and Mrs. Griffin (defendants/appellants), which covered a 110-acre tract of land until 1 December 1969. The Griffins maintain the Hayeses cancelled the option in September 1969. The Hayeses brought suit for specific performance. The trial court found for the Hayeses, and the Griffins appealed.

BROCK, Judge

Defendants' answer and evidence at trial, and the thrust of their arguments on this appeal, are centered upon their contention that plaintiffs had cancelled the option to purchase the tract of land by subsequent oral agreement.

In the absence of a definite parol rescission or abandonment of rights under an option contract, an abandonment or waiver of such rights is to be inferred only from positive and unequivocal acts and conduct which are clearly inconsistent with the contract. In our opinion, there is no evidence in this case of acts or conduct by plaintiffs which would justify the jury in finding that plaintiffs had positively and unequivocally acted inconsistent with the contract. Therefore, no instruction by the judge upon this principle of law was required.

Affirmed.

Discussion Questions

1. What was the option period?
2. Why does the offeror not allow the exercise of the option?
3. Was the option rejected?
4. What type of proof of option rejection is necessary?

The jurisdictions are split on the answers to the questions raised by the option holder's premature rejection. One view is that rejection is rejection, that is, an option is an offer that terminates once rejected by the option holder (offeree). The majority view is that a premature rejection has no effect on the option, that is, that the option continues for the specified period unless the offer has materially changed position. Under this view, if the parties agreed to a partial refund and signed a mutual release terminating the option, then the offeror would be free to sell the property to another. Under the first view, release and refund would not be required for the offeror to be free to transfer the property.

In light of the split among the courts on how options are to be handled in the event of premature rejection, it is probably best for the parties to put a clause in their option agreement dealing with the problem of premature rejection, the offeror's rights in such circumstances, and the option holder's right of refund. Clarifying the result by agreement may prevent a tenuous legal position for the offeror and may be less costly for an offeree who is able to make an early purchase decision.

(11.3) Consider:

On 7 February 1988, A entered into negotiations with B for the purchase of B's farm. After consulting with an attorney and having the property appraised, B agreed to sell for $150,000. A and B agreed in writing that in exchange for $300 then received from A, B would hold the offer open for 9 months. After 6 months, A wrote B that he was no longer interested in buying the farm. Several days later, A received notice from B that he was negotiating with C to sell the farm for $250,000. A immediately called B, who suggested that if A would agree to pay $175,000 and conclude the deal within 10 days, then B would still be willing to sell to A. A protested that B was driving a hard bargain, but finally agreed by telegram that evening to buy the farm for $175,000 within 10 days. A purchased the farm as ag~~ ~ and then sought to recover $25,000 from B or alternatively to rescind the purchase (in other words, get out of the contract). What results and why?

The difficulty encountered with the early rejection of options indicates that careful drafting can eliminate many of the problems that may arise in the effective use of option agreements. The items in the following checklist should be included when negotiating and drafting option agreements:

- Legal description of the property.
- Proper names of the parties.
- Signatures of the parties.
- Length of the option.
- Beginning and ending dates of the option period.
- Amount of consideration to be paid.
- Destiny of the consideration if
    a. the option is exercised: Can it be a down payment?
    b. the option expires without acceptance: Does the offeror retain the money?
    c. the option holder rejects prior to expiration: Will there be a prorated refund?
    d. the property is destroyed during the option period.
    e. one of the parties dies.

- Recording of the option in the public records, and its removal if not exercised.
- Procedures and notifications required for exercise of the option.
- All terms or provisions of the sales contract:
  a. marketable title (type of deed, insurance, and so on).
  b. rights of lessees.
  c. presence of mortgages and attachment of new liens during the option period.
- Assignability of the option.

Options should not be confused with *earnest money* deposits accompanying offers by buyers for the purchase of real estate. Earnest money is appropriately named because it is customarily required to show the offeror's good faith and is actually part of the payment for the purchase price. Options generally come from sellers and are promises to hold offers open for periods of time. Payment for an option is not necessarily a payment of part of the purchase price. Furthermore, consideration is required for an option to be valid, whereas earnest money is not required for a valid contract to purchase (although it may be good business practice).

Acceptance

Acceptance is the conduct on the part of the offeree that indicates a willingness to assent to the terms of the offer. Acceptance is the second part of the so-called meeting of the minds requirement for formation of a contract. Like the offer, acceptance has certain requirements: (a) acceptance must be by the party with the power of acceptance; (b) it must be absolute, unequivocal, and unconditional; and (c) it must be communicated to the offeror.

Power of Acceptance The only party with the power of acceptance is the party to whom the offer is made. Offers are not transferable. An exception to this rule involves options, which are contracts for time, and are transferable as are any contracts. An assignment of an option right entitles the assignee to exercise the rights afforded by the option.

Absolute, Unequivocal, and Unconditional Acceptance This element of acceptance was already briefly explained in the section about the termination of offers. The offeree must accept the offer on the terms set forth by the offeror, and must not change the terms or condition acceptance upon some new or different terms. If the offeree does make any changes in the terms, then there is no acceptance; rather, a counteroffer has been made which the original offeror (now offeree) is free to accept or reject.

(11.4) Consider:

On 6 April 1955 a buyer and seller entered into a "preliminary agreement of purchase" for some Lincolnwood, Illinois, property. The price was to be $49,500, with a $2,000 earnest money deposit, $35,500 cash at closing, and assumption of a $12,000 mortgage. The contract was to be executed on a Chicago Real Estate Board sales contract form within 5 days of the seller's acceptance of the preliminary agreement. The sellers signed a purchase contract that was not a Chicago Real Estate Board form and which called for earnest money of $4,950. The buyer claimed there was no contract. The seller disagreed. What was the result?

Communication of Acceptance to the Offeror The signature on the purchase contract alone is insufficient acceptance: a copy of that agreement must be delivered to the offeror or the offeror's agent for a valid contract to exist.

Many times an offer will dictate how acceptance is to be accomplished. It may require acceptance to be by mail or personal delivery, or to be given within a certain period of time. The offeree must comply with these requirements for the acceptance to be valid; otherwise, noncompliance with the terms may be treated as a counteroffer.

Problem of Multiple Offers Because acceptance is effective upon communication to the offeror, an offeror who has made more than one offer may find two acceptances being communicated before one or both of the offers can be revoked. Thus, it poses a major legal risk for an offeror to have more than one offer outstanding. Consider the following sequence of events as an example:

- *Day 1.* Buyer A submits an offer to seller.
- *Day 2.* Seller counteroffers to buyer A. Buyer B submits an offer to seller.
- *Day 3.* Seller counteroffers to buyer B. Buyer A accepts. Before seller can revoke, buyer B accepts.

The seller in the example would have to convey the property to one buyer and pay damages for breach to the other buyer.

(11.5) Consider:

Cynthia has listed her home with We Sell 'Em Realty, Incorporated. Buyer A conveys a written offer of $83,000 to Cynthia on 1 March 1988. Buyer B conveys an offer of $84,000 to Cynthia on 2 March 1988. On 2 March 1988 Cynthia issues counteroffers of $85,000 to both A and B. On the counteroffers Cynthia adds the following: "This offer good until 4 March 1988, 6:00 P.M."

Suppose buyer A accepts on 3 March 1988 (written forms signed) and communicates the acceptance to Cynthia at 7:00 P.M. that day. Cynthia then contacts buyer B and says "I revoke the counteroffer." What is the result?

a. Suppose that before Cynthia contacts B, B contacts Cynthia and accepts at 2:15 P.M. (written forms signed). What would be result?

b. Suppose that B paid Cynthia $50 to hold the offer open until 4 March 1988, 6:00 P.M. What would be result?

c. Suppose same facts as b. except that B calls Cynthia at 1:00 P.M., 3 March 1988, and states "I reject," whereupon Cynthia receives A's acceptance. What would be the result?

Consideration

The third and final requirement for formation of a valid contract is consideration. *Consideration* is something of value given up by each party to the contract. In most cases involving a sale of real property, consideration is easily established: The seller gives up title to the property; and the buyer gives up money, assumes a mortgage, or both in order to pay for that property.

Consideration need not be money. As noted, the buyer's promise to take over a loan is sufficient consideration. Therefore, the traditional earnest money deposit received from buyers in a real estate transaction is not required for the contract to be valid and binding. Provided that both parties have promised to give something up in the transaction, those promises constitute sufficient consideration. However, earnest money does demonstrate sincerity and good faith on the part of the buyer, and may be used as a source of funds for damages in the event of a problem.

As already mentioned, the amount of consideration is not of legal concern to the courts, so long as there is consideration. Therefore, a promise to pay $5,000 for property worth $20,000 is a valid consideration provided that each party voluntarily agrees to the terms. The following case deals with the sufficiency of consideration in a real estate purchase agreement.

TRENGEN v. MONGEON

206 N.W.2d 284 (N.Dak. 1973)

On 9 May 1967 Louis and Margaret Mongeon executed a warranty deed conveying approximately 960 acres of land to their son Ernest and his wife, Pearl (defendant/appellee). The deed contained an acknowledgment of the receipt of $38,400 as consideration for the conveyance. At the same time, the parties entered into an agreement whereby Ernest and Pearl agreed to pay to Louis and Margaret the sum of $1,800 annually for as long as both or the survivor of them shall live. At the time of the agreement Louis was 87 and Margaret was 83. Ernest's sister, Elaine Trengen (plaintiff/appellant, as guardian for her parents), brought suit seeking to set the deed aside on the grounds of lack of consideration. The trial court found for Ernest and Pearl, and the sister appealed.

TEIGEN, Judge

In the present case the consideration is of an indeterminable value. Monetarily, payment of the sum of $1,800 was made in the fall of 1967, and that sum will continue to be payable on or before November 1 of every year for as long as both or the survivor of the plaintiffs shall live. Payments received by the plaintiffs to the present time total $10,800.

. . . *Since adequacy of consideration is not necessary to sustain a deed, and any valuable consideration, however small, is sufficient, the consideration need not equal the value of the property conveyed, especially where no creditor's rights are affected. Indeed, the merely nominal consideration of one dollar, which is frequently recited in deeds, evidences a sufficient consideration. So, where, as compared with the actual value of the property or interest received, the consideration is adequate, the deed will stand, whether such consideration be merely a valuable one without any monetary payment or a valuable one coupled with pecuniary advances. Adequacy of monetary consideration is not an important element in a conveyance which has for its principal purpose the conferring of a gift or endowment rather than financial gain. The adequacy of consideration is not to be viewed with hindsight, but it should rather be considered from the viewpoint of the parties at the time the deed was executed. The ordinary standard for testing the adequacy of consideration to support a transfer of property is not applicable to a deed conveying realty on condition that the grantee care for the grantor during the remainder of the grantor's life because of the uncertainty of life involved in such agreements. In considering the adequacy of consideration of a promise to care for and support a grantor for the remainder of his life in exchange for a conveyance of land, conditions existing at the time the contract is made are controlling, and subsequent events, such as the early death of the person to be cared for cannot be used to determine the adequacy of the consideration.*

The trial court also found that the plaintiff's love and affection for their son Ernest was both a motivating factor and part of the consideration for the transaction.

Natural love and affection has always been held to be sufficient consideration for a deed where the relationship of the parties is such as to justify the presumption that love and affection exists.

The love and affection the plaintiffs [parents] felt toward Ernest is evidenced by the fact that, as stated in the agreement, the land in question had been devised to Ernest by the wills of both Louis and Margaret, and nine days after the land was conveyed to Ernest and the defendant [Pearl], Louis and Margaret executed new wills, each of which contained this provision:

I have purposely omitted my son, Ernest Mongeon, as a devisee or legatee under this Will, for the reason that my [wife, Margaret Mongeon] [husband, Louis Mongeon] and I have made disposition of substantial farmlands to him during our lifetime for a fair consideration . . . [emphasis added].

We conclude that, in the absence of a finding of fraud or undue influence, the evidence is sufficient to support a finding that there was adequate consideration to uphold the conveyance of the land from the plaintiffs to Ernest and the defendant.

Judgment affirmed.

Discussion Questions

1. What was the relationship between Louis and Margaret and Ernest and Pearl?
2. How much land was conveyed?
3. What was the total price?
4. How was the price to be paid?
5. How old were Louis and Margaret at the time of the conveyance?
6. Was there consideration?

SPECIFIC REQUIREMENTS FOR THE REAL ESTATE CONTRACT

In addition to meeting the common law requirements just discussed, parties desiring to execute a valid real estate purchase contract must also meet certain specific requirements that apply to real estate contracts in particular. These requirements are: (1) that the contract be in writing; (2) that the signatures of the parties appear on the contract; (3) that the description of the property be included and adequate.

The Writing Requirement

As discussed in Chapter 9, contracts and deeds relating to the transfer of property must be in writing under what is termed the statute of frauds. Oral agreements for the transfer of property are unenforceable. Every state has some provision in its statute of frauds governing real estate contracts and the need for them to be in writing.

The writing need not be a formal contract: a contract and its terms may be pieced together from informal writings so long as all the requirements for formation are met and the necessary elements are present. The following case deals with this issue.

WARD v. MATTUSCHEK

330 P.2d 971 (Mont. 1958)

Otto and Frank Mattuschek (defendants/appellees) owned a ranch in Montana consisting of 3540 acres. Carnell, a real estate broker, discovered their interest in selling the ranch and the following instrument was executed:

PLAINTIFF'S EXHIBIT "A"
APPOINTMENT OF AGENT

I hereby appoint E. F. Carnell of Lewistown, Montana whose office is located in said City and State, my agent with the exclusive right to sell the following property:

Our Ranch property 3540 acres, T.23 & 22-R-19 & 20-Fergus County Mont.

———————

For the Sum of <u>$30,000</u>.

Conditions and terms of the sale are as follows:

Cash to seller. Possession Dec. 1–1953, seller retain 5% landowner Royalty. Seller pay 1953 taxes, seller transfers all lease land to buyer.

And I agree to furnish a title as outlined in the following paragraph:

A———————

A. An abstract of title showing a good merchantable title to said property together with a warranty deed properly executed.

Said sale may be made for a less amount if hereafter authorized by me; you are further authorized to receive a deposit on the sale price. I agree to pay a commission of $1000—on the sale price and the commission shall be payable as soon as the sale is made and a down payment has been made, or sale price paid in full at the time of sale, and, or as soon as a binder fee has been collected on the sale, whichever be first.

This authorization is to remain in effect and full force for 30 days and thereafter until revoked by me in writing.

Dated at Lewistown, Montana this 14th day of May 1953—

x <u>Otto Mattuschek</u>
x <u>Frank Mattuschek</u>

Carnell then met Ward (plaintiff/appellant), a prospective buyer, and accepted from him a check for $2,500 as a binder. The check looked as follows:

PLAINTIFF'S EXHIBIT "B"

1st   93-73
                                                                    921

Bank
Stock   First National Bank of Lewistown
Corporation

                Lewistown, Montana, May 20 1953   No. ____

Pay
To The   00
Order of _____ Red Carnell _____ $2500xx

————twenty five hundred and no/100————Dollars

                                                    s/s E. E. Ward

For down Payment on land

        Mattuschek

[Endorsement E. F. Carnell]

At the same time Carnell executed the following:

PLAINTIFF'S EXHIBIT "C"

(Defendant's Exhibit no. 1)

Real Estate	Fergus Realty	City Property
Insurance	213 Main St. Phone 598	Farms
Rentals	Lewistown, Montana	Ranches

                        May 20 – 1953—

        I hereby agree to buy the Mattuschek place in accordance with
the terms of the agreement between E. F. Carnell and the Mattuscheks.
Dated May 14, 1953.

                                                    /s/ E. E. Ward

        To Buy Or Sell—See "Red" Carnell

        Carnell drove to the ranch and advised the Mattuscheks of the sale. They asked if Ward would be willing to lease back the property. When the closing was attempted the Mattuscheks refused to convey the property, and the Wards filed suit seeking specific performance and damages. The trial court held the writings did not meet the statute of frauds requirements. Ward appealed.

FALL, District Judge

One of the questions presented is whether the writings (Plaintiff's Exhibits "A," "B" and "C") are sufficient to take the case out of the Statute of Frauds.

Few more fruitful sources of litigation can be found than that arising out of brokerage contracts relating to the sale of real estate.

Much of the briefs and a great part of oral argument was directed toward the question of the right of a real estate broker to enter into a contract for the sale of the seller's land. As we view it, for reasons hereinafter stated, that is not before this court on this appeal.

The note or memorandum must name the parties. It may consist of several writings.

The note or memorandum must contain all the essentials of the contract but may be stated in general terms.

With the foregoing principles of law in mind, an examination of Plaintiff's Exhibits "A," "B" and "C" shows the following:

The respondents Mattuscheks unqualifiedly and exclusively agreed in writing to permit Carnell for a period of thirty days to sell their ranch for $30,000 for which they agreed to pay Carnell a commission of $1,000. The terms of sale were succinctly but adequately stated in these words: "Cash to seller. possession Dec. 1–1953, seller retain 5% landowner, Royalty. seller pay 1953 taxes, seller transfers all lease land to buyer."

The acceptance of Ward was in writing (Plaintiff's Exhibit "C"), and accompanied by a check (Plaintiff's Exhibit "B") as a down payment. It was unqualified. It is difficult to conceive of a more clear-cut offer and acceptance in writing than is evidenced in the exhibits above set forth. This is not a situation of a broker making a contract for the seller at all—it is simply a situation of a buyer executing, in writing, an unqualified acceptance of a seller's offer to sell.

It is well established that a court, in interpreting a written instrument, will not isolate certain phrases of that instrument in order to garner the intent of the parties, but will grasp the instrument by its four corners and in the light of the entire instrument, ascertain the paramount and guiding intention of the parties. Mere isolated tracts, clauses and words will not be allowed to prevail over the general language utilized in the instrument.

The further question has been presented that the offer executed by the Mattuscheks fails insofar as this plaintiff is concerned because of lack of mutuality, i.e., that Ward did not sign the contract executed by the Mattuscheks. Ordinarily, both parties to a written agreement execute it, but that is not always necessary. "While an agreement signed by one party only, without other evidence of obligation on, or acceptance by, the other party, will ordinarily be regarded as unilateral, mutuality does not require that both parties sign the contract, and if a contract signed by one party is acted upon by the other a binding agreement may result."

This court has said: " . . . plaintiff contends that the letter, Defendant's Exhibit 1, is not a contract because it is signed by only one party, and hence lacking in mutuality. It is signed, however, by the only party affected and bound by it, and it constituted a written offer by plaintiff."

The two general rules as to the party or parties who must sign the memorandum are that a party not signing the memorandum cannot be charged on the contract, and that the only signature made necessary by the statute [of frauds] is that of the party to be charged, or, in other words, defendant in the action or the party against whom the contract is to be enforced. Mutuality of obligation is not essential to the validity of a contract, insofar as its compliance with the statute of frauds is concerned, and the fact that the contract may not be enforceable against one party, because not subscribed by him, is no defense to the other, by whom it is signed.

The rule was established soon after the enactment of the statute of frauds, that a contract, the memorandum of which was signed by the defendant, may be specifically enforced by a plaintiff who has not signed, notwithstanding because of the lack of such signature this contract could not be enforced against plaintiff, either in law or in equity, up to the time of the commencement of the suit, since the requisite mutuality is supplied by complainant's filing of his bill.

Nor can objection be made on the part of the defendants that their offer was not intended for this particular plaintiff and hence, fails for lack of mutuality. It is the rule that if the memorandum is otherwise sufficient it is binding for the purpose of satisfying the statute of frauds, "even though it is not intended for, or addressed, delivered, or known to, the other contracting party."

However, all this is somewhat beside the point for the reason that the plaintiff, as pointed out above, accepted the offer of defendants, in writing and without qualification.

Reversed.

ADAIR, Justice

I dissent.

The instrument designated "Appointment of Agent" between the real estate agent, E. F. Carnell, and signed by Otto and Frank Mattuschek is simply a thirty day listing agreement. It does not constitute a power of attorney. It does not authorize the real estate agent to execute or deliver in the name of the Mattuscheks any deed of conveyance or any Contract for sale and purchase. It is purely and simply an agreement between the real estate agent and the owners of the 3,540 acre ranch. Should the Mattuscheks wrongfully fail to perform their part of the agreement, the only loss to the real estate agent would be his commission of $1,000 to become due him upon a sale by the Mattuscheks of their property. Such would be the extent of the real estate agent's damage and it could be fully satisfied by the payment of money.

Discussion Questions

1. Who owns the property at issue?
2. Who is the broker?
3. Who is the buyer?
4. What three writings are submitted as evidence to satisfy the statute of frauds?
5. Is there an issue of Carnell's authority to enter into the agreement?
6. Is there sufficient writing to satisfy the statute of frauds?
7. Why does the dissenting justice disagree?

One of the exceptions to the writing requirement for land contracts under the statute of frauds is the doctrine of part performance. Under this doctrine, a party may be entitled to enforce an oral agreement for the sale of property if certain conduct can be established. Under Section 197 of the Restatement of Contracts, the party seeking to invoke the protection of the doctrine of part performance must establish one of the following:

1. That valuable improvements have been made to the property; or
2. That there has been full or partial payment of the purchase price *and* that the paying party has possession of the property.

The reasoning behind this exception is that establishing that either criterion has occurred provides some tangible physical evidence that an agreement exists. In other words, if a contract did not exist, why would the improvements have been made, or why was payment accepted and a party permitted to possess the property? While some states do not recognize the doctrine of part performance at all, the states that do recognize it require possession to be established. In addition, some states require payment, or improvements, or both. The following case illustrates the application of the doctrine of part performance.

RICHARDSON v. FIELDS
527 P.2d 708 (Oreg. 1974)

In 1961 the father of Nancy Richardson (plaintiff) and of Dellard Fields (defendant), along with his wife Dorothy Fields (appellant), purchased 10 acres of land near Grants Pass, Oregon. His payments were $50 per month. Soon after taking possession the father sold the property to Fields, who made the $50 payments, took possession of the property, and built a house on it. In 1967 Fields moved and rented the house to Kelley. Richardson alleged that in 1968 she and Fields entered into an oral agreement for her to buy the property for a price of $7,250.68, consisting of a down payment in the form of a boat, trailer, and three motors; plus payment of the mortgage; and $4,500 after the mortgage was paid. Fields took possession of the boat, trailer, and motors and sold them. Richardson moved onto the land, improved the road leading to the house, installed a hot water tank, wall gas furnace, bathroom fixtures, septic tank, and a drain field. They paid the taxes, insurance, and mortgage payments.

In 1973 Fields refused to give the deed to the property to Richardson or sign any contract or escrow instructions. Richardson brought suit. The trial court entered an order of specific performance on the basis of the doctrine of part performance, and Fields appealed.

LEAVY, Justice Pro Tem

One of the tests for ordering specific performance of an oral contract is that the proof must be clear, unequivocal and by a preponderance of the evidence. We hold that the plaintiff's proof meets that standard. Considering the testimony of the parties, along with their actions consistent with and pursuant to the terms of the oral agreement and the contents of the writing signed by defendants and the deed, we find that the terms are shown by full, complete and satisfactory proof to have been so precise that neither party could reasonably misunderstand them.

The appellant contends that because of unfairness and inequality of the terms and circumstances of the contract, a court of equity should refuse relief. The argument is based largely upon the 1968 contract price compared to evidence of 1973 market value. Ordinarily the fairness of a contract should be determined in light of the circumstances as they existed at the time of the making, and the adequacy of consideration for property should also be determined as of the making of the contract rather than according to the increased value at the time of trial. We find nothing inequitable about the price or other terms of the agreement.

Finally, appellant [Dorothy Fields] claims that she is the victim of a conspiracy to take her property for less than its value and that plaintiffs have taken undue advantage of the relationship of her husband as brother to plaintiff Nancy Richardson. She says that she is an uneducated woman who has been subjected to arguments, threats, misrepresentations and physical punishment, all of which show a lack of clean hands of plaintiffs.

We do not find that the plaintiffs were responsible for such actions nor that such actions caused appellant to enter the contract now being enforced, nor do we find her lacking in capacity. On the occasion when physical force was used, the suit had already been filed. The agreement had already been entered into and the documents evidencing it had already been signed. As we have noted, her husband conveyed his interest in the property to her shortly after the case was filed. The deed recites as consideration the sum of the one dollar and says, "Consideration consists additionally of love and affection and other value given." From the evidence before us we cannot say the appellant's difficulties with her husband can be blamed upon the plaintiffs to defeat their remedy of specific performance.

The decree requires that the contract be performed according to the terms of the agreement signed by the defendants. That writing has a date of January 31, 1972, and calls for interest at 6% on unpaid balances from that date. The plaintiff Nancy Richardson testified that in arriving at the oral agreement in February 1968 it was agreed that interest would be paid.

We find that interest at the rate of 6% per annum on unpaid balances should run from February 1, 1968, the date of the oral agreement, which also is the approximate date on which the plaintiffs began to treat the property as their own.

The decree is affirmed.

Discussion Questions

1. What is the relationship between Dellard Fields and Nancy Richardson?

2. What payment was made on the property?

3. What improvements were made?

4. Is there sufficient basis for enforcing the oral agreement?

5. What additional problem did Dorothy raise?

(11.6) Consider:

Hancock Construction maintained that it had an oral agreement to purchase property from Kempton & Snedigar Dairy. On the basis of the oral contract, Hancock had engineering studies done on the property and arranged to obtain a loan for $292,830. Kempton & Snedigar refused to go through with the contract alleging a defense of the statute of frauds. Hancock brought suit for specific performance relying on the doctrine of part performance. What was the result?

Signatures of the Parties

One requirement of a written contract is that the signatures of the parties must appear. If several writings are used to satisfy the contract requirement, the signatures of the parties must be found somewhere in each of those writings.

Perhaps the most important aspect of obtaining signatures for a contract is to make sure that all signatures necessary to bind the party appear. In the case of joint owners both signatures are necessary, and in many states the signatures of both husband and wife are required. The signature lines will generally appear as follows on a formal contract:

_____	_____
Purchaser or Buyer	Seller
_____	_____
Purchaser or Buyer	Seller

In the cases of business organizations such as partnerships and corporations, it is necessary to ensure that the parties signing possess sufficient authority to transfer property and that they properly indicate the capacity in which they are signing. (See Figure 9.1.) For example, a corporate officer signing for the corporation should have the following signature line:

ABC Company, Inc.

by _____
      Steven Doe, President

Attest _____
      John Doe, Secretary

An attest line (as shown in the preceding example) is also included if a second officer's signature is required.

Adequate Description of the Property

To satisfy the statute of frauds the property to be conveyed must be identified. Although in most states including the legal description is not required for the purchase contract, it is perhaps the best way to reasonably identify the property and avoid confusion. If the description used does not clearly indicate what land is being conveyed, then the writing will not satisfy the statute of frauds and the contract will be unenforceable. (See Chapter 8 for further discussion.)

TERMS OF THE PURCHASE CONTRACT

Satisfying the minimum requirements for the real estate purchase contract is not terribly troublesome for buyers and sellers. Most difficulties arise because the parties do not carefully set forth the details and terms of the sale. For although the statute of frauds permits the enforcement of fairly simple agreements, the desires of the parties may not be met unless the terms are clearly set forth in the agreement.

A complete contract begins with a careful review and inspection of the property. Figure 11.2 is a checklist for buyers to complete before purchasing any property.

Once the parties have completed their preliminary investigations and negotiations, it is necessary to execute a formal contract reflecting their desires. Many parties elect to sign a binder followed by a formal purchase contract. Such binders can be hazardous for two reasons: On one hand, the binder may be so loosely drafted that the parties really have no protections and no locked-in price or terms. On the other hand, the binder may be drafted carefully enough so as to legally bind the parties but it may not contain all the terms desired, and the parties may be bound by a general agreement not reflective of the details of their understanding. Therefore, it is best for the parties to have an agreement that irons out all their understandings and details, so that a contract based on their desires either will or will not go through. Each portion of the real estate contract is discussed in detail in the following sections. Although some portions may not be appropriate for every transaction, they are included to make purchasers and sellers aware of all possible contingencies.

Title and Introduction

The title of a purchase contract seems insignificant on its face, but the wrong title can lead to litigation if it creates an ambiguity or causes confusion about

Figure 11.2 *Checklist for Negotiating Real Estate Contracts*

1. Determine exact boundaries of buildings, driveways, and fences.
2. Determine easements and underground utilities.
3. Determine zoning laws and other governmental regulations applicable to property.
4. Determine future or present uses of surrounding property.
5. Determine quality of available utilities and fire protection.
6. Determine rights-of-way or easements if necessary for use of property.
7. Determine locations of schools, public transportation, churches, and shopping centers.
8. Determine physical condition of building: termites, plumbing, electric, and water in basement.
9. Determine traffic conditions on street and surrounding streets.
10. Determine possible changes in traffic and street structure (such as a proposed freeway).
11. Determine possible nuisances: factories, aircraft, playgrounds, smoke, fumes, and noise.
12. Determine title: judgments and assessments.
13. Determine status of inhabitants (if any).
14. Determine soil suitability if intention is to build.
15. Determine if seller is married or was previously married.
16. Determine utility costs.
17. Determine reputation of builder if new development, verify warranties, approval, conformity with Interstate Land Sales Full Disclosure Act (ILSFDA), bonding, and licensing of builder.
18. Determine if any warranty protection is available.
19. Determine whether any toxic wastes exist or have existed on the property and whether any environmental agencies have actions pending.
20. Determine whether the property is located in a natural hazard area: faults, flood-plains, or shifting soil.

the parties' intentions. For example, a contract in which a definite purchase is desired should not be labeled as an option. Such a title would only create a conflict between title and terms and could result in unnecessary litigation. Appropriate titles for a purchase contract are: "Agreement to Purchase and Sell Real Property"; "Contract for the Purchase of Real Property"; "Real Estate Purchase Contract and Receipt for Deposit"; or "Contract for the Purchase of Land." Nebulous titles such as "Agreement," "Commitment," or "Binder" should be avoided.

The purposes of the introduction are to reemphasize the type of document being executed and to establish the date of the transaction. The following are examples of introductory phrases:

1. This agreement to purchase and sell real property dated
   _____, 19___ . . .
2. This agreement made and entered into this _____ day of
   _____, 19___ . . .
3. This agreement entered into and executed in triplicate this
   _____ day of _____, 19___ . . .

Many standard forms begin with a clause such as "Received from _____ this _____, 19___, as Buyer who will take title. . . ." The difficulty with such a form is that it does not, at the outset, strongly establish the intent to be bound and agree to terms. The language begins the contract as if its major purpose were a receipt for a deposit, when in fact its major purpose is an agreement to buy and sell property.

Identification of the Parties

Following the introductory phrase in the purchase contract will be the identification of the parties. For example, the following language may be used:

This agreement made and entered into this _____day of _____, 19___, between _____, hereinafter referred to as "Seller," and _____, hereinafter referred to as "Buyer."

Many times, a contract hereinafter refers to a "party of the first part" and a "party of the second part," but using seller and buyer is clearer and also serves as an indicator of the parties' intent to enter into a purchase contract.

It is at this stage of the real estate transaction that the authority and exact names of the parties should be established. If such problems are handled before a binding agreement is signed, then the execution of the deed and proper transfer will be completed without the need for supplements to the contract or time extensions. In filling in the parties' names to a contract, the following information should be obtained:

1. Name: full name, aliases, and AKAs (also known as). How does seller's name appear on deed granting title?
2. Marital status.
3. If legal entity (corporation) is involved
   a. Place incorporated and proper corporate name.
   b. Name of president.
   c. Name of secretary.
   d. Authority of individual signing.

4. If partnership is involved
   a. Proper partnership name.
   b. Type of partnership (general or limited).
   c. Name of partner.
   d. Authority of partner.
5. If executor for estate is involved
   a. Name of estate.
   b. Executor's name and aliases.
   c. Executor's appointment and authority.
6. If agent acting for another is involved
   a. Name of agent and aliases.
   b. Authority of agent (power of attorney).

Many forms provide space for the buyer's and seller's addresses following their names. Such additional information further identifies the parties but is not required.

Holding and Taking of Title

Many purchase contracts set forth how the sellers currently hold title and how the buyers will take title. The parties could hold title as joint tenants, tenants in common, or tenancy by the entirety, or as community property. (See Chapter 15.) A clause setting forth the type of title would follow the buyer's name and would state: "Showing title vested as tenants in common"; "Taking title as tenants in common"; "Taking title as a general partnership"; or "Taking title as husband and wife and as joint tenants with right of survivorship." Again, establishing this type of detail in the purchase agreement saves time and avoids delays in the execution of the final paperwork.

It is also in this section of the contract that the parties should specify the type of deed to be furnished by the seller, such as warranty, or special warranty.

Property Identification

In most purchase contracts (other than those for acreage) the street address will be given, followed by a clause such as, "and more particularly described as" or "more fully described as" and then the legal description. In many cases, brokers or salespersons will take the description from the listing agreement; however, caution should be used in this practice because an error in the description can be made very easily. Perhaps the best source for the description is straight from the seller's deed.

Following the legal description, a general protection clause (found in many form contracts) should be inserted and reads as follows:

> . . . together with all the right, title, and interest of the seller in and to the land lying in the streets in front of or adjoining the above described property, to the center lines thereof respectively.

If any personal property is being conveyed, a notation should be made in the contract. A clause reading "together with the following personal property . . ." may be inserted along with a list of the personal property. This clause is particularly important in the purchase of multiunit dwellings. Since the standards for what constitutes a fixture may vary, it is best to list the property included if there is any doubt. It is important to verify that the seller actually owns the personal property and whether there are any Article 9 security interests in the property. (See Chapter 6 for a full discussion of security interests.) Identification of the property by serial number may serve to assure the buyer that the same personal property that was viewed will be acquired.

Because a deed transfers title to real property only, the conveyance of title to personal property should be handled through a different document. It is wise for the contract to include a provision for a bill of sale, which is in effect a deed for personal property. Through use of this separate device, title is passed without any issue of property transference.

If there are any title limitations over the property being transferred, such as assessments, easements, or rights-of-way, they should also be noted in the contract. In many forms, a general provision appears after the description, which reads: "subject to rights, rights-of-way, easements, including those for public utilities, water companies, alleys, and streets; assessments and other encumbrances of record." If there are restrictive covenants on the property, they too should be noted in the provision. If the seller needs to reserve or grant an easement, a clause to that effect should also follow the description. An example of a reservation clause is as follows:

> Reserving for the seller, his successors, and assigns, an easement for ingress and egress over _____ of tract no. ____, for a private roadway to be used in common with the owners of the lot.

Consideration

Purchase Price The consideration given by the buyer under the contract may be paid in many different ways but should be summarized in one lump sum as in the following examples:

1. The total consideration or purchase price for the property shall be
_____ dollars (\$ _____ .00).
2. The agreed upon purchase price is _____
dollars (\$ _____ .00).

The purchase price should then be broken down into its respective elements to indicate how it will be paid. The clause that introduces these elements should include the language "and shall be paid as follows" or "to be paid as follows."

Earnest Money As discussed earlier, this payment is not required for the validity of the purchase contract but does demonstrate the buyer's good faith. The amount should be indicated in the contract along with the name of the person who is to hold the deposit for the parties. For example, the following phrases could be used:

1. \$500.00 earnest deposit payable to Security Title.
2. \$500.00 cash or check drawn to the order of _____ to be held in escrow by _____.

Additional Down Payment In most transactions, the buyer will pay additional cash at the closing of the transaction and this should be listed as an element of the purchase price:

_____ dollars (\$ _____ .00) additional down payment to be paid to _____ at or before the close of escrow.

Financing This element of the purchase price is critical and must be carefully set forth. For example, a buyer is purchasing a home for \$110,000. The earnest money is \$1,000, the additional down payment is \$19,000, and the remaining amount to be paid is \$90,000. According to the flexibility of the parties, this \$90,000 of consideration may be paid in a number of ways. The payment methods most readily used are: (1) assumption of an existing mortgage, (2) purchase money mortgage by the seller, (3) new financing, or (4) any combination of the first three.

1. Assumption of an Existing Mortgage To pay the remaining \$90,000 of the purchase price, the buyer in the example could agree to assume responsibility of the \$90,000 mortgage on the property. This means that the buyer takes over the seller's payments on the property and becomes responsible for the entire \$90,000 debt. (The problems and liabilities of assumption are discussed in Chapter 12.) A sample clause providing for assumption follows:

As part of the total purchase price, the Buyer agrees to assume and pay the existing first mortgage on the property described above with

_____ (mortgagee) and having an approximate balance of _____ dollars ($ .00), with said balance to be established by Seller furnishing a mortgagee's statement with payments of principal, interest, taxes, and insurance of $_____ per month with an annual interest rate of ____% and running until _____, 19____.

Some drafters prefer to list the exact balance at drafting and provide for an update at closing. It is important that the monthly payments, rate, and ending date of the loan are accurate. If a listing agreement is available, the figures can be found there but should be verified with the seller.

If approval by the mortgagee is required for an assumption, then a clause stating, "subject to the mortgagee's approval" should be inserted. Furthermore, some states permit the mortgagee to increase the interest rate upon assumption, and such an increase should be set forth in the contract.

2. *Purchase Money Mortgage by the Seller* In some land transfers, the seller will act as the lender either by retaining title until the money is paid or by taking a mortgage on the property. In the example, if there were no mortgage to be assumed and the $90,000 still remained to be paid, the seller could finance the buyer's purchase. The language used would be as follows:

As part of the total purchase price, Seller agrees to take a purchase money note secured by a mortgage covering the above described property in the amount of _____ dollars ($ .00), with the principal amount of the note being that sum and the rate of interest being ____% per annum, with both principal and interest payable in the amount of $_____ on the ____ day of each month beginning on the ____ day of _____, 19____, and continuing until _____, 19____, when the balance shall be paid in full.

It is further agreed that the Buyer will execute the necessary note and mortgage reflecting these terms at or before closing on the property.

The seller may ask the buyer to furnish a balance statement or credit report as a condition to the granting of the note and mortgage.

3. *New financing* To complete payment of the purchase price, the buyer may agree to obtain new financing for the balance due ($90,000 in the example). At the time the parties agree to the terms of the sale, they may have no knowledge as to whether the buyer will be able to obtain financing. Thus, when new financing is used, it is necessary for this portion of the purchase contract to be phrased as a condition precedent to performance or contingency.

A condition or contingency is an event that must occur before the parties or one party is obligated to perform under the contract. If a condition precedent drafted into a contract never occurs, then the parties are not obligated to perform but are released from their contractual obligations. Although the contract is binding and creates legal obligations, conditions or contingencies control whether those obligations must be performed.

When a buyer is seeking to pay part of the purchase price with new financing, it is important that the contract contain a clause indicating that if the buyer is unable to obtain financing, then the buyer is excused from performing. At a minimum, such a conditional clause should contain the most important terms such as the principal amount, interest rate, maturity date, amount and frequency of installments, number of points (lender's commitment fee), and source of the financing (bank, trust company, or other source). Also, the clause should place time limitations on the buyer: "The loan application must be made within 14 days of the agreement," plus a maximum time for qualification. The following is a typical conditional financing clause:

> This agreement is subject to the Buyer's securing a new first mortgage loan on the property described in this agreement in an amount of not less than _____ dollars ($ .00) from (bank, savings and loan, Federal Housing Administration, or other source), principal and interest payable in equal monthly payments of not more than $_____ at an interest rate of not more than ____% per annum, said mortgage loan being all due and payable ____ years from date of consummating this agreement.

Many times conditional financing clauses give the buyer a specified period within which to obtain financing and then give the seller the opportunity to find financing for the buyer. Such an arrangement should have carefully drafted time limits and notification requirements.

In spite of careful drafting of financing conditions, interpretive problems can still arise when the financing obtained differs slightly from the language in the contract. The following case involves interpretive problems.

LUTTINGER v. ROSEN

316 A.2d 757 (Conn. 1972)

The Rosens (plaintiffs/appellees) contracted to purchase from the Luttingers (defendants/appellants) some property in Stamford for $85,000 and paid an $8,500 deposit. The contract contained the following contingency:

. . . *subject to and conditional upon the buyers obtaining first mortgage financing on said premises from a bank or other lend-* *ing institution in an amount of $45,000 for a term of not less than twenty (20) years and at an interest rate which does not exceed 8 1/2 percent per annum.*

The Rosens agreed to use due diligence in attempting to obtain such financing. The parties further agreed that if the Rosens were unsuccessful in obtaining financing as provided in the contract, and notified the Luttingers within a specific time, all sums paid on the contract would be refunded and the contract would terminate without further obligation of either party.

In applying for a mortgage that would satisfy the contingency clause in the contract the Rosens relied on their attorney, who applied at a New Haven lending institution for a $45,000 loan at 8-1/4 percent per annum interest over a period of 25 years. The Rosens' attorney knew that this lending institution was the only one that would at that time lend as much as $45,000 on a mortgage for a single-family dwelling. A mortgage commitment for $45,000 was obtained with "interest at the prevailing rate at the time of closing but not less than 8 3/4%." Since the commitment failed to meet the contract requirement, timely notice was given to the Luttingers and demand was made for the return of the down payment. The Luttingers' counsel thereafter offered to make up the difference between the interest rate offered by the bank and the 8-1/2 percent rate provided in the contract for the entire 25 years by a funding arrangement, the exact terms of which were not defined. The Rosens did not accept this offer and, on the Luttingers' refusal to return the deposit, an action was brought. From a judgment rendered in favor of the Rosens, the Luttingers appealed.

LOISELLE, Associate Justice

The defendants claim that the plaintiffs did not use due diligence in seeking a mortgage within the terms specified in the contract. The unattacked findings by court establish that the plaintiff's attorney was fully informed as to the conditions and terms of mortgages being granted by various banks and lending institutions in and out of the area and that the application was made to the only bank which might satisfy the mortgage conditions of the contingency clause at that time. These findings adequately support the court's conclusion that due diligence was used in seeking mortgage financing in accordance with the contract provisions.

The defendants assert that notwithstanding the plaintiffs' reliance on their counsel's knowledge of lending practices, applications should have been made to other lending institutions. This claim is not well taken. The law does not require the performance of a futile act.

The remaining assignment of error briefed by the defendants is that the court erred in concluding that the mortgage contingency clause of the contract, a condition precedent, was not met and, therefore, the plaintiffs were entitled to recover their deposit. "A condition precedent is a fact or event which the parties intend must exist or take place before there is a right to performance." If the condition precedent is not fulfilled the contract is not enforceable. In this case the language of the contract is unambiguous and clearly indicates that the parties intended that the purchase of the defendant's premises be conditioned on the obtaining by the plaintiffs of a mortgage as specified in the contract. From the subordinate facts found the court could reasonably conclude that since the plaintiffs were unable to obtain a $45,000 mortgage at no more than 8 1/2 percent per annum interest "from a bank or other lending institution" the condition precedent to performance of the contract was not met and the plaintiffs were entitled to the refund of their deposit. Any additional offer by the defendants to fund the difference in interest payments could be rejected by the plaintiffs.

Affirmed.

Discussion Questions

1. What was the purchase price?
2. Who was the buyer? Who was the seller?
3. What financing terms were set forth in the condition?
4. What financing commitment was obtained?
5. What did the Luttingers offer to do?
6. Did the Rosens have to take the offer?
7. Was the condition satisfied?
8. Were the Rosens required to apply at more than one institution?

(11.7) Consider:

Highlands Plaza, Incorporated, entered into an agreement to purchase property from Viking Investment Corporation. The purchase was conditioned upon Highlands obtaining a $125,000 mortgage on the property. Highlands was able to obtain the $125,000 only through a first and second mortgage with different institutions, but still sought to go through with the sale. Viking refused on the grounds that the financing condition was not met. Highlands has brought suit for specific performance. What is the result?

4. Combinations of Financing Methods The buyer can pay the purchase price through a combination of methods 1 to 3. Thus, in the same example of a buyer purchasing a home for $110,000, the financing might be arranged as follows: If the property was already mortgaged for $78,000, the buyer could pay $1,000 earnest money, put $19,000 down, and assume the $78,000 mortgage; and the seller could take a second mortgage and carry the remaining $12,000. This arrangement could be written in the contract as follows:

The purchase price of one hundred ten thousand dollars ($110,000.00) is to be paid as follows:

a. $ 1,000.00 Earnest money to be deposited with ABC escrow in the form of cash or check
b. $19,000.00 Additional down payment to be paid on or before the close of escrow
c. $78,000.00 Approximate balance of first mortgage with California Pacific Mortgage to be assumed by the buyer with monthly payments of principal, interest, taxes, and insurance of _____ due and payable on the ____ day of each month and an annual rate of ____%, with final payment being made on _____, 19____.
d. $12,000.00 Buyer agrees to execute note and second mortgage to seller on the above described property in the amount of $12,000 at a rate of ____% per annum

payable in monthly installments of _____
on the _____ day of each month beginning on the
_____ day of _____, 19____.

Property Reports

Often buyers contract to purchase property before actually knowing the condition (in detail) of the property. However, the contract may require, as conditions precedent to the buyer's performance, the furnishing of certain expert reports on the property. One such condition often inserted in the contract is the furnishing of a clean termite report. An example of such a clause is as follows:

> The Sellers shall, at their expense and prior to closing, furnish the Buyers with a certificate from a reputable exterminator (a) certifying that the building(s) are free and clear from infestation and any resulting damage caused by termites or other wood-boring insects, and (b) guaranteeing such status for a period of one year from the date of closing. If such infestation or damage is found, buyer shall have the option of terminating all rights and obligations under this contract or requiring the sellers to cure and/or repair any infestation or damage on the property caused by termites or other wood-boring insects.

Another type of report buyers may require in conditional form is a soil report, particularly in circumstances where buyers are purchasing land for development and construction. The quality of the soil will control the feasibility of constructing homes or other buildings on the property.

In recent years, it has become critical for buyers to verify the status of the property with respect to its condition and with regard to certain environmental concerns. In many transactions, it has become standard procedure for the parties to make inquiries of governmental agencies regarding the presence of toxic waste on the property or its previous use for toxic waste disposal. State and federal environmental agencies are asked to check their files to determine whether any actions or investigations regarding the property are pending or have been taken (see Chapter 22).

Also, many parties to purchase contracts will request geological reports to determine whether the property is a risk because of its location in a fault or floodplain.

Condition of the Premises

To provide assurance for the buyer that the property will not be substantially damaged between the time of purchase and the time of closing, a conditional clause on the property's condition should be put in the contract. In addition, any repairs the buyer feels must be made should also be included as conditions to the buyer's performance. The following clause would be appropriate:

> The Sellers agree to keep the property in the same condition as it exists as of the date of the contract. Sellers further agree to repair the following items: _____ _____
> _____. If such repairs are not completed or if the condition of the property has deteriorated, the buyers shall have the option of terminating all rights and obligations under this contract, or having said repairs made, or having conditions corrected at the sellers' expense, or requiring sellers to make said repairs or remedies.

In recent years, the issue of whether warranties are made from the seller to the buyer in the transfer of real property has become often litigated. The following article summarizes the history of home warranties and their current status to date.

HOMEOWNER WARRANTIES: IMPLICATIONS FOR BUYERS AND BUILDERS *Arizona Business,* April 1980

For most Americans, the purchase of a home is the single largest investment of a lifetime. This investment means that about 30 percent of a family's disposable income will be used to make monthly payments on the home. These substantial expenditures are being made by more and more Americans each year. Despite the magnitude of the investment and the numbers of Americans who are investing, investors have remained relatively unprotected. The Federal Trade Commission (FTC) estimates that 10 percent of new homes have major defects such as inadequate insulation or faulty plumbing.[1] In a survey of the Department of Housing and Urban Development (HUD), 42 percent of the families surveyed had unexpected repairs in the first two years of ownership costing an average of $500 each, and 11 percent had repair costs of over $1,000. The defects manifested themselves after some occupation in the home, with 55 percent occurring in the first six months and 80 percent occurring in the first year.

Caveat emptor has been the philosophy of the courts and legislatures in challenges by buyers on the quality of their home construction. However, with the advent of consumerism, even this long-standing philosophy is beginning to suffer the consequences of new theories for home buyer protection. In the late 1960s, courts began to develop means for buyers to recover damages when foundations sank, roofs leaked, and plaster cracked. The purpose of this article is to discuss the change

[1]Federal Trade Commission, "Housing Policy Session," November 6, 1978, pp. 1 and 38.

in the law on new home defects from *caveat emptor* to the current protective provisions now afforded home buyers and the effects of these protections on the homebuilding industry.

Traditional Theories

The doctrine of *caveat emptor* or "let the buyer beware" originally applied to real property purchases. In sixteenth century England the courts felt that a buyer had opportunities to inspect the potential purchase before closing, and defects could thus be located and corrected. The buyer's failure to inspect the property constituted a waiver of his right to correction. This notion of responsibility on the buyer also existed in the sale of goods. Problems with homes or goods, once the sale had occurred, left the buyer without remedy. Although in retrospect the doctrine seems harsh, it was a notion engrained in the legal system for over 300 years.

This doctrine of *caveat emptor* was fortified by another common law doctrine that was just as aged—the doctrine of merger. The doctrine, simply stated, is that once the buyer has received the deed transferring the property to him, any rights or duties that were in the sales contract but are not in the deed are lost.[2] Most standard real estate contract forms contain some warranties on "workmanlike" construction. However, since the deed would contain no promises or warranties regarding construction of the home, delivery of the deed would serve to waive the buyer's rights for contractual breach. The effect of the doctrine of merger is to prevent buyers from recovering damages where a contractual promise on construction was part of the original bargain.[3] The reason for the doctrine was to prevent recovery by buyers in reliance upon over zealous salespersons' statements. Any such statements are merged upon delivery of the deed, with the unfortunate side effect of all other promises being merged.

These traditional doctrines presented substantial barriers to those attempting recovery, and both the judiciary and the legislative branches recognized the need for some buyer protection. In spite of the recognition of need, protection for buyers had developed conservatively and slowly.

Federal, State and Local Regulations

Attempts to assist the home purchaser have been varied in approach and effect; on the local level, building codes have been enacted to ensure builder compliance with health and safety regulations and with certain minimum construction standards. State and local building codes regulate construction, electrical systems, plumbing, heating, mechani-

---

[2]See *Snyder* v. *Griswold*, 37 Ill. 216 (1865); *Weber* v. *The Aluminum Ore Co.*, 304 Ill. 273, 136 N.E. 685 (1922).

[3]It should be noted that the doctrine of merger is applicable only in situations where the delivery of the deed is contemplated as full performance. *Shelby* v. *Chicago* and E.I.R., 143 Ill. 385, 32 N.E. 438 (1892).

cal, energy, fire safety, fire prevention and gas installation. These codes are based, for the most part, on "model" codes written by private groups: The International Association of Plumbing and Mechanical Officials drafted the *Uniform Plumbing Code;* and the National Fire Protection Association drafted the *National Electrical Code.* The result of this proliferation of codes and code provisions has been increasingly strict and complex regulation.

An inevitable result of such regulation is an increase in cost to both builder and buyer—often an excessive increase. These cost increases were protested by consumers and builders, and Congress reacted with the Housing Act of 1949. Under the act, urban renewal grant decisions were made after the Department of Housing and Urban Development (HUD) determined whether the locality applying had encouraged housing cost reductions through the use of new materials and techniques and through elimination of restrictive code provisions. HUD was able to eliminate restrictive provisions in approximately 4,000 localities' codes until their power to do so was revoked in 1974.[4] The original idea was to lessen buyer protection to reduce costs; but since the 1974 revocation, HUD has avoided construction regulations with the exception of FHA and VA mortgage insurance requirements. HUD's aversion to regulation stems from the construction industry's reluctance to provide warranties or promises on quality construction. A HUD report on housing stated:

Normally, consumer protections involve some additional burdens on the lender, builder or the manager of the housing. Thus, builders have objected as to the existing requirement that they give the home purchaser a warranty against structural defects. . . . These and many other mortgage insurance requirements bear on whether a sponsor decides to use [mortgage] insurance, that affects production. Therefore, any proposed legislation for additional consumer protection or other benefits [for FHA houses alone] must be weighed against its possible curtailment of the use of the program.

The fear of desertion by builders has left HUD with the limited consumer protection for FHA buyers. This fear is also evidenced in HUD's reluctance to enforce a section of the National Housing Act. Section 518(a) of the act allows federal reimbursement to FHA homebuyers whose homes have structural defects.[5] Complaints have been received from attorneys across the country and other federal agencies on HUD's lack of enforcement.[6]

[4]See 42 U.S.C. §§1441 et seq. and 40 U.S.C. §§460 and 461.

[5]See 38 U.S.C. et seq. and 12 U.S.C. §1215 et seq.

[6]HUD's lack of enforcement of section 518(a) and 518(b) on low income houses is not justified by the statistics. Research indicates that 24 percent of newly constructed low income housing is defective and that two-fifths of that 24 percent have major defects affecting safety and health. Housing Policy, p. 13.

Private Action

Regulation has come from the builder-vendors themselves through the National Association of Homebuilders which developed its Home Owners Warranty program (HOW). The HOW program offers a method for settling claims and also offers insurance for builders who do not pay off valid claims. The effectiveness of HOW, however, is limited by the number of builders who subscribe.

A survey by a building magazine indicates that 79 percent of home buyers think a warranty is important while only 22 percent of the builders think such a guarantee is important.[7] Private action to enforce these warranties has been taken by individual builders both in the quality of construction and in follow-up repair.

These attempts to relieve home buyers are not universal in their coverage, however, and not always strong in their enforcement. The absence of effective public or private regulation sent the issue to the courts, resulting in legal remedies for affected homeowners.

Implied Warranty Theories

The void that exists through application of the common law and through lack of statutory and private remedies is being filled by laws that adopt the implied warranty theory, which basically promises consumers that the products they purchase are fit for ordinary purposes. This theory for the protection of home buyers is not a new one—it has existed in a different form under the Uniform Commercial Code (UCC). Although the code, adopted in virtually all the states, is applicable only to sales of goods, its theories have been carried over into other areas. Section 2-314 of the code gives to purchasers "an implied warranty of merchantability." The definition is as follows:

Unless excluded or modified, a warranty that the goods shall be merchantable is implied in a contract for their sale if the seller is a merchant with respect to goods of that kind.

The limitation on applicability to merchants is significant and the term is defined in section 2-104:

"Merchant" means a person who deals in goods of the kind or otherwise by his occupation holds himself out as having knowledge or skill peculiar to the practices or goods involved in the transaction or to whom such knowledge or skill may be attributed by his employment of an agent or broker or other intermediary who by his occupation holds himself out as having such knowledge or skill.

The application of this warranty to the sales of goods has had widespread effects. Recovery has been awarded for defective designs in cars, shattered glass, broken shoe heels, and other similar problems.

---

[7]"What Consumers Want in Housing," *Professional Builder*, December 1978, p. 70.

The strength of this notion has been carried over to landlord-tenant law where an implied warranty of habitability has developed. The warranty provides remedies for tenants who lease premises that are in such poor condition as to be uninhabitable. The landlord implies that the premises being leased are fit for human dwelling. Breach of the warranty entitles the tenant to rescind the lease agreement and to have prepaid deposits and rents refunded or the premises made habitable.[8]

With this extension to landlord-tenant, it was just one small step for the courts to apply the implied warranty theory to new housing. The warranty is one of habitability and fitness in new housing and, like its UCC counterpart, appears to apply only to builder-vendors, meaning that the builder-vendor is engaged in the construction business and the sale is commercial. The theory has already been adopted as law in about half the states. Basically stated, the theory holds builder-vendors liable for buyers' losses that result from construction defects. The warranty is not one that would require perfect construction but one that protects against defects that would not occur if reasonable construction methods had been used: waterproof basements under normal conditions, soil dense enough to hold the house, a roof that does not leak under normal conditions.

There are restrictions on application of the implied warranty. The warranty application has a requirement of privity which is a contractual relationship between the home purchaser and the builder. Purchasers of used homes would have no right of action against the builder.[9] Furthermore, the warranty has consistently been applied to single family dwellings and not to commercial construction.

Arizona and the Implied Warranty

Arizona just recently adopted as law the implied warranty of habitability theory in *Columbia Western Corp.* v. *Vela.*[10] The *Columbia* case dealt with the rights of several homebuyers who found, shortly after purchasing their new homes, that their soil was clay and their homes were sinking, cracking, and suffering other structural defects. These factual circumstances afforded the Court of Appeals the opportunity to consider the implied warranty theory applied by so many other courts. In the case, the plaintiffs, the Velas and the Martinezes, bought homes from Columbia Western Corporation, which was both the builder and seller of the homes that were covered by a Warranty of Completion required for VA financing.

[8]*Pines* v. *Perssion,* 14 Wis. 2d 590, 111 N.W. 2d 409, (1961); *Lemie* v. *Breeden,* 462 P. 2d 470 (Hawaii, 1969).

[9]In *Litwin* v. *Timbercrest Estates, Inc.* 37 Ill. App. 3d 956, 347 N.E. 2d 378 (1976) it was held that the original buyer cannot effectively assign his rights against the builder to the purchaser unless the defect has already been discovered by the original buyer.

[10]*Columbia Western Corp.* v. *Vela,* et al., 592 P. 2d 1295 (1979).

That warranty permitted the buyer, through written notice, to claim "substantial nonconformity" to home plans and specifications for a one-year period if defects were to occur. Columbia also provided an extended builder's warranty for an additional year.

Shortly after the plaintiffs purchased their homes, the walls began to crack. Columbia attempted repairs several times, but when repairs proved to be an inadequate solution, the plaintiffs ordered the repairs stopped and had an engineering firm examine their homes and the surrounding homes. The lab report indicated that the clay characteristics of the soil resulted in soil changes and were causing the cracking. The case went to trial, and the plaintiffs were awarded damages to the extent of the cost of repairs plus the decreased value of the property and attorneys' fees.

Columbia appealed, citing *Voight* v. *Ott*[11] for support since in that case, the Arizona Supreme Court held that implied warranties as to quality or condition do not apply to realty. The majority of the Court's opinion is spent distinguishing the *Voight* case from the case under consideration. Their initial observation summarizes the distinction, which is basically the difference between the sale of realty and the construction of realty: "In our opinion *Voight* is authority for the proposition that no implied warranties arise from the *sale* of realty, but is not dispositive of the issue of implied warranties arising out of the *construction* of new housing which ultimately becomes 'realty.' "

The Court goes on to point out three Arizona cases in which a contractor has been held to imply that the construction he undertakes, which will ultimately become realty, will be performed in a workmanlike manner. The cases involved an improperly constructed roof on a shed, improperly installed casting in a wall, and an improperly installed electrical system in a brick kiln. Although the cases do not deal squarely with the issue of builder-developer warranty, the court cites them arguably as cases in which a warranty was extended to realty and took the step so many other jurisdictions have taken to provide protection for buyers.

"Since World War II, homes have been built in tremendous numbers. There have come into being developer-builders operating on a large scale. Many firms and persons, large and small operators, hold themselves out as skilled in home construction and are in the business of building and selling to individual owners. Developers contract with builders to construct for resale. Building construction by modern methods is complex and intertwined with governmental codes and regulations. The ordinary home buyer is not in a position, by skill or training, to discover defects lurking in the plumbing, the electric wiring, the structure itself, all of which is usually covered up and not open for inspection."

The Court then held that on new-home construction, the builder-vendor implies and thus warrants that the construction was done in a workmanlike manner and that the structure is habitable.

[11]86 Ariz. 128, 341 P. 2d 923 (1969).

Implications and Effects

This new theory, which has been adopted as law in many states, has provided buyers with a means of recovery—the cost of which must be absorbed by someone, although the comfort of shifting expensive repairs to builders or insurance companies is short-lived since ultimately the cost of these repairs will be paid by the home buyer in the cost of a new home. However, warranties can also have an impact in providing incentives for builders to take precautions to ensure suitable construction.

With the adoption of protection comes the issue of whether these protective rights or warranties can be disclaimed in the construction contracts. Under the Uniform Commercial Code, the implied warranty of merchantability can be disclaimed by specific language such as "as is," "with all faults," or "there is no warranty of merchantability." Indeed such attempts have been made, but so far have been unsuccessful. In *City of Philadelphia* v. *Page,*[12] an attempted disclaimer was held invalid with the Court finding that such disclaimers would be valid only if conspicuously and clearly stated and intended by the parties.

Faced with these new buyer protections, builders may need to protect themselves. For example, the builder may want to take precautions by explaining the terms of the warranties in the written contract or in a statement signed by the buyer. The purpose of "walk-through" inspections should be explained to buyers so that buyer-caused claims can be minimized, at least for material. The implied warranty theory placed a burden on the construction industry to educate and clarify. Perhaps this burden may become a benefit as more and more builders follow the example of those who have established methods and routines designed to discover and repair defects as well as to improve the overall construction of their homes. The benefit is greater consumer satisfaction and an implied warranty in favor of homeowners that may indirectly benefit the builder-warrantors.

Conclusion

These required protections seem to place a tremendous burden on one industry; but by taking an affirmative stance with the buyer by saying, "You have these rights and you may enforce them in this manner," builders can psychologically and legally use these new protections to establish a better position for themselves and for the industry as a whole. No other industry has been required to provide so much protection for its customers. This factor can aid the new housing industry reputation, however, with continued efforts to educate and compensate new home buyers. Ultimately, the benefits of warranties to builders may outweigh the costs.

Marianne Jennings, *Arizona Business,* April 1980. Reprinted with permission.

[12]363 F. Supp. 148 (E.D. Pa. 1973).

Discussion Questions

1. What is the doctrine of *caveat emptor*?
2. What private standards exist on the quality of homes?
3. Has HUD regulated the quality of home construction?
4. What is HOW?

5. Who enjoys the protection of the implied warranty theory?
6. What was the breach of warranty in the *Columbia* case?
7. Can the implied warranty be disclaimed?

As noted in the article, the *implied warranty of habitability* protection is currently limited to purchasers of new homes, and is applied only to builders and vendors. The great number of cases decided on the issue have several consistent standards for habitability, summarized as follows:

1. It is possible for a new home to be in substantial compliance with building codes and still be uninhabitable.
2. The primary function of a new home is to shelter its inhabitants from the elements. If a new home does not keep out the elements because of a substantial defect of construction, such home is not habitable within the meaning of the implied warranty of habitability.
3. Another function of a new home is to provide its inhabitants with a reasonably safe place to live, without fear of injury to person, health, safety, or property. If a new home is not structurally sound because of a substantial defect of construction, such a home is not habitable within the meaning of the implied warranty of habitability.
4. If a new home is not aesthetically satisfying because of a defect of construction, such a defect should not be considered as making the home uninhabitable.

(11.8) Consider:

On basis of the article and the four statements on the warranty of habitability, determine whether the following defects would be a breach of the warranty. (Assume all buyers purchased new homes.)

a. A septic tank that does not function properly
b. Water seepage into a home
c. A mud slide damaging a homeowner's patio area
d. A cracked foundation
e. Cracked basement walls

Many states have passed statutes that specifically dictate when warranties are made and also codify the judicially afforded protection of the implied warranties. Over the past five years, the extent of the implied warranty protection has been extended. The following case is an illustration of that expansion.

RICHARDS v. POWERCRAFT HOMES, INC.

678 P.2d 427 (Ariz. 1984)

Richards and others (plaintiffs) purchased homes in the Indian Hills subdivision near Case Grande between 1975 and 1977. The houses had been built by Powercraft beginning in 1974. Richards bought his home, not directly from Powercraft, but as a repossessed home offered for sale by Farmers Home Administration (FHA).

After living in the home for a while, Richards discovered numerous defects including faulty water pipes; improperly leveled yards that resulted in pooling and flooding; cracking of interior and exterior walls; separation of floors from the walls; separation of driveways; and sidewalks, carports, doors, and windows that were stuck closed or could not be locked because of misalignment.

Powercraft was notified, and repair attempts brought only temporary relief.

Richards filed a complaint with the Registrar of Contractors. The Registrar found that Powercraft had failed to follow certain plans and specifications when building the homes and that it had failed to properly compact the soil beneath each home before the building began. Powercraft's license was revoked on 6 December, 1978.

Richards filed suit alleging a breach of the implied warranty that houses be habitable and constructed in a workmanlike manner. A jury awarded the plaintiffs $210,000. Powercraft appealed and the Court of Appeals reversed. Richards appealed.

GORDON, Vice Chief Justice

In setting aside the verdicts in favor of Richards, the Court of Appeals held that "there must be privity to maintain an action for breach of the implied warranty of workmanship and habitability." One basis cited for that holding was this Court's decision in *Flory v. Silvercrest Industries, Inc.*, 129 Ariz. 574, 633 P.2d 383 (1981). In *Flory*, we held that warranties implied pursuant to A.R.S. 44-2331 (the Arizona version of U.C.C. 2-314[2]) require privity. We specifically stated:

It is important to note that what we have said herein regarding the requirement of privity to recover for breach of warranty

under the Uniform Commercial Code is limited to those actions (Id. at 579, 633 P.2d at 388).

In the instant case, the warranty at issue is not implied pursuant to A.R.S. §44-2331. Rather, it is imposed by law. In *Columbia Western Corp. v. Vela*, 122 Ariz. 28, 592 P.2d 1294 (App. 1979), builder-vendors of new homes were held to impliedly warrant that construction has been done in a workmanlike manner and that the structure is habitable. The issue before us now is whether this implied warranty extends to subsequent buyers of the homes.

The courts of several states have

confronted this issue. Many of those courts have refused to extend the implied warranty of habitability to remote purchasers or to those not in privity with the builder-vendor.

Others, however, have rejected the imposition of a privity requirement and have allowed remote purchasers to maintain a cause of action against a builder-vendor for breach of the implied warranty of habitability.

We find the latter group of cases to be more in line with the public policy of this state and hold that privity is not required to maintain an action for breach of the implied warranty of workmanship and habitability.

We agree with the persuasive comments of the Wyoming Supreme Court in that:

[T]he purpose of a warranty is to protect innocent purchasers and hold builders accountable for their work. With that object in mind, any reasoning which would arbitrarily interpose a first buyer as an obstruction to someone equally deserving of recovery is incomprehensible.

In addition, such reasoning might encourage sham first sales to insulate builders from liability.

The implied warranty of habitability and proper workmanship is not unlimited. It does not force the builder-vendor to "act as an insurer for subsequent vendees." It is limited to latent defects which become manifest after the subsequent owner's purchase and which were not discoverable had a reasonable inspection of the structure been made prior to purchase. We adopt the standard set forth by the Indiana Supreme Court.

The standard to be applied in determining whether or not there has been a breach of warranty is one of reasonableness in light of surrounding circumstances. The age of a home, its maintenance, the use to which it has been put, are but a few factors entering into this factual determination at trial.

The burden is on the subsequent owner to show that the defect had its origin and cause in the builder-vendor and that the suit was brought within the appropriate statute of limitations. Defenses are, of course, available. The builder-vendor can demonstrate that the defects are not attributable to him, that they are the result of age or ordinary wear and tear, or that previous owners have made substantial changes.

In the present case, the plaintiffs met their burden and proved that the defect had its origin and cause in Powercraft. There was no indication that the original owners substantially changed the structure of the homes. The cracking of the exterior and interior walls, the separation of the floors from the walls, and the separation of the sidewalks, driveways, and carports from the homes were due to improper compacting done by Powercraft prior to building the houses coupled with an apparent systematic lack of reinforcement in the floors, walls, ceilings, and roofs of the houses. Such improper compaction and lack of structural reinforcement could not have been determined from a reasonable inspection prior to purchase. Each of the plaintiffs moved into their homes before the end of 1977. The defects became manifest only after extraordinarily heavy rains in early 1978. Therefore, all of the plaintiffs, whether or not in privity with Powercraft, are entitled to the jury verdicts rendered in their favor.

The decision of the Court of Appeals that the verdicts in favor of plaintiffs Richards be set aside is vacated; the verdicts in favor of plaintiffs are affirmed in all other respects.

Reversed.

Discussion Questions

1. What was wrong with the homes?
2. Did Richards purchase his home from Powercraft?
3. Is there privity between Richards and Powercraft?
4. Does the implied warranty protection apply?
5. Why does the court decide to extend the scope of warranty protection?
6. Was the nature of the defects part of the reason Richards is afforded warranty protection?
7. What will a builder have to prove to escape liability to a secondary purchaser?

If a buyer is not in a position of being protected by either a statutory or implied warranty, the purchase contract may still be drafted to afford protection in the event defects arise. One way to obtain such protection is to require the seller to purchase one of the available home warranty protection plans. Most policies for used homes will run for a period of a year, but varying coverage exists. The buyer should specify in the contract what type of protection is sought. Another protection can be obtained by requiring the seller to personally warrant the property. A sample seller's warranty clause follows:

> The Seller warrants that the plumbing, heating, air conditioning, and electrical systems in the buildings on the property are in good working order and condition, and will be in good working order and condition at the time of closing. In the event such items are not in working order at closing, the Seller agrees to deduct the cost of repair or replacement from the amount due from the buyer at settlement.

A seller may, on the other hand, not wish to warrant and may insist that the rather simple warranty disclaimer of "as is" appear in the contract.

Risk of Loss

In most jurisdictions, the risk of loss by fire or other casualty is with the buyer from the time the purchase contract is executed. Thus the buyer has an insurable interest at the time of the contract execution and may hold a valid policy on the property even though there is no title or possession.

However, in most cases the seller will maintain insurance on the property until the date of closing. To avoid the duplication of insurance and costs, it is quite important that the parties agree that the seller will maintain insurance on the property until closing. If the parties do agree to such an arrangement, the buyers should be added to the existing policy along with a notation establishing the buyer's interest in the property.

Recording the Contract

The purchase contract need not be recorded to be effective between the parties. The obvious danger is that without recording, the property may have liens attached and other interests recorded that would have priority over the buyer's interests. Nonetheless, throughout the country the recording of the sales contract is very uncommon. One reason for not recording is a very practical one: The contract has conditions and contingencies that might not be met; therefore, it is always subject to the buyer's default. If the recorded contract falls through, the seller is not free to sell to anyone else until a release is signed and the contract is somehow stricken from the records. Without the defaulting purchaser's signature on a release, clearing the contract could be an expensive matter requiring a court hearing. It is best to put a clause in the agreement prohibiting recording.

Assignment

It is within the discretion of the parties as to whether the contract rights may be assigned. As discussed earlier in the chapter, the death of a party once the contract has been executed does not terminate the parties' responsibilities; and in that sense the contract is assigned to executors, heirs, and devisees. Voluntary inter vivos transfers of the contract rights may be prohibited or controlled with the proper clause in the agreement. The following clause serves to restrict, but not prohibit assignments.

> The parties expressly agree and understand that the Buyer may not transfer or assign this Agreement without first obtaining the written consent of the Seller.

Possession

In most transactions possession is delivered when the closing of the property occurs, and the simple language providing for such is "Possession shall be delivered at the close of escrow." If the buyer is taking possession prior to closing, it may be necessary for the parties to draw up a simultaneous lease to cover the time when the buyer is in possession prior to ownership. A daily damage provision may be included for the seller's failure to deliver possession:

> In the event the seller does not surrender possession at the close of escrow, the seller shall pay to the buyer the sum of _____ dollars ($ .00) per day for each day until possession is surrendered to the buyer.

Closing Date and Escrow Instructions Although the purchase contract establishes the terms of the sale, it does not contain all the details for the execution of documents, transfer of title, and payment of money. The purchase contract will provide a date for the closing of escrow, such as in the following clause:

1. Closing shall take place within _____ days of the date of this agreement.
2. Closing shall be on _____, 19____.

In many states the closing is handled by a third party (see Chapter 13), and a contract is required among the buyer, seller, and third party to properly complete the transaction. It is necessary to have a clause in the purchase contract that requires the parties to execute such an agreement, and the standard forms provide:

> Buyer and Seller shall execute escrow instructions to fulfill the terms hereof and deliver the same to the escrow agent within 15 days of the date of execution of this agreement.

Also, if applicable a simple clause, such as "time is of the essence in the performance of this agreement," may be included to indicate the parties' intention that delays mean the contract will not go forward. This will save the parties later problems with extensions in the execution of the contract. Without an indication of the parties' intent, the courts are likely to permit reasonably timely performance that may not comply with the time limits the parties wished to be absolute.

Leases

It is important that the purchase contract establish the rights of lessees who might be in possession of the property at the time of closing. The existence of the lease and its status may be indicated by a simple clause following the description of the property as follows:

> Subject to that lease dated _____, 19____ between _____, lessor, and _____, lessee, and running until _____, 19____.

Apportionments

Unfortunately, the transfer of property cannot always be accomplished at times when taxes, insurance, and rent are due. Usually the property is transferred after the parties have prepaid insurance premiums or taxes or after they have received advance rent from lessees. To be absolutely fair to the parties, the amounts involved must be apportioned between the buyer and seller as of the transfer of title date. Specific clauses may be used for the apportionment of each type of fund, or a general apportionment clause may be used. The following are examples of specific types of clauses:

1. **PRORATION OF RENT**

    All rent on any and all portions of the property shall be pro-rated to the date of closing, with the seller receiving all rents due to the date of closing and the buyer receiving all rents due thereafter. All prepaid rents shall be prorated in the same manner.

2. **TAXES**

    All taxes due and owing on the property shall be prorated to the date of closing, with the seller paying all taxes due to the date of closing and the buyer paying all taxes due thereafter. Any prepaid taxes shall be prorated in the same manner.

A general clause includes all types of payments and receipts:

Prorations of taxes, interest, rents, and any assessments shall be as of the date of close of escrow.

Marketable Title

The clause on marketable title in the purchase contract is a condition precedent to the buyer's performance that requires the seller to deliver a certain quality of title. The clause may be very simple, requiring the seller to furnish a title insurance policy, or it may be demanding and restrictive, by requiring the seller to remove liens or obtain zoning changes. The following are examples of title clauses:

1. In the event title to said property herein described is found by a title insurance company to be unmarketable at the time of closing, the purchaser is excused from performance.

2. Seller agrees to deliver marketable title as evidenced by a standard form Owners Title Insurance Policy issued by a qualified title insurance company, subject only to: all covenants, reservations, conditions, and restrictions of record and utility easements; ordinances regulating the use and occupancy of said property; current undue taxes and taxes which may be a lien but the amount of which is not yet determined; nondelinquent assessments including assessments for improvements initiated but which have not yet become

liens; and any charges which may be assessed against the property by reason of its inclusion in any improvement district as of date of closing sale; and the unpaid balance of any mortgage or deed of trust of the seller.

3. Title to the premises shall be good and marketable and free and clear of all liens, restrictions, easements, encumbrances, leases, tenancies, and other title objections, and shall be insurable as such at ordinary rates by any reputable title insurance company selected by the buyer.

Although each of the clauses differs substantially, there is one term used in all of them: *marketable title*. The concept of marketable title is difficult to define, but generally it is a title that is free from reasonable doubt or controversy and which is not subject to any liens or encumbrances. An unmarketable title is one that has encumbrances, liens, or defects that could cause the purchaser to be subjected to adverse claims or litigation. The concept of marketable title was developed by the courts of equity, and the determination of whether a particular title meets the standard of marketability is made on a case-by-case basis. One general standard applied in reviewing the marketability of a title is, Would a prudent person accept this title in exchange for a fair purchase price? The following case involves the task of determining marketability.

KNIGHT v. DEVONSHIRE CO.
736 P.2d 1223 (Colo. 1986)

Warren A. Knight (plaintiff) and Carl Swanson entered into a contract for the sale and purchase of Swanson's real property located in Arapahoe County, Colorado, for $450,000 with an earnest money deposit of $40,000. The deposit was given to Devonshire Company (defendant) as broker for Swanson.

Pursuant to the contract, Devonshire obtained a title insurance commitment that included as an exception a mineral reservation in the United States government. When Knight received the commitment, he notified Devonshire that he considered the reservation a defect such as would render the title unmarketable. Knight demanded correction. Devonshire could not remove the exception but could only offer insurance for surface damage in the event the mineral rights were exercised. Knight did not accept the accommodation and demanded that his deposit be returned. Devonshire maintained it was ready to close and refused to return the deposit. Knight filed suit.

The trial court found for Knight and Devonshire appealed.

SMITH, Judge
A merchantable or marketable title in real estate is a title free from reasonable doubt. It means a title that is "reasonably free from such doubts as will affect the market value of the estate; one which a reasonably prudent person with knowledge of all the facts

and their legal bearing would be willing to accept."

To be marketable, a title must be such as to make it reasonably certain that it will not be called into question in the future so as to subject the purchaser to the hazard of litigation. Where no reasonably forseeable challenge to title or to the right of possession and quiet enjoyment of the property can be demonstrated, title will be determined to be marketable.

We view the decision in *Burke v. Southern Pacific R.R.*, 234 U.S. 669, 34 S.Ct. 907, 58 L.Ed. 1527 (1914), as being dispositive of the question of merchantability of the specific title in question here. That case, just as this one, involved a patent granting large tracts to the railroad. It contained a reservation, the language of which is in all material respects identical to the one here. The same reservation appeared in all patents issued to railroads between 1866 and 1904.

In *Burke,* the Supreme Court, after examining the public land laws of the United States, held that the issuance of such a patent constituted a conclusive determination by the Land Department that the lands granted were non-mineral in character. Those minerals which in fact did exist passed to the railroad, and title would not be defeated or diminished by a subsequent discovery of minerals. We interpret the *Burke* decision as holding that the "mineral lands" reservation contained in these patents, and specifically the one at issue here, is of no legal effect and, thus, void.

Under *Burke,* the only basis upon which the railroad's title to minerals could be attacked would be if the patent had been procured by fraud, and then only the government would have the right to bring an action to annul the patent. To commence such an action, however, the government would have had to file its petition within six years of the date the patent was issued.

In our view, the *Burke* court intended to dispel uncertainty as to the merchantability of title under patents containing the mineral lands exception. After reviewing and reaffirming prior decisions which had come to the same conclusions, the *Burke* court said:

Not only has the Land Department accepted them (the decisions) as determinative of the excepting cause now before us, but innumerable titles within the limits of the western railroad grants have been acquired with a like understanding and are now held in the justifiable belief that they are impregnable.

The patent in the instant case was issued in 1883 and granted described lands to the Union Pacific Railroad. This patent was issued pursuant to the congressional enactment of July 1, 1862, as amended in 1864, 1866, and 1869. Although the *Burke* case dealt with a patent issued under the enactment of July 27, 1866, we conclude its holding applies to this patent as well. The Supreme Court indicated the broad scope of its holding when it said:

The exclusion of mineral lands is not confined to railroad land grants, but appears in the homestead, desert-land, timber and stone, and other public land laws, and the settled course of decision in respect to all of them has been that the character of the land is a question for the Land Department . . . and that when a patent issues it is to be taken, upon collateral attack, as affording conclusive evidence of the non-mineral character of the land. . . ."

More recently, in *United States v. Union Pacific R.R.*, 353 U.S. 112, 77 S.Ct. 685, 1 L.Ed.2d 693 (1957), Justice Douglas noted the applicability of the *Burke* case to patents issued under the enactment of July 1, 1862. He cited specifically to *Burke* in distinguishing the validity of mineral reservations in grants of "rights-of-way" from the invalidity of mineral land exceptions in patents.

In light of the dispositive nature of the *Burke* holding, we perceive no foreseeable, or even remote, possibility of litigation here stemming from the patent's purported reservation of mineral rights.

Thus, we hold that the trial court erred in concluding that seller's title was unmarketable because of the possibility of litigation concerning the reserved mineral rights. Consequently, plaintiff's election not to proceed to closing based on this "defect" was a default under the terms of the contract, and he was not entitled to a return of his earnest money deposit.

Reversed.

Discussion Questions

1. What is the general rule on mineral rights and marketable title?
2. What is the worst that could happen if the mineral rights reservation were exercised?
3. What did the *Burke* case provide?
4. Was the title marketable?
5. Should Knight have proceeded to close?

In many purchase contracts, the seller is given a time limit within which to cure defects in title discovered before closing. For example, if the preliminary title report shows a defect, the seller may be given an extension on closing of 30 or 60 days to cure the defect.

(11.9) Consider:

The following clause is part of a sales contract for the purchase of real property.

"Title is to be conveyed free from all encumbrances except: Any state of facts an accurate survey may show, provided same does not render title unmarketable."

Upon a title search it was discovered that a telephone easement was recorded for the property, and that the height of the sidewalk on the property violated a city ordinance, although a waiver had been obtained for its construction. The title company offered to insure title except for the sidewalk waiver and the telephone easement. The buyers refuse to perform on the grounds of lack of marketable title. What is the result?

Remedies

Liquidated Damages It is probably best if the parties include a provision in the purchase contract to control what will happen if either party does not fulfill the obligations created under the contract. In most contractual provisions, the parties provide that the earnest money or deposit will be used for damages in the event of a breach by one of the parties. For this reason it is important to obtain a deposit large enough to cover damages. The following are examples of such clauses:

1. Should the undersigned Buyer fail to carry out this agreement, all money paid hereunder, including any additional earnest money, shall, at the option of the Seller, be forfeited as liquidated damages and shall be paid to or retained by the Seller, subject to deductions of broker's commission and disbursements, if any. In the event neither party has commenced a law suit within one (1) year after the closing date set forth herein, the broker is authorized to disburse the earnest money as liquidated damages, and if the seller has not notified the Buyer of election to consider the earnest money as liquidated damages within six (6) months of said closing date, broker is authorized to refund all earnest money to the Buyer.

   Should the Seller be unable to carry out this agreement by reason of a valid legal defect in title which the Buyer is unwilling to waive, all money paid hereunder shall be returned to the buyer forthwith, and this contract will be void.

2. PURCHASER'S DEFAULT

   In the event of a default by the Purchaser hereunder, Seller may elect to enforce the terms of this contract or declare a forfeiture hereunder and retain the deposit as liquidated damages.

   SELLER'S DEFAULT

   In the event of a default by the Seller hereunder, the Purchaser may elect to enforce the terms of this contract or demand and be entitled to an immediate refund of his entire deposit in full termination of this Agreement.

In most cases, the courts will enforce the earnest money retention as a valid *liquidated damages* clause; that is, a clause in which the parties agree on the amount of damages before any breach of contract occurs. However, the seller may not attempt to keep the earnest money deposit and collect actual damages in addition, for then the remedy would be viewed as a penalty and void. Also, the amount of liquidated damages must be reasonable or reflective of the potential loss the seller will suffer because of the buyer's breach.

Because of so much litigation over the validity of liquidated damage clauses, some states have passed statutes requiring that specific language be used in order to have a valid and enforceable provision for liquidated damages. Many of these statutes also require that the parties sign or initial the clause in the contract so that a court can be certain the parties were aware of its existence.

The following case deals with the issue of the reasonableness of a liquidated damage clause.

ROHAUER v. LITTLE
736 P.2d 403 (Colo. 1987)

Floyd D. and Joyce C. Little entered into a contract with Frank G. Rohauer for the sale of the Littles' home for $425,000. The contract provided for $20,000 in earnest money, which Rohauer deposited with the broker. The contract contained the following language:

3. *An abstract of title to said property, certified to date, or a current commitment for title insurance policy in an amount equal to the purchase price, at seller's option and expense, shall be furnished the purchaser on or before July 10, 1981. If seller elects to furnish said title insurance commitment, seller will deliver the title insurance policy to the purchaser after closing and pay the premium thereon.*

* * *

9. *Time is of the essence hereof, and if any payment or any other condition hereof is not made, tendered or performed as herein provided, there shall be the following remedies. In the event a payment or any other condition hereof is not made, tendered or performed by the purchaser, then this contract shall be null and void and of no effect, and both parties hereto released from all obligations hereunder, and all payments made hereon shall be retained on behalf of the seller as liquidated*

damages. In the event that the seller fails to perform any condition hereof as provided herein, then the purchaser may, at his election, treat the contract as terminated, and all payments made hereunder shall be returned to the purchaser; provided, however, that the purchaser may, at his election, treat this contract as being in full force and effect with the right to an action for specific performance and damages.

Rohauer had difficulty obtaining financing and through the broker made several alternative financing proposals to the Littles. These proposals were not acceptable to the Littles.

The title insurance commitment was obtained on 7 July 1981, but the Rohauers were not notified of the commitment until 15 July 1981. By that time, the Rohauers had stopped payment on the deposit check and had met with a lawyer. They did not close the sale. The Littles sold their home in November for $430,000.

The Littles kept the $20,000 earnest money deposit and the Rohauers brought suit for its return. The trial court found for the Littles and the appellate court affirmed. The Rohauers appealed.

QUINN, Chief Justice

The Rohauers contend that, even if they are contractually liable to the Littles, the trial court erred in enforcing the liquidated damages provision of the contract since the $20,000 earnest money greatly exceeded any actual damages suffered by the Littles. We are unpersuaded by their claim.

Unless the contract on its face establishes that the stipulated liquidated damages are so disproportionate to any possible loss as to constitute a penalty, the party challenging the liquidated damages provision bears the burden of proving that fact. The factors to be considered in determining whether an amount designated as liquidated damages is in reality a penalty, rather than a reasonable estimate of actual damages, are: (1) whether the parties intended to liquidate damages; (2) whether the amount of liquidated damages, when viewed as of the time the contract was made, was a reasonable estimate of the presumed actual damages that the breach would cause; and (3) whether, when viewed again as of the date of the contract, it was difficult to ascertain the amount of actual damages that would result from a breach.

In this case, we agree with the court of appeals that the liquidated damages provision was legally enforceable. Nothing in the record suggests that the parties did not intend the $20,000 earnest money to be retained by the sellers as liquidated damages in the event of a breach by the purchasers. Nor can we conclude that the stipulated amount of $20,000 was an un-

reasonable estimate of the actual damages likely to be incurred by the sellers as a result of the purchasers' breach of a $425,000 contract. When the contract was made it was not unreasonable for the parties to anticipate that if the sale to the Rohauers did not go through, it could take several months—during which the Littles would have to make mortgage and tax payments and maintain the property—before a new buyer could be found. Finally, it cannot be said as a matter of law that as of the date of the contract the amount of actual damages likely resulting from a breach was readily ascertainable. Although the Rohauers argue that the Littles' actual damages or net loss could have been easily calculated by subtracting from the Littles' expenses incurred as the result of the Rohauers' failure to close the additional $5,000 obtained by the Littles in the sale of their home in November 1981, this argument misses the mark. It is the difficulty in ascertaining damages at the time of the contract, not afterwards, that is relevant for purposes of enforcing a liquidated damages provision. That difficulty was quite obvious in this case.

Affirmed.

Discussion Questions

1. Describe the nature of the contract.
2. Was the time just before closing confusing? Why?
3. Did the Littles suffer $20,000 in damages?
4. Are the Littles permitted to keep the $20,000? Why?

Actual Damages In studying the language of the liquidated damage clauses quoted in the preceding section, it should be noted that the decision to keep the earnest money as damages is made at the discretion of the seller. In other words, the seller may elect to proceed and collect the actual damages sustained by the buyer's breach. Such damages could include all the monies expended by the seller in preparing for closing, such as the cost of reports. It could also include a commission to the broker or lost rental value if the property remains vacant or if a lease is terminated in anticipation of the buyer's takeover.

Likewise, the buyer may opt to collect actual damages for the seller's breach, which could include the costs of preparation for closing in the form of loan origination or commitment fees, appraisal fees, survey costs, and so on.

It is the burden of the party that is suing for actual damages to establish proof of the amount of the damages and that those damages were suffered as a result of the other party's breach.

If the action for actual damages is brought for nontimely performance in a time-is-of-the-essence agreement, the party bringing the action must show damages that resulted from delay. Examples of such damages are a higher interest rate on a loan, a loss of rent, and the cost of renting another property.

The *Uniform Land Transactions Act (ULTA)*, drafted for passage by the states in 1975, has several sections providing formulas for determining actual damages in the event of a breach of a land sales contract. For example, a seller reselling at a lower price than that provided in the breached contract is permitted to recover from the breaching buyer the difference in price plus the incidental costs of resale.

Specific Performance *Specific performance* is a remedy generally granted to buyers, whereby the court requires the seller to go forward with the transaction according to the terms of the contract. The remedy afforded the buyer is thus what the buyer was originally entitled to receive under the contract.

Generally, specific performance is not awarded to sellers who have breaching buyers: sellers are left to the remedies of actual damages or the collection of liquidated damages.

Rescission *Rescission* is a remedy that entitles the parties to rescind their agreement and return to the positions they were in before they entered into the contract. The buyer is given back any compensation paid and the seller is no longer obligated to sell the land. Rescission is most commonly used in cases where the seller is guilty of misrepresentation or fraud regarding the land or its condition. (See page 329 for a discussion of misrepresentation.)

(11.10) Consider:

The Willistons signed a purchase agreement for the construction and purchase of a new home from United Homes. The Willistons paid $1,000 earnest money. The contract provided that in the event the Willistons did not qualify for their loan of the property, only $800 would be returned and $200 would be retained by

United for paperwork and processing. The Willistons did not qualify and United kept $200. The Willistons maintain the retention of the $200 is unfair and illegal. What is the result?

Federal Regulations

A number of federal laws have been passed in recent years that require that certain provisions and disclosures be included as part of written land contracts. The two acts that require discussion are the Truth-in-Lending Act and the Interstate Land Sales Full Disclosure Act (ILSFDA).

Truth-in-Lending Act When the seller finances the buyer's purchase of the property, the seller is required under the Truth-in-Lending Act and its regulations (12 C.F.R. §226) to disclose to the buyer the cost of the financing including the annual percentage rate, the monthly payments, the number of payments, and the actual cost of paying over time. Chapter 12 discusses the details of financing disclosures.

Interstate Land Sales Full Disclosure Act In the 1960s because of an increase in available leisure time and disposable income, more and more Americans sought to purchase land for the construction of recreational, second, or vacation homes. Unfortunately, many purchases of such land were made sight unseen, with buyers purchasing mail-order lots. Most buyers had no idea of what they were purchasing but were led by colorful and often misleading brochures that depicted the property as part of a lush vacation spot, when in fact it was nothing but raw, undeveloped land often lacking roads, utilities, and water.

Because of the large number of frauds being perpetrated, Congress passed the *Interstate Land Sales Full Disclosure Act (ILSFDA),* (15 U.S.C. §1701 et seq.), which is a disclosure act regulating sellers of undeveloped properties while still permitting them to sell the land. The basic purpose of the act is to provide the buyer with full and accurate information so that the buyer is in an equal bargaining position when making the purchase decision. The ILSFDA is administered by the Office of Interstate Land Sales Registration (OILSR), a division of the Department of Housing and Urban Development (HUD).

1. Who is Covered Under the ILSFDA Since the ILSFDA is a federal enactment, it applies only to sales of land involving or affecting interstate commerce. Generally, the act applies to the sale or lease of fifty or more unimproved lots in interstate commerce. The act defines what constitutes interstate commerce in a negative manner by excluding those sales not covered under the act. The following types of sales are automatically excluded from coverage under the ILSFDA:

a. Sales of real estate pursuant to court order
b. Sales of securities by real estate investment trusts
c. Sales by governments or government agencies
d. Sales of cemetery lots
e. Sales of less than fifty lots
f. Sales of lots 5 acres or more in size
g. Sales of lots where there is a residential, commercial, or industrial building
h. Sales of lots zoned for industrial or commercial development
i. Sales of lots that exceed 10,000 square feet that will be sold for less than $100

These exemptions also apply to leases of the listed categories of property and do not require the seller to file for exemption.

However, there are several additional exemptions from the ILSFDA that do require filing with the OILSR. The limited sales exemption exempts developers who have not made more than twelve sales or leases during any of the last 5 calendar years and shall not exceed this limit in the future. The local offering exemption requires the developer to file and establish the following information:

a. Site contains less than 200 lots.
b. Promotional sales activity is directed only to local residents of the community. Advertisements appear only in newspapers in the county where the property is located; any billboards for advertising are within 15 miles of the lots; and brokers listing the property are in the same county as the lots or in an adjacent county.
c. Prospective buyers make on-site inspections of the lots before purchasing.
d. Sales contract (1) identifies who will be responsible for roads and utilities; (2) provides deeds free and clear of any blanket encumbrances; and (3) grants a rescission period of 3 business days.
e. Lots are not in flood-prone areas.

The residential subdivision exemption requires the developer to file and establish the following criteria:

a. County where the subdivision is located has specific minimum standards for subdivision development.

b. Every lot is on a paved public street constructed according to local government standards and is to be maintained by the local government.

c. Sales contract requires delivery of the deed to be made within 180 days after the contract is signed.

d. Title insurance policy has been issued.

e. Prospective buyers are able to inspect the lot prior to purchase.

f. Sales are not promoted by direct mail, telephone solicitations, or gifts.

g. Development is limited to single-family dwellings.

If a developer qualifies for these exemptions, forms for application are available from OILSR. Approval of the exemption is required prior to the initiation of sales activities.

2. *Contents of Filing Reports for Nonexempt Developers* If a developer is nonexempt, a *statement of record* must be filed. The statement of record must include the following information:

a. Names of the developers and their interests in the property

b. History of the developers including disbarment, disciplinary actions, indictments, and convictions relating to the sale of real property

c. Bankruptcies of the developers in the last 13 years

d. Pending litigation that may have an effect on the developers or the subdivision

e. Identification of other filings with OILSR

f. Legal description of the topography, climate, nuisances, subdivision map, permits, and licenses

g. Identification of agencies affecting licensing or permits for the land

h. General terms and conditions of the lot offer, including selling price and buyer's right of revocation for 48 hours

i. Access to nearby communities and roads

j. Availability of utilities; and if the utilities are developer-controlled, financial statements for the utilities

k. Recreation and common facilities and the costs of maintenance

l. Taxes and assessments

m. Whether there is any occupancy

n. Location of shopping facilities

o. Financial statements for the developers and the development

In addition to filing the statement of record, the developer is required to file a copy of the *property report*. A copy of the property report must also be given to every buyer before the buyer signs a contract for purchase. The report is set up in an easily understood question-and-answer format. It includes the same basic information as the statement of record but in a more readable manner. In addition, the property report must include certain statutory disclosures informing the buyer of the purpose of the report.

3. Penalties for Violation of ILSFDA Developers failing to comply with the disclosure requirements face both civil and criminal penalties. Parties who purchase from violating developers may sue the developers for damages, specific performance, or any other relief the court deems fair, just, and equitable. Purchasers may also sue to recover interest, court costs, attorneys' fees, appraisal fees and cost of travel to and from the lots. They are even permitted to recover for fraud or misrepresentation in the property report, whether or not they actually relied on the report. The criminal penalties for willful violations of the act are $5,000, 5 years' imprisonment, or both.

In addition to regulation by the ILSFDA, all developers (even those exempt under the federal act) may be required to comply with state land sales acts and disclosures. These state acts may also require the filing of reports and documents prior to the negotiation of sales.

MISREPRESENTATION

There are times when parties have all the elements of a contract and have executed a complete written agreement, but the contract is set aside because one of the parties was led into the agreement through a misrepresentation by the other party.

Misrepresentation can be innocent; that is, one party through misinformation or lack of knowledge provides the other party with inaccurate and misleading information. Misrepresentation can also be fraudulent, as when one party intentionally provides inaccurate information for purposes of inducing a sale. Finally, misrepresentation can occur because of a party's failure to disclose information that would have affected the purchasing decision. Upon discovery of misrepresentation, the party may seek to rescind the agreement. However, all types of misrepresentation require proof of the following common elements before legal action may be taken:

1. A statement of material fact has been made or omitted—the type of information involved would affect the buying decision.
2. There is reliance on the statement of fact—the buyer uses the fact in making the decision of whether to buy.
3. There is detriment—the buyer suffers through loss of property value or cost of repair.

The following case illustrates the application of the three elements in a case in which the misrepresentation was fraudulent.

NORDSTROM v. MILLER
605 P.2d 545 (Kans. 1980)

Carl and Cleo Nordstrom (plaintiffs) entered into a contract to purchase 480 acres of farm land from John Lee and Marilee Miller (defendants). The purchase price was $480,000. The advertisements for the property described it as "irrigated cropland" and stated that the property had two wells. One advertisement read:

480 acres of Prime Developed irrigation land located northwest of Garden City in Finnery County, Kansas. Two irrigation wells and approximately 14,000 ft. of underground pipe. This land is flood-irrigated and all runs are one-half mile long.
THIS IS ONE YOU HAVE TO SEE TO BELIEVE.

Robert Legere, a real estate broker, contacted the plaintiffs and showed them the property. Nordstrom inspected the land, the buildings, and the wells. The Nordstroms paid $15,000 down, sold their home and store in Colorado, and purchased the property and moved in on 2 March 1976.

During the summer of 1976, one of the irrigation wells went dry. On further investigation, Nordstrom discovered that insufficient water was available to supply either well and the farm could no longer be operated owing to its geological limitations.

Nordstrom confronted the defendants with the information and the defendants offered to drill another well and change the contract payment terms. The Nordstroms refused and brought suit for fraud and misrepresentation seeking rescission of the agreement. The trial court granted rescission but refused to award punitive damages. The defendants appealed.

HERD, Justice

The remaining issue is whether plaintiffs sustained the burden of proving fraudulent misrepresentation by the Millers. Actionable fraud includes an untrue statement of fact, known to be untrue by the party making it, made with the intent to deceive or recklessly made with disregard for the truth, where another party justifiably relies on the statement and acts to his injury and damage.

We have held fraud is never presumed and must be proven by clear and convincing evidence.

The evidence in this case reveals Miller advertised his land for sale as irri-gated land through advertisements of his own and those of this agent for which he is responsible as principal. He obtained the going price for irrigated land—$1,000 per acre. Evidence showed dry land was worth around $450–$500 per acre. Unrefuted evidence showed the irrigation wells both failed within 6 months of the effective date of the contract. The record also reveals there remained no sufficient recoverable irrigation water under the Miller land to operate it as an irrigated farm.

Turning now to the final elements needed to establish fraud, we are called upon to determine whether Miller knew the representations he made were false. If not, were the statements made with a reckless disregard for the truth?

There can be no doubt Miller knew his wells were producing from the Niobrara Formation, a limestone deposit known as a chalk aquifer. This formation lays below the Ogallala sand, the aquifer for much of the irrigation water in Colorado, Nebraska, Kansas, Oklahoma and Texas. The Niobrara has no porosity but where it erodes, it is capable of trapping water in cracks and crevices from perculation through a thin layer of Ogallala sand and gravel. If a driller is lucky he can sometimes tap a crack reservoir and obtain production in paying quantities until the deposit is depleted. Since there is no significant recharge and the supply is a subterranean pond, the small ponds, known as "crack wells," usually are short-lived and deplete without warning. This condition exists north of Holcomb where the Miller land is located. There are about 45 irrigation wells in Finney County producing from the Niobrara, most of them short-lived.

John Lee Miller drilled the south well in 1969 and the north well in 1971. Similar wells were going dry in the area. He knew his irrigated farm would be a dry land farm soon. Nonetheless, he advertised the land as an irrigated farm with two wells, pumping 2300 gallons per minute. He later admitted that figure did not represent the current gallonage being produced. The gallonage had decreased by the time the advertisements appeared. There is substantial, competent evidence to show he told Nordstrom the water production was from the Ogallala aquifer, when the source of the water supply was actually Niobrara.

Defendants next argue even if their representations were untrue, plaintiffs negligently failed to make inquiry about the nature and condition of the irrigation wells and are, therefore, stuck with their bargain.

They argue they asked Nordstrom to check the production of both wells with Lloyd Harkness, who drilled the wells. They also argue Carl Nordstrom is a knowledgeable buyer, having had farming and irrigation experience, and he could not rely on Miller's representation.

These arguments are without merit. The evidence is clear, convincing and uncontroverted that Nordstrom had had no experience with irrigation, except one year's work with water which was obtained from a surface reservoir and connecting ditch. Such is not comparable with the facts in the instant case. A subterranean water resource is a complicated geological study about which even the experts know too little. It could not be expected that one with no experience or education on the subject would anticipate or even recognize a problem.

"Where one party to a contract or transaction has superior knowledge, or knowledge which is not within the fair and reasonable reach of the other party and which he could not discover by the exercise of reasonable diligence, or means of knowledge which are not open to both parties alike, he is under a legal obligation to speak, and his silence constitutes fraud, especially when the other party relies upon him to communicate to him the true state of facts to enable him to judge of the expedience of the bargain" (cites omitted).

Defendants next argue plaintiffs are estopped to rescind because they remained in possession of the land after the suit for rescission was instituted.

The acts of the Nordstroms from the moment they discovered they had been misled are consistent with rescission and restoration to the status quo. Their continued possession of the real estate was dictated by the circumstances. They had sold their former home as the result of the fraud which induced the contract. Therefore, they had no place to go. While laboring under the mistaken belief they had purchased an irrigated farm, plaintiffs harvested the growing wheat, cut the hay, and planted milo. To say they must walk away from the farm and permit the growing crops to deteriorate, is a tortured, irrational interpretation of the rule. They had the duty to do equity, which in this case, involved preventing waste. This they did commendably and they should not suffer or be punished for their actions. We do not find acts or conduct on the part of plaintiffs that will defeat the remedy of rescission. Plaintiff's demeanor was proper under the circumstances and estoppel will not lie.

Affirmed.

Discussion Questions

1. What information about the farm was incorrect?
2. Should the buyers have been able to discover the problem from their inspection?
3. How was the property advertised?
4. Did the buyers act incorrectly in remaining on the farm?
5. What should the realtor have done? Does the realtor have liability here?
6. Is the contract rescinded?

(11.11) Consider:

The Nasons purchased a lot from the Voights, and after closing on the property, the Nasons discovered that it was located within a flooding plane which the Voights never disclosed to them. The Nasons wish to set aside the sale. What is the result?

KEY TERMS

offer
counteroffer
option
earnest money
acceptance
consideration
implied warranty of habitability
marketable title
liquidated damages

Uniform Land Transactions Act
(ULTA)
specific performance
rescission
Interstate Land Sales Full Disclosure
Act (ILSFDA)
statement of record
property report
misrepresentation

CHAPTER PROBLEMS

1. Tom received a flyer in the mail that read: "Auction of land parcels— 1/2 acre to 200 acres. Begins promptly at 8:00 A.M. Saturday. Be there to

shout your bid." Tom is curious and will attend. Has an offer been made?

2. Tom writes to Bob, "I offer to sell you my property, Blackacre, for $10,000 cash. This offer to remain open until June 1, 1988. /s/ Tom." Bob writes back on 2 June 1988, "I'll take the property on your terms. /s/ Bob." Tom refuses to sell. Bob says he must because there was no revocation. What is the result?

3. Susan writes to Jane, "I offer to sell you my San Juan Blackacre for $75,000 cash. This offer to remain open until December 28, 1988. /s/ Susan." On 1 December 1988 Jane writes to Susan, "I'll take San Juan Blackacre on your terms. /s/ Jane." Upon receipt of Jane's letter, Susan calls Jane and says, "I'm sorry, I already sold the property to Bob." Jane says, "I'll see you in court about this." What is the result?

4. The facts are the same as in question 3, except Susan called Jane to tell her of the sale to Bob on 30 November 1988 and Jane wrote on 1 December 1988, "I will take the property on your terms. I am warning you—I will hold you to your offer. /s/ Jane." Susan refuses to sell to Jane. What is the result?

5. Tilley writes to Hapsted, "I offer to sell you my farm, Greenacre, for $125,000 cash." Hapsted writes back, "I will take Greenacre. I assume the shed and corn bin are included." Do Tilley and Hapsted have a contract?

6. State which of the following defects would be covered under the implied warranty of habitability (assuming new-home purchasers):
   a. Defective air conditioning system
   b. Use of ungalvanized nails in walls
   c. Variations in the color of carpet (one color ordered)
   d. Sagging roof
   e. Lack of insulation.

7. Would a building encroachment render a title unmarketable?

8. Bert was selling his home in White Plains, New York, and Ernie was interested in buying it. While touring the home, Ernie observed substantial cracks in the walls and in the basement. Ernie did not ask about the cracks, and Bert did not mention them. Ernie purchased Bert's home, but after more cracking occurred and water was found in the basement, Ernie sought to rescind the purchase on the grounds of misrepresentation. What was the result? Why?

9. Bob signs a brief but enforceable contract to buy a single-family house from Sam for $40,000, giving a $1,000 deposit. Shortly thereafter Bob finds another house that he likes more and refuses to go through with

the deal. Discuss the parties' rights in each of the following circumstances:

a. Sam sells the house to Thurd for $46,000. Bob wants his deposit back.

b. Sam sells the house to Thurd for $31,000 and wants to recover his loss of $8,000 ($9,000 minus $1,000 deposit).

c. Sam wants to recover his loss but has not sold to anyone else.

d. Sam wants specific performance.

Would any of your answers be different if Bob's default were due to an unanticipated difficulty in getting financing, rather than a mere change of mind?

10. Design Craft Homes transfers homes it has built but not sold after 6 months to a subsidiary corporation called Home Craft Homes. Will buyers from Home Craft be entitled to their full year of warranty protection? Does the lack of privity prevent them from getting any warranty protection?

12

FINANCING IN THE TRANSFER OF REAL ESTATE

Edward Knudson owned a 9-acre ranch, adjacent to a country club, that was appraised at $900,000. Edward's monthly mortgage payments of $4,008 became too burdensome and he defaulted. The Mortgage Company, after public notice, sold the ranch for $214,460—a mere $5.66 more than the amount needed to satisfy the mortgage on the property. Edward wants to know, "Can they do that?"

Edward has found himself in the position of a defaulting debtor with the question of what the creditor may or may not do to attempt to collect the balance due on the loan. This chapter discusses the methods of financing the purchase of land, and the rights and remedies of borrowers and lenders under each method.

Obtaining funds to buy property is a critical element of the economy. The successful repayment of that financing not only affects the lender but is also partially responsible for the status of the national economy at any given time. Successful repayment is often dependent on the rights the lender retains in the property, or on the rights the lender is able to exercise with regard to the property, when a problem with repayment arises. There are various methods for affording the lender either constant or exercisable rights in the property, but perhaps the most common and well-known method is the mortgage. Alternative lender security methods include the deed of trust or trust indenture; the installment or land contract; the subdivision trust; and various combinations of these. Each method creates a different form of security for the lender, as well as different rights for both the borrower and the lender when the financing advanced for the purchase is not repaid.

THE MORTGAGE

Ancient civilizations such as in Egypt and Babylonia employed the concept of pledging property to finance its purchase or to secure loans for other purposes. Called *fiducia* in ancient Rome, the process of obtaining security in real property required the borrower to transfer title to the lender, who retained such title until the borrower had completely repaid the loan. Later, under the concept of *pignus*, the borrower retained title, but the lender was entitled to take possession at any time if the borrower defaulted.

Although the Roman concepts of *fiducia* and *pignus* were used later in Europe as methods for financing the purchase of real property, the term *mortgage* was not introduced into the English legal system until after the 1066 invasion of England by William I (William the Conqueror). *Mortgage* is derived from the French word *mort*, which means dead or frozen (to indicate that the borrower could not transfer the property freely), and *gage*, which means pledge.

The following is a current definition of mortgage from Black's Law Dictionary (1968):

> a pledge or security of a particular property for the payment of a debt or the performance of some other obligation, whatever form the transaction may take, but is not now regarded as a conveyance in effect, even though it may be cast in the form of a conveyance.

This basic definition applies to all forms of mortgages and mortgage theories adopted by each of the states. However, the details on the creation, enforcement, and rights of parties do vary; and these details are discussed in the following sections.

Parties to the Mortgage

A mortgage is a two-party relationship. The borrower who is buying or pledging property is referred to as the *mortgagor*. The mortgagor may be borrowing the funds to purchase the property being pledged, thus creating a purchase money mortgage. Alternatively, the mortgagor may be pledging property already owned as security for a loan obtained for reasons other than the purchase of property.

The lender who advances the mortgagor the funds for the loan is referred to as the *mortgagee*. In a mortgage relationship, one of these two parties (mortgagor or mortgagee) will hold title to the property and the other will have an interest in the property. Depending on the happening of certain events, a transfer of title from one party to the other may result.

Creation of the Mortgage Relationship

The Writing Requirement As with all documents relating to real estate transactions, the instrument creating a mortgage must be in writing. There are three reasons for this requirement: First, the mortgage creates and transfers a land interest, which must be evidenced in writing to comply with the statute of frauds. Second, the rights of the mortgagee in the property are to a certain extent protected by public notification of the mortgagee's interest. Such public notification comes through the recording of the mortgage instrument with the appropriate governmental unit—the same governmental unit where deeds (Chapter 9) and security interests (Chapter 6) are recorded. Finally, a mortgage creates a complex land interest and complex rights and remedies between the parties. Therefore, it is necessary to ensure that all interests, rights, and remedies are clearly established, and a written document is the only method whereby such clarification is possible.

The Underlying Debt Requirement

1. The Debt Instrument A mortgage is invalid unless executed for the purpose of securing some underlying debt. In other words, a mortgage cannot be enforced unless the mortgagor owes some debt to the mortgagee. Generally, and particularly in the sale and purchase of residential property, that underlying debt is evidenced by a *promissory note*. The promissory note is the actual contractual arrangement between the parties for the loan of funds. It is usually a very simple instrument specifying the principal amount, the rate of interest, and the payment terms. Also, the promissory note indicates that its payment is secured by a mortgage or deed of trust. Figure 12.1 is an example of a note secured by a mortgage.

      The promissory note usually contains terms that make it negotiable—a quality that enables the lender to easily transfer and sell the note to third parties. Also, the note contains various clauses relating to acceleration, default, and attorneys' fees. These provisions are closely tied to the rights afforded mortgagees and are discussed in conjunction with appropriate mortgage terms.

2. Regulation Z Perhaps one of the most significant concerns faced by all lenders in properly executing the note underlying a mortgage is whether the note complies with all applicable federal regulations. The *Truth-in-Lending laws* were passed by Congress in 1968 as part of the *Federal Consumer Credit Protection Act*. To carry out the basic provisions of the act, the Federal Reserve Board promulgated specific regulations on compliance, which are referred to in their entirety as *Regulation Z* (12 C.F.R. §226 et seq.). If Regulation Z is applicable in a mortgage

Figure 12.1 *Promissory Note*

$_____

City, State _____19____

_____

For value received _____

promise(s) to pay to _____

or order, at _____

the sum of _____

DOLLARS ($_____) in _____

installments of _____

DOLLARS ($_____).

    Should default be made in the payment of any installment when due, then the whole sum of principal and interest shall become immediately due and payable at the option of the holder of this note, with interest from date of such default at the highest legal rate until paid on the entire unpaid principal and accrued interest.

    Should any installment due hereunder not be paid as it matures, the amount of such installment which has matured shall, at the option of the holder of this note, bear interest at 10 percent per annum from its maturity date until paid.

    Principal and interest payable in lawful money of the United States of America.

    Should suit be brought to recover on this note _____ promise(s) to pay as attorneys' fees a reasonable amount additional to the amount found hereunder.

    The makers and indorsers hereof severally waive diligence, demand, presentment for payment and protest, and consent to the extension of time of payment of this note without notice.

    This note is secured by a mortgage upon real property.

_____   _____

_____   _____

transaction, certain disclosures must be made to the party or parties signing the note. Regulation Z applies to all businesses and individuals who are:

1. Offering or extending credit to consumers
2. Offering or extending such credit on a regular basis
3. Offering or extending credit either
   a. Subject to a finance charge or
   b. Payable by written agreement in more than four installments

4. Offering or extending credit primarily for personal, family, or household purposes

Therefore, lending institutions engaged in mortgage lending are subject to Regulation Z. The applicability of Regulation Z to brokers and other private parties participating in installment sales and other creative financing methods is discussed later in this chapter. The types of real estate transactions that are excluded from Regulation Z coverage are as follows:

1. Business transactions
2. Commercial transactions
3. Agricultural transactions
4. Organizational credit transactions
5. Credit transactions that involve more than $25,000 but which are not secured by real estate or a dwelling

If Regulation Z is applicable to a lender and the particular credit transaction involved, then the lender is required to make certain disclosures. Basically, the following information must be furnished to the borrower:

1. Annual percentage rate
2. Finance charge
3. Amount financed
4. Total payment amount
5. Number of payments
6. Amount per payment
7. When the payments are due
8. Late payment charges

Generally, these disclosures are made on a statement separate from the promissory note and mortgage documents. Figure 12.2 is an example of a Regulation Z disclosure statement for a mortgage-secured note. If the note has a variable interest rate, the disclosure form shown in Figure 12.3 is required under Regulation Z.

If the note is to be repaid under a graduated payment plan, then the disclosure statement must include a summary of the payments to be made and their amounts. For example, the following chart might be used to satisfy this portion of the Regulation Z disclosure requirements:

NUMBER OF PAYMENTS	AMOUNT OF PAYMENTS	WHEN PAYMENTS ARE DUE
12	$450.00	Beginning 12/1/83
12	$475.00	Beginning 12/1/84
12	$500.00	Beginning 12/1/85
12	$530.00	Beginning 12/1/86
12	$570.00	Beginning 12/1/87
12	$625.00	Beginning 12/1/88

Figure 12.2 *Sample Mortgage Disclosure Statement*

Mortgage Savings and Loan Assoc.

Date: April 15, 1981

Glenn Jones
700 Oak Drive
Little Creek, USA

ANNUAL PERCENTAGE RATE The cost of your credit as a yearly rate.	FINANCE CHARGE The dollar amount the credit will cost you.	Amount Financed The amount of credit provided to you or on your behalf.	Total of Payments The amount you will have paid after you have made all payments as scheduled.
14.85 %	$156,551.54	$44,605.66	$ 201,157.20

Your payment schedule will be:

Number of Payments	Amount of Payments	When Payments Are Due
360	$558.77	Monthly beginning 6/1/81

This obligation has a demand feature.

You may obtain property insurance from anyone you want that is acceptable to Mortgage Savings and Loan Assoc.. If you get the insurance from Mortgage Savings and Loan Assoc. you will pay $ 150-/year

Security: You are giving a security interest in:

☒ the goods or property being purchased.

☐ _____ .

Late Charge: If a payment is late, you will be charged $ N/A , 5 % of the payment.

Prepayment: If you pay off early, you may have to pay a penalty.

Assumption: Someone buying your house may, subject to conditions, be allowed to assume the remainder of the mortgage on the original terms.

See your contract documents for any additional information about nonpayment, default, any required repayment in full before the scheduled date, and prepayment refunds and penalties.

e means an estimate

Figure 12.3 *Sample Adjustable Rate Mortgage (ARM) Disclosure Form*

State Savings and Loan Assoc.

Anne Jones
600 Pine Lane
Little Creek, USA

Account number: 210802-47

ANNUAL PERCENTAGE RATE	FINANCE CHARGE	Amount Financed	Total of Payments
The cost of your credit as a yearly rate	The dollar amount the credit will cost you	The amount of credit provided to you or on your behalf	The amount you will have paid after you have made all payments as scheduled
15.07 %	$157,155.20	$44,002—	$201,157.20

Your payment schedule will be

Number of Payments	Amount of Payments	When Payments Are Due
360	$558.77	monthly beginning 6-1-81

Variable Rate

The annual percentage rate may increase during the term of this transaction if the prime rate of State Savings and Loan Assoc. increases. The rate may not increase more often than once a year, and may not increase by more than 1% annually. The interest rate will not increase above 19.75 %; Any increase will take the form of higher payment amounts. If the interest rate increases by 1 % in one year, your regular payment would increase to $594.51

Security: You are giving a security interest in the property being purchased.

Late Charge: If a payment is late, you will be charged 5% of the payment.

Prepayment: If you pay off early, you ☒ may ☐ will not have to pay a penalty.

Assumption: Someone buying your house may, subject to conditions, be allowed to assume the remainder of the mortgage on the original terms.

See your contract documents for any additional information about nonpayment, default, any required repayment in full before the scheduled date, and prepayment refunds and penalties.

e means an estimate

In addition to the preceding disclosures required for the financing of the property purchased, the following items must be included on the disclosure statement regardless of the type of loan or note involved.

1. Identity of the creditor
2. Demand feature of the note, if one exists
3. Prepayment penalties, if any
4. Whether the loan is assignable or transferable
5. Separate identification of credit insurance premiums

Although Regulation Z provides for a 3-day rescission period for security interests and second mortgages, the rescission period does not apply to *residential mortgage transactions,* which are defined in §226.2(a)(24) as:

> transactions in which a mortgage, deed of trust, purchase money security interest arising under an installment sales contract, or equivalent consensual security interest is created or retained in the consumer's principal dwelling to finance the acquisition or initial construction of that dwelling.

Thus the exception to the 3-day rescission period and notice of that period is for first notes and mortgages on property being purchased by a consumer for use as a residence. However, the consumer who executes a second note and mortgage on a property is permitted to cancel that transaction within the 3-day period. In this case the lender must disclose the right of cancellation and must also provide, in written form, procedures for exercising the right of cancellation. Figure 12.4 is a sample from the regulations.

One additional issue that lenders must be concerned with under Regulation Z is with the advertisement of the credit terms the lender has available. Regulation Z defines an *advertisement* as "a commercial message in any media that promotes, directly or indirectly, a credit transaction." Advertisements must be accurate and state only those terms that are actually available. Any advertisements including finance charges must also state those charges in terms of an annual percentage rate (apr). The apr is an expression of the cost of credit according to its yearly rate. Formulas for computing the apr are set forth in the regulation, along with tables that can be used in such computation.

Regulation Z also provides that if certain *triggering language* is used in advertisements, then additional disclosures must also be included. Triggering language includes:

1. Amount or percentage of any down payment
2. Number of payments or period of repayment
3. Amount of any payment
4. Amount of any finance charge

The additional disclosures that must be made in advertisements using triggering terms are as follows:

1. Terms of repayment
2. Annual percentage rate
3. Disclosures of any increases in payments or rates that may occur

Figure 12.4 *Sample Notice of Right to Cancel*

Your Right to Cancel
You are entering into a transaction that will result in a [mortgage/lien/security interest] [on/in] your home. You have a legal right under federal law to cancel this transaction, without cost, within three business days from whichever of the following events occurs last:
(1) the date of the transaction, which is _____; or
(2) the date you received your Truth in Lending disclosures; or
(3) the date you received this notice of your right to cancel.

If you cancel the transaction, the [mortgage/lien/security interest] is also cancelled. Within 20 calendar days after we receive your notice, we must take the steps necessary to reflect the fact that the [mortgage/lien/security interest] [on/in] your home has been cancelled, and we must return to you any money or property you have given to us or to anyone else in connection with this transaction.

You may keep any money or property we have given you until we have done the things mentioned above, but you must then offer to return the money or property. If it is impractical or unfair for you to return the property, you must offer its reasonable value. You may offer to return the property at your home or at the location of the property. Money must be returned to the address below. If we do not take possession of the money or property within 20 calendar days of your offer, you may keep it without further obligation.

How to Cancel
If you decide to cancel this transaction, you may do so by notifying us in writing, at

(creditor's name and business address)

You may use any written statement that is signed and dated by you and states your intention to cancel, or you may use this notice by dating and signing below. Keep one copy of this notice because it contains important information about your rights.

If you cancel by mail or telegram, you must send the notice no later than midnight of

(date)

(or midnight of the third business day following the latest of the three events listed above). If you send or deliver your written notice to cancel some other way, it must be delivered to the above address no later than that time.

I WISH TO CANCEL

_____   _____
Consumer's Signature   Date

Two examples of down payment triggering language are, "total move-in costs of $1,000" or "as low as 10 percent down." The phrase "30-year loan" is an example of a triggering term because it indicates the repayment period.

"Payable in monthly installments of $550" is triggering language related to the amount of the payments. Triggering language related to the finance charge includes, "total cost of credit is . . ." and "$50,000 mortgage with two points." Use of any of these phrases requires the advertising lender to include the additional information.

General language such as, "no down payment," "years to repay," and "monthly installments to suit your budget" may be used without triggering the additional disclosure requirements.

(12.1) Consider:

Harry and Wilma are purchasing their first home, which is to be constructed over the next 6 months. They will put down $10,000 and borrow the remaining $90,000 of the purchase price. First Savings and Loan will be lending the $90,000 to Harry and Wilma.

a. With what provisions of Regulation Z must First Savings and Loan comply?

b. Suppose that 1 year after moving in, Harry and Wilma decide to borrow money to construct a swimming pool. They sign a note and second mortgage with Hank's Bank. With what provisions of Regulation Z must Hank's Bank comply?

(12.2) Consider:

Do the following advertisements contain any triggering language requiring further disclosure?

a. NEW LISTING—Exciting three bedroom home. Excellent Northeast Mesa location. Pool and tennis court. Low rates and low down payment.

b. 5% DOWN, 12-1/2% INTEREST LOAN—Country style two bedroom and guest house.

3. Equal Credit Opportunity Act Mortgage lenders are also subject to the provisions of the *Equal Credit Opportunity Act (ECOA)*, (15 U.S.C. §1701), which prohibits lenders from refusing loans or discriminating in lending on the basis of sex, marital status, race, religion, or national origin. Penalties for violations include private suits as well as fines. Mortgage lenders must be cautious in reviewing loan applications and must base their decisions on issues of creditworthiness that can be substantiated.

4. Usury One additional problem lenders need to be concerned with in the creation of a debt underlying the mortgage involves the amount of interest charged. Most states have laws fixing the maximum interest rates that may be charged legally. If the lender charges a rate in excess of that statutory maximum, then *usury* is present. The usury rate varies significantly from state to state and also according to changes in the economic climate and the type of credit transaction involved.

Although most lenders would never use an interest rate that exceeds the statutory maximum, they may engage in usury by charging fees in addition to the interest collected on the loan. These fees include financier's charges and points. However, there are certain charges that may be made legally in addition to the maximum legal interest rate without having the loan made usurious. The following list explains such charges:

a. *Charges for costs actually incurred.* It is a general rule that additional charges by a lender for necessary expenditures actually made in rendering the loan will not make the transaction usurious. These charges include appraisal fees, credit report fees, survey costs, title search and insurance costs, recording fees, and actual costs incurred in the preparation of loan documents.

b. *Charges for commissions by loan brokers.* Brokers, in negotiating a loan between parties, may charge commissions even though the loan is negotiated for the statutory maximum; and the payment of such a commission will not render the loan usurious. By law, such a charge must be paid to a third party and not the lender.

c. *Standby commitment charges.* Often a builder will have obtained a construction loan for a project but will not have obtained permanent financing. Instead, the builder will usually arrange to have a standby commitment for permanent financing from a lender. Because the standby commitment requires the lender to produce the money upon the builder's demand, with no guarantee that the builder will make such a demand, the lender's funds are tied up for a period of time. The lender is permitted to charge a commitment fee in addition to the maximum legal interest rate for the loan because of the legitimate service rendered.

d. *Late charges.* Late fees are not considered usurious because of the expense, time, and paperwork involved in collecting and posting late payments.

e. *Government loan charges.* When a borrower seeks a government insured loan (such as a Federal Housing Administration [FHA] loan) there is additional paperwork involved, and the lender is required to pay a premium for government loan insurance. These expenses may be charged to the borrower in addition to the maximum legal interest rate without being considered usurious.

f. *Construction loan charges.* Construction lenders generally have more paperwork and tasks associated with their loans. The principal amount of the loan is paid in various installments as construction progresses, and the lender may be required to inspect before releasing funds. Also, additional paperwork is required to handle liens (e.g., mechanic's liens as discussed in Chapter 7) and payment of subcontractors and suppliers. Fees for these services may be charged in addition to the maximum legal interest rate without resulting usury problems.

g. *Life insurance premiums.* Many lenders require the borrower to maintain life insurance, with the benefits to be used to retire the note debt. Payment of the premiums for such insurance is not included in the computation of interest charges.

h. *Prepayment penalties.* The issue of whether early loan repayment charges are included in the total interest charges varies from state to state. However, even in states where prepayment penalties are not included in the interest rate, the amount of the charges may be limited by state statutes.

i. *Brundage clauses.* A Brundage clause requires the borrower to pay any tax that may be imposed on the lender's mortgage. However, in some states the loan will be usurious if the tax plus the interest charged exceeds the statutory maximum.

Each state provides that certain types of lenders and transactions are exempt from the usury laws. For example, all states with usury laws have some type of exemption for business loans, and many states exempt FHA insured loans from their usury statutes.

The penalties for charging a usurious rate vary from state to state. In some states the lender forfeits all interest and recovers only the principal. In other states the lender forfeits only that amount of interest above the maximum. In yet other states the entire contract is void, and the lender forfeits both interest and principal.

Recording A mortgage need not be recorded to be valid. However, an unrecorded mortgage gives rights only between the borrower (mortgagor) and the lender (mortgagee). In order to protect the mortgagee against others' rights or to give the mortgagee priority in relation to other creditors, the mortgage must be recorded in the government office where deeds and other documents affecting land interests are recorded. The process of recording gives the lender priority over subsequently recorded and unrecorded land interests. (See discussion of priorities later in this chapter.)

Title Theory Versus Lien Theory

Although all states permit the use of the mortgage to enable the mortgagee to secure repayment of the underlying debt by the mortgagor, each state has a different theory of how that security is accomplished. However, each of the state theories can be classified as a title theory, a lien theory, or an intermediate theory (a combination of the two).

Title theory states follow the idea that a mortgage actually gives the mortgagee some type of legal title to the property. This theory is the older of the two and is found primarily in the eastern states. Under title theory, the mortgagee has the right to possession and the right to collect rents on the property.

In *lien theory* states, the mortgagee has only a lien on the property and is entitled to possession and rents only upon foreclosure. Under this theory, the mortgagor actually holds title to the property. The lien theory is followed by the majority of states west of the Mississippi.

Some states follow an intermediate theory, which is a combination of the title and lien theories. In these states the mortgagee is entitled to possession and rents upon the default of the mortgagor. However, unlike the lien theory, the mortgagee is not required to wait until after foreclosure; and unlike the title theory, the mortgagee does not hold title until after completion of proceedings mandated by statute but short of full disclosure.

The following case illustrates the effect of a lien theory mortgage when a mortgagor is in default. The language of the court provides an excellent summary of the distinctions between the theories of mortgages.

GANBAUM v. ROCKWOOD REALTY CORP.
308 N.Y.S.2d 436 (1970)

SPIEGEL, Justice

Rockwood Realty (defendant), mortgaged property to Ganbaum and then sold the property to Edith Levine (defendant) who bought the property subject to the mortgage. When payments were not made on the property, Ganbaum filed a foreclosure suit and also sought to recover $31,180.64 in damages because Levine had retained rents and failed to pay taxes, sewer and water payments for two years prior to the time of the filing of Ganbaum's suit. The mortgage contained the following clause:

13. That the mortgagor hereby assigns to the mortgagee the rents, issues and profits of the premises as further security for the payment of said indebtedness, and the mortgagor grants to the mortgagee the right to enter upon and take possession of the premises for the purpose of collecting the same and to let the premises or any part thereof, and to apply the rents, issues and profits, after payment of all necessary charges and expenses on account of such indebtedness. This assignment and grant

348

shall continue in effect until this mortgage is paid. . . .

It is the law of New York that a mortgage gives the mortgagee only a lien upon the mortgaged premises. The common law doctrine that the mortgagee held title thereto or any incidents thereof has long ago been abolished. A clear indication of this was the abolition by the legislature in 1830 of the right of the mortgagee to maintain action in ejectment to recover possession of the mortgaged premises. . . . The mortgagee was thus left with only the remedy of foreclosure to obtain possession of the mortgaged premises.

The courts of this State have consistently upheld the principle that a mortgage creates no more than a lien upon the premises. Unless this is so, we must impute to the legislature (in abolishing the maintenance by a mortgagee of the action of ejectment) the vain formality of enacting a statute which can be rendered nugatory by the voluntary act of the person whose conduct the statute was designed to control.

In accordance with this policy, it has been held in New York, a deed conveying real property, absolute on its face, when the transaction is intended by the parties to be a mortgage, not only is treated as a mortgage, but is held in law to be a mortgage and not a conveyance. To reiterate, it is firmly the law of this State that a mortgage is merely a lien, which gives the mortgagee security and no more, and cannot, regardless of its form or the intention of the parties to the mortgage, transfer title to the mortgagee.

Defendant Levine, during the period relevant to the cause of action for rents, held title to the mortgaged realty.

Title to real estate is generally defined to be "the means whereby the owner of lands has the just possession of his property. Title means full, independent and fee ownership."

It is not shown that the interest of Defendant Levine in the mortgaged real property is less than that of a fee. The fee includes title, the right of possession, and the right to use for any purpose which may be lawful.

Certainly the title of Defendant Levine included, for the period in issue, the rights to the rents upon the realty and the right to apply those rents as she saw fit. As a mortgage cannot convey title to the mortgagee, the assignment of rents clause in Paragraph 13 of the mortgage herein sued upon cannot convey ipso facto to the mortgagee the right to the rents, which is an incident of title. Therefore, though Defendant Levine is bound by the terms of the mortgage, subject to which she acquired title to the subject premises, she is not liable to the plaintiffs for the rents collected by her prior to foreclosure nor for the use made of them. A contrary holding would subvert the firm principle of New York jurisprudence that a mortgage is merely a lien and cannot operate as a transfer of title.

The motion for summary judgment is granted.

Discussion Questions

1. Who is the mortgagor? Who is the mortgagee?
2. What does the mortgagee want in addition to foreclosure?
3. Is New York a title theory state or a lien theory state?
4. Who has title to the property?
5. Is the mortgagee entitled to the rents on the property during the period of default?

(12.3) Consider:

Realty Investors borrowed money from Anaconda Trust to purchase a 20-unit apartment complex that is located in a lien theory state. Realty gave Anaconda a mortgage on the property as security for the loan. Realty has rented all the apartments in the complex. Who is entitled to the rent received on the 20 units? Who would be entitled to the rent if the apartment complex were located in a title theory state?

Terms of the Mortgage

Only the minimum requirements for execution of a valid mortgage have been discussed to this point. However, as with contracts for the sale and purchase of real property and with brokerage agreements, there are many additional terms that may be included in the mortgage agreement and often should be included to protect and define the rights of the parties to the mortgage. Although many of these terms could also be a part of the underlying debt agreement, it is wise to have corresponding provisions in the documents of mortgage and promissory note.

Acceleration Clause Usually, the *acceleration clause* appears only in the promissory note. The purpose of the acceleration clause is to permit the mortgagee to accelerate the maturity date of the note in the event of a default by the mortgagor. The second paragraph in Figure 12.1 is a typical example of an acceleration clause. The acceleration clauses in that sample note are exercisable at the option of the holder of the note.

The reason virtually all mortgage notes contain an acceleration clause is that in their absence, the mortgagee does not have a powerful remedy upon the mortgagor's default. Without an acceleration clause, the mortgagee's only recourse for default would be a suit to collect the amount of payments missed or a partial foreclosure for the amount of the mortgagor's default. The mortgagee would thus be required to bring suit each time there was a default and would not be permitted to have one dispositive and final suit.

The acceleration clause is recognized as valid in all states and is also permitted in government insured loans for real estate.

Interest Acceleration Clause The interest acceleration clause also generally appears in the underlying note for the transaction. This clause allows the increase of the interest being paid on the debt to either the maximum amount permitted by law or some other amount established in the clause. This increase results when the mortgagor has defaulted on the payments. An example of the language used to create such a right follows:

Should default occur and acceleration of the full amount of the entire indebtedness is called for, interest on the entire amount of the indebtedness shall accrue thereafter at the maximum rate of interest then permitted under the laws of the state of _____ or continue at the rate provided herein, whichever of said rates is greater.

Balloon Payment Clause Usually, a mortgage is amortized over a certain number of years, so that the full amount of the mortgage loan and the interest are paid when the term of the mortgage has expired. For example, after 30 years of a typical residential 30-year mortgage, the mortgagor will have paid the full amount of the debt and interest due on the mortgage. However, when the mortgage contains a balloon payment clause, the result will not be the same.

Under a mortgage with a *balloon payment clause,* the mortgagor is still required to make periodic installment payments, but those payments do not fully amortize the amount of the loan; hence, the mortgagor will be required to pay the balance of the amount due at the end of the term of the mortgage. The lump sum due at the end of the mortgage term is called a *balloon payment.*

Although the balloon payment provision is very typical in commercial transactions, it is unusual and often prohibited in residential mortgages. For example, government insured loans cannot include balloon payment provisions.

Prepayment Penalty Clauses The mortgagee has the right to earn the interest on the money invested and loaned to the mortgagor for the term of the mortgage. Unless the note or the mortgage specifically provides, the mortgagor has no right to prepay the amount due on the loan in advance of the mortgage term.

Most mortgages will thus contain a clause that requires the mortgagor to pay a penalty in order to prepay the amount due on the loan. The penalty is justified on the grounds that prepayment makes it necessary for the lender to find a new investment outlet and to incur the expenses associated with finding and making that reinvestment. The penalty may apply to the entire period of the loan or may be applicable only during the first 5 to 10 years of the mortgage. The following is an example of a prepayment penalty clause:

In the event of a default hereunder, or in the event that said mortgagor desires by reason of sale or otherwise to prepay the total amount due and owing at the time of any of the above described prepayments, the mortgagee shall have the right to assess and collect a premium of _____ (_____%) of the then principal balance. The right of the mortgagee to assess and collect such premium shall continue for a period of 10 years from the time the amortization of the above described indebtedness begins.

The *prepayment penalty clause* is recognized as valid in all states; however, it should be noted that on certain types of government insured loans, a prepayment penalty cannot be part of the mortgage agreement or the note. Also, if loans are to be sold or transferred to certain government corporations, the loan arrangement cannot include a prepayment penalty.

Late Payment Clause To help the mortgagee receive payments on time and to avoid the problems of collecting payments after the agreed upon mortgage payment deadlines, late payment clauses are usually included in mortgage documents, promissory notes, or both. These clauses enable the mortgagee to charge a late fee for payments received a certain number of days after the due date. The purpose of the fee is to cover the bookkeeping expenses of having to post late payments. Late payment clauses are legal in all types of loans. The following is an example of a late payment clause from a mortgage:

> If any payment due hereunder is received later than fifteen days after the due date of the payment, a late charge of _____ (_____%) of the amount then overdue may be charged by the mortgagee for the purposes of defraying costs of collection and posting of the account.

Due-on-Sale Clause The *due-on-sale clause* is a provision in the mortgage agreement that is similar to the acceleration clause already discussed. The difference is that it takes effect not upon the default of the mortgagor, but upon the attempted sale of the property by the mortgagor to a buyer who will take over mortgage payments. The due-on-sale clause gives the mortgagee the right to call the entire balance of an indebtedness due and payable if the borrower sells the mortgaged property. The following is an example:

> TRANSFER OF THE PROPERTY; ASSUMPTION. If all or any part of the property or an interest therein is sold or transferred by Borrower without Lender's prior consent, excluding (a) the creation of a lien or encumbrance subordinate to this deed of trust; (b) the creation of a purchase money security interest for household appliances; (c) transfer by devise, descent, or by operation of law upon the death of a joint tenant; or (d) the grant of any leasehold interest of three years or less not containing an option to purchase, LENDER MAY, AT LENDER'S OPTION, DECLARE ALL SUMS SECURED BY THIS DEED OF TRUST TO BE IMMEDIATELY DUE AND PAYABLE. Lender shall have waived such option to accelerate if, prior to the sale or transfer, Lender and the person to whom the property is to be sold or transferred reach agreement in writing that the credit of such person is satisfactory to Lender and that the interest payable on the sums secured by this deed of trust shall be at such rate as the Lender shall request. If Lender has waived the option to accelerate provided in this paragraph and if the Borrower's successor in interest has executed a written assumption agreement accepted by Lender, Lender shall release borrower from all obligations under this Deed of Trust and note.

If Lender exercises the option to accelerate, Lender shall mail Borrower notice of such acceleration at least 30 days prior to the time Lender will declare such sums due and payable.

As interest rates increase, such a clause becomes more helpful to the mortgagee because mortgage notes at older, unprofitable rates can be eliminated and the outstanding funds reinvested at higher rates. However, the clauses do create problems for the mortgagor attempting to sell property in a period of high interest rates. If the buyer cannot take over an existing loan and the cost of borrowing is prohibitive, then the seller will experience great difficulty in transferring the property.

Because of the increase of interest rates during the 1970s and early 1980s, many lenders sought to enforce their due-on-sale clauses when mortgagors attempted to sell their property. Both buyers and mortgagors had objections to the legality of the clauses, and from 1970 until 1980 more than twenty different cases involving the issue of due-on-sale clauses were heard by state appellate courts. Some states recognized the clauses as valid while others declared them unenforceable.

Additional complications regarding the validity of the clauses arose because some lenders were regulated by the federal government, which had passed a regulation that permitted federal institutions to use and enforce the clauses in mortgage arrangements. State courts were thus making decisions affecting federal institutions, and the issue of preemption of federal law by state law became fundamental in the continuing judicial battles over the clauses.

The due-on-sale clauses were declared invalid by state courts when the lender automatically called the loan due upon transfer without establishing that the loan was somehow in jeopardy, meaning that the mortgagor was selling to a party who was incapable of making the payments, was insolvent, or had a credit rating that would cause a lender to refuse them a loan. Many states held that to permit lenders to automatically exercise such clauses was a restraint on alienation and contrary to public policy.

Those states recognizing the clauses as valid did so on two different bases: First, the clauses were often classified as forms of acceleration clauses; and because acceleration clauses in general were valid, the due-on-sale acceleration clauses were also valid. Second, some courts held that the mortgagee had the right to protect the investment made and therefore, upon transfer of the property, could choose to reinvest the funds elsewhere. Such a reinvestment was not contrary to public policy so long as the parties had agreed to the term in advance.

The validity of due-on-sale clauses has been decided at the federal level for application to federally chartered or insured lenders. In the following case, the United States Supreme Court decided the issue of whether due-on-sale clauses could be used by those institutions. This case also resolved the issue of preemption in this area. Note that the decision is limited to federal institutions; the state financial institutions are discussed on page 356.

FIDELITY FEDERAL SAVINGS AND LOAN ASSOC. v. DE LA CUESTA
458 U.S. 141 (1982)

Fidelity (defendant/appellant) loaned money to several buyers for the purchase of different parcels of property located in California and took deeds of trust in the properties as security for the loans. The deeds of trust all contained due-on-sale clauses. The deeds of trust also contained clauses that provided that the agreements be governed by "the law of the jurisdiction in which the property is located." California's courts had declared the due-on-sale clause invalid.

Moore, Whitcombe, and de la Cuesta (purchasers/plaintiffs/appellees) each purchased one of the properties in which Fidelity held the deeds of trust. Fidelity was not notified of any of the transfers by its mortgagors prior to the time of the transfers. When Fidelity discovered the transfers, it notified the purchasers that the due-on-sale clauses would be en-

forced. In lieu of exercising the clauses, Fidelity offered to consent to the transfers if the purchasers would agree to increase their loan interest rates to the prevailing market rate. The purchasers refused the offer on the loan increases, and Fidelity instituted nonjudicial foreclosure proceedings.

The purchasers filed suit alleging that Fidelity's exercise of the due-on-sale clauses violated California's ruling that such clauses were unreasonable restraints on alienation "unless the lender can demonstrate that enforcement is reasonably necessary to protect against impairment to its security or the risk of default."

The district court found for Fidelity, but the court of appeals reversed the decision. The California Supreme Court denied review, but the United States Supreme Court granted certiorari.

BLACKMUN, Justice

The Federal Home Loan Bank Board, an independent federal regulatory agency, was formed in 1932 and thereafter was vested with plenary authority to administer the Home Owner's Loan Act of 1933 (HOLA). Section 5(a) of the HOLA, 12 U.S.C. §1464(a)(1976 ed., Supp. IV), empowers the Board, "under such rules and regulations as it may prescribe, to provide for the organization, incorporation, examination, operation and regulation of associations to be known as 'Federal Savings and Loan Associations.' " Pursuant to this

authorization, the Board has promulgated regulations governing "the powers and operations of every Federal savings and loan association from its cradle to its corporate grave."

In 1976, the Board became concerned about the increasing controversy as to the authority of a federal savings and loan association to exercise a "due-on-sale" clause. Specifically, the Board felt that restrictions on a savings and loan's ability to accelerate a loan upon transfer of the security would have a number of adverse effects: (1) that "the financial security and stability of Federal associations would be endangered if . . . the security property is transferred to a person whose ability to repay the loan and properly maintain the property is inadequate"; (2) that "elimination of the due on sale clause will cause a substantial reduction of the cash flow and net income of Federal associations, and that to offset such losses it is likely that the associations will be forced to charge higher interest rates and loan charges on home loans generally"; (3) that "elimination of due on sale clauses will restrict and impair the ability of Federal associations to sell their home loans in the secondary mortgage market, by making such loans unsalable or causing them to be sold at reduced prices, thereby reducing the flow of new funds for residential loans, which would otherwise be available." The Board concluded that "elimination of the due-on-sale clause will benefit only a limited number of home sellers, but generally will cause economic hardship to the majority of home buyers and potential home buyers."

Accordingly, the Board issued a regulation, effective July 31, 1976, governing due-on-sale clauses. The regulation, now 12 CFR §545.8-3(f) (1982), provides in relevant part:

A federal savings and loan association continues to have the power to include, as a matter of contract between it and the borrower, a provision in its loan instrument whereby the association may, at its option, declare immediately due and payable sums secured by the association's security instrument if all or any part of the real property securing the loan is sold or transferred by the borrower without the association's prior written consent. Except as otherwise provided . . . in this section . . . exercise by the association of such option (hereafter called a due-on-sale clause) shall be exclusively governed by the terms of the loan contract, and all rights and remedies of the association and borrower shall be fixed and governed by that contract.

In the preamble accompanying final publication of the due-on-sale regulation, the Board explained its intent that the due-on-sale practices of Federal savings and loans be governed "exclusively by Federal law." The Board emphasized that "Federal associations shall not be bound by or subject to any conflicting state law which imposes different . . . due-on-sale requirements."

The pre-emption doctrine, which has its roots in the Supremacy Clause, U.S. Const., Art. VI, cl. 2, requires us to examine Congressional intent. Pre-emption may either be express or implied, and "is compelled whether Congress' command is explicitly stated in the statute's language or implicitly contained in its structure and purpose." Absent explicit pre-emptive language, Congress' intent to supersede state law altogether may be inferred because "the scheme of Federal regulation may be so pervasive as to make reasonable the inference that Congress left no room for the States to supplement it," because "the Act of Congress may touch a field in which the Federal interest is so dominant that the Federal system will be assumed to preclude enforcement of state laws on the same subject," or because "the object sought to be obtained by Federal law and the character of obligations imposed by it reveal the same purpose."

Even where Congress has not completely displaced state regulation in a specific area, state law is nullified to the extent that it actually conflicts with Federal law. Such a conflict arises when "compliance with both Federal and state regulations is a physical impossibility," or when state law "stands as an obstacle to the accomplishment and execution of the full purposes and objectives of Congress."

These principles are not inapplicable here simply because real property is a matter of special concern to the States: "The relative importance to the State of its own law is not material when there is a conflict with a valid Federal law, for the Framers of our Constitution provided that the Federal law must prevail."

Federal regulations have no less pre-emptive effect than Federal statutes. Where Congress has directed an administrator to exercise his discretion, his judgments are subject to judicial review only to determine whether he has exceeded his statutory authority or acted arbitrarily.

The questions upon which resolution of this case rests are whether the Board meant to pre-empt California's due-on-sale law, and, if so, whether that action is within the scope of the Board's delegated authority.

The California courts have limited a Federal association's right to exercise a due-on-sale provision to those cases where the lender can demonstrate that the transfer has impaired its security.

The conflict does not evaporate because the Board's regulation simply permits, but does not compel, Federal savings and loans to include due-on-sale clauses in their contracts and to enforce those provisions when the security is transferred. The Board consciously has chosen not to mandate use of due-on-sale clauses "because it desires to afford associations the flexibility to accommodate special situations and circumstances."

The California courts have forbidden a Federal savings and loan from enforcing a due-on-sale clause solely "at its option" and have deprived the lender of the flexibility given it by the Board.

The question remains whether the Board acted within its statutory authority in issuing the pre-emptive due-on-sale regulation. The language and history of the HOLA convince us that Congress delegated to the Board ample authority to regulate the lending practices of Federal savings and loans so as to further the Act's purposes.

HOLA did not simply incorporate existing local loan practices. Rather, Congress delegated to the Board broad authority to establish and regulate "a uniform system of savings and loan institutions where there are not any now," and to "establish them with the force of the government behind them, with a national charter."

Congress delegated power to the Board expressly for the purpose of creating and regulating federal savings and loans so as to ensure that they would remain financially sound institutions able to supply financing for home construction and purchase. The due-on-sale regulation was promulgated with these purposes in mind. The Board has determined that due-on-sale clauses are "a valuable and often an indispensable source of protection for the financial soundness of Federal associations and for their continued ability to fund new home loan commitments." Specifically, the Board has concluded that the due-on-sale clause is "an important part of the mortgage contract" and that its elimination "will have an adverse effect on the earning power and financial stability of Federal associations, will impair the ability of Federal associations to sell their loans in the secondary markets, will reduce the amount of home-financing funds available to potential home buyers, and generally will cause a rise in home loan interest rates."

The Board's analysis proceeds as follows: It observes that the Federal associations' practice of borrowing short and lending long—obtaining funds on a short-term basis and investing them in long-term real estate loans, which typically have a 25-to-30 year term—combined with rising interest rates has increased the cost of funds to these institutions and reduced their income. Exercising due-on-sale clauses enables savings and loans to alleviate this problem by replacing long-term, low-yield loans with loans at the prevailing interest rates and thereby to avoid increasing rates across the board.

Admittedly, the wisdom of the Board's policy decision is not uncontroverted. But neither is it arbitrary and capricious. As judges, it is neither our function, nor within our expertise, to evaluate the economic soundness of the Board's approach. In promulgating the due-on-sale regulation, the Board reasonably exercised the authority, given it by Congress, so as to ensure the financial stability of "local mutual thrift institutions in which people . . . invest their funds and . . . which provide for the financing of homes." By so doing, the Board intended to pre-empt conflicting state restrictions on due-on-sale practices like the one in California.

Affirmed.

Discussion Questions

1. Who holds the deeds of trust in the properties?
2. What did Fidelity offer to do in lieu of exercising the due-on-sale clauses?
3. Who passed the Federal regulation permitting the use and enforcement of due-on-sale clauses?
4. For preemption purposes, is a federal regulation given the same status as a federal law?
5. Are federal savings and loan associations to be governed exclusively by federal laws and regulations?
6. May Fidelity exercise its due-on-sale clauses in California?

On 15 October 1982 Congress enacted the *Garn-St.Germain Depository Institutions Act* of 1982 (called the *Garn Bill;* 12 U.S.C. §226), which provides that states may not restrict the enforcement of due-on-sale clauses with respect to real property loans except to protect home buyers who relied on due-on-sale restrictions and reasonably believed they had assumable loans. The Garn Bill created *window periods* to protect these types of buyers. Any loans issued during a window period enjoy protection from enforcement of due-on-sale clauses. The typical period runs from 1970 until the date of the Garn Bill. Therefore, buyers who purchased during a window period in a state that prevented enforcement of due-on-sale clauses are protected and have assumable mortgage loans. The Garn Bill is applicable to loans made by organizations other than federally chartered institutions, and it still permits lenders to exercise due-on-sale clauses if the buyer is not creditworthy. The Garn Bill also prevents the exercise of due-on-sale clauses of loans made after 15 October 1982 in transfers by mortgagors to relatives; in the creation of purchase money security interests (PMSIs); in the granting of leases of 3 years' duration or less; and in marriage dissolution transfers. The purposes of the Garn Bill were to aid buyers who might have relied on assumability and to clarify the types of transfers under which the due-on-sale clause may be enforced.

Types of Mortgages

Government Insured Mortgages—FHA and VA Mortgages The acronyms *FHA* and *VA* are used widely in advertisements, discussions, and news about the housing market. Both terms signify a government backed loan, which means that if the borrower defaults on repayment of the loan, the lender can recover the loan amount from the federal agency insuring the loan. The Federal Housing Administration and the Veterans Administration serve as the insuring agencies for these types of loans.

The loans are issued through savings and loan associations, mortgage companies, and banks but have many associated restrictions, most of which are imposed for the protection of the mortgagor. For example, the interest rate on such loans is set by the federal government, and the borrower must qualify for the loan through the insuring government agency. Also, the terms of the mortgage and note are regulated by the federal government, and certain types of clauses discussed above are prohibited. For example, as mentioned earlier, the balloon payment provision is prohibited in FHA and VA loans.

In addition to the benefits of the government's acting as an insurer, a mortgagee giving a government insured loan also enjoys the benefits of having a secondary market for these mortgages through government owned corporations. These government owned corporations, such as the *Federal National Mortgage Association (FNMA or Fannie Mae)*, the *Government National Mortgage Association (GNMA or Ginnie Mae)*, and the *Federal Home Loan Mortgage Corporation (FHLMC or Freddie Mac)*, purchase blocks of government insured mortgages and in some cases conventional mortgages. These secondary market corporations were created to encourage primary lenders to participate in the home mortgage market.

There are additional restrictions on government insured mortgages. For example, both FHA and VA carry maximum loan amounts, so that these loans are not available for higher-priced residences. Also, the borrower is required to pay the premium for the government insurance, which is .5 percent of the outstanding balance for the life of the loan. On FHA loans a certain minimum down payment is required, but on VA loans no down payment is required.

Because of climbing and high interest rates in recent years, many different types of FHA loans have been developed to enable buyers to qualify for and afford home purchases. For example, FHA introduced the graduated payment mortgage (FHA 245), which provided for a lower beginning monthly payment that is gradually increased each year over the next 5 years until reaching a level payment in the sixth year of the loan. Additional features were introduced by FHA for the purchase of low income housing, including lower interest rates and lower down payments, to help those in lower income brackets purchase homes.

Conventional Mortgages The *conventional mortgage* is a mortgage made by a private lender that is not insured by a government agency and, hence, not subject to the restrictions imposed on lenders seeking government insurance. The conventional mortgage may be offered by the same institutions offering FHA and VA loans.

Financing property by a conventional mortgage is different from financing by a government insured mortgage in that the interest rate will probably be higher; the down payment required will probably be greater; and the lender will be able to incorporate additional terms in the mortgage agreement such as balloon payments, due-on-sale clauses, interest acceleration clauses, and other terms restricted or regulated in government loans.

Purchase Money Mortgages The *purchase money mortgage* is one in which the funds are being borrowed to finance the purchase of the property, and the property is pledged as security for the loan. In most residential home purchases, the lender obtains a purchase money mortgage for the buyer, who borrows funds for the purchase of the residence.

Master Mortgages With all of the possible clauses that may be used in a mortgage, it is likely that the mortgage will be long and complex. Furthermore, a lender may be using the same mortgage forms for all mortgages given and will be recording the same document each time in the appropriate governmental office. To avoid this duplication of recording some states have enacted *master mortgage* statutes, which permit lenders to record one master mortgage. Then, to record a newly created mortgage, the lenders simply record a document that refers to the location of the recorded master mortgage, and which gives the description of the subject property.

Straight Term Mortgages A *straight term mortgage* is a mortgage in which there is no provision for the amortization of principal over a period of time. Rather, the borrower makes interest payments at various intervals and then repays the unpaid principal along with any accrued interest at the end of the term (usually 3 to 5 years). The balloon payment clause creates a form of a straight term mortgage. This type of mortgage can be used effectively by the seller in creative financing techniques. (See later.)

Subordinate or Wrap-around Mortgages A *subordinate mortgage* (or *wrap-around mortgage)* is created in property that is already subject to another mortgage. It has been used effectively by sellers who act as lenders for their buyers who cannot afford a loan from a commercial lender because of high rates. This type of mortgage is discussed in detail in the creative financing section of this chapter.

Anaconda or Dragnet Mortgages An *Anaconda mortgage* or *dragnet mortgage* contains a clause that provides that the mortgage secures all items of indebtedness that the mortgagor may, at any time during the period of mortgage, owe to the mortgagee. Under such an agreement, the lender may acquire all the debts of the mortgagor at a discount and then collect 100 percent through the mortgage transaction.

Adjustable Rate Mortgages A new trend in home financing is the *adjustable rate mortgage (ARM)*. The adjustable rate mortgage is one that has a fluctuating interest rate throughout the life of the loan. The fluctuations result from the loan's rate being tied to some index such as the FHA rate, the treasury securities index, or treasury bill rates. The fluctuations will vary according to the terms of the note or loan agreement, but the following factors should be covered to assure the borrower knows the extent of the fluctuations.

1. What index will be used? Short term indices (like treasury bills) tend to be more volatile. The only restrictions on use are that the index be public and not controllable by the lender.
2. What will be the margin? The margin is the difference between the index rate and the contract rate. In other words, the borrower's rate is the index plus the margin. The margin could be from 1% to 4%.
3. What adjustment period will be used? Will the ARM be adjusted every six months? Every year? Shorter periods are more beneficial for the lender.
4. Is there a rate cap? Is there a maximum interest rate for the loan?
5. If the loan is assumed, is the cap readjusted upon assumption?
6. Is the rate for loan qualifying different from the rate for the first year? If so, there may be negative amortization which means the monthly payments are low the first year but the size of the mortgage increases during that time.

Rights and Responsibilities of Mortgagor and Mortgagee

It is hoped that most of the responsibilities of the mortgagor and the mortgagee will be fully covered in the written and executed mortgage agreement between the parties. But in case the parties fail to specify all the necessary terms of their relationship, the law does provide certain rules for governing the relationship.

Rents and Leases The rights of the parties with regard to the rents received from the property will vary (as discussed earlier) according to whether the property is located in a title or a lien theory state. In the title theory states, the mortgagee has the right to the rents upon execution of the mortgage. In the lien theory states, the mortgagee is not entitled to rents or possession until after default and the successful completion of court proceedings for foreclosure.

However, in some lien theory states the parties are permitted to put a clause in their mortgage agreement that gives the mortgagee the right to possession and rents immediately upon default by the mortgagor. In other lien theory states, such a clause is treated as void.

In any state where the mortgagee is properly in possession of the mortgaged property and collecting rents, the mortgagee does have the responsibility for accounting to the mortgagor for the rents received during the period of possession. In some lien theory states, the rents received while the mortgagee is in possession must be applied to the reduction of the mortgage debt.

One final issue that remains in the area of the leasing of mortgaged property is that of the tenant's rights. The rights of tenants of mortgaged property will vary according to the time the lease was executed. For those leases that antedate the mortgage, the mortgagee is required to honor the tenant's rights, and such rights must be honored even when the mortgagee forecloses. In a postdated lease, the mortgagee is permitted to terminate the lease simply because of the mortgagor's default. Of course, the mortgagor and mortgagee could have a clause in the lease that made tenants' rights subject to all mortgages.

If a lease is entered into after the mortgage has been executed, then the mortgagee is permitted to extinguish the rights of the tenant upon default and foreclosure.

Both tenants and mortgagees should carefully scrutinize the other documents before entering into their transactions. For example, a tenant leasing subsequent to a mortgage execution should check the mortgage for termination and cancellation provisions to fully appreciate the rights available. A mortgagee taking a mortgage on property subject to existing leases should carefully review the terms of the leases prior to execution of the mortgage, to determine if any additional protections or clauses need to be built into the mortgage.

The following case illustrates the rights of mortgagor, mortgagee, and tenants upon default by the mortgagor. After reading the case, determine whether the result would be the same under the theory of mortgages followed by your state.

IN RE STUCKENBERG
374 F. Supp. 15 (Mo. 1974)

Stuckenberg, through a straw party, purchased a ranchette-style apartment building with five apartments under one roof. Stuckenberg purchased the property with funds from a note signed with First Federal, which was secured with a deed of trust on the property. Paragraph 7 of the deed of trust provided:

First Federal shall have power and authority to take possession of the said real estate and to manage, control and lease the same and collect all rents, issues and profits therefrom for the purpose of paying the note secured by the deed of trust.

The full amount of the loan was due in February 1969, and Stuckenberg defaulted on both the January and February 1969 payments. After the default, First Federal notified Stuckenberg's son of their intention to exercise their rights under paragraph 7 and requested information on the tenants, the rental amounts, and the rental due dates. First Federal then sent to Stuckenberg, his attorney, and all the tenants a notice of First Federal's rights under paragraph 7 and their intent to exercise those rights. A management corporation was hired by First Federal, and personal service of the letter was given to three of the five tenants in the building (the other tenants could not be reached).

Shortly after this notice, Stuckenberg filed for bankruptcy. First Federal claimed it was entitled to the rents after the default, but this contention was challenged because First Federal had not notified all tenants. The bankruptcy judge held that First Federal was entitled to the rents on three of the five apartments, and First Federal appealed.

REGAN, District Judge

The applicable Missouri rule is to the effect that after default, the mortgagee has the right to possession of the mortgaged property for the purpose of collecting rents and profits and applying them to the discharge of the mortgage debt, but that he is not entitled to rents "until the mortgagee enters into actual possession of the property or takes some equivalent action."

The theory advanced below was that First Federal only had actual possession with regard to those units for which notice was given prior to bankruptcy.

We start with the fact that the deed of trust covers a single parcel of real estate with but one building on it, so that basically the question is whether First Federal entered into possession of that building. Even though there was no specific affirmative consent by the bankrupt to the action of First Federal, the circumstances clearly evidence an implied consent on his part. Not only had notices of default theretofore been sent to the bankrupt but he was given a copy of the February 21 letter which expressly informed him not merely that First Federal intended to take possession but that it was then taking possession of the property as of that date.

. . . *where, as here, the owner is not in actual but constructive possession of the mortgaged premises, nothing more than the service of a notice, or demand made by the mortgagee upon the tenant, setting forth that he is exercising his rights of possession could be required. Certainly, the mortgagee is not required to remove the tenants and thus actually and physically place himself in possession.*

Under the totality of the facts in evidence, we believe that it would be anomalous to hold that First Federal took possession of only three units of the building, leaving the other two units in the bankrupt's possession.

The order of the Referee is modified to include First Federal's right to rents from the remaining two units.

Discussion Questions

1. Who is the mortgagor? Who is the mortgagee?
2. Describe the property mortgaged.
3. What did First Federal do upon default?
4. Who was served with personal notice and who served it?
5. Who was entitled to what rents according to the bankruptcy court?
6. What issue controlled whether First Federal was entitled to the rents?
7. Upon appeal, who is entitled to the rents?
8. What is the significance of paragraph 7?
9. Is the case in a title theory or lien theory state?

Property Covered by the Mortgage Unless otherwise specified, the mortgage will include all real property located on the land described in the mortgage document. The mortgage will thus cover all buildings, fixtures, easements, and any other items classified as real property.

Often mortgagees will include as a provision in their mortgage agreement an *after-acquired property clause.* The purpose of such a clause is to have the mortgage include any buildings, fixtures, or other attachments that might be made to the land subsequent to the time of the mortgage. The clause also protects the mortgagee in that substantial changes could occur in the structures already existing on the land or in additions to those structures, and a limited mortgage coverage would prevent the mortgagee from effectively exercising rights in that property.

To clarify the exact property included in the mortgage, the mortgagee should specify any questionable items that might be construed as personal instead of real property. The following clause is an example of a thorough inclusion clause (which can cover after-acquired clause property) that would follow the legal description of the property in the mortgage agreement.

> TOGETHER with all articles and fixtures used in occupying, operating, or renting the building on the premises, including but not limited to gas and electric fixtures, radiators, heaters, washers, driers, engines and machinery, boilers, ranges, elevators, escalators, incinerators, motors, bathtubs, sinks, pipes, faucets, and other heating and plumbing fixtures, air conditioning equipment, mirrors, cabinets, refrigerators, stoves, fire prevention and extinguishing devices, furniture, shades, blinds, curtains, draperies, drapery and curtain rods, rugs, carpets, and all other floor coverings, lamps, wall hangings and pictures, and all replacements thereof and additions thereto from this point on and such additions and replacements shall be deemed to form a part of the realty and are thus covered by the lien of this mortgage.

Transfers and Assignments In many property purchases made through the use of a purchase money mortgage, the mortgagor will not remain in possession or use of the property for the entire term of the mortgage. In residential and commercial transactions, it is often necessary for the original mortgagor to sell or transfer the mortgaged property. In the following sections, the methods of transfer and the rights and duties of the parties involved in the transfer are discussed.

1. The Assumption In many cases the original mortgagor's interest rate is lower than the rates available at the time the transfer of the property becomes necessary. Thus if the buyer can purchase the property by agreeing to assume the responsibility for repayment of the original mortgage, the seller will have a much better chance of being able to market the property at a good price.

The following factual example helps to illustrate how this method of transferring the mortgage debt as part of the purchase price of the property works:

Hal Wood purchased a small home for $43,500 in 1977. In 1980 it became necessary for Hal to sell the home. Hal had a mortgage balance of approximately $40,000 on the home, and he advertised to sell the home for $55,000. Bob Freeman has made an offer of $52,000, with Bob paying Hal $12,000 cash and agreeing to assume responsibility for repayment of the $40,000 mortgage.

The following is a diagram of the example:

FIRST MORTGAGEE ⟷ HAL WOOD, MORTGAGOR

BOB FREEMAN, BUYER

The transaction is a simple assignment of contract benefits and a delegation of contracts duties. Bob will enjoy the benefits of residing in the property but will assume responsibility for the mortgage payments. The transaction is referred to as an *assumption*, or, frequently, as a *cash-to-mortgage sale*, since Bob is paying enough cash down to be able to assume the mortgage.

The transaction raises several questions as to the liability of each of the parties involved. Bob, as the buyer or assignee, becomes liable on the mortgage by executing an assumption agreement. An assumption agreement specifies the amount of the mortgage balance, the name of the mortgagee, and that the buyer agrees to assume responsibility for repayment of the mortgage amount. Such an agreement does not, however, relieve the original mortgagor (Hal) of liability under the mortgage arrangement. The mortgagor remains liable for repayment of the debt and may be turned to if the buyer defaults. The mortgagee has the right to enforce repayment against either one of the parties and always retains the right of foreclosure in the event both parties default (discussed later). The buyer is primarily liable on the mortgage and the seller is secondarily liable so that the lender is required to proceed against the parties in a certain order.

The only way the mortgagor can be relieved of liability under the mortgage agreement is if the mortgagee consents to such a release. Many mortgages have provisions that require a release once the mortgagee has qualified or is satisfied with the purchaser and has consented in writing to the transfer and assumption.

Not all mortgages may be assumed and, as discussed earlier, many are subject to a due-on-sale provision, which effectively prevents the mortgagor from transferring the rights available under the mortgage.

2. The Subject-to Sale In a sale of property by a mortgagor to a buyer where the buyer takes *subject-to* the existing mortgage, the mortgagor remains personally liable on the mortgage; the buyer undertakes no personal responsibility for payment of the mortgage; and the property remains subject to the foreclosure rights of the mortgagee. In a subject to sale, the seller continues to be responsible for the payments on the mortgage. The mortgagee's rights are not affected by a transfer of property subject to its existing mortgage. The subject-to sale can be used very effectively in some of the creative financing techniques discussed later in the chapter.

3. Refinancing In some property sales where the cash-to-mortgage balance is too high for the buyer, the buyer will be required to finance the purchase of the property by borrowing the money under a new note secured by a new mortgage. When this occurs, the purchase of the property is being refinanced. The result is that the original mortgagee is paid the full amount due on the mortgage, the seller is given the cash difference between the sale price and the mortgage balance, and a new mortgage is created in the property. Upon payment, the seller is no longer liable and the mortgagee no longer has any rights in the property.

Satisfaction of the Mortgage As discussed earlier, a mortgage is valid only if it is supported by some underlying debt. Once that debt is repaid the mortgage is no longer valid and must be terminated. The termination of the mortgage and hence the mortgagee's interest is accomplished through the execution and recording of an agreement called a *satisfaction of mortgage.*

The satisfaction of mortgage requires only an adequate description of the property and the signature of the mortgagee (usually notarized). Figure 12.5 is an example of the simple language that may be used to satisfy the requirements for clearing title to the property of the mortgage.

Figure 12.5 *Satisfaction of Mortgage*

KNOW ALL MEN BY THESE PRESENTS: That the mortgage executed by

_____

to _____ dated _____ and recorded _____
in Docket ____ pages _____ in the Office of the County Recorder of
_____ County, _____, together with the debt thereby secured, is fully paid, satisfied, and discharged.

DATED THIS ____ day of _____, 19____

_____

MORTGAGEE

The satisfaction of the mortgage document should be recorded where all other land interests are recorded because it serves to clear the title of the mortgage lien in lien states or to vest title in the mortgagor in title states. All states have some type of statutory penalty that is imposed upon mortgagees who wrongfully refuse to execute a release or satisfaction of the mortgage. Ordinarily the penalty is minimal, but in some states the fine may be imposed on a weekly basis, such as $50 per week for each week the release or satisfaction is not given.

Default of the Mortgagor A *default* occurs when the mortgagor fails to comply with some provision of the mortgage agreement. Generally, default occurs when the mortgagor has failed to make timely payments in accordance with the schedule agreed to under the terms of the underlying note or in the mortgage agreement itself. However, it is possible for default to occur whenever the mortgagor breaches the agreement through violation of any of the other provisions of the mortgage. For example, most mortgagees require the mortgagor to maintain hazard insurance on the property and to make timely payments of taxes and assessments. Failure to comply with these provisions also constitutes a default.

In case the mortgagor engages in conduct that causes destruction, devaluation, or general decline of the property, there is usually a provision in the mortgage agreement that prohibits such activities, known as waste, and the mortgagee may declare such conduct to be a default.

It is important that the provisions in the mortgage agreement establish what constitutes default. Although all states afford remedies for mortgagees upon the mortgagor's default, very few of the statutes define what actually constitutes default. Therefore, the mortgagee must rely on the written mortgage agreement to establish the actual default of the mortgagor. Only upon establishing default is the mortgagee able to exercise the remedies afforded under mortgage law: foreclosure. The following is an example of a clause imposing rights and responsibilities on the mortgagor. The mortgage acceleration clause and default provisions are to be tied to violations of the provisions within this clause.

> THE MORTGAGOR, his heirs, administrators, executors, and assignees hereby covenant and agree with the mortgagee, its successors, and assigns to pay the principal sum of money and interest as above specified; to pay all taxes and assessments now due or that may hereafter become liens against said premises at least 10 days before penalty attaches thereto; to keep any buildings on said premises insured by companies approved by the mortgagee against loss by fire for at least the sum of _____ DOLLARS, and to deliver to said mortgagee the policies for such insurance with mortgage clause attached in favor of said mortgagee or its assigns; to pay when due, both principal and interest of all prior liens and encumbrances, if any above mentioned; and to keep said premises free and clear of all other prior liens and encumbrances; to commit or permit no waste on said premises and to keep them in good repair.

FORECLOSURE

Processes of Foreclosure

As mortgages existed initially in England, the mortgagor was required to make payment of the debt by a certain date. If the payment was not made, the mortgagor lost all right and interest in the property to the mortgagee. Today, upon the mortgagor's default it is quite possible that the mortgagor will lose all interest in the property, but the loss will not occur without substantial judicial procedures and notification plus a second chance or two for the mortgagor to regain the interest in the property.

Upon default, the mortgagee is entitled to foreclose on the property. This *foreclosure* may be accomplished in different ways according to state law. Each state has different procedures for the mortgagee to follow in exercising foreclosure rights, but basically the methods can be divided into two groups.

Judicial Foreclosure Under *judicial foreclosure*, the mortgagee is required to bring suit in the appropriate court to have the rights of the interested parties determined. The court then orders the sale of the property to satisfy the total amount then due and owing on the debt. If the mortgagee is to have good title pass through the judicial foreclosure sale, there must be proper compliance with all procedural requirements; otherwise the entire proceeding may be set aside.

1. Filing the Petition Judicial foreclosure begins with the mortgagee or the mortgagee's attorney filing a petition in the proper court, usually in the state and county where the property is located. The petition must adequately state the factual basis for the foreclosure action, including the dates and amounts of all defaults, the exact amount of principal then due on the underlying debt, and the requested relief such as a judicial sale.

2. Required Parties After the petition is filed, it must be served upon all parties who will be affected by the foreclosure action. In addition to the mortgagor, other parties included are tenants, second or junior mortgagees, holders of mechanic's liens, Article 9 secured creditors, any government agencies having tax claims, and all other statutory lienors. Determining the parties who need to be served with notice of foreclosure is best accomplished by conducting a search of the land records for all possible land interests.

3. Filing the Notice of Action (Lis Pendens) Because of court backlog and required statutory waiting periods, it may be some time before the foreclosure sale can actually be ordered and carried out by the courts. Public notification of the pending foreclosure is necessary to prevent the creation of additional interests in the property between the filing of the petition and the actual sale of the property. To accomplish this the mortgagee files a notice in the land records that an action has been filed. This notice is called a *lis pendens,* and it serves as adequate notification to all dealing with the property or the mortgagor that a foreclosure suit is pending. The notice is filed under all parties' names so that the records establish whose interest existed prior to the filing of the action.

4. Foreclosure Trial or Hearing The only elements required to be established at the actual hearing for foreclosure are that there has been a default and that the mortgage agreement authorizes the judicial action and sale. Generally, such a hearing is simply a formality and the mortgagor may not even appear to challenge the proceedings.

5. Strict Foreclosure Once the court finds that foreclosure is appropriate, an order for foreclosure will be entered. In strict foreclosure states, the judge enters an order that permits the mortgagor a certain time period (usually 3 to 4 months) within which to pay the total amount due and owing, and thereby reacquire the property in question. If the mortgagor is not able to pay the amount due within that time, the order provides for a sale of the property. The mortgagor thus loses forever all interest in the property and the right to reacquire the property.

6. Foreclosure with Statutory Redemption In other states, a sale will be held as soon as possible after the judge finds default and orders foreclosure, but the mortgagor is still given one last chance to redeem the property interest. For a statutory period ranging from 6 months to a year after the property is put up for sale, the mortgagor is given the right to pay the full amount due and regain right to the property (even if the property has in fact been sold). This right to pay the debt after the judicial sale is referred to as the *statutory right of redemption*. The effects of the statutory period are twofold: (1) to require the mortgagee to wait before closing the case file completely, and (2) to require the purchaser of the property to wait before actually obtaining full and complete title.

7. The Judicial Sale Upon order in most state courts, the mortgaged property is offered at a public sale for which notice has been published. The sale is carried out by an officer of the judiciary, such as a sheriff, and is conducted as an auction with the property being transferred to the highest bidder. In strict foreclosure states, the purchaser is given a sheriff's deed, which serves to convey title but does not include any warranties of title. The deed is only as good as the judicial procedures were proper. In statutory redemption states, the purchaser is given some type of document such as a certificate of sale as evidence of the purchase, but the purchaser cannot be given title to the property until the period of statutory redemption has passed. At the end of the statutory redemption period, the purchaser is given a *sheriff's deed* (also called a *judicial deed*).

Most challenges to foreclosure proceedings by mortgagors arise because of complaints about the manner in which the judicial sale is handled. To avoid such challenges, it is important that the sale be adequately advertised and that the bidding be conducted in a fair and proper manner. Often mortgagors feel that the price obtained for the property was inadequate. Such a complaint is seldom a basis for setting aside the transaction because the very nature of the transaction results in lower bids. This is especially true in states where redemption is possible and the investment is tied up for the statutory period with no guarantee of title being transferred.

(12.4) Consider:

Reconsider Edward Knudsen's question at the beginning of the chapter. Has the Mortgage Company acted properly?

8. The Soldiers and Sailors Relief Act (50 U.S.C. §501) This federal act can have a substantial effect on mortgage foreclosure proceedings. It requires that special notice be given to mortgagors who are currently in active military service. The act also permits the court to postpone foreclosure proceedings if the default of the mortgagor results from a pay reduction because of induction into the armed services.

The Soldiers and Sailors Relief Act was passed to protect those drafted into the military service from losing their homes while they served. The act provides further protection in statutory redemption states because the period of the mortgagor's active military service is not included in computing the statutory period. In other words, the period does not begin until active service terminates.

Foreclosure by Power of Sale Many states permit mortgagees to include in their mortgage agreements provisions that permit them to sell the property, upon the mortgagor's default, without the court proceedings. This *power of sale* is a characteristic of the deed of trust financing arrangement (discussed later).

Under this method of foreclosure, a rather quick and nonjudicial sale may be held. All states permitting foreclosure by this method have set up statutory procedures with which the mortgagee must comply before the sale is recognized as valid.

1. Notice and Advertisement All states recognizing the power of sale as a method of foreclosure require the mortgagee to furnish notice to all interested parties (the mortgagor, secondary or junior creditors, lienors, and so on) and also to advertise or publish notice of the impending sale, including time and place of the sale. In some states the notice of sale is so important that this method of foreclosure is referred to as *foreclosure by advertisement*. The notice and advertisement must be accomplished within a certain time period before the sale takes place. (Many states require that notice and advertisement be given 90 days prior to the date of sale.)

In many states recognizing power of sale, the ease with which foreclosure can be accomplished is not without some cost to the mortgagee. This is because in many states, the mortgagee loses the right to a deficiency action by exercising the power of sale. In other words, the mortgagee is entitled to a speedy foreclosure; but if the sale does not bring enough to satisfy the mortgagor's obligation, the mortgagee is not permitted to sue the mortgagor for the amount of the deficiency.

Because the power of sale foreclosure is not judicially instituted or supervised, mortgagors frequently bring challenges to the adequacy of notice, the conduct, and the propriety of the actual sale. The following case illustrates the types of problems that can arise in these nonjudicial procedures.

BLOCK v. TOBIN

119 Cal. Rptr. 288 (1975)

George Tobin and others (respondents) published notice that property subject to a deed of trust would be sold at a public auction to satisfy the secured obligation. Respondent Transamerica was the assignee of the original trust beneficiary, Anthony Cocciardi. The advertisement was placed by a foreclosure officer of Transamerica. It was planned that Cocciardi would bid on the property at the sale.

The sale was originally scheduled for 7 December 1972 but was postponed several times and eventually held on 12 January 1973. Tobin was substituted as trustee at the sale, and the property was sold for $26,700. The fair market value was $36,000. Block and others (appellants) were prospective bidders at the sale and brought suit challenging the legality of the sale. The trial court dismissed the suit and Block appealed.

CHRISTIAN, Associate Justice

Appellants have alleged that respondents knowingly made, or caused to be made, a false statement with knowledge of its falsity. The misrepresentation consists of respondents' notice indicating that a public auction was intended when, in fact, the property was to be sold secretly. A defendant who deceives the public by advertisements which are intended to induce reliance may be liable to any individual who reasonably relies on the misrepresentation. Appellants alleged: "[I]t was foreseeable that persons such as plaintiffs might suffer damage in the loss of advantages relative to purchasing of the subject real estate and might suffer damage by reason of the time, effort, and investigation expended in attempts and preparation to attempt to purchase said real estate if in fact defendants were to breach the duty to conduct the public auction." That language sufficiently alleges respondents' awareness that persons such as appellants might act in reliance on the notice of public auction. Respondents argue that they could not have formed an intention to defraud purchasers at the sale if, as alleged, they had never really intended to sell the property at public auction. But the alleged deceit was the fraudulent announcement of the public auction, not the making of false statements to induce the purchase of the property.

Appellants alleged that they had reasonably relied on the misrepresentation and that they had expended $600 in preparing their bid. Damages are not recoverable if the fact of damage is too remotely speculative or uncertain. But one may recover compensation for time and effort expended in reliance on a defendant's misrepresentation. Respondents argue that such losses should not be recoverable because they were the ordinary business expenses of a bidder at a trustee's sale. That would be so in the absence of a deceitful scheme; but it cannot be seriously contended that appellants would have devoted time and energy to prepare for the sale if they had known that the announcement of a public sale was spurious.

Appellants also seek to recover the difference between the fair market value of the property, $36,000, and the price actually paid by the beneficiary, $26,700. Appellants claim that they would have realized a profit of that amount if they had been the successful purchasers at the sale. But appellants have not alleged that they would have been the successful bidders had the public auction actually been held. Anticipated profits cannot be recovered if it is uncertain whether any profit would have been derived at all.

Appellants have also prayed for exemplary damages. In an action for fraud or deceit, a plaintiff may be entitled to recover punitive damages in addition to actual damages. Such damages may appropriately be awarded to deter a wrongdoer from defrauding the public.

Citing *Munger v. Moore,* 11 Cal. App. 3d 1, 89 Cal. Rptr. 323 (1970), and *Monolith Portland Cement Co. v. Tendler,* 206 Cal. App. 2d 800, 24 Cal. Rptr. 38 (1962), respondents claim that appellants have no standing to maintain this action for deceit. The *Munger* case does hold that a trustee or beneficiary may be held liable in damages to the trustor or his successor in interest for conducting an illegal, fraudulent or oppressive sale. The decision does not preclude recovery by a bidder as well, for damages sustained as a consequence of a trustee's deceit. In *Monolith,* supra, the court held that a judgment creditor, having only a lien, had no standing to attack the validity of a trustee's sale. Here, appellants do not sue derivatively; they allege damages personal to themselves.

Respondents also argue that it would be disruptive of the statutory scheme for sales of property under a trust deed to allow appellants to attack the validity of the trustee's sale. But the validity of the sale is not in controversy; the statutory procedure is not disrupted by allowing appellants to prosecute this action.

Finally, respondents contend that the absence of references to the rights of bidders in Civil Code §2924 et seq. suggests that a trustee owes no duty to prospective purchasers. It is true that Civil Code §2924h defines only the obligations, not the rights, of bidders. But the silence of the statute cannot be taken as taking away the rights which bidders would otherwise have to recover damages for deceit. We conclude that appellants have stated a cause of action for deceit.

Appellants also claim that the complaint stated a cause of action in alleging respondents' violations of several statutes which may apply to sales of real estate and to the actions of auctioneers. It is not necessary to reach those contentions; the real basis of appellants' claims, according to their allegations, is in the cause of action for deceit. The statutes relied upon either were not directed at the situation alleged by appellants or do not apply to acts which are already actionable if deceitful. No additional recovery would be achieved if a statutory violation were proved.

Finally, appellants assert that they were entitled to maintain their action to enforce the trustee's fiduciary duty to the trustor. A trustee under a deed of trust owes a duty to conduct the sale fairly and openly and to secure the best possible price for the benefit of the trustor.

Reversed on the deceit count and affirmed on others.

Discussion Questions

1. What allegations do the other bidders make?
2. Which one does the court find appropriate?
3. Was the sale "spurious"?
4. What are the damages?

2. Right of Redemption An additional distinction between the power of sale and foreclosure procedures is that under the power of sale, the debtor loses the statutory redemption period. The debtor has only up until the time of the sale to redeem the property. Once the property is sold at the advertised sale, full title is conveyed; and the debtor does not have a 6 month or 1 year period (as under judicial foreclosures) to redeem the property. Again, this distinction emphasizes the speed with which a nonjudicial procedure can clear the property of the debtor's interest.

3. The Soldiers and Sailors Relief Act This act also affords protection for those in active military duty from the power of sale foreclosure. Under the Soldiers and Sailors Relief Act, the procedures must simply be postponed for all those who qualify. The postponement runs for the period of active service.

Deed in Lieu of Foreclosure Chances are that before foreclosure procedures of any type are initiated by the mortgagee, substantial effort has been made to work with the mortgagor in an effort to correct the default. On government insured loans, the average duration of default before foreclosure is initiated is 6 months. If there is an effort by the mortgagor to correct the default—in most cases by making up back payments—the average duration of default before foreclosure is 10 months. Thus the lender works with the borrower before instituting proceedings. The mortgagor is encouraged to try to sell the property during this time in an effort to save any interest the mortgagor may have in the property.

After the mortgagee has extended all possible accommodations and there is no hope for recovery, the parties may still reach an agreement to avoid the costs and delays of foreclosure. The agreement the parties reach will be for the mortgagor to quitclaim the property to the mortgagee. Often the mortgagee will agree to pay the mortgagor for such a deed, although it may be a minimal amount such as $500. When the mortgagor turns over title in this manner, the transaction is called a *deed in lieu of foreclosure*. When the deed is signed over by the mortgagor, the underlying debt is canceled.

In some states, for the mortgagee to be a bona fide and protected purchaser, there must be some payment in addition to cancellation of the debt so that the mortgagee is a purchaser for value and entitled to full protection as a transferee.

It is also necessary that the transaction be free of coercion on the part of the mortgagee toward the mortgagor. The mortgagee must be able to establish that the mortgagor entered into the transaction voluntarily.

To avoid difficulties and questions about voluntariness, particularly if the mortgagor subsequently declares bankruptcy, the parties should sign an agreement explaining their transaction or at least have the mortgagor execute an affidavit explaining the reason for the transfer and the consideration being paid for it. Such an agreement will serve to answer any questions that might arise in subsequent proceedings.

Proceeds and Priorities Upon Foreclosure

One of the most important issues in mortgage law is the priority of parties holding interests in the mortgaged property. The priority of the parties will determine rights of foreclosure and will also determine who will be entitled to payment first upon sale of the mortgaged property at a foreclosure sale. Very often when a mortgagor defaults, there is more than one creditor with an interest in the property. The priority of the various creditors will determine the order of distribution of the proceeds from the sale of the property.

Recorded Interests As mentioned earlier a mortgage is valid even if not recorded, but only as between mortgagor and mortgagee. An unrecorded mortgage takes last position against any interests in the mortgaged property that are recorded either prior to the mortgage execution or subsequent to it.

If a mortgage is recorded, then the general rule for priority of interests is first in time is first in right. That is, the mortgage recorded first will enjoy priority over junior or second mortgages recorded later in time. Generally, the same rule applies for the priority of mortgage interests over other recorded land interests such as lien or security interests: If the mortgagee recorded the mortgage prior to the recording of these other interests, then the mortgagee will have priority. There are exceptions as discussed in Chapters 6 and 7. For example, purchase money security interests (PMSIs) in fixtures take priority over previously recorded mortgages if the PMSI is recorded before annexation of the fixture to the land or within 10 days after its annexation; and mechanics' liens take priority over previously recorded mortgages if work on the land began before the mortgage was recorded.

Multiple Debts and One Mortgage Many times a mortgagor who has executed several notes for a mortgagee will replace those notes with a single mortgage. Ordinarily, this type of transaction presents no priority problems if the mortgagee retains all of the notes. However, if the notes are transferred to various parties, questions of priority arise between these note holders, who are all secured by the same mortgage. In some states the rule is that the notes enjoy priority according to their maturity dates: first to mature has first priority. In other states the original note holder will always have rights subordinate to those who are transferees of the notes. In the remaining states, all notes have equal lien standing regardless of their maturity dates.

(12.5) Consider:

M gave a mortgage to C1, who recorded the mortgage that day (30 May 1988) at 8:00 A.M. in the county recorder's office. M had previously given a mortgage to C on 15 May 1988, which C recorded at 11:00 A.M. on 30 May 1988. Who, between C and C1 has priority?

Applications of Proceeds from Foreclosure The determination of priority among the various interest holders is the preliminary step in determining who will or will not be paid in the event foreclosure on the property becomes necessary. It is very likely that only a minimal amount will be received at a foreclosure sale— perhaps simply the amount of the outstanding debt. However, the order of the distribution of funds is as follows:

1. Payment of the costs of sale: court costs, fees, notice and publication costs, and so on
2. Payment of the mortgage debt having first priority
3. Payment of any junior liens, claims, or mortgages in the order of their priority
4. If there is any surplus, it is distributed to the mortgagor

Although the preceding list makes the law appear fairly clear as to the order of distribution, there are times when the issue becomes complicated because of the types of mortgages involved and the clauses found in them. The following case illustrates some of the issues that can arise.

BOB PARROTT, INC. v. FIRST PALMETTO BANK
211 S.E.2d 401 (Ga. 1974)

First Palmetto Bank (bank/defendant/ appellee) held a first mortgage in the property upon which foreclosure was instituted and which was sold pursuant to a judicial sale. Bob Parrott, Inc. (subordinated lender/plaintiff/ appellant) held second and third mortgages in the same property.

The bank's mortgage did not contain a dragnet provision. The bank foreclosed on the property in question on 6 February 1973 when the amount due and owing on the obligation was $37,543.56. At the foreclosure sale, the subordinated lender bid $1.01 higher than the bank and acquired the property. This bid resulted in an amount remaining in the bank's possession that was $4,291.76 in excess of the initial obligation to the bank and that was secured by the sold property. The subordinated lender made demand for the surplus, but the bank refused to surrender the amount on the grounds that the debtor owed the bank a greater amount on other debts that made no reference to the property. The bank's bid at the sale was for an amount that covered the sums due under the first mortgage plus these independent, unsecured debts.

CLARK, Judge

Where the deed to secure debt identifies a particular debt, it cannot be extended to cover other debts except by a new agreement between the parties, subject to the rules governing recording and priorities. Accordingly, the priority possessed under the foreclosed first loan debt is expressly limited to the specific obligation that was thereby secured, in the absence of an "open-end" (dragnet) clause.

The holder of a subordinate loan may claim surplus funds accruing from the foreclosure of the first loan. The money received in a foreclosure sale stands for the land and therefore such surplus funds retain the character of real estate in so far as junior lienholders whose liens were divested by the sale are concerned.

The obligation of making proper distribution of the proceeds were placed upon the Bank. The funds are to be applied first to costs incurred in the sale, attorneys' fees, and principal plus interest of the secured indebtedness. Any surplus remaining after these items must be paid over to the grantor or his assignee. Mere knowledge of the existence of other claims will not justify him

The subordinated lender brought suit to recover the amount retained by the Bank. The Bank claimed priority by possession. The trial court found for the bank, and the subordinated lender appealed.

in withholding payment unless such claimants file appropriate proceedings to subject the funds in his hands.

Thus, the surplus funds here could have been applied by the bank to the other debts owing to it excepting for the claim and notification thereof made by the Subordinated Lender. Under the authorities . . . it is clear that the Subordinated Lender had priority over the Bank as to the surplus proceeds on the basis that these funds were substituted for the land when the foreclosure divested the liens of the second and third loans held by Subordinated Lender and the independent debts were not included in the foreclosed security instrument.

Any surplus arising on the sale of a security for a debt may be recovered in an action for money had and received by the person entitled thereto, whether the original debtor or subsequent mortgagee, and a junior mortgagee, after refusal of the senior mortgagee to deliver over surplus proceeds, may forego his lien and rely wholly on the action for the money received.

Reversed.

Discussion Questions

1. Who is the first mortgagee?
2. Who holds the second and third mortgages?
3. How much was the first mortgagee's debt?
4. How much was received at the sale?
5. Who was the high bidder at the sale?
6. Who was given the excess received at the sale?
7. Why was the excess claimed by two parties?
8. Who is given the proceeds by the court? Why?

There are some exceptions to the general priority rules of first in time is first in right. One such exception relates to the priority of liens for federal and state taxes. Although the mortgage recorded prior to the filing of the lien will enjoy priority, the expenses associated with foreclosure may be subordinate to the tax lien filed prior to foreclosure.

(12.6) Consider:

A foreclosure sale on a parcel of property took place on 11 September 1983. The amount received from the sale is $75,000. The following list indicates the parties holding interests in the property sold. Distribute the funds according to the priority of the parties.

- First Federal: balance of $32,000 due on note secured by mortgage recorded 21 January 1981
- Great Western: balance of $8,000 due on note secured by mortgage recorded 16 October 1982
- Federal tax lien: balance of $22,000 due, with notice of lien recorded on 5 January 1983
- First Federal's costs and expenses of foreclosure: $5,000
- Judgment lien against the property owner for $10,000 recorded 23 December 1982
- American Finance: purchase money security interest in solar water heater, filed before attachment in 1 December 1982, in the amount of $3,000

Postforeclosure Remedies—The Deficiency Judgment

In many cases the sale of the mortgaged property at a foreclosure sale does not bring sufficient funds to satisfy the mortgage debt and expenses associated with the foreclosure. Therefore many states allow a *deficiency judgment*, or allow the mortgagee to collect the deficiency from the mortgagor in the form of a personal judgment in addition to the permitted foreclosure process.

In some states a personal judgment is given against the mortgagor at the same time the court enters the decree of foreclosure. In other states an action for deficiency cannot be brought until the foreclosure sale is held and the exact amount of the deficiency is known. In yet other states a deficiency judgment is not permitted in certain types of mortgages, particularly in purchase money mortgages for residential property.

Statistics indicate that deficiency actions, particularly in the case of residential purchase money mortgages (even where permitted), are not frequently used because of the appearance of taking more from debtors who have just lost their residences to foreclosure (from Howard Rudnitsky, "Arms Race," *Forbes*, May 7, 1984, p. 34).

In some states mortgagees are required to proceed in a certain manner in order to preserve their rights to deficiency judgments. That is, the mortgagee must establish that the security for the underlying note was exhausted or that the foreclosure remedy has been pursued. In some states, if the mortgagee proceeds directly on the note in order to obtain a personal judgment against the mortgagor, the right of foreclosure is forfeited.

DEEDS OF TRUST

The typical mortgage involves only two parties: the mortgagor and the mortgagee. The *deed of trust* (also known as the trust deed form of securing debts with real property) is a type of mortgage or security agreement that includes three parties. In this arrangement, the property owner (buyer/trustor) conveys title to a third party (trustee) who then holds title for the benefit of the lender (beneficiary).

This three-party financing arrangement holds several advantages for the lender. First, the lender in most states has the right of foreclosure in the event of default, but without proceeding through the courts (called the *power of sale*). The power of sale is generally exercised by notice to the trustor and publication of the proposed sale date. Although there is a statutory minimum waiting period before the sale may be conducted, it is a much shorter period than that required for foreclosure. Also, exercising the power of sale is less costly than instituting and conducting judicial foreclosures.

A second advantage for the lender is that the lender's involvement can be kept secret, since only the trustee's name need appear in the records. Further transferees of the note can also keep their indentities a secret.

Another advantage is that the deed of trust facilitates the borrowing of large sums. Sales of bonds and other debentures by corporations to many parties can be secured by one deed of trust on corporate property, which will be held by a third party.

Relationship to Mortgages

Even though a deed of trust may be used instead of a mortgage to secure an underlying debt, the rights and relationships of the parties with the exception of foreclosure remain the same. That is, the trustor still has the obligations of timely payment, nonwaste, insurance, and so on. Furthermore, the deed of trust contains the same types of clauses and provisions discussed under the mortgage sections of this chapter.

The lender must be cautious about the language used to create the deed of trust so that the proper relationship is set up, or in many states the setup will be treated as a mortgage. Perhaps the most important idea to be included in the deed of trust instrument is the notion of the separation of title. The actual title to the property is held by a third party, the trustee, and upon satisfaction of the debt the title must be conveyed to the trustor.

A provision in the deed of trust, which provides that the deed of trust becomes null and void upon satisfaction of the debt, has caused many courts to rule that the instrument was instead a mortgage.

In mortgages the mortgagee is given the right of foreclosure in the event of default. In deeds of trust the trustee is given the power of sale. As already discussed, there are definite time advantages associated with the power of sale. There is also the benefit of the elimination or limitation of the redemption rights of the trustor. Under the deed of trust, the borrower is usually given a right of reinstatement, which is the right to pay the amount due and owing the trustor at any time prior to the sale time and thereby redeem the property. The distinction between this right and the right of redemption is that reinstatement must take place prior to the sale. Under a deed of trust the sale terminates all rights of the trustor; under a mortgage the period of redemption actually begins at the time of the sale and runs for 6 months to a year afterwards. Strict foreclosure applies to mortgages, not deeds of trust.

In some states reinstatement requires the trustor to pay only the amount due in back payments plus costs and expenses. In other words, when the power of sale is exercised the right of reinstatement may be exercised without the trustor paying the full, accelerated amount of the loan then due. This type of provision permits borrowers to reinstate more easily.

Duties and Responsibilities of the Trustee

The trustee in a deed of trust financing arrangement is acting for the benefit of both parties and is therefore required to act impartially. The trustee is under no duty to check title or verify recording of the trust instrument, but is merely the administrator responsible for carrying out the financing arrangement according to the terms set forth.

In many states a statute specifies what parties are permitted to serve as trustees in a financing arrangement. In all states recognizing this form of financing, the trustee must be someone other than the lender. Typically, those authorized to serve as trustees are lawyers, brokers, title insurers, and escrow companies.

When conflicts arise between the parties or when a default has occurred, it is the responsibility of the trustee to honor the provisions of the trust agreement and conduct a sale pursuant to the terms of the agreement and according to any statutory procedures provided in the state where the property is located.

(12.7) Consider:

Fill in the chart to indicate the distinctions between mortgages and deeds of trust. Be sure to list under the mortgage sections the provisions applicable in title theory and lien theory states.

	NUMBER OF PARTIES	TITLE	REMEDIES UPON DEFAULT	RIGHT OF REDEMPTION
MORTGAGES				
DEEDS OF TRUST				

INSTALLMENT LAND CONTRACTS

The *installment land contract* is an alternative method of financing the purchase of property to a mortgage or a deed of trust. It is frequently used when the buyer is unable to obtain financing, when the buyer cannot come up with a large enough down payment, or when the rate at which financing can be obtained is simply exorbitant. Often called a *contract for deed* or a *long-term land contract*, the installment contract is also used to finance the purchase of property in areas where lenders have been reluctant to lend because of problems with maintaining their interest in the secured property.

Each state has different statutes and regulations regarding the land contract, but all states follow the basic nature of this method of financing the purchase of property. The installment land contract is not a purchase contract in which earnest money is received and whose primary purpose is to establish the rights and responsibilities of the parties between the time the agreement is reached and the closing of the transaction. Rather, the installment land contract is an agreement covering the parties for the life of the debt, which is being carried by the seller and repaid by the buyer. The installment land contract may not be executed until the date of closing.

The Forfeiture Aspect

One of the unique features of the installment land contract is that in some states the seller has a very strong remedy in the event of the buyer's default: *forfeiture*. In other words, some states recognizing the validity of installment contracts provide that if the buyer defaults, the buyer will forfeit all interest acquired in the property to the seller.

The forfeiture takes place without judicial procedures and within a certain period of time after the default. For example, some states provide that if a defaulting buyer has paid less than 20 percent of the property's purchase price, then that buyer's interest is forfeited within 30 days after the notification of the default. The 30 days is deemed to be a grace period during which the buyer has the opportunity of redemption by paying what is then due and owing. The length of the grace period varies according to the amount of payment made by the buyer; in some states it may last up to a year.

A seller who wishes to exercise the forfeiture provisions must be cautious in accepting late payments from the buyer. If the seller has been customarily accepting late payments, then the forfeiture provisions cannot be invoked on the basis of late payments unless the seller provides the buyer with notice of the reinstatement of timely payments. In order for the forfeiture statutes to be constitutional, some form of notice of default and intent to exercise forfeiture rights must be given to the defaulting buyer.

Some states still require a form of foreclosure proceedings for a forfeiture of interest to take place. In these states the courts have been concerned with the protection of the buyers; thus they have required sellers to give buyers a chance for redemption rather than subject them to the time limits of strict forfeiture.

Title Problems

When a mortgagee is involved in financing the purchase of property, chances are that the mortgagee will verify that there is good title vested in the seller of that property, for a clean title is the secret to the stability of the mortgagee's security. However, in an installment contract there is no third party involved who may be interested in protecting the business. The parties have only to deal with each other, and there is a good chance that title will not be examined. Thus many buyers using the installment method of finance may find that they have purchased property with tax liens and other possible deficiencies that would ordinarily be discovered by the lender.

Furthermore, without the involvement of a third party lender, many buyers neglect to record the installment contract. Thus their rights become subject to other interests that may be recorded after the fact. The time span of the contract may also create problems with title because bankruptcy could occur, the vendor could pass away, and title issues would exist in the transference of the credit.

For the seller of the property, the recording of the land contract can present problems if the buyer defaults and forfeits all interest in the property. The seller would have a recorded land contract as a defect on the title to the property, and a quiet title action would be required to remove the cloud of the forfeited contract from the records.

Tax Consequences

One of the benefits of using the installment method of financing the purchase of property is that the seller may defer recognition of gain made on the sale of the property to the buyer. By meeting certain requirements set forth in the Internal Revenue Service regulations, the seller avoids having to report an entire gain on the sale of property in 1 year. The specific tax benefits available in installment sales are discussed in Chapter 17 but have been limited significantly under the Tax Reform Act of 1986.

Regulation Z Application

The seller in an installment contract is required to comply with certain disclosure requirements if Regulation Z (12 C.F.R. §226) is applicable to the property sale. Many lots for second or resort homes are purchased on an installment basis and hence regulation is applicable.

The seller covered by Regulation Z must be certain to comply with two major disclosure provisions under the regulations. First, the buyer must be notified of the right of rescission. For example, in the purchase of nonprimary residential property, the buyer is entitled to the 72-hour rescission period and must be given a form to sign indicating that the right exists and how it can be exercised.

The seller must also be concerned with disclosing all minimum requirements for a closed-end transaction under Regulation Z. (Minimum disclosure requirements were discussed earlier and include such information as the amount of the payments, the number of payments, the annual percentage rate, and so on.)

A Sample Contract

Figure 12.6 is a sample installment contract that covers all necessary provisions such as late payments, Regulation Z disclosures, and action in the event of forfeiture. An installment contract may also be part of a two-document transaction that includes a promissory note.

Figure 12.6 Sample Installment Contract

PURCHASE AGREEMENT

This agreement, made and entered into by _____, a _____ corporation, hereinafter referred to as SELLER, and _____ and _____, his wife, of _____, hereinafter referred to as PURCHASER.

WITNESSETH: Seller has executed a warranty deed this date to _____to hold and retain for Purchaser for Lot No. _____, _____ Subdivision, as per plat record recorded in the Registrar's Office for _____ County, _____.

Purchaser agrees to pay the sum of $_____ for said lot, of which $_____ is herewith paid in cash. The balance of the purchase price of $_____, which includes interest at the rate of _____% per annum, is represented by an installment note signed by Purchaser of even date, said note being payable in monthly installments as recited therein.

Upon Purchaser's payment of the full amount of the balance due under said installment note, _____ shall execute a warranty deed conveying full title to Lot No. _____ as described above to Purchaser.

Purchaser shall have the right to prepayment with respect to such installment note without penalty. No policy of title insurance shall be furnished in connection with the warranty deed issued except at the Purchaser's request.

Purchaser shall pay all general and special taxes and charges hereinafter assessed on said lot or lots. Risk of loss or damage to the premises shall be on Purchaser following the date hereof. Seller insists upon a uniformly clean and attractive appearance of the lots herein sold, and therefore Purchaser agrees to keep weeds

Figure 12.6 *(continued)*

and vegetation cut and not to permit rubbish or debris to accumulate on the premises.

Default in any of the Purchaser's obligations hereunder shall entitle the Seller or its successors to proceed upon any of the provisions contained in this obligation, the installment note, or under any of the statutory protections afforded installment sellers under the laws of the state of _____.

This is the entire agreement between the parties and no understanding or agreements exist between the parties other than this agreement except for the installment note mentioned herein.

The Purchaser acknowledges receipt of a copy of this document, a copy of the installment note, a copy of the Regulation Z disclosure statement, and a copy of the notice of right to cancel statement.

IN WITNESS Whereof, the parties sign this agreement this ____ day of _____, 19____.

_____

SELLER

_____

BUYER

Discussion Questions

1. What type of deed will be given to the purchaser?
2. Will a title insurance policy be furnished?
3. Who will hold title while the installment note is being paid?
4. Is there a prepayment penalty?
5. Is a provision made for late payments?

SUBDIVISION TRUSTS

The *subdivision trust* is available only in a limited number of states. This method of financing is a three-party arrangement that involves a trust relationship, but the parties have different roles than in the deed of trust financing arrangement. Both the buyer and the seller are beneficiaries of a trust managed by a third party trustee. The seller transfers title to the property to the trustee, and the buyer and seller execute a note or other contract that contains the payment terms and other provisions governing the parties' relationship.

In addition the parties will execute a trust agreement that will contain the provisions explaining the duties and responsibilities of the trustee, who will hold title to the property. The trust agreement in this method of financing is critical because it will determine when the trustee may take action and how payments are to be made. In essence, the trust agreement determines how effective the seller's security in the property will be. The diagram shows the subdivision trust relationship.

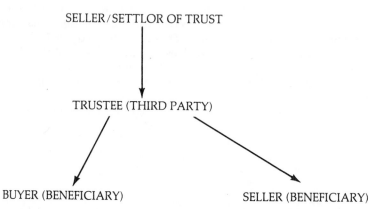

SELLER/SETTLOR OF TRUST

TRUSTEE (THIRD PARTY)

BUYER (BENEFICIARY)   SELLER (BENEFICIARY)

If the buyer defaults on the payments due, the trust agreement will provide the trustee with the right of sale of the property, or perhaps with the right of reconveyance of title to the seller with a forfeiture of the buyer's interest in the property. This method of financing permits the seller quick relief in the event of a buyer default.

Typically this method of financing is used by developers (buyers) with great ideas but little cash for the development of land parcels. Under this arrangement the buyer and seller have the protection of a third party holding title, and the benefit of having the trust continue once the developer is able to sell or lease the development; thus, both buyer and seller can benefit from the profits obtained upon completion of the development. The trust agreement may thus provide that the seller is not only paid a certain amount for the property, but is also entitled to collect a certain portion of the development profits after the buyer begins to earn on the investment.

An example of a subdivision trust arrangement is when a farmer sells a substantial portion of prime-location real estate to a shopping center developer. During the construction of the shopping center, the farmer would take minimal or no payments for the property. Upon completion of the shopping center, the leasing of the property, and the collection of rents and perhaps percentages of the sales of tenants, the farmer would collect the purchase price of the property, an additional share of the profits received for a certain period of time, or both. The relationship is shown in the diagram.

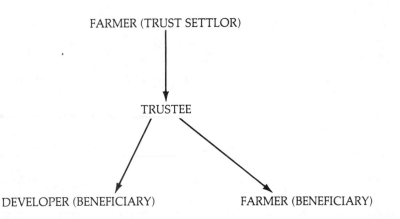

FARMER (TRUST SETTLOR)

TRUSTEE

DEVELOPER (BENEFICIARY)   FARMER (BENEFICIARY)

In many of the states recognizing the subdivision trust as a method of financing the purchase of property, the rules on foreclosure, redemption, power of sale, and reinstatement rights are simply inapplicable. Rather, the parties are governed only by the law of trusts for that jurisdiction. Thus the parties are often free to insert provisions in their trust agreements for the trustee to follow in the event of nonpayment or any other form of default.

CREATIVE FINANCING

Economic conditions in the 1970s and early 1980s resulted in high interest rates and the creation of financial barriers to the purchase and ownership of residential, income-producing, and commercial properties. These barriers were high down payments and high monthly payments, which effectively prevented many willing buyers from participating in the real estate market. To ease some of the burden and open the market, many lenders, sellers, buyers, and brokers instituted methods of financing the purchase of property that combined traditional methods, created new methods, and often combined the two. In the following sections, some of the methods used quite frequently are discussed.

Shared-appreciation Equity-participation Financing Mortgages

The *shared-appreciation mortgage* or *equity-participation financing* is a creation of the commercial lender that involves a trade-off: the lender offers lower monthly interest rates in exchange for a share in the appreciation of the property pledged as security. Under this approach the lender will finance a loan at say 10 percent as opposed to 12 percent and, upon the borrower's sale of the property, will receive some percentage of the profit made—usually no more than 40 percent. The lender thus experiences a gain on the transfer of the property, and the buyer enjoys the benefit of lower monthly payments by giving up a portion of the property appreciation.

Wrap-around Mortgages

This type of financing arrangement is used in the purchase of property that already has financing not subject to a due-on-sale clause upon transfer. The wrap-around mortgage is similar to an assumption except that the seller is afforded more security.

For example, suppose that a residence is being sold for $85,000, and there is an existing mortgage balance of $50,000 on the property. The buyer can afford to put $10,000 down. In an assumption, the buyer would then assume the $50,000 obligation, and the seller would take a second mortgage on the property to secure the buyer's repayment of the $25,000 to him. Under a wrap-around arrangement, the buyer simply takes title to the property subject to the mortgage. The buyer is given a loan by the seller for $75,000, which is secured by an all-inclusive mortgage. The seller will continue to make the payments on the $50,000 loan, and the buyer will make payments to the seller on a full $75,000 at a lower than market rate. The seller will retain that portion of the buyer's monthly payment that is above the amount due on the $50,000 mortgage.

One way the seller can make a profit on the transaction is to charge a higher rate on the entire wrap-around mortgage. Thus, if the $50,000 loan is at 9 percent, then the seller could carry the full $75,000 at 12 percent and would make 12 percent on $25,000 and an additional 3 percent on the original $50,000 obligation.

Exchanges or Trades

In a property exchange, the parties involved swap the equity in their properties as a means of purchasing each other's property. This type of financing is used more commonly in commercial transactions. It is frequently used when employees in the same firm are being transferred to each other's respective location. Each needs a house in the other's location, and the equities are simply swapped as a means of purchase.

The primary concern of the parties to a property exchange is that the equities are even. If the equities in the exchanged properties are not even, then one of the parties must pay the other the difference in cash.

Lease Purchase Agreements

If it is difficult for the buyer to obtain financing at the time the parties desire to enter into a transaction and if the seller does not wish to become involved in carrying the buyer's purchase, the parties may enter into an agreement of sale and simultaneously execute a lease agreement. The purchase agreement will have a delayed closing date.

The parties will agree to the purchase price and to a future date for closing the sale when financing will be more reasonable. Usually the buyer will make a deposit toward the down payment and will also make monthly rental payments to the seller. The amount of the monthly rental payments will cover at least the underlying mortgage debt for which the seller is responsible, and it may exceed that amount as a benefit to the seller carrying the lease or as partial payment of the eventual down payment that will be required.

With the *lease-purchase mortgage*, the buyer has a definite purchase price locked in at the current market prices as well as the opportunity to wait for better loan terms. The seller enjoys the tax benefits of leasing the property (discussed in Chapter 17) and has a sale guaranteed at some future date. The seller also has the generally afforded remedy of retaining the buyer's deposit in the event the sale is not executed or the buyer terminates the lease.

A variation of this method of financing is the lease with an option to buy. Under this type of arrangement, the parties do not actually enter into a purchase contract, but the buyer is given the right to exercise an option to purchase at any time during the period of the lease. The parties' agreement may also provide that the rental payments may be used toward the down payment if the option to purchase is exercised.

The Broker, Regulation Z, and Creative Financing

Creative methods of financing carry with them complexities that require the assistance of brokers and lawyers in making the methods work effectively for both parties in the transaction. In addition, these methods of financing may also carry with them hidden legal pitfalls for the broker assisting a seller or a buyer in arranging the method of financing.

The broker who is regularly involved in the arrangement of credit must meet all of the disclosure requirements under Regulation Z. *Regularly* involved in credit arrangements means that the broker has participated in the arrangement of credit for "more than 5-secured by a dwelling" financing arrangements, or for more than twenty-five transactions in which a dwelling was not used as credit. However, all of these transactions must meet the basic Regulation Z criteria of a finance charge or financing payable in more than four installments for the broker to be required to comply.

If compliance with Regulation Z is required, the broker must see that the buyer is furnished with all of the disclosure statements discussed earlier for closed-end transactions.

The brokers should also consult with an attorney to determine whether the acts of individual salespersons in arranging credit transactions can be attributed to them in determining whether they have met the transaction criteria for application of Regulation Z. Thus a broker may be required to make disclosures if the salespersons working in the same office have met the criteria for the firm as a whole.

A CONCLUDING WORD ON FINANCING

The many complexities and loopholes of all the methods of financing discussed in this chapter are potentially costly to one or both of the parties to the transaction. It is important that all parties involved in the financing arrangement for the purchase of real property examine the following areas before entering into an agreement, so that problems and pitfalls can be avoided initially rather than encountered during the course of performance.

- Is there some form of security for loan repayment?
- What constitutes default under the agreement? Is it defined?
- Are late payments permitted? Is it possible for the acceptance of late payments to cause rights to be waived?
- Is Regulation Z compliance required? Who must comply?
- Are there other secured interests in the property? Who has priority?
- May the security instrument be recorded for protection?
- If there is a default, will the debtor be given some type of grace period?
- What happens if the property is transferred?
- What tax benefits or implications exist?
- Does the written document (or documents) reflect all desires and intents?

KEY TERMS

mortgage	usury
mortgagor	title theory
mortgagee	lien theory
promissory note	acceleration clause
Truth-in-Lending laws	balloon payment clause
Federal Consumer Credit Protection Act	balloon payment
Regulation Z	prepayment penalty clause
residential mortgage transactions	due-on-sale clause
advertisement	Garn-St. Germain Depository Institutions Act
triggering language	Garn Bill
Equal Credit Opportunity Act (ECOA)	window periods
	FHA

VA
Federal National Mortgage
    Association (FNMA; Fannie
    Mae)
Government National Mortgage
    Association (GNMA; Ginnie
    Mae)
Federal Home Loan Mortgage
    Corporation (FHLMC; Freddie
    Mac)
conventional mortgage
purchase money mortgage
master mortgage
straight term mortgage
subordinate mortgage
wrap-around mortgage
Anaconda mortgage
dragnet mortgage
adjustable rate mortgage (ARM)
after-acquired property clause
assumption
cash-to-mortgage sale
subject-to sale
refinancing

satisfaction of mortgage
default
foreclosure
judicial foreclosure
lis pendens
statutory right of redemption
sheriff's deed
judicial deed
Soldiers and Sailors Relief Act
power of sale
foreclosure by advertisement
deed in lieu of foreclosure
deficiency judgment
deed of trust
power of sale
installment land contract
contract for deed
long-term land contract
forfeiture
subdivision trust
shared-appreciation mortgage
equity-participation financing
lease-purchase mortgage

CHAPTER PROBLEMS

1. A purchased B's home through a cash-to-mortgage arrangement with A assuming B's $40,000 Federal Housing Administration (FHA) loan. Three months after the purchase, A has lost his job and is unable to meet the monthly payments. The mortgagee has turned to B for the payments and B protests, claiming he is no longer liable on the underlying mortgage note. The mortgagee, complying with proper procedures, forecloses on the property and sells it for $25,000. The mortgagee is now interested in obtaining a deficiency judgment and has therefore sued both A and B. Has the mortgagee acted properly under the circumstances? Is B correct about his liability? Is a deficiency judgment possible under the circumstances? Would it make any difference if a deed of trust arrangement were involved?

2. The following summarizes the sequence of events involved on a parcel of property located in Nevada and owned by the Lundgrens:

30 November 1970. The Lundgrens executed a note in favor of Nevada Wholesale Lumber in the amount of $7,767.44, secured by a deed of trust, with Title Insurance and Trust Company as trustee.

8 May 1972. The Lundgrens, without notifying Nevada Wholesale, conveyed fee simple title to Rampart Corporation.

6 December 1972. The Lundgrens executed a second note to Nevada Wholesale for $12,126.99. The note was secured by a dragnet clause in the 30 November 1970 deed of trust.

16 January 1973. Rampart Corporation executed a note and deed of trust to Myers Realty.

7 February 1973. Nevada Wholesale recorded a notice of default and election to sell the property.

12 February 1973. Nevada Wholesale filed suit on the $12,126.99 note.

28 June 1973. Default judgment was awarded Nevada Wholesale on suit and the land was attached.

17 August 1973. Myers Realty filed notice of foreclosure on its deed of trust from Rampart Corporation.

Assuming the sale of the property does not bring enough to satisfy all parties in the transactions, who has priority?

3. Stadium Apartments, Incorporated, applied for a loan from Prudential Insurance Company. The loan was eligible for FHA insurance, and Prudential made application for such insurance. The FHA issued a commitment for insurance, and the mortgage on the property was executed on the appropriate FHA forms. The mortgage contained the following provision:

   "The Mortgagor, to the extent permitted by law, hereby waives the benefit of any and all homestead and exemption laws and of any right to a stay or redemption and the benefit of any moratorium law or laws."

   Stadium Apartments defaulted and Prudential assigned the mortgage to the FHA. The FHA obtained a default judgment foreclosing on the mortgage, but the district judge framed the decree to allow for the 1-year period of redemption provided under Idaho law. The FHA objected on the grounds of the above provision. Is Stadium Apartments entitled to the period of redemption under state law?

4. W. J. Minderhout has entered into a lease agreement with Coast Bank under which Minderhout will lease an office building (worth $200,000) from Coast for rental payments of $25,000 per year. The agreement also provides that at the end of the 10-year lease period established in the

agreement, Minderhout will have the option to purchase the building for $40,000. Minderhout wishes to know if the arrangement is a mortgage or a lease and what rights both he and Coast will have in the event he defaults on the lease payments.

5. Seven Palms Motor Inn obtained financing from Commerce Mortgage Company for the purchase of a motel. Commerce secured the purchase through a duly recorded mortgage on the property, which contained an after-acquired property clause. Seven Palms then contracted, through a security agreement perfected by the filing of the financing statement, with Sears, Roebuck and Company for the purchase of drapery rods, drapes, and matching bedspreads for each of the rooms in the motel. Seven Palms defaulted and Commerce foreclosed. Sears claimed priority in the items they furnished, since the items were personal property. Commerce claimed the items were fixtures and were covered by the mortgage. What was the result?

6. Dr. Lindsey Scott purchased an office building and borrowed the funds for the purchase from Amato, Incorporated. Amato took and recorded a mortgage on the property. Scott had hired Essex Cleaning Contractors to perform janitorial services in the building. Scott defaulted, and Amato took possession of the building and collected and retained all rents. Amato did not pay Essex, contending that Scott had entered into the contract with them and that Scott was therefore liable even after Amato took possession. Scott maintains Amato enjoyed possession and benefits and was therefore liable to Essex. What is the result?

7. Which of the following types of provisions in mortgages or deeds of trust are illegal?
   a. Balloon payments
   b. Interest acceleration clauses
   c. Prepayment penalties
   d. Due-on-sale clauses

8. Do any of the following statements contain triggering terms that require further disclosure under Regulation Z?
   a. "$70,000 balance payable in 120 monthly installments"
   b. "Total interest payments are $40,000 less"
   c. "FANTASTIC ASSUMPTION TERMS AVAILABLE"
   d. "Assume low interest FHA loan"

9. Define the following terms:
   a. Brundage clause
   b. Dragnet or Anaconda clause
   c. Subdivision trust

10. A construction lender had an obligation to loan $250,000 to a builder/mortgagor. The mortgage was recorded upon execution of the note. The funds were to be dispersed to the mortgagor as follows: 20 percent when the foundation was set, 20 percent when the building was roofed in, 20 percent when the interior plaster was set, 20 percent when the certificate of occupancy was issued, and 20 percent 30 days later. Will the lender have priority at the time of recording or at the time and amount of each advance?

13

CLOSING THE DEAL

Founder of Escrow Firm Admits Swindles of $183,874
Escrow President Uses Clients' Deposits for Loans

The settlement or closing is the time when the property transaction is actually completed. Many items in completing performance of the contract must be done simultaneously, and it is sometimes difficult for the parties to coordinate them. Therefore, the parties involve an independent third party to handle the actual consummation of the real estate transaction. This third party acts as an agent for the parties in the purchase and sale transaction by handling all the necessary paperwork and transfers in order to furnish the seller with funds, the buyer with title, and the lender (if one is involved) with the appropriate security.

The actual transaction of closing varies according to the portion of the country in which the property is located and may also vary significantly from state to state. In some states the buyer and seller sit down face-to-face with the lender and the third-party agent in order to close the transaction. In other states only one party is present. In yet other states the parties sign documents in advance and independently of each other, and the closing takes place at a definite time and date with neither party present.

Although the general description of closing seems simple, there are in fact many documents, rights, and responsibilities involved. As the introductory headline emphasizes, the *escrow* or closing arrangement presents opportunities for fraud and substantial losses on the parts of the parties involved.

The purpose of this chapter is to explain the process of closing from the requirements for setting it up, to the work required to close, and to the relationships and liabilities of the parties involved.

THE ESCROW SETUP

The Parties

The escrow setup generally involves three or four parties. The buyer and seller who set up the escrow arrangement are the first two parties. If there is a lender involved either in the financing or assumption of financing of the property, the lender is also a party to the transaction. The final party is an independent party who handles the collection of necessary documents and the actual transfer of funds, and title.

The independent party is usually a title company in those states having title insurers. Other states have actual escrow companies, which serve only as agents for property closings. The independent party may also be an attorney, an insurance company, or any other type of individual or firm authorized by state law to serve as an agent for closing.

As the introductory headline made clear, the party chosen to act as the escrow agent should be carefully screened so that the parties do not subject themselves to a substantial loss because of the agent's lack of integrity. There is nothing that requires a buyer or seller to use a particular company or escrow agent for closing; and if one side has objections or reasons for doubt as to the agent's honesty, such objections and reasons should be made before the transaction is turned over to the escrow agent. Perhaps it would be worth the time of the buyer, seller, or lender to do some background checking on the proposed agent through government and private records such as those of the Better Business Bureau. Such checks would reveal past complaints, potential criminal actions, and the names of those dissatisfied with prior services of the agent.

Since the transfer of property inevitably involves the transfer of large sums of money, such sums should not be turned over to an agent who has not been recommended or at least checked.

Requirements for Setting Up the Escrow

Valid and Enforceable Contract for Purchase and Sale of Real Estate An escrow or closing arrangement is set up to formally carry out the provisions of a real estate contract; therefore, for an escrow to be valid there must be an underlying valid contract between the parties. Without such a contract, the third party is only carrying out an agency relationship that has no binding effect on either of the parties since there is no direct contractual relationship between them. Many parties attempt to consummate a sale quickly by going directly to escrow instructions, but such a timesaving step can be costly in that there is no enforceable contract between buyer and seller—only an agency contract between the escrow agent and the buyer and seller.

Deposit of Deed with the Escrow Agent This requirement emphasizes a more general requirement for a valid escrow, which is that the parties set up the transaction as irrevocable. Irrevocability requires that the parties are not permitted to withdraw their funds and documents at will, but that such withdrawals or returns will occur only if the provisions in their contract and escrow instructions are not met. If the seller is free to revoke the deed at any time or if the buyer is able to withdraw the funds at any time, the transaction could never be closed and the agent's responsibilities would be frustrated and liabilities complicated. Obviously, this requirement necessitates that the seller deposit the deed with the escrow agent in a validly executed form so that the agent is able to transfer title.

Valid Escrow Instructions Even the irrevocable depositing of the deed with the third party will not create an escrow unless the agent and the other two or three parties execute a contract called *escrow instructions,* which will direct the agent or third party on the hows, whens, and whats of closing the property transaction. As will be discussed later in the chapter, the third party is authorized to do only what is specified in the contractual escrow instructions; without instructions, the third party has no authority for consummating a sale.

Contents of the Escrow Instructions

Mandatory Matters Because the escrow involves the transfer of a land interest, the authority of the third party must be in writing. In addition there are several items that must be included in every set of escrow instructions to make them enforceable. These mandatory items include the following:

1. Name of the agent, third party, or depository
2. Names of the buyer (buyers) and seller (sellers) and their proper designation (partnership, corporation, married couple, single person, and so on)
3. Legal description of the property to be transferred
4. Purchase price of the property
5. Conditions of transfer and payment
6. Allocation of expenses, costs, insurance, taxes, assessments, and so on
7. Signatures of the buyer and seller

Recommended Provisions In both brokerage contracts and contracts for the sale of property, the minimum requirements do not always provide for the contingencies that can arise in the process of closing a property transaction. It is therefore wise for the parties to include additional provisions to govern various aspects of closing. Although many states and regions have customs in the area of property closings, it is often a dispute over such customs that results in expensive and time-consuming litigation.

1. Allocating Costs The escrow instructions should specify who will pay which costs associated with closing the transaction. Again, there are many customs for such allocations, but it is much easier and legally binding to list such cost breakdowns as part of the escrow instructions. The following list is indicative of the typical costs associated with closing that should be assessed by the parties in the transaction:

1. Escrow fee
2. Fees for title search, title abstract, title insurance, and attorneys' fees associated with title
3. Recording fees for the deed, mortgage, deed of trust, and any other documents required to complete the transaction
4. Mortgage transfer or release fees
5. Loan origination fees
6. Termite inspection report
7. Appraisal or survey fees
8. Credit report fees
9. Loan discount points
10. Attorneys' fees for drafting documents and so on

By agreeing to the allocation of costs in advance, the parties avoid possible confusion and delay in the closing process. However, the parties should be familiar with any restrictions the lender has placed on the payment of closing costs. For example, with certain government insured loans, federal regulations specify which party must pay certain parts of the costs listed above. With some government loans, the seller is required to pay the loan discount points.

2. Prorating Prepaids Property transfers do not usually occur at times when taxes, insurance premiums, and rents are due. At the time of nearly every closing, the seller has prepaid taxes or insurance but will not enjoy the property for the period for which payment has been made. Thus a seller may have paid a $120 insurance premium in January that covers insurance on the property until June, with the property being transferred to the buyer in March. The escrow instructions should provide how those funds will be *prorated* so that the buyer pays for the coverage from March until June.

In many areas there are formulas that are customarily used to prorate prepaid amounts as to the date of transfer. Basically the formulas follow along one of two general theories. Theory 1 breaks the year into 360 days with 12 months of 30 days each. Theory 2 holds that the year consists of 365 days and prorates prepaids on a daily basis of 1/365th of the total annual cost. Thus, assuming the closing took place on 15 March in the example above, under theory 1 the seller would receive a credit of $70 or 3 months at $20 plus 1/2 month at $10. Under theory 2 the seller would receive a credit of $.66 per day (240/365). Taking the number of days from 15 March to 30 June the total credit would be $70.62 (107 × $.66).

(13.1) Consider:

A seller has prepaid both taxes and insurance on the property about to be transferred. The taxes are $600 per year and the insurance premiums are $300 per year. The seller prepaid both in January for the entire year through 31 December. The closing on the property will take place on 15 March, and the parties wish to know what formulas can be used to prorate these prepaids. Explain the results to them under both the 360-day year and the 365-day year formulas.

3. *Documents to Be Delivered by Each Party* Although a minimum requirement for escrow is that the seller deposit the deeds for transfer, there are other documents associated with the property transfer that both seller and buyer must deposit for the closing to take place. The following list is not comprehensive but is indicative of the detail that should be provided in the escrow instructions:

1. By the seller:
   a. Title documents: abstract, opinion, and insurance
   b. Most recent tax bill
   c. Insurance policies
   d. Plans and specifications for original construction and modifications
   e. Warranties on any appliances, heating systems, and so on
   f. Uniform Commercial Code (UCC) bulk sale affidavit if business transfer
   g. Soil, termite, and other property condition reports including reports from environmental agencies
   h. Keys

    i. Notes, mortgages, deeds of trust, UCC Article 9 security agreement and financing statements

    j. List of tenants and copies of leases

    k. Building code inspection and compliance

2. By the buyer:
    a. Earnest money check
    b. Loan commitment
    c. List of defects to be remedied prior to closing
    d. Corporate authorization if corporate buyer is involved

3. By the lender:
    a. Mortgage, deed of trust, and promissory note
    b. Truth-in-lending statement (see Chapter 12)
    c. Real Estate Settlement Procedures Act (RESPA) statement (see later for discussion)
    d. Required forms if Federal Housing Administration (FHA) or Veterans Administration (VA) loan
    e. Required inspections if FHA or VA loan

4. Cancellation Provisions Because the escrow agent is permitted to consummate the transaction only upon the completion of certain conditions specified in the instructions, it follows that if those conditions are not met the parties are excused from their performance under the contract and the entire escrow arrangement must be canceled.

Many states have provisions for cancellation, but it is best for the parties to specify when cancellation may occur and how such cancellation is to be accomplished. In drafting the cancellation clause, the parties should carefully specify three items: First, the grounds for cancellation should be set forth. The grounds may be a simple statement such as "if either party fails to comply with the terms hereof," or they may be specifically listed. Second, the parties should specify the method of cancellation. The parties are free to agree as to what form the cancellation notice should take (in writing for example); and how such notice is to be delivered (either personally, through the escrow agent, or by mail). Third, the cancellation clause should include time specifications: when the cancellation takes effect and whether the other party will be allowed a certain amount of time within which to comply before the cancellation becomes effective.

5. Sale of Personal Property If any personal property such as appliances or furniture is being transferred with the property, the parties should so specify in their agreement. Also, the seller should furnish the escrow agent with a bill of sale in order to transfer title to the property. The bill of sale should accurately describe the property being transferred, preferably including model number and serial number if available. If furniture is being transferred, as in the sale of an apartment complex, the description should be as specific as possible including the size, color, and purpose of the furniture; for example, "one 96-inch green and yellow plaid living-room sofa." The bill of sale should also include warranties from the seller that the seller has title to the property and is authorized to transfer title, and that there are no liens or encumbrances on the transferred property.

6. Relationship Between the Purchase Contract and the Escrow Instructions In the majority of real estate transactions, form agreements are used for both the purchase contract and the escrow instructions. One difficulty that can arise from using form agreements that are not carefully cross-compared is that they may include contradictory terms. Often the parties will have problems in complying with their conditions, and the contract may specify a remedy or procedure different from the remedy or procedure specified in the escrow instructions. The question of which document is controlling becomes a critical one, and the answer varies from state to state. Some states hold that the escrow instructions control, since they were executed later in time and can be viewed as superseding the contract. Other states hold that the contract is better evidence of the parties' intent, since the escrow agreement is merely a set of instructions to a third party and not the true purchase and sale agreement. The following case illustrates one state's solution to the conflict in agreements.

ALLAN v. MARTIN
574 P.2d 457 (Ariz. 1978)

Kirby and Felicienne Allan (defendants/appellants), both licensed real estate agents, approached George and Pamela Martin (plaintiffs/appellees) about purchasing the Martin's property which was located in Mesa, Arizona. The Martins wished to sell the property to obtain funds to complete and move into a home they were building in the mountains. The parties entered into a purchase and sale contract which provided that escrow would close on or before 31 July 1974. The Martins needed the funds by that date so that their mountain home could be completed and they could be in it before the cold weather began. Escrow instructions were prepared by a title company and signed by both parties.

The closing did not take place on 31 July but the Martins agreed to a 15-day extension. The Martins checked with the title company on 15 August, the last day of the extension, and discovered that the money necessary to purchase their property had not been deposited into escrow. The Martins sent a telegram to the Allans which read, "Due to delay in the sale to you of our home we will no longer sell as the contract expired 7-31-74." The Allans received the telegram on 15 August.

The next day the Martins signed a "thirteen day letter," which instructed the title company to cancel the escrow if the Allans did not comply with the escrow instructions within 13 days from the date of the letter. The 13-day provision for notice and compliance was part of the escrow instructions. The Martins indicated that they believed the 13-day notice was given only for the purpose of canceling the escrow. The Allans complied within 13 days, but the Martins refused to sell. The Martins brought suit seeking cancellation of the contract. The trial court found for the Martins, rescinding the contract and awarding them $1,000 in damages. The Allans appealed.

HAYS, Justice

A contract to sell real estate and an escrow arrangement are not the same thing. There must exist a binding contract to sell the real estate which is the subject of the escrow, or the escrow instructions are unenforceable. An escrow primarily is a conveyancing device designed to carry out the terms of a binding contract of sale previously entered into by the parties. Therefore, the escrow instructions are not a part of the underlying real estate sales contract and the terms of the instructions cannot alter or modify the sales contract unless the parties specifically and clearly state such alteration or modification in writing with specific reference to the fact it changes the original contract.

The appellants (Allans) base their appeal almost entirely upon a fine print form provision in the escrow instructions:

CANCELLATION
16. If either party, who has duly performed hereunder, elects to cancel these instructions because of the failure of the other party to comply with any of the terms hereof within the time limits provided herein, said party so electing to cancel shall deliver to Escrow agent a written notice to the other party and Escrow agent demanding that said other party comply with the terms hereof within thirteen days from the receipt of said notice by Escrow agent or that these instructions shall thereupon become cancelled.

This term clearly applies only to the procedure for cancelling the escrow instructions; it has nothing to do with how and under what circumstances the real estate contract may be rescinded. The time for performance of the contract was the date designated in the contract for the close of escrow. The latest date agreed upon by the parties was August 15, 1974. The sales contract stated that time was of the essence, and appellees [Martins] informed appellants that the time for the closing of the transaction was very important to them. The latest date for closing was a bargained for term, clearly material in this case. The cancellation provision in the escrow instructions cannot be construed to permit the appellants to perform their contract obligation any later than August 15, 1974.

On August 15 the appellant still had not complied with the sales contract; the money to purchase the property had not been delivered to the escrow agent. When time for performance is material to a contract and one party fails to perform by the contract deadline date, the other party may treat the contract as ended. Thus, when the purchase price was not paid into escrow on the last day agreed upon for closing, the appellees had the legal right to refuse to convey their property and to cancel the contract. They notified appellants they were exercising this right by telegram on August 15.

When appellees exercised their right to treat the contract as ended, the escrow instructions became unenforceable because there was no longer a binding contract to sell the property which was the subject of escrow. The "thirteen day letter" cancelling the escrow then became only a formality to prove that the escrow was now void. The fact that the quoted provision on cancellation of the escrow instructions gives a party thirteen days to comply with the terms of the escrow does not mean that one may belatedly comply with the breached sales contract when the nonbreaching party has given notice that he elects to treat the contract as ended. Nothing in the escrow instructions can revive an already dead underlying contract.

Appellants also urge that by signing the "thirteen day letter" appellees elected the escrow cancellation remedy and thus are bound to convey the property because appellants met their obligations under the escrow within thirteen days. As explained previously, this is incorrect because the escrow was already void at the time the letter was issued and also because the escrow cancellation procedure does not apply to a sale contract.

The verdict and judgment are affirmed.

Discussion Questions

1. Who are the buyers in the transaction? Who are the sellers?
2. What was the original closing date as provided in the purchase contract?
3. Why was a timely closing important to the Martins?
4. What happened when closing did not occur on the original closing date?
5. What happened when closing did not occur on the second date?

6. What is the significance of the "thirteen day letter" in the escrow instructions?
7. Did the Allans comply with the 13-day provision?
8. Is the 13-day provision controlling?
9. Which document controls, the contract or the escrow instructions?

In addition to the unilateral cancellation provision in the escrow instructions, the parties may wish to provide methods for cancellation by mutual agreement. A form should be used explaining the parties' mutual action, releasing them from liability, and providing for the return or distribution of deposited funds.

The provisions in the escrow instructions for the distribution of funds and costs in the event of cancellation should be consistent with the contractual provisions. Otherwise the parties should insert a clause in the escrow instructions indicating their intent to have the escrow instructions control. For example, the following clause could be used to give the escrow instructions control so that cancellation procedures, forms, and refunds are clearly established.

> In the event of any conflict in the provisions of these escrow instructions and the underlying sales agreement, it is the intent and desire of the parties that the terms of these escrow instructions be controlling.

7. Contingencies for Closing In this portion of the escrow instructions the parties must carefully set forth all requirements that must be met before the escrow agent may deliver title to the buyer and funds to the seller. The contingencies vary significantly from transaction to transaction, but there are many examples that appear repeatedly in both residential and commercial transactions. For example, a requirement that the seller establish compliance with building codes and zoning restrictions may be a condition to the consummation of the sale. As discussed in Chapter 11, delivery of marketable title is a condition to the completion of the sales transaction on all land transfers.

Other contingencies that may be required are the assignment of all lease and service contracts associated with the property, the furnishing of a favorable pest report, evidence of repair of items agreed to be repaired by the seller, the furnishing of an architect's certificate of completion on a newly constructed building, the completion of a final property inspection, the verification of boundaries by survey, and for business sales the furnishing of audited financial statements. The number and types of contingencies are limitless, but in drafting the escrow instructions, all parties should think of how they can be fully protected before transfer occurs to avoid any surprises once the escrow agent has carried forth the actual transfer of title and payment of funds.

RESPONSIBILITIES OF THE LENDER IN CLOSING—THE REAL ESTATE SETTLEMENT PROCEDURES ACT

As noted in the preceding discussion of the documents required for closing, the lender, if one is involved, must furnish certain documents for the transaction to be completed. The lender will furnish the promissory note, the truth-in-lending disclosures statement, and also the document that will be recorded to evidence the lender's security: the mortgage or deed of trust. However, the lender may be required to make further disclosures and comply with additional provisions created and required under a federal act passed in 1974: the *Real Estate Settlement Procedures Act (RESPA)*, (12 U.S.C. §2601 et seq.). If the lender is covered under RESPA, then additional forms, paperwork, and procedures are required before the closing of the transaction is permitted to take place.

Purpose of RESPA

The Real Estate Settlement Procedures Act was passed by Congress in reaction to evidence obtained through hearings that indicated buyers of residential property were surprised at closings with additional fees and expenses that were not disclosed to them in advance. The result was that neither buyers nor sellers could meet these substantial additional costs, or if they could meet them there was a loss on the expected return on the sale. The first section of RESPA (12 U.S.C. §2601 et seq., or Regulation 10) states the four purposes of the act:

1. To provide more effective advance disclosure to home buyers and home sellers of settlement costs;

2. To eliminate kickback or referral fees that tend to increase the costs of settlement services;

3. To reduce the amounts buyers are required to pay into escrow for taxes and insurance; and

4. To reform local record keeping and land title information.

Application of RESPA

The Real Estate Settlement Procedures Act is applicable to "federally related mortgages," which is defined to include the following types of mortgages:

1. Those secured by a first lien on residential property (including condominiums and cooperatives) designed principally for occupancy by one to four families;

2. Those made by any lender whose deposits are secured partially or in their entirety by any branch, agency, or portion of the federal government;

3. Those loans made by any lender that will be insured by some branch of the federal government;

4. Those loans intended to be sold on the secondary market to any corporation of the federal government (Fannie Mae, Ginnie Mae, Freddie Mac; see Chapter 12); and

5. Those loans made by lenders investing $1 million or more per year in residential real estate loans.

From the list it is clear that RESPA applies to virtually all residential loans. However, RESPA does not apply to second mortgages, purchases of property involving 100 acres or more, and home improvement loans. Loan commitments are covered by RESPA, and lenders are required to furnish the RESPA information upon issuing a loan commitment.

Disclosures Under RESPA

The Buyer's Information Handbook When a lender covered under RESPA receives a loan application, the applicant must be furnished with borrower's information handbook within 3 days. The handbook may be printed by the lender or purchased from the *Department of Housing and Urban Development (HUD)*—the agency responsible for enforcing RESPA. Written by HUD, the handbook includes explanations of RESPA, the selection of an escrow agent, the role of the real estate broker, and the lender's responsibilities. It also contains sample disclosure forms and explanations for fees charged.

Good Faith Estimate of Settlement Costs As originally passed, RESPA required lenders to make advance disclosures of closing costs to buyers. However, an amendment to the act calls for the lender to make only an estimate of the charges expected at closing. The items required in the good faith estimate are as follows:

- Sales and brokers' commissions
- Loan origination fees
- Loan discount
- Appraisal fee
- Credit report
- Lender's inspection fee
- Mortgage insurance application fee
- Assumption fee
- Interest (from date of closing to first payment)
- Mortgage insurance premium
- Settlement or closing fee
- Abstract or title search

- Title examination
- Title insurance binder
- Document preparation
- Notary fees
- Attorneys' fees
- Title insurance (with breakdown of lender's and owner's coverage)
- Recording fees
- City and county taxes and stamps
- State tax and stamps
- Survey
- Pest inspection
- Application or commitment fee

Because all transactions will not include all of the fees listed, RESPA requires the lender to make a good faith estimate for only those figures that the lender "anticipates the buyer will pay at settlement based upon the lender's general experience as to which party normally pays each charge in the locality." Those charges that could arise but are contingent must also be disclosed to the buyer as possibilities, as well as a figure for the charge if it is assessed.

Although HUD offers no precise formula for determining what constitutes a good faith estimate, the estimate must be expressed as a dollar amount. The only other standard for determining compliance is that the estimate must bear "a reasonable relationship to the charges the buyer is likely to experience at closing." In the case of figures that may change substantially between application and closing (such as points), HUD suggests that the lender also include a disclosure regarding the possible fluctuation with the good faith estimate.

While HUD has not provided a standard form for use by the lender in making the good faith estimate, it is permissible for the lender to use HUD's Uniform Settlement Statement (USS; discussed in the next section). Figure 13.1 is a sample of one lender's good faith estimate form. Specifically, RESPA requires that the good faith estimate meet the following four criteria:

1. The form must be clear and concise;
2. The form must include the lender's name;
3. The form must include the following statement or its equivalent in boldface type:
   THIS FORM DOES NOT COVER ALL ITEMS YOU WILL BE REQUIRED TO PAY IN CASH AT SETTLEMENT, FOR EXAMPLE, DEPOSIT IN ESCROW FOR REAL ESTATE TAXES AND INSURANCE. YOU MAY WISH TO INQUIRE AS TO THE AMOUNTS OF OTHER SUCH ITEMS. YOU MAY BE REQUIRED TO PAY OTHER ADDITIONAL AMOUNTS AT SETTLEMENT; and
4. The names of the charges in the estimate should be identical or as near as possible to the names used in the Uniform Settlement Statement.

Note that both the handbook and the good faith estimate must be delivered within 3 days of loan application regardless of whether the lender ultimately approves the loan of the applicant.

Uniform Settlement Statement and Advance Disclosure The purpose of the *Uniform Settlement Statement (USS)* required under RESPA is to provide the buyer with a final summary and explanation of all costs paid at the closing. Upon request, the buyer is permitted to inspect the USS 1 day in advance of the settlement. If the request is made, then the escrow agent must furnish the buyer with a completed USS. Any buyer who does not request the USS in advance is entitled to receive a copy at the time of closing, or if the buyer is not present at closing, as soon as is practicable thereafter.

The form used for the USS was developed by HUD, and a filled-in sample appears in Figure 13.2. All of the charges listed on the form must be disclosed. In some circumstances the buyer will be required to pay a fee before closing, but such a fee is required by the lender not by HUD. In cases of outside payment, such as for pest inspection, the cost must still be noted on the USS but will be followed by the abbreviation *poc* (paid outside closing).

The USS is not required if the buyer is to pay one flat fee at closing, so long as the fixed fee is given to the buyer as a dollar amount at the time of the loan application. This exemption is generally applicable in situations where the buyer is purchasing a new home from the developer, who is offering fixed closing costs as an incentive for purchase.

Figure 13.1 *Sample Good Faith Estimate of Closing Costs*

Pima Savings

Borrower _____

Property Address _____ Loan Term_____

Type of Loan _____ Loan Amount_____ Int. Rate _____

GOOD FAITH ESTIMATE

In accordance with the Real Estate Settlement Procedures Act (RESPA) of 1974, outlined below are your **ESTIMATE** costs in connection with the above referenced transaction.

	Buyer	Seller
DOWN PAYMENT	$_____	
CLOSING COSTS:		
Broker's Commission	$_____	$_____
FHA-VA Loan Discount or Points	$_____	$_____
Origination Fee or Service Charge	$_____	$_____
Initial Private Mortgage Insurance Premium	$_____	$_____
Appraisal Fee	$_____	$_____
Inspection Fee	$_____	$_____
Escrow or Settlement Fee	$_____	$_____
Owner's Title Policy		$_____
Title Insurance - Lenders Coverage (ALTA)	$_____	$_____
Recording Fees	$_____	$_____
Credit Report Charges	$_____	$_____
Tax Service Contract	$_____	$_____
Document Preparation Fee	$_____	$_____
Termite Inspection	$_____	$_____
Buydown	$_____	$_____
	$_____	$_____
TOTAL CLOSING COSTS:	$_____	$_____
IMPOUNDS OR PREPAID ITEMS:		
First Year's Insurance Policy Plus _____ months	$_____	$_____
Taxes	$_____	$_____
MIP or PMI	$_____	$_____
Initial or Prepaid Interest From C.O.E. _____ TO _____	$_____	$_____
	$_____	$_____
TOTAL IMPOUNDS:	$_____	$_____
TOTAL MOVE-IN COSTS (Down Payment + Closing Costs + Impounds)	$_____	$_____
ESTIMATED MONTHLY PAYMENT:		
Principal and Interest	$_____	$_____
MIP or PMI	$_____	$_____
Taxes	$_____	$_____
Insurance	$_____	$_____
	$_____	$_____
TOTAL	$_____	$_____

NOTE: This form does not necessarily cover all items you may be required to pay in cash at settlement. It does, however, ESTIMATE the amount you will likely pay to the best of our knowledge as of the date of application.

Provided that I qualify financially for a loan, I (we) understand that the terms of any commitment to make a loan which may be issued hereafter shall only be binding to Pima as follows:

Funds shall be committed for a period of _____ days from the date the Loan _____.

Interest rate and Service charge shall be committed for a period of _____ days from the date the Loan _____.

In the event the permanent real estate loan does not close within the time period referred to above, and Pima is no longer accepting applications for this type of credit, I (we) understand that Pima is under no obligation to extend its commitment to make my (our) loan. Should I (we) request Pima to issue a new commitment to extend credit after the expiration date of this commitment, the terms of the loan shall be renegotiated and I (we) must requalify if deemed necessary. I (We) understand that if Pima agrees to issue a new commitment to extend credit, Pima may, at its option, require my (our) loan to be closed at Pima's current market rate with such service charges as are in effect for my (our) particular category of loan at the time.

I (We) have received a copy of the Good Faith Estimate, HUD Booklet, Financial Privacy Notice, and Consumer Handbook on Adjustable Rate Mortgages.

Pima Savings & Loan

Agent/Processor _____

Signature _____

Phone _____ Date _____

Date _____

Signature _____

Date _____

Source: Appears courtesy of Pima Savings.

Figure 13.2 Sample Uniform Settlement Statement

HUD-1 (3-86)

Form Approved
OMB No. 2502-0265

A. U.S. DEPARTMENT OF HOUSING AND URBAN DEVELOPMENT

B. TYPE OF LOAN

1. X FHA   3. __ FMHA   3. __ CONV. UNINS.
4. __ VA   5. __ CONV. INS.

6. File Number   55156ns

7. Loan Number   0056720

8. Mortgage Ins. Case No.

TICOR TITLE INSURANCE

SETTLEMENT STATEMENT

C. NOTE: *This form is furnished to give you a statement of actual settlement costs. Amounts paid to any by the settlement agent are shown. Items marked "(P.O.C.)" were paid outside the closing; they are shown here for informational purposes and are not included in the totals.*

D. NAME OF BORROWER:
TERRY H. JENNINGS AND
MARIANNE M. JENNINGS

E. NAME OF SELLER:
STAPLEY CONSTRUCTION

F. NAME OF LENDER:
WESTERN AMERICAN MORTGAGE
728 E. McDowell   Phoenix, AZ

G. PROPERTY LOCATION:
1261 E. Hale, Mesa, AZ

H. SETTLEMENT AGENT: Pioneer National Title Ins. Co.
PLACE OF SETTLEMENT: 144 S. Mesa Dr. Mesa, AZ 85202

I. SETTLEMENT DATE: 1-31-88

J. SUMMARY OF BORROWER'S TRANSACTION		K. SUMMARY OF SELLER'S TRANSACTION	
100. GROSS AMOUNT DUE FROM BORROWER:		*400. GROSS AMOUNT DUE TO SELLER:*	
101. Contract sales price	43,500.00	401. Contract sales price	
102. Personal property		402. Personal property	
103. Settlement charges to borrower *(line 1400)*	425.00	403.	
104.		404.	
105.		405.	
Adjustments for items paid by seller in advance		*Adjustments for items paid by seller in advance*	
106. City/town taxes to		406. City/town taxes to	
107. County taxes to		407. County taxes to	
108. Assessments to		408. Assessments to	
109.		409.	
110.		410.	
111.		411.	
112.		412.	
113.		413.	
114.		414.	
115.		415.	
120. **GROSS AMOUNT DUE FROM BORROWER**	43,925.00	420. **GROSS AMOUNT DUE TO SELLER**	
200. AMOUNTS PAID BY OR IN BEHALF OF BORROWER:		*500. REDUCTIONS IN AMOUNT DUE TO SELLER:*	
201. Deposit or earnest money	3,923.74	501. Excess deposit *(see instructions)*	
202. Principal amount of new loan(s)	40,000.00	502. Settlement charges to seller *(line 1400)*	
203. Existing loan(s) taken subject to		503. Existing loan(s) taken subject to	
204.		504. Payoff of first mortgage loan	
205.		505. Payoff of second mortgage loan	
206.		506.	
207.		507.	
208.		508.	
209.		509.	
Adjustments for items unpaid by seller		*Adjustments for items unpaid by seller*	
210. City/town taxes to		510. City/town taxes to	
211. County taxes 1-1 to 1-23	1.26	511. County taxes to	
212. Assessments to		512. Assessments to	
213.		513.	
214.		514.	
215.		515.	
216.		516.	
217.		517.	
218.		518.	
219.		519.	
220. **TOTAL PAID BY/FOR BORROWER**	43,925.00	520. **TOTAL REDUCTION AMOUNT DUE SELLER**	
300. CASH AT SETTLEMENT FROM/TO BORROWER		*600. CASH AT SETTLEMENT TO/FROM SELLER*	
301. Gross amount due from borrower (line 120)	43,925.00	601. Gross amount due to seller (line 420)	
302. Less amounts paid by/for borrower (line 220)	43,925.00	602. Less reduction in amount due seller (line 520)	
303. CASH (FROM) (TO) BORROWER	00.00	603. CASH (TO) (FROM) SELLER	

CAT NO. FF00112
ES 355 (10/86)

Page 1

Figure 13.2 (continued)

		PAID FROM BORROWER'S FUNDS AT SETTLEMENT	PAID FROM SELLER'S FUNDS AT SETTLEMENT
L.	SETTLEMENT CHARGES		
700. TOTAL SALES/BROKER'S COMMISSION:			
BASED ON PRICE $ @ %			
Division of Commission (line 700) as follows:			
701. $ to			
702. $ to			
703. Commission paid at Settlement			
704.			
800. ITEMS PAYABLE IN CONNECTION WITH LOAN			
801. Loan Origination Fee %		385.45	14.55
802. Loan Discount %			1,600.00
803. Appraisal Fee to			15.00
804. Credit Report to			
805. Lender's Inspection Fee to		14.30	
806. Mortgage Insurance Application Fee to		(25.00)	∅
807. ~~XXXXXXXXXX~~ tax service			15.00
808. bring down			13.00
809. photo fee			10.00
810.			
811. WAMCO funding for landscaping			25.00
812.			
813.			
814.			
900. ITEMS REQUIRED BY LENDER TO BE PAID IN ADVANCE			
901. Interest from 1-30 to 2-1 @$ 9.32 /day (- days)		18.64	
902. Mortgage Insurance Premium for months to			
903. Hazard Insurance Premium for years to Farmers			90.00
904.			
905.			
1000. RESERVES DEPOSITED WITH LENDER			
1001. Hazard Insurance 2 months @ $ 7.50 per month		15.00	
1002. Mortgage Insurance 1 months @ $ 16.61 per month		16.61	
1003. City property taxes months @ $ per month			
1004. County property taxes months @ $ per month			
1005. Annual assessments months @ $ per month			
1006. months @ $ per month			
1007. months @ $ per month			
1008. months @ $ per month			
1100. TITLE CHARGES			
1101. Settlement or closing fee to Pioneer National Title Ins. Co.			59.50
1102. Abstract or title search to			
1103. Title examination to			
1104. Title insurance binder to			
1105. Document preparation to			
1106. Notary fee to			
1107. Attorney's fee to			
(includes above items numbers:			
1108. Title insurance to Pioneer National Title Ins. Co.			283.50
(includes above items numbers:			
1109. Lender's coverage $			
1110. Owner's coverage $			
1111.			
1112.			
1113.			
1200. GOVERNMENT RECORDING AND TRANSFER CHARGES			
1201. Recording fees: Deed $:Mortgage $:Release $			22.00
1202. City/county tax/stamps: Deed $ Mortgage $			
1203. State tax/stamps: Deed $ Mortgage $			
1204.			
1205.			
1300. ADDITIONAL SETTLEMENT CHARGES			
1301.			
1302.			
1303. SRVWUA			2.50
1304.			
1305.			
1306.			
1307.			
1308.			
1400. TOTAL SETTLEMENT CHARGES (enter on lines 103, Section J and 502, Section K)		425.00	2,150.05

HUD

BUYER _____   SELLER _____

BUYER _____   SELLER _____

CAT. NO. FF00113
ES 3551 (10-86)   Page 2

Penalties for Failure to Make Disclosures The Real Estate Settlement Procedures Act does not provide any express penalties for failure to make the disclosures. Enforcement of the disclosure requirements depends on suits by individuals who believe they have been injured by noncompliance with the disclosure requirements. Since 1975 there have been several suits filed by individual buyers claiming injury for lack of proper disclosures, and federal district courts have taken jurisdiction in hearing these cases.

Relationship of State Laws The act invalidates only those state laws that are inconsistent with its provisions. Thus it is possible for lenders and escrow agents to be required to comply with even higher standards of disclosure and possible penalties if their states' laws require further disclosures and procedures. Lenders must comply with both RESPA and any applicable state regulations and statutes.

Prohibited Conduct Under RESPA

Another stated purpose of RESPA was to eliminate the kickback and referral costs, which were increasing the cost of closing for buyers. Thus, certain forms of conduct between members of the real estate industry are now prohibited under RESPA.

Kickbacks and Unearned Fees Prior to the passage of RESPA, it was common practice for escrow agents to pay fees for business referred to them by lenders, brokers, and salespersons. Such fees were often payable in the form of a percentage commission. However, RESPA prohibits the giving or accepting of "any fee, kickback, or thing of value" for the referral of business. Therefore, cash payments, special discounts, stock, and special prices are all prohibited.

Requiring the Use of a Specific Title Company The act also prohibits sellers from requiring "as a condition to selling the property, that title insurance be purchased by the buyer from any particular title company." This provision was passed to regulate developers who were given substantial discounts in their title policies in exchange for the promise to send all of their purchasers to the title insurer for their policies.

Penalties Unlike the disclosure sections of RESPA, the prohibition sections contain specific penalties for violation. The penalty for violating the kickback section is a fine of $10,000, 1 year of imprisonment, or both; plus liability to the harmed party in the amount of three times the kickback paid or received; plus court costs and attorneys' fees. The penalty for requiring the use of a particular title company is three times the amount charged for the title insurance (paid to the buyer), plus court costs and attorneys' fees. The treble recovery is permitted even if the charge for the policy was reasonable and conformed to charges acceptable within the area. The following case deals with an issue of whether a RESPA violation took place.

U.S. v. GRAHAM MORTGAGE CORP.
740 F.2d 414 (6th Cir. 1984)

From September 1975 through May 1979, Graham Mortgage Corporation (GMC/defendant) provided Rose Hill Realty, Inc. with interim financing of Rose Hill's purchase, rehabilitation, and resale of Detroit-area residences. For each loan it received, Rose Hill agreed to refer to GMC two mortgage loan applicants from its brokerage business in addition to referring the purchaser of the rehabilitated house. In turn, GMC, when making FHA or VA mortgage loans to purchasers of the rehabilitated residences sold by Rose Hill, charged Rose Hill fewer points than it charged other sellers. To recoup the income lost through the reduction in points charged to Rose Hill, GMC increased the points charged to sellers of residences referred to Rose Hill and financed by FHA or VA loans.

Richard E. Chapin, executive vice president and director of GMC;

Thomas P. Heinz, a vice president and manager of GMC; and Manford Colbert, president of Rose Hill Realty, were charged along with GMC with violations of Section 8(a) of RESPA. Section 8(a) provides:

No person shall give and no person shall accept any fee, kickback, or thing of value pursuant to any agreement or understanding, oral or otherwise, that business incident to or a part of a real estate settlement service involving a federally related mortgage loan shall be referred to any person.

The defendants moved at the trial court to have the indictment dismissed on the grounds that the making of a mortgage loan is not "a real estate settlement service." The district court denied the motion to dismiss and the defendants appealed.

PECK, Senior Circuit Judge

In reviewing a question of statutory interpretation, we first turn to the language of the statute. Where the language of the statute is ambiguous and can be interpreted to support readings either imposing or not imposing criminal liability on individuals for particular conduct, the court must turn to the legislative history of the statute. "If the legislative history fails to clarify the statutory language, our rule of lenity would compel us to construe the statute in favor of . . . [the] criminal defendants in this case."

Section 8(a) of RESPA prohibits the payment or receipt of fees, kickbacks, or things of value in exchange for referrals of "business incident to or part of a real estate settlement service involving a federally related mortgage loan" (12 U.S.C. §2607[a]). Section 3(3) of RESPA defines the term "settlement services" as follows:

[T]he term "settlement services" includes any service provided in connection with a real estate settlement including, but not limited to, the following: title searches, title

examinations, the provision of title certificates, title insurance, services rendered by an attorney, the preparation of documents, property surveys, the rendering of credit reports or appraisals, pest and fungus inspections, services rendered by a real estate agent or broker, and the handling of the processing, and closing of settlement (12 U.S.C. §2602[3]).

The critical textual question is whether this definition of "settlement services," which does not expressly include within its scope the making of a mortgage loan, properly may be construed to do so implicitly.

The government advances a simple argument in support of its position that the language of §3(3) of RESPA provides for the treatment of the making of a mortgage loan as a settlement service. The government first contends that the definition of "settlement services," by its own terms, does not purport to contain an exhaustive list of settlement services, but rather denotes "any service provided in connection with a real estate settlement" (12 U.S.C. §2602[3]). The government then contends that the making of a mortgage loan is a service in the sense that it satisfies a borrower's need or demand for money. The government concludes that because the making of a mortgage loan is the service essential to a real estate settlement, it must be incidental to the settlement and fall within the scope of the definition in §3(3) of RESPA.

There can be little question that the list of settlement services contained in §3(3) of RESPA was not intended by Congress to be exhaustive. The language of the definition that the term includes, "but [is] not limited to," the services listed constitutes an explicit recognition that the list was not intended to be exhaustive. Accordingly, the Seventh Circuit upheld a conviction for splitting charges in violation of 12 U.S.C. §2607(b) based, in part, on its determination that a county counterman's han-

dling of Torrens filings is a settlement service for purposes of RESPA even though the service is not included in the list. The determination that the list of settlement services in §3(3) of RESPA is not exhaustive, however, does not render the government's argument persuasive. The issue before this court is not whether the list in §(3) of RESPA is exhaustive; rather, the issue before this court is whether the making of a mortgage loan constitutes the provision of a service "in connection with a real estate settlement."

In arguing that the making of a mortgage loan is a service provided incident to a settlement, the government appears to rely on what it contends is an ordinary meaning of the term "service," viz., that "service" denotes the supplying of some demand or need. Because the making of a mortgage loan supplies the need for money in connection with a real estate settlement, the government concludes that the making of a mortgage loan is a real estate settlement service. The problem with this argument is that, as the government concedes, the meaning of the term "service" varies depending upon the context in which the term is used.

Because of the illumination provided by the list of settlement services in §3(3) of RESPA, we need not rely upon any purported common understanding of the term "service," assuming that such an understanding exists. Our examination of the illustrative list of services included in §3(3) of RESPA indicates that the common thread running among the listed services is that each is an ancillary or peripheral service that, unlike the making of a mortgage loan, is not directly related to the closing of a real estate sale covered by RESPA. As §8(a) of RESPA makes explicit, referrals of "business incident to or a part of a real estate settlement service" are prohibited only where the settlement involves a federally related mortgage loan. Accordingly, unlike the services listed in §3(3), the making of a mortgage loan is central to any transaction covered by RESPA. In light of the centrality of the making of a mortgage loan to any RESPA-covered transaction, Congress's failure to specify the making of a mortgage loan in listing settlement services seems inexplicable unless the omission was intended. In short, because the government furnishes no convincing explanation of the absence of the pivotal activity of the making of a mortgage loan from the list of settlement services in §3(3) of RESPA, it is more likely that the omission was intentional than accidental.

In sum, neither the plain language of the relevant section nor the structure of RESPA affords an unambiguous reading that requires the imposition of criminal liability on the conduct alleged in the indictment. Accordingly, we turn to the legislative history of the statute.

As an initial point, the HUD-VA Report, although indicative of the problems which Congress intended to address by RESPA, was more concerned with the abuses involved in the real estate conveyancing industry that with those involved in real estate financing. More significantly, the report, provided to Congress two years prior to the enactment of RESPA, provides no indication as to the scope of the statute as enacted.

In settling upon the broader language of the Senate version, we do not believe that Congress intended to bring real estate financing within the scope of settlement services for purposes of RESPA. Instead, the following statement by Senator Proxmire indicates that the decision reflected an intention to expand the coverage not to the making of a mortgage loan but rather to the activities of realtors:

It should also be noted that the conference report retains the broader definition of settlement charges included in the present law. This definition has been interpreted by HUD to include real estate sales commissions. Congress attempted, in 1972, to exclude real estate commissions from the definition of settlement charge but no legislation was enacted. The National Association of Realtors contacted members of the conference committee on S. 3164 and urged them to exclude real estate commissions from the definition of settlement charges.

However, the conference committee gave no consideration to this request. As a result, real estate commissions along with all other settlement charges are subject to HUD's regulatory authority under section 701.

Accordingly, we conclude that the legislative history lacks the clarity and force to compel the conclusion that Congress intended to treat the making of a mortgage loan as a settlement service when it enacted RESPA.

In light of our holdings that the language of RESPA is ambiguous with respect to the issue of whether the making of a mortgage loan is a settlement service and that the statute's legislative history does not direct any resolution of that issue, "the rule of lenity mandates judgment for the [defendants]."

Reversed.

Discussion Questions

1. What type of payments or arrangements were made between the realty and the mortgage company?

2. Did someone else have to bear the cost of that arrangement?

3. What does the court use to determine

whether making a mortgage loan is a settlement service?

4. Is the language clear?

5. What does the legislative history reveal?

6. Does the court find that a mortgage is a "settlement service"?

7. Did the defendants violate the spirit of RESPA?

(13.2) Consider:

Security Escrow kept $250,000 in an account with Southwestern Savings and Loan at no interest. Southwestern was a substantial residential mortgage lender in the area and had all of its borrowers use Security Escrow to close their residential purchases. Would this present any problems under RESPA?

Limitations on Escrow Deposits Under RESPA

The final purpose of RESPA was to eliminate the excessive prepaids and deposits required of buyers before escrow could close. The reasons for the prepaid amounts required by lenders was to make sure that the property was insured and that tax liens did not arise immediately after closing. For the buyer the prepaids were forced savings, but they also created difficulties in coming up with the cash necessary for closing. To solve this conflict, RESPA limits the amount that the lender may require to be deposited at the time of escrow and also limits the amount which may be required monthly.

At escrow, the maximum payment is calculated as the amount that would normally have been paid into escrow from the date the charge would have been last paid until (but not including) the date of the first full mortgage payment, plus the equivalent of 2-months' payment. For example, suppose annual taxes on the property are $1,200 (or $100 per month), due on 30 April. Closing on the property will occur on 15 July, and the first full mortgage payment will be made on 1 September. Under RESPA the maximum deposit would be $600, computed as follows: $100 would be paid on May, June, July, and August 1 before the first full mortgage payment is due, for a total of $400. The 2-month cushion is $200, so the total is $600.

After settlement, RESPA prohibits the lender from requiring large monthly deposits for taxes and insurance. Monthly payments for taxes and insurance are limited to 1/12 of the amount that will become due during the year on such charges.

There are no civil or criminal penalties stated in RESPA for violation of these deposit limitations, but there have been several suits by harmed buyers in which federal district courts have taken jurisdiction and have held that the buyers do have a civil remedy under the act for their actual damages.

(13.3) Consider:

The Calhouns are purchasing property, and the taxes on the property are $600 per year and the insurance is $300 per year. Both taxes and insurance are due on 30 June. Closing on the property will take place on 15 September, with the Calhoun's first mortgage payment due on 1 November. How much is the lender permitted to be paid at closing? How much may the lender require in monthly deposits?

THE ESCROW AGENT'S RESPONSIBILITIES

Perhaps the greatest area of concern and liability in the closing process lies with the party responsible for conducting the closing: the third party or escrow agent. The difficulty with the role of the escrow agent is that the relationship is not a true agency, since both parties' interests are carried forth by the agent. A trust relationship is not established because a trust is not created. The unique position of the agent in closing is established by a series of duties and responsibilities created specifically for this arrangement necessary for real estate transfers.

Escrow Agent's Duty to Follow Instructions

The escrow agent is given an assignment to perform according to the provisions established in the escrow instructions. The agent can do no more and no less than what is specified in that agreement because the only authority possessed by the agent is that given in the escrow instructions. Agents exceeding their authority are liable, and agents not performing the required functions are also liable. For example, if an agent is required to pay all tax liens on the property before turning funds over to the seller and fails to do so, the agent is liable to the buyer for the amount of the tax liens.

The escrow agent often faces the same difficulties the buyer and seller face if it is not made clear which document controls—the escrow instructions or the contract. In the absence of a provision to the contrary, the agent must follow only the terms and conditions set forth in the escrow instructions, for that is the only agreement to which the agency is a party. The following case illustrates this principle of limiting the duties of the agent to the escrow instructions.

DELSON L. CO. v. WASHINGTON ESCROW CO., INC.

558 P.2d 832 (Wash. 1976)

The material facts are undisputed. Washington Escrow (defendant/appellant) made partial payments of Delson Lumber Company's (plaintiff/appellee) funds on a timber purchase in violation of the escrow instructions. The underlying earnest money agreement required the seller to provide title that was "free of encumbrances, or defects, except those of record." The escrow instructions of both seller and buyer provided, "Timber to be free and clear of all encumbrances except: BLANK."

On 18 January 1974 Washington Escrow sent a letter to Delson Lumber's counsel enclosing the escrow instructions, a preliminary title report, and copies of the earnest money agreement and timber deeds. The letter commented on three outstanding encumbrances and suggested what was necessary to clear title. On 19 January 1974 Delson Lumber's counsel advised Washington Escrow that he would have Delson Lumber execute the escrow instructions and the timber deed and obtain the check to close the matter. Delson Lumber's counsel

also wrote a letter reminding Washington Escrow of the provision in the instructions requiring the title insurance company to insure the timber free of all liens and encumbrances.

On 21 January 1974 Delson Lumber sent the escrow instructions, an executed deed, and a check for $25,819.77. The cover letter contained a reminder of the title provision.

Washington Escrow made disbursement from the funds deposited in spite of the fact that the timberlands were subject to three real estate contracts of record. Delson Lumber notified Washington Escrow of its intent to cancel unless clear title was furnished. Washington Escrow sought to force closure and Delson Lumber brought suit. The trial court awarded summary judgment to Delson Lumber, and Washington Escrow appealed.

PEARSON, Judge

An escrow holder occupies a fiduciary relationship to all parties to the escrow and owes the same duty of fidelity that an agent or trustee owes to its principal.

As a general rule, an escrow agent becomes liable to his principals for damages proximately resulting from his breach of instructions, or from his exceeding the authority conferred on him by the instructions.

The undisputed facts disclose that Washington Escrow breached its instructions and paid out escrowed funds without assuring that plaintiff would receive the requisite title. Any doubt or uncertainty about its duty arising from the inconsistency between its instructions and the underlying earnest money agreement could and should have been resolved before defendant proceeded to close the transaction.

Defendant relies upon cases which hold that conflicts between escrow instructions and the underlying agreement should

be controlled by the latter agreement; or that where ambiguities are created by differences in the two agreements they should be construed together; or that escrow agreements do not take the place of the agreement for sale, but are a vehicle for carrying it to its completion.

Those rules may be applicable where the dispute concerns the immediate parties to the underlying agreement of sale. They should not, however, be used to diminish the duty of an escrow holder to act strictly in accordance with the provisions of the escrow agreement. For the latter agreement is the controlling instrument between the escrow [agent] and his principal.

Furthermore, the letter from plaintiff's counsel at the inception of the transaction should have resolved any uncertainty with reference to plaintiff's intention that the escrow instructions were to control. At the very least, defendant was put on notice of the conflicting instruments and should have resolved the conflict before proceeding with the closure of the transaction.

We hold that liability attaches to the escrow where it improperly parts with the escrowed funds. The measure of damages is the sum improperly paid whenever the underlying transaction is not consummated and the benefit of the bargain is lost.

Judgment affirmed.

Discussion Questions

1. Who was the purchaser under the earnest money contract?
2. What type of title provision was contained in the earnest money contract?
3. What type of title provision was contained in the escrow instructions?
4. Was the escrow agent aware of the conflict in the documents?
5. Which document did the escrow agent follow?
6. Were there title defects?
7. Did the escrow agent act properly?
8. In the event of a conflict between the escrow instructions and the underlying purchase contract, which should the escrow agent follow?
9. Is this decision inconsistent with the *Allan* case?

Escrow Agent's Fiduciary Responsibilities

Along with the duty of following instructions, the escrow agent also has the responsibility of acting for the benefit and only in the best interests of the parties to the transaction. The agent cannot jeopardize either party's rights by closing for the sake of obtaining the closing fee if the required terms and conditions of the instructions have not been met. The consequence of the breach of this fiduciary responsibility by the agent will be the imposition of liability by the party who experiences a loss as a result of the agent's conduct.

Embezzlement of deposited funds by the escrow agent is definitely a breach of the fiduciary duty, but the problem is that usually the agent has disappeared or the funds cannot be recovered from the agent. This lack of remedy leaves the parties to the underlying sales contract to determine who will absorb the loss of the embezzled funds. The risk of loss will be determined according to the degree of compliance with the contract contingencies. That is, if the buyer has complied with all contingencies and the money has been deposited with the agent, then title to the money technically belongs to the seller and the seller would absorb the loss. Likewise, if the money has been deposited but the contingencies necessary for transfer have not been completed (e.g., the buyer does not qualify), title to the funds (and hence the risk of loss) would remain with the seller.

Escrow Agent's Duty of Care

The escrow agent has a duty to exercise reasonable care and skill in the performance of the closing function. Thus an agent is expected to understand and comply with title procedures, insurance documents, and recording requirements. In other words, the agent is held to the professional standards of those who are involved in the real estate industry and familiar with its terms and procedures. The following case illustrates the difficulties an escrow agent can encounter as a result of an oversight.

U.S. LIFE TITLE v. BLISS

722 P.2d 356 (Ariz. 1986)

William R. Bliss (appellee) agreed to sell George P. Salemo, Jr. (and later his nominee Catherine Salemo, his wife), a piece of residential property in the Phoenix area for $795,000. U.S. Life Title Company of Arizona (appellant) was employed as the escrow agent for the transaction. Written escrow instructions were executed and delivered to U.S. Life Title.

The buyer's agent gave a certified check for $114,023.80 to U.S. Life Title at the time of closing. The certification was forged and Chase Manhattan Bank, on which the check was drawn, refused payment. Before the forgery was discovered, U.S. Life Title delivered the closing documents, including the deed, from Bliss to Salemo and disbursed $74,422.28 to Bliss.

U.S. Life Title recorded a lis pendens and brought suit against Salemo for the amount of the forged check.

The suit was later amended to include Bliss as an additional defendant on the grounds of an indemnity provision in the escrow instruction.

After the forgery was discovered, on October 22, Bliss purchased a home from the Tillotsons and as part payment assigned the note he had received from Salemo. That note was secured by a deed of trust on the property. Tillotson foreclosed on the deed of trust and resold it to Bliss who in turn sold it to another buyer for $755,000. Thus Bliss received $49,745 from Salemo through escrow and $74,422.28 at closing and then recovered the property that he had sold. Bliss therefore received benefits of $310,000 to $375,000 from the various transactions.

On Bliss' motion for summary judgment, the case was dismissed and U.S. Life Title appealed.

BIRDSALL, Presiding Judge

In his motion for summary judgment and on appeal, Bliss contends: (1) that the appellant cannot prevail because it violated its fiduciary duties under the escrow instructions; (2) that the escrow instructions were not followed because the appellant closed the transaction, including delivery of the deed, before the terms of the sale had been performed; (3) that Salemo had not performed because the check was not honored and the appellant should not have accepted mere delivery of the check as performance; (4) that the appellant should have verified with the bank that the check was good even though it purported to be certified; and (5) that he orally requested the appellant's escrow officer to secure verification from the bank. As to his last contention, the evidence before the trial court on the motion for summary judgment confirms that Bliss made this request, that the escrow officer made several unsuccessful attempts to contact the bank, and that the appellant closed anyway on the strength of the certification. The evidence further shows that other checks tendered by Salemo during the transaction had been dishonored and that appellant had notice of this fact. The appellant submitted evidence that the escrow industry practice in the community was to accept, as good and genuine, and as payment, a certified check. The appellant also points to the following provision in the escrow instructions:

12. Direct that all money payable hereunder be paid to Escrow Agent which, upon receipt thereof, shall deposit such funds in a general escrow account in one or more banks doing banking business in Arizona. Disbursement of any funds may be made by checks of Escrow Agent. Escrow Agent shall be under no obligation to disburse any funds represented by check or draft, and no check or draft shall be payment to Escrow Agent in compliance with any of the requirements hereof, until it is advised by the bank in which deposited that such check or draft has been honored, unless Escrow Agent specifically agrees in writing to accept liability for the sufficiency thereof.

The appellant argues that it never agreed in writing, or otherwise, to accept liability for the sufficiency of the check.

We must decide whether the appellant is entitled to proceed on an indemnity theory.

The escrow instructions provided that the seller (Bliss):

Will deliver to Escrow Agent a deed of the property from Seller to Buyer to be held by Escrow Agent until the terms hereof have been performed, at which time it shall deliver said deed to Buyer.

This is the very essence of escrow; and the purpose for having an independent escrow agent. The terms included a requirement that the buyer (Salemo) pay the amount required at closing. Salemo did not perform. The only payment made for closing was the check with the forged certification. When U.S. Life Title proceeded with the closing, including delivery of the deed, it breached the quoted provision of the escrow agreement. The title company assumed the risk when it elected to close on the strength of the check. Paragraph 12 is no defense. While it may be argued that the title company did not "agree to accept liability for the sufficiency of the check" in so many written words, it did more than that. It accepted the worthless check as payment and closed the transaction. This was, at least, the equivalent of an agreement to be responsible.

An indemnitee, the title company here, may not recover for losses arising from its own breach of contract unless the indemnity agreement so provides in clear and unequivocal terms. The indemnity provision of the escrow agreement contained no such language. It read:

SELLER AND BUYER:
9. Will indemnify and save harmless Escrow Agent against all costs, damages, attorney's fees, expenses and liabilities which it may incur or sustain in connection with these instructions or the escrow or any court action arising therefrom and will pay the same upon demand.

If the appellant's breach is viewed as negligence, it would also be precluded from recovery by indemnification. The duties of an escrow agent are defined in the escrow agreement and must be strictly construed.

Affirmed.

Discussion Questions

1. Who were the parties in the original property transaction?
2. What was the problem with the certified check?
3. What was the purpose of the lis pendens?
4. How much loss did Bliss experience as result of the transaction?

5. What clause in the escrow instructions is critical?
6. Who will bear the loss of the certified check?
7. How could the problem have been prevented?

KEY TERMS

escrow
escrow instructions
prorated
Real Estate Settlement Procedures
    Act (RESPA)

Department of Housing and Urban
    Development (HUD)
Uniform Settlement Statement (USS)

CHAPTER PROBLEMS

1. Herbert Walsh is the owner of some valuable commercial/industrial acreage located near a municipal airport. Sam Stanton is interested in purchasing the property and informs Walsh that he has deposited $25,000 with First American Escrow, along with signed escrow instructions to purchase the property for a total cash price of $750,000. If Walsh signs the escrow instructions, do the parties have an enforceable contract?

2. Gladys Pickrell entered into a contract to purchase property from the Wades for $40,000. Pickrell and the Wades signed a purchase and sale agreement and also signed escrow instructions that would permit closing upon Pickrell's qualifying for a loan. Pickrell deposited $1,500 earnest money with the escrow agent. A judgment creditor of Pickrell garnished the earnest money prior to Pickrell's qualifying for the loan. The Wades protest that the money belonged to them. What is the result?

3. Saxon had a contract to purchase property located on Mundy's Mill Road in Clayton County, Georgia. The escrow instructions provided that closing would take place upon the completion of a survey report indicating the acreage was 5.59 acres. When Saxon went to close, the survey report was not completed, but he was assured by the escrow officer that the land contained the proper acreage and that the report was simply a formality. Saxon closed, but after closing, the survey report revealed the property contained only 4.74 acres. Saxon is suing the escrow agent and company. Are there any grounds for liability?

4. First Trust was the escrow agent designated to handle a property closing for Reinhold as seller and Cazalet as buyer. Escrow instructions were executed and provided for payment to Reinhold in one lump sum upon the satisfaction of certain contingencies. Shortly after the instructions were executed, Cazalet wrote to First Trust and asked that payment be made in three installments rather than in a lump sum and that payment be delayed. First Trust complied with Cazalet's letter and Reinhold objected. What was the result?

5. Ace Title Company pays fees to brokers (who refer business to them) for arranging for appraisers, loan applications, and title reports. It is customary for brokers to perform these services anyway as part of earning their commission. Is there a violation of RESPA?

6. Prepare a good faith estimate of closing costs and a settlement statement from the following information:

    Sales price. $70,000.00

    Term of loan. 30 years

    Loan. $63,000; 90 percent FHA loan; $450.00 origination fee; 2 percent discount

    Principal and interest. $652.00

    FHA insurance. 1 percent

    Location of property. 5730 E. Grand Ave., Mesa, AZ 85203; Maricopa County

    Tax information. $1,200 per year for city, county, and state taxes; taxes due 1 July 1988

    Estimated settlement date. 15 June 1988 with first payment on 1 August 1988

What additional information is needed to complete the good faith estimate and settlement statement?

7. Which of the following loans and lenders would be subject to RESPA?
    a. A loan for a single-family dwelling by First Federal Savings and Loan
    b. A loan for the purchase of one condominium unit for use as a residence in a complex consisting of 450 such units
    c. A loan for the purchase of a twenty-unit apartment complex by a bank insured by the Federal Deposit Insurance Corporation (FDIC)
    d. A loan secured by a second mortgage for the construction of a swimming pool in the backyard of a residence
    e. A loan for the purchase of a cooperative that was formerly an apartment

8. Who of the following is not permitted to serve as an escrow agent in a land transaction closing?
   a. The lender
   b. An attorney
   c. The title insurer
   d. An escrow company

9. Discuss the propriety of the following under RESPA:
   a. An estimate of closing costs that is $4,000 lower than the actual costs of closing
   b. A broker requiring a seller to use a particular title company

10. If a conflict exists between the purchase contract and the escrow instructions, which document is controlling?

14

TRANSFERRING REAL ESTATE AFTER DEATH—WILLS, ESTATES, AND PROBATE

Let's talk of graves, of worms, and epitaphs;
Make dust our paper, and with rainy eyes
Write sorrow on the bosom of the earth.
Let's choose executors and talk of wills.

—William Shakespeare,
King Richard II *Act III, Scene 2*

The value of property owned by an individual can be significantly reduced if that individual dies without a will, or dies with a will that fails to clarify the disposition of the property and to take advantage of the tax breaks available for property distribution at death. The purpose of this chapter is to discuss the methods whereby title to property is transferred at death as well as the processes and tax implications involved in such transfers.

THE LAW OF WILLS, ESTATES, AND PROBATE

In all areas of law relating to real estate discussed thus far, it has been clear that the specific laws for various subjects often vary significantly from state to state. This degree of variation is greatly exaggerated in the law of wills, estates, and probate. In fact, the states can vary significantly on every aspect of probate law, and an entire series of texts would be required to fully explain all of the variations that exist in that area of the law. This chapter does not attempt to explain each state's provisions but deals with the subject in general terms.

However, there is a uniform law in the area, called the *Uniform Probate Code (UPC)*, which by 1988 had been adopted in some form by more than one-fourth of the states[1] and was being considered by three other states. Because of the likelihood of expanded adoption of the UPC and because of its simplicity, the provisions of this code are discussed throughout the chapter.

INTESTATE ESTATES

If a person dies without a valid will or fails to dispose of certain items of property in a will, the person is said to have died *intestate* or partially intestate. In the case of an intestate death, the property of the decedent is distributed according to the state's law on *intestate succession*. The method of distributing the intestate's property differs between each of the states, but in all states it is controlled by the decedent's familial situation at the time of death.

Intestacy with a Surviving Spouse

Generally, each state statute begins by attempting to leave the property of the decedent to the closest living relatives. All state intestacy statutes begin by giving all or some portion of the property to the surviving spouse if there is one. In some states the surviving spouse will share the amount of the estate with any surviving children. As early as 1670, England's statute of distribution gave one-third of the intestate's property to the surviving spouse and two-thirds to the surviving children.

Under the UPC, if the decedent is survived by a spouse but no children, all property goes to the spouse. If the decedent is survived by a spouse and children, all of whom are children of the surviving spouse, the spouse is still entitled to all of the property. However, if the decedent is survived by a spouse and children, all of whom are not children of the surviving spouse, then the spouse receives one-half of the estate and each of the children receives an equal portion of the remaining half.

Intestacy with No Surviving Spouse but with Issue

Although there are variations, if the intestate has no surviving spouse but does have surviving children, the intestate property is distributed among those children. Again, England's early statute of distribution provided that if there was no surviving spouse, all property went to the children.

Most states tend to follow the theory that it is better for the property to

---

[1]Alaska, Arizona, Colorado, Hawaii, Idaho, Louisiana, Maine, Minnesota, Montana, Nebraska, New Jersey, New Mexico, North Dakota, Pennsylvania, Utah, and Wisconsin.

pass down to growing generations than to pass it back to older generations. Under the UPC, if the decedent has no surviving spouse but does have surviving issue, the estate property passes to the issue. Because the UPC uses the term *issue* to include children, grandchildren, and other direct lineal descendants of the intestate, it carries the presumption that where possible the property should pass to future generations.

(14.1) Consider:

Ralph married Cora in 1949. Ralph and Cora had two children, Steven and Alice. Cora died in 1959, and Ralph married Susan in 1963. Ralph and Susan had two children, Alan and Erica. Ralph has just died intestate and his estate is valued at $300,000. How would Ralph's property be distributed under the intestacy laws of your state? How would it be distributed under the UPC?

Intestacy with No Surviving Spouse or Children

It is in the circumstance where a person dies intestate with no spouse and no children that the states begin to vary significantly in the way the intestate property is distributed. There are basically four groups of relatives remaining to whom the property can be distributed: (1) parents, (2) brothers and sisters and their issue, (3) grandparents, and (4) uncles and aunts and their issue. In some states the method of distribution is controlled by the degree of relationship of each of these relatives, so that the closest relative in a step diagram receives most or all of the estate.

Under the UPC the property is given first to the parents. If the parents have predeceased the intestate, the property is given to brothers and sisters of the decedent. If the brothers and sisters have predeceased the intestate, but left issue (nieces and nephews of the decedent), then the issue is entitled to the property. If there are no surviving relatives in any of the preceding groups, then the UPC requires that one-half of the decedent's property be distributed to the decedent's maternal grandparents and their issue (aunts, uncles, and so on) and the remaining half be distributed to the decedent's paternal grandparents and their issue.

(14.2) Consider:

Ron, a single young man, has just passed away. Survivors include his parents, a brother, a sister, both sets of grandparents, and two uncles. How would Ron's property be distributed under the laws of intestacy of your state? How would it be distributed under the UPC?

Intestacy with No Surviving Relatives

All states have some provision governing the destiny of the property of a decedent who has no surviving relatives. At some point in all of the state statutes the property will go to the state, or some public fund, or *escheat* to the state. The degree to which a state statute permits distant relatives to inherit varies. Under the UPC, the property will escheat if there are no lineal descendants of the maternal or paternal grandparents; thus, the UPC does not permit second or collateral heirs to inherit.

The escheat provisions of state intestate statutes are often referred to as *laughing heir statutes* because an escheat is required before distant heirs, who may not have known the decedent, inherit the decedent's property.

Intestacy Terminology and Special Provisions

There are some terms and special provisions used in intestacy statutes that affect how the property is distributed. The following sections define and discuss some of those terms and provisions.

Per Stirpes Versus Per Capita Distribution Very often an intestate will leave relatives who are entitled to receive property under the law, but the relatives hold different degrees of relationship to the decedent. In order to distribute the property fairly, most states specify the proportion that the different degrees of heirs are entitled to receive.

Under a *per capita* theory of distribution, all parties take an equal share of the decedent's property. Some states follow a per capita theory for all relatives entitled to property. In other states the per capita method of distribution is used only if all the heirs bear the same degree of relationship to the decedent. For example, if Bob, a widower, died and left three children all of whom are entitled to his property under the state's intestate distribution provisions, then each child would receive one-third of Bob's estate under per capita distribution.

Under *per stirpes*, parties receive a portion of the estate that is proportional to their degree of relationship. Suppose that in the preceding example Bob died leaving two living children and two grandchildren who have survived their parent (Bob's third child). The relationships of the parties is shown in the diagram.

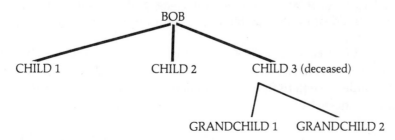

Under per stirpes distribution, children 1 and 2 would each receive one-third of Bob's estate. Grandchildren 1 and 2 would receive one-sixth each (half of one-third). Because the grandchildren hold a lesser degree of relationship to Bob and receive their share through their parent, they receive less of the estate than the children.

(14.3) Consider:

H and W were married in 1939. They had four children, A, B, C, and D. H died in 1980 and left all of his property to W. W passed away 2 months ago, intestate. A died in 1979 but had three children, X, Y, and Z. B, C, and D are alive at the time of W's death. B has one child, R; and C has two children, T and S. How would the property of W be distributed in your state? How would the property be distributed by per stirpes distribution under the UPC?

Relatives by Marriage In most states, relatives by marriage other than the surviving spouse are not entitled to receive property through intestate distribution. Stepchildren, nieces, nephews, and spouses of predeceased children are all part of this excluded group.

Half-blood Relatives No state has a provision that absolutely excludes half-blood relatives of the intestate from taking a share under the statutory scheme of distribution. Many states and the UPC treat a half-blood relative the same as a full-blood relative. Other states have provisions requiring the half-blood relatives to take a lesser proportion of the estate than the full-blood relatives.

Posthumous Heirs At common law and under all state statutes and the UPC, children of the intestate born after the intestate's death are still treated as heirs. Some states stipulate that the *posthumous heir* must be born within 10 months of the decedent's death in order to be treated an heir. The states vary significantly on posthumous relatives who are not children of the decedent or lineal descendants of the decedent. Some states do not permit any such posthumous relatives to take property under intestate distribution; other states stipulate that these relatives must be in the embryonic stages of development at the time of the intestate's death to be eligible to take property.

Illegitimate Children Under the UPC and in all states illegitimate children who have not been adopted by anyone are treated as natural children of their mothers and are entitled to inherit from their mothers and their mothers' relatives. Unless legitimized, these children are not treated as the natural children of their fathers.

Adopted Children The legislative trend has been for adopted children to be treated as the natural children of the parents adopting them. The UPC also follows this doctrine for purposes of intestate distribution.

Aliens Aliens are entitled to receive property through intestate distribution. Their citizenship is not an issue in their right to inherit.

Convicts A convict is permitted to inherit property and have it distributed through intestate succession at the time of death. Conviction status does not result in the escheat of the convict's property to the state.

Murder Under the UPC and in most states, an heir convicted of murdering the intestate is not entitled to the intestate share of property that ordinarily would be awarded. State provisions vary as to the type of conviction required before the inheritance is lost.

Advancements At common law, the doctrine of *advancements* required that any gifts to heirs made by the intestate while alive had to be subtracted from that heir's share before distribution of the intestate estate was made. For example, suppose 3 heirs were entitled to receive equal shares of a $90,000 estate. If one heir had received $10,000 as an inter vivos gift, that heir would get only $20,000 under the doctrine of advancements. The remaining two heirs split the extra $10,000. Some states still follow the doctrine but it is not recognized under the UPC.

Property Interests Not Passing by Intestate Succession Some estates in land will not transfer by intestate distribution because of their characteristics. These interests, which were discussed in Part I, are: life estates, joint tenancies, tenancies by the entireties, and rights under dower and curtesy (discussed in Chapter 15). These interests automatically pass title at the time of death of one of the parties involved and thus are not subject to the rules of intestacy. Life insurance benefits also pass according to the party or parties named as beneficiaries under the policy, and the distribution of proceeds is not governed by the laws of intestacy.

Simultaneous Death In cases of accidents and air disasters it is frequently true that a husband and wife, who would ordinarily receive each other's estates, will perish together or will die under circumstances where it is impossible to tell who predeceased the other. Some states have survival period requirements that must be met before an heir may inherit through intestate distribution. Under the UPC, heirs must survive by 120 hours before they are permitted to inherit. The reason for survival clauses is efficiency. For example, a husband might survive his wife in an auto crash by only a few hours or a day and then pass away. In the absence of a survival provision, the property of the wife would pass to her husband's estate which would in turn pass according to the remaining rules of intestate succession. With a survival provision, the property of each would be directly distributed to those next in line.

Some states have passed a uniform law related to the UPC, the *Uniform Simultaneous Death Act (USDA)*, which provides that if a married couple dies under circumstances where it is impossible to determine the order of their deaths, then property of each spouse is distributed as if the other spouse had predeceased them. Thus, the wife's property would be distributed as if she died without a surviving spouse and the husband's property would be distributed in the same manner. Again, the purpose of the statute is to avoid the multiple distributions that might be required if the order of death had to be determined.

WILLS

Purpose of a Will

A *will* is a series of written instructions that sets forth what will be done with the decedent's property upon death. The will cannot serve to transfer any property so long as the maker of the will (testator) is alive. As discussed in the intestacy section, the law does provide for the distribution of property in the event of an intestate death, but the law's method of distribution may not be desirable or may not be the wish of the decedent.

A will can expedite the distribution of property. Under the UPC, the procedures provided for probating a will require a minimal number of court appearances and substantially reduce paperwork, court costs, and attorneys' fees.

A will also may more accurately reflect the decedent's desires. For example, the will can name who will be responsible for handling and distributing the property, who should be appointed as guardian for minor children, who will make the funeral arrangements, and what type of funeral arrangements are to be made.

Trusts to protect the income of minor children and trusts to save on estate taxes assessed at the time of death may also be created by a will.

Without a will, it is possible that the intestate distribution of property will be inequitable or even that the distribution will include someone who has not been particularly close to the decedent.

Requirements for a Valid Will

The requirements for executing a valid will vary from state to state as significantly as do the methods of intestate distribution. However, all of the states deal with the following topics in their provisions that govern the requirements for a will: writing, testamentary capacity, signature, witnesses, and acknowledgment.

Writing Like all other documents conveying interests in real property, a will is generally required to be in writing to be recognized as valid. The writing requirement is true for wills even if the testator is not disposing of any real property in the will. A few states do recognize oral or *nuncupative wills*, but often such wills are limited to the disposal of personal property and must be created under circumstances of near death. In many states the nuncupative will requirements are similar to the gift in contemplation of death (gifts causa mortis) requirements.

Perhaps the most frequently litigated issue under the writing requirement is the issue of whether the document actually constitutes a will or is an attempt to substitute some other document for a will. The following sections discuss the validity of such will substitutes.

1. Holographic Will Most wills are thought of as formally typed documents drafted by attorneys, backed by blue paper, and written in very formal language. However, there are other types of writings that can qualify as wills that have none of those characteristics. Many states and the UPC recognize the holographic will as valid. The *holographic will* is a will that is written entirely in the handwriting of the testator and signed by the testator.

Some states require that the holographic instrument be witnessed to be valid, while others recognize the will as valid so long as it is signed. In many cases, letters with proper execution have qualified as wills for the testator. One problem with the holographic will, particularly in states where the will need not be witnessed, is establishing the authenticity of the handwriting and the signature as that of the testator. The long-lasting probate battle over the will of millionaire Howard Hughes was the result of trying to establish whether the several purported holographic wills were authentic.

2. Contracts to Make Wills and Joint or Mutual Wills Often, particularly between husbands and wives, contracts will be executed for the parties to make *joint* or *mutual wills* that will serve to dispose of the property belonging to the two in a certain way. Such expression of intent cannot be changed or revoked by either party through a change in the will provisions unless the change is mutually agreed upon.

The contract to make the wills cannot itself be recognized as a will. However, once the wills are executed the terms of both the agreement and the wills can be enforced, and each party is bound to abide by them even after the death of one of the parties to the agreement.

To be enforceable, the agreement to make a will must be supported by consideration. Such consideration is furnished in the case of husband and wife by their mutual relinquishment of the right to distribute their property according to their desires.

A joint will is a will in which the same document is executed by different parties as their own will. Mutual wills are the separate wills of parties that are reciprocal in their provisions and are probably based on a mutual agreement, understanding, or contract to make a will. States vary in their recognition of the validity of joint wills, but all states recognize and enforce mutual wills and their provisions.

One of the issues often arising in the case of a mutual will is whether its provisions can be revoked. The provisions can be revoked with the mutual consent of the parties but cannot be revoked unilaterally.

3. Content of the Writing There are no requirements for specific provisions in a valid will (with the exception of execution requirements discussed later). However, all persons executing wills should remember the purpose of their wills and clearly set forth their intentions and desires for the distribution of their property and the handling of their affairs upon death.

Generally, wills can be broken down into the following topics, although the topics and their content may vary from state to state and according to the needs of the testator's family:

1. *Declaration clause.* Declares the age, capacity, and residence of the testator and that the document is a will;
2. *Definition clause or clauses.* Lists wife, husband, children, and so on. Defines terms such as children and issue;
3. *Funeral and burial arrangements' clause.* If desired, specifies funeral procedures;
4. *Debt clause.* Provides for payments of all debts, estate and inheritance taxes, and so on;
5. *Appointment clause or clauses.* Appoints the party responsible for the administration of the estate. May also specify the powers of the appointed person;
6. *Gift clause or clauses.* Disposes of the estate property, by either specific dispositions or a general disposition; and
7. *Execution and signature clauses.* (See discussion later in this chapter.)

Testamentary Capacity There are two requirements for *testamentary capacity*: age capacity and mental capacity.

1. Age Capacity Every state has a statute that fixes the minimum age requirement for executing a valid will. In most states the age of testamentary capacity is the age of majority, which in most states is 18 or 21. The age computation is made at the time the will is executed; thus age capacity is required before a valid will can be executed and is not determined as of the time of death.

2. Mental Capacity Many wills begin their declaration clause with, "I _____, being of sound mind. . . ." This establishes the mental capacity requirement for the execution of a valid will, which is that the testator must be of sound mind. Mental capacity is not synonymous with intelligence, logic, or distributing property only to relatives. Rather, mental capacity is established when the testator is able to understand the following:

1. The nature or extent of his or her property;
2. What persons would be the natural recipients;
3. What disposition is being made of the property;
4. The relationship between items 1 to 3; and
5. How to form an orderly distribution of property.

Thus, the presence of eccentricity or old age is insufficient in and of itself to establish a lack of testamentary capacity. Each case on testamentary capacity presents a different set of factual circumstances and requires the court to apply each of the five factors listed according to the familial situation of the individual testator. The following case illustrates how the determination of testamentary capacity is made.

IN THE MATTER OF THE WILL OF EMMETT J. KING
342 S.E.2d 394 (N.C. 1986)

On 9 August 1983, Mr. Emmett King was taken to the emergency room at Halifax Memorial Hospital with a leaking abdominal aneurysm. He was in extreme pain and suffering from shock from the loss of blood. He was given considerable pain medication including meperidine (Demerol), morphine, and diazepam (Valium). Meperidine and morphine both may decrease mental awareness.

He was placed on a respirator with an intratracheal tube and taken to intensive care. At about 1 PM, Delores King, one of King's daughters, visited him with Jeff Crowder, King's grandson. Jeff went to the waiting area and asked Patsy West and Rhoda Joyner to come and witness a codicil (an addition to a will—see page 444) King was executing. When they went in, Delores read the codicil to King and asked him if he understood that he was giving Jeff his business and the real property on which it was located. King nodded that he did. Delores helped guide King's hand across the document for a signature. Patsy and Rhoda signed as witnesses. The witnesses indicated Mr. King was aware of them and what was happening. The codicil was executed at 1 PM, and King died at 2:15 PM. Dr. Richard Frazier, King's doctor, said that King was in a semicoma during most of the morning and had been sedated. Dr. Frazier believed that King would have been incapable of knowingly executing the document.

PHILLIPS, Judge

Appellants' main argument is that the evidence does not show that the codicil was executed in the manner that the law requires. A codicil must be executed with the same formalities as attend the execution of a will. Those formalities, set out in G.S. 31-3.3, are as follows:

(a) An attested written will is a written will signed by the testator and attested by at least two competent witnesses as provided by this section.

(b) The testator must, with intent to sign the will, do so by signing the will himself or by having someone else in the testator's presence and at his direction sign the testator's name thereon.

(c) The testator must signify to the attesting witnesses that the instrument is his instrument by signing it in their presence or by acknowledging to them his signature previously affixed thereto, either of which may be done before the attesting witnesses separately.

(d) The attesting witnesses must sign the will in the presence of the testator but need not sign in the presence of each other.

Appellants contend that because of his illness and the medications received that the testator could not have the mental awareness that is necessary for the execution of a testamentary document; and they argue at considerable length, mostly upon the premise that Mr. King did not know what was going on, that there was no evidence, express or implied, that the testator intentionally signed the codicil, that he signified to the attesting witnesses that

Prior to the execution of the codicil, King's wife, children, and grandchildren received his estate. With the codicil, Jeff (appellee) got most of it. The trial court found the will and codicil to be valid, and Thomas King, a son (appellants), appealed.

the instrument was his, or that the codicil was signed by the attesting witnesses in his presence.

Nevertheless, a review of the record leads us to conclude that though the evidence as to the testator's mental capacity and awareness might fairly be regarded as weak, it was sufficient to support the verdict and its weight was for the jury. The witnesses to the codicil and Jeff Crowder testified that he did know what was going on and had sufficient mental capacity, in their opinion, to execute the will. While Dr. Frazier may have been better qualified than the lay witnesses to testify as to the testator's mental awareness and capacity, the jury was not obliged to accept his testimony over theirs and he did not see the testator at the time crucial to this case, as they did. Too, the terms of the codicil were consistent with the intention, expressed several times according to the testimony, to give his interest in the linen business to his grandson that had been helping him in it. That the testator received physical assistance in making his mark does not affect the validity of the instrument, and whether he was too weak to resist his daughter's actions, as appellants contend, was another question of fact for the jury.

The evidence that he made his mark on the codicil in the presence of the witnesses indicates that the instrument was his, and is sufficient to imply a request that they attest his signature. In short the evidence before the jury tended to show, as they found, that the codicil was executed in accordance with all the requirements of our law and we cannot say that the learned trial judge, who heard the testimony and observed the demeanor of the witnesses, abused his discretion in letting the verdict and the judgment entered thereon stand.

Affirmed.

Discussion Questions

1. What did the original will provide?
2. When was the codicil executed?
3. Who was present?
4. What changes did the codicil make?
5. What was the medical opinion regarding King's capacity?
6. Did Mr. King have capacity?

(14.4) Consider:

Grace Supplee executed a will on 29 July 1965 that divided her property among her brother, her niece, and her stepdaughter. The will was executed after Grace had suffered several heart attacks and had a guardian appointed for the management of her affairs. Grace had indicated to her neighbors that her property was to go to her stepdaughter.

Upon Grace's death, the stepdaughter contested the will on the grounds that Grace lacked testamentary capacity.

The reason for the difference between Grace's will and what she had told neighbors was that while she was in a home recuperating from the heart attacks, her stepdaughter was in charge of maintaining her apartment. When Grace returned home and found several items missing she concluded that her stepdaughter had taken them and therefore left her less under the will.

The stepdaughter was able to establish that she did not take the property. Did Grace have testamentary capacity?

Signature All states require, as part of the formal prerequisites for a valid will, that the will be signed by the testator. The signature requirement is straightforward when the testator is able to sign. However, there are circumstances when the testator, because of disease or hospital equipment, is unable to personally sign the will. In these circumstances and under the UPC, the testator may direct someone else to sign the will so long as the testator acknowledges the will and is present at the signing of it.

Those who are unable to write may still authenticate a will by placing an X on the signature portion of the will, witnessed by others as being placed by the testator.

The signature of the testator should appear at the end of the will to make clear what portions and provisions were intended to be included in the will. As a matter of practice or law, the testator should also initial each page of the will to prevent pages from being added or altered after the execution occurs.

(14.5) Consider:

Joseph Treitinger was a nearly blind widower when he executed his will at age 85. His signature began to the left of the signature line on the last page of the will and then slanted to the left and into the body of the will. Joseph also made an X on the signature line. His signature was witnessed. Joseph's heirs are now challenging the validity of the signature. What is the result?

Witnesses The witness requirements for a valid will vary from state to state. The number of witnesses required for a valid will is either two or three; under the UPC, the requirement is two. In addition some states require that the witnesses be disinterested parties; that is, the witnesses must not be beneficiaries under the will. This requirement of having disinterested witnesses is not imposed under the UPC. Often the issue of whether the witnesses are disinterested arises because of indirect benefits obtained.

(14.6) Consider:

George Baxter Gordon executed a will that provided that the Church of Christ of New Boston, Texas would receive a substantial amount of his property. The will was executed with two members of the church serving as witnesses for the will. Upon George's death, several heirs contested the admission of the will to probate on the grounds that the witnesses were interested parties. What was the result?

Many states not only prescribe the number and quality of witnesses required for the execution of a valid will but also specify the manner in which the witnesses witness the transaction. For example, some states require that all of the witnesses be present in the same room at the time the testator signs the will, and that the witnesses sign in the presence of the testator and in the presence of each other. Other states and the UPC do not require the witnesses to actually witness the signing by the testator so long as the testator indicates the signature is authentic before the witness signs.

Acknowledgments Many states and the UPC provide all testators with the opportunity to execute a *self-proving will*. In a self-proving will, the signatures of the testator and the witnesses are notarized following a clause that is a form of affidavit for the parties. If the proper acknowledgment procedures are followed then the will is presumptively valid, meaning that there is a presumption that the will was validly executed and meets all formalities required for proper execution. The following clause is an example of an acknowledgment clause used in a UPC state. The clause is inserted in the will after the testator and the witnesses have already signed.

STATE OF _____)

)SS. ACKNOWLEDGMENT/AFFIDAVIT

County of _____)

We, _____, _____, and _____, the Testator and the witnesses, respectively, whose names are signed to the foregoing instrument, being first duly sworn, do hereby declare to the undersigned authority that the Testator signed and executed the instrument as his Last Will and Testament and that he signed willingly, and that he executed it as his free and voluntary act for the purposes therein expressed, and that each of the witnesses, in the presence of the Testator, signed the will as witness and that to the best of their knowledge the Testator was at that time eighteen or more years of age, of sound mind, and under no constraint or undue influence.

Testator _____

Witness _____

Witness _____

Subscribed and sworn to and acknowledged before me by _____, the Testator, and subscribed and sworn to before me by _____, and _____, witnesses, this _____ day of _____, 19___.

Notary_____

Will Contests

The validity of a will may be challenged by anyone who might have an interest in the estate of the decedent—someone named in the will or an heir omitted from the will. Some of the grounds for such challenges have already been discussed. For example, it is possible to have a will set aside if the testator lacked testamentary capacity. Or a will may be set aside if the formalities of execution were not met, as in the cases where the witnesses were interested parties or where there were no witnesses. Lack of the testator's signature is another ground for having the will set aside.

However, one very common ground for having a will set aside that has not yet been discussed is that of *undue influence*. Under this type of contest, the party challenging the will does not dispute the valid execution of the will or the testator's capacity, but rather raises the defense that the will was not executed of the testator's own free will and choice—that someone else was directing the testator.

Undue influence is a difficult concept to define. It need not amount to force but must be something more than advice, persuasion, and kindness. The following elements must be established for the court to set aside a will on the grounds of undue influence:

1. The testator must be established as a person who could be subject to undue influence;
2. A party must be shown to have had the opportunity to exercise undue influence;
3. A party must have been disposed to exercise undue influence; and
4. There must be a will that reflects the results of undue influence.

Undue influence, like testamentary capacity, is based on the factual circumstances in each individual case. Classically, the finding of undue influence occurs when an elderly party becomes dependent on a friend or relative for assistance in day-to-day living, then executes a will leaving all or the majority of their estate to that person while other relatives are ignored in the testamentary disposition.

Relationships of dependency and trust are called confidential relationships. In many states there is a presumption that undue influence was involved in the execution of a will if there is a confidential or fiduciary relationship between the testator and the party who is a major beneficiary and who also procured the execution of the will. The next case involves this issue.

IN RE ESTATE OF MALNAR

243 N.W.2d 435 (Wis. 1976)

Frances Malnar (testatrix), a widow, was 74 and suffering from advanced liver disease. Frances had no children but had a sister in Yugoslavia and several nieces and nephews who were the children of her two brothers who had predeceased her. Frances was on good terms with her nieces and nephews, corresponded with them throughout the year, and had visits from them on occasion.

Frances could speak very little English and could write only her name. Her native language was Croatian.

In July 1971 Frances executed a

will, which left most of her property to her nieces and nephews and a $100 gift to a Catholic church. One of her nephews was named executor of the will.

Frances had severe health problems and was hospitalized a number of times for gastrointestinal bleeding. When she returned home from hospital stays, she was helpless and was assisted by Genevieve Malnar (proponent) with groceries, trips to her doctor, and so on. Genevieve was the wife of Frances's husband's nephew and the daughter of Mary Mishka, a 30-year friend of Frances. Genevieve visited Frances two to three times per month and talked with her on the phone on a daily basis.

In July 1972 Frances gave Genevieve a power of attorney, and Genevieve used it to open a checking account and pay bills for Frances.

On 18 June 1973 Frances was hospitalized for liver failure and remained hospitalized or in a nursing home until her death. During this period she was visited frequently by Mary Mishka. On 30 July 1973, Gene-vieve brought her mother's attorney to Frances in the nursing home for the purpose of drafting a will. Frances had used a different attorney for her original will and for Genevieve's power of attorney and did not know the attorney Genevieve brought to the home.

With the attorney present, Genevieve and Frances spoke in Croatian about the disposition of Frances's property. Genevieve then told the attorney that the entire estate was to go to her. The attorney did not speak Croatian. The attorney drafted the will, and then Genevieve arranged for the execution and helped prop up Frances so that she could sign an X to the will.

Upon Frances's death, Genevieve petitioned to have the will admitted to probate. The nieces and nephews presented the original will and challenged the second will on the grounds of undue influence. The trial court found undue influence and refused to admit the second will to probate, and Genevieve appealed.

HEFFERNAN, Justice

Ordinarily, the test of undue influence on a testatrix is fourfold: (1) Was there opportunity to influence, (2) was there a disposition to influence, (3) was there susceptibility to influence, (4) was a coveted result obtained. An opponent to the will must prove each of these elements by clear, satisfactory, and convincing evidence.

Undue influence may also be proved under a second approach. Where the relationship between the testatrix and the principal beneficiary is "confidential or fiduciary" in nature, that fact, "coupled with the existence of 'suspicious circumstances,' " is enough to create the presumption or inference of undue influence.

An examination of the record in the instant case clearly shows that the opponent of the will was entitled to invoke the presumption of undue influence. Genevieve Malnar was given a power of attorney for Frances Malnar in July, 1972. Thus, there was a fiduciary relationship between the proponent—sole beneficiary—and the testatrix. Furthermore, there existed a confidential relationship between testatrix and the person who engaged in procuring the drafting of the will and who took the benefit thereunder—Genevieve Malnar. Frances Malnar relied heavily on Genevieve Malnar for transportation, maintaining her household, assisting her in taking medication, making translations for her, and assisting her in financial matters. These factors indicate the presence of a confidential relationship.

The record is also replete with suspicious circumstances surrounding the execution of the will. Proponent procured the drafting of the will and participated in the drafting and execution of the will in which she was the sole beneficiary. The attorney who drafted the will was not the personal attorney of the deceased. Rather, he was the attorney of the proponent's mother and had never met the testatrix. Proponent did all of the translation required in the execution of the will. Genevieve told the attorney Frances had no sisters when she did have one living in Yugoslavia. There was no explanation given for the sudden change in the attitude of the testatrix from that expressed in the 1971 will, which bequeathed her estate to nieces and nephews as well as leaving money to the church of which she was a member. The will was made in haste—the discussion of the terms of the will and its execution were completed on the same day. The testatrix was in such a weak and debilitated condition that she had to be held up in bed and even then did not have the strength to sign her name. At the funeral, Genevieve told one of the nephews that she knew Frances left a will naming her a personal representative, but did not know the contents of the will. None of the nieces and nephews had been informed of the seriousness of the testatrix's condition in the summer of 1973 or that the testatrix was considering making another will, despite that fact that proponent knew that testatrix was near death. Rather, proponent waited until after testatrix's death to inform the nieces and nephews of what had transpired.

The basis for the undue influence presumption lies in the ease in which a confidant can dictate the contents, and control or influence the drafting, of a will either as the draftsman or as one who procures the drafting.

Once the presumption was established, the burden of persuasion shifted to the proponent, Genevieve Malnar, to introduce sufficient evidence to rebut the presumption.

In attempting to satisfy her burden of persuasion, Genevieve Malnar introduced evidence indicating that testatrix was a strong-willed woman who was not susceptible to influence.

We find the presence of undue influence was established by the great weight and preponderance of the evidence.

Affirmed.

Discussion Questions

1. Who is challenging the will on the basis of undue influence?
2. Is Genevieve of any relation to Frances?
3. What things did Genevieve do for Frances?
4. What did Genevieve do with the power of attorney?
5. Whose lawyer drafted the second will?
6. Who translated for the lawyer during the drafting of the will?
7. Who helped in the execution of the will?
8. How long did it take to draft and execute the will?
9. What does the court say is the basis for the undue influence presumption?
10. Was undue influence present?

(14.7) Consider:

James G. Newkirk left his wife and daughter in 1951. Shortly thereafter he met Pauline Knight and began living with her; they held themselves out as husband and wife in all places where they resided. In 1952 Newkirk executed a will that left all of his property to Pauline and made no provision for his wife or daughter except the following clause:

> Third: I have a daughter, Joan Janick, who is married, and for whom I have heretofore provided, and I do not wish her to participate in my will.

> Newkirk died in 1964 and Pauline presented the will for probate. Newkirk's daughter challenged the will on the grounds of undue influence because the will had been made less than a year after Newkirk left and was made at a time when he was still married and had a child to provide for. What was the result?

Disinheritance and Limitations on Distribution

Most states have provisions that prevent *disinheritance* of certain family members. In fact, all states have some protections for the surviving spouse. Thus, although a will may purport to disinherit a surviving spouse, the surviving spouse will be entitled to one or more of the following depending on the state's system of property allocation between husband and wife:

1. *Dower.* In some states the wife is entitled to a certain portion of her husband's estate. If she is not provided for in the will, she will still receive her statutory dower percentage.
2. *Curtesy.* In some states the husband is entitled to a portion of the wife's estate, and the result will be the same as in the dower situation above.
3. *Community property.* In community property states the surviving spouse is entitled to half of the community property even if the testator spouse has attempted to disinherit by the terms of the will.
4. *Homesteads, exemptions, and family allowances.* Most states have some provision that requires that the home and often specific personal property (usually furnishings) pass to the family (spouse and children) of the decedent. These items are thus given to the family regardless of disinheritance provisions in the will. Also, many states provide for an allowance to be given to the spouse and children of the decedent for the purposes of support during the probate of the estate.

In some cases the surviving spouse has been provided for in the will but would be entitled to receive more under the afforded statutory protections.

Under these circumstances, many states permit the surviving spouse to elect whether to take what was provided under the will or to take the statutory share as provided by the applicable protections. The election must be formally filed as part of the probate proceedings, usually within a certain limited period.

Relatives other than the surviving spouse may be disinherited. Testators who disinherit relatives should be cautious in making sure that all property is given to others because if there is any unbequeathed property it is still possible that the disinherited relative will inherit under the laws of intestate succession. In addition, some states require a clause in the will naming the disinherited relative and the testator's intent to disinherit that relative. Even when such a clause is not required, it may aid in the determination of capacity, by showing that the testator was aware of the familial situation. The clause also aids in interpretation by showing the specified intent of the testator.

Living Wills

In recent years the term *living will* has been used extensively. A living will is a document that verifies the wishes of the testator to be taken off artificial life-support systems when there is no reasonable prospect of recovery. States that recognize living wills have statutory requirements for their validity. For example, disinterested witnesses and specific language are required in many states. Whatever requirements a state has must be followed if the living will is to be valid.

Revocation of Wills

A will can be revoked in several different ways: (1) by physical destruction of the document, (2) by execution of a subsequent document, or (3) by operation of law.

Revocation by Physical Destruction Revocation can be accomplished by some act of mutilation or destruction of the will document by either the testator or by someone acting on behalf of the testator and at the testator's request. In addition to the physical destruction of the document, the testator must have accompanying intent to destroy the will. The degree of destruction and the permissibility of partial destruction varies according to state law. For example, some states recognize the crossing out of portions of a will as a revocation of that portion of the will, whereas other states treat such an act as a destruction of the entire will.

The types of acts sufficient for physical destruction include cutting, tearing, burning, and writing *void* or *canceled* across the will. If there are copies of the will, some states provide that the destruction of one of the copies constitutes revocation of the will, while other states require the destruction of the original.

The following case illustrates the point of law that the physical act of destruction must be accompanied by the intent to revoke the will for the revocation to be effective.

IN RE ESTATE OF BOGNER
184 N.W.2d 718 (N.D. 1971)

On 13 February 1956, Philip Bogner made his last will and testament. One portion of the will gave a one-half interest in some real and personal property to his daughter Helen Bogner Fallgren and her husband, Curtis Fallgren. At the time of the execution of the will, Helen and Curtis were married and had eight children. From 1946 to 1956, Curtis was employed by Philip and received a salary of $5,800 as well as a furnished home.

In 1956, the Fallgrens moved to Oregon to run a poultry ranch that had been purchased using a loan on an insurance policy Philip had purchased for Helen. Philip repaid that loan when it was evident the Fallgrens would not. Sometime thereafter, a physician and Helen told Philip that Curtis had been involved in depraved moral conduct including incestuous relationships with one of his daughters and that such activity had continued for a number of years.

Helen obtained a divorce from Curtis in 1965 on the grounds of infidelity and returned home to North Dakota with her children to live with her father. Bogner told several people including a family counselor, his sis-

ter, and one of his employees that he was going to disinherit his son-in-law. Bogner died on 3 September 1968, and portions of his will read as follows:

THIRD: To my daughter, Helen Bogner Falgren and her husband Curtis Falgren, *or to the survivor of them* . . .
SIXTH: I appoint my daughter, Helen Bogner Falgren, to be my Executrix under this Will, and if she fails or ceases to act, I appoint Curtis Falgren Sr., husband *of my daughter, Helen Bogner Falgren, to be the Executor and successor Trustee of the trust hereinabove provided. If my daughter does not survive me, or dies before a grandchild of mine attains the age of 21 years, without having appointed a guardian of the persons and estates of my grandchildren, I appoint* Curtis Falgren, Sr. *to be guardian of the persons of such grandchildren and of their estates. (Emphasis added.)*

Lines had been forcefully drawn through the emphasized words. The obliterations did not exist at the time the will was originally executed. The trial court found Philip had revoked the will and Curtis appealed.

PAULSON, Judge

Section 56-04-01, N.D.C.C., provides that a will may be revoked in whole or in part. Such revocation can be accomplished by burning the will, tearing it, concealing it, obliterating it, or destroying it, with the intent of revoking the same. Furthermore, there is a presumption that obliteration of a will was effected by the testator where the will had been in the custody of the testator, where after his death the will was found among his personal effects, and where the obliteration fell within any of the statutorily prescribed modes of revocation. In the instant case, in Paragraph Three and in Paragraph Six of Mr. Bogner's Last Will and Testament there were lines drawn which obliterated certain portions of those paragraphs of his will. The will was found in the safe located in Mr. Bogner's business office in Dickinson. The will was found in a metal container among other personal effects and papers belonging to Mr. Bogner. The will was in Mr. Bogner's possession until his death. Thus it was Mr. Fallgren's burden to rebut the presumption that the obliterations were made by Mr. Bogner. Mr. Fallgren has failed to rebut this presumption, since he has produced no evidence which would indicate that this presumption is rebutted. The lines drawn through the name "Curtis Falgren" and the surrounding words constitute an obliteration within the meaning of the North Dakota statute. *Black's Law Dictionary* (4th ed., 1951), states that "Lines drawn through the signatures of the witnesses to a will amount to an 'obliteration,' though the signature is discernible." Thus, obliteration is an erasure or a blotting out of written words. Section 56-04-01, N.D.C.C., further requires that this obliteration must be done with the intent and for the purpose of revoking those portions of a will so obliterated. Section 56-04-03, N.D.C.C., allows obliteration on the face of a will to be either partial or total, and revocation is complete when a material part is so obliterated as to show an intention to revoke. While the above authority indicates that proof of an intent may be assumed from the fact that the obliteration occurred, in the instant case it is proper to show other facts and circumstances, including the declarations of the testator which would indicate that it was his intent to revoke a portion of his Last Will and Testament. In addition, §56-05-01, N.D.C.C., requires that a will is to be construed according to the intention of the testator and that this intent must have effect as far as possible. Thus, in the in-

stant case, the county court and the district court would have been derelict if they had not received evidence as to the proof of intent, and construed such evidence when giving effect to the will. Since it is proper to consider the evidence with reference to Mr. Fallgren's infidelity and the subsequent divorce from Mr. Bogner's daughter, and its profound impact on Mr. Bogner, certainly such evidence would buttress the presumption that Mr. Bogner obliterated those portions of his Last Will and Testament concerning his ex-son-in-law as to any prospective inheritance that Mr. Fallgren might receive under Mr. Bogner's will.

Having determined that Philip Bogner obliterated those contested portions of his will, we are confronted with the next issue, which is: Did Mr. Bogner intend to add any further dispositive language to his will, and, if so, can his intent to make further disposition become effective in view of the last part of §56-04-03, N.D.C.C., which provides:

[B]ut when, in order to effect a new disposition, the testator attempts to revoke a provision of the will by altering or obliterating it on the face thereof, such revocation is not valid unless the new disposition is legally effected.

Mr. Bogner made no attempt to make a substitute provision either on the will in question or by the addition of a codicil or by the drafting of any other instrument which could be construed as being a new disposition. In fact, Mr. Bogner deleted the name of Curtis Fallgren from Paragraph Three of his Last Will and Testament so that the devise and bequest then left an undivided one-half interest to Mr. Bogner's daughter, Helen; and the remaining undivided one-half interest, which previously had been bequeathed and devised to Curtis Fallgren, was revoked. The obliterations found in Paragraph Six of Mr. Bogner's will, wherein the name of Curtis Fallgren was obliterated as a secondary executor and as a guardian, also are valid because the evidence supporting the intent to revoke the bequest and devise contained in Paragraph Three is equally applicable to Paragraph Six of Mr. Bogner's will; and for the further reason that each of the parties concedes that no additional dispositive language was needed because of the fact that no property is passing pursuant to the provisions of Paragraph Six. This particular issue is of no significance because Mrs. Helen Bogner Fallgren has qualified as the executrix and has assumed the guardianship pursuant to Paragraph Six of Mr. Bogner's will. Thus the second part of §56-04-03, N.D.C.C., is not applicable, as there was no new disposition to which legal effect had to be given in the form of dating, signatures, and attestation, in order to comply with the provisions with reference to the execution and attestation of a codicil or a will.

Finally, it must be decided whether or not the undivided one-half interest originally devised and bequeathed to Curtis Fallgren is to pass under the will or by the laws of intestacy; and if it passes under the will, does Mr. Bogner's daughter become the beneficiary, who, originally, was to receive an undivided one-half interest by Paragraph Three of the will; or should it become a part of the residuary estate. This Court held, in *In Re Glavkee's Estate,*

76 N.D. 171, 34 N.W.2d 300, 301 (1948), in paragraphs 1 and 7 of the syllabus:

1. The sole purpose of the court in construing a will is to ascertain the intention of the testator as the same appears from a full and complete consideration of the will, when read in light of the surrounding circumstances. If that intent can be ascertained and is not violative of some rule of law which exists for the purpose of limiting the power of the testator to dispose of his property as he wishes, such intent must prevail.

7. The making of a will gives rise to a presumption against intestacy, or that the testator intended to die intestate as to any part of his property, and in the absence of an indication in the will to the contrary, the testator is presumed to intend to dispose of his entire estate.

Since there is no evidence in the case at bar which would rebut the presumption that Mr. Bogner did not wish the property mentioned in Paragraph Three of his will to pass by the laws of intestacy, we hold that the property in question should pass pursuant to the provisions of the will, and that this property should inure to his sole heir at law, his daughter, and that she would then be the sole legatee and devisee to that portion of the estate bequeathed and devised in Paragraph Three of Mr. Bogner's Last Will and Testament.

Affirmed.

Discussion Questions

1. What did the original will provide?
2. What was the nature of the relationship between Bogner and his daughter and her family?
3. What happened to sour the relationship?
4. What action did Bogner take with respect to the will?
5. Did he tell anyone what he was doing?
6. Did he partially revoke his will?

Attempted revocation of a will by interlineation or the addition of the terms *void* or *cancelled* to the will document will be recognized as cancellation when sufficient intent to revoke is shown.

(14.8) Consider:

Charles Uhl executed a will in 1946, and upon his death it was found in his safe-deposit box. The will contained a number of interlineations and markings made by Uhl in colored pencil, including a notation in the left-hand margin of the first page that stated, "Revise whole mess."

Uhl's sister visited him while he was alive and they found the will. His sister told him the will would not be valid and Uhl replied, "The will is still good and is good anywhere. Oh, nuts! I am going to make a new one. I will get it done. Don't worry about it."

When the will was offered for probate, the sister objected because her share was small and she contended the will had been revoked. What was the result?

Revocation by Execution of a Subsequent Document A will can be revoked by the subsequent execution of any of a number of instruments. A second will serves to revoke a prior will. An addition to a will (called a *codicil*), which may contain provisions inconsistent with the original will, also serves to revoke certain portions of the will. And a subsequent contract or agreement that so provides also serves to revoke a will. Revocation by a subsequent document is valid only if the subsequent document is executed with the same formalities required for the execution of the original will.

Generally, a subsequent will contains a clause that provides that the testator "hereby revokes any prior wills and codicils." However, such a clause need not be present for the subsequent will to serve as a revocation of the preceding will. The will that is latest in time of execution serves to revoke prior wills.

In jurisdictions that recognize holographic wills, a holographic will or codicil can serve to revoke a prior formally executed will so long as the holographic instrument complies with all validity requirements.

Revocation by Operation of Law Most states have provisions that require the revocation or partial revocation of a will when the familial circumstances of the testator change between the time of the will's execution and the testator's death. For example, many states provide that divorce automatically serves to revoke a will at least with regard to property left to the former spouse. In other states, marriage after the execution of the will entitles the new spouse to at least an intestate share of the property.

Perhaps one of the most common partial revocations of wills occurs when testators have children after execution of the will but before death, so that such children are not provided for under the provisions of the will. Children born or adopted after will execution are called *pretermitted* children. Many states provide that these children are entitled to receive the amount they would have received through intestate succession.

PROBATE

Purpose of Probate

Probate is the name given to encompass all legal proceedings required to accomplish the passing of title of the decedent's property to those for whom it was intended. Probate involves determination of the existence of a valid will and any defenses to the will, the existence of heirs if no will exists, the proper construction of the will, the collection of the decedent's assets, the payment of debts, and the distribution of the estate. The procedures and the terminology for the procedures vary from state to state, but the basic processes discussed in the following sections apply to all states.

Appointment of Party to Administer the Probate

In every state, some party or parties will be appointed responsible for carrying out all administrative details involved in probating an estate. Various terms are used by the states for this administrative party. If the decedent died intestate, the party is often called an *administrator* or *administratix.* If the decedent died testate, the party is often called an *executor* or *executrix.* Under the UPC, the party is called a *personal representative* regardless of whether the decedent died testate or intestate.

No matter which name is given to the administrative party, their role is the same: carrying out of all transfers, payments, and distributions involved in the probate of the estate. In many cases, because these parties are responsible for substantial sums and valuable property, they will be required to post a bond for the period of the estate's administration. Under the UPC and in most states, the requirement of a bond can be waived in the testator's will or by statute, particularly in cases where the sole beneficiary will act as the personal representative. Waiving the bond can mean a substantial savings in the cost of administering the estate.

The party appointed to this position varies. If the decedent died testate, then the party named in the will is appointed personal representative. If the party appointed in the will is unable to serve or if the decedent died intestate, then the court is required to appoint a party. Most states have statutes specifying who qualifies as a personal representative and the order of preference for appointment. For example, in many states the surviving spouse has first priority for appointment.

The Application for or Opening of Probate

Probate proceedings are opened by the filing of an application or petition with the appropriate court. The appropriate court is generally the probate division or probate court located in the area of the decedent's domicile. However, other courts may have jurisdiction. For example, if the decedent owned property in a second jurisdiction, the probate court in that area would also be entitled to receive an application or petition for probate. In the case of an estate located in multiple jurisdictions, one probate court will serve as the court for hearings, petitions, and so on, and the other courts will then recognize those proceedings as dispositive with regard to the property distribution and will carry out that court's orders.

Parties who may apply or petition for the opening of probate include heirs, devisees, persons entitled to appointment as personal representatives, and creditors. Basically, any party with an interest in the estate may apply or petition for the estate to be opened.

The application or petition will include a filing of the document alleged to be the will if the decedent died testate. It will either seek to have the will admitted to probate or to have the determination made that the decedent died intestate. The applicant or petitioner is required to serve notice upon potential heirs and interested parties that application has been filed, and the notice includes a hearing date. Because the purpose of the hearing is to determine the validity of the will, any persons wishing to challenge its admission to probate must prepare to present evidence at the hearing. Many of the cases in this chapter involved appeals from hearings wherein a will was found to be valid or invalid.

Collection of Assets

Once the will is admitted to probate or the finding of intestacy has been made, it becomes the job of the personal representative to collect the assets of the estate. Most states and the UPC require the personal representative to file an inventory with the court within a certain period after appointment. The inventory is also sent to heirs and devisees, and its purpose is to fully disclose the extent of the estate and to serve as a beginning reference point for the accounting of the personal representative.

It is the responsibility of the personal representative to collect all debts due to the estate and to make sure that all property to which the decedent held title is obtained.

Determination and Payment of Debts

In addition to collecting and reporting assets, it is the responsibility of the personal representative to determine what valid debts exist and should be paid. Most states require the publication of a notice of probate in a public newspaper to alert creditors of their need to file a claim with the estate. For example, under the UPC the personal representative is required to publish notice of the opening of probate once a week for 3 weeks in a newspaper of general circulation. Creditors then have 4 months from the time of first publication to file a claim with the estate or have their claim forever barred from collection.

Once the personal representative receives a creditor's claim, the decision is made to allow and pay the claim or to disallow it. If a claim is disallowed, the creditor always has the opportunity to bring suit against the estate for the purpose of having a judicial determination on the validity of the claim.

Distribution of the Estate

Whether the decedent died testate or intestate, the determination must be made as to who will be entitled to what portions of the estate after creditors' claims, taxes, and administration expenses have been paid.

In the case of intestacy, the court will hold a hearing or trial for the adjudication of heirs. In the case of a testate estate, the court may still be required to construe the provisions of an ambiguous will, and a hearing or trial will be required for that interpretation. In interpreting a will, the court's primary rule is to follow the intent of the testator. If such intent is not clear from the words in the document itself, then extrinsic evidence may be used to clarify the intentions of the testator. In determining intent on specific provisions, the court will examine the overall purpose and intent conveyed by the testator in the will as an entire document.

After the determination of heirs and the interpretation of the will, the property will be distributed to the appropriate parties. Different terms are used to describe the types of gifts given to heirs of the decedent. A gift of real property is called a *devise* and the recipient a *devisee;* a gift of money is called a *legacy* and the recipient a *legatee;* a gift of personal property is called a *bequest* (general term that includes legacies).

Occasionally, certain circumstances arise that make the distribution of gifts impossible. For example, a testator may have left a specific item of property or a legacy to an heir who has predeceased the testator. In the absence of the testator's provision or a state statute that permits such a gift to go to the heirs of the predeceased recipient, the gift will *lapse,* become part of the residuary estate, and revert to those who are entitled to that portion of the estate. If there is no clause devising the residuary estate, then the specific gift would be distributed according to the laws of intestacy.

Also, there are times when a testator has left a specific item of property to an heir; and although the heir is still in existence, the property is not. For example, a testator may have left a "1982 Honda Accord to my nephew Ralph." If the testator does not own the Honda Accord at death, then the gift adeems or fails completely. This doctrine of *ademption* will apply regardless of the intention of the testator.

Closing of Probate

Once all of the preceding steps have been accomplished, the personal representative may proceed to close the estate. The closing of the estate may require a hearing or may be accomplished, as under the UPC, by the informal filing of a closing inventory and accounting. Once the proper procedures have been complied with and the required hearings held, the estate is closed and cannot be reopened for the purposes of relitigating creditors' and heirs' claims. The closing of the estate thus operates as an estoppel for future actions in the absence of any fraud or wrongdoing in the administration of the estate, and assuming proper compliance with all procedural requirements.

Estate Tax Implications

The transfer of property from the decedent to the heirs may involve the payment of taxes on the parts of the estate and the heirs. There are several types of taxes that may be involved in the passage of title to property through probate. First, there is the possible estate tax at both the federal and state levels. Before a tax may be imposed upon an estate at either level, the estate must have a certain minimum value. For example, the minimum value of estates subject to taxation at the federal level is now $600,000.

The amount of tax due on an estate subject to taxation is computed according to tables provided by the federal government, and certain deductions are allowed before the taxable value is actually determined. For example, at the federal level there is a marital deduction given for a probate transfer of property between spouses for the entire amount of the estate.

In addition to a tax on the estate, there may also be an inheritance tax imposed on the heirs. Inheritance tax is computed as a certain percentage of the amount received by the heir. It should be noted that the inheritance tax is not an obligation of the estate; it is an obligation of the heir.

The time limitation for filing a federal estate tax return is 9 months, which can be extended upon an estimation of no tax or a payment of the amount estimated to be due.

KEY TERMS

Uniform Probate Code (UPC)
intestate
intestate succession
escheat
laughing heir statutes
per capita
per stirpes
posthumous heir
advancements
Uniform Simultaneous Death Act
   (USDA)
will
noncupative will
holographic will
joint will
mutual will
testamentary capacity
self-proving will

undue influence
disinheritance
living will
codicil
pretermitted
probate
administrator
administratrix
executor
executrix
personal representative
devise
devisee
legacy
legatee
bequest
lapse
ademption

CHAPTER PROBLEMS

1. Define the following terms:
   a. Codicil
   b. Administrator
   c. Testatrix
   d. Personal representative
   e. Intestate
   f. Ademption
   g. Devise
2. Sam, at age 90, had three children and seven grandchildren. With the help of his attorney, Hubert Levin, Sam executed a formal will leaving all of his property to Hubert. Hubert was no relation to Sam but had helped Sam with the management of his affairs since the death of Sam's wife when Sam was 85. Sam died at age 93. The children and grand-

children have challenged the probate of the will on the grounds of undue influence. What is the result?

3. Bob wrote in his holographic will: "leave all my property, except my land in Pleasantville, to my three children." However, the will failed to dispose of the land in Pleasantville. Bob is survived by his wife and three children (all children of their marriage). Who is entitled to the land in Pleasantville?

4. William and Margaret Pearl Phillips, husband and wife, executed a joint will for the disposition of their property. The will contained the following clause:

> It is the intention of the testators that the surviving testator shall have the right by codicil to change the bequests of equal division referred to said testator's heirs, but may not change the bequests to the heirs of the first deceased testator.

William died first and Margaret drafted a codicil, which changed the distribution of the property to William's heirs. Upon her death, William's heirs challenged the admission of the will to probate on the grounds that the codicil violated a joint contract to make a will. What is the result?

5. D. W. Elmer died testate, and a provision in his will was as follows:

> THIRD: I make no provision for my brothers, Jake N. Elmer, Henry Elmer, nor for my sisters, Lena Elmer, Rachel Martell, and Marie Brown, all of whom are financially so fixed that they can well live without any benefits from my estate.

Unfortunately, D. W. did not dispose of all of his property under the provisions of the will. To whom will the property be given?

6. Linda Cravens had executed a valid formal will and then 2 years later executed a holographic codicil that substantially revoked provisions of the formal will. Upon her death, several heirs challenged the validity of the formal will on the basis of the holographic codicil, which operated as a revocation. What was the result?

7. Ben B. Boddy had executed a formal will but after his divorce printed the word "void" in letters varying from 1 to 3 inches in height in three places across the first page and again across the second page of the two-page will. "Void" was written on all paragraphs except the attestation clause and a clause appointing an attorney as the executor. The probate of the will is challenged on the ground that Boddy revoked it. What is the result?

8. Andrew, age 60, made a formal, typed will leaving all of his property to his wife, Wilma. The will was valid in all respects; however, only one

witness had signed it. Steven, Andrew's son, claimed this will was void due to insufficient witnesses. Is Steven correct? Why or why not?

9. Tom is in the hospital and is dying, having suffered a stroke that has left him partially paralyzed. Tom's will has been prepared for him (he is of sound mind), but Tom cannot control the movement of his hand to sign or make a mark on the will. Tom's wife guides his hand over the paper, making an X. Is the will valid?

10. Wilma has passed away intestate and is survived by the following relatives: her mother, Catherine; her sister, Chris; her granddaughter, Elizabeth (daughter of Wilma's deceased daughter Jill); a grandson, Joe (son of Wilma's living daughter Buddy); daughter Buddy; and a single daughter, Diane. Who is entitled to Wilma's estate?

III

REAL ESTATE OWNERSHIP— METHODS, PROBLEMS, AND RESPONSIBILITIES

15

CO-OWNERSHIP OF REAL ESTATE

In 1955 Mrs. Ora Coleman purchased a lot in Scottsdale, Arizona. In 1963 Mrs. Coleman caused the property to be transferred to herself and her son, John Coleman, as joint tenants with right of survivorship. In 1971 Mrs. Coleman quitclaimed her undivided one-half interest to her daughters: Hazel Register, Mildred Jo Parry, Mabel Hart, and Mary Jennings. Mrs. Coleman passed away in 1975, and the daughters brought suit for partition in 1977. John Coleman opposed the partition on the grounds that Mrs. Coleman and he had an oral agreement under which John would keep the property but would pay $2,000 to Hazel and $1,000 to the other sisters upon Mrs. Coleman's death. The sisters claim the joint tenancy was severed. Who wins?

It is not unusual for more than one person to own a tract of land or portion of real estate. Married persons generally hold title to their home together. In the case of real estate partnerships, the partners will together hold title to the property. (In some states the partnership may hold title to the property; see Chapter 24.) When children inherit property from a deceased parent they become co-owners of a parcel or parcels of property. Since so much of real property ownership consists of ownership by more than one person, it is necessary to understand the forms and rights of *co-ownership*. The questions to be answered in this chapter are, How can title be held among several owners? What are the rights of each of the owners? What are the responsibilities of each of the owners? What action or actions may be taken in the event difficulties arise between or among the parties?

METHODS OF CO-OWNERSHIP

In this chapter, four methods of co-ownership are discussed: tenancies in common, joint tenancies, tenancies by the entirety, and tenancies in partnership. The marital co-ownership rights of dower, curtesy, and community property are also covered, later in the chapter.

455

Tenancies in Common

When parties hold title to property as *tenants in common* they hold separate interests in a single portion of property. The tenants in common may hold equal or unequal shares in the land. For example, two tenants may hold a one-half interest in a tract of land or they may hold a one-third/two-thirds portion of the property. Tenants in common may acquire their interests at different times and may convey their interests to others. For example, if X and Y hold title to a piece of property and X passes away leaving, by will, his property to sons W and Z, then Y, W, and Z are all tenants in common.

Under a tenancy in common, each tenant is entitled to equal possession of the whole of the property. If the land is separated then the parties are neighbors as opposed to co-owners; and if the property is currently possessed by one owner with the idea that the other or others will possess it in the future then a presently possessed interest and future interests have been created.

In the majority of states, the language necessary to create a tenancy in common is simply, "To A and B." When this language is used, A and B will each have a 50 percent interest in the property. To create unequal interests, the amount of ownership must be specified. For example, "One-third of the above described property to my son B and two-thirds of the same to my daughter C," would be the language needed to create a tenancy in common with different shares or interests in the property.

Joint Tenancies

For a *joint tenancy* to exist four conditions, referred to as *unities*, must be met. They are unity of time, unity of title, unity of interest, and unity of possession. Although unities are not required for the creation or existence of a tenancy in common, they must be present for both joint tenancies and tenancies by the entireties.

Unity of Time This condition means that joint tenants must take their title to the property at the same time. For example, if O conveyed Blackacre to A and B on 30 December 1987, then A and B meet the unity of time requirement because they acquired their interest at the same time. However, if O conveyed half of Blackacre to A on 30 December 1987 and then conveyed the other half to B on 30 June 1988, A and B cannot be joint tenants because they acquired their interests at different times. They are tenants in common.

In some states this unity of time requirement presents problems when one party owns property prior to marriage and then after marriage seeks to hold the property with a spouse as joint tenants. For example, suppose Jane owns a home prior to marriage and upon marrying Bob seeks to transfer the property so that she and Bob will hold the property as joint tenants. If Jane transfers the property, then the unity of time is not satisfied because Jane would have acquired her interest previously. This problem is overcome by setting up what is called a *straw-man* transaction. In this straw-man transaction, Jane transfers the property to a third party (the straw-man), who then transfers the property back to Jane and Bob. Jane and Bob have thus satisfied the requirement of unity of time for joint tenancy. Although this transaction is simply procedural, it is necessary if this unity is to be satisfied. Some states have eliminated the requirement of unity of time in circumstances like Jane and Bob's, and have passed statutes indicating the straw-man transaction need not be conducted for the joint tenancy to be valid.

Unity of Title Parties are not joint tenants unless they derive their title from the same source or grantor. For example, if O conveys Blackacre to A and B, A and B can be joint tenants. However, if B then conveys his interest to C, A and C cannot be joint tenants since A derived her title from O and C derived his title from B. A and C are tenants in common.

Unity of Interest This unity requires that joint tenants have equal interests in the property. For example, A and B each holding a one-half interest qualifies for joint tenancy. However, if A holds a one-third interest and B holds a two-thirds interest, A and B can be only tenants in common.

Unity of Possession This requirement is for a valid tenancy in common as well. Under unity of possession, the parties must have equal rights to possess the property, and one party cannot dispossess the others of the land. If the land is divided either geographically or by time (into present and future interests; see Chapters 2 and 3), then the parties are no longer co-owners and unity of possession is lost. For example, if O conveys Blackacre to A for life and then to B and C, B and C may be any type of tenant in the future, but they are not joint tenants with A because their interest in the property is divided.

A joint tenancy also differs from a tenancy in common in the area of transferability of interest. Tenants in common may convey their shares at any time and may also dispose of their interest by will or have it passed by intestate succession. Joint tenants have the right of survivorship, meaning that upon the death of one tenant, the remaining tenant or tenants acquire the deceased tenant's share. This right of survivorship gives the final surviving tenant full title to the property. Some states do not permit married persons to hold title to property as joint tenants. But joint tenancy of residential property is ideal for married persons because upon the death of one spouse, the title can be cleared and the property transferred with relative ease, and in some states without probate (see Chapter 14).

Because joint tenancy carries with it this aspect of survival, many states require that the intent to create a joint tenancy be made clear through the language chosen. Some states even have statutes that specify the language that must be used to create a joint tenancy validly. For example, language such as "To A and B not as tenants in common and not as a community property estate, but as joint tenants with right of survivorship," is characteristic of the type of specificity required to create this form of co-ownership. Some states require the use of the phrase "right of survivorship" in creating a valid joint tenancy. Because each state has its own requirements, caution should be used in drafting deeds and contracts to ensure compliance. The following case deals with the language used and the intention of the parties in the creation of a co-ownership interest.

EDWARDS v. MILLER
378 N.E.2d 583 (Ill. 1978)

Beginning in 1958 and ending 17 years later, Rita Louise Edwards (plaintiff/appellee) and Glen Miller (defendant/appellant) lived together in a relationship akin to husband and wife. Rita's three children (one of whom was alleged to be Glen's) resided with them during that period. Both worked during the relationship, and in 1969 Glen acquired a parcel of property known as the Thebes property. The deed was a joint tenancy deed and named Glen and Rita Louise Miller as the tenants.

When the parties had a falling out, Glen attempted to sell the property but could not without Rita's signature. He alleged that it was only a temporary gift and that he had used his name for Rita to avoid embarrassing her. Rita alleged Glen's intentions were made clear by the proper language in the deed and brought suit to have the joint tenancy severed and her interest granted to her. The lower court found for Rita, and Glen appealed.

JONES, Justice

It is well settled that instruments which purport to create joint tenancies presumably speak the whole truth and those who claim adversely thereto must, in order to prevail, prove by clear and convincing evidence that a gift was not intended.

His testimony revealed that in putting the deed in both names, he was influenced by his desire to provide for ownership in plaintiff after his death. This is not the type of evidence which can be equated with a clear rebuttal of the intent to make a gift. At most, defendant's evi-

dence indicated that he desired to have unbridled control over the property during his lifetime. He apparently felt that he could create a joint tenancy which only conferred the interests he approved of. This is not the law. Moreover, we feel that although the plaintiff was not defendant's legal wife, the evidence that she contributed towards its purchase strengthens the presumption of a gift of the joint tenancy interest. Consequently, plaintiff has an undivided one-half interest in the parcel of real estate.

Affirmed.

Discussion Questions

1. Who are the joint tenants?
2. What is their relationship?
3. What type of deed was used in the acquisition of the Thebes property?

4. Why is the joint tenancy challenged?
5. Is there a valid joint tenancy?

When joint tenants convey their interests to parties outside the tenancy, the joint tenancy is severed. For example, if A and B own property as joint tenants and B conveys his interest to C, then A and C are tenants in common because the unities of time and title have not been met. If there are more than two joint tenants, the result is slightly different. For example, if A, B, and C are joint tenants and C conveys her interest to D, then D holds a one-third interest as a tenant in common with A and B, but A and B remain joint tenants.

(15.1) Consider:

A and B are tenants in common. B has passed away leaving his widow, W, as his only heir. What is the effect of B's death? Who now holds title to the property? Would the result be different if A and B were joint tenants?

yes

Tenancies by the Entirety

A *tenancy by the entirety* requires the presence of the same four unities as for a joint tenancy plus one additional unity: unity of person. Unity of person requires that the tenants be married.

Tenancy by the entirety also carries with it the right of survivorship; thus spouses are not permitted to dispose of the property by will. Severance of this tenancy requires the signature of the nonsevering spouse, and the property itself may be subject to dower and curtesy rights (discussed later in the chapter). Upon divorce of the parties (or dissolution of the marriage), tenancy by the entirety is severed. In some states this results in a conversion to joint tenancy, while in other states it results in a conversion to tenancy in common.

Each state recognizing tenancy by the entirety has language requirements for its creation. Many parties make the mistake of not using the correct language, so that it eventually becomes necessary to have a court interpret what type of estate was granted. The following case is an example of such a situation.

CARVER v. GILBERT

387 P.2d 928 (Alaska 1963)

Carver (defendant/appellant) received title to a piece of property from Fred T. Gilbert, who had acquired title to the property with his wife from a warranty deed that described them as "Fred T. Gilbert and Patricia Gilbert, husband and wife . . . grantees." Patricia died intestate prior to Fred's grant to Carver. Mark (plaintiff/appellee), the only living issue of the marriage, brought suit seeking to recover a portion of the property on the grounds that title was held by his parents as tenants in common. Carver maintained that their interest was held in a tenancy by the entirety. The lower court ruled that a tenancy in common existed, and Carver appealed.

AREND, Justice

The parties agree that at common law it was presumed that a conveyance to husband and wife created a tenancy by the entirety even in the absence of language of survivorship or reference to that kind of tenancy. The appellant claims that this presumption can be changed only by statute clearly in derogation of the common law and that such a statutory change has never been enacted in Alaska. The appellee, on the other hand, insists that the presumption has been changed by the Alaska statute which provides for a presumption of tenancy in common unless the parties "expressly declare" the conveyance shall be in joint tenancy.

The appellant contends and cites authority to support the contention that joint tenancy and tenancy by the entirety constitute distinct estates and that the statute has no application to a conveyance to husband and wife, for they take as tenants by the entireties. We, however, favor the view of another line of authorities, holding that tenancy by the entirety is but a species of joint tenancy, their incidents being identical.

This being the case, the statutory presumption favorable to tenancy in common "unless it is expressly declared" in the conveyance that the grantees shall take as joint tenants, must be taken to apply to tenants by the entirety. So, to overcome the presumption that a man and woman named as grantees in a conveyance and described therein as "husband and wife" shall take as tenants in common, the conveyance must declare that they shall take as tenants by the entirety with right of survivorship.

Judgment affirmed.

Discussion Questions

1. Who are the co-owners in the grant at issue?
2. How did Carver become involved?
3. Who is Mark Gilbert?
4. Who has title if a tenancy in common exists? If a tenancy by the entirety exists?
5. What statutory provision is involved?
6. What distinction does the court make between joint tenancies and tenancies by the entirety?
7. What type of interest was granted?

Tenancy in Partnership

A *tenancy in partnership* exists either when partners have contributed property to the partnership or when the partnership has purchased property with partnership funds. The partners hold title to such property as co-owners or as tenants in partnership. A tenancy in partnership has the characteristics of a joint tenancy. Upon the death of one of the partners, the remaining partners are entitled to the deceased partner's share. Heirs and devisees of the partner have no rights to the partnership property itself but they may be entitled to payment for the value of the deceased partner's share or interest in the partnership.

A tenancy in partnership also has characteristics common to all of the tenancies. Each partner has the right to possession and use of the property for partnership purposes, and one partner cannot dispossess the other partners or the partnership of the property. In many states transfer of partnership requires the signature of all partners. Parties engaging in a land transaction with a partner should verify how title is held and whether the partner has authority to transfer the property.

CREDITORS' RIGHTS AND CO-OWNERSHIP

Because there is more than one method of co-ownership, creditors' rights in property vary. The extent of the creditor's rights in terms of repossession and sale are limited according to the rights of the cotenant. In a tenancy in common, tenants may mortgage, lien, or pledge their share of the property; and in the event of one tenant's default on the underlying debt, the creditor could become a tenant in common or could sell the tenant's portion of the property to satisfy the debt. It is important to recognize that tenants may pledge only so much of the property as they own and that a creditor cannot foreclose on the entire property when one of the tenants defaults.

Creditors who accept pledges of property from joint tenants must realize the limitation of their interests. Because the estate is subject to survivorship, it is possible that their security will be lost if their debtors predecease other joint tenants. If a joint tenant defaults on an underlying debt secured by joint tenancy property, the creditor takes possession and title by foreclosure (or other method) and thus becomes a tenant in common.

In a tenancy by the entirety, creditors have no rights in the property unless the underlying debt is a joint debt of the husband and wife. Thus a creditor cannot validly enforce a pledge of the property made unilaterally by one of the spouses.

A creditor taking only a partial property pledge from a co-owner should be aware of problems in priority that may arise if later all tenants pledge their interests to another creditor. In those circumstances, it is possible that the first partial creditor will be second in priority to a later full pledge creditor.

Figure 15.1 compares the tenancies—their creation, transfer, and creditor relations.

(15.2) Consider:

A and B are joint tenants in an undeveloped piece of property. B has borrowed $20,000 from First National Bank and has pledged his interest in the property as security. B dies, and there is not enough money in his estate to satisfy First National's $20,000 debt. First National now wishes to become a tenant in common with A. What is the result? Would the result be different if A and B were tenants in common?

Figure 15.1 *Comparison of Methods of Co-ownership*

CHARAC-TERISTICS	METHOD OF CO-OWNERSHIP			
	Tenancy in Common	*Joint Tenancy with Right of Survivorship*	*Tenancy by the Entireties*	*Tenancy in Partnership*
Unities		1. Time 2. Title 3. Interest 4. Possession	1. Time 2. Title 3. Interest 4. Possession 5. Person (marriage)	3. Interest 4. Possession 5. Person (partners)
	4. Possession			
Transferability	Inter vivos Testamentary transfer	Inter vivos (severs tenancy) No testamentary transfer	One spouse cannot sell Surviving spouse	One partner could sell Title goes to surviving partners
Creditors' Rights	Rights survive debtor Creditor can become tenant in common	Limited to rights of survivorship Creditor can become tenant in common	Must be debt of husband and wife	Only partnership debts

Rights and Responsibilities of Cotenants

Rents Since in all of the tenancies each tenant has the equal right of possession, nonpossessing tenants are not allowed to collect rent from the tenant who is in possession of the property. However, the possessing tenant does not have the right to exclude the other tenants from the property (see discussion on partition and ouster). If the tenant in possession is collecting rents and profits from third parties who are using the property, such receipts should be shared with the other tenants. Although this right of equal sharing is part of common law, presently all states allow the possessing tenant to retain all rents and profits.

Expenditures When cotenants do not pay equal amounts for the purchase of property, most courts have ruled that the shares in the property are not equal and have apportioned title according to the portion of the purchase price contributed.

Some payments are necessary to keep the land or its title clear, for example taxes and mortgage payments. Cotenants are required to share in these expenses according to their proportionate share of title in the property. The proportion of these payments may be offset, in some states, if one of the cotenants has been in exclusive possession.

Expenditures for improvements are made solely at the discretion of the improving cotenant; there is neither a right to require contribution from the other tenants nor a right to offset costs by reducing the portion of mortgages and taxes paid by the improving cotenant. Expenditures for repairs are treated in the same manner because of the difficulty in trying to distinguish between repairs and improvements.

Partition and Ouster Partition is the physical division of co-owned property whereby co-owners become adjoining landowners or neighbors. Severance, on the other hand, merely changes the form of co-ownership. Partition results in separate owners of adjoining parcels of land.

A partition can be made voluntarily when co-owners agree upon a geographical division of the property or it can be made by a court when circumstances require. The following circumstances require the partition of co-owned property: (1) when one tenant has dispossessed the other tenant or tenants and refuses to allow access (ouster), (2) when a tenant refuses to contribute for necessary expenditures, (3) when a tenant refuses to distribute rents and profits earned from exclusive possession (at common law) or, (4) when other circumstances arise where the court deems a partition appropriate (such as feuding relatives).

If it is impossible or illogical to physically divide the property, a court may order the property sold and the proceeds divided among the cotenants according to their proportionate interests. For example, if a piece of property has water on only one portion, a division would be unfair but a sale would allow the parties to realize the value of their interests.

(15.3) Consider:

X and Y own equal shares of a 1-acre parcel of land in the White Mountains of Arizona. Y has built a cabin on it at a cost of $22,000. Y has also managed to rent the cabin for 50 of the 52 weeks in 1988 at $250 per week. Mortgage payments on the cabin are $220 per month. Utilities vary from summer to winter but average about $90 per month. Taxes on the property are $40 per month with the cabin, but were $20 without it. Insurance is $120 per year. X has demanded an equal share of the profits. Y refuses but says X is responsible for half of the mortgage, utilities, taxes, and insurance. What is the result? Would the result be different depending upon what type of tenancy exists?

MARITAL PROPERTY RIGHTS—CO-OWNERSHIP BY MARRIAGE

In every state, there are provisions to protect married persons holding title to property with their spouses. Tenancy by the entirety is one example, and other provisions and protections include dower and curtesy rights in some states and community property rights in other states.

Dower Rights

Under common law, *dower rights* existed for the protection of a widow. The common law rule was that a widow is entitled to a one-third interest for her life in any and all real property her husband owned at any time during their marriage.

Because dower rights applied to all real property owned during the entire course of a marriage, no one could safely take property from a married man unless his wife executed an instrument releasing her dower interest in the property. If such a release was not obtained, the wife could upon her husband's death claim a one-third interest in property once held by her husband—regardless of how many times ownership had changed since the husband held title. This right of dower is sometimes referred to as *inchoate* dower because it existed only if the wife survived the husband. If she predeceased her husband, all dower rights terminated.

Because of the probable confusion and complications, many states have changed dower rights to simply protect a surviving spouse by requiring that one-third to one-half of the deceased spouse's property of any character (real or personal) be given to the surviving spouse. Such statutes help prevent the problem of disinheritance by giving some property to the surviving spouse, but outright instead of in the form of a life estate interest. Some states have homestead exemptions that provide the surviving spouse with a minimum amount of property such as a residence, some personal property, a living allowance, and vehicles. This minimum amount is given to the surviving spouse before any distributions of property and before any creditors' obligations are satisfied.

Curtesy Rights

Curtesy is a surviving husband's protection that, at common law, gave the husband a life estate in all real property owned by his wife during their marriage. However, the curtesy rights existed only if there were issue born of the marriage. This right has been modified by the states today, and the above-discussed statutory protections now passed eliminate dower and curtesy but still protect surviving spouses.

Community Property

Community property is a system of ownership by spouses that has Spanish origins and that exists, in some form, in eight states: Louisiana, Texas, New Mexico, Arizona, Nevada, California, Idaho, and Washington. In these states, unless the parties agree and specify otherwise, property is held as community property.

The basic principle governing this system of co-ownership is that both partners in the marriage work for the benefit of the community and do so on an equal basis and therefore own half of all property acquired during the course of the marriage. This half ownership principle is true regardless of whether the spouses were employed or unemployed during the course of the marriage. In some states this basic principle has been applied in cases where the parties were not married but lived as husband and wife. Courts in community and noncommunity property states have allowed unmarried cohabitants rights in their partner's property acquired during the course of cohabitation. The basis for allowing these property recoveries has been a contract, express or implied, or a quasi-contract found to exist between the unmarried partners. Perhaps the most famous of these cases was the following case from the community property state of California, wherein the court recognized the rights of unmarried cohabitants.

MARVIN v. MARVIN

557 P.2d 106 (Calif. 1976)

Michelle Triola Marvin (plaintiff/appellant) began living with Lee Marvin (defendant/appellee) in October 1964. Michelle claimed that she and Lee entered into an oral agreement, that provided that while they lived together they would combine their earnings and efforts and would share equally in any property accumulated during the period of their cohabitation. They also allegedly agreed they would hold themselves out to the public as man and wife and that Michelle would be a companion, homemaker, housekeeper, and cook for Lee.

Shortly after entering into this oral agreement, Michelle gave up her career as a singer to be a full-time companion, housekeeper, and cook to Lee.

Michelle and Lee lived together until May 1970, and at that time Lee "compelled" Michelle to leave the household. During the period of their cohabitation, Lee had acquired substantial real estate and personal property including motion picture rights that totaled over $1 million. From May 1970 until November 1971, Lee provided support but at the end of that time ceased all support payments.

After Lee stopped payments, Michelle brought suit alleging she had a contract entitling her to half of the property acquired during her cohabitation with Lee and sought to have a constructive trust imposed upon that half of the property.

The trial court rendered judgment for Lee on the grounds that Michelle's complaint failed to state a cause of action, and Michelle appealed.

TOBRINER, Justice

Numerous other cases have upheld enforcement of agreements between nonmarital partners in factual settings essentially indistinguishable from the present case. . . . The fact that a man and woman live together without marriage, and engage in a sexual relationship, does not in itself invalidate agreements between them relating to their earnings, property, or expenses. Neither is such an agreement invalid merely because the parties may have contemplated the creation or continuation of a nonmarital relationship when they entered into it. Agreements between nonmarital partners fail only to the extent that they rest upon a consideration of meretricious sexual services. Thus the rule asserted by defendant, that a contract fails if it is "involved in" or made "in contemplation" of a nonmarital relationship, cannot be reconciled with the decisions.

Defendant secondly relies on the ground suggested by the trial court: that the 1964 contract violated public policy because it impaired the community property rights of Betty Marvin, defendant's legal wife until a final divorce decree awarded in January, 1976. Defendant points out that his earnings while living apart from his wife before rendition of the interlocutory [temporary] decree were community property under the 1964 Code and that defendant's agreement with plaintiff purported to transfer to her a half interest in that community property. But whether or not defendant's contract with plaintiff exceeded his authority as manager of the community property, defendant's argument fails for the reason that an improper transfer of community property is not void ab initio [from its inception], but merely voidable at the instance of the aggrieved spouse.

In the present case, Betty Marvin, the aggrieved spouse, had the opportunity to assert her community property rights in the divorce action. The interlocutory and final decrees in that action fix and limit her interest. Enforcement of the contract between plaintiff and defendant against property awarded to defendant by the divorce decree will not impair any right of Betty's, and thus is not on that account violative of public policy.

Defendant's third contention is noteworthy for the lack of authority advanced in its support. He contends the enforcement of the oral agreement between plaintiff and himself is barred by Civil Code section 5134, which provides that "All contracts for marriage settlements must be in writing. . . ." A marriage settlement, however, is an agreement in contemplation of marriage in which each party agrees to release or modify the property rights which would otherwise arise from the marriage. The contract at issue here does not fall within that definition, and thus is beyond the compass of Section 5134.

In summary, we base our opinion on the principle that adults who voluntarily live together and engage in sexual relations are nonetheless as competent as any other persons to contract respecting their earnings and property rights. Of course, they cannot lawfully contract to pay for the performance of sexual services, for such a contract is, in essence, an agreement for prostitution and unlawful for that reason.

But they may agree to pool their earnings and to hold all property acquired during the relationship in accord with the law governing community property; conversely they may agree that each partner's earnings and property acquired from those earnings remains the separate property of the earning partner. So long as the agreement does not rest upon illicit meretricious consideration, the parties may order their economic affairs as they choose, and no policy precludes the courts from enforcing such agreements.

We believe that the prevalence of nonmarital relationships in modern society and the societal acceptance of them, marks this as a time when our courts should by no means apply the doctrine of unlawfulness of the so-called meretricious relationship to the instant case.

We conclude that judicial barriers that may stand in the way of a policy based upon the fulfillment of reasonable expectations of the parties to a nonmarital relationship should be removed. As we have explained, the courts now hold express agreements will be enforced unless they rest on an unlawful meretricious consideration. We add that in the absence of an express agreement, the courts may look to a variety of other remedies in order to protect the parties' lawful expectations.

The courts may inquire into the conduct of the parties to determine whether that conduct demonstrates an implied contract or implied agreement of partnership or joint venture, or some other tacit understanding between the parties. Finally, a nonmarital partner may recover *in quantum meruit* for the reasonable value of household services rendered less the reasonable value of support received if he can show that he rendered services with the expectation of monetary reward.

The judgment is reversed.

Discussion Questions

1. How long did the nonmarital relationship between Michelle and Lee last?
2. During what period of the relationship was Lee still married to Betty?
3. What oral agreement did Michelle allege existed, and what were the terms of the agreement?
4. Will the court enforce the oral agreement?
5. What form of consideration for agreements between nonmarital partners would be illegal?
6. Will implied agreements ever be enforced?
7. What recovery will be permitted *in quantum meruit* for a nonmarital partner?

If community property law is applicable to a marriage relationship, then all property acquired during the course of the marriage is classified as community property and is half owned by each spouse. However, the spouses may still have some separate property to which they hold complete title. For example, any property owned prior to marriage that is brought into the marriage is separate property. Also, gifts and inheritances received by individual spouses during the marriage are separate property. Thus, if a wife received an inheritance from her father, the money would be her separate property and would not belong to the community.

Debts are also considered community obligations, and each spouse is responsible for 50 percent of the debts entered into for the benefit of the community.

Those dealing in real estate in community property states need the signature of both spouses for the listing, mortgaging, improvement, or sale of real property. Real estate partnerships operating in these states must obtain a waiver from the spouses of all partners, so that the property can be transferred without the risk of a spouse's interest being exercised at a later time. In noncommunity property states, the same practice should be followed for dower and curtesy rights.

One of the benefits of the community property system is that both spouses acquire some property rights during the course of the marriage. In noncommunity property states, marriage for a lifetime does not guarantee a 50 percent share of the property acquired during the marriage. To equalize the states' laws on marital property, the *Uniform Marital Property Act* has been drafted and is being considered by several states for possible adoption. The purpose of the act is to bring community property principles to noncommunity property states.

Antenuptial Agreements

In recent years, and particularly with second marriages, many couples have entered into agreements minimizing or waiving their marital property rights.

These agreements, called *antenuptial agreements,* are subject to strict review by courts. The agreements are examined to determine if they are fair and also whether the parties entered into them voluntarily. The following case involving two well-known partners discusses the validity of their antenuptial agreement.

DELOREAN v. DELOREAN

511 A.2d 1257 (N.J. 1986)

John Z. DeLorean (husband/plaintiff) and Cristina DeLorean (wife/defendant) entered into an antenuptial agreement on 8 May 1973 (only a few hours before they were married) that provided the following:

[A]ny and all property, income and earnings acquired by each before and after the marriage shall be the separate property of the person acquiring the same, without any rights, title or control vesting in the other person.

The potential assets (such as future earnings) could have exceeded $20 million and practically all of them are in the name of the husband. With-

out this agreement and considering that the marriage lasted 13 years and resulted in two minor children, the wife would ordinarily be entitled to 50 percent of the marital assets at the time of divorce.

On the husband's petition for divorce, the wife alleged that the agreement was invalid because she was not given full information about the extent of her husband's financial affairs before she signed and that her husband exercised undue influence on her in getting the agreement signed. The trial court upheld the validity of the agreement, and Mrs. DeLorean appealed.

IMBRIANI, J.S.C.

Initially, it is clear that "antenuptial agreements fixing post-divorce rights and obligations [are] . . . valid and enforceable" and courts should "welcome and encourage such agreements at least 'to the extent that the parties have developed comprehensive and particularized agreements responsive to their peculiar circumstances' " (*D'Onofrio v. D'Onofrio,* 200 N.J.Super. 361, 366, 491 A.2d 752 [App.Div. 1985]). In determining whether to enforce an antenuptial agreement there are at least three requirements that have to be met.

First, that there was no fraud or duress in the execution of the agreement or, to put it another way, that both parties signed voluntarily. The wife alleges she did not sign voluntarily because her husband

presented the agreement to her only a few hours before the marriage ceremony was performed and threatened to cancel the marriage if she did not sign. In essence she asserts that she had no choice but to sign. While she did not have independent counsel of her own choosing, she did acknowledge that before she signed she did privately consult with an attorney selected by her husband who advised her not to sign the agreement. Yet, for whatever reasons, she rejected the attorney's advice and signed.

While her decision may not have been wise, it appears that she had sufficient time to consider the consequences of signing the agreement and, indeed, although she initially refused to sign it, after conferring with her intended spouse and an attorney, she reconsidered and decided to sign it. Concededly, the husband was 25-years older and a high-powered senior executive with General Motors Corporation, but she was not a "babe in the woods." She was 23-years old with some experience in the modeling and entertainment industry; she had experienced an earlier marriage and the problems wrought by a divorce; and she had advice from an attorney who, although not of her own choosing, did apparently give her competent advice and recommended that she not sign. While it may have been embarrassing to cancel the wedding only a few hours before it was to take place, she certainly was not compelled to go through with the ceremony. There was no fraud or misrepresentation committed by her husband. He made it perfectly clear that he did not want her to receive any portion of the marital assets that were in his name. At no time did she ever make an effort to void the agreement and, of course, it was never voided. Under these circumstances the court is satisfied that the wife entered into the agreement voluntarily and without and fraud or duress being exerted upon her.

Second, the agreement must not be "unconscionable." This is not to say that the agreement should be what a court would determine to be "fair and equitable." The fact that what a spouse receives under an antenuptial agreement is small, inadequate or disproportionate does not in itself render the agreement voidable if the spouse was not overreached and entered into the agreement voluntarily with full knowledge of the financial worth of the other person. So long as the spouse is not left destitute or as a public charge the parties can agree to divide marital assets in any manner they wish. Mrs. DeLorean presently enjoys substantial income from her employment as a talk-show television hostess and was given a life interest in a

trust of unknown amount created by Mr. DeLorean, which he testified had assets of between $2 and $5 million. She will not be left destitute. The court is unaware of any public policy which requires that the division of marital assets be made in what the court believes to be fair and equitable if the parties freely and voluntarily agree otherwise. In the final analysis it is for the parties to decide for themselves what is fair and equitable, not the court. So long as a spouse had sufficient opportunity to reflect on her actions, was competent, informed, and had access to legal advice and that of any relevant experts, a court should not, except in the most unusual case, interject its own opinion of what is fair and equitable and reject the wishes of the parties. Since the wife voluntarily agreed to this division of the marital assets and she will not become destitute or a public charge, the agreement is not unconscionable.

Third, the spouse seeking to enforce the agreement made a full and complete disclosure of his or her financial wealth before the agreement was signed. Obviously, one cannot make a knowing and intelligent waiver of legal and financial rights unless fully informed of all of the facts; otherwise one cannot know what is being waived. The husband asserts that the wife acknowledged that she received a full and complete disclosure of his financial wealth because the agreement states:

Husband is the owner of substantial real and personal property and he has reasonable prospects of earning large sums of monies; these facts have been fully disclosed to Wife.

However, that statement is not very meaningful and is insufficient to satisfy his obligation to make a full and complete disclosure of his financial wealth. While several states hold that a full and complete disclosure is not synonymous with a detailed disclosure, those cases can be distinguished because they impose upon each spouse a duty to inquire and investigate into the financial condition of the other. However, as far as this court can ascertain, New Jersey imposes no such duty.

A conflict arose as to precisely what financial information was disclosed by Mr. DeLorean. However, the court is satisfied that even if it accepted as true the testimony of Mr. DeLorean he did not satisfy his legal obligation to make a full and complete disclosure.

While the wife was aware that Mr. DeLorean was a person of substantial wealth, there was no way that she could have known with any substantial degree of certainty the extent of his wealth. This is important because one can appreciate that while a wife might waive her legal rights to share in marital assets of $1 million, she might not be willing to do so if she knew the marital assets were worth $20 million. And the suggestion that Mrs. DeLorean had a duty to investigate to ascertain the full nature and extent of his financial wealth is both unfair and unrealistic. How many people when about to marry would consider investigating the financial affairs of their intended spouse? How many people would appreciate or tolerate being investigated by an intended spouse? And how many marriages would be cancelled when one of the parties is informed of an investigation being conducted by the other? Such a requirement would cause embarrassment and impose a difficult burden.

The only way that Mrs. DeLorean could knowingly and intelligently waive her legal rights in Mr. DeLorean's assets was if she was fully and completely informed what they were. And for Mr. DeLorean to merely state that he had an interest in a farm in California, a large tract of land in Montana, and a share in a major-league baseball club fell far short of a full and complete disclosure.

However, it is argued that California, not New Jersey, law should be applied. When the agreement was executed the parties had substantial contacts with California and reasonably expected to retain many of them which, indeed, has been the case. For these reasons the law of California must be applied in this case. California does not treat a party to an antenuptial agreement as a fiduciary. As this court reads California law, the disclosures made by John DeLorean appear to be sufficient.

Affirmed.

Discussion Questions

1. When was the antenuptial agreement signed?
2. Describe the circumstances surrounding the signing of the agreement.
3. Was Mrs. DeLorean represented by her lawyer at the time the agreement was signed?
4. What is the extent of the assets involved?
5. Why does the court use the term "babe in the woods"?
6. Is the agreement under California or New Jersey law?
7. Was there undue influence?
8. Is the agreement valid?

CO-OWNERSHIP—A NOTE OF CAUTION

Whether a party is a seller, buyer, or creditor, the status of property co-owners must be determined. Questions to be answered before entering into an obligation regarding the co-owned property are:

1. Who are the co-owners?
2. What type of co-ownership exists?
3. Is one co-owner authorized to transfer title or to give a lien?
4. How much of an interest does the co-owner have?
5. Are additional signatures (spouses') required?

KEY TERMS

co-ownership	tenancy in partnership
tenants in common	dower rights
joint tenancy	curtesy
unities	community property
straw-man	antenuptial agreements
tenancy in the entirety	Uniform Marital Property Act

CHAPTER PROBLEMS

1. In 1983 Samuel Shapiro died, leaving a large parcel of land to his nephew and his nephew's wife through the following language: "To Allen and his wife, Mary, as joint tenants and not as tenants in common." Allen has died and by will left half of the property given by Samuel to his son. Mary claims the parcel belongs to her. What is the result?

2. A, B, and C were partners in the operation of a grocery store. The partnership's major assets were the store and the land on which it was located. C has passed away, and the executor of C's estate now wants to sell the estate's one-third interest in the store and the land. A and B claim they now own the land. What is the result?

3. Rick, Bob, and Ryan own a 40-acre parcel as joint tenants with right of survivorship. Rick conveyed his interest to Russell; then Bob passed away and conveyed his interest to his wife in his will. Who owns the 40-acre parcel, in what capacity, and in what portions?

4. Bill bought a house on 3 September 1988 for $60,000 with $5,000 down and a $55,000 mortgage. On 5 November 1988 Bill was married and deeded the property to "William H. Smith and Jane D. Smith, husband and wife, not as tenants in common, and not as community property

estate, but as joint tenants with right of survivorship." What type of co-owners are Jane and Bill?

5. Betty and Barbara purchased a home together and agreed to split the monthly mortgage payments. Barbara has left and now Betty must make the payments alone. If they are tenants in common, what rights does Betty have?

6. Nieman was arrested for possession of marijuana, and the arresting San Francisco inspector then went to Nieman's home. Tompkins, who was Nieman's joint tenant, allowed the inspector to enter and search the premises. A considerable amount of marijuana was discovered and used in the prosecution of Nieman. Nieman alleged the marijuana obtained from his property could not be used in evidence because the search was illegal. The police maintained the evidence was admissible because the joint tenant had given consent. What was the result?

7. Mrs. Smyth and her children were tenants in common of a 30,000-acre parcel of land. Through a 99-year lease, Mrs. Smyth conveyed to White the right to remove rock asphalt from the property in exchange for a royalty of $.25 per ton. The children demanded a share of the royalties. What was the result?

8. Mr. and Mrs. Michalski owned a parcel of land as tenants in common and entered into an agreement whereby neither would mortgage their interests and whereby a partition, regardless of circumstances, was prohibited. Is such an agreement valid?

9. Mr. Lichtenstein and his son, Albert, owned a department store in downtown Corpus Christi. Because of their disagreements over leasing, payments, and maintenance, the two sought to have their tenancy in common partitioned. The court found the property could not be fairly and equitably divided and ordered a sale with the distribution of proceeds to the Lichtensteins. Was the court correct in its action?

10. The following clause was written in a deed: "To Nathan H. Palmer and Alice E. Palmer as joint tenants, and not as tenants in common, to them and their assigns and to the survivor, and the heirs and assigns of the survivor forever." What type of cotenancy was created?

11. Determine the result in the introductory chapter problem.

16

ZONING

Nectow's land was zoned by the city of Cambridge as R-3, which was a zoning area permitting dwellings, hotels, clubs, churches, schools, philanthropic institutions, greenhouses, and gardening. Immediately adjoining Nectow's land were railroad yards and industrial plants. Nectow has brought suit against the city alleging the zoning ordinance was too broad and deprived him of his property without due process of law. Will Nectow win?

As the problem indicates, local governmental bodies may pass laws to control the use of land within their jurisdiction. These laws are grouped into one term describing their regulatory effect: *zoning*. The zoning on a piece of property can affect its value, price, and marketability. Knowing and understanding the zoning on a piece of property is a preliminary inquiry for any buyer. In this chapter the following questions are answered: What is zoning? What types of zoning exist? What terms are used in zoning and zoning procedures? Are all forms of zoning constitutional? Is it possible to change or make exceptions?

PURPOSES

Each community is divided into areas, districts, or zones in which certain types of activities are permitted and others prohibited according to their classification. Zoning may control items such as the height of buildings or whether apartments as opposed to single-family dwellings may be constructed. In some cases zoning prohibits construction of buildings altogether, such as when construction of homes on a mountainside is prohibited. Zoning has been used in many cities as a method of controlling community development. A *general* or *master plan* for the community is developed and then zoning ordinances are passed according to the plan, so that the community develops in an orderly fashion and the

474

problems and nuisances that result from residential areas being too close to factories are effectively precluded.

Zoning laws are for the most part ordinances passed by a local governmental entity such as a city or town. These entities act under an enabling statute that is general in character. In most cases the enabling statute is based on the *Standard State Zoning Enabling Act,* which was drafted by the United States Department of Commerce in the 1920s. This act authorizes the local governmental entities to pass zoning laws that "lessen congestion . . . promote safety . . . prevent overcrowding . . . avoid undue concentration of population . . . and promote health and general welfare."

AUTHORITY

The purposes of the final authorization to "promote health and general welfare" are to grant broad authority to local government and also to establish the source of that authority. The source of authority for zoning laws is found in the police power clause of the United States Constitution, which provides that governments exist for the promotion of the health, safety, morals, and general welfare of people and that governmental bodies may promote these goals through regulation of the individual citizens. Thus, zoning laws passed for the general welfare purpose fit within this constitutional framework.

Restrictions on the exercise of police power are that the zoning laws passed must, in fact, serve some public health, safety, or morals interest, and that zoning laws cannot be arbitrary or discriminatory. (These issues are discussed later under the subheading Methods.) Another constitutional issue raised when zoning ordinances were first enacted was whether restrictions on use constituted a taking without due process of law as required under the Fourteenth Amendment (see Chapters 1 and 19). The Fourteenth Amendment constitutionality of zoning was at issue in the following landmark case.

VILLAGE OF EUCLID, OHIO v. AMBLER REALTY CO.
272 U.S. 365 (1926)

Ambler Realty (plaintiff/appellee) is the owner of a 68-acre tract of land located in the west part of Euclid, Ohio. The tract abutted Euclid Avenue to the south and Nickel Plate Railroad to the north. Adjoining this tract, as part of Euclid's adopted compre-hensive zoning plan, were residential tracts on the east and on the west.

Euclid's plan had six use classes denominated U-1 to U-6, three height districts denominated H-1 to H-3, and four districts denominated A-1 to A-4. Ambler's tract fell under U-2, U-3, and

U-6. The allowable uses under these classes are as follows:

U-2. Single-family or two-family dwellings, public parks, passenger stations, farming, and noncommercial greenhouses

U-3. Everything in U-2 plus apartment houses, hotels, churches, schools, public libraries, museums, private clubs, community center buildings, hospitals, sanitariums, playgrounds, recreation centers, city hall, and court houses

U-6. Everything in U-1 to U-5 plus sewage disposal plants including incineration, scrap yards, aviation fields, cemeteries, crematories, penal and correctional institutions, insane and feeble-minded institutions, oil and gas storage, public utilities, and manufacturing and industrial operations of any kind

Ambler brought suit challenging the constitutionality of the zoning ordinances on the grounds that the ordinances were a derogation of Section 1 of the Fourteenth Amendment and that Ambler was being deprived of liberty and property without due process of law. The lower court found the ordinances to be unconstitutional and the village of Euclid (defendant) appealed.

SUTHERLAND, Justice

Before proceeding to a consideration of the case, it is necessary to determine the scope of the inquiry, . . . the tract of land in question is vacant and has been held for years for the purpose of selling and developing it for industrial uses, for which it is especially adapted, being immediately in the path of progressive development; that for such use it has a market value of about $10,000 per acre, but if the use be limited to residential purposes the market value is not in excess of $2500 per acre.

It is specifically averred that the ordinance attempts to restrict and control the lawful uses of appellee's land, so as to confiscate and destroy a great part of its value and that the various zones applied serve to lessen the property's value for either residential or industrial purposes.

The question is . . . as stated by appellee: Is the ordinance invalid, in that it violates the constitutional protection "to the right of property" in the appellee by attempted regulation under the guise of the police power, which is unreasonable and confiscatory?

The ordinance now under review, and all similar laws and regulations, must find their justification in some aspect of the police power asserted for public welfare. The line which in this field separates the legitimate from the illegitimate assumption of power is not capable of precise delimitation. It varies with circumstances and conditions. A regulatory zoning ordinance, which would be clearly valid as applied to the great cities, might be clearly invalid as applied to rural communities.

Here, the exclusion is in general terms of all industrial establishments, and it may thereby happen that not only offensive or dangerous industries will be excluded, but those which are neither offensive nor dangerous will share the same fate. The inclusion of a reasonable margin, to insure effective enforcement will not put upon a law, otherwise valid, the stamp of invalidity. Such laws may also find their justification in the fact that, in some fields, the bad fades into the good by such insensible degrees that the two are not capable of being readily distinguished and separated in terms of legislation. It cannot be said that the ordinance in this respect "passes the bounds of reason and assumes the character of a merely arbitrary fiat."

The exclusion of places of business from residential districts is not a declaration that such places are nuisances or that they are to be suppressed as such, but it is part of the general plan by which the city's territory is allotted to different uses, in order to prevent, or at least reduce, the congestion, disorder, and dangers which often inhere in unregulated municipal development.

The matter of zoning has received much attention at the hands of commissions and experts, and the results of their investigations have been set forth in comprehensive reports. These reports, which bear every evidence of painstaking consideration, concur in the view that the segregation of residential, business and industrial buildings will make it easier to provide fire apparatus suitable for the character and intensity of development in each section; that it will increase the safety and security of home life, greatly tend to prevent street accidents, especially to children, by reducing the traffic and resulting confusion in residential sections, reduce noise and other conditions which produce or intensify nervous disorders, preserve a more favorable environment in which to rear children, etc.

If these reasons, thus summarized, do not demonstrate the wisdom or sound policy in all respects of those restrictions which we have indicated as pertinent to the inquiry, at least the reasons are sufficiently cogent to preclude us from saying, as it must be said before the ordinance can be declared unconstitutional, that such provisions are clearly arbitrary and unreasonable, having no substantial relation to the public health, safety, morals, or general welfare.

Decree reversed.

Discussion Questions

1. Who owns the tract of land involved and what is its size?
2. What was the intended use of the property?
3. What was the effect of the zoning ordinances on the property?
4. Can the validity of zoning ordinances vary from city to city?
5. What public welfare purposes for zoning were given by the court?
6. Is Euclid's zoning plan constitutional?

The *Euclid* case established that zoning is constitutional in general, and that the zoning process is permissible under the exercise of police power, and that resulting decreases in land values do not constitute a taking of property requiring compensation. Although it is possible that zoning ordinances as applied to particular tracts of land within a city may be unconstitutional, such determinations must be made on a case-by-case basis. The following case deals with the issue of whether a zoning ordinance as applied to a particular tract of land is valid.

SMOOKLER v. TOWNSHIP OF WHEATFIELD
232 N.W.2d 616 (Mich. 1975)

Bernard Smookler and his wife (plaintiffs/appellees) purchased a 123-acre tract of land at the intersection of Jolly and Meridian Roads in Wheatfield Township in 1968. Ninety acres were used for agriculture and 1.5 acres were rented to a tenant for residential use. Two years later they requested a zoning change from rural agricultural to mobile home park with a 300-foot strip for commercial zoning. The planned mobile home park would be called Wheatfield Acres Mobile Home Park, would include 5 units per acre, and would have 535 total units.

The 1970 census put the population of Wheatfield Township at 1117 with 325 housing units. The township is 36 square miles with 18,297 acres and only about 5 percent developed. There are three residential areas in the township with most of them located in the northern part. The proposed park would be in the northwest section.

At the time of the application, Wheatfield had one commercial development: a gas station along Interstate 96. The township had no police or fire department and relied on the adjoining cities, counties, and the state for such services. There are no mobile home parks in the township and nothing that could be characterized as low-cost housing.

There is no master plan for the township but there has been some discussion of creating mobile home parks.

The Zoning and Planning Commission denied the plaintiffs' application, stating that the area would be better for residential use: there would be an added burden to police and fire services, added burden to the schools, and no benefit to the surrounding community.

The Smooklers appealed the Commission's decision to the trial court. There the Smooklers and the Commission stipulated that there would be no traffic problem nor any problems with the sanitary or sewage systems. The Smooklers alleged at the trial court that the decision of the Commission was evidence of a preconceived scheme to eliminate or prohibit mobile home parks.

The trial court found for the Commission and the Smooklers appealed. The appellate court reversed and the Commission appealed.

WILLIAMS, Justice

Plaintiffs have properly borne the burden of proof in demonstrating that the Wheatfield Township Zoning Ordinance Amendment No. 2, purporting to permit mobile-home parks in the township is, in fact, exclusionary on its face.

Critical is the fact that there is no reference to any actual territory to which this zoning applies. The net result is that there is no land in the township zoned for mobile-home parks and consequently they are excluded.

The fact situation presented by the instant case does not vary substantially from those this Court examined in the past. Therefore, we find no reason to disturb solid past precedent, and find the Wheatfield Township zoning ordinance invalid as it effectively excludes mobile home parks from the area.

Similar ordinances were expressly disapproved by this Court in cases including *Gust v. Canton Twp.*, 337 Mich. 137, 59 N.W.2d 122 (1953); 342 Mich. 436, 70 N.W.2d 772 (1955); *Dequindre Development Co. v. Charter Twp. of Warren*, 359 Mich. 634, 103 N.W.2d 600 (1960); *Smith v. Plymouth Twp. Building Inspector*, 346 Mich. 57, 77 N.W.2d 332 (1956); and *Knibbe v. City of Warren*, 363 Mich. 283, 109 N.W.2d 766 (1961).

In all these cases, the townships were as relatively undeveloped as Wheatfield Township. Reasons proferred for the denial of rezoning or building requests included the lack of school, police, water, and sewage facilities. Exclusionary zoning devices included prohibition of trailer parks except by special permission as well as that employed in the instant case. Most directly on point are *Dequindre* and *Knibbe*.

When we invalidated the Warren township ordinance in *Dequindre*, there was one mobile-home park "bursting at the occupational seams" (359 Mich. 634, 636, 103 N.W.2d 600), already in the jurisdiction. However, the chancellor's findings, approved by this Court, were that:

> [T]he city of Warren does not intend to permit trailer parks now or in the future. It is operating in the same way now that it operated under the ordinance prior to its amendment, which originally, in effect, prohibited trailer parks by making no provision therefor, and which condition induced the amendment to the ordinance in providing a R-4 classification, which defendant now ignores by non-observance of its intent . . . even though such ordinance has permitted R-4 zoning classification since September 1955, a period of nearly 3 years, there is no instance in which either the Township Board or the City Council has approved a rezoning to R-4" (359 Mich. 634, 638-639, 103 N.W.2d 600, 602).

Thus, the Court disapproved "the outright prohibition of trailer coach parks by the selective administration of a local ordinance" (359 Mich. 634, 640, 103 N.W.2d 600, 603).

The same legal principle was enunciated in *Knibbe*, where Warren refused permits authorizing water, sewer and electrical services to permit extension of plaintiffs' mobile-home park (apparently the one "bursting" at the seams in *Dequindre*), as the "defendant has in effect, again prohibited trailer parks by, on the one hand, making them lawful and on the other by failing to give substance to their intent by not zoning any property within the city limits to an R-4 district . . . the refusal of the defendant to rezone any parcel to R-4, regardless of location and suitability . . . is arbitrary and capricious . . ." (363 Mich. 283, 285, 109 N.W.2d 766, 767).

There is no good reason to reject this established precedent, nor does defendant offer any persuasive means of distinguishing these holdings. That the proposed mobile-home park will dramatically increase population of the township is not a sufficient reason. In a community as undeveloped as Wheatfield Township, any kind of development would increase population substantially. Insofar as affecting municipal services, the Court of Appeals properly noted in *Pederson v. Harrison Twp.*, 21 Mich. App. 535, 175 N.W.2d 817 (1970):

> The snow removal, law enforcement, fire protection and sewer problems, averred to by the defendant, are anticipatory; and there is no proof that these problems would prove insuperable.

In *Green v. Lima Twp.*, 40 Mich. App. 655, 199 N.W.2d 243 (1972), the Court of Appeals quoted with approval the holding of the Pennsylvania Supreme Court in *National Land & Investment Co. v. Easttown*

Twp. Board of Adjustment, 419 Pa. 504, 532, 215 A.2d 597, 612 (1965), that, "A zoning ordinance whose primary purpose is to prevent the entrance of newcomers in order to avoid future burdens, economic and otherwise, upon the administration of public services and facilities cannot be held valid."

That older inhabitants of an area are afraid of being outvoted by newcomers is, of course, a political problem, and one not properly handled by the jurisprudence of the state.

We hold, therefore, that the Amendment 2 to the Wheatfield Township zoning ordinance is invalid as exclusionary.

Affirmed.

Discussion Questions

1. How much land is involved?
2. What is the proposed use of the land?
3. What types of changes would such a use bring about?
4. What problems did the Commission claim existed with the proposed development?
5. What types of services did the township have?
6. What was the extent of the township's commercial development?
7. Was the Commission justified in denying the permit?

(16.1) Consider:

Agins owned property in the city of Tiburon, Marin County, California. Tiburon and Marin County are wealthy residential suburban areas. Agins' property consists of 5 acres of ridge land with a view of San Francisco Bay. An ordinance of Tiburon permits a maximum of five dwellings on Agins' property. Agins sought to develop the property with condominiums and brought suit alleging the zoning was arbitrary and not justified under the police power of the city. What was the result?

METHODS

Once a governmental entity has been given authority to enact zoning ordinances, that authority may be used in many different ways and with many different combinations of restrictions. Generally, the governmental body begins, pursuant to the Standard State Zoning Enabling Act, with a master plan in which it divides the geographical area into an appropriate number of districts with varying shapes that will help carry out the purposes of traffic control, safety, and so on. Once these districts are decided upon, the governing body may then proceed to pass ordinances for each district. Similar situations must be treated uniformly; for example, all zoning districts must be subject to the same rules and regulations.

The following sections address the types of rules and regulations a governmental body might choose in setting up its zoning structure.

Use Restrictions

Generally, land use is regulated by zoning ordinances. Uses can usually be classified into four categories: residential, commercial or business, industrial, and agricultural. A city may divide these categories into several subcategories, as when residential is divided into R-1 for single-family dwellings, R-2 for duplex houses, R-3 for apartments, mobile homes, or similar structures. Industrial districts may be classified according to the nature of the industry with respect to noise, waste, activity, danger, odor, and so on. When various degrees of each category are established, the number 1 is usually associated with the most restrictive land use as in the example of R-1, which included only single-family dwellings.

Zoning classifications may be cumulative or noncumulative. In a *cumulative classification*, the lesser restricted areas allow all of the activities permitted in more restricted areas. Thus if cumulative zoning existed in the example, then R-2 districts would allow single-family dwellings as well as duplex houses, and R-3 districts would allow single-family dwellings, duplex houses, apartments, and mobile homes. This type of zoning was described in the *Euclid* case, which appears earlier in the chapter.

Cumulative zoning also permits high-ranked activities in low-ranked districts. (Classifications are ranked 1. residential–single family; 2. residential–multiple family; 3. residential–apartment; 4. commercial–office; 5. commercial–business; 6. industrial.) For example, an area zoned commercial could have residential uses within it under cumulative zoning. However, the reverse does not apply. Thus, no industrial or commercial activity would be permitted in residential areas.

In a *noncumulative classification*, only the activities specified by the applicable zone are permitted. For example, in R-2 areas, there would be no single-family dwellings. Also, if an area is zoned industrial or commercial, there can be no residences under a noncumulative system. Noncumulative zoning serves to prevent nuisance actions by prohibiting the existence of homes and apartments in industrial areas.

In developing their zoning systems, local governments are restricted only by the constitutional restraint of legitimate purpose and reason for the exercise of their police power. One of the issues that has been raised repeatedly in challenging the validity of zoning ordinances is whether zones limited to single-family dwellings can be permitted, with the effect of eliminating other less-costly forms of housing and thus precluding a portion of the population from residing in certain areas. The following case raises this issue.

VILLAGE OF BELLE TERRE v. BORAAS

416 U.S. 1 (1974)

Belle Terre is a village with an area of less than 1 square mile near the State University of New York at Stonybrook. In 1973 its population of 700 resided in 200 homes. Belle Terre passed an ordinance that permitted the construction of single-family homes only and prohibited households consisting of more than two unrelated persons. Boraas rented out a home he owned to six college students, and suit was brought for an injunction ordering Boraas to comply with the ordinance. Boraas defended on the grounds that the ordinance was unconstitutional. The district court found the ordinance to be constitutional. The Court of Appeals reversed.

DOUGLAS, Justice

The present ordinance is challenged on several grounds: that it interferes with a person's right to travel; that it interferes with the right to migrate to and settle within a State; that it bars people who are uncongenial to the present residents; that it expresses the social preferences of the residents for groups that will be congenial to them; that social homogeneity is not a legitimate interest of government; that the restriction of those whom the neighbors do not like trenches on the newcomers' privacy; that it is of no rightful concern to villagers whether the residents are married or unmarried; that the ordinance is antithetical to the Nation's experience, ideology, and self-perception as an open, egalitarian, and integrated society.

We find none of these reasons in the record before us. The ordinance is not aimed at transients. It involves no procedural disparity inflicted on some but not on others. It involves no "fundamental" right guaranteed by the Constitution, or any rights or privacy. We deal with economic and social legislation where legislatures have historically drawn lines which we respect against the charge of violation of the Equal Protection Clause if the law be "reasonable, not arbitrary" and bears a rational relationship to a possible state objective.

It is said, however, that if two unmarried people can constitute a "family," there is no reason why three or four may not. But every line drawn by a legislature leaves some out that might well have been included. That exercise of discretion, however, is a legislative, not a judicial, function.

The ordinance places no ban on other forms of association, for a "family" may, so far as the ordinance is concerned, entertain whomever it likes.

The regimes of boarding houses, fraternity houses, and the like present urban problems. More people occupy a given space; more cars rather continuously pass by; more cars are parked; and noise travels with crowds.

A quiet place where yards are wide, people few, and motor vehicles restricted are legitimate guidelines in a land-use project addressed to family needs. This goal is a permissible one. The police power is not confined to elimination of filth, stench and unhealthy places. It is ample to lay out zones where family values, youth values, and the blessings of quiet seclusion and clean air make the area a sanctuary for people.

Reversed.

Discussion Questions

1. Where is the village located?
2. What does the zoning ordinance at issue provide?
3. What violation of the ordinance occurred?
4. On what basis is the ordinance challenged?
5. What interest is found to be served by the court?
6. Is the ordinance constitutional?

One of the difficult social issues resulting from the single-family zoning regulation is that of group homes for the mentally retarded. The following case provides the United States Supreme Court view on the issue.

CLEBURNE v. CLEBURNE
473 U.S. 432 (1985)

In July 1980, Jan Hannah purchased a building at 201 Featherston Street in the city of Cleburne, Texas, with the intention of leasing it to Cleburne Living Center (CLC) for the operation of a group home for the mentally retarded. It was planned that thirteen retarded men and women would live in the home under the constant supervision of CLC staff members. The house had four bedrooms and two baths; a half bath was to be added.

The City of Cleburne informed CLC that a zoning regulation that required special use permits for "hospitals for the insane or feeble-minded, or alcoholic (sic) or drug addicts, or penal or correctional institutions" applied because the group home would be considered a "hospital for the feeble-minded." CLC submitted a permit application. After a public hearing, the City Council voted three to one to deny the special permit.

CLC filed suit in Federal District Court alleging that the zoning ordinance was discriminatory in violation of the equal protection rights of its potential residents. The District Court held that the ordinance and its application were constitutional. CLC appealed. The Court of Appeals reversed, holding that mental retardation was a quasi-suspect classification and that the ordinance was invalid under intermediate-level scrutiny. The city appealed.

WHITE, Justice

The Equal Protection Clause of the Fourteenth Amendment commands that no State shall "deny to any person within its jurisdiction the equal protection of the laws," which is essentially a direction that all persons similarly situated should be treated alike. Section 5 of the Amendment empowers Congress to enforce this mandate, but absent controlling congressional direction, the courts have themselves devised standards for determining the validity of state legislation or other official action that is challenged as denying equal protection. The general rule is that legislation is presumed to be valid and will be sustained if the classification drawn by the statute is rationally related to a legitimate state interest. When social or economic legislation is at issue, the Equal Protection Clause allows the States wide latitude, and the Constitution presumes that even improvident decisions will eventually be rectified by the democratic processes.

The general rule gives way, however, when a statute classifies by race, alienage, or national origin. These factors are so seldom relevant to the achievement of any legitimate state interest that laws grounded in such considerations are deemed to reflect prejudice and antipathy—a view that those in the burdened class are not as worthy or deserving as others. For these reasons and because such discrimination is unlikely to be soon rectified by legislative means, these laws are subjected to strict scrutiny and will be sustained only if they are suitably tailored to serve a compelling state interest.

Legislative classifications based on gender also call for a heightened standard of review. That factor generally provides no sensible ground for different treatment. "[W]hat differentiates sex from such non-suspect statuses as intelligence or physical disability . . . is that the sex characteristic frequently bears no relation to ability to perform or contribute to society."

We have declined, however, to extend heightened review to differential treatment based on age:

While the treatment of the aged in this Nation has not been wholly free of discrimination, such persons, unlike, say, those who have been discriminated against on the basis of race or national origin, have not experienced a "history of purposeful unequal treatment" or been subjected to unique disabilities on the basis of stereotyped characteristics not truly indicative of their abilities.

. . . [W]here individuals in the group affected by a law have distinguishing characteristics relevant to interests the State has the authority to implement, the courts have been very reluctant, as they should be in our federal system and with our re-

spect for the separation of powers, to closely scrutinize legislative choices as to whether, how, and to what extent those interests should be pursued. In such cases, the Equal Protection Clause requires only a rational means to serve a legitimate end.

Against this background, we conclude for several reasons that the Court of Appeals erred in holding mental retardation a quasi-suspect classification calling for a more exacting standard of judicial review than is normally accorded economic and social legislation. First, it is undeniable, and it is not argued otherwise here, that those who are mentally retarded have a reduced ability to cope with and function in the everyday world. Nor are they all cut from the same pattern; as the testimony in this record indicates, they range from those whose disability is not immediately evident to those who must be constantly cared for. They are thus different, immutably so, in relevant respects, and the States' interest in dealing with and providing for them is plainly a legitimate one. How this large and diversified group is to be treated under law is a difficult and often a technical matter, very much a task for legislators guided by qualified professionals and not by the perhaps ill-informed opinions of the judiciary. Heightened scrutiny inevitably involves substantive judgments about legislative decisions, and we doubt that the predicate for such judicial oversight is present where the classification deals with mental retardation.

Second, the distinctive legislative response, both national and state, to the plight of those who are mentally retarded demonstrates not only that they have unique problems, but also that the lawmakers have been addressing their difficulties in a manner that belies a continuing antipathy or prejudice and a corresponding need for more intrusive oversight by the judiciary. Thus, the Federal Government has not only outlawed discrimination against the mentally retarded in federally funded programs, but it has also provided the retarded with the right to receive "appropriate treatment, services, and habilitation" in a setting that is "least restrictive of [their] personal liberty." In addition, the Government has conditioned federal education funds on a State's assurance that retarded children will enjoy an education that, "to the maximum extent appropriate," is integrated with that of nonmentally retarded children.

Especially given the wide variation in the abilities and needs of the retarded themselves, governmental bodies must have a certain amount of flexibility and freedom from judicial oversight in shaping and limiting their remedial efforts.

Our refusal to recognize the retarded as a quasi-suspect class does not leave them entirely unprotected from invidious discrimination. To withstand equal protection review, legislation that distinguishes between the mentally retarded and others must be rationally related to a legitimate governmental purpose. This standard, we believe, affords government the latitude necessary both to pursue policies designed to assist the retarded in realizing their full potential, and to freely and efficiently engage in activities that burden the retarded in what is essentially an incidental manner.

We turn to the issue of the validity of the zoning ordinance insofar as it requires a special use permit for homes for the mentally retarded.

The constitutional issue is clearly posed. The city does not require a special use permit in an R-3 zone for apartment houses, multiple dwellings, boarding and lodging houses, fraternity or sorority houses, dormitories, apartment hotels, hospitals, sanitariums, nursing homes for convalescents or the aged (other than for the insane or feebleminded or alcoholics or drug addicts), private clubs or fraternal orders, and other specified uses. It does, however, insist on a special permit for the Featherston home, and it does so, as the District Court found, because it would be a facility for the mentally retarded. May the city require the permit for this facility when other care and multiple-dwelling facilities are freely permitted?

It is true, as already pointed out, that the mentally retarded as a group are indeed different from others not sharing their misfortune, and in this respect they may be different from those who would occupy other facilities that would be permitted in an R-3 zone without a special permit. But this difference is largely irrelevant unless the Featherston home and those who would occupy it would threaten legitimate interests of the city in a way that other permitted uses such as boarding houses and hospitals would not. Because in our view the record does not reveal any rational basis for believing that the Featherston home would pose any special threat to the city's legitimate interests, we affirm the judgment below insofar as it holds the ordinance invalid as applied in this case.

The District Court found that the City Council's insistence on the permit rested on several factors. First, the Council was concerned with the negative attitude of the majority of property owners located within 200 feet of the Featherston facility, as well as with the fears of elderly residents of the neighborhood. But mere negative attitudes, or fear, unsubstantiated by factors which are properly cognizable in a zoning proceeding, are not permissible bases for treating a home for the mentally retarded differently from apartment houses, multiple dwellings, and the like. It is plain that the electorate as a whole, whether by referendum or otherwise, could not order city action violative of the Equal Protection Clause.

Second, the Council had two objections to the location of the facility. It was concerned that the facility was across the street from a junior high school, and it feared that the students might harass the occupants of the Featherston home. But the school itself is attended by about 30 mentally retarded students, and denying a permit based on such vague, undifferentiated fears is again permitting some portion of the community to validate what would otherwise be an equal protection violation.

The other objection to the home's location was that it was located on "a five hundred year flood plain." This concern with the possibility of a flood, however, can hardly be based on a distinction between the Featherston home and, for example, nursing homes, homes for convalescents or the aged, or sanitariums or hospitals, any of which could be located on the Featherston site without obtaining a special use permit.

The same may be said of another concern of the Council—doubts about the legal responsibility for actions which the mentally retarded might take. If there is no concern about legal responsibility with respect to other uses that would be permitted in the area, such as boarding and fraternity houses, it is difficult to believe that the groups of mildly or moderately mentally retarded individuals who would live at 201 Featherston would present any different or special hazard.

Fourth, the Council was concerned with the size of the home and the number of people that would occupy it. The District Court found, and the Court of Appeals repeated, that "[i]f the potential residents of the Featherston Street home were not mentally retarded, but the home was the same in all other respects, its use would be permitted under the city's zoning ordinance." Given this finding, there would be no restrictions on the number of people who could occupy this home as a boarding house, nursing home, family dwelling, fraternity house, or dormitory. The question is whether it is rational to treat the mentally retarded differently. It is true that they suffer disability not shared by others; but why this difference warrants a density regulation that others need not observe is not at all apparent.

The short of it is that requiring the permit in this case appears to us to rest on the irrational prejudice against the mentally retarded, including those who would occupy the Featherston facility and who would live under the closely supervised and highly regulated conditions expressly provided for by state and federal law.

The Supreme Court affirmed the invalidity of the statute but used a different test in reaching the result.

Discussion Questions

1. What zoning ordinance was at issue?
2. Was the zoning ordinance passed to deal directly with group homes for the mentally retarded?
3. What standard of review does the Supreme Court use?
4. Is the ordinance valid?
5. What long-term implications does the case carry?

Intensity Zoning

Intensity zoning regulates the extent to which an area zoned at a certain level may be put to that level's use. Intensity regulations generally take the following forms:

1. Building height limitations
2. Setbacks for buildings (minimum distance between the street or sidewalk and the structure)
3. Minimum lot sizes (may be total square feet or minimum length and width)
4. Maximum structures per area (often called density—specifies, for example, the number of houses that may be built in an R-1 tract)
5. Floor area ratios (sets a maximum amount of floor area per lot. For example, a 10-to-1 ratio would permit a 10-story building to occupy an entire lot or a 20-story building to occupy half the lot.)

Aesthetic Zoning

The purpose of *aesthetic zoning* is to control or improve the beauty of a city or other area subject to a zoning plan. Zoning that exists purely for aesthetics is not valid in a majority of the states. However, if the alleged aesthetic control can be tied to or coupled with a health or welfare purpose, then the aesthetic control is valid. More and more, courts are recognizing the public interest in aesthetic controls and upholding their validity. For example, an aesthetic zoning ordinance may prohibit the construction of homes on the side of a mountain to prevent the beauty of the mountain from being destroyed. However, if it can be established that there is too much risk in constructing homes on the mountainside because of possible slides that would not only destroy the homes but could injure others at the foot of the mountain and require city safety and rescue equipment, then the ordinance is more of an exercise of police power for safety reasons than an aesthetic control.

Many of the aesthetic zoning provisions deal with architectural design. The following case deals with this type of ordinance and the issue of its validity.

STATE OF MISSOURI EX REL. STOYANOFF v. LADUE
458 S.W.2d 305 (Mo. 1970)

The Stoyanoffs (plaintiffs) sought to build a home of an ultramodern design in Ladue, Missouri. The home was to be built in a neighborhood in which all of the homes were of two-story conventional architectural design such as Colonial, French, or English.

The city of Ladue has a zoning ordinance that requires that a proposed structure

. . . *conform to certain minimum architectural standards of appearance and conformity with surrounding structures, and that unsightly, grotesque and unsuitable structures, detrimental to the stability of value and the welfare of surrounding property, structures and residents, and to the general welfare and happiness of the community, be avoided, and that appropriate standards of beauty and conformity be fostered and encouraged.*

The city denied the Stoyanoffs a permit to build the home on the basis of evidence that the proposed residence would reduce the market value of the homes in the area.

The Stoyanoffs filed suit alleging the ordinance was unconstitutional because of its vagueness and also because the powers being exercised exceeded the city's constitutional police power. The lower court held the ordinance was unconstitutional.

PRITCHARD, Commissioner

It is argued that the ordinance is invalid and unconstitutional as being an unreasonable and arbitrary exercise of the police power. It is argued that a mere reading shows the ordinance is based entirely on aesthetic factors. The argument ignores the further provisos in the ordinance: ". . . and that unsightly, grotesque and unsuitable structures, detrimental to the stability of value and the welfare of surrounding property, structures and residents, and to the general welfare and happiness of the community, be avoided, and that appropriate standards of beauty and conformity be fostered and encouraged." The proposed residence does not descend to a "patently offensive character." Nevertheless, the aesthetic factor taken into account by the city's Architectural Board is not to be considered alone. Along with that inherent factor is the effect that the proposed residence would have on property values in the area. In this time of burgeoning urban areas, congested with people and structures, it is certainly in keeping with the ultimate ideal of general welfare that the Architectural Board, in its function, preserve and protect existing areas in which structures of a general conformity of architecture have been erected. The area under consideration is clearly, from the record, a fashionable one.

If by the term "aesthetic considerations" is meant a regard merely for outward appearances, for good taste in the matter of the beauty of the neighborhood itself, we do not observe any substantial reason for saying that such a consideration is not a matter of general welfare. The beauty of a fashionable residence neighborhood in a city is for the comfort and happiness of the residents, and it sustains in a general way the value of the property in the neighborhood.

In the matter of enacting zoning ordinances and the procedures for determining whether any certain proposed structure or use is in compliance with or offends the basic ordinance, it is well settled that the courts will not substitute their judgments for the city's legislative body, if the result is not oppressive, unreasonable or arbitrary. The denial of a building permit for a highly modernistic residence in this area where traditional Colonial, French Provincial and English Tudor styles of architecture are erected does not appear to be arbitrary and unreasonable when the basic purpose to be served is that of the general welfare of persons in the entire community.

Reversed.

Discussion Questions

1. What zoning ordinance is at issue?
2. Who wishes a building permit and what is to be constructed?
3. Where is the home to be constructed?
4. What will be the effect of the construction?

5. Is the zoning ordinance only for aesthetics?

6. Is the ordinance unconstitutional?

Aesthetic zoning has been used to preserve historical towns and portions of cities by controlling the type of architecture, its repair, and alteration. These types of zoning ordinances have been held valid not only because they serve to preserve historical areas but also because they preserve the tourist business for the localities.

(16.2) Consider:

The city of Baltimore passed an ordinance to regulate signs in the commercial district of Baltimore. The ordinance was designed to achieve uniformity in all signs in the commercial district. Signs that would hang over the sidewalks were prohibited. Swartz and ten other firms doing business in the commercial district filed suit seeking to enjoin enforcement of the ordinance on the grounds that it had no purpose other than aesthetics and was, therefore, unconstitutional. What was the result?

Exclusionary Zoning

Exclusionary zoning was at issue in the *Smookler* case, where zoning was being used to exclude others from the community and prevent increases in population. Such ordinances, as established in the *Smookler* case, are invalid. However, for ordinances to be invalid, it must be shown that they are a permanent block to any use of the land within the locality. Restrictions on the rate of development so that services and governmental organization can grow at an equal rate serve a legitimate public interest and are permissible forms of regulation.

Exclusionary zoning may also be used to prevent certain types of land use. The *Belle Terre* case is an example of an ordinance seeking to eliminate all but single-family dwellings. These types of ordinances are valid.

Interim Zoning

It may take a city or town some time to make a study and develop a master plan upon which to base zoning regulations. In the time it takes for such study and planning, developers may enter the community and develop segments so that any plan adopted will be frustrated. To alleviate this problem, cities and towns may adopt *interim* or *hold zoning* to prevent uncontrolled development before a comprehensive plan and ordinances are adopted. The interim zoning may be as simple as a requirement of approval before construction or development begins. This prior approval gives the city or town government discretionary control before permanent zoning takes effect.

Social Issue Zoning

In *social issue zoning*, zoning ordinances are used as a tool in battling social issues. For example, zoning ordinances have been used to disperse adult theaters and bookstores. In *Young v. American Mini Theaters*, 427 U.S. 50 (1976), the United States Supreme Court held that zoning ordinances may classify these types of businesses differently from other movie houses and bookstores for safety purposes, thus upholding the dispersement treatment required by the ordinances at issue in the case. In the following case, the United States Supreme Court dealt with the issue of the validity of an ordinance regulating adult theaters.

CITY OF RENTON v. PLAYTIME THEATRES, INC.
475 U.S. 41 (1986)

The city of Renton, Washington (appellant), has a zoning ordinance that prohibits adult motion picture theaters from locating within 1000 feet of any residential zone, single- or multiple-family dwelling, church, park, or school. Playtime Theatres, Inc. filed an action in federal district court seeking a declaration that the Renton ordinance violates the First and Fourteenth Amendments. The District Court found for Renton and the Ninth Circuit reversed. The city of Renton appealed.

REHNQUIST, Justice

In our view, the resolution of this case is largely dictated by our decision in *Young v. American Mini Theatres, Inc.* There, although five Members of the Court did not agree on a single rationale for the decision, we held that the city of Detroit's zoning ordinance, which prohibited locating an adult theater within 1000 feet of any two other "regulated uses" or within 500 feet of any residential zone, did not violate the First and Fourteenth Amendments.

The Renton ordinance, like the one in *American Mini Theatres*, does not ban adult theaters altogether, but merely provides that such theaters may not be located within 1000 feet of any residential zone, single- or multiple-family dwelling, church, park, or school. The ordinance is therefore properly analyzed as a form of time, place, and manner regulation.

Describing the ordinance as a time, place, and manner regulation is, of course, only the first step in our inquiry. This Court has long held that regulations enacted for the purpose of restraining speech on the basis of its content presumptively violate the First Amendment. On the other hand, so-called "content-neutral" time, place, and manner regulations are acceptable so long as they are designed to serve a substantial governmental interest and do not unreasonably limit alternative avenues of communication.

At first glance, the Renton ordinance, like the ordinance in *American Mini Theatres*, does not appear to fit neatly into either the "content-based" or the "content-neutral" category. To be sure, the ordinance treats theaters that specialize in adult films differently from other kinds of theaters. Nevertheless, as the District Court concluded, the Renton ordinance is aimed not at the content of the films shown at "adult motion picture theatres," but rather at the secondary effects of such theaters on the surrounding community. The District Court found that the City Council's "predominate concerns" were with the secondary effects of adult theaters, and not with the content of adult films themselves.

In short, the Renton ordinance is completely consistent with our definition of "content-neutral" speech regulations as those that "are justified without reference to the content of the regulated speech." The ordinance does not contravene the fundamental principle that underlies our concern about "content-based" speech regulations: that "government may not grant the use of a forum to people whose views it finds acceptable, but deny use to those wishing to express less favored or more controversial views."

We also find no constitutional defect in the method chosen by Renton to further its substantial interests. Cities may regulate adult theaters by dispersing them, as in Detroit, or by effectively concentrating them, as in Renton. "It is not our function to appraise the wisdom of [the city's] decision to require adult theaters to be separated rather than concentrated in the same areas. . . . [T]he city must be allowed a reasonable opportunity to experiment with solutions to admittedly serious problems. Moreover, the Renton ordinance is "narrowly tailored" to affect only that category of theaters shown to produce the unwanted secondary effects.

Respondents contend that the Renton ordinance is "under-inclusive," in that it fails to regulate other kinds of adult businesses that are likely to produce secondary effects similar to those produced by adult theaters. On this record the contention must fail. There is no evidence that, at the time the Renton ordinance was enacted, any other adult business was located in, or was contemplating moving into, Renton. In fact, Resolution No. 2368, enacted in October 1980, states that "the City of Renton does not, at the present time, have any business whose primary

purpose is the sale, rental, or showing of sexually explicit materials." That Renton chose first to address the potential problems created by one particular kind of adult business in no way suggests that the city has "singled out" adult theaters for discriminatory treatment. We simply have no basis on this record for assuming that Renton will not, in the future, amend its ordinance to include other kinds of adult businesses that have been shown to produce the same kinds of secondary effects as adult theaters.

Finally, turning to the question whether the Renton ordinance allows for reasonable alternative avenues of communication, we note that the ordinance leaves some 520 acres, or more than five percent of the entire land area of Renton, open to use as adult theater sites. The District Court found, and the Court of Appeals did not dispute the finding, that the 520 acres of land consists of "[a]mple, accessible real estate," including "acreage in all stages of development from raw land to developed, industrial, warehouse, office, and shopping space that is criss-crossed by freeways, highways, and roads."

Respondents argue, however, that some of the land in question is already occupied by existing businesses, that "practically none" of the undeveloped land is currently for sale or lease, and that in general there are no "commercially viable" adult theater sites within the 520 acres left open by the Renton ordinance. The Court of Appeals accepted these arguments, concluded that the 520 acres was not truly "available" land, and therefore held that the Renton ordinance "would result in a substantial restriction" on speech.

We disagree with both the reasoning and the conclusion of the Court of Appeals. That respondents must fend for themselves in the real estate market, on an equal footing with other prospective purchasers and lessees, does not give rise to a First Amendment violation. And although we have cautioned against the enactment of zoning regulations that have "the effect of suppressing, or greatly restricting access to, lawful speech," we have never suggested that the First Amendment compels the Government to ensure that adult theaters, or any other kinds of speech-related businesses for that matter, will be able to obtain sites at bargain prices. In our view, the First Amendment requires only that Renton refrain from effectively denying respondents a reasonable opportunity to open and operate an adult theater within the city, and the ordinance before us easily meets this requirement.

In sum, we find that the Renton ordinance represents a valid governmental response to the "admittedly serious problems" created by adult theaters. Renton has not used "the power to zone as a pretext for suppressing expression," but rather has sought to make some areas available for adult theaters and their patrons, while at the same time preserving the quality of life in the community at large by preventing those theaters from locating in other areas. This, after all, is the essence of zoning. Here, as in *American Mini Theaters,* the city has enacted a zoning ordinance that meets these goals while also satisfying the dictates of the First Amendment.

Reversed.

Discussion Questions

1. Does the Renton ordinance regulate the content of speech?
2. Is the Renton ordinance overly broad?
3. What does "content-neutral" mean?
4. Does the ordinance apply only to adult theaters?
5. Is the ordinance constitutional?

(16.3) Consider

The city of Southborough, Massachusetts, passed a zoning ordinance that prohibited the operation of abortion clinics within the town. Framingham Clinic attempted to establish a clinic that would perform first trimester abortions and challenged the ordinance. Is the regulation permissible? *Framingham Clinic, Inc. v. Board of Selectmen,* 367 N.E.2d 606 (Mass. 1977)

PROCEDURAL ASPECTS

Adoption of Zoning Regulations

As already stated, local governments obtain their authority for zoning from an enabling act, and most states have adopted some form of the Standard State Zoning Enabling Act. This act consists of nine basic sections summarized as follows:

- *Section 1—Grant of power.* In this section the governmental unit is given the authority to zone on the basis of a need to preserve health, safety, morals, and the general welfare of the community. It is a broad grant of authority intended to give the governmental unit its full constitutional range of power.
- *Section 2—Districts.* In this section the governmental unit is given the authority to divide its area of jurisdiction into any size, shape, and number of districts for purposes of regulating activities or structures in those districts.
- *Section 3—Purposes in View.* This section requires the governmental unit to exercise its power under Section 2 pursuant to a master plan designed to provide all areas with adequate safety protection, schools, water, sewage, parks, and all other amenities.
- *Section 4—Method of Procedures.* In this section the governmental unit is authorized to establish procedures for adopting and amending zoning regulations. This section requires that a public hearing, with 15-days' advance public notice, be held before any zoning regulation is enacted.
- *Section 5—Changes.* This section specifies that changes in zoning may be made but can be stopped if 20 percent or more of the owners of lots in the area in question oppose the change. The 20 percent may also include those who own lots within a certain distance of the area subject to the change. The distance (in feet) is left blank, to be determined by the adopting governmental unit. The distance of 200 feet is typical.
- *Section 6—Zoning Commission.* This section establishes the right of the governmental unit to appoint a commission to set up the original zoning plan on the basis of studies of the area.
- *Section 7—Board of Adjustment.* The purpose of this section is to allow the local governments to set up a board that can, in cases and circumstances they deem appropriate, make exceptions to the zoning regulations in particular areas, so long as the exceptions are in keeping with the idea of the master plan and basic district division. These exceptions are called *variances* under the act.
- *Section 8—Enforcement.* In this section the local governmental body is authorized to call zoning violations misdemeanors and to provide for penalties of either fines or imprisonment. Also, the local governmental body is authorized to bring suit to stop construction or use of property that is in violation of the zoning regulations; in other words, to seek an injunction for violative activity.
- *Section 9—Conflicts.* This section serves to clarify which set of laws will govern in the event two governmental units have established zoning for

the same area; for example, if a county has adopted zoning for the county, but the cities within the county have adopted their own zoning ordinances. This section provides that city ordinances will be controlling to the extent they are more strict than the county ordinances.

The Standard State Zoning Enabling Act was drafted in 1922, revised in 1926, and at one time was adopted in most states. Today, although it is still the law in the majority of states by far, it provokes some dissatisfaction. The American Law Institute has drafted a Model Land Development Code which some states have adopted as supplement to the Standard State Zoning Enabling Act. Although there may be slight variations in adoption forms, the preceding sections summarize the basic ideas, theories, and practice of zoning in local governmental units. The zoning control must be in the hands of a public body, and not subject to individual discretion, as discussed in the following case.

FIRST BAPTIST CHURCH OF BISBEE v.
ARIZONA STATE LIQUOR BOARD
716 P.2d 81 (Ariz. App. 1986)

Shepherd's Inn, Inc. applied for a retailer's liquor license with the Arizona State Liquor Board. The Board approved the application despite the opposition of the First Baptist Church and the Bisbee City Council.

An Arizona statute (A.R.S. §4-207 [A][1]) provides as follows:

A. No retailer's license shall be issued for any building whose exterior walls are within three hundred horizontal feet of a public or parochial school building or church building in which services are regularly conducted unless, in addition to the other requirements of this chapter:

1. The issuance of such license is recommended for approval by the governing body of each public school or the individual or board holding title to the property of each parochial school or church located within three hundred horizontal feet of the proposed location, and

2. The issuance of such license is recommended for approval by the governing body of the city or town if located within the corporate limits, or by the board of supervisors if located in the unincorporated area of the county.

The trial court found that the Board's decision violated the statute, and Shepherd's Inn appealed.

BIRDSALL, Judge

The Board's action was arbitrary and capricious because the proposed liquor establishment was within 300 feet of the church. The only evidence before the Board was that the distance from the nearest exterior wall of the applicant's building to the church building was less than 300 horizontal feet. The Board could not have lawfully considered measurements from and to other beginning and ending points. Thus, the evidence of the distance from the doorway of the applicant's building to the doorway of the church had to be disregarded. Likewise, the distance from the nearest exterior wall of the church to the doorway of the applicant's building (including the distance down a stairway of the latter) had to be disregarded, as well as a measurement from the farthest exterior wall of the applicant's premises to the wall of the church. Nor could the Board disregard the statutory requirement of a horizontal measurement and take the hills and valleys between the two buildings into account. The only proper evidence before the Board showed the horizontal distance to be from 264.78' to 270'9". At least five different persons, including two qualified surveyors, reported these distances. In fact, if a Sunday school building on the church premises had been considered, the distance would have been even less.

We believe that the language of the statute is clear and unambiguous. "Exterior walls" must be interpreted to mean the nearest walls of the two buildings. Otherwise, the measurement would depend on the size of the buildings. If either were large enough and the furthest exterior walls were used, for example, the buildings could be adjacent to each other. The points from which the measurement is to be made are certain, and the distance to be measured is horizontal, meaning "in a place parallel to the horizon" (*Webster's New Collegiate Dictionary*, 1973). "Horizontal" means along the shortest straight line, and not along the course of a highway or along the usually traveled way, or along or upon the surface of the ground.

Since neither the church nor the city had recommended approval of the license, and the inn would have been located within the prohibited 300 feet, the trial court correctly found that the Board's decision was in complete disregard of the legislative requirements.

Reversed and remanded.

Turning now to the constitutional question, we believe it is important and necessary to hold subsection (A)(1) of the statute unconstitutional because the disapproval by the church may have affected the vote of the city council. By giving the church a veto power over the issuance of the liquor license, A.R.S. 4-207(A)(1) is unconstitutional.

We believe that that portion of the statute may, however, be severed from the remainder. The legislature may constitutionally provide that no liquor license may be issued within a reasonable distance of a church unless the city council approves. In the instant case, because the applicant's premises were within 300 feet and the city council did not recommend approval, the trial court correctly ruled that the Board abused its discretion in granting the license. However, the city council's action may very well have been influenced by the absence of church approval. A council member might have thought that there was no point in voting to approve a license because city council approval was an idle act absent additional · church approval.

We were advised in oral argument that the superior court judgment was stayed pending this appeal. The liquor license was issued and Shepherd's Inn has been serving liquor. We believe we should continue that stay pending a new presentation of the matter to the Bisbee City Council, so that its members may vote with the knowledge that church approval is unnecessary.

We remand to the Arizona State Liquor Board with directions to request that the Bisbee City Council hold a new hearing and advise the Board of the results. If the council recommends approval, that will validate the issuance of the license. If the council does not recommend approval, the Board shall rescind the license.

Discussion Questions

1. What is the content and purpose of the statute at issue?
2. Who opposed the license?
3. Is the statute constitutional?
4. What concerns did the court have about the statute?

Exceptions from Zoning Regulations

Section 7 of the Standard State Zoning Enabling Act provides for a board of adjustment and allows the board to grant exceptions or variances for use in zoned districts. An application for a variance to the board of adjustment must show two things:

a. That the petitioning party would suffer an undue hardship if the ordinance is enforced
b. That the granting of the variance will not be excessively disruptive of the surrounding land or the master plan

Factors considered by boards in making their variance decisions include: the effect of the use on surrounding land; the benefit to the public of the varied use; whether the property for which the variance is sought is different in its surface character from other property in the district; whether loss will be experienced if the variance is not granted; and whether the master plan's purposes would be defeated through the grant of the variance.

One of the most frequently approved variances involves an exception to building height restrictions. Building height may be limited by ordinance, but it may be economically beneficial to the community and not a burden on surrounding property to permit a large business to build a multistory building in a single-story zoned district.

Another frequently used term that allows an exception to the zoned use is *special permit*. Under a special permit, the board makes an exception such as for the construction of a church or school in a residential area provided certain restrictions or conditions are met. Whether a variance or special permit will be granted is within the discretion of the board and is, more or less, a matter of opinion.

If a variance or special permit is denied, the party or parties seeking the variance have the right to seek judicial review of the board of adjustment's decision on the grounds of abuse of discretion, constitutionality, or arbitrariness. Figure 16.1 summarizes the procedural aspects of zoning.

Nonconforming Uses

A *nonconforming use* is the use of property in a way prohibited by a zoning ordinance passed after the use already existed. An example would be a store or

Figure 16.1 *Zoning Process*

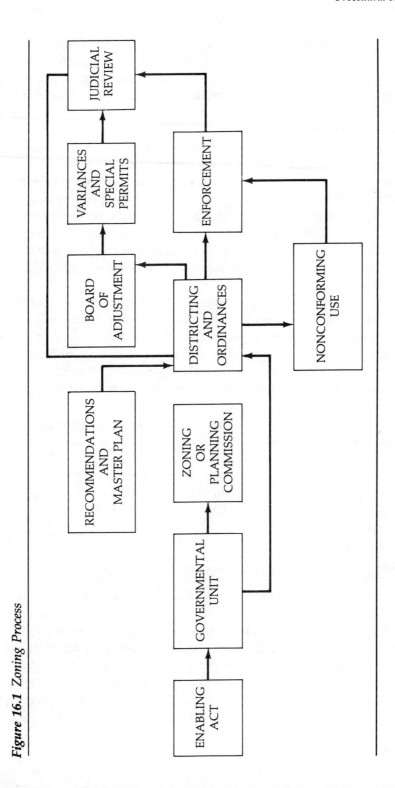

business operating in an area that has just been zoned residential. Most zoning ordinances permit the continuation of such uses even though the ordinances would prohibit a new store or similar use from beginning. A nonconforming use also occurs when an existing building does not meet subsequently passed ordinances, such as a building of several stories located in an area that subsequently prohibits multistory buildings.

For a nonconforming use to be immune from newly passed zoning ordinances, it must be in existence at the time the zoning is passed. Furthermore, the activity or structure cannot be expanded but must remain limited to the extent of the nonconforming use at the time the zoning was passed.

A right to nonconforming use can be lost if the nonconforming activity is abandoned or if the nonconforming building is destroyed by fire or natural events. The zoning ordinances may specify a time period for abandonment and may also specify what constitutes destruction for purposes of ending a nonconforming use.

Recently, many local governments, in an effort to carry out their community planning objectives, have sought to eliminate nonconforming uses over time and have passed ordinances that require amortization of nonconforming uses. These amortization sections require nonconforming uses to be eliminated over a specified period—usually 5 years. Amortization periods allow landowners some time to convert their property to appropriately zoned activities or buildings.

Some courts have even declared certain nonconforming uses to be nuisances and have had them eliminated by legal action for nuisance. Thus, through the actions of surrounding landowners, nonconforming use can be eliminated by court injunction. For example, a smelting plant in a residential area could easily be enjoined as a nuisance and the problem of nonconforming use eliminated. Reread the *Hopper* case in Chapter 1 (page 11) for a review of zoning exceptions.

CONCLUSIONS AND RECOMMENDATIONS

From the information and cases in this chapter it is not difficult to see that the issue of zoning can be controlling in the value of property and is certainly controlling in the use to be made of property. Before land is purchased or before construction is begun, a zoning check should be made. In addition, surrounding tracts and plats should be checked to see the effects of growth and expansion and also the resulting effect on property values. Finally, the master plan should be evaluated to determine any future problems and possible changes or variances that might affect the land's value. When it comes to the issue of zoning, there can never be enough research.

KEY TERMS

zoning	interim zoning
general plan	hold zoning
master plan	social issue zoning
Standard State Zoning Enabling Act	zoning commission
cumulative classification	board of adjustment
noncumulative classification	variances
intensity zoning	special permit
aesthetic zoning	nonconforming use
exclusionary zoning	

CHAPTER PROBLEMS

1. The city of Mesa's planning and zoning board passed an age-restrictive ordinance that, in certain districts, required residents to be a minimum of 50 years of age. Mesa's population consists of about 50 percent retired individuals and is a winter haven for retired individuals from other states. Much of the city's economy is derived from their activities. A young couple seeking to buy a home in one of the districts has challenged the ordinance on the grounds that it exceeds the police power because it serves no public interest. What is the result?

2. New Orleans passed an ordinance governing its historical Vieux Carré section that detailed the types of structures and their repair, maintenance, and alteration permissible in the area. The ordinance has been challenged on the grounds that it exceeds the police power. What is the result?

3. A city has recently passed an ordinance that prohibits the operation of "vehicle graveyards" in any district where they will be visible from the highway. An owner of one of these vehicle junkyards has challenged the ordinance as unconstitutional. What is the result?

4. Du Page Trust Company wished to erect an apartment building in a single-family residential district in Glen Ellyn, Illinois. A special permit was refused, and Du Page challenged the ordinance on the grounds that its effect was to keep out lower-income individuals from the town. What was the result?

5. Stockton applied to the board of adjustment of the town of Sea Girt for a special permit to operate a hotel. The permit was granted by the board of adjustment without a public hearing. Kramer, an adjoining property owner, brought suit alleging the granting of the special permit without a public hearing was improper. What was the result?

6. Manning applied to the board of adjustment of Avon Lake, Ohio, for a special permit to operate a service station on a piece of property located on the edges of a residentially zoned district on one side and a commercially zoned district on the other side. The permit was denied, and Manning appealed the decision as arbitrary and capricious. What was the result?

7. An ordinance of Lake County permitted certain nonconforming uses to continue after the passage of zoning laws. Included in the nonconforming uses permitted were buildings for which "construction programs" had begun. A nonconforming use was permitted for an office building already under construction in a residential neighborhood; however, it was denied for a similar building not yet under construction, although plans had been drawn and a contractor hired. The firm denied use brought suit challenging the arbitrary ordinance. What was the result?

8. Westfield's house was in an area zoned for single-family dwellings. She sought a variance to convert her home into four apartments and was denied. Westfield sued, challenging the validity of the ordinance and the refusal of the variance. What was the result?

9. The city of St. Louis passed an ordinance that required all for-sale signs posted on properties within the city to include an indication of the zoning for the property. Green failed to place the zoning on the sign for one of his listed properties and was convicted of a misdemeanor. Green appealed the conviction on the grounds that the ordinance was an excess exercise of power by the city. What was the result?

10. An ordinance of the city of Palo Alto, a college town, prohibits two or more persons from living together in a single-family residential district unless they are related by blood, marriage, or legal adoption. A tenants' union has brought suit challenging the validity of the ordinance. What is the result?

17

TAX ASPECTS OF REAL ESTATE OWNERSHIP AND TRANSFER

Taxes are what we pay for a civilized society.

–Oliver Wendell Holmes, Jr.

There are three different types of taxes affecting land ownership and transfer. The tax of ownership is commonly called property tax and is paid for a certain period at a rate based on the value of the property. Income tax rates can be affected by real estate ownership and property transfer, helping to make real estate a good investment. Finally, estate, gift, or inheritance tax (or all three) is paid when property is transferred after the death of the owner (see Chapter 14). The purpose of this chapter is to discuss property taxes and income tax as it relates to real estate ownership and transfer. Questions to be answered include, What is property tax? How is the amount of property tax determined? What happens if property taxes are not paid? Can the amount of the property tax be contested? What effects on income does the sale of property have? Can owning property offer income tax deductions and credits? Are there any exemptions for gains made from the sale of property?

PROPERTY TAXES

Purpose

The taxing of property has been documented as existing as early as 596 B.C., when the city of Athens levied a tax on the owners of all property within the

501

city. Roman property taxes at one time applied to both real and personal property. During the reign of Henry II in England, a 10 percent tax rate was applied to all "rents and movable properties." In 1697 the first "land tax" was levied in England. When the colonists arrived in North America, they brought with them and exercised three forms of taxation: polls, property, and faculty (income earning capacity).

In all of these historical cases, the purpose of levying the tax was to support the government. Property taxes in the United States currently account for 88 percent of the tax revenues of local governments and finance about half of all local government expenditures (Lindholm, *Property Taxation USA*, 1976). Thus, the property tax has been a long-standing source for most local governmental units. The advantages of property taxes are that there is always property to tax and failure to pay results in a lien or the eventual sale of the property (discussed later in the chapter).

Assessment

The tax *assessment* is the estimation of the value of all parcels of land for the purposes of taxation. The amount of tax is calculated on the basis of a predetermined factor, such as $10 per $1,000 valuation. Property owners pay at the same rate but pay different amounts depending on the assessed value of their property. For example, if the tax rate is $10 per $1,000 of valuation and a property is valued at $100,000, then the tax would be $1,000. However, someone with property valued at only $50,000 would pay property tax of $500.

The real property tax is thus called an *ad valorem tax* because it increases as property values increase. It is not based on ability to pay or on the amount of services received from the governmental agency that administers the property tax revenues. This type of taxation has been held constitutional so long as the uniform rate structure just illustrated is applied.

To administer the tax program, each county has a tax *assessor* or other official prepare a list of all properties in the county and their owners. This list is often referred to as a *property tax roll* and includes all property that will be subject to the tax. Once the list is completed, it becomes the job of the assessor (who is usually an elected official) to determine the valuations for all properties on the list.

Many assessors prepare land value maps to outline various areas for purposes of assessing values. Thus the location of schools, shopping, transportation, and other factors affecting land values can be easily determined. In arriving at the final figure for assessment, the assessor may use any of the methods or combinations of methods used by appraisers in their valuations such as comparable property sales prices, replacement cost, or potential rental income. The assessment figures vary significantly from state to state because each state has its own wording as to the basis for assessment value.

The assessment of property involves a great deal of discretion, and many criticisms of the property tax are aimed at this part of the system. However, assessed values tend to be lower than market values, and a recent survey indicated that the average national assessment figure for properties was 29 percent of market value (Holland, *The Assessment of Land Value*, 1979).

The timing of an assessment can affect the assessment figure. Furthermore, many assessors' offices are limited in the amount of time and personnel that can be devoted to the assessment task. In many areas, assessments are not done on an annual basis but biennially or as infrequently as every 3 or 4 years. The frequency of evaluations will affect the amount of revenue raised since property values tend to rise.

In some cases, raw land is being assessed, but a subdivision or some other type of development is imminent because of surrounding property usage. Some assessments will value the property as if it were capable of being in use at the time (the highest and best-use concept) and will, of course, cause a higher tax on the property. Sometimes this type of future value assessment serves to force development because the owner of raw land cannot afford the assessed value tax.

Other factors that may be considered in the assessment process are:

1. Market value: what a willing seller would pay a willing buyer through a private sale;
2. Original cost of acquisition;
3. Cost of any improvements; and
4. Amount of rent currently received.

Exemptions from Assessment and Tax All states have some land exempt from assessment and tax. Land exempted must include federal properties unless there is consent from the federal government. Some states that have large amounts of federal lands receive a percentage of profits from mineral operations on the land, but these receipts are not the equivalent of what a property tax would have yielded. State and local government property is also generally exempt from assessment and taxation. Examples include governmental buildings, parks, and preserves. Most states provide tax exemptions for properties held by nonprofit and charitable institutions. The definitions of exempt organizations vary from state to state.

Some states have used their property tax structure to attract new business to the state. For example, businesses may be given a 5- or 10-year exemption from payment of tax or they may be taxed at a lower rate. This type of favorable treatment can affect decisions made by companies on the placement of plants or storage facilities.

Objections to Assessed Value The due-process clause requires all states to give property owners the opportunity to object to or protest the assessed values of their properties. All procedures for protesting assessed value are statutory and include several basic steps:

1. Property owners must be notified of the assessed value of their property.
2. Property owners must be given a reasonable amount of time after assessment to gather information and prepare a protest.
3. Property owners must have a procedure for filing a protest and must be given instructions for the hows and whens of such a filing.
4. The local governmental body must provide a hearing forum: an administrative body or some form of judicial review for the property owners' presentations of protests.
5. Property owners have the burden of proof, during the hearing, to show the overvaluation of their property.

Property owners are entitled to all of the above procedural protections before the tax on the property becomes due and owing. No tax can be constitutionally imposed or made final until the property owner has had the opportunity to object. Once the hearing has been held and an adverse decision rendered, the property owner must pay the taxes but may then seek judicial review of the administrative action and challenge the assessment and tax in court. The following case deals with the sufficiency of due process in the taxpayers' challenge procedures.

BATH CLUB, INC. v. DADE COUNTY
394 So.2d 110 (Fla. 1981)

Dade County's property appraisal adjustment board (defendant/appellee) assessed the value of the property of the Bath Club (plaintiff/appellant), and the Bath Club brought a trial court action challenging the assessments. The trial court refused to reduce the assessments, and the Bath Club appealed on several grounds, one of which was that the board's authority to appoint special masters to take testimony and make recommendations denied procedural due process since taxpayers could not appear and offer testimony.

ENGLAND, Justice

. . . [T]he Club asserts that the statute which allows the Board to appoint special masters to take testimony and make recommendations on which "the board may act upon without further hearing . . ." denies procedural due process. The Club argues that the Board is merely a "rubber stamp" of the special masters; another contention made without record support. In any event, "due process is met if one adequate method of judicial review of the orders of administrative agencies is set up and such method may be made exclusive by statute." Viewing the statute as a whole, we see that taxpayers desiring to challenge their ad valorem real property tax assessments are afforded not only notice and an opportunity to be heard at an administrative level but an absolute right to a trial de novo in the circuit court. The statute obviously provides taxpayers with procedural due process.

Affirmed.

Discussion Questions

1. Who is challenging their assessment?
2. How are assessments made in Dade County?
3. What is the basis of the appeal?
4. Is the assessment valid?

Collection of Taxes

Accompanying the assessment notice given to all property owners is information on the rate of tax, the total amount of tax due, and the date the tax is due. Most states provide a grace period and then a period during which the tax may be paid along with a penalty. In the case of residential properties subject to a mortgage or deed of trust, the mortgagee or trustee or their assigned servicing agent generally pays the taxes for the property owner through monthly withholdings included in mortgage payments according to the initial loan agreement.

Tax Liens Because property tax is not a personal obligation but an obligation of the property, the nonpayment of the tax may result in a lien on the property. Once the tax is not paid, it becomes purely a procedural responsibility for the enforcement agency to execute and file a lien upon the property. Each state's statutes must provide for the procedure of translating nonpayment of property taxes into a lien and must authorize some official or agency to execute the lien; in other words, all *tax lien* procedures are regulated by state statute. In some states, nonpayment results in an automatic lien on the property without any action of filing or recording. In these states, title cannot be cleared or insured until the tax records are checked to be sure there are no property tax delinquencies.

The effect of a tax lien, in most states, is to make all other liens and mortgages inferior and to give the tax lien first priority for payment above all other prior-existing liens. The tax lien may be removed only by payment of the tax due plus any delinquencies and statutory penalties that may accrue through nonpayment. (See Chapter 7 for a discussion of other liens.)

Tax Sales Since property tax is not a personal tax and the state's enforcement is through the tax lien, the procedure for collecting on a lien is sale of the property, with proceeds being distributed according to priority of parties with security in the property. The authority to foreclose on a lien or sell property for satisfaction of delinquent taxes is within the authority of local governments. The key factor in the *tax sale* of real property is compliance with due-process requirements. In other words, before a tax sale may be held, adequate notice must be given to property holders and the property holders must be given an opportunity to respond to the proceedings.

Satisfaction of due-process requirements does not mandate that there be judicial proceedings prior to the tax sale. Thus the local government need not obtain a judgment against the property before proceeding to a tax sale. Although the procedures for tax sales vary from state to state, they usually begin with the filing of notice, the delivery of notice to the property owner, and the publication of notice of sale.

When the sale is held, anyone may be present and bid, for the sale is required to be public. The proceeds from the sale are applied first to satisfy the taxes due, interest accrued during nonpayment, any applicable penalties, and the costs of the sale. After those amounts have been satisfied, payment is made according to the priority of any parties having security in the property. (See Chapters 6, 7, 9, and 12 for a complete discussion of priorities.)

In most states the tax sale is not a final resolution of the property owners' rights, for there usually exists a right of redemption in the delinquent property owner. This right may be exercised in two ways, but whichever method a state follows, it is important to understand that purchase of property at a tax sale does not result in a taking of full and complete title. The rights obtained by a buyer at a tax sale are subject to the property owner's right of redemption. In other words, the owner of the property is given a certain period of time within which to pay amounts due and redeem or regain the property.

Under one method of redemption the buyer is given a deed to the property, but the deed conveys only defeasible title. This means that at any time during the statutory redemption period, the title of the buyer can be defeated if the property owner is able to pay all amounts due in taxes, interest, penalties, and costs. Once the statutory period expires, the defeasible title becomes full fee simple title. The statutory period varies from state to state in a range of 6 months to 6 years.

Under the other method of redemption the buyer at a tax sale is given only a certificate of sale, which is simply evidence of the purchase. Once the redemption period has expired, the buyer is given a deed to the property.

Under either method, the deed given is called a *tax deed* and is issued by the appropriate tax agency or official in the jurisdiction. The deed will usually indicate that all steps required for a tax sale have been complied with and that the agency or official has the right to conduct the tax sale. However, the tax deed, like a sheriff's deed, has no warranties either express or implied; and the buyer's title is only as good as the agency's or official's compliance with all requirements for a valid tax sale. If there is noncompliance, the buyer runs the risk of having the sale set aside by a property owner who has been denied due process.

(17.1) Consider:

Connor failed to pay the property taxes on his half acre of undeveloped property because he protested the valuation and assessment of the property as excessive. When Connor received notice of a pending sale of his property for taxes, he protested on the grounds of unconstitutionality. Was Connor correct?

INCOME TAX AND REAL PROPERTY

Although income tax is a personal tax and is not tied to ownership of property but earning of income, real estate ownership and transfer does affect the net income of an individual. The most significant reform in the tax laws since their inception is the *Tax Reform Act of 1986* (or *TRA* as it is commonly known). TRA has been called the Internal Revenue Code of 1986 because of the sweeping reforms it has made in the tax laws. One of the goals of the act was "revenue neutrality," or the elimination of special deductions and shelters that had been afforded to certain industries. One of the industries hardest hit by revenue neutrality was the real estate industry. Many of the specifics of the act, such as the new rules on depreciation and passive losses, cut right to the heart of the tax shelters that real estate afforded. Although a complete review of all the changes in the TRA is impossible, the following sections provide a summary of the most important changes in the tax laws that have affected real estate.

Passive Activity Rule—A Blow to Real Estate Investments

One of the benefits that real estate investments and syndications had to offer was tremendous loss write-offs for investors. In investments in which depreciation deductions were quite high, real estate investors could enjoy significant losses within the first few years. The TRA includes a new section from the *Internal Revenue Code (IRC)*, §469, which provides that net passive losses from trade or business activities cannot be deducted against income from other sources.

Section 469 established three classifications for income and losses: passive; active; and portfolio. Portfolio income is basically dividend income and is not a concern in terms of real estate investments. Passive and active income refer to income from a business and *active income* exists when the taxpayer "materially participates" in the business as in those situations where the taxpayer earns a wage from the business or owns the business as a sole proprietor. *Passive income* results from partnership earnings from real estate investments. Indeed, the TRA carries a presumption that all income from real estate partnerships is passive. Since most real estate investments are in the form of limited partnerships, the TRA has eliminated the extra benefit real estate investors once had of being able to use their real estate losses to offset other income. The losses, often called *suspended losses*, may be carried forward indefinitely but cannot be used to reduce other income. For example, a loss on a real estate investment could not be taken against the active salary income of the individual investor.

The section applies to individuals, estates, trusts, personal service corporations, and most closely held corporations. Even a taxpayer who materially participates in real estate rental activity can deduct only up to $25,000 in losses from other income.

Material or active participation is not defined in the act and is left to the regulations. However, it is clear that active participation is more than just management activities as defined elsewhere in the Internal Revenue Code. There is, however, an exception for low-income housing investments that permits the $25,000 deduction even when the taxpayer does not materially participate in the activity. Also, the intent of Congress in allowing these exemptions was to offer some relief for the moderate-income investor. The $25,000 exemption is reduced (never below zero) by 50% of the taxpayer's adjusted gross income that exceeds $100,000. Thus, those taxpayers whose adjusted gross income exceed $150,000 do not enjoy the $25,000 exemption. The effect of these *passive loss* changes are illustrated in the following example:

Taxpayer has an investment interest in three rental properties (definitely passive). The performance results on the properties are as follows:

PROPERTY	YEAR	INCOME/LOSS
1	1	($50.00)
	2	($100.00)
	3	($30.00)
2	1	($10.00)
	2	($20.00)
	3	($19.50)
3	1	($90.00)
	2	0
	3	($40.50)

Taxpayer has passive income as follows:

1	$30.00
2	$90.00
3	$150.00

For year one, taxpayer has a loss of $120 ($150 less the $30 in income). For year two, taxpayer has an additional $30 in losses. In year three, there is no loss.

(17.2) Consider

What would be the result if taxpayer had $150 in income in year one? (Other figures remain the same.) Discuss the results if taxpayer had $150 in income in year two.

In addition to not being able to take the losses against personal income, taxpayers will have to allocate the carry-forward losses according to the proportions for each passive activity. Hence, the carry-forward loss in year one is $40 to property one, $8 to property two, and $72 to property three.

(17.3) Consider

Suppose that the taxpayer in the previous example had all three investments in low-income housing. Would the result be different? Suppose that the taxpayer lived as the manager and did all maintenance work at property one and held no other job. Would the result be different?

The At-Risk Rule

Before TRA, real estate investment activities were not subject to the *at-risk rules.* However, §465 was passed to limit losses by requiring taxpayers to be "at-risk" to take the losses. The provision has also been a blow to the real estate tax shelter industry. Prior to TRA, real estate investors were at-risk for the amount of any property or money they contributed as well as a pro rata share of any borrowed funds such as lines of credit or nonrecourse notes even though the investors had no personal liability for repayment of such borrowed funds. Under the TRA, real estate investors are at-risk for only those borrowed funds for which they have personal liability. The amount a taxpayer has at risk is the initial capital contribution plus any borrowed amounts as long as the taxpayer has personal liability for repayment or has pledged property that is not used in the activity as collateral for the loan. Even these two tests will not put the taxpayer at-risk if the lender is also involved in the activity in some way other than as a creditor. Again, this loophole was closed to eliminate the interest losses being taken in real estate syndications when the syndicating entity or partnership was the lender for the operating partnership. Thus the investors were not really at risk when the syndicator was the lender.

If the taxpayer is not at-risk, the losses must be taken from that activity and not from other income. Again, the losses can be carried forward indefinitely.

Investment Interest—Another Limitation

In still another blow to the real estate tax shelter business, TRA closed a potential loophole by applying the same principles to the deductibility of interest. Interest for indebtedness on a taxpayer's investment activity can only be deducted from the taxpayer's investment income generated by non-passive investment. Thus investment interest is deductible only if the indebtedness money is used to purchase any property held as a nonpassive investment.

The Home Interest Deduction

After much debate, Congress permitted the deductibility of home mortgage interest plus that of one other residence (that the taxpayer uses as a second home under IRC definitions) to continue. The TRA also continues to permit the deductibility of taxes on those properties. However, TRA does limit the amount of debt that qualifies for the interest deduction. Because of economic changes, many homeowners were refinancing their residences at lower rates but were also taking advantage of the low-cost funds by pulling out their equity in the home in addition to refinancing the original mortgage. The amount of interest that is deductible in a refinancing is the amount the taxpayer paid plus any improvements. If the taxpayer takes out more equity than the basis in the house, the interest attributable to that portion of the loan is not deductible as home mortgage interest. For example, homeowner A bought her home for $70,000 and has landscaped and added a pool at a cost of $12,000. The market value of her home is $100,000 but she can only refinance $82,000 to have the full amount of the loan interest be deductible. If she borrows more, she will be required to fill out a special form breaking out the deductible interest from the nondeductible interest.

In addition, an original loan amount has interest deductible only to the extent of the fair market value of the home. Both of these interest deduction limitations were designed to prevent manipulation of one of the few real estate tax benefits that remained in the IRC. For example, this provision prevents someone from buying a home for $120,000 and financing $150,000 in an attempt to obtain a loan with deductible interest. With the gradual elimination of the personal debt interest, closing this loophole became important.

Installment Sales

IRC §453C was added by the TRA and limits the use of the installment sales method of reporting income from certain property sales. Although the section does not apply to personal residence sales (hence the wrap-around mortgage can remain as an effective means of financing), it does apply to business sales. It eliminates the deferral aspect of installment sales that the IRC carried in the past that permitted the seller to carry forward the gains made by the sale of the property. Such deferrals continue to be available for installment sales of personal use (residence) property.

Depreciation Changes

One of the expenses that contributed significantly to the attractive paper losses of real estate syndications was that of depreciation. Accelerated methods for depreciating property gave real estate investors substantial losses over short periods. The TRA generally modifies the *accelerated cost recovery system (ACRS)* that had also become a significant part of real estate tax shelters. ACRS permitted a rapid depreciation to allow for substantial operating losses because of the large deduction for an expense that is not out-of-pocket. ACRS has basically been replaced with a system which establishes classes of property for determining depreciation periods and rates. Under the original ACRS program, real property was depreciated over a 15-year period. In 1986, that depreciation period was increased to 19 years. Under TRA, property purchased after 1986 will be depreciated over 27.5 years if it is residential real estate and over 31.5 years for non-residential real estate. The TRA also permits only a straight line computation of depreciation and disallows the 175 percent declining balance that so rapidly accelerated the depreciation and hence, tax benefits, of owning real estate during the early 1980s. There are more rapid schedules for low-income housing.

In addition to these changes, the TRA repealed the benefits of the *investment tax credit* with some transitional protections afforded for certain types of property. The tax credit was a substantial benefit because of the direct tax write-off but is now extinct.

Capital Gains

Congress eliminated the special deduction on capital gains. *Capital gains* result when property is sold at a profit after a designated holding period. Prior to TRA, 60 percent of the capital gain on a sale was not reportable as income. TRA eliminated that 60 percent deduction so that capital gains are reported at their full rate. In 1987, however, Congress did provide for a cap on the amount of tax on capital gains.

Tax Benefits of Ownership

While the TRA took away much of the benefit of real estate tax shelters, it allowed many of the benefits of real estate ownership to remain. For example, interest on homes is still deductible, as are property taxes. Depreciation rates have been slowed but still remain deductible and a tax benefit. While the disproportionate benefits have been removed, the tax benefits of real estate still remain in a modified form.

CONCLUSIONS AND RECOMMENDATIONS

A practical note for the discussion on property taxes is that the amount of taxes must be verified and a title search should be done (to determine whether there are any tax liens involved) before any transactions on the property are completed. For property owners, notice should be taken of assessment and valuation notifications, so that any discrepancies can be properly and timely challenged.

Regarding the effect of real estate ownership on income tax, buyers and sellers should always investigate the tax consequences of their real estate transactions before entering into contracts. In some cases the sale may be structured to maximize benefits. In the case of property ownership, the parties should be certain that all possible deductions are being taken so that the return on their investment is maximized.

No property transaction is complete without a tax-effect investigation—both on the property and the income of the parties involved.

KEY TERMS

assessment

ad valorem tax

assessor

property tax role

tax lien

tax sale

tax deed

Tax Reform Act of 1986 (TRA)

Internal Revenue Code (IRC)

active income

passive income

suspended losses

passive loss

at-risk rules

accelerated cost recovery system (ACRS)

investment tax credit

capital gains

CHAPTER PROBLEMS

1. Galena Oaks Corporation constructed apartment units for the purpose of renting them. Because of a factory shutdown in the area, most of the tenants left and the apartments were difficult to rent. Galena sold the

units and treated the gain as capital. The IRS claims the gain is ordinary income. What is the result?

2. Otis and Ethel Wade are considering purchasing a second home in the Catskills. The home will be an A-frame cabin, and they plan to spend 6 to 10 weeks plus 5 to 6 weekends there per year. Currently, the Wades own a home in New Rochelle and have paid off 10 years of their 30-year mortgage. They wish to finance the purchase of the cabin but are concerned that the interest may no longer be deductible. Offer Otis and Ethel an explanation of what TRA did to interest deductions on second homes.

3. Myron and Glenda Warren are interested in refinancing their home. The home has been appraised at $150,000. They bought the home for $97,500 and added a pool for $10,000. Their landscaping cost $7,500, and drapes and flooring cost $3,000. The lender will refinance up to 80 percent of the appraised value. The Warrens want to be certain the full amount of their loan is deductible. How much can they finance and still have fully deductible interest?

4. Roberta Hathaway is a limited partner in a partnership that runs a shopping center. The center had a loss of $600,000 during its first year because tenants were difficult to find. Roberta's share of the loss is $50,000. She will have personal income of $62,000. Can she take the loss, and if so, how much?

5. Suppose that Hathaway was a limited partner in a HUD low-income housing development. Would the result be different?

6. Will the general partner/operating partner in the shopping center be able to deduct his $200,000 portion of the loss? What additional information would you need?

7. A and B each own homes in the same area. A's home is 1550 square feet, and B's home is 2200 square feet. Although the rate of tax is the same, B's assessment is higher than A's. B claims these valuations are unfair because the lots are of the same size and are in the same neighborhood. Is B correct?

8. With reference to problem 7, if B wishes to protest the assessment, what procedures must be followed?

9. A purchased a parcel of property at a tax sale and was given a certificate of sale. A wishes to construct a building on the property, but no lender will lend on the basis of the certificate. Explain why.

18

THE LANDLORD–TENANT RELATIONSHIP

Who is responsible for paying the damages caused by a fire in my apartment—I or my landlord?

What happens if I move out early—before my lease expires?

Can my landlord, without my permission, enter my apartment while I'm gone?

All of the above questions are frequently asked by tenants leasing apartments, homes, and trailers from those who own the property. Although a rental agreement seems like a simple transaction—the tenant pays the rent and the landlord allows the tenant to live on the premises—there are many rights and responsibilities of both parties, which should be clearly understood by them before execution, during performance, and after termination of the lease agreement. This chapter answers the questions, What types of lease agreements exist? What terms should be included in the lease agreement? What rights and responsibilities do each of the parties have? In answering these questions, common law and majority views will be discussed along with the provisions of the Uniform Residential Landlord Tenant Act (URLTA), which has been adopted in fifteen states. This chapter concentrates on residential leases and Chapter 23 deals with commercial leases. The residential tenant has more protections and rights than the commercial tenant.

TYPES OF TENANCIES

The four types of tenancies that existed at common law are discussed in detail in Chapter 2 and are tenancy for years, periodic tenancy, tenancy at will, and tenancy at sufferance.

Tenancy for Years

In a *tenancy for years* (sometimes called a *tenancy for a term*), the parties have agreed that the lease is to run for a specific period of time. A tenancy for years may run for as short as 4 months or as long as 99 years—the length is a matter of agreement between the parties. At the end of the specified period, the lease terminates.

Periodic Tenancy

A *periodic tenancy* is created when the parties agree that rent will be accepted for specific rental periods on a period-at-a-time basis. The length of the period for a periodic tenancy is determined by the time for which the rent is paid. For example, if a landlord accepts rent on a weekly basis, then a week-to-week tenancy results. Accepting rent on a monthly basis results in a month-to-month tenancy. Unless changed by statute, a period tenancy is generally terminated by one of the parties giving a full period's notice of intention to terminate. Thus, on the month-to-month tenancy, a notice of a full month would be required to properly terminate the leasehold relationship.

Often a periodic tenancy will result upon the termination of a tenancy for years, when the tenant does not leave the premises and the landlord continues to accept rent, for example, on a monthly basis. This would be a month-to-month tenancy.

Tenancy at Will

In a *tenancy at will*, a tenant is in possession of the property without any agreement, such as for rent or term of lease. This type of tenancy exists in situations where a lease which should have been in writing (under the Statute of Frauds) but is not, and the tenant still takes possession of the property. Because no valid lease agreement exists, the tenant is there at the will of the landlord. A tenancy at will is converted to a periodic tenancy by the landlord's acceptance of a period's rent.

Tenancy at Sufferance

A *tenant at sufferance* has no right to possession of the property and is in possession only until the landlord orders the tenant's removal. A tenancy at sufferance exists during the time between the expiration of a lease and when the landlord accepts a rental period that begins a periodic tenancy. During this time, the tenant is in possession at the sufferance of the landlord and may be asked to leave at any time. Also, a tenancy at sufferance may exist whenever any of the three types of tenancies end and the tenant remains in possession of the property.

(18.1) Consider:

Walter Epren had a 2-year lease on a service station. At the end of the 2 years, the landlord did not ask Walter to leave and Walter remained, continuing to pay rent on a monthly basis. Just last week, the landlord notified Walter that he would have to be out in 2 months. Walter wishes to know his rights. Using the information just presented and the information in Chapter 2, determine Walter's rights.

TERMS OF THE LEASE AGREEMENT

The Need for a Lease Agreement

Although many leases arise from informal arrangements between the parties, it is best to have a formal lease agreement. There are several reasons why a formal lease agreement will prove beneficial to the parties. First, in many states lease agreements of certain durations must, under the Statute of Frauds, be in writing. The typical requirement for a lease to be in writing is if it runs for a period longer than 1 year. In some states the writing requirement may be imposed at 6 months.

To satisfy the Statute of Frauds, the writing may be informal—in the form of a letter, memorandum, or series of documents. The basics needed are the parties, the signatures of the parties, a description of the leased premises, the term of the lease, and the amount of the rent. The following case deals with the issue of compliance with the Statute of Frauds in a lease agreement.

WILLIAM HENRY BROPHY COLLEGE v. TOVAR
619 P.2d 19 (Ariz. 1980)

Brophy College (plaintiff/appellant) was a devisee in the will of Anastasia Nealon and received title to two parcels of real property through the probate of her will: lots 2337 and 2339 located on East McDowell Road in Phoenix. The Tovars (defendants/appellees) claimed the right to occupy these lots under a purported lease agreement they had with Nick Mercer (purported to be the husband of Anastasia). The Tovars operated an adult bookstore and theater on the premises.

In 1977 most of the property on lots 2337 and 2339 was destroyed by fire and Brophy College gave the Tovars notice of the right of termination on lot 2337 and notice of termination of a periodic tenancy on lot 2339. The notice on 2337 was pursuant to a lease agreement that permitted the tenant to terminate if there was a fire; and the notice for lot 2339 was a period's notice to terminate the periodic tenancy on that lot.

The Tovars claimed there was a lease for lot 2339 included in the lease for lot 2337, since there was a longhand addition to the lease that stated,

"These premises primarily for expansion of Empress Theater 2339 E. McDowell." During their occupancy, the Tovars had spent $1,500 making improvements on lot 2339, including a stage, dressing room, sign, and carpeting. They did not use lot 2339 for 6 to 8 months prior to the fire because of poor business but did pay rent for its use. Tovar testified that he and Mercer had orally agreed that the lease on lot 2337 applied to lot 2339.

The Tovars failed to vacate the premises, and Brophy College brought action in forcible detainer to require the Tovars to leave. The trial court found for the Tovars, and Brophy College appealed.

EUBANK, Presiding Judge

Basically appellants assert that appellees are in possession only as tenants from month to month; that the tenancy was properly terminated; and that the appellees have no further right to possession. They also say that appellees' claimed oral lease of 2339 is void under the Statute of Frauds, and that there is no memorandum thereof sufficient to comply with the statute.

Appellees claim they are entitled to possession of 2339 under either of two theories. One, they have an oral lease with appellants' predecessor in title, which they have partly performed to a sufficient extent to take the lease out of the Statute of Frauds. Two, the written lease of 2337 contains certain handwritten notations which constitute a sufficient "memorandum" within the meaning of the Statute of Frauds to extend the provisions of the 2337 lease to both sets of premises, and thus to create a lease of 2339. . . .

. . . [W]e have no trouble agreeing with the trial court that the Statute of Frauds, A.R.S. §44-101, applies to the purported oral lease of 2339. That section provides in part as follows:

No action shall be brought in any court in the following cases unless the promise or agreement . . . , or some memorandum thereof, is in writing and signed by the party to be charged . . . 5. Upon an agreement which is not to be performed within one year from the making thereof. 6. Upon an agreement for leasing for a longer period than one year.

The minimum essential terms that must appear in the memorandum itself in order to make it sufficient to establish a lease are identification of the property to be leased, the term of the lease, and the rental agreed on.

The only writing claimed to constitute any memorandum here is the series of handwritten notations which were added to the typed lease for 2337. Examination of these notations indicates that they do not in any sense unequivocally set forth the premises to be rented, the rent promised to be paid, or the term of the lease, the essentials for a lease stated above. In our opinion they are clearly insufficient to constitute a memorandum which complies with the Statute of Frauds.

The oral lease is therefore void, unless appellants are estopped from asserting the statute because of appellees' part performance in reliance thereon. Whether this doctrine is labeled "estoppel" or "part performance" does not affect the ultimate result of its application, which is that a party may be precluded from asserting the Statute of Frauds as a defense when he has induced or permitted another to change his position to his detriment in reliance on an oral agreement which could be within the Statute.

In order to take an oral contract out of the Statute of Frauds under this doctrine, the part performance alleged must be unequivocally referable solely to the oral contract. Here, appellees relied on possession, payment of rent, and the making of improvements. Appellants claim that this part performance was not referable solely to the oral lease but instead was merely consistent with appellees' month to month tenancy. Appellees remained in possession and paid rent both before and after the claimed oral lease, and it is true that both of these acts are consistent with a month to month tenancy except for that period of about 6 to 8 months when they continued to pay rent when not using the premises. Payment during that period, we believe, is inconsistent with a month to month tenancy and instead reinforces appellees' claim that they were in possession under a long term lease. Also, their making of improvements of value approaching that of five months' rent is inconsistent with a monthly tenancy and referable, as we see it, to a longer term. We therefore find as a matter of law that the uncontradicted evidence is sufficient to establish part performance of the alleged oral lease by appellees in reliance thereon, and that appellants are estopped from asserting its invalidity under the Statute of Frauds.

The judgment and order are affirmed.

Discussion Questions

1. Who originally owned the property?
2. Who entered into the lease agreement?
3. Who owns the property now?
4. Who are the tenants and how is the property used?
5. What types of leases existed?
6. Was the lease on lot 2339 in writing?
7. What are the exceptions to the Statute of Frauds writing requirement in Arizona?
8. Are any of the exceptions met?
9. What is the significance of the 6- to 8-month period during which lot 2339 was not used?
10. Who prevails?

As the *Brophy* case indicates, if a lease required to be in writing is not in writing, there are exceptions honored by most states as substitutes for writing. But it should be noted that establishing those rights often takes litigation as in the *Brophy* case.

(18.2) Consider:

Edson was in need of a small store for the operation of his video-game repair service. He contacted Perry Development, and Ron Perry indicated that a small store was available in the Westwood Way Plaza and that Edson could rent it for a 3-year term. Perry wrote a letter to Edson confirming the location of the store, the dates of the lease term, the rent, and to whom the rent would be paid. After Edson had occupied the shop 3 months, he received a notice from Perry that the lease would terminate at the end of the fourth month. Edson objected, but Perry maintained that a lease for longer than a year must be in writing, and without a writing Edson was a month-to-month tenant only. Edson wishes to know his rights.

Even though the statute of frauds requires only that leases of certain durations be in writing, all leases should be in writing so that the parties' rights and responsibilities are clearly established. In addition to the minimum requirements for a written lease already mentioned, there are many issues and details upon which the parties should agree before entering into or performing under a lease. In the following sections, various terms and areas of difficulties pertaining to leases are discussed. If the parties do not deal specifically with these issues in a written lease agreement, statutory or common law provisions will apply and the parties may not be afforded the protection or obtain the results they expect.

Habitability

At common law, when tenants leased property the doctrine of caveat tenant applied: tenants leased the premises at their own risk and there were no warranties, covenants, promises, or guarantees that the premises were habitable. The common law did not impose an obligation on the landlord to deliver habitable premises. The effect of this was that many tenants were entering into leases for uninhabitable properties. They were then obligated to the lease and faced with the often difficult task of obtaining repairs and services from the landlord.

To prevent the devastating effects of this doctrine, particularly in areas where there were housing shortages, many cities and state legislatures enacted laws that require landlords to deliver premises to tenants in habitable condition. For example, the following sample regulatory language would prohibit the rental of uninhabitable premises.

> No persons shall rent or offer to rent any habitation, or the furnishings thereof, unless such a habitation and its furnishings are in a clean, safe and sanitary condition, in repair, and free from rodents or vermin.

The effect of a regulation such as this is to make a lease for uninhabitable premises void and thereby excuse the tenant from performing by it.

Even in jurisdictions without a statute that applies specifically to leases, some tenants have been excused from performing lease agreements on other grounds. Leases of premises found to have building or fire code violations have been held void, and courts have excused tenants from performing on the grounds of illegality. For example, in *Pines v. Perssion* 111 N.W.2d 409 (Wis. 1961), four college students leased a home for use as their residence for the school year. The landlord promised that the premises would be repaired in time for the start of the fall semester. When the four tenants arrived for the fall semester, the home was in a state of complete disrepair. An attorney advised the students to have the home inspected, and a building inspector found many violations including inadequate wiring, broken plumbing, faulty stair handrails, and lack of windows and screens. The court excused the students from performing on the grounds that the violations of the building code made a lease of the premises void.

Under a third and final theory for requiring landlords to deliver habitable premises, some states have ruled that an *implied warranty of habitability* exists in all lease agreements. The following is a landmark case in which the issue of this modern implied warranty was involved.

LEMLE v. BREEDEN

462 P.2d 470 (Hawaii 1969)

Mrs. Breeden (defendant/appellant) owned a house in the Diamond Head area of Honolulu, which she rented to Lemle (plaintiff/appellee) for $800 per month for the periods from 22 September 1964 to 20 March 1965 and from 17 April 1965 to 12 June 1965. The terms were agreed to on 21 September 1964, and that day Lemle paid Breeden's agent $1,900 for a deposit and prepaid rent.

The dwelling consists of several structures containing six bedrooms, six baths, a living room, kitchen, dining room, garage and saltwater swimming pool. The main dwelling is constructed in Tahitian style with a corrugated metal roof over which coconut leaves have been woven together for a grass shack effect. The house is relatively open without screening on windows or doorways.

Lemle, his wife, and four children moved into the home on 22 September 1964. That evening it became abundantly evident to Lemle that there were rats within the main dwelling and on the roof. During the night and the next 2 nights, Lemle and his family were sufficiently apprehensive of the rats that they slept together in the downstairs living room. They saw and heard rats on all 3 nights.

On 23 September 1964 Breeden's agent hired a firm to exterminate the dwelling and Lemle himself set traps, but the next 2 nights were no better. After the 3 nights, Lemle and his family left the dwelling and sought the refund of their $1,900. Upon Breeden's refusal to return the money, Lemle brought suit. The trial judge found there was an implied warranty of habitability and ordered Breeden to return the money plus interest. Breeden appealed.

LEVINSON, Justice

The rule of caveat emptor in lease transactions at one time may have had some basis in social practice as well as in historical doctrine. . . . Yet in urban society where the vast majority of tenants do not reap the rent directly from the land but bargain primarily for the right to enjoy the premises for living purposes, often signing standardized leases, as in this case, common law conceptions of a lease and the tenant's liability for rent are no longer viable.

In the law of sales of chattels, the trend is markedly in favor of implying warranties of fitness and merchantability. The reasoning has been (1) that the public interest in safety and consumer protection requires it, and (2) that the burden ought to be shifted to the manufacturer, who, by placing the goods on the market, represents their suitability and fitness. The manufacturer is also the one who knows more about the product and is in a better position to alleviate problems or bear the brunt of any losses. The same reasoning is equally persuasive in leases of real property.

The application of an implied warranty of habitability in leases gives recognition to the changes in leasing transactions today. It affirms the fact that a lease is, in essence, a sale as well as a transfer of an estate in land and is, more importantly a contractual relationship. From that contractual relationship an implied warranty of habitability and fitness for the purposes intended is a just and necessary implication. Legal fictions and artifical exceptions to wooden rules of property law aside, we hold that in the lease of a dwelling, such as in this case, there is an implied warranty of habitability and fitness intended.

Here the facts demonstrate the un-inhabitability and unfitness of the premises for residential purposes. For three sleepless nights the plaintiff and his family literally camped in the living room. They were unable to sleep in the proper quarters or make use of the other facilities in the house due to the natural apprehension of the rats which made noise scurrying about on the roof and invaded the house through the unscreened openings.

The defendant makes much of the point that the source of the rats was the beach rocks and surrounding foliage. She contended that this exonerated her from the duty to keep the house free of rats. While it is not clear where the rats came from, assuming that they did originate from outside the premises, the defendant had it within her power to keep them out by proper and timely screening and extermination procedures. But to begin such procedures after the plaintiff had occupied the dwelling and to expect that he have the requisite patience and fortitude in the face of trial and error methods of extermination was too much to ask.

When the premises were vacated, they were not fit for use as a residence. Nor was there any assurance that the residence would become habitable within a reasonable time.

Affirmed.

Discussion Questions

1. Who is the landlord? Who are the tenants?
2. Describe the property being leased.
3. What are the terms of the rental agreement?
4. How much was paid initially?
5. What problem did the tenants experience?
6. How long did the tenants stay on the property?
7. Why did the tenants leave?
8. Can the tenants have their money returned and be excused from the lease?
9. What theory is applied and what precedent is used for its application?

Not all states have passed statutes on habitability or follow the idea of implied habitability as established in the *Lemle* case. Therefore, tenants desiring protection against uninhabitable premises in states not affording protections should provide for habitability as a term for performance in their lease agreement. The clause may be simple, as the following language indicates: "Owner (landlord) agrees to deliver premises to tenant in a fit and habitable condition."

If the tenant has the opportunity to inspect the premises prior to entering into the lease agreement, a clause may be added requiring the landlord to make certain repairs and adjustments prior to the tenant's taking possession. To the just-mentioned habitability clause, the following language might be added: "Owner (landlord) agrees to repair the following or make the following changes prior to the date of the tenant's possession: . . ." The following case discusses a refinement of the tenant's rights under the implied warranty of habitability.

ARMSTRONG v. CIONE
736 P.2d 440 (Hawaii 1987)

Adam Armstrong (plaintiff/appellant) rented Apartment 103-A located at 441 Kanekapolei Street in Honolulu from Jack Cione (defendant/appellee). The apartment was originally part of a 2-bedroom unit within a cooperative building called the Waikiki Regent, which was constructed in 1959 and contained nine identical units. The apartment resulted from a conversion of one of the 2-bedroom units into two 1-bedroom units, 103-A and 103-B, by a previous owner.

In 1981, Cione rented 103-A to Tom Cesar who occupied it until March 1982. Armstrong had been a guest of Cesar's on many occasions and took over the apartment in March 1982.

On 12 April 1982, Armstrong's right hand and wrist were injured when a glass panel in the apartment's shower door shattered as he attempted to close it. The shower door was installed when the apartment was originally built and was constructed of three glass panels with hinged aluminum frames on an aluminum track. Safety glass was not used.

Cione says he was unaware of a crack in the door and Armstrong knew the door was difficult to close but never complained to Cione about the problem.

The trial court found for Cione and Armstrong appealed.

HEEN, Judge

A cause of action for a breach of implied warranty of habitability is based upon an entirely independent legal theory and involves different legal issues from those in a cause of action for negligence. Under the law of implied warranty of habitability, the defect or unsafe condition "must be of a nature or kind which will render the premises unsafe, or unsanitary and thus unfit for living therein" (*Kline v. Burns*, 111 N.H. 87, 92, 276 A.2d 248, 252 [1971]). The premises must be substantially unsuitable for living so that the breach of the warranty would constitute a constructive eviction of the tenant. Not "every transient inconvenience of living attributable to the condition of the premises will be a legitimate subject of litigation. The warranty is one of habitability and is not a warranty against all inconvenience or discomfort." A cause of action for negligence against a landlord on the other hand is based upon an injury to person or property caused by the landlord's breach of a duty to maintain the rental premises in safe condition.

The jury's verdict was not "irreconcilable" and the cases cited by Plaintiff in support of his argument are inapposite. The jury apparently found that Defendant was negligent because the shower door was unsafe, but that the shower door did not render the apartment uninhabitable so as to cause a constructive eviction and, therefore, there was no breach of implied warranty of habitability. The denial of the motion for new trial was properly granted.

Affirmed.

Discussion Questions

1. Was the apartment originally part of the building's construction?
2. Was anyone aware of a problem with the door?
3. Was the landlord aware of the problem?
4. Does the problem fit the requirements of breach of the implied warranty of habitability?
5. Would the result have been different if Cione had been aware of the problem?
6. Does Armstrong's living there so long hurt his case?

(18.3) Consider:

Del Bosco purchased a car dealership and the property on which it was located. Included in the real property was a one-bedroom house, which was occupied by a 60-year-old widow who had paid the previous owner $65 per month for rent out of her total monthly income of $123. Del Bosco allowed the widow to remain but indicated no repairs would be made. A building inspector inspected the home, found it to be in "atrocious" condition, and ordered Del Bosco to make the repairs within 60 days or occupation of the premises would be unlawful.

At the end of the 60 days, no repairs had been made and the widow withheld her rent. Del Bosco was warned to make the repairs but he instead decided to level the building. He brought an action to have the widow evicted for nonpayment of rent. The widow claimed the nonpayment was due to the uninhabitable condition of the property and maintained she could not be evicted. What was the result?

Deposits

Most tenants are required to make some type of deposit when initially entering into a lease agreement. The types of deposits include the security deposit, the cleaning deposit, and prepaid rent.

Security Deposit The deposit most frequently made is the *security deposit*. The purpose is to protect the landlord in the event of property damage or in the event a tenant terminates a lease agreement early. The money held on deposit as security may be used to cover expenses or damages.

In some states, security deposits are regulated to a great extent; while in other states, it is the responsibility of the parties to agree on the purpose and effect of the security deposit. For example, under the *Uniform Residential Landlord Tenant Act (URLTA)* there is a provision that limits the amount of a security deposit that the landlord is permitted to demand. Section 2.101(a) provides, "A landlord may not demand or receive security, however denominated, in an amount or value in excess of (one) month['s] period."

Once landlords have obtained a security deposit, they will remain in possession of it until the termination of the underlying lease agreement. There are considerable differences between the states as to landlords' uses and obligations regarding security deposits received by tenants. The common law rule is that the landlord is a debtor to the tenant for the security deposit and is free to use the funds as if they were the landlord's own. However, some states have enacted legislation requiring landlords to pay tenants a minimum amount of interest (such as 5 percent) for the time the deposit is held. Some states also require landlords to keep the security deposits in special trust accounts and maintain and submit periodic records of their balances and deposits received.

States also differ on their definitions of what constitutes a security deposit. For example, in some states prepaid rent is considered part of the security deposit, and in other states the landlord is not required to follow security deposit procedures on funds labeled prepaid rent.

The security deposit may encourage a tenant to perform according to the terms of the lease; for if the tenant breaches the lease agreement, the landlord may according to the lease provisions keep the security deposit as liquidated damages. Parties to a lease are free to agree on damage provisions, and a liquidated damage clause is an advance agreement between the parties of how a breach will be determined and what the breach damages will be. The lease may provide that the liquidated damages for breach will be the security deposit. For example, if a tenant leases an apartment for $300 per month for a 6-month period and abandons the premises at 4 months, the landlord is entitled, with a proper liquidated damage provision in the lease, to keep the security deposit as damages for early termination by the tenant. When early termination occurs, it is uncertain whether the landlord will suffer any damages (the apartment could be rerented the next day or could sit vacant for the remaining 2 months of the terminated tenancy). Thus, an agreement to keep the security deposit as damages is a valid liquidated damage clause because it is unclear how much the damages (if any) will be.

In some states and under the URLTA, the landlord's retention of a security deposit, for whatever reason, is subject to regulation. Sections 2.101(b) and 2.101(c) of the URLTA provide:

> (b) Upon termination of the tenancy property or money held by the landlord as prepaid rent and security may be applied to the payment of accrued rent and the amount of damages which the landlord has suffered by reason of the tenant's noncompliance with section 3.101 all as itemized by the landlord in a written notice delivered to the tenant together with the amount due [14] days after termination of the tenancy and delivery of possession and demand by the tenant.
>
> (c) If the landlord fails to comply with the above subsection (b) or if he fails to return any prepaid rent required to be paid to the tenants under this Act, the tenant may recover the property and money due him together with damages in an amount equal to [twice] the amount wrongfully withheld and reasonable attorneys' fees.

It is important to note that if the landlord chooses the remedy provided by the above sections (that of keeping the security deposit), then the landlord is limited to the amount of the security deposit as damages. To attempt to collect actual damages as well as keeping the security deposit as damages would be assessing a void penalty for breach. Thus, a landlord is not entitled to both liquidated and actual damages. Furthermore, as provided by the URLTA, retention of the security deposit requires the landlord to account the reasons and the amounts to the tenant.

Leases should specify what amounts are being taken and for what purposes. The following language is an example of the type of clause necessary to establish that funds are being taken as a security deposit:

> SECURITY: In order to guarantee Resident's faithful performance of the terms and conditions contained herein, Resident hereby deposits with owner the sum of $_____ as a security deposit to be applied to the payment of accrued but unpaid rent and any other damages suffered by reason of Resident's noncompliance or breach of any terms and conditions of the Rental Agreement.

If there are no statutory provisions governing security deposits in the state, the parties should specify in the lease agreement their rights to the security deposit, including procedures and time limitations for its use and return and its effect as a provision for liquidated damages.

(18.4) Consider:

Barbara Kent and her roommate Sheila Barnes have signed a 9-month lease on an apartment. The rent is $350 per month, and the roommates were required to make a $500 security deposit. At the end of 4 months, they decide to move to a house closer to their places of employment. The apartment owner is unable to lease the apartment for 3 months, and the apartment is vacant for that time. Discuss the use of the security deposit to cover damages according to the laws of your state.

Cleaning Deposits In addition to security deposits, which are intended to secure rental payments, landlords may require tenants to make other deposits before occupying the leased property. A *cleaning deposit* is a typical lease requirement and may take the form of a nonrefundable fee that all tenants are required to pay. Under the URLTA, a nonrefundable cleaning deposit must be stated as such in the lease agreement. The following is a sample clause from a lease: "Additionally, Resident hereby pays the sum of $_____, which is a NON-REFUNDABLE decorating fee." The fees paid may be called cleaning, refurbishing, redecorating, or restoration fees but they all require advance disclosure of retention under the URLTA.

Some cleaning fees are taken with the idea that they will be used, if necessary, at the time the tenant vacates the premises. The theory behind this type of deposit is that tenants will have greater incentive to keep the premises clean and well-maintained and not destroy items of property. For example, some leases contain addendums that specify cleaning costs to be assessed if, at the end of the lease and upon the landlord's inspection, specific cleaning tasks are necessary. Specific items such as drapery cleaning or wall repainting may be specified as a dollar amount, so that tenants will know the potential assessments in advance.

Prepaid Rent Many landlords require tenants to pay the first and last months' rent prior to taking possession of the property. Such a provision is for the protection of the landlord in the event the tenant vacates the premises without paying rent. However, the URLTA and many other states' provisions limit the amount of prepaid rent or total deposits that may be required of the tenant initially, and the limit may be as small as 1-1/2 times the monthly rent. The lease agreement or an addendum to it should specify exactly what amounts are being received from the tenant, and the purpose and application of those amounts.

Amount of Rent

In addition to specifying the amount of prepaid rent, the lease agreement should specify the monthly rental fee. The amount of rent becomes more of an issue in commercial leases where landlords are entitled to portions of profits. (See Chapter 23.) Residential lease agreements should specify how much rent is to be paid, the date the rent is due, to whom the rent is to be paid, and if there are any fees associated with late rental payments. The following is a sample rental fee clause that includes the necessary terms for rental payments.

> RENTAL: The rental shall be $_____ per month, plus sales tax thereon at the rate in effect from time to time, payable in advance on the FIRST day of each month at the on-site manager's office. An equitable pro-ration of the first month's rent shall be made if the term of this Rental Agreement commences other than on the first day of the calendar month. A late charge of $2.00 per day shall be added as additional rent to any monthly rent payment not paid in full on or before the due date. A $10.00 fee will be charged for all checks returned from the bank unpaid. Management reserves the right to demand that all sums due under the lease be paid in cash and to return any check previously accepted by Management and demand cash.

Practical items such as returned checks and late payments are covered in the clause and help eliminate many of the issues that arise in rental payments.

Lease Term

The portion of the lease agreement that specifies the term may simply state the beginning and ending dates of the lease. However, additional language is necessary if the tenant is to be given the option to renew. The option to renew should specify when the option must be exercised, how it is to be exercised, and how the rental amount for the option period is to be computed. In addition, the length or maximum length of the option period should be specified.

An option may be created and exercised in the informal manner of a periodic tenancy. Thus the lease term clause might also provide for the effect of a holdover tenant, the rent that will be due, and how the tenant may be required to leave. For example, the following clause would take care of the problems associated with an implied option to renew arising through the hold-over tenant:

> HOLDOVER: Either Management or Resident may terminate this Rental Agreement at the end of the above-stated term by giving to the other at least thirty (30) days prior written notice, but in default of such notice this Rental Agreement shall continue on a month-to-month basis until terminated by either party by giving to the other written notice at least thirty (30) days prior to the end of a monthly rental period.

In this clause the parties have specified how termination is to occur properly. One additional item that should be specified in this type of clause is to whom the notice of termination or option to renew is to be given, and whether it must be done in writing and mailed or in writing and personally given to the designated party.

Attorneys' Fees

In spite of careful drafting and execution of lease agreements, there is still the possibility of litigation. All leases should make provisions for the payment of costs and attorneys' fees in the event litigation on the lease becomes necessary. The following clause is an example of an attorneys' fee provision:

> If legal action is necessary to enforce compliance with this Rental Agreement, and judgment is rendered against Resident, Management shall be entitled to recover reasonable attorneys' fees in an amount determined by the court, and the amount of said award shall be regarded as accrued rent.

In states where attorneys' fees cannot be collected in contract actions, these clauses are unenforceable.

One of the problems with the preceding provision from a tenant's standpoint is that it is one-sided and affords fees for a prevailing landlord but not for a prevailing tenant. Another type of clause, which benefits both parties, is as follows:

> In the event legal action is necessary for the enforcement of rights and obligations granted under this agreement, the prevailing party shall be entitled an award including attorneys' fees and all attendant court costs regardless of the stage to which the legal action proceeds.

Rules and Regulations

Particularly in apartment complexes, it is necessary for smooth functioning of joint facilities and for each tenant's peaceful enjoyment of the property that all residents comply with certain rules and regulations on the use of the property. Under the Uniform Residential Landlord Tenant Act (URLTA) and most state statutes, landlords are permitted to promulgate rules by which tenants must abide for the smooth operation of the rented property. Section 3.102 of the URLTA states:

    (a)   A landlord, from time to time, may adopt a rule or regulation, however described, concerning the tenant's use and occupancy of the premises. It is enforceable against the tenant only if:

        1.   its purpose is to promote the convenience, safety or welfare of the tenants in the premises, preserve the landlord's prop-

erty from abusive use or make a fair distribution of services and facilities held out for the tenants generally;

2. it is reasonably related to the purpose for which adopted;

3. it applies to all tenants in the premises in a fair manner;

4. it is sufficiently explicit in prohibition, direction or limitation of the tenant's conduct to fairly inform him of what he must or must not do to comply;

5. it is not for the purpose of evading the obligations of the landlord;

6. the tenant has notice of it at the time he enters into the rental agreement, or when it is adopted.

(b) If a rule or regulation is adopted after the tenant enters into the rental agreement that works a substantial modification of his bargain it is not valid unless the tenant consents to it in writing.

Rules and regulations may be incorporated into the lease agreement in three ways:

1. They may actually be written into the section of the lease agreement on the applicability of rules and regulations.

2. They may be incorporated as an addendum or a schedule to the lease agreement.

3. They may be mentioned in the lease agreement as existing. In this case, it is specified that compliance is required and that the tenant has been given a copy of the rules and regulations or that they are posted in an accessible location.

The types of rules and regulations that are typical and meet the standards of the URLTA are hours of pool use, use of laundry facilities, parking regulations, and noise and pet restrictions.

As noted in the URLTA section quoted earlier, rules may be changed after a lease agreement is executed and still be enforceable against existing tenants. The tenants must be given notice of the change of rules; and so long as the change does not alter the basics of the lease agreements, it is applicable to both existing and subsequent tenants occupying the premises. A notice of change should be sent directly to each tenant.

Landlord's Right of Access

Although landlords own the property, tenants have the exclusive rights of possession even as against the landlords so long as a valid lease agreement exists. This principle of exclusive possession was applied at common law and has been codified in many states to protect tenants from landlords' unauthorized entry onto leased premises. For example, the following provisions appear in Section 3.103 of the URLTA:

(a) A tenant shall not unreasonably withhold consent to the landlord to enter into the dwelling unit in order to inspect the premises, make necessary or agreed repairs, decorations, alterations or improvements, supply necessary or agreed services or exhibit the dwelling unit to prospective or actual purchasers, mortgagees, tenants, workmen or contractors.

(b) A landlord may enter the dwelling unit without consent of the tenant in case of emergency.

(c) A landlord shall not abuse the right to access or use it to harass the tenant. Except in case of emergency or if it is impracticable to do so, the landlord shall give the tenant at least (2) days' notice of his intent to enter and enter only at reasonable times.

(d) A landlord has no other right of access except (1) pursuant to court order (2) as provided by section 4.202 and section 4.203 (b) or (3) unless the tenant has abandoned or surrendered the premises.

Basically, under the URLTA and other similar state statutes, the landlord is required to give advance notice and must be entering the dwelling unit for the purpose of repair, cleaning, or redecorating.

In the lease agreement, the parties are free to agree to other terms of entry and arrangements for entry, and in most states these terms will be enforceable so long as the tenant has not been required to give up any statutorily protected rights. Figure 18.1 is a sample residential lease.

Assignments and Subleases

Assignments and *subleases* are similar in that they both bring third parties into the landlord–tenant relationship. However, there is a distinction between the two processes: In an assignment, tenants actually transfer their leasehold interests to third parties who will take over all obligations and assume all benefits associated with the original lease. In a subleasing arrangement, the tenants give up only a portion of their leasehold estate. For example, a tenant with a 3-year lease sublets the leased premises to someone who resides there while the tenant is studying in Europe for 1 year. But if the tenant remains in Europe and the other party takes over the remaining 1-1/2 years on the lease, then an assignment has occurred. Regardless of the label the parties give to the transfer of interest, the issue of whether an assignment or a sublease has occurred is one for the courts.

A leasehold interest at common law was freely alienable; thus, both

Figure 18.1 Sample Residential Lease

BUILDING MANAGEMENT SERVICES, INC. Scottsdale, Arizona INCOME PROPERTY MANAGEMENT	TOTAL MONTHLY RENTAL		COMPLEX NAME	
	Apartment Rent			
			INDIVIDUAL'S NAME(S)	

BMS USE ONLY	DEPOSIT REQUIREMENTS		Furniture			
	Security		* Other			
	Preparation Fee		TOTAL RENTAL (Sub Total)		APARTMENT NO.	APARTMENT TYPE
	PET ___ Pets @ $ ___		Tax			
	TOTAL DEPOSIT		TOTAL MONTHLY PAYMENT		TERM OF LEASE BEGINNING DATE	ENDING DATE

*Utility adjustments to be inserted when and if applicable.

APARTMENT RENTAL AGREEMENT

Building Management Services, Inc., as manager and agent (hereinafter called "Management") for the Owner, hereby rents to Resident(s), and Resident(s) hereby rents from Owner, apartment #___ of _____ Apartments, located at _____ to be used solely for the purpose of a personal residence by___ persons, upon the following terms and conditions:

1. TERM: The term of this agreement shall be ____ months, commencing and ending on the dates indicated above.

2. RENTAL: The rental shall be $_____ per month, plus sales tax thereon at the rate in effect from time to time, payable in advance on or before the FIRST day of each month at the on-site manager's office. An equitable proration of the first month's rent shall be made if the term of this Rental Agreement commences other than on the 1st day of the calendar month. A late charge of $2.00 per day shall be added as additional rent to any monthly rent payment not paid in full on or before the due date. A $15.00 fee will be charged for all checks returned from the bank unpaid. Management reserves the right to demand that all sums due under this lease be paid in cash and to return any check previously accepted by Management and demand cash.

3. SECURITY: In order to guarantee Resident's faithful performance of the terms and conditions contained herein, Resident hereby deposits with Owner the sum of $_____ as a security deposit, to be applied to the payment of accrued but unpaid rent and any other damages suffered by reason of Resident's NON-compliance or breach of any of the terms and conditions of the Rental Agreement. Additionally, Resident hereby pays the sum of $_____ which is a NON-REFUNDABLE preparation fee. Resident understands and agrees that without Management's written consent, the security deposit may not be used by Resident as credit for rent owed prior to the termination or expiration of this Rental Agreement. Owner shall hold the security deposit in his personal savings or checking account, and interest, if any, accrued on such deposit shall belong to the Owner.

4. UTILITIES: Resident shall be responsible for contracting for electrical power service for the subject unit at the commencement of the tenancy and shall be responsible for maintaining such service and paying all deposits and fees required by the utility for such service throughout the entire tenancy. Management may require proof of transfer of the electrical service by time of movein. Management is not responsible for arranging for electrical service, nor for any charges for such service during the entire tenancy. If, for any reason, Resident fails to maintain electrical service at any time during the tenancy or fails to meet payment obligations for the same, Management may, at its option, treat such non-payment as a non-payment of rent and may proceed with remedies allowed as to non-payment of rent under provisions of A.R.S. Sec. 33-1368 or other provisions allowed by law or in equity.

5. CARE OF PREMISES:
(a) Resident shall not decorate or alter the leased premises without permission in writing from Management. Further, Resident shall comply with all State statutes and City ordinances which are applicable to the premises. Resident has carefully inspected the premises and finds them to be in a clean, rentable, undamaged condition except as may be noted otherwise at the end of this Rental Agreement. (Schedule D, Apartment Inventory and Damages). Neither the Owner nor Management shall be liable to Resident or Resident's licensees and invitees for any damage to person or property caused by the act or neglect of any other resident or non-resident at the apartments, and Resident, having inspected the premises, accepts the same as suitable for the purposes for which they were rented.
(b) Resident agrees to exercise reasonable care in his use of the premises and to maintain and redeliver the same in clean, safe and undamaged condition, free from unsightly debris, equipment or decor. Resident agrees to pay for all repairs, replacements and maintenance caused by his misconduct or negligence, or that of his family, pets, licensees, and invitees, and, at Management's option, such charges shall be paid immediately or regarded as additional rent to be paid no later than the monthly rent payment date next following such repairs.
(c) Resident shall maintain the leased premises in a clean and safe condition at all times.
(d) The leased premises is for residential use only. No business or commercial enterprise may be conducted from or upon the leased premises.

6. HOLDOVER: Either Management or Resident may terminate this Rental Agreement at the end of the above-stated term by giving to the other at least thirty (30) days prior written notice, but in default of such notice this Rental Agreement shall continue on a month-to-month basis until terminated by either party giving to the other written notice at least thirty (30) days prior to the end of a monthly rental period.

7. ACCESS: Resident shall not unreasonably withhold consent to Management, or Management's authorized representatives, to enter the premises to inspect the same, make necessary or agreed repairs, decorations, alterations, or improvements, supply necessary or agreed services or exhibit the premises to prospective or actual purchasers, mortgagees, residents, workmen or contractors. Resident hereby agrees that his notification to Management of service or maintenance requirements within his premises simultaneously grants authority to enter said premises at times determined by Management for the specific and sole purpose of that requirement during all reasonable hours. Management shall otherwise give Resident at least two days notice of its intent of access except in cases of emergencies, or where notice would be impractical, or where the Resident has abandoned the premises or has failed to properly maintain the premises.

8. ABANDONMENT: "Abandonment" means absence of Resident from the dwelling unit, without notice to Management for at least 7 days, if rent for the unit is outstanding and unpaid for 10 days and there is no reasonable evidence, other than presence of the Resident's personal property, that the Resident is occupying the unit. Such abandonment shall not constitute "surrender" without consent of Management. In the event of abandonment, Management shall be entitled to all remedies at law or in equity, including those under A.R.S. Sec. 33-1370. Additionally, if any personal property abandoned by Resident is determined by Management to be of less value than the cost of moving, storage and conducting a sale thereof, Management may destroy or otherwise dispose of any or all of the abandoned property.

9. ATTORNEY'S FEES: In the event of legal action to enforce compliance with this Rental Agreement, the prevailing party may be awarded court costs and reasonable attorney's fees.

10. WAIVER: Time is expressly made of the essence with respect to Resident's performance of any term or condition of this Rental Agreement. Waiver by Management or its agents of any covenant or condition, or the giving of consent or approval with respect to any act of Resident which required the approval or consent of Management, shall not be deemed to waive or render unnecessary Management's consent or approval to or of any subsequent act by Resident. In addition to the foregoing, it is specifically understood and agreed that Management's acceptance of any rental payment which is less than the entire amount of rent then due shall not consequent partial payment unless, upon accepting said partial payment, Management, or its authorized agent, expressly and in writing then and there agrees with Resident not to terminate by virtue of receiving but a partial payment; and, without such a written agreement, the terms of this paragraph shall be deemed repeated and remade upon the payment of each rental installment due hereunder, whether or not the payment thereof is partial, and the acceptance of any rent owed hereunder, whether in whole or in part, shall not be deemed a waiver of any preceding breach by Resident of any term or provision of this Rental Agreement.

11. MISCELLANEOUS:
(a) Resident shall have the privilege of termination of this Rental Agreement due to permanent change of employment assignment outside the Phoenix metropolitan area, provided Resident notified Management of his intent to terminate this Rental Agreement, in writing in a form provided by Management, thirty (30) days prior to actual vacation of the premises. Such a termination shall be at the end of a monthly rental period, and the notice to terminate this lease shall be accompanied by a copy of the Resident's orders to be transferred outside the Phoenix metropolitan area.

Figure 18.1 (continued)

(b) Owner and/or Management may discontinue any and all facilities furnished and services rendered by Owner and/or Management not expressly covenanted for herein or required to be supplied under the Arizona Residential Landlord/Tenant Act, it being understood that they constitute no part of the consideration for this Rental Agreement.

(c) Where there is more than one Resident under this Rental Agreement, rent and other charges shall, when paid by check, be paid in totem by a single instrument. Where there is more than one Resident, the full refundable portion of any security deposit for the Apartment unit may be returned to any one of such Residents.

(d) This Rental Agreement shall be binding upon the parties hereto and their respective heirs, executors, successors and assigns. All rights given therein to Management shall also extend and inure to the benefit of the Owner of the apartments, or to any other person designated by Owner and/or Management as the recipient of said rights, and their respective assigns and successors in interest. Resident may not assign this Rental Agreement or sub-let the premises, in whole or in part, without the prior written consent of Management. Each of the obligations imposed on Resident hereunder or in the Rules and Regulations is to be regarded as material in nature and the violation of any one or more of such obligations shall entitle Owner to exercise any and all available remedies, including the termination of this Rental Agreement and recovery of stipulated damages.

12. RESIDENT HOUSE RULES: The rules provided in Schedule "B" are for the mutual benefit of all residents. Schedule "B" is deemed a part hereof of this lease and violations or breaches of any rule shall constitute a default hereunder.

13. DISCLOSURE: In compliance with the provisions of Arizona Revised Statutes 33-1322, it is hereby disclosed to Resident that the Manager of these apartment premises is Building Management Services, Inc., located at 3225 N. 75th Street, Suite 4, Scottsdale, Arizona 85251. Said Manager is authorized to act for the Owner for purposes of services and receiving notices. To be effective, all notices provided for herein shall be in writing and shall be delivered to the Manager at the address indicated above and to the Resident at the residential unit leased herein. Notices shall be sent by certified mail, return receipt requested, or personally delivered and receipted for, or as otherwise provided in Arizona Statutes 33-1313.

14. INDEMNIFICATION: Management shall not be liable for any damage or injury to tenant, or any other person, or to any property, occurring on the premises, or any part thereof, or in the common areas thereof, unless such damage is the proximate result of gross negligence or unlawful act of management, its agents, or employees. Resident agrees to hold management harmless from any and all claims for damages no matter how caused, except for injury or damages for which management is legally responsible.

15. SUBORDINATION: This Rental Agreement is and shall remain subordinate to any ground lease, mortgage, deed of trust, agreement for sale, or other encumbrance now existing or hereafter to be placed upon the unit and to any modifications, extensions, replacements and advances in connection therewith.

16. SEVERABILITY: Should any provisions of this Rental Agreement be held to be void, invalid or unenforceable, the same shall not affect any other provisions contained herein.

17. INSURANCE: Resident agrees to carry a Homeowner/Tenant's Insurance Policy with the minimum limits of liability in the amount of $50,000.00 for bodily injury and personal damage liability and adequate coverage to insure all interior furnishings and appliances, decorations, and other items provided by Management, as well as to insure the Resident's own personal property.

18. BANKRUPTCY: This Apartment Rental Agreement, and any rights arising out of this tenancy, shall not become an asset in bankruptcy. In the event a petition is filed by or against Resident, or if a receiver is appointed as to the assets of Resident, this lease shall, at the election of Management, terminate and Management may proceed to recover possession of the subject unit.

SCHEDULE "A"   SECURITY DEPOSIT REQUIREMENTS

Listed below is the procedure necessary to assure the return of the refundable portion of your security deposit:

After fulfilling all terms and conditions as outlined in this agreement, resident shall:

Step A: Thirty (30) days prior to vacating your apartment notify your manager in writing of your intention to vacate your apartment and fill in and sign the Manager's copy of the "Notice of Intention to Vacate" form provided you at the time.

Step B: At the time you are vacating the apartment:

1. The apartment must be left in a clean and rentable condition. Use the checklist provided by the Manager.
2. There will be a charge for any damage to the apartment and furniture located therein which is not deemed to be normal wear and tear.
3. Return your keys at the moveout time. A lost key charge of $5.00 will be assessed for each mail box and apartment key not returned.
4. Your apartment will be inspected after you have vacated the premises by you and the Manager. All of the refundable deposit(s) due you will be mailed as required by law, to the address furnished on the "Deposit Request".

SCHEDULE "B"   RESIDENT HOUSE RULES

1. All tenancies commence at 10:00 a.m. and terminate at 10:00 a.m.
2. The sidewalks, driveways, passages and common areas shall not be obstucted nor used for any purpose other than inress and egress to and from units.
3. Resident agrees that Management has the right to control the method and manner of parking in the parking spaces in and around the premises, and to designate what portion of the premises may be used by the Resident, his family and guests, for parking, and to tow away and store at the Resident's expense any vehicle parked by Resident, his family or guests, in spaces not so authorized by Management. Resident acknowledges that Management is not responsible for vehicles, or other items kept or stored outside the unit, and Resident hereby waives any claims against Management for damages or loss in connection herewith. No disabled or unregistered motor vehicle shall be allowed on the premises of the community for more than 48 hours. No repair work or washing of vehicles on the premises is permitted without consent of the resident manager. "Head-in" parking is required in all parking spaces.
4. Signs, advertisements or notices by the Resident shall not be painted or affixed upon any part of the building, outside or inside, nor shall any article be suspended outside the buildings or placed on the window sills thereof. Do not install any outside aerials, wires or equipment in connection with any radio or television or make any outside installation.
5. Please conduct yourself and your guests in such a manner that you will not disturb your neighbor's peaceful enjoyment of our community. Noisy, disorderly or offensive conduct, or conduct annoying or disturbing to other tenants shall be grounds for termination of occupancy. Excessive vocal or instrumental music will not be permitted.
6. Pets are prohibited in the buildings or on grounds anytime, except by written consent of the Management and subject to special rules outlined in a separate agreement.
7. Resident will replace or pay for (at Management's option) breakage, loss or damage done to furniture, drapes, carpeting, kitchen utensils, glass, locks, keys or other items in the unit. Locks may not be altered or changed without prior written consent of Management.
8. The pools are for the exclusive use of Residents. Rules and regulations regarding use of swimming pools are posted and must be complied with. Children under age 18 must be accompanied by a resident adult at all times when on grounds, in the pools, or in the recreation building. Use of pool facilities by guests requires advance permission of Management. Management may deny use of the pool to anyone for reasonable cause.
9. All gates must be kept closed except when in continuous use.
10. Clothes lines shall not be permitted nor shall laundry be hung over patios or balconies or railings. Along the same lines, you may use your own draperies as long as they have a white liner. Do not put up tinfoil, signs, paper or obstructions in the windows.
11. Digging in any area is prohibited.
12. Laundry facilities shall be left clean after each use.
13. Trash is to be placed in dumpsters located conveniently around the grounds.
14. Overnight house guests or residents must be limited to two (2) persons for two (2) nights only, except by prior permission by Management. Additional rent may be assessed in the amount of $5.00 per day, per person.
15. Efficient and prudent use of utilities is required.
16. These rules are subject to change by Management upon resonable notice.
17. The Management reserves the right to require cash, certified or cashier's checks in the payment of any amount due under the Agreement.
18. By entering into possession, each Resident agrees to be bound by these rules. Any breach hereof shall be deemed a default by Resident under the terms of his Rental agreement or occupancy. Management may deny use of such remedies provided by law as Management shall elect to pursue.
19. This agreement shall be subject to, if applicable, the current resident vacating the premises as scheduled.

THE RESIDENT MANAGER IS ONLY AUTHORIZED TO EXECUTE A MONTH TO MONTH RENTAL AGREEMENT ON BEHALF OF MANAGEMENT. ANY AGREEMENT EXECUTED BY THE RESIDENT MANAGER IN EXCESS OF A MONTH-TO-MONTH TENANCY IS VOID. ALL RENTAL AGREEMENTS FOR TENANCIES GREATER THAN MONTH TO MONTH MUST BE EXECUTED BY AN OFFICER OF BUILDING MANAGEMENT SERVICES, INC. AT THE CORPORATE OFFICES SITUATED AT 3225 NORTH 75th STREET, SCOTTSDALE, ARIZONA.

I HAVE READ, UNDERSTOOD AND ACCEPTED THIS AGREEMENT, AND SIGN AND ACKNOWLEDGE RECEIPT OF A FULLY EXECUTED COPY OF THIS

_____DAY OF _____ 19____

_____

Resident Manager   Resident

By _____

Building Management Services, Inc. Corporate Office   Resident

Source: Courtesy of Building Management Services, Scottsdale, Arizona.

subleases and assignments were permitted and honored. However, the parties may restrict transfers through the terms of their agreement. For example, some leases declare any transfer void, although the enforceability of such a provision is questionable. Another type of transfer restriction is a provision whereby tenants forfeit their leasehold interests if they attempt to transfer those interests to others. Under this type of provision, the assignment or sublease is not void, but the landlord has terminated both the original party's interest and the subtenant's or assignee's interest. Finally, the lease agreement may simply contain a provision by which the tenant promises not to sublet or assign. If the tenant violates the provision and the landlord has resulting damages, those damages are collectible from the breaching tenant. In some leases the sublease or assignment is not prohibited, but the tenant is first required to obtain the landlord's approval for the transaction. If the landlord does not approve, one of the other types of provisions just mentioned would take effect. The following clause is an example in which prior consent is required: "Resident may not assign this Rental Agreement or sublet the premises, in whole or in part, without the prior written consent of management."

This consent to assignment was established as an ongoing right by the 1603 *Rule in Dumpor's Case*, which provided that if the landlord consented to one assignment, all other assignments were also deemed valid. In other words, at common law, once the landlord waived rights to prohibit an assignment the right to prohibit was lost. Most states have abolished the effect of this rule.

Rights and Responsibilities of Parties to a Lease Assignment Although an assignment is a complete relinquishment of the tenant's leasehold interest, the tenant's obligations do not end by the making of an assignment. The tenant remains obligated to the landlord; if the assignee does not perform according to the terms of the lease agreement, the original tenant will be liable for damages.

The assignee is not responsible for the obligations of the original tenant unless the assignee assumes these obligations. The assumption of responsibilities is not generally a problem since the assignee will be the recipient of the benefits— the right to the leasehold interest. The assignee does have the right to require the landlord to perform according to the terms of the lease agreement and also has the right of suit in the event of nonperformance. If an assignment is to be permitted, the lease agreement should specify all details on assignment, such as methods of payment and communication.

The assignor remains liable for performance on the contract and is not released from obligations simply because a third party is now involved. In the event of nonperformance or breach, the landlord has an election for suit between the original tenant and the assignee. Although the landlord does not have privity of contract with the assignee, the landlord is still obligated to perform obligations as established by law or by the original parties' lease agreement.

Rights and Responsibilities of Parties to a Sublease In a sublease, the subtenant becomes a tenant of the original lessee and not a tenant of the landlord. There is no legal relationship between landlord and subtenant, and thus there are no rights of enforcement by one party against another. Any rights the parties have must be exercised indirectly through the tenant with whom they have a contractual relationship. For example, if a landlord who is required to maintain insurance on the leased premises fails to do so and a subtenant loses property because of it, the subtenant could proceed against the tenant. Although the tenant could then proceed against the landlord for recovery, the subtenant would have no direct cause of action against the landlord. This is because the landlord's obligation to insure is one to the tenant and not to the subtenant.

Unconscionability

As with most consumer contracts of the 1980s, leases are subject to judicial standards of fairness in language and bargaining power. Under the Uniform Residential Landlord Tenant Act (URLTA) a rental agreement is unconscionable if the tenant is required to waive any of the rights, remedies, or protections afforded under the act (Section 1.103).

In many court decisions, a popular issue in unconscionability is the determination of the validity of exculpatory (hold harmless) clauses in lease agreements, in which landlords attempt to hold themselves harmless for injuries, damages, or other resultant problems that occur while tenants are in possession of the property. The legal effect of such clauses is discussed in the next section.

Other areas in lease agreements found unconscionable by courts include excessive cleaning deposits, excessive assessment of cleaning fees, excessive security deposit requirements, prohibitions on the right to organize, and waivers of judicial process. The basic standard in all cases is one of bargaining power and fairness to the parties involved.

RIGHTS AND RESPONSIBILITIES OF THE PARTIES TO A LEASE AGREEMENT

Absent an assignment or sublease, there are two parties to a lease agreement and each has certain required responsibilities of performance and certain rights. In discussing the responsibilities of one party, the rights of the other party in the event those responsibilities are not performed must be discussed, so that the magnitude of the lease agreement can be appreciated.

Responsibilities of Landlords and Rights of Tenants

Maintenance of the Premises At common law, a lease was viewed as a transfer of a land interest with no obligation of maintenance and repair for the landlord once the tenant began the leasehold interest or lease period. Just as the doctrine of habitable premises has changed considerably, so has the doctrine governing the landlord's duty of repair. Several theories have now been used by courts or codified by states that require the landlord to keep the leased premises in repair. The theories are constructive eviction, self-help, tort liability, and lease termination.

1. Constructive Eviction One theory used to require repairs and thereby insure the tenant of continued habitability is the doctrine of *constructive eviction*. For this doctrine to apply, the tenant must be able to establish that the landlord had an obligation to repair either through a covenant in the lease agreement or through some statutory or judicially imposed duty. Under URLTA Section 2.104, the following duties are imposed upon the landlord:

(a) A landlord shall:
  (1.) comply with the requirements of applicable building codes materially affecting health and safety;
  (2.) make all repairs and do whatever is necessary to put and keep the premises in fit and habitable condition;
  (3.) keep all common areas of the premises in a clean and safe condition;
  (4.) maintain in good and safe working order and condition all electrical, plumbing, sanitary, heating, ventilating, air-conditioning and other facilities and appliances, including elevators, supplied or required to be supplied by him;
  (5.) provide and maintain appropriate receptacles and conveniences for the removal of ashes, garbage, rubbish and other waste incidental to the occupancy of the dwelling unit and arrange for their removal; and
  (6.) supply running water and reasonable amounts of hot water at all times, reasonable heat [between [October 1] and [May 1]] except where the building that includes the dwelling unit is not required by law to be equipped for that purpose, or the dwelling unit is so constructed that heat or hot water is generated by an installation within the exclusive control of the tenant and supplied by a direct public utility connection.

Once the tenant has established that the landlord was responsible for maintenance of the premises, the tenant must also prove that the landlord has failed to perform according to the statute or agreement. Furthermore, it must be shown that the failure to perform has made it difficult or impossible for the tenant to continue living on the premises. Under the doctrine of constructive eviction, the tenant in these circumstances is evicted constructively by the landlord, and by moving out is excused from performance of the lease. The greatest problem with the doctrine is that the tenant must move out for the doctrine to apply. In areas where housing shortages exist, particularly low-cost housing shortages, this requirement of moving out imposes hardships. In some states the courts have permitted tenants who can establish all of the elements of constructive eviction to fix the problem areas and remain in the leased premises, deducting the cost of the repairs from their rent.

2. *Self-help* Common law did not permit the *repair and deduct* self-help method of remedying leased premises in disrepair. However, under the URLTA, this remedy of *self-help* had been adopted by an increasing number of states. Section 4.103 of the act provides:

> (a) If the landlord fails to comply with the rental agreement or Section 2.104, and the reasonable cost of compliance is less than ($100), or an amount equal to (one-half) the periodic rent, whichever amount is greater, the tenant may recover damages for breach under Section 4.101 (b) or he may notify the landlord of his intention to correct the condition at the landlord's expense. If the landlord fails to comply within (14) days of being notified by the tenant in writing or as promptly as conditions require in a case of emergency, the tenant may cause the work to be done in a workmanlike manner and, after submitting to the landlord an itemized statement, deduct from his rent the actual and reasonable cost or the fair and reasonable value of the work, not exceeding the amount specified in this subsection.
>
> (b) A tenant may not repair at the landlord's expense if the condition was caused by the deliberate or negligent act or omission of the tenant, a member of his family, or other person on the premises with his consent.

Under this section of the URLTA, the tenant is given the statutory right to repair and deduct property problems that are not self-induced. Notice must first be given to the landlord under the URLTA provisions.

3. *Tort Liability* In the absence of the statutorily or judicially imposed self-help right, tenants have another theory under which to correct problems and recover the cost from the landlord. In some decisions, the tenant has not been permitted to repair and deduct but has been permitted to repair and recover in tort for the damages caused or alleviated through the tenant's corrective actions. The difficulty with this remedy is that it necessitates legal action by the tenant for recovery to be possible. The following case involves the issue of the landlord's tort liability for disrepair.

GARCIA v. FREELAND REALTY, INC.

314 N.Y.S.2d 215 (1972)

Garcia (plaintiff) lived in a tenement house in the East Harlem section of Manhattan with his two young children. The paint in one of the rooms and in the bathroom was flaking off the walls, and Garcia's children were eating the paint and the flakes. When Garcia made several complaints to the landlord (defendant), the landlord did not remedy the problem. Garcia then expended $29.53 for materials and $70 for labor to replaster and repaint the walls in the rooms. He brought suit for the recovery of these amounts from his landlord.

The court took judicial notice of the fact that the peeling paint and plaster contained lead which, if ingested by children, could cause lead poisoning leading to mental retardation and death.

GOODELL, Judge

The issue here, in light of the uncontested facts, is whether a recovery by the plaintiff is barred as a matter of law in view of the common law rule that the landlord, in the absence of an express covenant, is not obligated to repair or paint.

The practical question that faced the plaintiff, was whether he was bound to sit by and do nothing despite the landlord's inactivity . . . or whether he should take prompt steps to prevent irreparable damage to his children and charge the cost to his landlord.

In these circumstances, the plaintiff had the right to remove the menace to the health and life of his children and to charge the cost to the landlord for the following reasons:

While it has been held that making of repairs by a tenant does not entitle the tenant to reimbursement from the landlord in the absence of an express covenant by the landlord, the landlord is nevertheless liable for injuries suffered by the tenant or members of his family as a result of the landlord's failure to make repairs.

It cannot be said now, with positiveness, what the result might have been had the condition in the plaintiff's apartment continued unchanged. It does seem fair to conclude, however, that had the condition continued unchanged, after notification had been given to the defendant, as testified to by the plaintiff, and had the plaintiff's children become, as a result, the victims of lead poisoning, that in those events a tort action might have been instituted by the plaintiff on behalf of his children and himself to recover damages for resultant injuries suffered.

The plaintiff, therefore, by his act, prevented the commission of an actionable tort that might have resulted from inaction. If damage based upon the commission of a tort is an appropriate award, then . . . it is proper and desirable to reimburse a plaintiff for the reasonable cost of preventing or averting the commission of a tort after the defendant has had a reasonable opportunity to act and failed to do so in circumstances calling for action on his part. As Prosser has said in his discussion of "prevention":

The "prophylactic" factor of preventing future harm has been quite important in the field of torts. . . . While the idea of prevention is seldom controlling, it very often has weight as a reason for holding the defendant responsible.

In the circumstances of this case involving the concurrent conditions of an immediate threat to health and life of children and a critical shortage of housing, it is my view that the prevention of an actionable tort by the plaintiff warrants his reimbursement for the cost of materials and the reasonable value of labor applied to the accomplishment of that result.

Judgment for the plaintiff.

Discussion Questions

1. Who is the tenant? Who is the landlord?
2. What corrective action did the tenant take and why?
3. What is the plaintiff's theory for recovery?
4. What amount is sought?
5. Is the decision limited to a particular type of factual situation?

If a tenant is able to exercise any of the rights and remedies afforded by self-help statutes, implied covenants, or tort liability, it is possible that the landlord may, in response to the tenant's action, retaliate with eviction. Because the purposes of these theories would be defeated if eviction resulted, the Uniform Residential Landlord Tenant Act (URLTA) and many state statutes provide that landlords may not engage in retaliatory eviction against tenants who choose to exercise their self-help rights. For example, Section 5.101 of the URLTA provides that a tenant cannot be evicted and that a tenant's rental fee cannot be raised or his or her services decreased as a result of any of the following: (1) filing a complaint with housing authorities, (2) organizing or joining a tenant's union, or (3) using self-help procedures and remedies. If a tenant has engaged in these activities, there is usually a period during which the landlord's eviction would be presumptively retaliatory. For example, the URLTA presumptive retaliatory period is 1 year after the tenant has engaged in any of the protected activities. The effect is that it becomes the landlord's burden to establish that the tenant was evicted for reasons other than the exercise of statutorily protected rights. Naturally, the presumption can be overcome or held inapplicable in cases where the tenant has not paid rent or has in some way breached the lease agreement.

4. Lease Termination A final option available to a tenant faced with a lease of uninhabitable premises is to treat the state of disrepair as constructive eviction, vacate the premises, and regard the lease and the obligation to pay rents as terminated. This right of termination through constructive eviction was a common law right that exists in all states in common law or statutory form. In the event a statute regulates constructive eviction, it is important for the tenant to comply with all procedural requirements before vacating the premises.

(18.5) Consider:

Ralph Ogden is leasing a 3-bedroom home and is having difficulty with insect infestation. The insects include poisonous black widow spiders, and Ralph is concerned about the safety of the premises for his preschool children. Ralph has told the landlord of the problem, but no exterminator has been sent in the 2 weeks since the landlord was informed. Ralph wishes to know his rights, and, more specifically, whether he may hire an exterminator and then deduct the cost of extermination from the monthly rent.

Maintenance of the Common Areas Regardless of any state's position on the landlord's responsibility to maintain individual dwelling units, all states obligate the landlord to maintain the common areas of a building. Common areas are areas used by all tenants, such as staircases, halls, and laundry facilities. Although tenants may not be entitled to terminate their leases for disrepair of these areas, the landlord will be held liable for injuries resulting from the disrepair. The following case deals with the liability of a landlord for an accident involving a tenant in a common area.

LEWIS v. W. F. SMITH & CO.
390 N.E.2d 39 (Ill. 1979)

Mary Lewis (plaintiff/appellee) fell on the icy stairs of her apartment building in December and, because of injuries to her leg, was unable to return to her waitress job until March. There was no railing along the stairway on which she fell.

Lewis brought suit against the owner, W. F. Smith (defendant/appellant), for damages caused by his alleged negligence in not clearing the stairway of snow and ice and in not providing a handrail.

The jury awarded Lewis $16,832.75, and the landlord appealed.

MEJDA, Justice

Defendants first contend that the trial court erred in denying their motions for a directed verdict in that they have no duty to remove the ice and snow from the stairs and that the absence of handrails alone was not sufficient to be considered the proximate cause of plaintiff's injury.

Ordinarily, in the absence of a contract, there is no duty on the part of a landlord to remove natural accumulations of ice and snow from common areas that remain under his control. Plaintiff has not claimed that defendants were under a contractual duty to maintain the stairway. Rather, she predicates her action solely on the common law duty of a landlord to exercise ordinary care in the maintenance of a stairway and contends that the janitor failed to remove the ice when it was his job to do so.

For plaintiff to recover on the basis of accumulation of ice and snow, she must show the defendants in some way caused an unnatural accumulation or that they aggravated a natural condition. The evidence discloses that the janitor merely sprinkled salt on the steps and did not attempt to chip away at the ice until a day or two after the storm. The mere sprinkling of salt, which may cause the ice to melt, although later it refreezes, has not been found to be the kind of act which aggravates a natural condition and leads to liability on the part of the landlord.

Nor can the fact that the janitor did not remove the ice be the basis of liability. Plaintiff maintains that the janitor failed to do his job, and that liability therefore attaches. However, the duty of the janitor to remove the ice was a duty that was owed to his employer, not to plaintiff.

Consequently, we find that plaintiff has made no showing of any duty or breach of duty on the part of defendants with regard to the removal of ice and snow from the stairs.

We do not agree, however, with defendants' contention that they were entitled to a directed verdict with regard to the absence of handrails. We conclude that there is evidence which can support the conclusion that the absence of the handrails caused plaintiff's injury. Defendants had a duty to put handrails alongside the stairway, as was required by the city ordinance admitted into evidence. Plaintiff testified that there was nothing to hold onto as she fell.

Affirmed.

Discussion Questions

1. What injury occurred and where did it occur?
2. What is alleged to have caused the accident?
3. Is the landlord liable? If so, on what basis?

Liability to Third Parties In addition to the tenants, there are other parties who may enter the common areas of leased property or who may enter the dwelling units of tenants as guests. For injuries occurring to third parties in the common areas, the landlord is liable in the same way as with tenants—the landlord is expected to exercise reasonable care in the maintenance of common areas.

The landlord's liability for injury to third parties while the third parties are actually in a dwelling unit varies according to the terms of the lease agreement. If the landlord has accepted the burden of repair and upkeep but fails to meet that burden, then resulting injuries to third parties are the responsibility of the landlord. On the other hand, if the tenant has undertaken the responsibility of repair and upkeep, then such injuries to third parties are the responsibility of the tenant.

Sometimes both the landlord and the tenant are liable. For example, in a case where the landlord is to maintain and a nonremedied problem exists (such as a loose step), the tenant must warn third parties of the problem until the landlord has the chance to repair. If the tenant fails to warn visitors of the problem during the interim, both landlord and tenant could be held liable.

If the leased premises have code violations, the landlord is responsible for injuries to third parties resulting from such violations. Furthermore, even if the landlord has no statutory or contractual duty to repair, it is his or her responsibility to warn the tenant of any hidden defects and to post notices for third parties who might enter the property. The following case deals with the issue of a landlord's liability for dangerous animals kept on the leased premises by a tenant.

BRADY v. SKINNER
646 P.2d 310 (Ariz. 1982)

Margaret Skinner (defendant/appellee) owned two adjacent parcels of land. She lived on one and leased the other to Bud Wellington on a month-to-month basis. The Bradys (plaintiffs/appellants) lived on the other side of Wellington. Skinner gave Wellington permission to keep two mules on the property. One was named Martin Luther and the other was named King. King acted like a typical, ornery mule. Basically he did not like anyone and would put his ears back and shy away when anyone got close to him. On the other hand, Martin Luther acted more like a horse than a mule. He was playful and friendly. The mules were docile and neither mule had ever kicked, bitten, or tried to injure anyone. They were no more dangerous than any other mules, but like other mules, they were unpredictable.

One day Arthur Brady, Jr., who was 4-years-old at the time, was kicked by one of the mules. No one seems to know which mule kicked him. The Bradys filed suit, and from the trial court's granting of a motion for summary judgment for Skinner, the Bradys appealed.

HOWARD, Chief Judge

Appellants rely on *Uccello v. Laudenslayer*, 118 Cal. Rptr. 741 (1975). This case holds that a duty of care arises when the landlord has actual knowledge of the presence of a dangerous animal and has the right to remove the animal by retaking possession of the premises. Assuming arguendo we would follow *Uccello*, we find that case is simply inapplicable to the facts here. *Uccello* holds that the landlord must have actual knowledge of the dangerous propensities of the animal. The mules here were not dangerous animals. They were domesticated animals. As far as mules are concerned it must be shown that the defendant knew or had reason to know of a dangerous propensity of the one animal in question.

Since neither mule had ever attacked, injured or kicked anyone, it is sheer speculation on appellants' part when they assert that the boy was probably kicked by King. Aside from this speculation, this case differs from *Uccello* because there was no showing of any dangerous propensities on the part of the mules.

Appellants also assert that Skinner would be liable under the doctrine of attractive nuisance. . . . The doctrine of attractive nuisance is limited to the possessor of the land.

Affirmed.

Discussion Questions

1. Who is the landlord? Who is the tenant?
2. Who are the Bradys?
3. What animals are involved?
4. Were the animals known to be dangerous?
5. What injury occurred?
6. Is the landlord responsible? Explain.

Use of Exculpatory Clauses To attempt to avoid liability to both tenants and third parties, landlords frequently include exculpatory or hold-harmless clauses in leases. These clauses provide the landlord will not be liable for any injuries or damages occurring on the premises because of the landlord's negligence or the negligence of any other parties. Although the clauses can be found in many lease agreements, their legal effect is minimal. In other words, landlords cannot by provisions in agreements hold themselves harmless for injuries caused by their failure to maintain the premises or comply with building and safety codes. The courts have interpreted such clauses, at least in residential leases, to be unconscionable and unenforceable, or in some decisions, void. Some states have enacted specific statutes that prohibit exculpatory clauses; and in states that have adopted the Uniform Residential Landlord Tenant Act (URLTA), the section on unconscionability has been used to invalidate exculpatory clauses. The following is an example of an exculpatory clause in a residential lease:

> Lessor and his Agent shall not be liable for any damage or inconvenience to either person or property, that may be sustained by Lessee, his family, invitees, licensees, or guests on or about the premises herein leased, including damage or inconvenience resulting from breakdown or delays.

Landlords may take two precautions to help reduce their potential liability for injuries caused to tenants and visiting third parties. The first precaution is for landlords to obtain adequate insurance. The second is for leases to specify who is responsible for repair and maintenance. A repair and maintenance clause may alleviate the effect of repair and deduct actions by tenants and may also serve to determine who is liable in the event disrepair causes an injury to a third party. The following is an example of a repair and maintenance clause specifying this area of responsibility for the parties.

> Resident shall maintain the unit in a clean, neat, and undamaged condition and in particular shall comply with all obligations of local building codes, maintain the premises that he occupies in a clean and safe condition, dispose of all ashes, rubbish, garbage, and other waste in a clean and safe manner, keep and use all plumbing, electrical, sanitary, heating, ventilating, air-conditioning, and other facilities and appliances in a clean and reasonable manner, and generally conduct

himself, and require other persons on the premises with his consent to conduct themselves, in a manner so as not to disturb his neighbors nor in any way deface, damage, or otherwise destroy any part of the premises. The Owner shall at all times comply with the requirements of applicable building codes, make all repairs necessary to keep the premises in fit and habitable condition, keep all of the common areas in a clean and safe condition, and maintain in a good and safe working order all plumbing and electrical facilities supplied by Owner.

(18.6) Consider:

Benson was a lessee in a building owned by Centennial Mills. A water pipe in the building burst and water poured into Benson's apartment, destroying Benson's furniture, clothing, appliances, rugs, and draperies. It has been established that the pipe burst as the result of faulty maintenance. Benson has brought suit against Centennial to recover damages for the loss of personal property. Centennial's defense is an exculpatory clause in the lease, which says the landlord is not responsible for such damages. What is the result? On the day the pipe burst, Benson had a guest staying with him, and the guest's personal property was also damaged. Does the guest have any rights against Centennial?

Rights of Landlords and Responsibilities of Tenants

Landlords have several basic rights under the lease agreement which, in turn, constitute the tenants' responsibilities under the agreement. The purpose of leasing property is to have the property produce income; thus, fundamental is the right of landlords to receive timely rental payments pursuant to the terms of the lease agreement.

In the past few years, many cities have attempted to impose rent controls on landlords. The following case provides the United States Supreme Court view on such controls.

FISHER v. CITY OF BERKELEY CALIFORNIA
475 U.S. 260 (1986)

In June 1980, the city of Berkeley passed an initiative entitled "Ordinance 5261-NS, Rent Stabilization and Eviction for Good Cause Ordinance" (hereinafter Ordinance). The stated purposes of the ordinance were:

to regulate residential rent increases in the City of Berkeley and to protect tenants from unwarranted rent increases and arbitrary, discriminatory, or retaliatory evictions in order to help maintain the diversity of the Berkeley community and to ensure compliance with legal obligations relating to the rental of housing. This legislation is designed to address the City of Berkeley's housing crisis, preserve the public peace, health and safety, and advance the housing policies of the City with regard to low and fixed income persons, minorities, students, handicapped and the aged.

To accomplish the goals, the Ordinance enacted strict rent controls. All rental properties (23,000) in Berkeley were given a base rate as of the May 1980 rental rate and increases were permitted only pursuant to an annual general adjustment of rent ceilings by the Rent Stabilization Board or pur- suant to a special petition approved by the same board. Failure to comply with the rent ceilings could result in suits by the tenants, the withholding of collected rents from the landlord, criminal penalties, or a combination.

Shortly after the Ordinance was passed, a group of landlords (appellants) brought suit in California Superior Court challenging the ordinance as unconstitutional because it preempted federal antitrust laws. The Superior Court upheld the ordinance, and the Court of Appeals reversed. The California Supreme Court held that there was no conflict between the Ordinance and the Sherman Act. The landlords appealed.

MARSHALL, Justice

Recognizing that the function of government may often be to tamper with free markets, correcting their failures and aiding their victims, this Court noted that a "state statute is not pre-empted by the federal antitrust laws simply because the state scheme may have an anticompetitive effect." We have therefore held that a state statute should be struck down on pre-emption grounds "only if it mandates or authorizes conduct that necessarily constitutes a violation of the antitrust laws in all cases, or if it places irresistible pressure on a private party to violate the antitrust laws in order to comply with the statute."

Appellants argue that Berkeley's Rent Stabilization Ordinance is pre-empted because it imposes rent ceilings across the entire rental market for residential units. Such a regime, they contend, clearly falls within the per se rule against price fixing, a rule that has been one of the settled points of antitrust enforcement since the earliest days of the Sherman Act. That the prices set here are ceilings rather than floors and that the public interest has been invoked to justify this stabilization should not, appellants argue, save Berkeley's regulatory scheme from condemnation under the per se rule.

Certainly there is this much truth to appellants' argument: Had the owners of residential rental property in Berkeley voluntarily banded together to stabilize rents in the city, their activities would not be saved from antitrust attack by claims that they had set reasonable prices out of solicitude for the welfare of their tenants. Moreover, it cannot be denied that Berkeley's Ordinance will affect the residential housing rental market in much the same way as would the philanthropic activities of this hypothetical trade association. What distinguishes the operation of Berkeley's Ordinance from the activities of a benevolent landlords' cartel is not that the Ordinance will necessarily have a different economic effect, but that the rent ceilings imposed by the Ordinance and maintained by the Stabilization Board have been unilaterally imposed by government upon landlords to the exclusion of private control.

The distinction between unilateral and concerted action is critical here. Adhering to the language of §1, this Court has always limited the reach of that provision to "unreasonable restraints of trade effected by a 'contract, combination . . . or conspiracy' between separate entities." The ordinary relationship between the government and those who must obey its regulatory commands whether they wish to or not is not enough to establish a conspiracy. Similarly, the mere fact that all competing property owners must comply with the same provisions of the Ordinance is not enough to establish a conspiracy among landlords.

There may be cases in which what appears to be a state- or municipality-administered price stabilization scheme is really a private price-fixing conspiracy, concealed under a "gauzy cloak of state involvement." This might occur even where prices are ostensibly under the absolute control of government officials. However, we have been given no indication that such corruption has tainted the rent controls imposed by Berkeley's Ordinance. Adopted by popular initiative, the Ordinance can hardly be viewed as a cloak for any conspiracy among landlords or between the landlords and the municipality. Berkeley's landlords have simply been deprived of the power freely to raise their rents. That is why they are here. And that is why their role in the stabilization program does not alter the restraint's unilateral nature.

Because under settled principles of antitrust law, the rent controls established by Berkeley's Ordinance lack the element of concerted action needed before they can be characterized as a per se violation of §1 of the Sherman Act, we cannot say that the Ordinance is facially inconsistent with the federal antitrust laws. We therefore need not address whether, even if the controls were to mandate §1 violations, they would be exempt under the state-action doctrine from antitrust scrutiny.

Affirmed.

Discussion Questions

1. Is there preemption of the Berkeley Ordinance by the federal antitrust laws?
2. What arguments do the landlords make on their behalf?
3. Who is setting rent prices?
4. Do the landlords have any control?
5. Is the Ordinance constitutional?

Tenants have an obligation to make timely rental payments according to the method and place of payment specified by the landlord. If a tenant does not make timely payment, there has been a breach of the lease agreement, and the landlord is permitted to take steps to minimize damages. Under URLTA Section 4.201, the landlord must give the tenant a written notice of nonpayment that states that the lease terminates within a specified period after receipt of the notice if rent is not paid. Although some states have changed the time constraints, the URLTA specifies that if rent is not received within 14 days from the time the tenant receives the notice of nonpayment, the lease will terminate within 30 days from receipt of the notice. Assuming that rent is not paid within the notice grace period, the landlord will have a terminated lease and a tenant still in possession of the property.

Most states provide specific procedures for having nonpaying tenants evicted from leased premises. Two names for this procedure are *forcible detainer* and *action for dispossession*. A distinct feature of these specialized procedures is that the defenses a tenant may assert are limited, so that the landlord is not kept in litigation for long periods while the tenant remains in possession of the property. For example, tenants may assert reasons for nonpayment that are justified under their states' landlord–tenant acts. Under the URLTA, defenses to nonpayment of rent are the landlord's failure to supply heat or water or the tenant's exercise of the right to repair and deduct for maintaining habitability of the premises. However, the right of asserting these defenses for nonpayment is limited to states that have recognized the right of habitability as being interrelated to the payment of rent and the existence of a valid lease agreement. In states not recognizing the doctrine of habitability, uninhabitability is not a defense to a landlord's action for possession. The following case involves a habitability issue in an action for dispossession for nonpayment of rent.

PARK HILL TERRACE ASSOCIATES v. GLENNON ET AL.
369 A.2d 938 (N.J. 1977)

Park Hill (respondent/plaintiff) owns an apartment complex of 100 units located in the borough of Fort Lee. Central air conditioning is provided. The form lease agreement for the tenants provides that in the event air conditioning, heat, and hot water cannot be furnished for reasons beyond the landlord's control, the tenants' obligations under the leases do not change.

Glennon and fifty-two other tenants (defendants/petitioners) withheld portions of their August 1975 rent because the air-conditioning system was inoperative. The tenants had written to the management of the building in May about the air conditioning. An expert testified that the apartments without air conditioning would rent for 20 percent less.

When the tenants withheld portions of their rent, Park Hill brought summary dispossess actions against several of the tenants. The landlord was given a judgment at the trial court level, and the tenants appealed.

PER CURIAM

The first question is whether the failure of an air conditioning unit with its consequent discomforts can breach the implied covenant of habitability. As delineated in *Marini v. Ireland*, 256 A.2d 526 (1970), every unpleasant condition found in a dwelling unit will not affect habitability. Many dwellings in this state are not air conditioned. We are not addressed to any authority which categorically assays air conditioning as an element of habitability. The condition complained of must be of a quality to render the premises uninhabitable in the eyes of a reasonable person. Respondent landlord argues that air conditioning in this case was but an amenity and that "air conditioning is but a luxury." We do not deem it controlling that the leasing contract contemplated the providing of air conditioning and that the rentals were higher because of it. There are many instances of breaches of the leasing agreement which would not affect habitability and thus would not be relevant in a dispossess action although they might very well be proper basis for a separate cause of action for breach of contract. The following list of factors is suggestive for determining habitability:

1. Has there been a violation of any applicable housing code or building or sanitary regulation?
2. Is the nature of the deficiency or defect such as to affect a vital facility?
3. What is its potential or actual effect upon safety and sanitation?
4. For what length of time has it persisted?
5. What is the age of the structure?
6. What is the amount of rent?

7. Can the tenant be said to have waived the defect or be estopped to complain?
8. Was the tenant in any way responsible for the defective condition?

On this record we perceive sufficient credible evidence to support the trial judge's finding that the air conditioning failure for the stated days affected the habitability of the involved premises.

It is now settled that the covenant on the part of a tenant to pay rent and the covenant, be it express or implied, on the part of a landlord to maintain the premises in a habitable condition are for all purposes mutually dependent. Thus, now, in an action by a landlord for unpaid rent a tenant may plead by way of defense and set-off the landlord's breach of his continuing obligation of an adequate standard of habitability.

Reversed.

Discussion Questions

1. What defect in the property is alleged?
2. How much rent did the tenants pay?
3. Who brought suit?
4. What defense do the tenants allege?
5. Are the premises habitable?

6. Do the tenants succeed with their defense?
7. What factors does the court list for determining breach of the warranty of habitability?

In seeking dispossession for nonpayment of rent, landlords must be able to establish that they have not waived their rights to timely payment. That is, if they have waited until the eighth day of the month for rent due on the first and have accepted the late payment, they will be bound by the delay period in the future unless they serve tenants with formal notice of the intent to exercise the right to timely payment.

In some states, landlords are afforded other remedies for nonpayment of rent. For example, in some cases a tenant abandons the premises and leaves personal property. Some states give the landlord a lien, an interest, or a right to possession of that personal property. Although some landlords attempt the private remedy of changing locks for a truly short dispossession action, the courts have invalidated such conduct on the grounds that the tenant has been denied due process.

In some cases, a tenant stops paying rent upon vacating the premises prior to the expiration of the lease term. The landlord has possession of the premises but no tenant to produce rental income. In these circumstances, the landlord has a right of action for breach of contract against the tenant to collect the lost rents and associated expenses of the property sitting vacant. However, most states do require the landlord to mitigate damages, which means that if it is possible, the landlord must rent the premises and recover from the tenant only for the period during which the apartment was vacant.

(18.7) Consider:

If a tenant abandons a leased apartment after performance of 3 months on a 6-month, $350-per-month lease, and the landlord is able to rent the apartment for 1 of the 3 remaining months, what are the landlord's damages?

Nonpayment of rent is the typical reason for a landlord's action for dispossession, but any breach of the rental agreement by the tenant may result in a termination notice and dispossession action by the landlord. Examples of other breaches include breaking the rules and regulations, failing to maintain the premises according to the lease agreement, and performing illegal activities on the premises.

Tenants are also under obligation to use the landlord's property in such a way that is not destructive or deteriorative of its future value. In the absence of express agreement or permission, tenants cannot destroy vegetation, reconstruct buildings, or destroy existing structures. Their basic right is use without change or destruction. The parties to the lease should agree in advance on the addition of fixtures and what will happen to the fixtures at the end of the lease term, so that their placement or removal is not interpreted to be waste of the landlord's property.

CONCLUSIONS

From the discussion and cases in this chapter it is not difficult to reach the conclusion that a detailed lease agreement is a necessity for the landlord–tenant relationship. In negotiating that lease, the following factors should be provided for, or at least considered:

1. What is the lease term? Must the lease be in writing? (Usually leases for longer than 1 year must be in writing.)

2. When the lease expires, is there an option to renew? Can a month-to-month tenancy then exist?

3. How much notice, if any, is required for termination by both the landlord and the tenant?

4. Are there provisions for attorneys' fees? Does the tenant waive any legal rights?

5. Are pets and children permitted? Are water beds permitted?

6. Are there rules and regulations on noise, pool use, and so on?

7. Is there an exculpatory clause? If so, what is its effect?

8. Who is responsible for maintenance in the dwelling unit and in the common areas?

9. What provision is made for fixture placement and removal?

10. Are assignments and subleases permitted?

11. When may the landlord enter the tenant's dwelling unit without permission?

12. How much is required in deposits? What is the purpose of each deposit? Are deposits refundable?

13. How are utilities paid?

14. Is there a warranty of habitability? Do any items need repair or replacement prior to the beginning of the lease term?

15. Are there late penalties for rental payments?

Although the list does not include all areas that should be covered in the lease, it serves as a checklist for the areas causing both landlords and tenants the most problems and the most litigation.

KEY TERMS

tenancy for years
tenancy for a term
periodic tenancy
tenancy at will
tenancy at sufferance
implied warranty of habitability
security deposit
Uniform Residential Landlord
    Tenant Act (URLTA)

cleaning deposit
assignments
subleases
Rule in Dumpor's Case
constructive eviction
repair and deduct
self-help
forcible detainer
action for dispossession

CHAPTER PROBLEMS

1. K. M. S. Investments hired a resident apartment manager for one of their complexes and did a very cursory background check. A female tenant and her girlfriend were violently sexually assaulted by the newly hired manager. Upon his arrest, it was discovered that he had a history of committing violent crimes. The victims have filed suit against K. M. S. for their injuries. Discuss the liability of K. M. S. to each of the women.

2. Dow Chemical leased residential property to several families. The properties were surrounded by a dike that drained water from Dow's plant. The dike ran through the backyards of each of the tenants' properties. In the summer of 1971 heavy rains caused a break in the dike, and the water flow caused damage to the cars and other personal property of the tenants. The tenants sued Dow, claiming their damages were the result of Dow's faulty maintenance of the dike. Dow claimed the maintenance became the responsibility of the tenants, since the dike was on their properties. What was the result?

3. Elmer owned sixteen rental cabins, and Mike and his family rented six of them on a month-to-month basis for $900 per month. The rental fee included gas, electricity, and water. Elmer failed to pay the gas bill, and the result was that Mike and his family had to live without gas for 40 days. Since the cabins had gas heat, Mike and his family were cold and uncomfortable for that 40-day period. Mike then withheld rent for the next 40 days to make up for the time they were required to live without heat. Elmer has brought suit to have Mike and family removed for nonpayment of rent. What is the result?

4. Southall Realty brought an action for dispossession against Mrs. Brown for nonpayment of rent on her apartment. Mrs. Brown defended on the grounds that she owed no rent because the apartment had several building code violations and was uninhabitable. Southall Realty countered by maintaining Mrs. Brown still continued to reside there. What was the result?

5. Engels, a university freshman, rented an apartment from W. E. Woold on a 1-year lease at $600 per month. After 3 months in the complex, Engels decided the tenants were not obtaining proper service and that their rights were being infringed. Engels organized a tenants' union, which over 50 percent of the tenants joined. Engels held a meeting in his apartment. The day after the meeting, Engels' air conditioner no longer worked. Engels called the manager and asked that it be repaired, but the manager said it was Engels's responsibility to repair. Engels

called a local repair service and had the unit repaired at a cost of $75, which Engels deducted from his next month's rent. When Engels refused to pay the $75 upon demand by Woold, Woold brought an action for dispossession. Under the URLTA, who will win?

6. Ella terminated her 6-month lease agreement at the end of 3 months by abandoning her apartment. Her monthly rent was $400. Although the landlord had several opportunities to rent the apartment he refused, stating, "Why hassle with another tenant when I can sue and collect the $1,200 from Ella?" Is the landlord correct in his assumption?

7. Alex, concerned with security, looked all over New York City for an apartment and eventually signed a 2-year lease in a building where the landlord had personnel at the door 24-hours per day. Two months into the 2-year lease, Alex received written notification that due to rising costs, the door personnel would be terminated at the end of the next month. Alex claims the landlord has breached the lease and wishes to be excused so that he may reside in another building. What is the result?

8. Because of the landlord's refusal to fix a window in their apartment, the Haineses have had unusually high heating bills. They wish to know if they can either have the window repaired and deduct the repair costs from their rent or deduct the additional heating costs from their rent. Explain to them their rights under the URLTA.

9. Because of a walkout of elevator workers, the elevators in a large apartment complex could not be maintained and were shut down. Tenants were forced to use the stairs in the thirty-five floor building. The tenants have agreed to pay only 50 percent of their rent because of the nonavailability of elevator service. Are the tenants acting properly?

10. Answer the three questions posed at the beginning of the chapter according to the URLTA.

19

CONSTITUTIONAL ISSUES IN REAL ESTATE OWNERSHIP

The Stovers were residents of the city of Rye, living in a 2-1/2 story dwelling in a residential district. When taxes were raised, the Stovers ran a clothesline from their front porch to the trees in their front yard along Forest Avenue. Each year for the next 5 years, the Stovers put up a new clothesline in protest of the taxes. Three lines ran from the front porch to the trees along Forest Avenue, and three lines ran from the porch to the trees along Rye Beach Avenue (the street alongside the Stovers' property.) The clotheslines contained old clothing, rags, underwear, and scarecrows.

The city of Rye passed an ordinance prohibiting clotheslines in side or front yards unless a permit was obtained on the basis of hardship. The Stovers were denied a permit but still continued to hang the clotheslines. They were charged with violating the ordinance and were convicted. The Stovers claim the ordinance is an unconstitutional deprivation of due process. Are they correct?

Throughout the prior chapters of this book, it has been emphasized that owning real property consists of rights that are afforded various forms of protection. Owning and transferring title to real property also includes certain constitutional rights that entitle property owners to certain guarantees with regard to their property ownership. The purpose of this chapter is to discuss the constitutional protections afforded real property owners and purchasers.

LAND TITLE AND CONSTITUTIONAL ISSUES— EMINENT DOMAIN

The right of a governmental body to take title to property for a public use is called *eminent domain*. This right is established in the Fifth Amendment to the

Constitution and may also be established in various state constitutions. Private individuals cannot require property owners to sell their property, but governmental entities can require property owners to transfer title for public projects for the public good. The Fifth Amendment provides, "property shall not be taken for a public use without just compensation." Thus, for a governmental entity to exercise properly the right of eminent domain, three factors must be present: public purpose, taking (as opposed to regulating), and just compensation.

Public Purpose

To exercise eminent domain, the exercising governmental authority must establish that the taking is necessary for the accomplishment of a government purpose. When eminent domain is mentioned, use of property for highways and schools is thought of most frequently. However, the right of the government to eminent domain extends much further. For example, the following uses have been held to constitute public purposes: the condemnation of slum housing (for purposes of improving city areas), the limitation of mining and excavation within city limits, the declaration of property as an historic landmark, and the taking of property in order to provide a firm that is the town's economic base with a large enough tract for expansion.

According to the United States Supreme Court, the public purpose requirement for eminent domain is to be interpreted broadly, and "the role of the judiciary in determining whether that power [eminent domain] is being exercised for a public purpose is an extremely narrow one." (*United States ex rel. T.V.A. v. Welch*, 327 U.S. 546 [1946].)

Taking or Regulating

For a governmental entity to be required to pay a landowner compensation under the doctrine of eminent domain, it must be established that there has been a *taking* of the property. Mere regulation of the property does not constitute a taking—as established by the *Village of Euclid* case in Chapter 16. Rather, a taking must go so far as to deprive the landowner of any use of the property. In the landmark case of *Pennsylvania Coal v. Mahon*, 260 U.S. 393 (1922), the Supreme Court established standards for determining a taking as opposed to mere regulation. At that time Pennsylvania had a statute that prohibited the mining of coal under any land surface where the result would be the subsidence of any structure used as a human habitation. The owners of the rights to mine subsurface coal brought suit challenging the regulation as a taking, and the Supreme Court ruled in their favor, holding that the statute was more than regulation and, in fact, was an actual taking of the subsurface property rights.

Because of the vast amount of technology that has developed since that case was decided, there are many new and subtly different issues in what constitutes a taking. For example, in some areas the regulation of cable television companies is an infringement on air rights. Such specialized areas of real estate rights are particularly difficult to resolve. In the following more recent case, the Supreme Court was faced with the same issue of regulation versus a taking under eminent domain.

LORETTO v. TELEPROMPTER MANHATTAN CATV CORP. ET AL.

458 U.S. 100 (1982)

A New York statute required landlords to permit cable television companies to install cable facilities on landlords' property so that tenants could subscribe to cable television services. Teleprompter Manhattan CATV (defendant/appellee) installed its equipment on the roof and side of Loretto's (plaintiff/appellant) building. The equipment was to permanently occupy Loretto's property and Loretto was paid the usual $1 fee to which a landlord is entitled upon installation of such equipment. Loretto filed suit alleging that this minor but permanent physical occupation of her property constituted a taking under the Fifth Amendment without just compensation. The New York Court of Appeals ruled the installation did not constitute a taking, and Loretto appealed.

MARSHALL, Justice

The Court of Appeals ruled that the law serves a legitimate police power purpose—eliminating landlord fees and conditions that inhibit the development of CATV, which has important educational and community benefits. Rejecting the argument that a physical occupation authorized by government is necessarily a taking, the court stated that the regulation does not have an excessive economic impact upon appellant when measured against her aggregate property rights, and that it does not interfere with any reasonable investment-backed expectations. In a concurring opinion by Judge Gabrielli, it was stated that the law works a taking but concluded that the $1.00 presumptive award, together with procedures permitting a landlord to demonstrate a greater entitlement, afford just compensation.

We conclude that a permanent physical occupation authorized by government is a taking without regard to the public interests that it may serve. Our constitutional history confirms the rule, recent cases do not question it, and the purposes of the Takings Clause compel[s] its retention.

In *United States v. Pewee Coal Co.*, 341 U.S. 114 (1951), the Court unanimously held that the Government's seizure and direction of operation of a coal mine to prevent a national strike of coal miners constituted a taking, though members of the Court differed over which losses suffered during the period of Government control were compensable. The plurality had little difficulty concluding that because there had been an "actual taking of possession and control," the taking was as clear as if the Government held full title and ownership. . . . In *United States v. Central Eureka Mining Co.*, 357 U.S. 155 (1958), by contrast, the Court found no taking where the Government had issued a war-time order requiring nonessential gold mines to cease operations for the purpose of conserving equipment and manpower for use in mines more essential to the war effort. . . . The Court reasoned that "the Government did not occupy, use, or in any manner take physical possession of the gold mines or the equipment connected with them." The Court concluded that the temporary though severe restriction on use was justified by the exigency of war.

The historical rule that a permanent physical occupation of another's property is a taking has more than tradition to commend it. Such an appropriation is perhaps the most serious form of invasion of an owner's property interests.

Constitutional protections for rights of private property cannot be made to depend on the size of the area permanently occupied.

This Court has consistently affirmed that States have broad power to regulate housing conditions in general and the landlord–tenant relationship in particular without paying just compensation for all economic injuries that such regulation entails. In none of the cases, however, did the government authorize permanent occupation of the landlord's property by a third party. Consequently, our holding today in no way alters the analysis governing the State's power to require landlords to comply with building codes and provide utility connections, mailboxes, smoke detectors, fire extinguishers, and the like in the common area of a building. So long as these regulations do not require the landlord to suffer the physical occupation of a portion of his building by a third party, they will be analyzed under the multi-factor inquiry generally applicable to non-possessory governmental activity.

Our holding today is very narrow. We affirm the traditional rule that a permanent physical occupation of property is a taking. In such a case, the property owner entertains an historically rooted expectation of compensation, and the character of invasion is qualitatively more intrusive than perhaps any other category of property regulation.

The issue of the amount of compensation that is due . . . is a matter for the state courts.

The judgment of the New York Court of Appeals is reversed.

Discussion Questions

1. What regulation is at issue?
2. What form of physical occupation of property is alleged?
3. Was Loretto paid for the occupation?
4. What public purpose did the New York Court of Appeals find existed?
5. The Supreme Court cites two cases in reaching its decision—what are they? What were their facts? What were the decisions?
6. In determining whether a taking has occurred, what is the significance of physical occupation?
7. What distinction is offered between television equipment and items such as smoke alarms and fire extinguishers?
8. How much compensation will Loretto be paid?

Recently, the courts have been faced with the issue of whether zoning regulations serve to limit the use of land so much that the result is a taking. The following is a landmark case in determining the impact of zoning regulations.

556

NOLLAN v. CALIFORNIA COASTAL COMMISSION
107 S.Ct. 3141 (1987)

James and Marilyn Nollan own a beachfront lot in Ventura County, California. A quarter-mile north of their property is Faria Park, an oceanside public park with a public beach and recreation area. Another public beach, known as "the Cove," lies 1800 feet south of their lot. A concrete seawall approximately 8 feet high separates the beach portion of the Nollan's property from the rest of the lot.

The Nollans originally leased their property with an option to buy and had only a small bungalow (504 square feet) located on the lot. The Nollan's option to purchase was conditioned on their promise to demolish the bungalow and replace it. To do that, the Nollans had to apply for a coastal development permit from the California Coastal Commission. They filed for such a permit and proposed construction of a three-bedroom home similar to other residences in the area.

The Nollans were informed that their application was on the calendar and the staff had recommended approval provided that the Nollans allow a public easement to pass across their property to make it easier for the public to get to the Cove and Faria County Park.

The Nollans filed suit with the Ventura County Superior Court asking them to invalidate the easement condition. The court agreed and remanded the matter to the Commission for a full hearing. The Commission found the new house would block the view of the beach and also inhibit the public psychologically from using the beach.

The Nollans filed another suit and said the condition constituted a taking of their property. The trial court agreed and remanded to the Commission. The Commission appealed, and the appellate court reversed. The Nollans appealed to the United States Supreme Court.

SCALIA, Justice

Had California simply required the Nollans to make an easement across their beachfront available to the public on a permanent basis in order to increase public access to the beach, rather than conditioning their permit to rebuild their house on their agreeing to do so, we have no doubt there would have been a taking. To say that the appropriation of a public easement across a landowner's premises does not constitute the taking of a property interest but rather, "a mere restriction on its use," is to use words in a manner that deprives them of all their ordinary meaning. Indeed, one of the principal uses of the eminent domain power is to assure that the government be able to require conveyance of just such interests, so long as it pays for them. Perhaps because the point is so obvious, we have never been confronted with a controversy that required us to rule upon it, but our cases' analysis of the effect of other governmental action leads to the same conclusion. We have repeatedly held that, as to property reserved by its owner for private use, "the right to exclude [others is] one of the most essential sticks in the bundle of rights that are commonly characterized as property."

Given, then, that requiring uncompensated conveyance of the easement outright would violate the Fourteenth

Amendment, the question becomes whether requiring it to be conveyed as a condition for issuing a land use permit alters the outcome. We have long recognized that land use regulation does not effect a taking if it "substantially advance[s] legitimate state interests" and does not "den[y] an owner economically viable use of his land." The parties have not elaborated on the standards for determining what constitutes a "legitimate state interest" or what type of connection between the regulation and the state interest satisfies the requirement that the former "substantially advance" the latter. They have made clear, however, that a broad range of governmental purposes and regulations satisfies these requirements.

The Commission argues that among these permissible purposes are protecting the public's ability to see the beach, assisting the public in overcoming the "psychological barrier" to using the beach created by a developed shorefront, and preventing congestion on the public beaches. We assume, without deciding, that this is so—in which case the Commission unquestionably would be able to deny the Nollans their permit outright if their new house (alone or by reason of the cumulative impact produced in conjunction with other construction) would substantially impede these purposes, unless the denial would interfere so drastically with the Nollans' use of their property as to constitute a taking.

The Commission argues that a permit condition that serves the same legitimate police-power purpose as a refusal to issue the permit should not be found to be a taking if the refusal to issue the permit would not constitute a taking. We agree. Thus, if the Commission attached to the permit some condition that would have protected the public's ability to see the beach notwithstanding construction of the new house—for example, a height limitation, a width restriction, or a ban on fences—so long as the Commission could have exercised its police power (as we have assumed it could) to forbid construction of the house altogether, imposition of the condition would also be constitutional. Moreover (and here we come closer to the facts of the present case), the condition would be constitutional even if it consisted of the requirement that the Nollans provide a viewing spot on their property for passersby with whose sighting of the ocean their new house would interfere. Although such a requirement, constituting a permanent grant of continuous access to the property, would have to be considered a taking if it were not attached to a development permit, the Commission's assumed power to forbid construction of the house in order to protect the public's view of the beach must surely include the power to condition construction upon some concession by the owner, even a concession of property rights, that serves the same end. If a prohibition designed to accomplish that purpose would be a legitimate exercise of the police power rather than a taking, it would be strange to conclude that providing the owner an alternative to that prohibition which accomplishes the same purpose is not.

The evident constitutional propriety disappears, however, if the condition substituted for the prohibition utterly fails to further the end advanced as the justification for the prohibition. When that essential nexus is eliminated, the situation becomes the same as if California law forbade shouting fire in a crowded theater, but granted dispensations to those willing to contribute $100 to the state treasury. While a ban on shouting fire can be a core exercise of the State's police power to protect the public safety, and can thus meet even our stringent standards for regulation of speech, adding the unrelated condition alters the purpose to one which, while it may be legitimate, is inadequate to sustain the ban. Therefore, even though, in a sense, requiring a $100 tax contribution in order to shout fire is a lesser restriction on speech than an outright ban, it would not pass constitutional muster. Similarly here, the lack of nexus between the condition and the original purpose of the building restriction converts that purpose to something other than what it was. The purpose then becomes, quite simply, the obtaining of an easement to serve some valid governmental purpose, but without payment of compensation. Whatever may be the outer limits of "legitimate state interests" in the takings and land use context, this is not one of them. In short, unless the permit condition serves the same governmental purpose as the development ban, the building restriction is not a valid regulation of land use but "an out-and-out plan of extortion."

Justice Brennan argues that imposition of the access requirement is not irrational. In his version of the Commission's argument, the reason for the requirement is that in its absence, a person looking toward the beach from the road will see a street of residential structures including the Nollans' new home and conclude that there is no public beach nearby. If, however, that person sees people passing and repassing along the dry sand behind the Nollans' home, he will realize that there is a public beach somewhere in the vicinity. The Commission's action, however, was based on the opposite factual finding that the wall of houses completely blocked the view of the beach and that a person looking from the road would not be able to see it at all.

Even if the Commission had made the finding that Justice Brennan proposes, however, it is not certain that it would suffice. We do not share Justice Brennan's confidence that the Commission "should have little difficulty in the future in utilizing its expertise to demonstrate a specific connection between provisions for access and burdens on access," that will avoid the effect of today's decision. We view the Fifth Amendment's property clause to be more than a pleading requirement, and compliance with it to be more than an exercise in cleverness and imagination. As indicated earlier, our cases describe the condition for abridgement of property rights through the police power as a "substantial advanc[ing]" of a legitimate State interest. We are inclined to be particularly careful about the adjective where the actual conveyance of property is made a condition to the lifting of a land use restriction, since in that context there is heightened risk that the purpose is avoidance of the compensation requirement, rather than the stated police power objective.

We are left, then, with the Commission's justification for the access requirement unrelated to land use regulation:

Finally, the Commission notes that there are several existing provisions of pass and repass lateral access benefits already given by past Faria Beach Tract applicants as a result of prior coastal permit decisions. The access required as a condition of this permit is part of a comprehensive program to provide continuous public access along Faria Beach as the lots undergo development or redevelopment.

The Commission [believes] that the public interest will be served by a continuous strip of publicly accessible beach along the coast. The Commission may well be right that it is a good idea, but that does not establish that the Nollans (and other coastal residents) alone can be compelled to contribute to its realization. Rather, California is free to advance its "comprehensive program," if it wishes, by using its power of eminent domain for this "public purpose," but if it wants an easement across the Nollans' property, it must pay for it.

Rewriting the argument to eliminate the play on words makes clear that there is nothing to it. It is quite impossible to understand how a requirement that people already on the public beaches be able to walk across the Nollans' property reduces any obstacles to viewing the beach created by the new house. It is also impossible to understand how it lowers any "psychological barrier" to using the public beaches, or how it helps to remedy any additional congestion on them caused by construction of the Nollans' new house. We therefore find that the Commission's imposition of the permit condition cannot be treated as an exercise of its land use power for any of these purposes.

Reversed.

Discussion Questions

1. What was the proposed use of the Nollans' land?
2. What condition did the Commission wish to impose?
3. If the Commission could not have the condition, were they willing to grant the permit?
4. Is the condition a taking of the Nollans' property?
5. What arguments did the Commission make?

Just Compensation

The final requirement for the proper exercise by a governmental entity of the right of eminent domain is that the party from whom the property is being taken be given *just compensation*. The issue of just compensation is difficult and is always a question of fact. Basic to this determination is that the owner is to be compensated for loss and that the compensation is not measured by the governmental entity's gain. In *United States v. Miller* 317 U.S. 369 (1943), the Supreme Court held that, in cases where it can be determined, fair market value is the measure of compensation. And in *United States ex rel. T.V.A. v. Powelson*, 319 U.S. 266 (1943), the Supreme Court defined fair market value to be "what a willing buyer would pay in cash to a willing seller."

Possible problems in applying these relatively simple standards include peculiar value to the owner, consequential damages, and greater value of the land because of the proposed governmental project. Basically, the issue of just compensation becomes an issue of appraisal, which is affected by all the various factors involved. Thus, in determining just compensation, the courts must consider factors such as surrounding property values and the owner's proposed use.

(19.1) Consider:

The Commonwealth of Massachusetts, in need of an interim facility for women prisoners who have been released from state prison but not yet entitled to full release, condemned a motel located near the court complex for the purpose of supplying the shelter necessary. There are several individuals opposed to the taking of the property. The owner of the motel protests on the ground that a public purpose is not being served. The surrounding restaurant, business, and motel owners protest on the same grounds as well as on grounds that the resulting devaluation of their property and loss of income constitutes a taking of their properties for which they must be compensated. The motel owner objects further when the appraised value and compensation offer are reduced for the resulting effects on surrounding properties. Discuss the issues of public purpose, the regulating versus taking of surrounding lands, and just compensation.

CONSTITUTIONAL ISSUES
IN LAND-USE RESTRICTIONS

The use of land is restricted through zoning requirements (Chapter 16), future interests (Chapter 3), and covenants or restrictions in deeds that control the use of the property being transferred (Chapter 25). Because the right to the full use and enjoyment of one's property has been protected so carefully, any imposed restrictions are subject to judicial scrutiny. All three forms of restrictions have met with constitutional challenges, and these are discussed in the following sections.

Zoning

Some constitutional challenges to zoning have already been discussed. For example, in the *Village of Euclid* case the constitutionality of zoning was upheld, and it was mandated that restricting use did not constitute a taking requiring compensation under eminent domain. Also, in the *Village of Belle Terre* case, the Supreme Court upheld a city's right to restrict property use to single-family dwellings under the public welfare interests of traffic, noise, and congestion control. However, in *Cleburne v. Cleburne*, 473 U.S. 432 (1985), (see Chapter 16), the court ruled that a zoning ordinance had gone too far in its regulation; that a constitutionally protected right had been infringed upon; and that the regulation prohibiting group homes for the mentally retarded was invalid.

The grounds for challenges to zoning ordinances are limited only by the rights afforded in the Constitution; thus, many zoning cases involve constitutional issues. The following two cases involve a constitutional issue raised by zoning ordinances that are different from those discussed to this point.

FRAMINGHAM CLINIC, INC. v. BOARD OF SELECTMEN
367 N.E.2d 606 (Mass. 1977)

Southborough, Massachusetts (defendant/appellee) passed a zoning ordinance that prohibited the operation of abortion clinics within that town. Framingham Clinic (plaintiff/appellant), which attempted to establish a gynecological clinic that would perform first-trimester abortions, brought suit challenging the validity of the ordinance. The lower court found for Southborough, and Framingham Clinic appealed.

KAPLAN, Justice

We hold for the plaintiffs. The ordinance is invalid. The conclusion becomes clear when attention is paid to the constitutionally protected rights of a woman in respect to termination of her pregnancy (and the correlative rights of an attending physician or a health facility), as expounded by the Supreme Court of the United States in the line of cases beginning with *Roe v. Wade.*

The ordinance would have the effect of banishing from the town any clinic in which first-trimester abortions, themselves admittedly lawful, were performed. But clinics offering other lawful medical procedures could locate themselves and carry on in this or any other industrial park district that might appear on the town map. This indicates strongly that discrimination was at work against the constitutional right.

The desires of members of the community to disfavor an "abortion clinic"— desires which, reflexively, may cause these persons to see an economic detriment to themselves in the existence of the clinic— cannot extenuate such a violation. The report of the Southborough planning board about public sentiment was thus an irrelevancy, and a dangerous one, for that way would lie the extinction of many liberties which are, indeed, constitutionally guaranteed against invasion by a majority.

Neither could Southborough justify its own exclusionary rule by saying that a woman might overcome it by going elsewhere in the Commonwealth. May a "fundamental" right be denied in Worcester County because it remains available in Suffolk or Barnstable? Such a proposition cannot seriously be maintained. The picture of one community attempting thus to throw off on others would not be a happy one.

Reversed.

Discussion Questions

1. What does the ordinance at issue provide?
2. Who is challenging the ordinance?
3. Is abortion a constitutionally protected right?
4. Of what relevance is the public sentiment report?
5. Does the fact that other towns permit abortions have any effect?
6. Is the ordinance constitutional?

CITY OF CHICAGO v. SCANDIA BOOKS, INC.
430 N.E.2d 14 (Ill. 1981)

In 1977 the city of Chicago (plaintiff/ appellee) passed zoning ordinances that included the following:

Section 3. Definitions
A. Adult Book Stores. An establishment having as a substantial or significant portion of its stock in trade, books, magazines, films for sale or viewing on premises by use of Motion Picture devices or any other coin-operated means, and other periodicals which are distinguished or characterized by their emphasis on the matter depicting, describing or relating to "Specified Sexual Activities," or "Specified Anatomical Areas," or an establishment with a segment or section devoted to the sale or display of such material.

The operation of adult bookstores was prohibited in all areas except those zoned C-2 commercial.

In June 1980 Robert Eggert, a police officer with the city of Chicago, was sent to investigate Scandia Books' (defendant/appellant) Broadway Book Shop located on North Broadway. The store was divided into two parts by a swinging door and a counter. In the front area of the store there were racks containing magazines such as *Time*

and *Life*, Bibles, and paperback books. In the back area there were rubber paraphernalia, and magazines and books pertaining to heterosexual and homosexual acts.

Officer Eggert took photographs of the store, which showed booths that contained adult films, a wall displaying books on lesbianism, and an area where rubber products were displayed. Eggert viewed a peep show, which portrayed a female and male engaged in intercourse. Two peep shows were offered per booth, and there were six booths in the store.

The city brought suit seeking a permanent injunction against Scandia Books for the operation of the adult bookstore in an area not zoned for such a business. The trial court ruled that the regulated uses of the ordinance had been violated and enjoined further use of the premises as an adult bookstore.

Scandia Books appealed on grounds that Section 3A is so vague and indefinite as to violate the due process clauses of both the United States and Illinois constitutions, and that their First Amendment rights were being infringed.

JOHNSON, Justice

The test for an ordinance which affects first amendment rights is:

A government regulation is sufficiently justified if it is within the constitutional power of the Government; if it furthers an important or substantial governmental interest; if the governmental interest is unrelated to the suppression of free expression; and if the incidental restriction on alleged First Amendment freedoms is no greater than is essential to the furtherance of that interest.

Applying this test to the instant case, we hold that the right of the City to reasonably regulate and restrict the location of certain uses, whether business, residential or industrial is clear. Further, the ordinance in question was enacted by the City to deter the decrease in property values, increase in crime, neighborhood decline, and the adverse effect on business and residential districts caused by the influx of adult bookstore businesses. The primary control or regulation of the Ordinance is the prevention of concentration of these kinds of uses [adult] in any one area. Chicago has provided that no adult use shall be located within 1000 feet of any zoning district which is zoned for residential use. Thus, the restrictions on first amendment freedoms is no greater than is necessary to further Chicago's interest in the protection of its citizenry and neighborhoods.

In support of their claim that the provision of the Ordinance which defines adult bookstores is vague, defendants point to the words, "substantial or significant" as being unconstitutionally vague. We find defendants' argument without merit. The word "substantial" as used in the definition of adult bookstores is not so indefinite as to render the Ordinance void and unenforceable. That term has been construed as having an ascertainable meaning in numerous statutory schemes. Additionally, the definition of an adult bookstore in the Ordinance includes an establishment with a segment or section devoted to the sale or display of adult material. Clearly, the record shows that defendants' bookstore contained a section devoted to the sale or display of adult material.

We cannot say that the Ordinance is so vague as to violate the due process clause of the Illinois or United States Constitutions. The language in question gave defendants a sufficiently definite warning and fair notice as to the forbidden conduct regulated by the Ordinance.

Accordingly, the issuance of the injunction is affirmed.

Discussion Questions

1. What did the ordinance at issue regulate?
2. What type of business was Scandia Books operating?
3. What constitutional challenges to the ordinance are made?
4. What is the test for validity of zoning in a First Amendment argument?
5. What were the city of Chicago's purposes in enacting the ordinances?
6. What portion of the ordinance is challenged as vague?
7. Is the ordinance unconstitutionally vague?
8. Does the ordinance violate the First Amendment?

(19.2) Consider:

A state has passed a law prohibiting the operation of stores "engaging primarily in the sale of drug paraphernalia." When an injunction is issued against the operator of a store selling items such as papers, clips, and pipes, the operator appeals on grounds that the statute is unconstitutionally vague. What is the result?

Future Interests

Although fee simples determinable and fee simples subject to conditions subsequent do restrict the use and transferability of property, the courts have not intervened in these land interests unless the restrictions have violated any of the fundamental rights afforded by the Constitution. One type of restriction that has been subject to constitutional constraints is the restriction on use according to race. The following case deals with the validity of a race restriction in the form of a fee simple determinable.

CAPITOL FEDERAL SAVINGS AND LOAN ASSOCIATION v. SMITH
316 P.2d 252 (Colo. 1957)

The predecessors to Capitol Federal's (plaintiff) title to the property at issue had taken title with the restriction that the lots involved never be sold or leased to colored persons. The grants provided that if the lots were ever sold or leased to colored persons, then title would automatically vest in the other lot owners (defendants/appellants).

Capitol Federal financed the purchase of one of the lots by Carmelita and Whitney Armelin, "colored persons of Negro extraction." The other lot owners (or their heirs) claimed they now held title because of the violation of the restriction. Cap-

itol Federal, together with the Armelins (plaintiffs/appellees), brought suit to have title quieted, alleging that the restriction was in violation of the United States Constitution.

The trial court held that Capitol Federal and the Armelins were title holders, and the court cleared their title and barred any enforcement of the restriction by the other lot owners. The trial court further held that the restrictive covenant violated the Fourteenth Amendment of the United States Constitution. The lot owners appealed.

KNAUSS, Justice

Covenants such as the one here considered whether denominated "executory interests" or "future interests," as urged by counsel for defendants cannot change the character of what was here attempted.

Counsel for the defendants contend that the covenant created a future interest in the land known as an executory interest. They assert "Such interest vested automatically in the defendants upon the happening of the events specified in the original instrument of grant, and the validity of vesting did not in any way depend upon judicial action by the courts. The trial court's failure and refusal to recognize the vested interest of the defendants, and its ruling that the defendants have no title or interest in or to the property, deprived defendants

of their property without just compensation and without due process of law." We cannot agree. No matter by what ariose terms the covenant under consideration may be classified by astute counsel, it is still a racial restriction in violation of the Fourteenth Amendment to the Federal Constitution. That this is so has been definitely settled by the decisions of the Supreme Court of the United States. High sounding phrases or outmoded common law terms cannot alter the effect of the agreement embraced in the instant case. While the hands may seem to be the hands of Esau to a blind Isaac, the voice is definitely Jacob's. We cannot give our judicial approval.

In *Shelley v. Kramer*, 334 U.S. 1, the Supreme Court of the United States said:

We hold that in granting judicial enforcement of the restrictive agreements in these cases, the States have denied Petitioners the equal protection of the laws and that, therefore, the action of the state courts cannot stand. We have noted that freedom from discrimination by the States in the enjoyment of property rights was among the basic objectives sought to be effectuated by the framers of the Fourteenth Amendment. That such discrimination has occurred in these cases is clear. Because of the race or color of these petitioners they have been denied rights of ownership or occupancy enjoyed as a matter of course by other citizens of different race or color. The Fourteenth Amendment declares "that all persons, whether colored, or white, shall stand equal before the laws of the States, and, in regard to the colored race, for whose protection the amendment was primarily designed, that no discrimination shall be made against them by law because of their color."

Because the language of the United States Supreme Court suggested that private racially restrictive covenants were not invalid per se, it was believed for some time that an action for damages might lie against one who violated such a covenant. A number of states adopted this position, and awarded damages against those who, contrary to their agreements, had made sales of property to negroes or other persons within excluded classes. This problem came to the attention of the Supreme Court of the United States in *Barrows v. Jackson*, 346 U.S. 249, where it was held that although such a grantor's constitutional rights were not violated, nevertheless the commodious protection of the Fourteenth Amendment extended to her and she could not be made to respond in damages for treating her restrictive covenant as a nullity.

Because the United States Supreme Court has extracted any teeth which such a covenant was supposed to have, no rights, duties or obligations can be based thereon.

The judgment is affirmed.

Discussion Questions

1. Who are the plaintiffs and what interest do they have in the property in question?
2. What restriction has been placed on the property?
3. What happens if the restriction, according to its terms, is violated?
4. Who are the defendants and what interest do they hold in the property?
5. What future interest is alleged to exist?
6. What is the basis for challenging the validity of the restriction?
7. Is the restriction constitutional?
8. Will compensation be paid for the loss of a land interest?

All-adult Covenants

In many areas, particularly in retirement communities, land purchases are subject to a restrictive covenant that allows only persons above the age of 18 or 21 to reside in a particular area: an *all-adult covenant*. The validity of these all-adult covenants and communities has been an issue before the courts, and the following case is one of those judicial reviews.

SCHMIDT v. SUPERIOR COURT
742 P.2d 209 (Calif. 1987)

Teri Lynn Schmidt and her sister and daughter (plaintiffs) wanted to purchase a mobile home in a mobile home park managed by Valley Mobile Park Investments (defendants). The purchase was conditioned on Valley's acceptance of the Schmidt's application for space. Valley rejected the application citing a rule that permitted only persons age 25 or older to live in the park. Schmidt then brought suit alleging that their constitutional rights as well as the Unruh Civil Rights Act had been violated. The trial court dismissed the case. The Court of Appeals ruled that the mobile home park was not specifically designated for senior citizens and reversed. Valley appealed.

MOSK, Justice

The central question in this case is whether a mobilehome park has the right to restrict residence to adults. Defendants contend that section 798.76 disposes of the issue. That section is embodied in an article of the Mobilehome Residency Law relating to the transfer of a manufactured house (§798.70-798.80). When a mobilehome is to remain in the park, management has the right to prior approval of the purchaser, although it may exercise its right only on narrow grounds (§798.74). Management may also require the purchaser to adhere to the terms of a rental agreement (§798.75). Section 798.76 adds that "The management may require" that such a purchaser "comply with any rule or regulation limiting residence to adults only." There is no doubt that plaintiffs are or aspire to be "purchasers" of a mobilehome. Defendants urge us to hold that when the Legislature permitted a mobilehome park to enforce a rule limiting residence to "adults," it meant exactly what it said.

Plaintiffs nevertheless urge us to look to the legislative intent behind section 798.76. They argue that in spite of ordinary meaning, other statutes and public policy compel the conclusion that the section's reference to "adults" must be construed to mean "senior citizens."

Plaintiffs contend that the Unruh Civil Rights Act (§51 et seq.) requires a construction of "adults" to mean senior citizens. Section 51 declares that "All persons . . . no matter what their sex, race, color, religion, ancestry, or national origin are entitled to the full and equal accommodations, advantages, facilities, privileges, or services in all business establishments of every kind whatsoever." We held in *In re Cox* (1970), 3 Cal.3d 205, 216, 90 Cal.Rptr. 24, 474 P.2d 992, that the identification of particular bases of discrimination in section 51 is illustrative rather than restrictive. In *Marina Point, Ltd. v. Wolfson* (1982), 30 Cal.3d 721, 180 Cal.Rptr. 496, 640 P.2d 115, a majority of this court held that the Unruh Act prohibited the blanket exclusion of families with children from an apartment complex. *Marina Point* observed, however, that age-based restrictions might be permissible when they reflect a compelling societal interest. By way of example, the opinion suggested that a housing facility specifically designed to meet the needs of older citizens would not violate the prescripts of the Unruh Act.

Rather than viewing section 798.76 as an exception to the general provisions of the Unruh Act, plaintiffs contend that we must construe the section to be consonant with the act. Understanding "adults" to only refer to senior citizens, they urge, would accomplish that result: mobilehome parks would be barred from age discrimination unless they catered specifically to senior citizens. But such a construction would render section 798.76 entirely without effect, because the section would then merely restate the restrictions of the Unruh Act.

Here, plaintiffs' proposed reading would render the entire statute superfluous; nothing new or significant would have been added by its adoption. To give meaning to section 798.76 we must conclude that "adults" refers to adults and that the Legislature intended the section to be an exception to the general prohibitions of the Unruh Act.

Plaintiffs attempt to avoid this conclusion by suggesting that the Unruh Act has been elevated to what might be described as quasi-constitutional status, and that it is therefore entitled to great deference. They also place much emphasis on the state's public policy of providing affordable housing for families. We do not dispute that the Unruh Act is entitled to appropriate respect and that the provision of housing to middle- and lower-income families is a matter of serious public concern. Nor do we doubt that mobilehomes are an increasingly important source of shelter for the growing number of this state's citizens unable to afford the traditional single-family suburban house. But the Unruh Act is legislative in origin. Even though it expresses an important public policy, as a legislative enactment the act does not override inconsistent subsequent legislation. What the Legislature giveth, it legitimately taketh away.

For these reasons we hold that when it enacted section 798.76, the Legislature meant exactly what it said: the management of a mobilehome park may require that the mobilehome purchaser who is to remain in the park comply with a rule limiting residence to adults, i.e., to persons 18 years of age or older. We now turn to plaintiffs' claim that as so construed the statute runs afoul of their constitutional rights.

Plaintiffs contend that a statute authorizing mobilehome parks to cater exclusively to adults violates equal protection of the laws. California's equal protection clause is substantially the equivalent of the federal guarantee, although the state protection possesses an independent vitality that may, in a given case, lead to a different result.

Defendants argue at length that there can be no constitutional violation here because there is no state action. It is incontrovertible that the mandate of the equal protection clause applies only to actions taken, directly or indirectly, by the government itself. The exclusion of children from a mobilehome park is normally a purely private act to which the requirements of equal protection do not adhere. But the gravamen of plaintiffs' claim is that the statute, by drawing a distinction between children and adults, is unconstitutional. While defendants' private act may not trigger equal protection scrutiny, the Legislature's adoption of a statute that discriminates on its face is plainly state action.

State equal protection analysis, of course, has traditionally proceeded on either of two levels of judicial scrutiny of a challenged governmental action, depending on the importance of the interest to be protected and the likelihood of discrimination against a particular group.

In the area of economic regulation, the high court has exercised restraint, investing legislation with a presumption of constitutionality and requiring merely that distinctions drawn by a challenged statute bear some rational relationship to a conceivable legitimate state purpose. [Citations.] On the other hand, in cases involving "suspect classifications" or touching on "fundamental interests," the court has adopted an attitude of active and critical analysis, subjecting the classification to strict scrutiny. [Citations.] Under [this standard], the state bears the burden of establishing not only that it has a compelling interest which justifies the law but that the distinctions drawn by the law are necessary to further its purpose.

Plaintiff first invites us to hold age classifications "suspect," thus requiring us to strictly scrutinize section 798.76. We cannot accept the invitation. Courts that have considered the issue have declined to extend heightened review to differential treatment based on age.

Nor are we persuaded that we should interpret the California equal protection clause to require strict scrutiny of age-based classifications. The rationale for according a particular group the status of suspect class is that it comprises a "discrete and insular" minority that may need protection from the whims of those who wield political power. A suspect class is one "saddled with such disabilities, or subjected to such a history of purposeful unequal treatment, or relegated to such a position of political powerlessness as to command extraordinary protection from the majoritarian political process."

Children are, in the first place, not a discrete and insular group. The line between relevant age differences is neither fundamentally fixed nor predetermined, but rather may be drawn at various points on the continuum from infant to centenarian, depending on the purpose of the distinction. Furthermore, everyone living a normal lifespan goes through every stage. Those

in charge of the political process are unlikely to discriminate against adults, since they are themselves part of this group. And they are equally unlikely to impermissibly burden the young—all were themselves children at one time, most have or had children, and virtually all will be dependent on a younger workforce to produce their ultimate social security benefits. Finally, young people have none of the stigma generally associated with a suspect class. The troubling persistence of racism, although often masked by a rhetoric of tolerance, leaves no doubt that even today many racial or ethnic groupings are treated at times as inferiors by the dominant culture. Minors are not stigmatized in this fashion. If anything, children are highly valued; the virtues of the family are extolled by political figures, sanctified by religious organizations, and subsidized by income tax laws.

Plaintiffs next contend that the exclusion of nonadults from a mobilehome park infringes on their right to privacy. They argue that defendants' rule divides people into two classes—those with children and those without—in regard to their fundamental right to live together as a family. Thus, under either a due process or a "fundamental interest" equal protection analysis, plaintiffs insist that strict scrutiny be applied.

Under the federal Constitution governmental action that directly creates a substantial burden on a family's right to live together must be strictly scrutinized. Because defendants' rule in the matter before us or its implementation is plainly not state action, we must focus instead on the legislative enactment of section 798.76 to determine whether it so burdens plaintiffs' right to privacy.

We note, first, that the statute does not directly regulate the family, but merely draws a distinction between adults and nonadults. It does not authorize a mobilehome park to impose restrictions on who lives with whom, aside from insisting that they all exceed a stated age. And the impact on the family is also indirect in that the statute simply allows, rather than mandates, age-based restrictions. In addition, the effect of the statute on familial privacy is relatively insubstantial. It may be, as plaintiffs claim, that all the mobilehome parks in the area in which they live have similar rules. But the doctrine of familial privacy does not go so far as to guarantee them a fundamental right to live together in a mobilehome in a location of their choosing. Furthermore, it appears that before they attempted to buy the mobilehome in defendants' park, the family lived together nearby and that they continue to reside, the family intact, in the same general area. Because the statute thus has only an indirect and minimal impact on plaintiffs' right to privacy, strict scrutiny is not appropriate.

Plaintiffs contend that under our construction section 798.76 is an invalid restraint on alienation. The contention is without merit. The rule against restraints on alienation (§711) is not absolute, but bars only unreasonable restraints. We note as an initial matter that section 798.76 does not in any way restrain the right of a mobilehome owner to sell his unit to whomever he chooses, including those who are not adults. The Mobilehome Residency Law simply requires that a purchaser desiring to maintain a mobilehome in a park must agree to abide by the terms of the rental agreement (§798.75) and to comply with any rule or regulation limiting residence to adults only (§798.76). This is not a restraint on alienation, but merely a limitation on whether a purchaser may rent a space in the park. To the extent that the restriction may inhibit sales to younger buyers or families with children, it is merely a byproduct of a statute that is reasonable exercise of legislative power. The minimal impact of requiring adherence to legitimate provisions in a rental agreement, which applies only when the mobilehome is to remain in the park, does not unreasonably interfere with the right of sellers to alienate their mobilehomes.

Reversed.

Discussion Questions

1. What restriction was placed on residence in the mobile home park?
2. How does the restriction differ from other restrictions?
3. How does the court deal with the issue of providing housing for families?
4. Is the mobile home park restriction unconstitutional?
5. Do results on these restrictions differ in retirement states?

(19.3) Consider:

The Judds purchased a home in a subdivision in Arizona that was designated as one for those age "55 and over." The restrictions on the subdivision also provide that children over the age of 18 only can reside with their parents. The Judds' daughter was recently divorced and has asked to live with them for a few months until she is financially stable again. The Judds' 12-year-old granddaughter will also be moving in. Can the neighbors obtain a court order to require the daughter and granddaughter to move out? *Riley v. Stoves*, 526 P.2d 749 (Ariz. 1974)

(19.4) Consider:

On the basis of the *Schmidt* case and the cases cited therein, determine the constitutional validity of the following:

a. A city ordinance requiring all-adult residences only.

b. A city zoning master plan that designates certain areas as adult-only residential areas.

c. A state statute that prohibits landlords from refusing to rent property located in all-adult subdivisions to families with children.

CONSTITUTIONAL ISSUES IN THE TRANSFER OF PROPERTY

One of the major issues in the transfer of property is the requirement that transfers of title be available to all regardless of race, sex, color, or national origin. The Fair Housing Act was passed in 1968 (42 U.S.C. §3601 et seq.), and §3604a provides that it is

> unlawful to refuse to sell or rent after the making of a bona fide offer, or to refuse to negotiate for the sale or rental of, or otherwise make unavailable or deny, a dwelling to any person because of race, color, religion, sex or national origin.

The basis for this statutory regulation is the Equal Protection Clause of the Fourteenth Amendment. As discussed in Chapter 1, the Fourteenth Amendment requires that all citizens be treated equally in the application and enforcement of state laws. The Fourteenth Amendment is the basis for many of the racial, religious, and national origin discrimination cases. The purpose of the amendment is to guarantee all an equal opportunity to be treated alike under state laws.

However, when the issue involved is private action as opposed to the application of state laws to individuals, the Fourteenth Amendment is not applicable. In other words, the Fourteenth Amendment does not prohibit private discrimination, and legislation to prevent private discrimination is required to fill that gap. The Fair Housing Act is an example of a statute passed to prevent private discrimination. The act applies not only to sellers of properties, but also to real estate brokers and salespersons, mortgage lenders, property insurers, and property appraisers. In the following sections, the techniques for discrimination and their validity are discussed.

Blockbusting

Blockbusting is a method of controlling the racial composition of neighborhoods and is usually attributed to the actions of real estate brokers or salespersons. For example, in *United States v. Mitchell*, 327 F. Supp. 476, (N.D. Ga. 1971), a real estate agent went from house to house in a neighborhood, informing the residents that "negroes were coming into the neighborhood" and that houses should be sold as quickly as possible. The result was that all of the white residents in the neighborhood sold their homes, and the neighborhood became all-black. Mitchell was convicted of violating the Fair Housing Act.

Steering

Steering is another form of property transfer discrimination that is generally attributed to real estate brokers and salespersons. It is an attempt to direct buyers to specific sections of town that are labeled as either *white* or *black* areas. In *Zuch v. Hussey*, 394 F. Supp. 1028 (E.D. Mich 1975), salespersons found to have violated the act made statements such as, "Do you read the newspapers? Even the police are afraid to live in the area and they are supposed to protect the rest of us," and "You wouldn't want that home, the coloreds have moved in pretty good there." In the same case, salespersons discouraged black buyers from buying in white areas by temporarily taking homes off the market. Through these tactics (which were declared illegal), several real estate firms were able to maintain racially segregated neighborhoods in the Detroit area for a period of time.

Redlining

Redlining is the refusal by a lender to lend or an insurer to insure on property because of its location within a predetermined geographic area. The name for this practice arose because lenders and insurers were literally drawing red lines on maps around areas in which property loans and insurance should not be made or should be made on less than favorable terms. The Fair Housing Act and many state statutes prohibit redlining; in many cases they require lending institutions to submit loan figures so that an agency can verify the institutions' lending records. For example, federal institutions are required to submit loan figures under the Home Mortgage Disclosure Act (12 U.S.C. §§2801 et seq.). Also, the Community Reinvestment Act of 1977 (12 U.S.C. §§2901 et seq.) imposes an affirmative obligation on federal financial institutions to meet the community's loan needs regardless of property location or area condition.

Redlining can occur in a number of different ways. The most obvious is when lenders openly refuse to make loans in particular areas. Other more subtle processes still classified as redlining include the arbitrary variation of loan application processes and loan terms. For example, redlining can consist of requiring a higher down payment, higher closing costs, minimum loan amounts, lowered percentage of loan amount to appraised value, or under appraisal of property. The determination of whether a lender has made a predetermined lending decision on the basis of property location is a question of fact requiring litigation. The following case involves the issue of whether a lender was engaging in redlining.

LAUFMAN v. OAKLEY BUILDING & LOAN CO.
408 F. Supp. 489 (Ohio 1976)

The Laufmans (plaintiffs) attempted to purchase property in an area of Cincinnati that was changing in racial composition from white to black. Oakley Building and Loan (defendant) denied the Laufmans' loan application on grounds that the neighborhood was declining and they would not have sufficient security by taking a mortgage on the property located there. The Laufmans filed suit alleging that Oakley Building and Loan had violated the Fair Housing Act.

PORTER, District Judge

In the present case, plaintiffs allege that they were denied a loan because of the racial composition of the neighborhood in which the home was located. We agree that this alleged conduct interferes with the plaintiffs' rights to equal housing opportunity protected by the Fair Housing Act.

The fact that it was not the plaintiffs' own race, but the race of the people who resided in the neighborhood does not exempt the defendants from application of the Act.

In this connection, we believe that the remarks made during oral argument by counsel for the Federal Home Loan Bank Board are notable:

Considering the brief time that's available, I'd like to start by refuting or attempting to refute a couple of points made by counsel for defendants. First, counsel points out that regulations of the Federal Savings and Loan Insurance Corporation discourage savings and loans from making investments or making loans in "declining neighborhoods," and he used that term several times. I suggest that's the gist of what the Bank Board was trying to make illegal in its regulations, was the feeling on the part of a great many lenders that a racially integrated neighborhood per se must be a declining neighborhood and per se must be a bad credit risk. There is nothing in the Board's regulations or in the Board's policies which mandates an association to make a bad loan as long as the criteria they use for making the loan are legitimate business criteria, such as the credit wor-

thiness of the borrower, the marketability, the salability of the security property, including the neighborhood in which it's located which has a bearing on its salability, the diversification of the institution's assets. All these things are legitimate criteria. But the facts have shown over the years, it's been shown time and again that a neighborhood which had changed from white to black or a neighborhood that is racially integrated, particularly an older neighborhood within city limits of an established and older city need not be a declining neighborhood, and that often a contributing factor to the decline is the re-

fusal of lenders to provide credit for the purchase of these homes or for the rehabilitation of them. So, we take issue with the defense, not on whether or not a financial institution is obligated to make loans in a declining neighborhood, but on the judgment that a declining neighborhood necessarily results when a neighborhood becomes racially integrated.

The foregoing statement constitutes a completely satisfactory statement of the relevant policies and regulations which we also believe are firmly supported by the law.

We find that the plaintiffs have stated a cause of action under the Fair Housing Act.

Discussion Questions

1. In what type of neighborhood is the property that the plaintiffs wish to purchase?
2. What conclusions cannot be drawn (under the Fair Housing Act) regarding a racially integrated neighborhood?
3. Can location of property in a declining neighborhood be a reason for denying a loan?
4. Was the defendant guilty of redlining in this case?

Although redlining is generally associated with lenders, it can become an issue in setting appraisal values. In the following case the appraisal standards of the American Institute of Real Estate Appraisers were challenged as violative of the Fair Housing Act.

UNITED STATES v. AMERICAN INSTITUTE OF REAL ESTATE APPRAISERS
442 F. Supp. 1072 (Ill. 1977)

The United States filed suit against two organizations, the American Institute of Real Estate Appraisers (AIREA) and the Society of Real Estate Appraisers (defendants) for violation of the Fair Housing Act. The suit alleged that since the effective date of the Fair Housing Act, these two or-

ganizations had engaged in unlawful discriminatory practices by promulgating standards that have caused appraisers and lenders to treat race and national origin as negative factors in determining the value of dwellings and in evaluating the soundness of home loans. The suit further alleged

574

that the organizations failed to take adequate steps to correct the continuing effects of past discrimination and ensure nondiscrimination by appraisers and lenders, whose practices are subject to the influence of the organizations.

The United States sought injunctive relief, and after extensive negotiations the United States and the AIREA agreed not to litigate the matter; instead, they asked for the approval of a settlement order, which would include the adoption of the following statements as policies of the AIREA:

1. It is improper to base a conclusion or opinion of value upon the premise that the racial, ethnic or religious homogeneity of the inhabitants of an area is necessary for maximum value.

2. Racial, religious or ethnic factors are deemed unreliable predictors of value trends or price variance.
3. It is improper to base a conclusion or opinion of value, or a conclusion with respect to neighborhood trends, upon stereotyped or biased presumptions relating to race, color, religion, sex or national origin or upon unsupported presumptions relating to the effective age or remaining life of the property being appraised or the life expectancy of the neighborhood in which it is located.

Opelka and others, as members of the AIREA, brought suit challenging the settlement order on grounds that appraisal was not within the coverage of the Fair Housing Act and that the AIREA has no authority to enter into such a settlement.

LEIGHTON, District Judge

The first and fundamental objection is that the court lacks jurisdiction (to approve the settlement) because the Fair Housing Act does not apply to appraisers. . . . [T]he court takes this opportunity to hold that the Fair Housing Act does apply to appraisers of real estate. . . . The principal argument advanced is that the sections of the Fair Housing Act do not mention appraisers. Section 3604 provides in pertinent part:

It shall be unlawful—
(a) To refuse to sell or rent after the making of a bona fide offer, or to refuse to negotiate for the sale or rental of, or otherwise make unavailable or deny, a dwelling to any person because of race, color, religion, sex or national origin.

It shall be unlawful to coerce, intimidate, threaten, or interfere with any person in the exercise or enjoyment of, or on account of his having exercised or enjoyed, or on account of his having aided or en-

couraged any other person in the exercise or enjoyment of any right [granted under this Act].

It is clear from the plain language of the provisions that appraisers are not exempted from their coverage; both sections are unrestricted with respect to the class of persons subject to their prohibition. The "otherwise make unavailable or deny" language has been applied to a variety of conduct to prohibit all practices which have the effect of denying dwellings on prohibited grounds. For example, the Act applies to racially exclusionary land use practices by a municipality. It applies to "redlining" by financial institutions. It applies to delaying tactics and discouragement of rental applications used by resident managers and rental agents, and top management and owners who fail to set objective and reviewable procedures for rental applications.

The "or interfere with" language has been similarly broadly applied to reach all practices which have the effect of interfering with the exercise of rights under the Act. The Act requires a liberal construction if the statute is to prohibit effectively "all forms of discrimination, sophisticated, as well as simple-minded." Given a broad interpretation of these provisions, it becomes clear that the United States has stated a claim for relief under their terms. The promulgation of standards which cause appraisers and lenders to treat race and national origin as a negative factor in determining the value of dwellings and in evaluating the soundness of home loans may effectively "make unavailable or deny" a "dwelling" and may interfere with persons in the exercise and enjoyment of rights guaranteed by the Act.

The settlement order is approved.

Discussion Questions

1. Who are the defendants in the case?
2. What does the settlement order provide?
3. Who is challenging the settlement?
4. What is the basis of the challenge?
5. Does the Fair Housing Act apply to appraisers?

(19.5) Consider:

Great Eastern Bank has been sued by several members of the Navajo Tribe for redlining on home loans located on the reservation. Great Eastern has supplied statistics indicating that over 75 percent of all home mortgage loans on reservation property end in default and foreclosure. Is Great Eastern's statistic a valid basis for denying future reservation loans?

DUE PROCESS AND REAL PROPERTY

Throughout the preceding chapters, the concept of due process has been mentioned in connection with different topics. For example, mortgage foreclosures require prior notice to the mortgagor, and the opportunity for the mortgagor to object, before title to or interest in financed property may be taken away. With respect to real property taxes, landowners must be given opportunities to object to and be heard on the valuations of their properties. Tax sales require advance notice to the property owner and an opportunity for redemption. All of these protections are afforded through the Fifth and Fourteenth Amendment's due process clauses of the Constitution, which require that before there is any deprivation of a property interest, the parties must be given opportunities to be heard and to object. Due process protections may be satisfied through judicial or administrative proceedings, so long as the opportunity to be heard is afforded.

In this chapter, only a few issues of constitutional law affecting real property rights were discussed. The opportunities for constitutional challenges to real property rights and procedures are as limitless as the field of constitutional law. Basically, the areas of constitutional law affecting real property are concerned with the issues of fairness, the deprivation of rights in existing property, or the right to own property. Constitutional protections offer security for property owners holding title and provide potential property owners opportunities for purchase.

KEY TERMS

eminent domain
taking
just compensation
all-adult covenant

blockbusting
steering
redlining

CHAPTER PROBLEMS

1. General Motors (GM) advised the city of Detroit that in 1 year it would shut down its Cadillac and Fisher Body Plants, which were both located within city boundaries. The reasons given for the closures were GM's need for a more modern plant and inability to find a 500-acre plot within the city on which to construct it. Faced with the potential of serious fiscal problems the impending shutdowns would bring, Detroit began looking for a 450- to 500-acre rectangular plot with access to long-haul railroad lines and a highway. The city came up with a vacant Dodge plant surrounded by 1,362 homes and began procedures to take the homes by eminent domain. In court, twenty home owners challenged the taking as unconstitutional, because no public purpose was involved. The city of Detroit maintained the taking was an essential part of a public program "to alleviate and prevent conditions of unemployment." Is the taking constitutional?

2. William G. Haas & Company purchased land and procured a site permit from the city of San Francisco for the construction of a high-rise project. Haas had paid in excess of $1.5 million for the property. The site permit was later invalidated because of violations of the Environmental Quality Act and later because of the rezoning of the property, which prohibited high-rise projects in the area. Haas brought suit claiming the rezoning and the imposition of other land-use restrictions diminished the value of his property to such an extent that the regulations constituted a taking. What was the result?

3. The village of Arlington Heights, Illinois refused to rezone a portion of property located within city limits so that the property could be used for the construction of federally financed low-cost housing. Several black citizens sued, alleging the effect of the rezoning was to prohibit low-income (predominantly black) families from moving into the area and that the refusal to rezone constituted a violation of the Fair Housing Act. What was the result?

4. Midwestern Indemnity refused to write insurance policies for homes located in neighborhoods that were predominantly black. Midwestern's reasons were high theft, vandalism, and arson rates in the areas, and they had the areas marked on maps in their offices. Several black home owners brought suit, alleging the insurer was redlining. Midwestern maintains insurers are not subject to the Fair Housing Act. What is the result?

5. The Harpers (a black family) purchased a home with financing through Union Savings Association. During the first year, two of the Harper's payment checks bounced but were immediately covered. Mr. Harper then lost his job and attempted to work out an interim payment schedule with Union. Union refused and foreclosed on the property. An examination of Union's records reveals that it was the first time Union had refused an interim payment plan for a temporarily unemployed borrower. Harper filed suit, alleging Union had violated the Fair Housing Act. Union maintains the Fair Housing Act is applicable only to purchases of homes and loans, not foreclosures. What is the result?

6. The city of Phoenix announced the taking of sixty homes located near the airport for the purpose of expanding the airport runways to support increased traffic. The home owners claim that the appraisals should reflect the commercial value of their property because of the closer proximity to the airstrips. The city of Phoenix maintains that value is determined before the change. What is the result?

7. In 1927, W. T. Shore and T. C. Wilson gave property to the city of Charlotte "so long as the property was used for municipal parks, golf courses, or playgrounds for whites only." Several black citizens have brought suit, alleging the restriction is unconstitutional. What type of interest was created, and what is the result?

8. The District of Columbia condemned several pieces of property so that a public housing project could be constructed. The owners of the property contest the taking as an improper exercise of eminent domain. What is the result?

9. The town of Hempstead passed an ordinance that prohibited dredging and pit excavating within its city limits. The rationale for the ordinance

was prevention of noise, prevention of road destruction, and safety of citizens. The owners of one of the pits object to the zoning as a taking and wish compensation for the loss of the right to mine. What is the result?

10. In reference to the chapter opening, is the city of Rye's clothesline ordinance valid?

IV

MARKETING REAL ESTATE AND COMMERCIAL REAL ESTATE

║20║

CONSTRUCTION AND CONSTRUCTION FINANCING

> *If a builder builds a house for a man and does not make its construction firm, and the house which he has built collapses and causes the death of the owner of the house, the builder shall be put to death.*
>
> *—Hammurabi's Code*

The construction of a building is a process that brings together nearly all aspects of real estate law covered to this point. Construction carries with it a great deal of uncertainty, limitless unforeseen possibilities, and tremendous liability for errors. To study the law of construction is to study the law, for construction brings together every aspect of contract, tort, and real property law. In a single chapter, coverage of *construction law* would be impossible. In this chapter, only a few of the typical problem areas are discussed; expert consultation and advice would be necessary for specific problems. The questions answered in this chapter are, Who are the parties in a construction project? Are there standardized procedures and forms for use in a construction project? How are risks in construction projects allocated? What are the more important problem areas that should be covered in a construction contract? What are the steps involved in obtaining construction financing?

PARTIES TO A CONSTRUCTION PROJECT

Since reference will be made to the various parties in a construction project, it is necessary to clearly set forth who those parties are:

1. The *owner* owns the land on which the building is being constructed.
2. The *construction lender* finances the project during the construction period.
3. The *permanent lender* or *lender* carries the mortgage on the property once construction is completed. (The permanent lender pays the construction lender's loan once construction is complete.)
4. The *general* or *prime contractor* or the *builder* is responsible for the coordination of the construction.
5. The *architect* may work with the general contractor or owner in making sure the building is constructed properly.
6. The *subcontractors* (usually a large group) perform individual projects for the construction. Subcontractors are responsible for separate jobs such as the electrical system, the heating and cooling system, and the roof.
7. The *suppliers* (a form of subcontractor) do no actual construction work but are usually a large group consisting of all businesses that supply materials for use in the construction project.
8. The *surety* or *sureties* stand as *guarantors* for either payment or performance according to the terms of the owner's contract or the contracts of subcontractors and suppliers.
9. The *insurer* for the owner, the contractor, or any other party stands liable in the event of destruction of the project during its course.
10. The *governmental supervisor* is the party who must be consulted or who must inspect as the project progresses.

From the list of the parties alone, it is easy to see why construction law is a complicated area of law.

THE CONSTRUCTION CONTRACT

Formation of Contracts

The formation of construction contracts is nearly a standardized procedure. The owner sends out a *bid notice*, which is an invitation for offers. General contractors then have the opportunity to bid on the project. Before bidding, general contractors will notify subcontractors of their intent to bid; thus subcontractors are given an invitation to make their offers for subcontract work.

The subcontractors' submissions of bids to the general contractor for their portion of the work is an offer. The general contractor's submission of a bid with the incorporated subcontractors' bids to the owner is an offer. When the owner reviews the bids, makes a decision, and notifies the chosen general contractor, there is a contract between the owner and the general contractor.

Much of the bidding, particularly between subcontractors and general contractors is done orally as a matter of practice. Although industry practice allows and encourages such oral commitments, when a lawsuit results on the bid or the contract, difficulties in proof do arise; and one party may find itself at the mercy of the other party's denial of a conversation or contradiction of a figure or term. A good practice is to require written verification of terms within a certain period of time, so that there is some basis for the general contractor's bid for the project. Figure 20.1 summarizes the flow of legal events in the formation stage of the construction contract.

In this system of bidding, there is a period of time that can be dangerous for the general contractor. It is possible for the owner to notify the general contractor of acceptance of the bid, and have the general contractor bound to perform, before the general contractor has had the chance to accept the offers of the subcontractors on which the bid was based. Thus, the general contractor is bound to perform for the bid price even though there are as yet no contractual commitments from the subcontractors. Since the subcontractors can revoke their offers at any time prior to acceptance, they could in this case revoke their offers after the general contractor is contractually bound to perform.

To avoid this problem, the general contractor has several alternatives. First, in the invitation for bids the general contractor could specify that once submitted, a bid is irrevocable. Second, the general contractor could make ac-

Figure 20.1 *Legal Relationships in the Bidding Process*

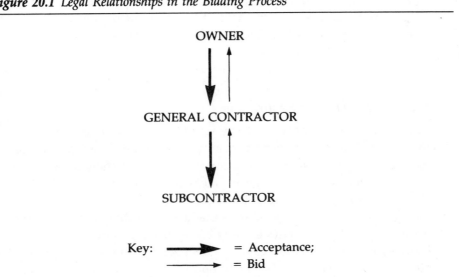

OWNER

GENERAL CONTRACTOR

SUBCONTRACTOR

Key: = Acceptance;
   = Bid

ceptance automatic upon the owner's acceptance of the general contractor's bid. Finally, the courts have used the doctrine of promissory estoppel to require subcontractors to perform according to their bids once the general contractor has relied upon the bids. Reliance is construed to be use of the subcontractors' bids in the general contractor's bid to the owner.

(20.1) Consider:

Gordon, a general contractor, was submitting bids to the city's port authority to construct a bridge in the city. Coronis submitted a bid as subcontractor for the structural steel work. After the city had accepted Gordon's bid, but before Gordon notified Coronis, Coronis revoked its bid and refused to perform. Gordon had to hire another subcontractor, Elizabeth Iron Works, to do the steel work at an additional $53,000. Gordon has sued Coronis to recover the $53,000. What is the result?

Form Contracts

Although construction projects are complex and detailed, similar problems seem to arise regardless of the size of the individual project or its location. For this reason, many standard or form contracts have been developed. For example, the American Institute of Architects has developed several form agreements that can be used between the architect and owner, the owner and general contractor, and the subcontractors and the general contractor. Other standard forms that are widely used and accepted are those of the Associated General Contractors and the National Society of Professional Engineers. These forms can be time-saving, but any special problems or needs should be integrated into the body of the contract through an addendum or provision.

Payment and Payment Assurances

Because of the large number of parties involved and the need for money to flow down from its source to the general contractor, subcontractors, and suppliers, payment of the parties is a major issue in the construction contract and in construction litigation. Indeed, the payment problem is the basis for the mechanic's lien system. (See Chapter 7.)

There are several problem areas that arise and should be covered in the payment portion of all contracts existing between the parties. The first is when payment is to be made. In most cases, payments are made periodically after the architect or project manager has had an opportunity to inspect the work. After inspection, an architect's certificate is issued, and the certificate authorizes the release of a certain portion of the funds.

The next problem area is that of who is to receive the payment once it is authorized. Too many times, the general contractor is paid but the subcontractors are not, with the result that the owner may face liens for nonpayment. In the following case, the problem of nonpayment of subcontractors is discussed.

SASSER & COMPANY v. GRIFFIN
210 S.E.2d 34 (Ga. 1974)

Griffin (defendant/appellant/owner) contracted with Sanford and Space (general/prime contractor) for the construction of a high-rise apartment building. Sasser and Company (plaintiff/appellee/subcontractor) contracted with Sanford and Space to do the plumbing, heating, and air-conditioning work in the building. The project was to be completed by 1 April 1971, but Sasser did not complete its work until August 1971.

The subcontract provided that Sanford and Space were to pay Sasser "as the work progresses, based on estimates and certificates of the Architects or Contractor and payments will be made from money received from the owner only and divided Pro Rate amount [sic] all approved accounts of subcontractors and material." These words were struck from the heating and plumbing contract and there was substituted after the word *made* "by 20th of each month following, less 10% retained until completion of job. Subcontractor will be paid by Contractor for approved work in place even though payment by the Owner has been withheld from Contractor for reasons not the fault of the subcontractor." The air-conditioning contract did not contain the above change but had added to it, "Payment within 10 days of receiving money from owner—approximately 20th of the month."

In July 1971 the designing architect certified the project as complete and ordered the release of all retained funds to Sanford and Space. Griffin denied approval of the project but claimed full payment of Sanford and Space. When Sasser was not paid, he recorded mechanics' liens on the property and filed suit.

From a trial court judgment for Sasser, Griffin appealed.

EBERHARDT, Presiding Judge

None of the owners has a contractual liability, jointly or otherwise, to plaintiff since they were not parties to the subcontracts between plaintiff and Sanford and Space, but this does not prevent the establishment of a lien by a subcontractor under Georgia law.

Sanford and Space . . . have defended against plaintiff's action on the contract on two grounds: (a) payment by owners to Sanford and Space was a condition precedent to latter's liability to plaintiff under the terms of both subcontracts, and owners had not paid all sums due under the prime contract; and, (b) plaintiff had breached the subcontract by not completing performance by the time required in the prime contract.

The language in the amendment of the plumbing and heating subcontract clearly shows that the parties intended for plaintiff to be paid independently of payments received from the owners by Sanford and Space. While the owners deny approval of the entire project, they do not dispute the plaintiff has completed his performance under the subcontract. That contract is to be enforced as written. It is the duty of the courts to construe and enforce contracts as made and not to make them for the parties. We are not at liberty to revise a contract while professing to construe it.

There is, however, no such amendment to the air conditioning subcontract, and it provides "payments will be made from money received from the owner only" and "payment within 10 days of receiving money from owner—approximately 20th of the month."

A provision in a contract may make payment by the owner a condition precedent to a subcontractor's right to payment if "the contract between the general contractor and the subcontractor should contain an express condition clearly showing that to be the intention of the parties."

. . . The condition is clearly expressed in this subcontract.

Sanford and Space cannot successfully defend their nonpayment of plaintiff on the ground that plaintiff breached the contract by not completing his work in time. Late performance may constitute a breach of contract by the plaintiff, but the remedy is not nonpayment; it is recoupment or what is now a counterclaim. And while it is true that, on acceptance of the work by the owner after the building contractor has rendered the entire service for which he has contracted, the contractor is authorized to proceed to collect the balance due him by the terms of the contract, any damage to the owner resulting through the negligent performance of the contract by the contractor is a matter for recoupment. This same rule applies to actions ex contractu, between contractor and subcontractor, and for damages alleged to have been caused by delay in completion of construction.

Therefore, the plaintiff is entitled to summary judgment against Griffin as to the establishment of the lien, in the amount claimed, and against Sanford and Space as to payment due under the plumbing and heating contract.

Affirmed.

Discussion Questions

1. Diagram the relationships of the parties in the case, following Figure 20.1 as an example.
2. What work is at issue?
3. What changes were made in the subcontracts?
4. When did Sasser complete the work?
5. Does late performance have any effect on Sasser's claim?
6. Is the lien filed by Sasser against Griffin's property proper?
7. Does Sanford and Space's problems with Griffin excuse its nonpayment of Sasser?

To avoid some of the problems occurring in the *Sasser* case, the parties can take protective measures to assure their payment and the performance by other parties to the contract. General contractors are entitled to payment as their work is completed and may stop performance if payment is not made, so that work stoppage is a means of security for them. To further assure payment, general contractors usually have the benefit of a three-party arrangement, whereby the funds are held by a third party (examples of third parties used are lenders, architects, escrow companies, attorneys, trustees, and banks) and released upon the architect's certification of adequate completion. With the three-party system, the general contractors know the funds exist—it is simply a matter of performance to have them released.

Owners can also use the three-party system to assure performance by the general contractor. Most standard contracts with such an arrangement permit the withholding of a certain amount of the payment due to cover defective work, late performance, or the general contractor's failure to pay subcontractors and suppliers. The withheld amount is typically 10 percent of the contract price and also 10 percent of each installment made during the construction period.

As noted in the *Sasser* case, general contractors can protect themselves against the subcontractors for the owner's nonpayment through the use of a *flow-down clause*. Under a flow-down clause, the general contractor is not required to pay the subcontractors until the owner has paid the general contractor.

In most projects, the parties do not limit themselves to these internal protections but rather seek and require some outside guarantee or assurance that payment and performance will occur. This outside assurance comes in the form of bonds issued by sureties for a premium. There are two types of bonds used in a project. The first is a *performance bond*, which the general contractor must usually obtain for the owner. Under this type of bond, the surety will be responsible to the owner for damages (in the amount of the bond) if the general contractor does not perform according to the terms of the contract.

The second type of bond is the *payment bond*, which the subcontractors may require the general contractor to obtain. Under this type of bond, the surety agrees to pay the subcontractors for their work (again, in the amount of the bond) if the general contractor does not.

Contract Price

Usually the price in a construction contract is fixed and covers the entire project. Other forms of pricing include *unit pricing*, in which the contract is broken down into units. For example, excavation could be one unit in a project. Framing could be another unit. The overhead costs for the project would be divided among the units according to the amount of time and/or cost involved in each unit. The unit system makes the payment division easier. Another form of pricing that leaves many variables and can create problems is the *cost plus formula*, in which the general contractor recovers whatever the cost of construction is along with a predetermined percentage or amount for profit. The difficulty with the cost plus system is determining what costs are reimbursable as project costs and what costs are the general contractor's cost of doing business: personnel salaries, equipment, and other overhead items.

After the price or price formula is determined and construction begins, there are two possible problem areas that may affect the price paid for the project by the owner. These areas are changed circumstances and work order changes.

Changed Circumstances The general contractor's bid on a project is based on assumptions about the project location, soil content, weather analysis, and other variable factors. If significant, unanticipated changes occur in those assumptions, the general contractor's costs will increase. With these cost increases, the issue arises of whether the price of completion will also increase. A clause in standard form contracts provides for price increases when: (1) there are concealed conditions below the surface of the ground or concealed conditions in any existing structure at variance with those conditions indicated by contract; and (2) there are unknown physical conditions at the site of an unusual nature, differing materially from those ordinarily encountered and generally recognized as part of the work provided for in the contract. Other conditions that are considered unusual and unknown are unseasonal or unusually bad weather conditions, labor problems, and material shortages. Even without a changed circumstances provision in the contract, the contractor is entitled to obtain an increased price if costs are greater because of misrepresentation of conditions by the owner in the bid information, the negotiations, or the contract.

Change Orders The second type of situation in which a contractor may increase the project price is through a *change order*. Because of circumstances or preferences, the owner may wish to change plans and specifications that represent additional costs to the contractor. Also, the contractor may discover during the course of construction that additional work is necessary and will want authorization for the work so that additional compensation can be paid. A typical change order clause will provide as follows:

> A change order is a written order to the contractor that is signed by the owner and the architect, issued after execution of the contract, authorizing a change in the contract sum or contract time. The contract sum and contract time may be changed by change order only.
> The owner, without invalidating the contract, may order changes in the work within the general scope of the contract, the contract sum and the contract time being adjusted accordingly.
> The contractor, provided he receives a written order signed by the owner, shall promptly proceed with the work involved.

The United States government's change order clause provides as follows:

> [I]f the change causes an increase or decrease in the cost of, or the time required for, performance of any part of the work under this contract, whether changed or not changed by such order, an equitable adjustment shall be made in the contract price or delivery schedule or both.

In some cases, the parties fail to comply with change order procedures in spite of contract provisions and change forms. The issue that arises is whether the contractor is still entitled to be compensated for the additional work performed. This issue of payment for extra work without formal authorization is discussed in the following case.

FLETCHER v. LAGUNA VISTA CORPORATION
275 So.2d 579 (Fla. 1973)

Laguna Vista Corporation (plaintiff/appellee/general contractor) had a contract with Fletcher (defendant/appellant/owner) for the construction of 204 garden apartments. The architectural firm of Allen Frye and Associates worked on the project also. The contract between Laguna Vista and Fletcher was the standard American Institute of Architects form, with the price being a stipulated sum.

Numerous changes were made during construction, and near the end of construction Laguna Vista presented to Fletcher change orders with Frye's signatures for the payment of an additional $67,112.45 for additional work done in the completion of the apartments. When Fletcher refused to sign the change orders or pay the additional amounts, Laguna Vista filed a lien to collect the amount claimed and then brought suit to foreclose on the lien.

The trial judge ruled for Laguna Vista, and Fletcher appealed.

RAWLS, Judge

Once the parties have reduced their understanding to a written contract, their conduct is governed by the agreement and the contract is looked to in determining the rights and obligations of the party. Here appellants and appellee chose to consummate their agreement concerning the construction of a $2,000,000-plus apartment complex in a voluminous printed form contract mass-produced by the American Institute of Architects. This document states . . . that the stated contract price of $2,000,000 plus is final and subject only to an increase or decrease by a change order. A change order is defined . . . as a written order to the contractor signed by the owner and the architect. If the contract stopped here it would be clear that the stated contract price could only be increased if appellant-owner agreed in writing. But the contract goes on and states . . . that the contractor can make a claim for an increase in the contract sum and if the owner and the contractor cannot agree on the amount then the sum shall be determined by the architect.

As is vividly illustrated by the above review, the printed A.I.A. contract is replete with ambiguities, contradictions, and is an attempt to give all things to both parties. In such a situation the manner in which the parties themselves have interpreted the contract through their course of dealings is of utmost importance. The record in this case is filled with testimony to the accord that both appellants and appellee had relied on architect Frye to make adjustments in the contract sum and had abided by his decision. Appellants knew that there would be at least a slight overage in the sums spent by appellee for overhead but had never objected. Appellants accepted decreases in the cost of millwork which were incorporated into a change order signed only by architect Frye and the contractor. The parties themselves have interpreted the contract to allow an increase and a decrease in the contract sum with only the written signature of architect Frye. Even if the contract does not grant this authority to architect Frye, the parties through their course of dealings have interpreted and modified the document so as to place in the hands of architect Frye the final authority to authorize increases and decreases in the contract sum.

The judgment appealed is affirmed.

Discussion Questions

1. Diagram the relationship of the parties and their roles.
2. What form agreement was used?
3. What provision was made for changes in the contract?
4. Whose signature was on the change orders?
5. Whose signature was on the millwork cost reduction that Fletcher approved?
6. Is Laguna Vista entitled to the cost increases?

Substantial Performance by the Contractor

Construction contracts present the unique problem of how to determine when the contractor has performed well enough to satisfy the terms of the contract. Because of the nature of construction, certain variations may occur between the plans or specifications and what is actually built. Change orders at the time of the slight modifications can alleviate the problems, but in the event such orders are not obtained the issue of substantial performance exists. The doctrine of *substantial performance* provides that a contractor may recover for completed projects in spite of variations between the plans and the actual finished product. The following questions must all be answered affirmatively in order to establish substantial performance:

1. Is the construction for practical purposes just as good?
2. Was the minor breach by the contractor nonmalicious?
3. Can the owner be compensated for the substitution or error made by the contractor?

An example of circumstances in which substantial performance is appropriate is when the wrong color scheme or cabinetwork is installed in a home or office. The owner may not be as happy, but the error meets the three criteria, and the contractor will be paid the contract price less an adjustment for the owner to be compensated or have the work redone.

Even when the contractor completes the work according to plans and specifications, the liability does not stop with payment by the owner. The contractor is liable for errors in construction and poor workmanship; and in spite of attempts to disclaim such liability in contract exculpatory clauses, public policy will not permit contractors to excuse themselves from injuries and damages resulting from their negligence.

In home construction, the contractor is required for 1 year (in most states) to repair or replace faulty construction problems under the implied warranty. (See Chapter 11.)

Compliance with Building Codes

One of the critical requirements for adequate performance by a contractor is that the structure comply, in all respects, with state and local building codes. Building codes may restrict building height, ceiling height, window placement, fire sprinkler systems, exits, lighting, and materials. Contractors are presumed to be familiar with building codes and will be liable for cutting costs by not complying with the minimum requirements.

Delays

One of the most frequently litigated issues in construction law is that of nontimely performance of a construction project. To avoid this area of litigation, the parties may include several provisions in their agreement to establish the rights and duties of the parties regarding delays. The contract should first specify whether delays are permissible or whether time is of the essence. If delays are impermissible, damages for delay should be specified so that the clause has some enforcement power.

If delays are permissible, the parties should specify procedures for notifying each other about the likelihood of delay and the length of the delay. In addition, the reasons for delay that are permissible may be specified. In some contracts a section specifies what constitutes an excusable delay and what constitutes an inexcusable delay. Specifics such as strikes, weather, and shortages of materials may be included.

Some contracts contain a provision that disallows the collection of damages in the event of a contractor's delay. Most courts faced with the issue of the validity of these clauses have upheld them as valid so long as the parties have equal bargaining power.

Arbitration

The inclusion of an arbitration clause in a construction contract is a critical decision for the parties. The advantages to arbitration are a more prompt settlement of disputes, informal proceedings, and reduced expense. Some of the disadvantages are that there are no prehearing discovery devices in arbitration, so that the evidence at the hearing comes as a surprise, and that often the hearing officer may not be familiar with the peculiarities of the construction industry or the particular case.

If an arbitration clause is to be included, the following topics should also be addressed:

1. Time limitations for hearings
2. What issues may be arbitrated
3. Who will serve as arbitrators
4. Amount limitations for arbitration
5. Where hearing will be held
6. Types of remedies arbitrator may award
7. What form or forms the arbitration may take
8. Whether prearbitration or prehearing discovery is permitted
9. Standards of proof for hearings
10. Whether the decision can be appealed

CONSTRUCTION FINANCING

There are several peculiar problems which arise in construction financing that should be noted. The first is obtaining a construction lender. The cases and discussion in this chapter serve as indicators of the difficulties of seeing a project through to its completion, and the construction lender will not be repaid unless the project is seen through to completion with full payment.

In many cases, construction lenders obtain some security before agreeing to make the construction loan to the owner, by requiring the owner to obtain a permanent lender or loan commitment. With this early commitment, the construction lender knows the funds will be repaid upon completion of construction.

The construction lender must also be cautious in recording its mortgage on the property. To obtain priority, the lender must record the mortgage or deed of trust prior to the commencement of construction. For in most states, if construction work has begun, suppliers and mechanics will have priority over the lender, since their liens go back to the start of construction. (See Chapter 7 for a complete discussion of liens.)

Finally, the construction lender will want to take steps to assure that the funds end up with the proper parties. Releases should be controlled according to completion and architect certification. Lien waivers should be obtained in exchange for payments. If the title becomes clouded with liens, the permanent lender has a basis for backing out of the commitment and the construction lender will not be paid.

RECOMMENDATION

Construction projects are complicated tasks requiring large numbers of parties functioning in different capacities with varying interests in the project. From the pitfalls discussed in this chapter, it is not an overstatement that one party who should not be left out of the construction project is the attorney—an attorney for each of the parties, so that each party's rights are protected and their responsibilities made clear.

KEY TERMS

owner	guarantors
construction lender	insurer
permanent lender	governmental supervisor
lender	bid notice
general contractor	flow-down clause
prime contractor	performance bond
builder	payment bond
architect	unit pricing
subcontractors	cost plus formula
suppliers	change order
surety	substantial performance
sureties	

CHAPTER PROBLEMS

1. Christiansen Brothers, Incorporated, a general contracting firm, was hired by Washington State University (WSU) for the construction of two buildings. In their contract the parties included a "no damages for delay" clause. Christiansen was 9 months late in completing the buildings, and WSU sought damages on the grounds that the no-damages for delay clause was unconscionable considering the extent of the delay. What was the result?

2. Burr, a general contractor, was bidding on a plant project for General Motors. Burr had two bids from electrical subcontractors. One was from

Corbin-Dykes and the other from White Sands. White Sands agreed to do the project for $4,000 less than Corbin-Dykes' bid if it could do the work in conjunction with another project it had in the area. Burr used Corbin-Dykes' bid and was awarded the project. However, Burr contracted with White Sands because they could do the work in the same amount of time at $4,000 less. Corbin-Dykes brought suit on the grounds of promissory estoppel and sought to force Burr to pay them. What was the result?

3. Gough agreed to put up the trusses on a Kinney Shoe Store that Chuckrow was building as general contractor. Gough put up the trusses, but later that day, thirty of the thirty-two erected trusses fell down. Gough put them back up and demanded additional compensation. Chuckrow refused, saying that the trusses fell down because of Gough's poor workmanship. Gough maintained that they fell down because of faulty plans and specifications. What was the result?

4. What is the difference between a fixed price contract and a unit price contract?

5. The city of Markland sought bids for the construction of a sewage treatment plant. In the bid notices the city provided that all bidders were responsible for investigation of the site, the soil, and any unusual construction problems. A general contractor wishes to know if such a clause is valid. Discuss.

6. In question 5, what effect would the clause have if the city had unique knowledge of a construction problem with the land where the plant is to be built?

7. St. Paul Dredging Company had a contract with the state of Minnesota that included a provision for delay damages. Because of a quiet title action, St. Paul was enjoined from entering the property until the title problem was judicially resolved. St. Paul was late in performing and the state deducted the late penalties from their payment to St. Paul. St. Paul objects. What is the result?

8. Modern Plumbers remodeled the three bathrooms in Jones's home. Two of the three bathrooms were done according to the plans, but in the third bathroom Modern installed a beige-colored bathtub instead of a cream-colored one. Jones wishes to know if this is substantial performance. What is the result?

9. If a construction mortgage is filed after excavation, who will have priority in foreclosure?

10. What is the difference between a payment bond and a performance bond?

21

MULTIUNIT HOUSING

-Reprinted by permission: Tribune Media Services.

During the past decade, increases in construction costs and interest rates have resulted in an era of creativity in both the financing of home purchases and in the types of homes being purchased. The housing style of the 1970s—the condominium or townhouse—developed and experienced tremendous growth. This growth was in response to an increasing number of people who desired the tax benefits of home ownership but were operating under income constraints, or who did not need a full-size home, or who did not want the upkeep of a single-family dwelling. The number of housing starts consisting of condominium construction has nearly doubled since 1979, and condominiums and townhouses are expected to make up nearly half of all housing starts by the end of the decade (Practicing Law Institute, *Condominium and Cooperative Conversions*, 1980). The tremendous growth is reason in itself for a study of the rights and responsibilities of the parties owning this and other new forms of real property interest. In this chapter, the following questions are answered: What are the definitions of and distinctions between condominium, townhouse, cooperative, and time-sharing properties? How is each of these multiunit housing arrangements created? Who is responsible for the common areas? How do multiunit developments function?

DEFINITIONS AND DISTINCTIONS

The four methods of ownership covered in this chapter have one thing in common: they are not traditional real estate ownerships. However, different rights and obligations are associated with each.

Condominiums

A *condominium* can take many physical forms—it can be a townhouse, an apartment, or part of a free-standing duplex house. However, the physical form of the condominium has no effect on the owner's legal status or rights. The owner owns a fee simple interest in the actual dwelling unit and is entitled to all the rights of a fee simple holder: the condominium may be sold, leased, or mortgaged and is subject to foreclosure, power of sale, and homestead rights. The owner is also given an undivided joint interest in all of the common areas of the building. Thus, the owner of a condominium unit in the form of an apartment in a multistory building would have an undivided interest in areas such as the halls, stairs, lobby, and any recreational facilities.

Although the condominium unit owner has an interest in the common areas, only the actual dwelling unit may be mortgaged or pledged; and creditors of the unit owner may foreclose only on a per unit basis, not on the entire unit. Also, although the unit owner holds a fee simple interest, there may be restrictions on the use and decoration of the condominium unit. These restrictions are imposed through the deed of the condominium or through other documents created for the smooth functioning of the multiunit development (discussed later in the chapter).

Cooperatives

Ownership of a *cooperative* is not a fee simple ownership of real estate. A cooperative is a living arrangement in which the dwellers own an undivided joint interest in the land and buildings that make up the cooperative. Ownership is most likely held by the cooperative as a nonprofit corporation, with each cooperative unit assigned a certain number of shares in the corporation. Thus, a unit dweller does not own a real estate interest, but owns a share or shares in a corporation that owns the entire complex. Accompanying this share ownership are the rights to a lease of the dwelling unit and to exclusive occupancy of that unit. In essence, the corporation of which the tenant is a shareholder, is the landlord for all units in the cooperative.

Another distinction between the cooperative method of land interest ownership and traditional fee simple ownership is the possibility that the cooperative shareholder may be restricted in the transfer of shares. Although cooperative unit owners may be free to sell their leasehold interests or shares, they may be required to offer their interests first to the corporation and may even be restricted in how the property can be disposed of upon their death. In the following case, the court deals with the issue of such restrictions.

GALE ET AL. v. YORK CENTER COMMUNITY COOPERATIVE, INC.
171 N.E.2d 30 (Ill. 1961)

Gale and four other families (plaintiffs/appellants) are members of the York Center Community Cooperative (defendant/appellee), a subdivision of seventy-two families located just south of Lombard, Illinois. The nonprofit corporation is the legal title holder to all real estate located within the subdivision, and each member has the right to perpetual use and occupancy of his or her dwelling.

Each member is subject to the transfer restrictions of the membership agreement. Under those restrictions, a member who wishes to withdraw from the corporation must give written notice of the intent to do so to the board of directors. The corporation then has a 12-month option period in which to purchase the membership. The corporation may purchase the membership at a price specified by several formulas in the membership agreement. If the corporation does not exercise its option within 12 months, then the membership may be sold on the open market.

If the open market purchaser is not acceptable to the corporation, it has 90 days to redeem the membership. If this right of redemption is not exercised within 90 days, then the purchaser acquires a full membership interest. The board of directors may give written approval to any transfer to preempt these procedures.

Upon death of a member, membership passing by will or descent to a son, daughter, spouse, or parent may be approved automatically by the board of directors. If the membership passes to another party who does not wish to remain a member, the board has 12 months to purchase the interest.

Members wishing to obtain financing for their properties are given a deed to their property; but after financing is obtained, they must reconvey the property to the corporation.

The plaintiffs filed suit alleging that the restrictions on their right to transfer their memberships violate the rule against restraints on alienation of property and are void. The lower court held the restrictions to be valid and ordered the five families to reconvey their properties to the corporation. The families appealed.

HOUSE, Justice

It seems to us the agreements show a studied effort on the part of the association to retain some voice in the selection of new members and at the same time to give its members as much freedom as possible in alienating their interests. Experience shows this to be the only way to keep cooperative housing cooperative. As necessary as these restrictions may be to cooperative housing, it must be determined whether they violate the rule against restraints on alienation.

It should be noted at the outset that the rule has not had a logical and consistent development. This seems to be due to the fact that such restraints vary greatly in form, and the application of the rule has turned largely on such considerations as the kind of property involved, the quality of the interest, and the form of restraint.

While other reasons are sometimes given for the rule, it seems to call for no other than that of sound public policy. Restraints on alienation keep property out of commerce, they tend to concentrate wealth, they may prevent the owner from consuming the property except as to the income from it, they may deter the improvement of the property and they may prevent creditors from satisfying their claims. Against these and other social and economic disadvantages to the public, the only benefit that would often accrue from such restraints is the satisfaction of the capricious whims of the conveyor. Thus, as a general rule, restraints on alienation are void even though they are limited in time. Such a restraint may be sustained, however, when it is reasonably designed to attain or encourage accepted social or economic ends.

We are of the opinion that the utility of the restraints in this agreement outweigh the injurious consequences to the public, if any. The legislature has given its approval to ownership of residential property on a cooperative basis by providing that not-for-profit corporations may be organized for this purpose. The restrictions on transfer of a membership are reasonably necessary to the continued existence of the cooperative association. This demonstrates the social utility of the partial restraints and might of itself be a basis for sustaining them. In addition, however, enforcement of the restraints in question would not appear to produce injurious consequences to the public. They would not tend to keep the property in the same family and concentrate wealth, but would seem to some extent to prevent retention by one family. The member is not prevented from liquidating his interest and therefore consuming the property. Creditors are not prevented from satisfying their claims. Cooperative ownership of residential property in this country seems to be increasing in popularity, and the extent to which these partial restraints would keep property out of commerce is entirely problematical.

Affirmed.

Discussion Questions

1. What restrictions on transfer have been imposed?
2. How is a mortgage arranged?
3. Are restraints on alienation generally valid?
4. What two factors are examined in de-

termining the validity of a restraint on alienation?

5. Are the cooperative's membership restraints valid?

Townhouses

The owner of a *townhouse* owns the land on which the townhouse is located, the actual dwelling unit, and an undivided joint interest in the common elements of the development such as a swimming pool, clubhouse, and so on. Actual ownership of the land on which the townhouse is located distinguishes this form of multiunit housing from the others, where there is simply ownership of space. It is possible for the owners in a townhouse development to form a corporation or a home-owners' association, so that each unit owner would also own a share in the corporation. More information on the organization and structure of townhouse developments is discussed later in the chapter.

Hybrids

In some states, hybrid forms of ownership can be found under various labels, such as *patio homes, garden homes,* and *attached homes.* In these hybrid forms, the owners may own the land and the entire dwelling unit but will have a party wall agreement for the joint walls between properties. The laws governing these hybrids vary from state to state. In some states joint wall properties are treated as townhouses, while in others they are labeled condominiums.

Time-Sharing Properties

In resort areas, the concept of *time-sharing* ownership or recreational ownership has become popular. The owner of a time share owns a fee simple interest but can exercise the right of possession for only a limited period of time each year and during the same period of time each year. For example, a time share may be the right to the use of a two-bedroom apartment in San Diego from 1 June to 8 June every year in perpetuity. This right of use may be transferred *inter vivos* or by will or intestate succession. The limitation on the property is the time of use. In addition to the right to use the dwelling unit, the owner is also given the right to use all common areas, including any recreational facilities such as pools, game rooms, and saunas.

Some states permit a method of time-sharing ownership known as the *recreational lease,* whereby the owners have the same rights of use but are lessees paying over time for the right of use. Generally, these recreational leases have rent escalation clauses that increase the rent according to some scale over the perpetual period of the lease.

The complexities of multiunit housing ownership and the liability for defects are demonstrated in the following case.

ROUNDTREE VILLAS ASSOCIATION, INC. v.
4701 KINGS CORPORATION
321 S.E.2d 46 (S.C. 1984)

Roundtree Villas Association, Inc. (plaintiff/respondent/Regime) is a nonprofit corporation whose primary function is to own and administer the common elements of the condominium project called "Roundtree Villas." Roundtree Corporation, Inc. (defendant/builder) was the original owner of a parcel of real estate that filed a deed under the Horizontal Property Act. Republic Mortgage Investment Services, Inc. (defendant/appellant/lender) was the financier of the project. Mortgage Investment Services, Inc. (defendant/appellant/lender's advisor) was an advisory service employed by Republic Mortgage, the lender. Fred B. Hallmark (defendant/architect) was employed by the builder with the lender's approval. Miles and Teal Builders (defendants/contractors) were the builders for the project. 4701 Kings

Corporation (defendant/seller) was a company created by the lender to accept title to the mortgaged property in lieu of foreclosure.

The condominium project was constructed at a time when money was short and sales were slow. The builder sold what he could, and then, 4701 Kings Corporation took over the property. Shortly after the acquisition, the owners of the units began to complain about problems with the units' roofs and balconies. The lender attempted to remedy the problems, but only with stop-gap measures. The problems continued.

The Regime filed suit for breach of the implied warranty of habitability and sought damages for the repair of the roofs and balconies. The jury entered a verdict against the lender and the lender appealed.

LITTLEJOHN, Chief Justice

The litigation is typical of many actions growing out of the depressed economy of the mid 1970s. In recent years, it has not been unusual for substantial construction undertakings to meet with financial disaster. Traditionally, as here, those parties most responsible for substantial loses [sic] cannot respond to a judgment and, accordingly, aggrieved parties seek a "deep pocket." Attempting to solve the complex issues of fact and of law is somewhat like attempting to unscramble an egg. The court strives to do justice which oftentimes must be only approximate. When justice cannot be meted out exactly, we do that which is next best—try to bring an end to the dispute.

The rights and authority of the Regime must be gleaned from the Horizontal Property Act and from the master deed. From these, we may determine (1) the property owned by the individual condominium owners and (2) the rights of the Regime. The Regime owns the common elements. Section 27-31-20, definitions, reads, in part, as follows:

[f] "General common elements" means and includes: . . . (2) The foundations, main walls, roofs, halls, lobbies, stairways, and entrance and exit or communication ways; . . .
[g] "Limited common elements" means and includes those common elements which

are agreed upon by all the co-owners to be reserved for the use of a certain number of apartments to the exclusion of the other apartments, such as special corridors, stairways, elevators, sanitary services common to the apartments of a particular floor, and the like; . . .

We have no trouble in finding that the roofs are common elements which must be maintained by the Regime and, accordingly, the Regime has a right to bring a cause of action as relates to roof defects. Neither the Act nor the deed imposes upon the Regime the duty to maintain balconies or the authority to bring a cause of action for alleged balcony defects. The Regime contends, in its brief, that:

The Master Deed and By-Laws make the Association responsible for the common elements. The definition in the Master Deed states that patio walls and load bearing interior walls and partitions are included in the common elements. The Respondent [Regime] considers the term "patio" to be synonymous with balcony and therefore considers the testimony concerning damages under the responsibility of the homeowners association.

We disagree with this analysis. Patio walls simply are not synonymous with balconies and balconies are not common element property. The trial judge should have held as a matter of law that the Regime had no standing to sue for damages to property not encompassed in the term "common element."

We will now discuss each of the four causes of action.

The gravamen of the Regime's contention in the first cause of action is that the Lender and the Lender's Advisor are liable for construction defects. At the appropriate times, the Lender and the Lender's Advisor moved for a directed verdict and for judgment notwithstanding the ver-

dict as to the first cause of action. They argued that, as a matter of law, they could not be held liable for the negligent or reckless construction of the roofs and balconies. The trial judge overruled the motions and charged the jury, in essence, that certain Defendants, including those here appealing, could be held liable for negligent and reckless construction.

There is no applicable statutory law. This court has, however, on previous occasions in recent years imposed new duties and responsibilities upon the sellers of real estate. We have not heretofore been confronted with a case wherein the purchaser has attempted to impose liability upon a lending institution because of faulty construction. We refuse to extend such liability now.

The builder of a house is entitled to make his own contract with the construction company. In like fashion, a lending institution is entitled to make its own contract with one who is building a house. Traditionally, lenders, in making a construction loan, make periodic inspections to assure that the construction loan advancements are being applied appropriately. This is fundamentally for the protection of the lending institution and does not impose upon the lending institution a duty to see that the builder is getting a job free of defects. Both the lender and the borrower have a common interest in seeing that the construction company builds a building free of defects but absent a contract the builder has no common law duty to protect the lender and the lender has no common law duty to protect the builder.

The Regime in its second cause of action alleges that the Lender and the Lender's Advisor undertook to repair the roofs and did so in a negligent manner proximately causing damages. We have held hereinabove that their involvement was not such as to make them liable for negligence on the part of the Builder, Ar-

chitect or Contractors. They were not active participants in the building enterprise
during the initial construction and prior to
1977. We hold however that, when the
Lender, in effect, took over the project and
undertook to market the units through a
corporation it had created and when it undertook to repair defects which existed to
promote sales, a common law duty to use
due care arose (Restatement [Second] of
Torts §323). On this matter there was a jury
issue, but only as relates to the common
elements. Under this cause of action the
Lender and the Lender's Advisor may only
be held liable for any damages proximately caused by the alleged negligent
repair, but not for any original damages
proximately caused by the negligence of

the Builder, Architect or Contractor. We
hold therefore that a new trial must be held,
restricted to the alleged negligent repairs
of common element property only. This, of
course, excludes the balconies.

In the third and fourth causes of action, the Regime asserts it should recover
because of a breach of either express or
implied warranties or both. A warranty of
either kind is, in effect, a contract. A search
of the record reveals nothing that would
warrant a finding that these appealing Defendants entered into any warranty agreement expressly or by implication. This is
not to say that warranties did not exist, only
that these particular appealing Defendants did not enter into any warranty
agreements.

Remanded.

Discussion Questions

1. Describe the complex relationships among the parties.
2. Why is there a distinction between the roof repairs and the balcony repairs?
3. Who brought the suit for breach of implied warranty?
4. Is a lender liable for construction defects?
5. If you were a buyer of a unit, what would you want to know about the seller?

APPLICABLE LAWS

Each state has its own statutes to govern each of the methods of real property ownership just discussed, and the statutes vary significantly from state to state. This concept of individual ownership of parts of buildings did not exist until the 1950s because of the relative ease with which single-family dwellings could be built or purchased. Puerto Rico passed the first applicable laws in 1958 with the adoption of its Horizontal Property Act.

In 1961 Congress authorized the Federal Housing Administration (FHA) to insure mortgages on condominium units; subsequently, the attractiveness of condominiums was substantially enhanced, and state laws were passed. At the end of 1963, thirty-nine states had some form of legislation, and by 1969 all states had adopted some form of regulation on condominium and townhouse developments.

The Uniform Condominium Act has been adopted by three states, but most state statutes are recognizable by the name *horizontal property regimes* or *horizontal property acts*. In some of these statutes, the definitions and applicable laws of condominiums and townhouses vary from the discussion in this chapter. It is important to check the state statutes when dealing with these methods of real property ownership.

CREATION OF MULTIUNIT HOUSING

Creation of a Condominium

A condominium development must be created carefully for several reasons. First, the ownership structure in the development has two levels: all unit owners hold fee simple title and an undivided interest in the condominium common areas. Second, much of the success of the condominium development depends on the development's organizational structure and the control that the organization has on the modification of units, collection of fees, neighborhood courtesies, and so on. Finally, in many states when an apartment complex is converted to condominiums, laws require adequate notification procedures and set limitations on conversion costs. The documents and steps typical to the creation of a condominium development are discussed in the following sections. (Note that the steps and documents may vary from state to state.)

Declaration of Condominium or Master Deed The prerequisite for the creation of a condominium development is the fee simple ownership of a lot or lots of an existing building or buildings. This fee simple ownership may be held by an individual, several individuals, or a corporation. The owner (or owners) begin the condominium development by drafting and recording a master deed or a declaration of condominium. This *master deed* describes the real property involved and states the number of units located therein. Every deed to every condominium unit owner will refer to this master deed for a complete legal description of the unit owner's interest. In some states this initial document is called a *declaration of horizontal property regime and covenants*. In general terms, and with state variations, the declaration contains the following items:

1. Legal description of the property
2. Detailed description of the building or buildings making up the complex and the number of stories, basements, and units
3. Mailing address of each unit and a physical description including the number of rooms, method of access, and other identifiable characteristics
4. Detailed description of the common areas

5. Limitations on the use of common areas
6. Monetary value of the buildings and each unit
7. How votes are to be assigned: per unit basis or per value basis
8. Restrictions on land use; for example, all-adult restrictions
9. Name and address of legal representative for the development
10. Voting procedures
11. Methods for amending the declaration of condominium

Although the items in the list appear to be routine, it should be noted that once the declaration is filed, it becomes a permanent reflection of the rights of all unit owners; and variations in the uses and structure of the property are not permitted unless the amendment procedures specified in the declaration are followed.

Incorporation Although it is not authorized in all states, the next step is the incorporation of the development. There are valid reasons for incorporation: Title to the common areas can be held by the corporate entity, with each unit owner having a share or interest in the corporation. This corporate ownership of the common areas alleviates some of the liability problems discussed later in this chapter. Corporate ownership also affords an opportunity for a system of controlling the common areas through voting with rules on meetings, methods of voting, quorums, and so on. One of the difficulties with condominium living is the inability of unit owners to agree on operations. Corporate ownership of common areas provides the parties with rules for determining operational methods. When disputes arise, there are far more legal precedents in corporate law than there are rights and procedures afforded under a *declaration of condominium*.

Bylaws Once the declaration and incorporation (if desired) are complete, the condominium developer must adopt *bylaws* for the unit owners. Part of the purpose is to provide rules and regulations for the unit owners and for the day-to-day operation of the units. The bylaws also include the rules for the home-owners' association, which is the governing body for the dwelling units once the developer has sold all units and withdrawn. An effective home-owners' association is responsible for dealing with issues of noise, property use, property upkeep, and maintenance of the common areas.

The bylaws are generally drafted by the developer but may be adopted by the unit owners once the developer has sold all of the units. The bylaws should contain rules for the following areas:

1. Composition of a governing board or committee for the association and the methods and requirements for election of its members.

2. Details for meetings, such as place, time, notice, quorum, and voting requirements.

3. Procedures for day-to-day maintenance authorizations, equipment replacements, and routine repairs.

4. Amount of any association fees to be collected from unit owners for maintenance of common areas, and so on, the methods for collecting such fees, and the penalties for late payment or nonpayment. (In some states, the association is entitled to a lien on the unit owner's property in the event of a failure to pay association fees.)

5. Procedures for amending the bylaws.

6. Use restrictions, such as adult-only restrictions and limitations on transfer and rental.

The following case illustrates how strictly the rules on paying association fees are followed.

JOHNSON v. FIRST SOUTHERN PROPERTIES, INC.
687 S.W.2d 399 (Tex. 1985)

Jay Johnson (appellant) purchased a condominium in November 1978 but failed to pay the monthly maintenance fee after August 1979. The Condominium Declaration for his condominium apartments provided that the home-owner's council has a lien on each apartment for any unpaid assessments and authorized the council to enforce the lien through "non-judicial foreclosure through a power of sale."

Using the authority in the declaration of condominium, First Southern (appellee) foreclosed on Johnson's unit. Johnson claimed he enjoyed a homestead exemption protection and that the council could not foreclose. The trial court found for First Southern and Johnson appealed.

ROBERTSON, Justice

Appellant first argues that the forced sale for payment of debts violated his constitutional homestead protections. He reasons that since this lien does not fall into any of the listed exceptions to the ban on forced sales of homesteads, the foreclosure was invalid. While appellant has presented a correct statement of Texas homestead law, several more basic principles come into play in this case. The shelter of a homestead is not unassailable. Rather, a right, such as a lien, may prevail over a homestead claim if such right exists before the land becomes a homestead.

The critical question then is whether the assessment lien "existed" prior to appellant's claim of the apartment as his homestead.

In the instant case, appellant signed the papers relating to the purchase of the apartment on October 13, 1978, and moved in on November 1, 1978; consequently the interim rules come into play. The deed and the deed of trust represented that he took the apartment subject to the declaration, which declaration designated that the homeowner's council had an assessment lien. This, of course,

606

amounted to a prior relinquishment of appellant's homestead claim. We therefore hold that the assessment lien constituted a valid pre-existing debt which would overcome the homestead claim.

Under a second theory, appellant contends that the declaration violated the Condominium Act effective at the time of purchase. He suggests that the Act did not authorize non-judicial foreclosure, and in fact provided that the sole remedy was to be a preferential payment upon sale of the unit. Consequently, he argues that the declaration providing for non-judicial foreclosure is invalid.

Neither the Act nor the declaration state that the remedies found in the Act are exclusive. The Act provides a framework to be utilized, if desired, but co-owners may certainly establish remedies in addition to those in the Act. See Tex. Rev. Civ. Stat. Ann., art. 1301a §3 (1980) (repealed and now located at Tex. Prop.Code Ann. §§81.001 et seq. [Vernon Supp. 1983]). Appellant's points contesting the substantial validity of the foreclosure are overruled.

Affirmed.

Discussion Questions

1. Why was the foreclosure initiated?
2. What gave authority for the foreclosure?
3. What exemption does Johnson claim?
4. Can there be a foreclosure for the nonpayment of association fees?
5. Are the fees given a higher priority than the mortgage on the property?

Many bylaws have been subjected to judicial review because of item 6 provisions—restrictions on use and transfer of condominiums. Of particular concern in this area has been the adult-only bylaw, which limits sale and occupancy of units within the development to persons over the age of 12, 18, or in some cases even 60. However, as noted in Chapter 19 such restrictions are constitutionally valid. In the following case, another state court faces the same issue.

FRANKLIN v. WHITE EGRET CONDOMINIUM
358 So. 2d 1084 (Fla. 1980)

White Egret Condominium Development (plaintiff/appellee) had association rules that prohibited ownership of a unit by more than one family. Furthermore, the declaration prohibited children under the age of 12 from residing in a unit for more than a 2-week period.

Marvin Franklin purchased one of the units in White Egret in his name or "nominee." Marvin's brother, Norman, was to have a half interest in the unit conveyed to him, and both Franklins (defendants/appellants) applied for membership in the association and approval of ownership. Both Franklins were nonresidents of the state and testified that they were buying the unit so that their families would have a place to stay when visiting Florida.

Norman's application was denied because he had a child under the age of 12, but Marvin conveyed to Norman a half interest in the unit despite the denial. White Egret brought suit seeking to have the conveyance to Norman set aside. The trial court ordered Norman to reconvey his interest to Marvin, and both Norman and Marvin appealed.

KOVACHEVICH, Associate Judge

This point on appeal questions the holding of title jointly by defendants. Ownership by the two defendant blood brothers was permissible. Article C specifically allows joint ownership of condominium apartments: "Membership may be held in the name of more than one owner . . ." In the entire article there is no mention of any limits upon the amount of owners or the character of the group that might own the apartment; the word "family" is not even mentioned in the provision. It speaks not to the manner of use but specifically to the number of owners. The court should not now aid the plaintiff in reading a new and unstated restriction into the unqualified language of its own condominium document.

The next point questions what a "single family" is. Defendants contend that they were members of a single family and the use to which they put the condominium apartment was that of a single family residence. Article XXII prohibits use for any other purpose than as a "single family residence." The word "family" has been used to describe a number of different sets of relationships and there is no consensus as to exactly what a family is.

The confusion surrounding the definition of the term "family" must be taken into account when interpreting the restrictions in the instant case, sub judice. As a restriction on the fee use of property the single family rule must be "strictly construed in favor of a free and unrestricted use of real property." Substantial ambiguity or doubt must be resolved against the person claiming the right to enforce the covenant. A restrictive covenant must be read in the context of the entire document in which it is contained. When the "single family residence" restriction is read in conjunction with the context of the joint ownership provision, the two sections are inconsistent, and inherently ambiguous. Even if one were to consider that the defendants constitute two separate families, the use to which they put the apartment was that of a single family dwelling; according to the record herein, each of the defendants alternated their stays on the premises.

The final point on appeal that we find has merit relates to a restriction in condominium documents against children under the age of twelve (12) as an unconstitutional restriction and violation of defendant Norman Franklin's rights to marriage, procreation, and association, and violation of his right to equal protection of the laws.

Article XXIII prohibits children under the age of twelve (12) from residing on the condominium premises. This was the reason given by plaintiff for its disapproval of Norman Franklin's membership application. The instant case involves a number of rights which the Supreme Court of the United States has labeled "fundamental": the right to marry, and the right to procreate, and the right to marital privacy. This restriction is an unconstitutional violation of this defendant's right to marry and procreate. Further, no compelling reason has been shown for refusing to allow children under twelve (12) to reside in the condominium. It seems difficult to comprehend that change that occurs on a child's twelfth birthday which suddenly renders him fit to live in the condominium, and the plaintiff has offered no explanation regarding the same. Additionally, the plaintiff provides for a designation of children guests and has certain families with children under twelve (12) residing on the premises. Thus the enforcement of the restriction is not only unsupportable by a compelling inter- est but is obviously unreasonable, since the plaintiff seeks to selectively and arbitrarily enforce the restriction. Even if the rule were valid, such unequal enforcement would be a violation of equal protection.

We find that the trial court erroneously ordered defendant Norman Franklin to transfer his interest in the apartment to defendant Marvin Franklin, and reverse the lower court and remand for the entry of a final judgment in favor of defendants.

Discussion Questions

1. What bylaws are at issue?
2. What relationship exists between the defendant joint owners?
3. What was the purpose of the defendants' purchase of a condominium and in what manner will they use it?
4. How is *single family* interpreted in the case?
5. What rights do the defendants allege are violated by the minimum age requirement?
6. Is the minimum age restriction enforceable? Why or why not?
7. Are the defendants permitted to hold title jointly?

In many bylaws, provision is made for the creation and operation of an architectural control committee. Its purpose is to maintain uniformity in the appearance of condominium units. Particularly with regard to freestanding units, it is important that the units remain somewhat similar in appearance and that owners' changes in colors, structure, or appearance not detract from the overall appearance of the development. The architectural control committee reviews proposed construction changes and then either approves or disapproves them. It may also be given the responsibility for periodically checking the neighborhood to ensure that unauthorized and unapproved changes are not being made.

(21.1) Consider:

The bylaws of the Villa Nueva Condominium Association included the following provision:

> Occupancy in the High Rise portion of the project shall be limited to persons 18 years of age or older. The term *occupancy* refers to a continuous occupancy for a period of 14 days or more.

A potential buyer wishes to know if the provision is valid, and if it is whether it is possible to have it eliminated from the bylaws.

Regulations Still another document (or documents) should be created in the establishment of a condominium development: the regulations for operation of the condominium development. Because condominium living is similar to renting and many condominiums are converted apartment buildings, occupants must be governed by regulations in order to assure smooth functioning of the unit. The regulations should contain provisions on items such as pets and the use of the pool, laundry room, and other recreational rooms and equipment. It is perhaps also necessary for the bylaws to contain provisions for the development of and amendment to the regulations. Many bylaws or regulations also establish enforcement procedures. For example, committees may be placed in charge of enforcement, or enforcement may be placed in the hands of the officers or directors of the condominium organization. Legal action for violations may be established in the rules as well as a provision for recovering attorneys' fees from a violating occupant.

Conversion Restrictions Because of the large number of conversions of apartments to condominiums, many states have passed statutes and regulations requiring minimum notice periods before conversions can take place. The purpose of *conversion restrictions* is to give tenants the opportunity to decide whether to purchase the condominium unit in which they live or to move. Tenants thus have the opportunity to plan and are not forced into a rapid decision on the conversion issue. The typical notice requirement of conversion statutes is 120 days. Also, most statutes provide that if within the notice period the tenant declines the offer to purchase the condominium unit, then the tenant must be given an additional period of time within which to vacate the premises. Many conversion statutes require that such tenants be permitted to live out existing leases at their option.

Deeds The final documents needed for condominium creation are the individual deeds for each unit, which will be given to buyers to evidence their ownership. Condominium deeds should comply with all requirements for real property deeds (see Chapter 9) in addition to the following specifics:

1. Legal description (includes a reference to the declaration of condominium and where it is recorded)
2. Mailing address

3. Use restrictions (may be a reference to another document)
4. Title warranties

Creation of a Cooperative

Because a cooperative is a different type of real property interest, the documents needed for its creation vary from the documents necessary for a condominium creation. The basic documents include the articles of incorporation and evidence of incorporation (certificate of incorporation or corporate charter), the bylaws, and the proprietary lease.

Articles of Incorporation and Evidence of Incorporation Since ownership of a cooperative is really ownership of an interest in a corporation, the first documents necessary for formation of a cooperative are the incorporation papers. These documents vary according to state corporation law. Most states do require the filing of articles of incorporation before a certificate of incorporation or corporate charter is issued. The following information is generally required for incorporation:

1. Corporate name
2. Purpose of the corporation
3. Share structure, including classes, value, voting rights, transferability, number of authorized shares, and capital structure
4. Name of legal agent or representative
5. Structure of the board of directors and makeup of initial board
6. Corporate duration
7. Names of officers
8. Provisions for amendment to the articles

Bylaws The bylaws for a cooperative are similar to the bylaws for both corporations and condominiums—their purpose is to specify how the operation is to be run. The bylaws provide the details for meetings, including place, time, notice, quorums, and voting requirements. Finally, the bylaws contain the procedures for transferring ownership rights to cooperative members and usually provide instructions for developing and executing the proprietary lease.

Proprietary Lease A *proprietary lease* is very similar to an ordinary lease in that many of the topics and issues arising in the landlord–tenant relationship are covered. However, the following factors distinguish a proprietary lease from an ordinary lease:

1. *Length.* If the proprietary lease provides for a termination date at all, the date will be a long time into the future. Otherwise, the termination of the lease is tied to the transfer of the tenant's interest in the cooperative corporation.

2. *Rent.* No provision for rent is made in a proprietary lease; instead, the tenant pays a maintenance fee to the board of directors or officers. A provision is made for possible increases in the maintenance fee and may even provide for percentage increases according to a cost of living scale.

The proprietary lease should also cover certain contingencies, such as the owner's option to sell if maintenance fees increase substantially and the owner's rights in the event the cooperative unit is uninhabitable for a period of time.

Creation of Townhouses

As already discussed, a townhouse is different from a condominium in that the real property on which the townhouse is located is part of the owner's interest. In many states another difference exists in the procedures for creating a townhouse development. In the following sections, the various documents needed for this method of multiunit development are discussed.

Declaration of Covenants, Conditions, and Restrictions Similar to a master deed or declaration of condominium, the *declaration of covenants, conditions, and restrictions (CCRs)* is the first step in developing a townhouse area. The CCR contains all of the rights and responsibilities of the individual owners. Since the CCR is recorded, everyone is presumed to know its content even though it may not have been read. Once recorded, the CCR serves as constructive notice of the operation and regulations of the development. Many times, all-adult restrictions are part of the CCR. In the event of a conflict, the CCR is the final authority for correcting ambiguities or clarifying legal rights.

Articles of Incorporation The decision to incorporate is discretionary in some states as simply a more convenient way of holding title. Other states require that a corporation must be formed to hold title to common areas, and each owner is given a certain percentage share of the corporation. The articles are not recorded with the land records but are usually found in the state's corporate formation document section.

Bylaws The bylaws deal with the need for smooth day-to-day functioning of the development, with attendance to repairs and maintenance and compliance with all restrictions. Although the bylaws set up voting procedures, such procedures must be consistent with the articles of incorporation to be valid. The bylaws may also establish various committees to aid in the enforcement of restrictions—an architectural control committee, for example.

Regulations The purpose of the regulations in a townhouse development is the same as those for a condominium development: to keep common facilities in repair and reasonably available to residents in the development.

Creation of Time-Sharing Interests

Recreational Leases A time-sharing interest may take the form of a recreational lease, a proprietary lease, or a limited fee simple interest. A recreational lease is a financing device that allows the lessee to spread out over time the payment for use of another's recreational property. The lease may be a true lease with a landlord–tenant relationship between the parties or it may depend more strictly on the terms of the agreement. Ninety-nine-year leases or those without a specific termination date are more likely to be proprietary leases and for a cooperative form of ownership. Leases where the rental payment is determined according to a formula that is based on expenses of operation are also more likely to be proprietary leases and for a cooperative form of ownership. Thus, time-sharing interests may be landlord–tenant relationships or they may be cooperative interests.

Time-sharing interests may also be interests in perpetuity but limited in use to a specified period during each year. Thus, it is possible for a time-sharing interest to be a fee simple interest with limited use rights.

In any of the arrangements, the documents should specify responsibilities and the liabilities for cost of maintaining the premises.

LIABILITY ISSUES IN MULTIUNIT HOUSING

Owners of single-family dwellings buy insurance to cover liabilities they may have for injuries occurring on their premises. Thus, with single-family dwellings it is clear that there is liability in ownership, and it is also clear that the liability rests with the home-owner. It is the owner's responsibility to maintain and repair the premises. However, in multiunit housing arrangements, the nature of multiple ownership makes the issues of liability and responsibility less clear.

Contractual Liability of Unit Owners

There are three issues of contractual liability for owners of multiunit housing that are of major concern and which should be clarified by anyone seeking to purchase, develop, or rent a multiunit housing project or unit. These issues are: (1) the liability of owners for unpaid bills of the developer, (2) the liability of owners for assessment and maintenance fees, (3) and the liability of owners for improvement and repair costs of common elements and individual units.

Liability for Unpaid Bills of the Developers Generally with multiunit developments, there comes a time when control of the development is turned over to a corporation, a home-owners' association, or a board of directors for operation. The point in time at which this turnover is made varies—some articles of incorporation or bylaws provide for a number turnover point (e.g., when 3/4 of all units have been sold) while others provide for an absolute point (when all units have been sold). When control is turned over to the development residents, the developer is not only no longer in control but also is no longer responsible for maintenance and repair costs.

One possible problem with turnover is when all construction elements of the development are not owned free and clear (when there are outstanding debts). In most cases, the developer would be responsible for payment of such obligations, since the corporation or home-owners' association probably would not have existed at the time of the debt contract. However, there are potential problems in spite of the developer's liability. First, the developer may not be able to pay, and fixtures may be repossessed from the development or liens may be placed on it. Second, even if the developer can pay, a lawsuit may be required to establish liability. Problems such as these are exemplified in the following case.

20 EAST CEDAR CONDOMINIUM ASSOCIATION v. LUSTER ET AL.
349 N.E.2d 586 (Ill. 1976)

Melvin R. Luster and Harold E. Friedman (defendants/appellants) formed a partnership to convert the 20 East Cedar property from rental property to condominium units. Deeds to each unit provided purchasers with title for the designated unit plus an undivided percentage of the "common elements." In each sales agreement, the partnership agreed to complete certain repair and rehabilitation work in the building.

In 1970 (during the conversion process) Luster and Friedman leased a canopy from White Way Electric Sign and Maintenance Company, with a down payment of $6,128 and 60 monthly payments of $261.76 each. The canopy was ornamental and was installed at the front entrance of the 20 East Cedar building.

In 1973 the unit owners formed their own association, and Luster and Friedman were relieved of their responsibilities. After the release, the unit owners discovered the liability remaining on the canopy lease as well as several other unpaid expenses incurred by Luster and Friedman in the rehabilitation of the building.

The association (plaintiffs/appellees) brought suit, seeking a complete accounting and monetary relief from Luster and Friedman. The trial court ordered Luster and Friedman to pay for the canopy, and Luster and Friedman appealed.

O'CONNOR, Justice

Defendants made a contract with plaintiffs which is unambiguous in its terms. The first page of the contract in question specifies that Holmkvist (an association member) purchased without encumbrance thereon his apartment as well as "1.5985% of the ownership interest in the 'common elements' of the 'property.'" . . . In paragraph 4 the "common elements" are defined as ". . . all portions of the 'property' except the units." Property, in turn, is defined as ". . . all the land, property and space comprising the Parcel, all improvements and structures constructed or contained therein or thereon, including the building and all easements, rights and appurtenances belonging thereto, and all fixtures and property intended for the mutual use, benefit or enjoyment of the unit owners." Additionally, a rider is attached to this contract which, in provision R-3 provides, inter alia, that all repairs and rehabilitation work set forth in an attachment to the contract titled "Schedule B" have been or shall be fully completed on or before delivery of the deed. Schedule B, in turn, lists a wide assortment of improvements, ranging from boiler repair to pigeon proofing. Under the heading "Front Entrance" there is the notation: "New canopy installed Fall, 1970." There is no indication in the purchase contract itself or in any of the riders or attachments that the plaintiffs would have to pay the cost of these improvements in addition to paying the purchase price of the condominium unit. On the contrary, the contract clearly outlines improvements promised by the seller to the purchaser as an inducement for the sale. The terms of this contract are controlling. They carefully set forth improvements which defendants contracted to make prior to selling to plaintiffs their condominiums. There is no necessity to go beyond the four corners of the contract.

Order and judgment affirmed.

Discussion Questions

1. Who converted the rental property to condominium units?
2. What were the terms of the canopy lease?
3. When was the canopy leased?
4. When did the home-owners' association take over?
5. What was the significance of schedule B in the purchase contract?
6. Who is liable for the canopy lease?

Liability for Assessment and Maintenance Fees In multiunit housing, all unit owners are responsible for the costs of maintaining common areas. Funds for the costs of repair and maintenance come from the assessment of monthly fees and perhaps periodic capital assessment payments made by the unit owners. The amount of these fees may be specified in the declaration or bylaws and may be subject to change upon a vote or according to a formula included in the declaration or bylaws.

Every unit owner is required to pay these fees. In many cases, the fees are paid to the mortgagee, who in turn pays the association (since the mortgagee has an interest in keeping the property, which is held as security, well-maintained). If an owner does not make the required maintenance or assessment payments, the association may have several alternatives, depending upon the particular state law. One alternative is to cut off services to the unit: running water, heat, and so on. Another alternative is to place a lien on the unit. (See *Johnson* at p. 605.)

Liability for Improvement and Repair Costs of Common Elements Whenever a multiunit housing development undertakes the improvement or repair of common elements, the owners are liable for the costs. Some of the issues arising in this area of liability are what constitutes a common element, whether limitations on amount of liability exist, and how assessments for such repairs can be changed, agreed to, or modified. Ideally, all of these issues are resolved in the bylaws, articles of incorporation, or declaration so that improvements do not become major legal issues. The following case is an example of the difficulties that can arise when unclearly defined actions on improvements are taken.

CASITA DE CASTILIAN, INC. v. KAMRATH
629 P.2d 562 (Ariz. 1981)

Casita de Castilian, Incorporated (plaintiff/appellee), is a nonprofit corporation formed to serve as the council of co-owners for Casita de Castilian condominium development. The Kamraths (defendants/appellants) owned a condominium in the development and had refused to pay $4,397 in past due assessments plus $765 in late penalties. The Kamraths claimed that their unit needed roof repairs at a cost of $2,393, and they counterclaimed for that amount in Casita's suit for the past due assessments. The Kamraths claimed that Casita did not have proper authority for the assessments on grounds that provisions were made only in the bylaws and that Casita was responsible for the roof maintenance. From a judgment for Casita for the full amount due, the Kamraths appealed.

BIRDSALL, Judge

The issues on appeal are:

1. Are the bylaws of the corporate council of co-owners a proper instrument in which to provide for maintenance of the common elements of the condominium?

2. If so, is it necessary that all the co-owners agree to such bylaw provisions?

3. Does a requirement that each individual owner maintain his own roof, a common element, satisfy A.R.S. Section 33-561 which requires the council

of co-owners to make provisions for maintenance of common elements?

A.R.S. §33-551(6)(b) provides in part that "general common elements" includes ceilings and roofs except as may be specifically otherwise provided for in the recorded declaration. A.R.S. §33-553(4) provides that the recorded declaration shall contain a description of the common elements. The declaration for this condominium describes the common elements as all of the real property committed to the regime except the individual units. Thus by reason of the statute the roofs are a common element. While the statutes do not require that the declaration speak in any way to maintenance, the declaration does recite that it is adopted, in part, "to provide for the maintenance of the common elements." However, there is no provision which fixes any responsibility for this maintenance.

Thus, we have no requirement in the statutes that the declaration fix responsibility for the maintenance of the common elements and the declaration is silent on this point. Likewise the articles of incorporation say nothing about such maintenance. As stipulated, the bylaws do fix such responsibility. The original bylaws make appellee responsible for maintenance of all the common elements. The amended bylaws make the individual member liable for maintenance and repair of the roof covering each apartment owned. Correspondingly, the corporation's maintenance responsibility excludes the roof covering. Article IV(A) of the declaration obligates all owners to pay assessments to meet the expenses of maintaining the common elements. Appellants argue this obligates the appellee to perform such maintenance. We disagree. This provision placed a burden on the individual owners to pay such assessments as are properly levied. It does not obligate the council to do the main-

tenance. We cannot read into that provision an obligation which is not there. We hold that the bylaws are a proper instrument in which to provide for maintenance of the common elements.

On the second issue, whether all co-owners must agree on a provision for maintenance of a common element, we find nothing in the statute requiring such unanimity.

The declaration provides that decisions and resolutions shall require approval of a majority of the owners. Appellee's articles of incorporation which were filed prior to the execution of the declaration and are referred to therein, provide for the enactment of bylaws by the board of directors governing the use of all common elements as well as for other corporate purposes. They further provide that a majority of the members (co-owners) may change or repeal the bylaws.

We believe that either of the bylaws provisions adopted here satisfy the statutory requirement that the appellee "make provisions for the maintenance of the common elements."

In 1977 the National Conference of Commissioners on Uniform State Laws approved the Uniform Condominium Act. 7 U.L.A. 97. This uniform law contains much different language than the Arizona Statute . . . regarding the maintenance of common elements. Section 3-107 states in part:

Except to the extent provided by the declaration . . . the association is responsible for maintenance, repair and replacement of the common elements, and each unit owner is responsible for maintenance, repair and replacement of his unit.

A 1980 amendment of this uniform act did not change the wording of this provision. Arizona has not adopted the uniform act or its language.

We hold . . . that the majority of condominium owners may provide for the maintenance of a common element by in- dividual owners. As a result appellants were not entitled to recover on their counterclaim.

We affirm.

Discussion Questions

1. Who filed suit, and what was the basis for the suit?
2. What was the basis for the counterclaim?
3. Where were provisions made for common elements in the condominium development?
4. What was required for an amendment to the bylaws?

5. Could the association exclude the roofs as common elements?
6. Who wins at the appellate level?
7. What does the Uniform Condominium Act provide regarding the case issue?
8. What is the significance of the declaration of condominium in this case?

(21.2) Consider:

The Island House Association, Incorporated, a home-owners' association formed for the operation of the Island House condominiums and villas, assessed each unit for maintenance fees. They required condominium owners to pay more for maintenance than villa owners because the condominium building was larger, had more units, and required more frequent repairs. The provision for fees was in the bylaws and had been voted on by the owners and approved by a majority. Thiess, a condominium owner, refused to pay his fees and claimed the assessment was inequitable and unfair. What was the result?

Tort Liability of Unit Owners

Individual Units Each unit owner is responsible for the maintenance and safety of his or her dwelling unit and is thus liable for torts occurring within it. A unit owner is expected to have insurance on the dwelling unit, just as a home-owner is expected to have insurance on the single-family dwelling.

Common Areas A major issue in multiunit housing law and a major concern for owners of these units is the liability for injuries occurring in common areas. If the development has a corporation, such as a nonprofit home-owners' association, then that corporation should carry insurance for liability in the common areas. Regardless of incorporation, the owners of the dwelling units are liable together and individually (jointly and severally) for torts occurring in common areas. The corporate organization with insurance simply makes the liability easier to bear, and the premium costs can be part of the assessment to each unit owner.

The liability for injuries occurring in common areas extends to visitors, repair persons, governmental personnel (such as fire and medical personnel), and any others authorized to be on the premises, including unit owners. The responsibility of maintaining common areas extends to the responsibility for injuries resulting from faulty repair or lack of maintenance.

Because of the potential liability to all who might be within the common areas, associations for multiunit housing should carry liability insurance to assure coverage and prevent the liability of individual owners for such torts.

The following article provides a summary of liability issues and insurance questions with regard to condominiums.

Understanding Condominium Claims

Associations and Insurance

Depending on the individual Declaration requirements, policies and statutes, a typical situation will require the unit owner to insure the contents of his or her own unit, while the association insures the common elements and limited common elements. Who insures the walls, floors and ceilings and the related fixtures, improvements and alterations that are actually within the unit will vary from Declaration to Declaration. The coverages may also be different. Early condominiums often required the association to insure such interior walls, floors and fixtures; however, conflicts within the commercial property forms available in the 1960s created insurable interest problems. New Association forms, such as the Special Multi-Peril Condominium General Building Form, (MP 00 81, Ed. 12-79) were needed to comply with Declarations containing such requirements. Such an association form includes not only the walls and fixtures of the unit, but may include even the unit refrigerators, air conditioners, ranges, dishwashers and clothes washer/dryer, for none of which the association has a real insurable interest.

Other Declarations reserve these items, or some portion of them, for the unit owner to insure. The standard Condominium Unit Owners Form (HO-6, Ed. 7-77) provides coverage for the "additions, alterations, fixtures, improvements or installations which are part of the building within the unfinished interior surfaces of the perimeter walls, floors and ceilings . . ." but only for $1000. This amount may be increased by use of the HO 31 endorsement.[1]

[1]Other HO endorsements increase amounts of liability, or cover a unit owner's assessment by the association of any loss not covered by the association's coverages, if a covered peril or liability is involved. Obviously, a loss such as that caused by earthquake or flood would not be included.

The Adjustment Problem

If a fire occurs within a unit and causes damage throughout the condominium common elements and in other units, there are many factors the adjuster must take into consideration:

• Exactly who is the "insured?" Even if the adjuster's insurer represents the association, if the Declaration *and* the policy both require the association to insure walls or fixtures or appliances within the individual units, those unit owners who have sustained loss may also be insureds. The policy and the Declaration will define this factor, and the unit owner may be an "additional named insured."

• Suppose the fire occurred when Unit Owner A was cooking, and negligently allowed the fire to occur. The unit owner, who may also be an "insured" for purposes of walls, fixtures, or even the range in which the fire developed, may also be the party against whom the other unit owners have a subrogation claim for their personal property damage. If their damage also includes interior walls and fixtures which the association insures, the adjuster may be handling for three or more insured parties. The Declaration document and policies resolve some potential conflict with either hold-harmless agreements or subrogation waiver clauses. Many condominium Declarations call for "cross-liability" or subrogation waiver endorsements within their liability policies.[2]

• The Declarations often also specify the individual or association officer or trustee who is authorized to file the proof of loss or execute agreement on behalf of the association, or to receive the insurance proceeds. Often, if the association has a mortgage or other lien on the common elements, the Declaration will also specify how proceeds may be payable.

• Where there are overlapping interests in the adjustment, the adjuster must analyze the Declaration and the policy to be certain that he or she is proceeding properly. May the individual unit owner execute a claim under the association policy if that policy covers property which is actually the sole property of the unit owner? Such a question can be particularly problematical where there is a deductible involved. For example, if a Declaration or statute calls for the association to insure the interior wall surfaces, carpets, fixtures and appliances *originally installed* within the units, and a unit owner has a kitchen fire which damages only the tile, appliances, walls and ceiling of that unit, must the association pay the deductible on that loss? What if the unit owner has replaced the original wall coverings and the range with more expensive items? Will the association policy still respond? Each of these matters must be examined carefully, in light of the Declarations, the statutes, or any case law that may affect the situation, and, more importantly, the insurance contracts as well. Which policy—the association's or the unit owner's—is "primary" and which is "excess"? If the association policy has a

---

[2]Obviously, in a situation where both unit "additions and alterations" and the association's own building coverages are under the same policy, there would be no subrogation. These arrangements are not necessarily standard, however, and each situation must be individually evaluated.

deductible of $5000, and the unit owner has only $1000 coverage on such property, must the association pay the deductible? Endorsements may be added to unit or association policies which clarify some of these issues.

The condominium adjustment process is just as complex for liability claims, and losses involving other lines of coverage. As more and more litigation focuses attention on possible mistakes by the officers of condominium associations, director and officer liability coverage claims are becoming more frequent. The confusion surrounding subrogation and cross-liability between unit owners and their association occasionally falls into gaps in the comprehensive design of the Declarations, but this may be clarified by the policies. Association officers also have fiduciary and fidelity exposures, and many condominiums employ large numbers of maintenance men, gardeners, secretaries and others, for whom worker's compensation and other coverages are needed. Additionally, there are liability exposures to the general public, who may visit the condominium.

No adjustment of a condominium loss can be considered without careful study of the involved documents and all insurance policies of the parties involved in any way in the loss. The condominium claim assignment is challenging and frequently frustrating. It requires every adjusting skill; successful settlement of a condominium claim is the mark of experience.

Reprinted with permission from *Crawford Risk Review.*

RECOMMENDATIONS

Like other real estate purchases, multiunit housing can be a good investment, but it is important to study before buying. The following questions should be answered before an investment is made.

For a condominium conversion:

1. What is the status of the building? What repairs are necessary? Who will make the repairs? Who will pay for the repairs?
2. When will the developer turn over control of the building operation? Who or what organization will control the building operation at that point? What system of government, maintenance, and repair has been set up?
3. Is there a provision to opt out (back out) if the units do not sell?
4. Will the developer finish repairs? Are there any outstanding liens?

For an existing development:

1. Is there an association? If so, how does it work and is it effective?
2. Are there assessments? If so, how much are they, and do the unit owners pay them?
3. What provisions for operations and restrictions are made in the declaration, charters, bylaws, and regulations?
4. Are the common areas well-maintained?
5. What elements are included in the common areas, and what elements are the responsibility of individual unit owners?
6. How do other unit owners feel about the assessments and how the development is functioning?
7. Are there any pending lawsuits?
8. Is there adequate insurance coverage for the common areas?
9. Are the units rented or owner-occupied?

For any type of multiunit purchase:

1. Is it possible to obtain financing?
2. What type of ownership interest is being obtained?
3. Are there restrictions on transferability?
4. Are there use and age restrictions?
5. Are the units subject to architectural control?

The quality of a multiunit investment is tied to the quality of the investor's investigation of the development—the investigation can never be too thorough.

KEY TERMS

condominium
cooperative
townhouse
patio homes
garden homes
attached homes
time-sharing
recreational lease
horizontal property regimes
horizontal property acts

master deed
declaration of horizontal property
    regime and covenants
declaration of condominium
bylaws
conversion restrictions
proprietary lease
declaration of covenants,
    conditions, and restrictions
    (CCRs)

CHAPTER PROBLEMS

1. What should be included in a declaration of condominium?

2. What is the difference between a cooperative and a condominium?

3. What is the difference between a townhouse and a condominium?

4. The Stoves live in a condominium development that prohibits persons under the age of 21 from living in any unit for a period exceeding 2 weeks. The Stoves, who wish to adopt a child, claim the restriction is unconstitutional. If the Stoves challenge the restriction, what will be the result?

5. Mayfair Engineering Company developed a condominium project, which had a declaration stating that thirty-five parking spaces were to be assigned, one to each unit, and that the spaces were part of the common areas. Mayfair then proceeded to sell the units, offering to transfer a parking space to each purchaser for additional consideration. Park and other buyers maintained Mayfair could not charge an additional fee for use of a common area. What was the result?

6. Robb, a resident of North Townehome Park, installed evaporative coolers in the windows of his townhouse, and the home-owners' association complained, citing architectural nonconformity. Is it permissible to prevent such an installation or require it to be removed?

7. Kaufman planted four trees in front of his townhouse in an area between the sidewalk and the street, which was designated as a common area in the declaration. Kaufman's neighbors, whose view was obstructed by the trees, complained. The home-owners' association then brought suit to have the trees removed, since Kaufman had no authority to plant them in a common area. What was the result?

8. The declaration of the Seagate Condominium Association contained a restriction that prohibited owners from leasing their units without first obtaining permission from the association. Duffy brought suit, alleging such a restriction was invalid. What was the result?

9. Silver purchased a condominium unit in a new building and less than 6 months after moving in, he and several other owners discovered that their air-conditioning units were defective. They sued the developer on a breach of implied warranty for new home construction. The developer maintained that the warranty applied only to single-family sales. What was the result?

10. If a postal employee slips and falls on the stairway in a condominium project, who is liable for injuries?

22

ENVIRONMENTAL LAW

Where there's smoke, there's liability.

–CIGNA Corporation ad slogan
(Reprinted with permission
from the Cigna Corporation

Frezzo Brothers, Incorporated, is a Pennsylvania firm engaged in mushroom farming at a location near Avondale. To produce their mushrooms, Guido and James Frezzo (the two family members responsible for the operation of the business), used a growing medium that consisted of fermented hay and horse manure. White Clay Creek, which flowed alongside of the Frezzo operation, was considerably polluted, and upon analysis the pollutants were found to consist mainly of horse manure. There had been no rain in the area, and the Environmental Protection Agency charged the Frezzos and their corporation with willfully discharging manure into the stream. The Frezzos claim the right to use the stream as riparians, and the United States government claims environmental regulations will control over common law rights. Who wins?

As the example indicates, there are times when governmental regulations conflict with the common law rights associated with real property ownership. However, property rights are subject to the restrictions imposed by governmental statutes and regulations. This chapter discusses both the governmental restrictions on land use and the governmental protections for landowners. The following questions are answered: What types of governmental regulations affect property use and ownership rights? Who is responsible for enforcing governmental regulations and what penalties exist for violation of the regulations? In the event of conflicts between common law rights and governmental regulations, which group of laws will control?

623

624

STATUTORY ENVIRONMENTAL LAWS

At the federal level, most environmental laws can be placed in one of three categories: those regulating air pollution, those regulating water pollution, and those regulating land pollution. In addition, the federal regulatory scheme has several laws affecting property rights that do not fit into these categories but are discussed in this section.

Air Pollution Regulation

The Early Legislation The first legislation dealing with the problem of air pollution passed in 1955 and was the *Air Pollution Control Act*. The act accomplished two purposes: to have the Surgeon General study the problems of air pollution and to declare that the responsibility for clean air was to be assigned to the states. The 1955 act did very little to control or take steps to control the problem of air pollution.

Federal regulation in this area began in 1963 with the passage of the *Clean Air Act*. Under this enactment, the Department of Health, Education and Welfare (HEW) was given the authority to convene conferences to settle pollution problems affecting more than one state. Little action was taken under the 1963 enactment; and to encourage greater involvement in the air pollution issue, Congress passed the *Air Quality Act* in 1967. Under this act, HEW was authorized to oversee the states' adoption of air quality standards and the implementation of those plans. Again, this legislation proved ineffective, for by 1970 no state had adopted a comprehensive plan.

1970 Amendments to the Clean Air Act—New Standards Because the states did not take action in the area of air pollution, Congress passed the 1970 amendments to the Clean Air Act (42 U.S.C. §7401); these amendments constituted the first federal legislation with any real authority for enforcement. Under the act, the *Environmental Protection Agency (EPA)* was authorized to establish air quality standards and once those standards were developed, states were required to adopt implementation plans to achieve the federally developed standards. These *state implementation plans (SIPs)* had to be approved by the EPA and adoption and enforcement of the plans were no longer discretionary but mandatory. The implementation plans, to obtain EPA approval, had to meet deadlines for compliance with the EPA air quality standards and thus the Clean Air Act established time periods for achieving air quality.

The air quality standards set by the EPA specify how much of a particular substance in the air is permissible. It was up to each state to devise methods for meeting those standards. The first step taken by the states was to measure existing air content of substances such as sulfur dioxide, carbon monoxide, and hydrocarbons. Based on the results, the states then took appropriate steps to reduce the amounts of those substances that exceeded federal standards.

In industrialized states, nearly all manufacturers were required to install pollution equipment. Installation of such equipment proved to be the subject of many suits because industries claimed the equipment substantially increased costs and that it was often technologically infeasible for companies to install equipment meeting the standards. Many companies filed suit seeking a delay in equipment installation until pollution control devices could be perfected or at least reduced in cost. The results of the argument for technological infeasibility varied. The following case involves the issue in an enforcement action brought against a manufacturer.

FRIENDS OF THE EARTH v.
POTOMAC ELECTRIC POWER COMPANY
419 F. Supp. 528 (D.C. 1976)

Potomac Electric operated a plant in the District of Columbia (the Benning Road facility) that had coal-fired stoker boilers that emitted visible smoke. The Friends of the Earth, a citizens' group, brought suit under the Clean Air Act seeking a declaration that Potomac (PEPCO/defendant) was in violation of the act and an order for their compliance with the act and all pertinent regulations. Following the Friends' (plaintiffs') motion for partial summary judgment, the following opinion and decision were made.

BRYANT, District Judge

. . . PEPCO asserts that the alleged technological and economic infeasibility of the absolute prohibition on visible emissions constitutes a defense to a charge of violation of the regulation. PEPCO relies principally on *Buckeye Power, Inc. v. EPA,* 481 F.2d (C.A. 6, 1973), to sustain this contention. The question of whether a violator may in certain circumstances raise a defense of economic or technological infeasibility was explicitly left open by the Supreme Court in *Union Electric,* 427 U.S. 246 (1976). The Court's reasoning and findings however totally undermine the rationale of the *Buckeye* court, leaving its holding without persuasive effect. The *Buckeye* court examined the legislative history of the 1970 Clean Air Act amendments and found that Congress did not intend plant shutdowns in the face of failure to meet the requirements of SIPs. The Supreme Court, in contrast, found that the Act is meant to be "technology-forcing," and that public health had been given absolute priority over continued operations of noncomplying polluters. The *Buckeye* court further articulated the rationale underlying its holding as follows:

Since we have determined that there could not have been an adequate hearing on individual claims such as those presented by the petitioners herein prior to approval of the state plans, the claims can be as-

serted as a defense in either federal or state enforcement proceedings (481 F.2d at 173).

The Supreme Court, however, held that such individual claims were wholly irrelevant to the Administrator's decision to approve or disapprove a state plan, and that such claims could rather be considered by the state in formulating the plan. Since the underlying premise of the *Buckeye* court has been found to be faulty, its holding cannot be given effect in the present case. And finally, despite the *Buckeye* court's reading of the legislative history of the 1970 amendments, that legislative history clearly contemplates that the Act's requirements be technology-forcing, and plainly reflects a congressional intent that claims of technology and economic infeasibility not constitute a defense to adjudication of violations of applicable SIP requirements.

This does not mean that each source

that is genuinely unable to comply with every requirement of an SIP must inevitably be closed; in formulating equitable relief the court must always exercise discretion and balanced judgment. While this judgment must give dominant weight to the public health interests protected by the Act, the court might for example, upon a finding of prior good faith efforts at compliance by the source, place it on a tight compliance schedule with shutdown specifically ordered if compliance had not been effected by a certain date. Whether such an extension of the original SIP requirements may be permitted will depend on the circumstances of each case, again with the public health criteria of the Act as primary guidelines. It may also of course be relevant to consider what relief plaintiffs actually seek; in the present case, they seek not shutdown but the maximum compliance possible given the current state of pollution control technology.

The court found PEPCO in violation and required a trial to determine remedies.

Discussion Questions

1. What violation of the Clean Air Act has occurred?

2. What defense does PEPCO allege for the violations?

3. Is PEPCO's defense valid?

4. When is technological/economic infeasibility to be considered?

5. What is meant by the phrase *technology-forcing*?

6. Must the PEPCO facility be shut down?

1977 Amendments When the 1977 amendments to the Clean Air Act were passed, businesses were given some relief from the technology-forcing requirement of the original act. Under these amendments, compliance by businesses could be extended if it could be established that closure would result in high levels of unemployment in the area. These economic effects were to be considered only in issues of compliance and not in the actual setting of air quality standards.

With the 1977 amendments also came authority for the EPA to regulate business growth in an attempt to achieve air quality standards. With this authority, the EPA classified two types of areas in which business growth could be contained. One type of area was called a *nonattainment area* and included those areas with existing, significant air quality problems, the so-called dirty areas. The second classification was for the clean areas and was called *prevention of significant deterioration areas (PSD areas).*

EPA Economic Controls for Nonattainment Areas For nonattainment areas, the EPA developed its *Emissions Offset Policy* that requires three elements before a new facility can begin operation in a nonattainment area.

1. The new plant must have the greatest possible emissions controls. In some cases this means the plant will be required to meet standards higher than existing standards.
2. The proposed plant operator must have all other operations in compliance with standards.
3. The new plant's emissions must be offset by reductions from other facilities in the area. These offsets have to be greater than the new emissions.

In applying these elements, the EPA follows the *"bubble concept,"* which examines all the air pollutants in the area as if they came from a single source. If it can be shown that a new plant will have no net effect on the air in the area (after offsets from other plants), then the new facility will not be subject to a veto.

Although the EPA did not regulate initially the construction of plants in areas already meeting air quality standards, environmentalists' protests and suits brought about the EPA regulations as to PSD areas. Basically, the purpose of PSD regulations is to permit the EPA to have the right to review proposed plant constructions prior to their construction. In their submissions for EPA review, the plant operators will be required to establish that there will be no significant effect on air quality and that emissions will be controlled with appropriate devices.

The following case shows the extent of power the EPA has in its attempts to clean up the air.

DRESSMAN v. COSTLE
759 F.2d 548 (6th Cir. 1985)

When Congress passed the 1977 amendments to the Clean Air Act, states were required to have an implementation plan by 1979 that would have them meet national ambient air quality standards (NAAQS) not later than 1982. The plan was to be approved by the EPA. If states did not comply with these requirements, the EPA could impose a moratorium on construction of new major stationary sources of pollution.

The state of Kentucky has three of its counties classified as nonattainment areas: Boone, Campbell, and Kenton counties. The EPA disapproved Kentucky's SIP and imposed a construction moratorium in those counties. The trial court upheld the moratorium and Kentucky appealed on the grounds that a moratorium was beyond the authority of the EPA as well as violative of the U.S. Constitution.

BROWN, Senior Circuit Judge

The petitioners (Kentucky judge executives of the affected counties) contend the EPA's actions in disapproving the SIP and invoking the moratorium were arbitrary and capricious or not according to law, and they urge this court to set aside the sanctions imposed by the Administrator.

When reviewing an EPA action concerning a SIP, this court's standard of review is an extremely narrow one. We must determine whether the EPA followed the proper lawful procedures and acted within its statutory authority when it promulgated its final rulemaking and whether that rulemaking is constitutional.

The Act provides that any state that does not have an approved SIP is subject to the construction moratorium. When Kentucky did not comply with the statute, the Administrator disapproved the Commonwealth's SIP, as he was statutorily mandated to do, and he properly imposed the construction moratorium in nonattainment areas, namely Boone, Campbell and Kenton counties.

The petitioners contend that the Administrator's actions were unconstitutional because they deprived the counties of valuable property rights without due process. The petitioners maintain they should have received an adjudicatory-type hearing before the Administrator by rule disapproved the Commonwealth's SIP and imposed the construction moratorium.

The Administrator's disapproval of Kentucky's SIP and imposition of the construction ban constitute rulemaking under the Administrative Procedures Act. Such rulemaking may be done without violating constitutional due process.

The petitioners also claim that the EPA is contravening their Tenth Amendment rights.

It is undisputed that air pollution is a severe national problem. Congress has exercised its power under the Commerce Clause to regulate directly air pollution. We find that the EPA's invocation of the construction moratorium was clearly a constitutional exercise of Congress' power under the Commerce Clause.

Affirmed.

Discussion Questions

1. What penalty was imposed on the state of Kentucky?
2. What objections were raised to the penalty?
3. Why was the penalty imposed?
4. What is the authority for such stiff regulation?

New Forms of Pollution—Acid Rain One of the more recent air quality issues relates to the problem of *acid rain*. Sulfur dioxide pollution from factories and coal-fired electricity generating plants is believed to be carried long distances and cause acid rain, which can damage lakes, fish, and trees. The most extensive acid rain and resulting environmental damage is found in the northeastern United States and eastern Canada. A bill to further control sulfur dioxide pollutants has been proposed in Congress in each of the last three sessions and a number of states have passed legislation designed to control acid rain.

The following case is one of the first to deal with the issue of acid rain liability.

STATE OF NEW YORK v. THOMAS
613 F. Supp. 1472 (D.C. 1985)

In 1981, Douglas M. Costle, then administrator of the EPA, sent a letter to former Secretary of State Edmund Muskie that stated in part that "acid deposition is endangering public welfare in the U.S. and Canada." The plaintiffs, including the state of New York and the Sierra Club, brought suit under the Clean Air Act. They alleged that the letter was sufficient proof to require regulation of acid rain and the modification of state implementation plans to include provisions for acid rain. Both sides submitted motions for summary judgment.

JOHNSON, District Judge

Section 304 of the Clean Air Act . . . provides that "any person" may commence a civil action to compel the Administrator to undertake action under the Act which is not discretionary. Under section 302 of the Act, person is defined to include "an individual, corporation, partnership, association [or] State. . . ." Thus, all of the plaintiffs who have joined in this action have statutorily cognizable claims.

The citizen group plaintiffs sue on behalf of themselves and on behalf of their members "who reside in areas throughout the midwestern and northeastern states and eastern Canada and breathe air pollution and suffer the other types of acid rain damages which are the subject of this action." Defendants argue that plaintiff associations have failed to allege that the associations or their members had been adversely affected by the inaction of the Administrator, relying principally on *Sierra Club v. Morton*, 405 U.S. 727, 92 S.Ct. 1361, 31 L.Ed.2d 636 (1972) and *Warth v. Seldin*, 422 U.S. 490, 95 S.Ct. 2197, 45 L.Ed.2d 343. These cases, however, do not prove defendants' contention. In *Sierra Club v. Morton*, plaintiff sued to obtain judicial review of action by the United States Forest Service approving recreational development in the Sierra Nevada Mountains. The Supreme Court denied standing to the plaintiff because it "failed to allege that it or its members would be affected in any of their activities or pastimes. . . ." In the present case, however, the plaintiffs have alleged not only that emissions from the polluting states have adversely affected eastern Canada, but also have alleged and supported with documentation that its members live, work, vacation, or own property in eastern Canada.

Moreover, in *Warth,* the Supreme Court recognized that an association may assert the rights of its members, but denied standing to the associated because none of them have sufficiently alleged cognizable injury. In this case, plaintiff associations have alleged with particularity that many of its members have suffered or will suffer concrete harm as a result of the putatively illegal inaction. Unlike *Warth,* which involved a tenuous causal link between the alleged illegality and the alleged harm, the present case involves alleged inaction which, if cured, may lead directly to reduced emissions and thus reduced harm. Plaintiffs have quite clearly stated that "respirable particulates and deposition of acidic materials are causing substantial and irreversible damage to the health and welfare of the people of the plaintiff states, plaintiff organizations, and the individual plaintiff."

The individual plaintiffs, with the exception of Representative Ottinger, also have alleged material facts sufficient to enable them to proceed as plaintiffs in this action. These plaintiffs own property in the Muskoka Lake area of Ontario and allege that their "air and water quality and personal property have been damaged by air pollution emitted from certain Midwestern States." Although defendants have countered that these plaintiffs have failed to specify any adverse effects that have impaired the use of their property, the Court is of the opinion that this is not required. Plaintiffs have alleged that their health and property have been placed in jeopardy by the pollutants. Further, the fact of their presence in a geographical region harmed by the Administrator's alleged inaction is sufficient to confer upon them a cognizable interest.

In addition to presenting properly cognizable claims in their representative or individual capacities, plaintiffs also have

alleged cognizable direct injury sufficient to meet the constitutional requirement of direct injury. Environmental harm is a legally redressable injury.

Since emissions from polluters in the midwestern United States may cause damage to air quality, water quality, and property in Canada, areas in which plaintiffs' citizens or members live, work, vacation or own property, plaintiffs have alleged threatened or actual injury sufficient to establish standing.

Article III requires that the injury complained of be fairly traced to the challenged action and that the harm involved be likely to be redressed by judicial intervention. As plaintiffs correctly noted, traceability and redressability "are inseparable in the present case because the relief plaintiffs seek is an order compelling the EPA to end the very inaction which is the cause of plaintiffs' injuries." These questions are problematic in the area of acid precipitation because of political and scientific dispute over the extent to which acid rain causes damage to aquatic ecosystems, terrestrial ecosystems, animal health, human health, or artifacts.

The task before the Court now is to determine if the requirements of section 115 have been satisfied and, if so, what action is required by the Administrator under the statute.

In order to trigger invocation of section 115, the Administrator must have "reason to believe that any air pollutant or pollutants emitted in the United States cause or contribute to air pollution which may reasonably be anticipated to endanger public health or welfare in a foreign country. . . ."

The IJC Report [International Justice Commission study on acid rain], upon which Administrator Costle in part based his decision, concludes that:

transmission of toxic and hazardous substances to the Great Lakes via long range atmospheric transport and deposition is a serious problem which requires further research efforts and control measures. . . . All parts of the Great Lakes watershed are now receiving precipitation containing 5 to 40 times more acid than would occur in the absence of atmospheric emissions.

Based on these findings, the Commission recommended "appropriate actions to substantially reduce atmosphere emissions of sulphur and nitrogen oxides from existing as well as new sources. . . ."

The Clean Air Act does not specifically state what is necessary for the Administrator to have "reason to believe," but the IJC Report would have afforded Costle ample basis upon which to conclude that air pollutants in the United States contribute to acid precipitation occurring in Canada such that it could reasonably be anticipated that the public health and welfare of Canada would be endangered. Indeed, that is exactly what Costle believed, for he specifically stated that "the IJC Report confirms that acid deposition is endangering public welfare in the United States and Canada and that the United States and Canadian sources contribute to the problem not only in the country where they are located but also in the neighboring country."

Defendants argue that Costle's findings are ambiguous and do not satisfy the requirements of section 115. They contend that Costle only made the finding that "the cumulative effects of Canadian and the United States emissions are creating a risk of public harm in Canada." This argument, however, cannot be reconciled with Costle's statements. In the letter to Senator Mitchell, Costle stated:

The relative contribution of U.S. and Canadian emission sources to acid deposition problems in the U.S. and Canada varies widely from location to location. . . . Surveys conducted over the past several years establish that there is a significant flow of these pollutants across the U.S.–Canadian border in both directions. Thus, we can say with some certainty that emission sources in the U.S. contribute significantly to the atmospheric loadings over some sensitive areas in Canada and that emission sources in Canada contribute significantly to the loadings over some sensitive areas in the United States.

It was based on this information that Costle had reason to believe that "U.S. and Canadian sources contribute to the problem not only in the country where they are located but also in the neighboring country." Therefore, this requirement of the statute is satisfied.

Summary judgment for plaintiffs.

Discussion Questions

1. How did the suit originate?
2. Who has brought the suit?
3. Is there sufficient proof for the implementation of regulations?

4. Do the plaintiffs have sufficient injury to bring the suit?
5. What will be required as a result of the decision?

Water Pollution Regulation

Early Legislation Federal legislation on the control of water pollution has been in existence since as early as 1899, but its effect has not always been significant.

The first act to be passed that was specifically directed at the problem of polluted waters was the *Water Pollution Control Act of 1948*. Until this enactment, the matter of water pollution was left to state and local governments.

(22.1) Consider:

Union Electric Company is an electric utility company servicing St. Louis and large portions of Illinois and Iowa. It operates three coal-fired generating plants in metropolitan St. Louis which are subject to sulfur dioxide restrictions that are part of the state of Missouri's implementation plan. Union Electric did not seek review of the implementation plan but applied for and obtained variances from the emissions limitations. When an extension for the variances was denied, Union Electric challenged the implementation plan on the grounds that it was technologically and economically infeasible and should therefore be amended. Under the *PEPCO* case, will Union Electric succeed in having the plan amended? See *Union Electric Co. v. EPA*, 427 U.S. 246 (1976).

The 1948 act made no significant change in this approach and only authorized the Surgeon General to study the problems of water pollution and then encourage the states to adopt and enforce implementation plans.

The first legislation to bring about federal involvement came with the enactment of the Water Pollution Control Amendments of 1956. Although this act did not set any standards for water pollution, it did authorize the Surgeon General to intervene in settling interstate water pollution problems and in the event there was no compliance with the settlement, authorized the attorney general to bring suit for enforcement.

In 1965, the first federal legislation on water quality standards was passed—the *Water Quality Act*. The act established a separate enforcement agency—the *Federal Water Pollution Control Administration (FWPCA)*—and required states to establish quality levels for the waters within their boundaries. Under the act, the states were permitted to designate or "zone" waters for certain uses and could thus vary the levels of water quality. For example, swimming waters would have higher standards than agricultural waters. After these designations or zones were established, states were then required to develop implementation plans to meet established standards for all zones. If a waterway did not meet zone standards, states were then required to control the discharges or pollutants being put into the waterway. Because the act contained few expeditious enforcement procedures, only about half of the states had developed their zones and standards by 1970 and none of the states were engaging in active enforcement of those standards with their implementation plans.

Owing to the states' lack of involvement and the burdensome enforcement procedures of the 1965 act, new legislation was needed to provide meaningful enforcement. That new legislation did not come in the form of a new act but in the rediscovery of an old act, the *Rivers and Harbors Act of 1899*. The name of the act is a partial explanation of its purpose: It prohibited the discharge of refuse into navigable rivers and harbors, which caused interference with navigation. Specifically, the act prohibited the release of "any refuse matter of any kind or description" into navigable waters in the United States without a permit from the Army Corps of Engineers. For a time, the act was used to control the issuance of permits and to prosecute those industrial polluters that were discharging without permit. A major problem with the use of this act was the lack of a general prohibition on what was released or the amount of releases, so long as a permit was obtained.

Present Legislation It was not until 1972 that meaningful and enforceable federal legislation was enacted with the passage of the *Federal Water Pollution Control Act of 1972* (33 U.S.C. §1401). Under this act, two goals were set: (1) swimmable and fishable waters by 1983 and (2) zero discharge of pollutants by 1985. The act was amended in 1977 to allow extensions and flexibility in meeting the goals and was renamed the *Clean Water Act*. One of the major changes brought about by the act was the move from local to federal controls of water pollution. Federal standards for water discharges were established on an industry basis and all industries, regardless of state location, are required to comply.

Under the act, all direct industrial dischargers are placed into twenty-seven groups and the Environmental Protection Agency (EPA) (now responsible for water pollution control since the FWCPA was merged into it) establishes ranges of discharge for each industrial group. The ranges for pulp mills will differ from those for textile manufacturers, but all plants in the same industry must comply with the same ranges.

The ranges of discharges permitted per industrial group are referred to as *effluent guidelines*. In addition, the EPA has established a specific amount of discharge for each plant within an industrial group, which is the effluent limitation. Finally, for a plant to be able to discharge wastes into water ways they must obtain from the EPA a *National Pollution Discharge Elimination System (NPDES) permit*. This type of permit is required only for direct dischargers, or *point sources*, and is not required of plants that discharge into sewer systems (although these secondary dischargers may still be required to pretreat their discharges). Obtaining a permit is a complicated process that not only requires EPA approval but also state approval, public hearings, and an opportunity for the proposed plant owners to obtain judicial review of a permit decision.

In issuing permits, the EPA may still prescribe standards for release.

Generally, the standards that are set depend upon the type of substance the discharger proposes to release. For setting standards, the EPA has developed three categories of pollutants: *conventional, nonconventional,* and *toxic.* If a discharger is going to release a conventional pollutant, the EPA can require it to pretreat the substance with the *best conventional treatment (BCT).* If the pollutant to be discharged is either toxic or nonconventional, then the EPA can require the *best available treatment (BAT),* which is the highest standard imposed. In issuing permits and requiring these various levels of treatment, the EPA need only consider environmental effects and not the economic effects on the applicant discharger.

(22.2) Consider:

Inland Steel Company applied for a permit from the EPA under the Federal Water Pollution Control Act of 1972. Although Inland was granted the permit, the EPA made the permit modifiable as new standards for toxic releases and treatment thereof were developed. Inland claimed the modification restriction on the permit was invalid because the EPA did not have such authority and also because Inland would be subject to every technological change or discovery made during the course of the permit. Inland filed suit. Was the restriction invalid? See *Inland Steel Company v. Environmental Protection Agency,* 574 F.2d 367 (7th Cir. 1978).

Solid Waste Disposal Regulation

Early Regulation The disposal of solid waste (garbage) has been a significant problem in the United States because of the long history and popularity of the open dumping method of disposal. As with other pollution issues, the disposal of solid wastes initially was perceived to be a problem of state and local governments. In 1965, Congress passed the *Solid Waste Disposal Act,* which provided money to state and local governments for research in solid waste disposal. In 1970, this 1965 act was amended with the passage of the *Resource Recovery Act.* It was this act that encouraged the recycling process by offering aid to local governments engaging in recycling projects. The act also provided funds for research and established guidelines for solid waste disposal, but the law had no real federal power or enforcement provisions.

Later Responses—Toxic Substance Control After several major open dumping problems, such as the Love Canal chemical dumping near Buffalo, New York, two federal acts were passed that granted some enforcement power to the federal government. The *Toxic Substances Control Act (TOSCA)* (15 U.S.C. §1601) was passed in 1976 and authorized the EPA to control the manufacture, use, and disposal of toxic substances. Under the act, the EPA is authorized to prevent manufacture of dangerous substances and stop the manufacture of substances found to be dangerous.

Also passed by Congress in the 1976 reaction to dangerous dumping practices was the *Resource Conservation and Recovery Act of 1976 (RCRA)* (42 U.S.C. §6901). The two goals of the act are to control the disposal of potentially harmful substances and to encourage resource conservation and recovery. A critical part of the act's control is a manifest or permit system that requires manufacturers to obtain a permit for the storage or transfer of hazardous wastes, so that the location of such wastes can be traced through an examination of the permits issued.

The Superfund In 1980, Congress passed the *Comprehensive Environmental Response, Compensation, and Liability Act (CERCLA)* (42 U.S.C. §9601), which authorized the president to issue funds for the clean-up of areas that were once disposal sites for hazardous wastes. Under the act, a *Hazardous Substance Response Trust Fund* is set up to provide funding for clean-up. If funds are expended in such a clean-up, then, under the provisions of the act, the company responsible for the disposal of the hazardous wastes can be sued by the federal government and required to repay the amounts expended from the trust fund. Often called the *"Superfund,"* the funds are available for governmental use but cannot be obtained through suit by private citizens affected by the hazardous disposals.

One of the most critical issues in the waste area is that of nuclear power plant wastes. The following case discusses that issue in relation to environmental concerns.

BALTIMORE GAS & ELECTRIC CO. v.
NATURAL RESOURCES DEFENSE COUNCIL
462 U.S. 87 (1984)

The Nuclear Regulatory Commission (NRC) has the responsibility of licensing nuclear power plants. In proceedings related to licensing criteria, the NRC decided that licensing boards should assume that the permanent storage of certain nuclear wastes would have no significant environmental impact and should not affect the decision of whether to license a particular power plant.

The Natural Resources Defenses Council (NRDC) is an environmental group that challenged the rule on wastes and its application to the license proceedings for the Vermont Yankee Nuclear Power Plant. The Court of Appeals found for NRDC and Baltimore Gas & Electric appealed.

O'CONNOR, Justice

We are acutely aware that the extent to which this Nation should rely on nuclear power as a source of energy is an important and sensitive issue. Much of the debate focuses on whether development of nuclear generation facilities should proceed in face of uncertainties about their long-term effects on the environment. Resolution of these fundamental policy questions lies, however, with Congress and the agencies to which Congress has delegated authority, as well as with state legislatures and, ultimately, the populace as a whole. Congress has assigned the courts only the limited, albeit important, task of reviewing agency action to determine whether the agency conformed with controlling statutes. As we emphasized earlier "administrative decisions should be set aside in this context, as in every other, only for substantial procedural or substantive reasons as mandated by statute . . . , not simply because the court is unhappy with the result reached."

The controlling statute at issue here is the National Environmental Policy Act. NEPA has twin aims. First, it places upon an agency the obligation to consider every significant aspect of the environmental impact of a proposed action. Second, it ensures that the agency will inform the public that it has indeed considered environmental concerns in its decision-making process. Congress in enacting NEPA, however, did not require agencies to elevate environmental concerns over other appropriate considerations. Rather, it required only that the agency take a "hard look" at the environmental consequences before taking a major action. The role of the courts is simply to ensure that the agency has adequately considered and disclosed the environmental impact of its actions and that its decision is not arbitrary or capricious.

The Commission has determined that the probabilities favor the zero-release as-

sumption, because the Nation is likely to develop methods to store the wastes with no leakage to the environment. The NRDC did not challenge and the Court of Appeals did not decide the reasonableness of this determination, and no party seriously challenges it here. The Commission recognized, however, that the geological, chemical, physical and other data it relied on in making this prediction were based, in part, on assumptions which involve substantive uncertainties. Again, no one suggests that the uncertainties are trivial or the potential effects insignificant if time proves the zero-release assumption to have been seriously wrong. After confronting the issue, though, the Commission has determined that the uncertainties concerning the development of nuclear waste storage facilities are not sufficient to affect the outcome of any individual licensing decision.

It is clear that the Commission, in making this determination, has made the careful consideration and disclosure required by NEPA. The sheer volume of proceedings before the Commission is impressive.

The Commission's decision to affix a zero value to the environmental impact of long-term storage would violate NEPA, however, only if the Commission acted arbitrarily and capriciously in deciding generally that the uncertainty was insufficient to affect any individual licensing decision. In assessing whether the Commission's decision is arbitrary and capricious, it is crucial to place the zero-release assumption in context. A separate and comprehensive series of programs has been undertaken to select the most effective long-term waste disposal technology.

A reviewing court must remember that the Commission is making predictions, within its area of special expertise, at the frontiers of science. When examining this kind of scientific determination, as opposed to simple findings of fact, a reviewing court must generally be at its most deferential.

We find the Commission's zero-release assumption to be within the bounds of reasoned decisionmaking required by the NEPA.

Reversed.

Discussion Questions

1. What assumption did the NRC make in licensing this plan?
2. Will the same assumption be made in all licensing decisions?
3. Does the NRC acknowledge the consequences if their assumption is wrong?
4. What standard is used to evaluate the assumption?
5. Is the assumption valid?

In 1986, CERCLA was amended by the *Superfunds Amendment and Reauthorization Act*. Under the amendments in that act, liability provisions were included and the EPA is now permitted to recover clean-up funds from those responsible for the release of hazardous substances. There are approximately 700 hazardous substances now covered. (They are listed at 40 C.F.R. §302.) Since the passage of the 1986 amendments, there has been judicial expansion of the concept of "responsibility." Clearly, those who release the substances are liable but that liability has been expanded to include those who purchase the property and did not perform adequate checks on the property's history and, as the following case illustrates, even lenders can be included as responsible parties.

UNITED STATES v. MARYLAND BANK & TRUST CO.

632 F. Supp. 573 (D.Md. 1986)

From 7 July 1944 to 16 December 1980, Herschel and Nellie McLeod owned a 117-acre piece of land located in the town of California, Maryland in St. Mary's County (referred to as the California Maryland Drum site or CMD site). During this period of ownership, Maryland Bank & Trust (MB&T) loaned money to the McLeods for the operation of his two businesses: Greater St. Mary's Disposal, Inc. and Waldorf Sanitation of St. Mary's, Inc. which were both trash and garbage

businesses. The record indicates that MB&T was aware of the nature of the businesses but it is unclear when it acquired its awareness.

During 1972 to 1973, the McLeods permitted the dumping of hazardous wastes on their property including lead, chromium, mercury, zinc, and ethylbenzene.

In 1980, the McLeod's son, Mark, obtained a loan from MB&T and purchased the 117 acres from his parents. Mark failed to make payments and MB&T instituted foreclosure proceedings in 1981 and bought the property at a sale in May 1982.

The EPA discovered the hazardous waste problems and conducted a clean-up of the site at a cost of $551,713.50. The EPA then demanded payment from MB&T. When payment was refused, the EPA (plaintiff) brought suit to collect the cost of the clean-up. Both sides moved for summary judgment on the case.

NORTHROP, Senior District Judge

CERCLA empowers the federal government to clean-up and otherwise respond to hazardous dump sites. The EPA has been delegated primary responsibility for this task.

"Response" actions undertaken by the EPA are financed primarily from the Hazardous Substance Response Trust Fund, commonly known as the "Superfund." The Act also authorizes the government to recover costs from certain "responsible parties" (Section 107). This section extends liability to four categories of persons: 1) current owners and operators of the hazardous substance facility; 2) past owners or operators of the hazardous substance facility at the time of the disposal; 3) persons who arranged for treatment or disposal of hazardous substances at the facility; and 4) persons who transported hazardous substances for treatment or disposal at the facility selected by them.

To establish liability, the government must establish the following:

1) The site is a "facility";
2) A "release" or "threatened release" of any "hazardous substance" from the site has occurred;
3) The release or threatened release has caused the United States to incur "response costs"; and
4) The defendant is one of the persons designated as a party liable for costs.

Defendant Maryland Bank & Trust does not dispute the fact that the first three elements of the prima facie case have been met by the United States. The question central to both the defendant's and the plaintiff's motions for summary judgment concerns the final element, specifically, whether Maryland Bank & Trust is an "owner and operator".

The Court initially turns to the question of whether MB&T falls within Section 107(a)(1). That section holds liable "the owner and operator" of the facility. It is undisputed that MB&T has been the owner of the facility since May 1982. The parties dispute whether the bank has been the operator of the facility since that time. The dispute over the term "operator" is not determinative, however, for the Court holds that current ownership of a facility alone brings a party within the ambit of subsection (1). Notwithstanding the language "the owner and operator", a party need not be both an owner and operator to incur liability under this subsection.

An examination of the legislative history, sparse as it is, and the lone relevant case convinces the Court to interpret the language of subsection (1) broadly to include both owners and operators. The House report explains the definition of operator as follows: "In the case of a facility, an 'operator' is defined to be a person who is carrying out operational functions for the owner of the facility pursuant to an agreement." By its very definition, an operator cannot be the same person as an owner. Therefore, a class defined as consisting of persons who are both owners and operators would contain no members. Such a definition would render section 107(a)(1) a totally useless provision.

The Court of Appeals for the Second Circuit recently held a current owner of a facility responsible for response costs under section 107(a)(1) even though that party had not owned the site at the time of the dumping and had apparently not "operated" the facility, *Shore Realty,* 759 F.2d 1032 (2d Cir. 1985). The court stated that "section 107(a)(1) unequivocally imposes strict liability on the current owner of a facility from which there is a release or threat of release, without regard to causation." This Court agrees.

MB&T contends that it is entitled to an exemption because it acquired ownership of the CMD site through foreclosure on its security interest in the property and purchase of the land at the foreclosure sale.

The exemption covers only those persons who, at the time of the clean-up, hold indicia of ownership to protect a then-held security interest in the land. The security interest must exist at the time of the clean-up. The mortgage held by MB&T (the security interest) terminated at the foreclosure sale of 15 May 1982, at which time it ripened into full title.

MB&T purchased the property at the foreclosure sale not to protect its security interest, but to protect its investment.

In conclusion, the Court grants the United States' motion for summary judgment.

Summary judgment for the United States.

Discussion Questions

1. Who originally owned the property and for how long?
2. How was the property used?
3. Who purchased the property?
4. How did MB&T become involved?
5. When did the EPA do the clean-up?
6. What interest did MB&T hold at the time of the clean-up?
7. Is MB&T liable?
8. What precautions should lenders take before loaning money for the purchase of property?

Many states have been concerned about hazardous waste disposal and have passed their own regulatory schemes to provide mechanisms and funding for clean-up and penalties for failure to follow their requirements. All fifty states have some form of hazardous waste regulation and the definitions of hazardous wastes as well as the penalties vary. Arizona includes garbage in its definition and Oregon establishes fines on the basis of a fee per animal destroyed as a result of the waste. The death of one mountain goat due to hazardous waste will cost the violator $3,500 in Oregon.

(22.3) Consider:

The Superfund has been used quite frequently since its inception. The result is that more funds are needed to keep it going. Congress has proposed expanding the tax used for funding to include all manufacturers. When expansion of the funding sources for the Superfund has been proposed in Congress, the businesses not currently subject to the superfund tax have opposed additional impositions on them. Do these firms have an obligation to assist in the clean-up? Can all firms claim that they do not affect the environment? Is the clean-up a general business obligation?

Environmental Quality Regulation

Environmental controls of air, water, and waste are directed at private parties in the use of their land. However, as part of the environmental control scheme, Congress also passed an act that regulates what governmental entities can do in the use of their properties. The *National Environmental Policy Act of 1969 (NEPA)* (42 U.S. §4321) was passed to require federal agencies to take into account the environmental impact of their proposed actions and to prepare an *environmental impact statement (EIS)* prior to taking any proposed action.

An EIS must be prepared and filed with the EPA whenever an agency sends a proposed law to Congress and whenever an agency will take major federal action significantly affecting the quality of the environment. The information required in an EIS is as follows:

1. The proposed action's environmental impact;
2. Adverse environmental effects (if any);
3. Alternative methods;
4. Short-term effects versus long-term maintenance, enhancement, and productivity; and
5. Irreversible and irretrievable resource uses.

Examples of federal agency actions that have required the preparation of EIS's include the Alaska oil pipeline, the extermination of wild horses on federal lands, the construction of government buildings such as post offices, and any highway construction built with federal funds.

The following case involves an issue of whether an EIS was required.

SIERRA CLUB v. UNITED STATES DEPARTMENT
OF TRANSPORTATION
753 F.2d 120 (D.C. 1985)

In 1983, the Federal Aviation Administration (FAA) issued two orders amending the operations specifications for Frontier Airlines, Inc. and Western Airlines, Inc. These amendments gave the airlines permanent authorizations to operate Boeing 737 jet airplanes (B-737s) out of Jackson Hole Airport, which is located within the Grand Teton National Park in Wyoming. These two airlines are the only major commercial carriers that schedule flights to and from Jackson Hole.

Private jets have flown into the

airport since 1960. Western Airlines has been flying into Jackson Hole since 1941. The airport is the only one in the country located in a national park and Congress has continually funded expansions and improvements of the once single dirt-runway airport.

In 1978, Frontier applied for permission to fly B-737s into the Jackson Hole Airport. The FAA released its EIS on the application in 1980. The EIS found that B-737s were comparable with C-580 propeller aircraft (the type then being used by Western and Frontier) for noise intrusion but were substantially more quiet than the private jets using the airport. The study also showed that fewer flights would be necessary since the B-737 could carry more passengers and that different flight paths could reduce noise. Based on this EIS, Frontier was given the right to use B-737s for two years. When Frontier applied for permanent approval, the FAA used the 1980 EIS statement and found that with flight time restrictions, the impact would not harm the environment.

The Sierra Club, a national conservation organization, brought suit for the failure to file an EIS for the 1983 amendments and for the use of national park facilities for commercial air traffic without considering alternatives.

BORK, Circuit Judge

We do not think the FAA violated NEPA by failing to prepare an additional EIS. Under NEPA, an EIS must be prepared before approval of any major federal action that will "significantly affect the quality of the human environment." The purpose of the Act is to require agencies to consider environmental issues before taking any major action. Under the statute, agencies have the initial and primary responsibility to determine the extent of the impact and whether it is significant enough to warrant preparation of an EIS. This is accomplished by preparing an Environmental Assessment (EA). An EA allows the agency to consider environmental concerns, while reserving agency resources to prepare full EIS's for appropriate cases. If a finding of no significant impact is made after analyzing the EA, then preparation of an EIS is unnecessary. An agency has broad discretion in making this determination, and the decision is reviewable only if it was arbitrary, capricious or an abuse of discretion.

This court has established four criteria for reviewing an agency's decision to forego preparation of an EIS. First, the agency must have accurately identified the relevant environmental concern. Second, once the agency has identified the problem, it must take a "hard look" at the problem in preparing the EA. Third, if a finding of no significant impact is made, the agency must be able to make a convincing case for its finding. Last, if the agency does find an impact of true significance, preparation of an EIS can be avoided only if the agency finds that changes or safeguards in the project sufficiently reduce the impact to a minimum.

The first test is not at issue here. Both the FAA and Sierra Club have identified the relevant environmental concern as noise by jet aircraft within Grand Teton National Park. The real issues raised by Sierra Club are whether the FAA took a "hard look" at the problem, and whether the methodology used by the agency in its alleged hard look was proper.

We find that the FAA did take a hard look at the problem. The FAA properly prepared an EA to examine the additional impact on the environment of the plan. The EA went forward from the 1980 EIS. The 1980 EIS, which was based on extensive research by Dr. Hakes of the University of Wyoming, noise testing by the FAA, and data derived from manufacturer information, showed that noise intrusions of B-737 jets over the level caused by C-580 propeller aircraft amounted to only 1 dbl near the Airport and decreased in proportion to the distance from the Airport. The agency, exercising its expertise, has found that an increase this minute is not significant for any environment. In addition, the EIS and Hakes studies were based on a worst case scenario, and it was determined that if certain precautions were taken the actual noise levels could be diminished greatly.

Petitioner (Sierra Club) argues that because Jackson Hole Airport is located within national parkland a different standard—i.e., individual event noise level analysis—is mandated. Both individual event and cumulative data were amassed in preparing the 1980 EIS on which the EAs were based. The fact that the agency in exercising its expertise relied on the cumulative impact levels as being more indicative of the actual environmental disturbance is well within the area of discretion given to the agency. We agree with petitioner that although noise is a problem in any setting, "airplane noise is fundamentally inconsistent with the type of recreational experience Park visitors are seeking" and should be minimized. Here the FAA found that a cumulative noise increase of 1 dbl or less is not significant—even for the pristine environment in which Jackson Hole Airport is located.

Given all of these facts, we think the FAA was not required to prepare yet another EIS before granting permanent authorizations for the use of B-737s.

The orders of the FAA are hereby affirmed.

Discussion Questions

1. What airport noise is at issue?
2. Who is involved in the case?
3. Was an EIS prepared?

4. What is the basis for the appeal?
5. What has the FAA allowed? Will the authorizations stand?

Other Federal Environmental Regulations

In addition to the previously major environmental laws, there are many other specific federal statutes that protect the environment.

Surface Mining The *Surface Mining and Reclamation Act of 1977* (42 U.S.C. §6907) requires those mining coal to restore land surfaces to their original conditions and prohibits surface coal mining without a permit.

Noise Control Under the *Noise Control Act of 1972* (42 U.S.C. §4901), the EPA, along with the Federal Aviation Administration (FAA) can control the amount of noise emissions from low-flying aircraft for the protection of landowners in flight paths.

Pesticide Control Under the *Federal Environmental Pesticide Control Act*, the use of pesticides is controlled. All pesticides must be registered with the EPA before they can be sold, shipped, distributed, or received. Also under the act, the EPA administrator is given the authority to classify pesticides according to their effects and dangers.

OSHA The *Occupational Safety and Health Administration (OSHA)* is responsible for the worker's environment. OSHA controls the levels of exposure to toxic substances and requires safety precautions for exposure to such dangerous substances as asbestos, benzene, and chloride.

STATE ENVIRONMENTAL LAWS

In addition to the federal enactments, thirty of the states have enacted some form of environmental law and have established their own environmental policies and agencies. Some states may require new industrial businesses to obtain a state permit along with the required federal permits for the operation of their plants. As noted earlier, all 50 states have some form of hazardous waste regulation.

ENFORCEMENT OF ENVIRONMENTAL LAWS

Federal environmental law can be enforced through criminal sanctions, penalties, injunctions, and suits by private citizens. In addition to the federal enforcement rights, certain common law remedies exist for the protection of property rights such as nuisance or trespass. This portion of the chapter discusses the various remedies available for environmental violations.

Parties Responsible for Enforcement

Although many federal agencies are involved with environmental issues, the Environmental Protection Agency, established in 1970, is the agency responsible for the major environmental problems of air and water pollution, solid waste disposal, toxic substance management, and noise pollution. The EPA is responsible for the promulgation of specific standards and the enforcement of those standards with the use of the remedies discussed in the following subsections. The Federal EPA may work in conjunction with state EPAs in the development and enforcement of state programs.

The *Council on Environmental Quality (CEQ)* was established in 1966 under the National Environment Protection Act and is part of the Executive Branch of government. Its role in the environmental regulatory scheme is that of policymaker. The CEQ is responsible for formulating national policies on the quality of the environment and then making recommendations to lawmakers regarding its policy statements.

In addition to these major environmental agencies, there are other federal agencies involved in environmental issues of enforcement such as the Atomic Energy Commission, the Federal Power Commission, the Department of Housing and Urban Development, the Department of the Interior, the Forest Service, the Bureau of Land Management, and the Department of Commerce. Basically, all federal agencies that deal with the use of lands, water, and air are involved in compliance with and enforcement of the environmental laws.

Criminal Sanctions for Violations

Most of the federal statutes discussed above carry criminal sanctions for violations. Figure 22.1 lists the penalties provided under each of the discussed acts.

In exercising its enforcement power, the EPA may require businesses to maintain records or to install equipment necessary to monitor the amounts of pollutants being released into the air or water.

The following case deals with the issue of criminal liability for environmental law violations.

UNITED STATES v. JOHNSON & TOWERS, INC.
741 F.2d 662 (3d Cir. 1984)

Johnson and Towers repairs and overhauls large motor vehicles. In its operations, Johnson uses degreasers and other industrial chemicals that

Figure 22.1 *Penalties for Violation of Federal Environmental Laws*

ACT	PENALTIES	PRIVATE SUIT
Clean Air Act	$25,000 per day, up to 1-year imprisonment, or both	Citizen suits authorized EPA suit for injunctive relief
Clean Water Act	$25,000 per day, up to 1-year imprisonment, or both	Citizen suits authorized EPA suit for injunctive relief
Resource Conservation and Recovery Act	$25,000 per day, up to 1-year imprisonment, or both	No private suits Hazardous Substance/Response Trust Fund for cleanup EPA suit for injunctive relief and reimbursement of trust funds

contain methylene chloride and tri-chlorethylene classified as "hazard-ous wastes" under the Resource Conservation and Recovery Act (RCRA) and pollutants under the Clean Water Act.

The waste chemicals from John-son's cleaning operations were drained into a holding tank, and when the tank was full, pumped into a trench. The trench flowed from the plant property into Parker's Creek, a tributary of the Delaware River. Un-der RCRA, generators of such wastes must obtain a permit from the EPA. Johnson had not received nor even applied for such a permit.

Jack Hopkins, a foreman, and Peter Angel, the service manager for Johnson, were charged with criminal violations of the RCRA and the Clean Water Act. Johnson was also charged and pled guilty. Hopkins and Angel pled not guilty on the grounds that they were not "owners" or "opera-tors" as required for RCRA viola-tions. The trial court agreed and dismissed all charges against Hop-kins and Angel except the criminal conspiracy charges.

The government appealed the dismissal.

SLOVITER, Circuit Judge

The single issue in this appeal is whether the individual defendants are subject to prosecution under RCRA's criminal pro-vision, which applies to:

any person who— . . . (2) knowingly treats, stores, or disposes of any hazard-ous waste identified or listed under this subchapter either—

(A) without having obtained a permit under Section 6925 of this title . . . or

(B) in knowing violation of any ma-terial condition or requirement of such permit.

If we view the statutory language in its totality, the congressional plan be-comes . . . apparent. First, "person" is defined in the statute as "an individual, trust, firm, joint stock company, corpora-tion (including a government corpora-tion), partnership, association, State, munici-pality, commission, political subdivision of a State, or any interstate body." Had Con-gress meant to take aim more narrowly, it could have used more narrow language.

Second, under the plain language of the statute, the only explicit basis for ex-oneration is the existence of a permit cov-ering the action. Nothing in the language of the statute suggests that we should infer another provision exonerating persons who knowingly treat, store or dispose of haz-ardous waste but are not owners or operators.

Finally, though the result may ap-pear harsh, it is well established that crim-inal penalties attached to regulatory statutes intended to protect public health, in contrast to statutes based on common law crimes, are to be construed to effec-tuate the regulatory purpose.

In summary, we conclude that the individual defendants are "persons" within the RCRA, that all elements of that offense must be shown to have been knowing, but that such knowledge, including that of the permit requirement, may be inferred by the jury as to those individuals who hold the requisite responsible positions with the corporate defendant.

The district court's dismissal is reversed and remanded.

Discussion Questions

1. Who is charged with criminal violations?
2. What violations are charged?
3. What violations did the lower court dismiss?
4. Did Congress intend to prosecute corporate employees?

5. Does the appellate court reinstate the charges?
6. What proof is required to show violations by the "persons" involved?

Civil Liability for Violations

Injunctive Relief Although the criminal sanctions imposed on violators may be costly, it is frequently more beneficial to landowners to have the polluting activity halted. As indicated in Figure 22.1, under each of the federal statutes, the EPA has the authority to bring suit for injunctive relief. In seeking injunctive relief, the EPA brings suit asking the court to order a business to stop an activity or other violation of one of the acts. In addition to the EPA power to seek injunctive relief, each of the federal acts (except NCRA) allows private citizens to bring suit for damages for violations and also for obtaining injunctive relief.

Common Law Relief In spite of the complex federal regulatory scheme as to the environment, the enforcement of private property rights and elimination of pollution has frequently come through private suits based on the common law doctrine of nuisance. A *nuisance* is defined as the use of one's property in such a manner that it interferes with others' use and enjoyment of their properties. (See Chapter 4 for more details.)

Typical activities that have been found to be nuisances are feedlot operations, oil refinery operations, and activities that create excessive noise and excessive traffic. If a suit is brought in nuisance, the plaintiff may seek either damages to compensate for property value loss or actual property damage or seek to enjoin the nuisance activity or both. Whether an activity will be enjoined depends upon a balancing test of the economic benefits of the activity versus the detrimental harm to other property owners.

In the following case, the court deals with a suit brought in nuisance and the issue of whether the activity should be enjoined.

HUBENTHAL v. COUNTY OF WINONA
751 F.2d 243 (8th Cir. 1984)

Albert J. Hubenthal leased approximately fifty-five acres of property in Winona County, Minnesota, to start a worm farming operation. Shortly thereafter, he began to collect large amounts of material including waste paper, cardboard, used tires, scrap wood, scrap metal, leather, and other building materials that he contends were essential to the farming operation.

The county attorney filed suit seeking to compel Hubenthal to clean up the property on the grounds that it was a public nuisance. After a hearing the lower court enjoined Huben-

thal from storing solid waste material that could be a "source of filth and sickness" and from maintaining a junkyard. The order gave Hubenthal thirty days to clean up and he failed to do so. Two months after the order was issued, county officials took three days to remove the materials accumulated from Hubenthal's farm. Hubenthal filed suit for trespass and violation of his due process rights.

PER CURIAM

Hubenthal contends the district court erred in dismissing his action because he presented a genuine issue of material fact as to whether an actual health hazard existed on his property. The state court found that Hubenthal's solid waste material created a potential home for rats, provided a breeding ground for mosquitos and that "larvae of the tree hole mosquito, a carrier of encephalitis, were found" there.

Hubenthal concedes that one mosquito larva and one bottle of human urine were found on the property, but argues that such a minimal finding provides no basis upon which the county could remove all of his treasured materials, including a quantity of soil and doubtless some worms.

Our review of the record discloses no genuine issue of material fact as to Hubenthal's maintenance of a health hazard. Obviously, an inventory of waste, salvage, and scrap materials, even if treasured and valuable to Hubenthal, kept in such fashion as to hold stagnant water and attract insects and vermin, is a health hazard.

Finally, Hubenthal argues that the county officials deliberately exceeded the scope of the court order by removing certain of the materials (notably dirt, worms, wood, hammer mills) from his property. As the district court indicated, there is nothing in the record to indicate that defendants acted deliberately or with reckless disregard of appellant's rights.

Affirmed.

Discussion Questions

1. What was Hubenthal's business?
2. What type of nuisance existed?
3. Why was Hubenthal's property cleaned up by others?

4. Were Hubenthal's rights violated?

Group Suits—The Effect of Environmentalists In many circumstances, private suits have had the most effect in terms of obtaining compliance with environmental regulations or in terms of abating existing nuisances affecting environmental quality. The reason for the success of these suits may be the ultimate outcome of the litigation—possible business shut-downs and at the least the payment of tremendous amounts of damages and costs.

In some cases, private suits have been brought by environmental groups that have the organizational structure and funding for the initiation and completion of such suits. In some cases, the environmental groups are formed to protest one specific action such as Citizens Against the Squaw Peak Parkway; other groups are national organizations that take on environmental issues and litigation in all parts of the country. Examples of these national groups include the Sierra Club, the Environmental Defense Fund, Inc., the National Resources Defense Council, and the League of Conservation Voters. Some environmental groups represent business interests in environmental issues, as does the Mountain States Legal Foundation, which becomes involved in presenting business issues when private organizations and individuals bring environmental suits.

These environmental groups have not only been successful in bringing private damage and injunctive relief suits, but have also been able to force agencies to promulgate regulations required under the federal laws and to enjoin projects where EISs should have been filed but were not.

THE CHANGING ENVIRONMENT

Because of changes in production and industry, environmental concerns have been exacerbated. The following article provides insight into those concerns.

The Lessons of Bhopal

Corporations, like humans, make mistakes. Some of these mistakes are costly and destructive, such as the accident at the Union Carbide plant in Bhopal, India, which killed more than 2,500 people and injured another 200,000. But, unlike humans, corporations do not easily learn from their mistakes; they simply repeat them in different forms.

As a result of the Bhopal accident, Union Carbide suffered public criticism, governmental scrutiny, and financial loss. So it is reasonable to expect Union Carbide to learn from mistakes made in Bhopal, and to develop more innovative responses to accidents. But the company's response to the accidental leak of aldicarb oxime from its Institute, West Virginia plant and to another accident in its South Charleston plant, on August 11 and 13, 1985, respectively, was similar in many respects to its response in Bhopal.

—Immediately after the Bhopal accident, local managers said that methyl isocyanate was a mild irritant and not lethal. In Institute, managers said that aldicarb oxime was a minor irritant and had no long-term effects.

Later, the public found out that both these substances were far more toxic than had been claimed by the company, and that little was known about their long-term effects.

—For weeks after the Bhopal accident, Union Carbide was reported to have held back information from the press, medical workers, and relief agencies. This was also true of the Institute accident. Company staff closed rank and responded to requests for information only through official press releases. In both cases the company was perceived as stonewalling requests for information.

—Both in Bhopal and in Institute, company managers failed to effectively warn the surrounding community about leaks, which led to *avoidable* injuries. In Bhopal, the community was never informed about the toxic materials used in the plant. At the time of the leak, a warning siren was switched on for a few minutes and then switched off. In Institute, operators waited for thirty-six minutes after the leak to switch on the warning siren.

—The causes of the accidents in Bhopal and Institute included failure in design and equipment and operator lapses. In Bhopal, the escaping toxic gases bypassed the flare tower and gas scrubber used for neutralizing them. In Institute, the flare tower and gas neutralizer failed to destroy the toxicity of escaping chemicals.

—In both Bhopal and Institute, the company behaved defensively and avoided admitting management mistakes. In Bhopal, the source of problems was local operating personnel. In Institute, the source of problems was the faulty computer system.

The reason a company does not learn from mistakes is that it possesses a rigid frame of reference that constrains decisions. Its frame of reference permits the company to selectively perceive problems and develop partial solutions. Managers generate inconsequential explanations for mistakes and then go about solving the wrong problems. The Bhopal accident was seen as a breach of safety systems and procedures. The company therefore decided to spend $5 million to improve safety at the Institute plant. Accidents at the Institute and Charleston plants were also seen the same way. After those accidents, the company promised to spend $50 million in safety improvements. Then, less than two weeks later, another accident occurred in the Charleston plant. Now the company announced plans to spend $250 million in safety improvements in all its plants. These expenditures are certainly necessary, but not sufficient for learning to handle hazardous systems safely.

To learn, a corporation must be willing to make fundamental changes in its frame of reference. This requires lowering defenses, accepting blame for past mistakes, taking responsibility, and risking failure. It requires basic changes in assumptions, decision processes, and types of information used by managers for doing risk analysis and making safety decisions. Managers need to develop new skills and ways of thinking about safety, social responsibility, and the environment. Methods for doing this are available, so we do not have to accept the company's view that, accidents will happen because "there are no zero risk systems" in the chemical industry.

"The Lessons of Bhopal" by Paul Shrivastava, *Business and Society Review.* Article reprinted with permission of *Business and Society Review,* a publication of the Walter E. Heller College of Business, Roosevelt University.

RECOMMENDATIONS

The implications of environmental laws on real property transactions are tremendous. Anyone seeking to purchase property for industrial use must be familiar with the air quality standards and release permit requirements in the area to determine if industrial use is possible, and if it is possible, if it will be more costly because of environmental constraints. Environmental law is one more area that must be thoroughly investigated before entering into an agreement for the sale or lease of property or for the construction of facilities on property already owned.

KEY TERMS

Air Pollution Control Act
Clean Air Act
Air Quality Act
Environmental Protection Agency (EPA)
state implementation plans (SIPs)
nonattainment area
Prevention of significant deterioration areas (PSD areas)
Emissions Offset Policy
bubble concept
acid rain
Water Pollution Control Act of 1948
Water Quality Act
Federal Water Pollution Control Administration (FWPCA)
Rivers and Harbors Act of 1899
Federal Water Pollution Control Act of 1972
Clean Water Act
effluent guidelines

National Pollution Discharge Elimination System (NPDES) permit
point sources
conventional pollutants
nonconventional pollutants
toxic pollutants
best conventional treatment (BCT)
best available treatment (BAT)
Solid Waste Disposal Act
Resource Recovery Act
Toxic Substances Control Act (TOSCA)
Resource Conservation and Recovery Act of 1976 (RCRA)
Comprehensive Environmental Response, Compensation, and Liability Act (CERCLA)
Hazardous Substance Response Trust Fund
Superfund

Superfunds Amendment and
  Reauthorization Act
National Environmental Policy Act
  of 1969 (NEPA)
environmental impact statement
  (EIS)
Surface Mining and Reclamation Act
  of 1977

Noise Control Act of 1972
Federal Environmental Pesticide
  Control Act
Occupational Safety and Health
  Administration (OSHA)
Council on Environmental Quality
  (CEQ)
nuisance

CHAPTER PROBLEMS

1. The U.S. Forest Service has granted several oil firms permits to explore 247,000 acres of "wild and ruggedly beautiful federal land" in Wyoming. The Sierra Club has brought suit seeking an injunction because no EIS was filed. Who will win?

2. A group of landowners situated near the Sanders Lead Company brought suit to recover for damages to their agricultural property from accumulations of lead particulates and sulfur oxide deposits released in Sanders production process. The landowners' property had increased in value because of its commercial potential in being close to the plant. Sanders employs most of the town residents in its operations. What common law and statutory rights do the landowners have and what relief can be obtained? (See *Borland v. Sanders Lead Co., Inc.*, 369 So.2d 523 [1979].)

3. Would the EPA need a warrant to examine the pollution control equipment and operations of a regulated facility? (See *CED'S Inc. v. EPA*, 745 F.2d 1092 [7th Cir. 1984].)

4. Reynolds Metal has been held to the same technological standards in its pollution control for can manufacturing plants as those applied to aluminum manufacturers. Reynolds claims the processes are different and that the technology is not yet available for can manufacturing. Does Reynolds have a point? (See *Reynolds Metals Co. v. EPA*, 760 F.2d 549 [D.C. 1985].)

5. The Mitchells lived in a residential section of Beverly Hills, Michigan, and sought to enjoin the operation of a nearby piggery. The pigs were fed in an open field and any garbage not eaten by the pigs was plowed under by tractors. The odors from the operation, particularly in the spring and summer, were such that the use and enjoyment of the Mitchells' property was impaired. Who will win? Are any federal statutory violations involved? (See *Mitchell v. Hines*, 9 N.W.2d 547 [Mich. 1943].)

6. Chasm Power Company was releasing steam and hot water from one

of its plants. The steam and water contained no pollutants, but the level of the water was raised significantly when releases were made into an adjoining stream. Downstream owners brought suit seeking injunctive relief. Who will win? (See *McCann v. Chasm Power Co.*, 105 N.E. 416 [N.Y. 1914].)

7. The Department of the Interior has proposed budget cutbacks in the National Wildlife Refuge System Budget. The Sierra Club says such cutbacks have significant environmental impact. Must the Department do an EIS? (See *Andrus v. Sierra Club*, 442 U.S. 347 [1978].)

8. What is the difference between an EA and an EIS?

9. Identify each of the following:
   a. EPA
   b. EIS
   c. NEPA
   d. BCT
   e. BPT

10. Would discharging manure into a stream be a violation of any environmental laws? (See *United States v. Frezzo Brothers, Inc.*, 602 F.2d 1123 [3d Cir. 1979].)

|23|

SHOPPING CENTERS

> 5. MINIMUM RENT. *Tenant agrees to pay to landlord as minimum rent due each month, without notice or demand, the monthly sum of four hundred dollars ($400.00) commencing April 1, 1984.*
>
> *In addition to the minimum rent set forth above, the tenant agrees to pay 1% of gross sale proceeds from the operation of the* LADD MARKET *in the above described premises.*
>
> *Ladd, the owner of Ladd's Market, has the preceding provision in his lease in a shopping center. Ladd is about to install some video games and wishes to know if they will be subject to the 1 percent gross sales provision.*

Ladd, not unlike many others who have leased shopping-center property, has found an issue that is not directly addressed by the ambiguous language of his lease. The shortcomings of lease language are one of many legal problems arising in the operation and rental of shopping-center property. In this chapter the following questions are answered: What is the nature of shopping-center operations? What provisions should be put in a shopping-center lease and what effects will those provisions have? What issues and facts should be examined before leasing shopping-center property?

The shopping center is a creation of the past 20 years. According to the International Council of Shopping Centers, there were fewer than 100 shopping centers in the United States in 1950. As of 1986, there were more than 20,000. Retail business in shopping centers makes up nearly three-fourths of all retail sales. The shopping center is thus a center for economic return; and if that return is to be maximized, the center and the leases in the center must be structured carefully. From the position of the shopping-center owner, the credit line and return depend on appropriate structure and effective leases. From the standpoint of the tenant, business return is maximized by an effective location and favorable lease terms. Both sides are thus benefited from an understanding of the legal implications of shopping-center operation.

The shopping center is an example of how the law is used to carry out marketing concepts. The idea behind the shopping center is for the large space or spaces in the center to be occupied by a major retail or grocery store in order to bring in business to the smaller units occupied by other types of businesses. These *anchor tenants* in the large spaces provide most of the traffic to the center. In many cases, anchor tenants pay a minimal or at least lower amount of rent than the other tenants. If the large spaces in the center go unoccupied, then all of the remaining tenants suffer. Tenants who occupy smaller units in the center do so with the idea that their services and goods will be unique to that center and that the landlord will not reduce their business by leasing to a competing venture in the same center. These ideas of traffic from anchor tenants and noncompetition are marketing tools that must be guaranteed by lease terms. Without the legal guarantees in the lease, the marketing idea of the shopping center would not work and many business failures would result. In the following sections, the suggested lease provisions for maximum protection of these marketing ideas are discussed.

SHOPPING-CENTER LEASE PROVISIONS— MAXIMUM PROTECTION AND MAXIMUM SALES

Lease Term

In Chapter 18 when terms of residential leases were discussed, the topic was easily covered because there is a beginning and ending date for a residential lease. In shopping-center leases, there are added problems that make defining the term of the lease more difficult.

The first problem that can arise in defining the lease term is determining the date that the lease term will begin because it is a frequent practice to have tenants committed to a shopping center before the center is actually built. Indeed, the developer may be able to obtain a construction loan or permanent financing only on the basis of a list of committed tenants, whose commitments are backed up in the form of executed lease agreements. In such cases the beginning date for the lease is tied to the construction completion date, which is subject to change. However, the tenant must have some idea of the lease commencement date for planning and inventory purposes.

Another issue to arise with beginning dates is whether the tenant is allowed to move in before actual completion of the unit or the common areas and, if so, when rent will become due. Because of the uncertainty involved, it is probably best for the parties to put an outside date in the contract, that is, a date by which there must be occupancy or the lease is terminated. With an outside date, contingencies such as noncompletion, bankruptcy, and delays are covered. The developer is not tied to a specific date of completion but has a range, and the tenant has a latest possible occupancy date for planning purposes. The lease may even provide an option for the tenant to extend the outside date if the date passes and the tenant still desires to continue with the lease.

In setting the beginning date in a shopping-center lease, the tenant should consider seasonal swings in purchasing and avoid commencing a lease during a slow period of the sales year. For example, retail outlets have higher sales from October through 1 January, so that commencing a lease in October would be wise. On the other hand, commencing a lease in February begins an obligation during a slow period, with a long wait for increased sales.

Rent

Again, in residential leases the rent was easily established as a fixed dollar amount per rental period. In shopping-center and commercial leases, the rental figure becomes more complicated as the developer seeks to share in the profits earned by the tenants.

Most shopping-center leases provide for a minimum rent: a figure set forth in the agreement that covers the basic costs of the developer, such as the mortgage, maintenance of the common areas, and so on. In addition to the minimum rent, there may be additional sums required of the tenants. These additional payments may be specifically explained or may be grouped in a section of the lease referred to as *adjustments* or *additional fees or costs*. In some centers, tenants are required to pay a fee for maintenance of the common areas. In others, tenants are required to pay a monthly advertising or promotional fee, which is used by the developer to advertise the existence of the center in general. For example, the developer might use the funds to advertise on television the existence of Green Valley Mall.

Another issue that arises in shopping-center leases is the problem of rent increases. Because these leases tend to run over longer periods of time, it is not economically beneficial to have the same rental rate apply for the full term of the lease. Thus, in many leases, a clause is included to provide for rental increases. The following is an example:

> In addition, the minimum rent as set forth above shall be subject to being increased by the percentage of increase, if any, in the Consumer Price Index—U.S. Average. All items and figures used will be those as published by the United States Department of Labor's Bureau of Labor Statistics. The base period, for purposes of such adjustment, shall be September of the year in which this Lease is executed. Each September following the commencement of rentals shall then be used for comparison purposes with any adjustment in Minimum Rent to be effective as of the next succeeding 1 January. In no event shall the

minimum rent be less than the sum or sums as specified above. Should the aforementioned index be discontinued, the parties shall select another similar index that reflects consumer prices, and if the parties cannot agree on another index, it shall be selected by binding arbitration.

Some leases contain *specific happenings increase provisions*. For example, a lease may contain a provision that allows a rent increase in the event the developer or landlord is required to pay increased taxes.

One of the largest issues in rental amounts in shopping-center leases is a provision that requires the tenant to pay the landlord a certain percentage of gross sales as rent in addition to a minimum rental fee. Such provisions are perfectly valid but often result in litigation because the parties have not clearly specified the terms of such a clause. When drafting a gross-sales provision, the parties should remember the following details to facilitate collection of the intended fees:

1. A definition of gross sales should be included and should specifically state what is and what is not included in the computation of gross sales.
2. Record-keeping obligations of the tenant should be specified, along with the landlord's right of examination and right to talk with the preparer and to have an independent auditor examine the records.
3. Details of how often the percentage is to be paid, when it is to be paid, and whether the tenant is required to submit periodic reports on sales, should all be included.
4. The landlord should have a covenant of secrecy for the right of access. That is, the landlord should be permitted to examine books and records, but should be subject to suit and damages if such information is disclosed to others.

In the following case, an ambiguity in a gross-sales lease provision is interpreted.

BORCHERT ENTERPRISES, INC. v. WEBB
584 S.W.2d 208 (Tenn. 1979)

E. H. Webb and Ann Thomas Webb (defendants/appellees) own a shopping center in Davidson County, Tennessee and leased one of the spaces in it to Scooter Stores, Incorporated, in 1971. In 1975 Scooter assigned the lease to Borchert Enterprises (plain-tiff/appellant). The Webbs approved the assignment, but various controversies arose between the parties, and Borchert filed suit. The Webbs counterclaimed for rent due under a clause in the lease, which required a payment of 2 percent of gross sales as additional rent. The clause provided as follows:

Lessee, in addition, agrees to pay to Lessor as additional rental a sum equal to two (2%) per cent of the gross sales in excess of Two Hundred Thousand ($200,000) Dollars per annum, excluding sales tax and money order sales, said payments to be made annually, within forty-five (45) days from each annual anniversary of this Lease. Lessee agrees to provide to Lessor annually a Certified Public Accountant's report of sales to substantiate the payments made hereunder.

SUMMERS, Judge

The cardinal rule for interpretation of contracts is to ascertain the intention of the parties and to give effect to that intention, consistent with legal principals. [sic] . . . It is the Court's duty to enforce contracts according to their plain terms. Further, the language used must be taken and understood in its plain, ordinary and popular sense.

The definition of a sale under T.C.A. 47-2-106(1) is: ". . . A 'sale' consists in the passing of title from the seller to the buyer for a price. . . ." In playing pinball machines there is nothing that passes from a seller to a buyer. This activity is considered an amusement and not a sale.

The sales that are reported to the state and on which sales tax is paid do not include receipts from pinball machines. At the time the lease was drawn up between the defendant and the original lessee, pinball machines were not in the lessee's place of business. We cannot say the parties contemplated the inclusion of revenue from pinball machines in gross sales. It was only

Borchert was engaged in the operation of a convenience market and installed several pinball machines. The Webbs contended that Borchert had failed to pay the 2 percent due on the pinball revenues, and Borchert contended that the revenue from the pinball machines was not included in the term *gross sales*.

The trial court held that the pinball income was part of gross sales, and Borchert appealed.

after the sublessee, the plaintiff herein, had been in possession of the property for several months that pinball machines were placed therein.

The term "gross sales" would appear to this court to be limited to transactions which are actually considered sales. Had the language in the lease been gross revenue, income, receipts, earnings, receivables or payments, this court would have no doubt that the income from the pinball machines would be included in computing additional rent due. However, the use of the word "sales" tends to limit the kind and quality of income to be used in calculating the additional rental.

From the testimony in the bill of exceptions we find that the plaintiff took no part in drafting the instrument in question. The defendants and Scooter Stores, Inc. negotiated the terms of this lease. It is also settled law in Tennessee that any ambiguity in a contract is settled against the drafter of the contract.

Therefore, this court sustains the assignment of error of the plaintiff and reverses that portion of the chancellor's ruling from which the plaintiff appealed. We find that the income received from the pinball machines should not be included as part of the "gross sales" referred to in the lease agreement.

658

Discussion Questions

1. Who is the lessor? Who is lessee?
2. Who is the sublessee?
3. What type of business is being operated?
4. What income is at issue?
5. Were the pinball machines in operation at the time of the sublease?

6. What definition does the court give for *sales?*
7. Who drafted the lease?
8. What language should have been included to cover all income?

Other topics that should be covered in the rental portion of a shopping-center lease include the place payment is to be made, to whom payment is to be made, whether there are penalties for late payment, and how much those penalties will be.

Security deposits are typical in commercial leases and can be substantial, so that the landlord is assured of payment. Because there is no uniform act on commercial leases, the parties should specify the purpose of the security deposit, whether it will be returned, on what grounds, if any, it can be retained, and whether there will be any time limits for returning the deposit upon termination of the lease.

Fixtures and Alterations

In most cases the premises being leased in a shopping center consist of walls, a roof, and a door. Generally, very little has been done to improve, finish, or decorate the interior of each retail space. Thus, it becomes a cost issue as to who will make the necessary improvements, alterations, and constructions to render the premises usable for a retail operation. It is generally the responsibility of the tenant to make the interior ready for operation because the landlord does not know the operation or needs of the tenant's business as well as does the tenant. This requirement of completion, plus any restrictions the tenant may have in altering the premises (because of building codes or the landlord's hesitancy or preference), should be set forth in the lease agreement. Thus, if the landlord wants limited or movable wall installation, such a restriction should be specified in the agreement.

An issue directly related to the tenant's responsibility of improvement and completion, is what happens to all the improvements the tenant has made once the lease is terminated. In other words, are the improvements treated as trade fixtures or do they become permanent fixtures and property of the landlord? Although there are legal guidelines for determining what is a trade fixture and what remains as the landlord's property (see Chapter 6), it is best for the parties to specifically provide for this.

One method of providing for all phases of tenant alterations is to place a provision in the lease that requires the tenant to obtain prior written approval of the landlord for all proposed alterations. Under this arrangement, the tenant supplies the landlord with a written proposal that includes specifications for what constitutes a fixture in the proposed alteration and what will remain the property of the tenant as a trade fixture.

Repairs and Warranties

The implied warranty of habitability or usability does not exist in commercial leases. Thus, if a tenant is to be guaranteed that the leased premises will be delivered with certain repairs, conditions, or improvements, a warranty for these items must be in the lease agreement. Problems such as faulty heating or air conditioning, leaking roofs, and broken windows should be described in the lease as repairs that are conditions precedent to the tenant's performance under the terms of the lease.

In addition to the initial condition of the premises, the parties should agree on which party will be responsible for maintenance. The landlord may want to specify that the obligation to repair does not arise until the tenant brings the condition of disrepair to the landlord's attention through a written notice. Some obligations of repair may be imposed upon the tenant, such as keeping trade fixtures in good working condition. For example, many tenants have an electronic sign outside their business; the obligation of repair and upkeep of that sign belongs with the tenant.

The parties may also wish to make a provision for emergency repairs— an authorization for immediate work in circumstances where the parties are unable to contact each other and the repair is absolutely necessary. Water leaks are an example wherein immediate action may save later costs and damage, and an emergency repair by either party without the other's approval can save money for both.

Use of the Premises

Operations Every shopping-center lease should contain provisions on operation of the tenant's business. Items that may be included that serve to bring continuity of operation are store hours (including days the facility is open), methods of in-store advertising (such as the use of windows for promotional ads), and outdoor sales. These types of regulations are particularly important in malls, since the doors to such facilities are locked at certain times.

Business Restrictions The makeup of a shopping center can be an important factor in its financial success. An appropriate mix of merchants will draw shoppers because they can accomplish more at one center with a good variety of stores. However, the proximity of the various businesses raises intense issues of competition, which have dotted the antitrust case law for the past 15 years. The lessees in the shopping center may want to control the makeup of the center or even the types of merchandise sold by each retailer. Indeed, in some instances, the anchor tenant stipulates that it must review and approve all potential lessees for a center. For example, in some leases, anchor tenants have clauses that disallow the leasing of space to discount merchants. This is to prevent the anchor tenant from being undersold on certain items because a store in the same center has been leased to a discount merchant of those items.

The issue that arises from these clauses that limit the types of business operations is whether the clauses violate federal or state antitrust laws. Many such clauses have been challenged by the Federal Trade Commission and the Justice Department in an effort to eliminate them. In the following case, the issue of use-restriction is critical.

CHILD WORLD, INC. v. SOUTH TOWNE CENTRE, LTD.
634 F. Supp. 1121 (S.D. Ohio 1986)

Child World, Inc. (plaintiff) operates large retail toy stores throughout Ohio and other states called "Children's Palace." South Towne Centre, Ltd. (defendant) is a limited partnership in the state of Ohio and leases space in its South Towne shopping center complex to a Children's Palace store. Section 43(A) of the lease, executed in February 1976, provided as follows:

Except insofar as the following shall be unlawful, the parties mutually agree as follows:
A. Landlord shall not use or permit or suffer any other person, firm, corporation or other entity to use any portion of the Shopping Center or any other property located within six (6) miles from the Shopping Center and owned, leased or otherwise controlled by the landlord (meaning thereby the real property or parties in interest and not a "straw" person or entity)

or any person or entity having a substantial identity of interest, for the operation of a toys and games store principally for the sale at retail of toys and games, juvenile furniture and sporting goods such as is exemplified by the Child World and Children's Palace stores operated by Tenant's parent company, Child World, Inc. at the demised premises and elsewhere.

The lease was a 20-year lease and was signed by Barbara Beerman Weprin, the sole general partner of South Towne. Mad River Ltd. is another limited partnership in which Weprin is the sole general partner. Mad River owns another parcel of land approximately one-half mile from the South Towne Center. On 24 December 1985, Mad River entered into an agreement to sell the parcel of land to Toys "Я" Us, Inc. Toys "Я" Us intends to construct a retail facility similar to the description in the above-noted lease clause. When Children's Palace was informed of the sale, they brought suit seeking to enforce the convenant not to lease or sell to a competitor of Children's Palace.

RICE, Circuit Judge

The consensus of the federal courts which have considered covenants in shopping center leases is one with which this Court can agree; namely, that the varying terms, conditions, and economic justifications for such restrictions render them inappropriate subjects for application of the per se rule. Defendants have not alleged nor proven anything about Section 43(A) of the lease which would indicate that it has only anticompetitive consequences. Indeed, in Finding of Fact #9, Defendants agree that Section 43(A) was negotiated as an inducement for Plaintiff to erect a Children's Palace store on Defendants' premises and to enter into a twenty-year lease. This economic justification for exclusivity clauses is among the primary reasons that clauses such as Section 43(A) have not been found to be per se illegal, but rather have been found consistent with the public interest in economic development. Such laws can induce tenants to establish stores and to enter into a particular marketplace, often then encouraging the entry of other, often smaller, merchants.

A number of factors have been considered by the courts which have excluded restrictive covenants in shopping center leases: (1) the relevant product and geographic markets, together with the showing of unreasonable impact upon competition in these markets, due to the restrictive covenant; (2) the availability of alternate sites for the entity excluded by the operation of such a covenant; (3) the significance of the competition eliminated by the exclusivity clause, and whether present or future competitors were the parties excluded; (4) the scope of the restrictive covenant and whether it varied depending on particular circumstances; and (5) the economic justifications for the inclusion of the restrictive covenant in the lease.

Defendants have made no attempt to address the majority of these factors and to introduce evidence as to the markets affected by Section 43(A), the nature of the competition in these markets, and the like. Rather, Defendants focus exclusively upon the breadth of Section 43(A) and its prohibition of sale or lease by Defendants to competitors of Plaintiff within a six-mile radius of the South Towne Centre shopping center. Defendants remind the Court that in none of the cases cited by Plaintiff was a restrictive covenant with a six-mile radius upheld under the rule of reason.

Due to the particular facts of this case, however, the Court needs not, and specifically does not, reach the validity of the six-mile limitation contained in Section 43(A). Regardless of possible overbreadth, a restrictive covenant challenged as unreasonable under Section 1 of the Sherman Act will be upheld to the extent that a breach of the covenant has occurred or is threatened to occur within a reasonable geographic area and time period. The parties have agreed, in Finding of Fact #12, that the parcel which Defendants seek to convey to Toys "Я" Us is approximately one-half mile from the Children's Palace store covered by the Lease. The Court finds that Section 43(A) is lawful and enforceable to the extent of one-half mile, as required by the facts of this case.

Defendants have the burden of establishing that Section 43(A), enforced to the extent of one-half mile, would constitute an unreasonable restraint of trade. Defendants have not, however, presented any evidence to discharge their burden of demonstrating unreasonableness. Furthermore, the facts in this case, both those proven by the parties and those of which the Court takes judicial notice, tend to underscore the reasonableness of Section 43(A) as applied. Considering the latter set of facts first, this Court is quite familiar with the area of Miami Township within which the South Towne Centre is located. The Court takes judicial notice of the manner in which the real property in the Centre's vicinity has been developed, the rate at which economic development has proceeded, and the physical relationship of shopping centers, one to another, in this area. These current economic and geographic characteristics, of which judicial notice is taken, are among the factors which tend, even apart from Defendants' failure to meet their burden of showing unreasonableness, to support the enforceability of Section 43(A) to the extent of one-half mile.

Turning to the impact which enforcement of Section 43(A), as applied in this case, would have upon the Defendants, the burdens of enforcement are not unduly great. As noted supra, Section 43(A) does not appear to preclude rental or sale, even within a one-half mile radius, to any number of stores which can compete with a Children's Palace toy and game store but which are not "copycat" stores. On the

financial level, there is testimony from a representative of Defendants in the record to the effect that the value of the parcel in question increases almost daily. Moreover, Defendants believe that they will have no difficulty in finding another purchaser, should Section 43(A) preclude their sale of the parcel to Toys "Я" Us.

Enforcement of Section 43(A) to the extent of one-half mile would also not appear to foreclose the entry of Toys "Я" Us into competition with Plaintiff's store in the environs of the South Towne Centre shopping center. In his deposition, J. Tim Logan indicated that, even were Section 43(A) upheld, presumably in its entirety, Toys "Я" Us would still establish a store in the vicinity of Plaintiff's store.

Other courts have believed that restrictive covenants of a scope of one-half mile or more, albeit less than six miles, are legitimate lures by landlords in order for shopping center tenants to enter particular marketplaces and to thereby enhance the economic development of the community. The public has surely benefited from the development of South Towne Centre. As a restriction of six miles appeared reasonable to Defendants' predecessors at the time of bargaining, enforcement of Section 43(A) of the Lease to the extent of one-half mile is consistent with that original calculation of value, and certainly reasonable.

Judgment for plaintiff.

Discussion Questions

1. Who leased what from whom?
2. What restrictions were there in the lease agreement?
3. How did Toys "Я" Us become involved?
4. Is the sale a violation of the anticompetition clause?
5. Is the same shopping center involved?

(23.1) Consider:

In its lease with the shopping-center developer, Ben Franklin Stores had a clause that prohibited the developer from leasing space in the center to another variety store. When the developer attempted to lease space to a Pay Less Drug Store, the owners of the Ben Franklin outlet brought suit to enjoin the lease. Pay Less and the developer claimed the Pay Less operation was sufficiently different to allow the lease and that to disallow it would constitute a restraint of trade in violation of federal antitrust laws. What was the result?

At this point, it is difficult to determine what clauses do or do not violate antitrust laws. Because the issues of the type of market, location, and competition vary from city to city, the validity of these clauses also varies. But for the most part, if the clauses are reasonably necessary for shopping center survival and are effective, they should be insisted upon by tenants.

Assignment of Leases

Most states readily permit the assignment of leases by tenants. But in nearly all shopping-center leases that have been drafted by the developer, assignments are prohibited unless approval from the developer is obtained. Even if a lease does not contain an assignment prohibition, the type of assignment may be severely limited by the use-restrictions clause. Since the tenant remains liable on the lease, the tenant would be responsible for a breach if an assignment were made to a retailer who sold goods that were unauthorized by the use provision.

In leases requiring developer approval, the issue often arises whether the landlord has unreasonably withheld consent to a tenant's wish to assign. In the following case, the issue of proper assignment and landlord approval is discussed.

MAGNA INVESTMENT v. BROOKS FASHION STORES
669 P.2d 1024 (Ariz. 1983)

Magna Investment (plaintiff/appellant) owns the El Con Shopping Center in Tucson, Arizona. In 1978 Magna entered into a lease agreement with Wiener Corporation, doing business as the Stamina, a men's clothing store. The lease provided that the premises "may be used and occupied only for the retail sale of young men's casual apparel and women's junior sportswear and accessories and related items" and for no other purpose or purposes without the prior written consent of the landlord "which consent Landlord agrees not to unreasonably withhold."

Wiener operated the store as a men's clothing store only, and Magna knew of the limited operation but did not object despite the clause in the lease agreement.

In 1981 Wiener assigned the lease to Brooks Fashion Stores (defendant/appellee), and at the time of the assignment had not obtained the written consent of the landlord. Brooks contacted Magna and informed them of the assignment negotiations, and Magna agreed to the assignment if Brooks would agree to an increase in rent. Brooks refused, and although Magna refused to agree to the assignment, Brooks moved in.

Brooks was a large corporation owning 475 stores and had gross sales in the center of $30,000 per month. Wiener owned only three stores and took in a substantially less amount in monthly sales.

Magna brought an action in forcible detainer to have Brooks removed from the premises. Magna's contention in the action was that a change from a men's clothing store to Brooks's operation of a women's clothing store interfered with Magna's attempts to obtain an appropriate "tenant mix" in the center. The trial court denied Magna's request for forcible detainer and found for Brooks. Magna appealed.

HOWARD, Chief Judge

Appellants' next contention is that it was not unreasonable in withholding its consent to assignment of the Wiener lease. Appellants appear to be asking this court to make its own decision on this issue. Appellants' reason for not giving its consent, that it wanted a men's store for proper tenant mix, was contradicted by the testimony that the lease would have been assigned if appellee had been willing to pay

more rent and by evidence that "the Stamina," from its inception, never operated according to the terms of the lease as both a men's and women's shop. The trial judge could have concluded that the reason for refusing which appellants gave at trial was a mere pretext and that the only reason they did not consent was because they wanted to extract more rent from appellee.

Affirmed.

Discussion Questions

1. Who were the landlord, the tenant, and the assignee?
2. What type of store was to be operated according to the lease provisions?
3. What type of store did Wiener operate?
4. What type of store did Brooks operate?
5. Did Magna consent to the assignment?
6. Who brought suit and what was the basis for the suit?
7. Could Magna prevent the assignment?
8. What is the effect of the "tenant mix" argument?

Common Areas

Several issues should be addressed in the shopping-center lease regarding common areas. The first is who is to be responsible for the upkeep and maintenance of the common areas. If the developer is to be responsible, any additional monthly fees for such maintenance should be clearly specified. The second issue is who is responsible for maintaining insurance on the common areas. Since many accidents could occur in these areas, it is helpful to establish liability as well. The final issue is how the common areas may be used by each tenant for advertising, sales, merchandising, and so on. The clauses covering this topic are the deed restrictions of the shopping center—the dos and don'ts of merchandising in the shopping-center common areas.

Some of the specific topics that may be covered in this area include whether the tenant is responsible for the costs for lighting or snow and ice removal in the parking lots. The tenant may wish to be specific about the necessary maintenance tasks, such as the landlord's responsibility for maintaining a clearly marked parking area with parking-space lines clearly painted. The maintenance of rest rooms and water fountains is also important. In drafting this portion of the lease, the concern is in making the shopping experience for the customer as fault-free as possible in all the areas in and leading to the shopping center.

Access

As in residential leases, commercial tenants have the right to the quiet use and enjoyment of their property, but on occasion, the landlord will need access. The lease should specify the hows and whens of the landlord's access, including when the landlord may enter the tenant's premises and for what purpose; how much notice is required before the landlord may enter, what form that notice must take, and how it is to be delivered; and whether notice provisions may be waived during emergency situations.

Destruction and Damage to the Premises

The parties need to make provisions for what would happen to their relationship in the event that accident or catastrophe destroys the shopping-center property. Several questions must be answered: If the premises are damaged or destroyed to the point of being unusable by the tenant, does the responsibility of rent abate? (During the time of nonuse, provision should be made for the tenant to stop paying rent.) May the tenant cancel the lease? At what point are the premises completely destroyed? Allowing the common law to cover these issues is inviting the ambiguity of the doctrine of impossibility and does not provide the parties with sufficient guidelines for their conduct.

In some cases, the parties incorporate into the lease an obligation of the landlord to rebuild the premises. Because of the unique nature of the shopping center, in which prime location can be the key to a successful business, this obligation to rebuild can be extremely important to the tenant. The tenant may not want to terminate the lease but may want to be back in business as soon as possible and can provide for time limitations on rebuilding. If a construction clause is imposed on the landlord, provision should also be made to require the landlord to carry appropriate insurance to cover reconstruction costs.

Breach

The last topic of concern to both parties in the shopping-center lease is what constitutes a breach and what the damages are in the event of a breach. For the landlord, nonpayment of rent is the major problem, and remedies should be specified. If the remedies are not specified, the law affords the same protections in commercial leases as it affords in residential leases. If rental payments are not made in a timely manner, the landlord may bring an action to dispossess the tenant. If the tenant breaches the lease agreement by terminating business prior to the lease expiration date, the landlord has the responsibility to mitigate the situation by trying to find another tenant. But the parties could specify otherwise and could provide for a liquidated damage figure. In cases of breaches in other areas (such as failure to maintain or failure to grant access), the parties may agree to submit matters to arbitration prior to suit.

If a suit is required, provision for payment of costs and fees to the winner should also be made in the lease agreement. The following is a standard clause for attorney's fees used in many lease agreements:

> In the event of any action at law or in equity between landlord and tenant and/or rights hereunder, the unsuccessful party to such litigation covenants and agrees to pay to the successful party all costs and expenses, including reasonable attorneys' fees and court costs, incurred therein by such successful party, and if such successful party shall recover judgment in any such action or proceedings, such costs, expenses, and attorneys' fees shall be included in and as a part of such judgment.

RECOMMENDATION

The shopping center represents a unique marketing concept but brings with it a unique set of legal problems from antitrust to liquidated damages to store hours. A checklist for shopping-center lease negotiations is a necessity, and the headings in this chapter can be used as a guideline in making sure all possible legal issues are covered. As is true with other areas of real estate, an investigation can never be too complete.

The following is a checklist for shopping center leases:

1. Amount of rent. If there is a profit-sharing arrangement, specify exact terms. Is it gross or net profit? What percentage? Where is it paid?
2. What competition will be permitted in the shopping center?
3. Who is responsible for maintaining the common areas? Who will carry liability insurance for the common areas?
4. Can the lease be assigned? Is approval for assignment required?
5. Who will make repairs? Who pays?
6. Who will make improvements?
7. Are there mandatory hours of operation?
8. Is there an understanding on fixtures? Who keeps them?
9. What deposits are required? Are they refundable?

KEY TERMS

anchor tenants
adjustments
additional fees or costs

specific happenings increase
provisions

CHAPTER PROBLEMS

1. What is an anchor tenant?
2. What types of controls should landlords cover in the use-provisions of a shopping-center lease?
3. How is assignment of a shopping-center lease related to the use-clause?
4. What topics should be covered in the rent clause of a shopping-center lease?
5. Is there an implied warranty of usability in a shopping-center lease?
6. What is the difference between a trade fixture and a fixture?
7. In shopping-center leases, who is generally responsible for the decoration and completion of the rented retail space?
8. What antitrust issues exist in use-clauses?
9. Who is responsible for accidents and injuries occurring in the common areas of a shopping center?
10. Determine the answer to the problem at the beginning of the chapter.

24

REAL ESTATE SYNDICATION

Real estate syndication is "togetherness" in the real estate investment field.

–Don G. Campbell
Register—Tribune Syndicate

Real estate investment can be a lonely and burdensome endeavor. If an investor invests alone, all of the decisions, work, and management problems fall to that one person, who may or may not be experienced in all three areas. The purpose of real estate syndication is to spread the burden of real estate investments. Not only are the burdens of management and work delegated, but the amount of risk in the investment is divided among the investors. Multiple investors invest small amounts, instead of fronting all of the funds for one large investment and accepting the accompanying larger risk. *Real estate syndication* is a generic term for ownership of real estate by multiple parties. For example, four partners investing $20,000 each in a small apartment complex have an easier investment burden than one investor putting $80,000 in that same complex. Real estate syndication allows a developer to acquire nonconventional funds for a development through groups of individual investors. The purpose of the syndication may be for the development of office complexes or apartments, or for acquiring land for development.

Before the Tax Reform Act of 1986 (TRA), tax shelter and real estate syndications were synonymous. Many predicted that the TRA would be the end of syndications. Even after TRA, however, the syndication industry is alive and well because developers with good ideas and little cash still need groups of investors to undertake projects. Large amounts of capital are more easily obtained through syndication than through commercial bank loans.

This chapter answers the questions, What types of real estate syndicates exist? How are these syndicates structured? What are the rights, responsibilities, and liabilities of the syndicate members? What legal pitfalls should be avoided in structuring and operating syndicates? The three types of real estate syndicates discussed in this chapter are partnerships, corporations, and investment trusts.

PARTNERSHIPS

The definition of a *partnership* can be found in several different sources. The *Uniform Partnership Act (UPA)*, which has been adopted in nearly all states and which governs general partnerships, defines a partnership as a voluntary "association of two or more persons as co-owners in a business for profit." Under the Internal Revenue Code (a critical source for a definition, since many partnerships are formed for maximizing tax benefits), the definition of a partnership is "a syndicate, group, pool, joint venture, or other unincorporated organization" (26 U.S.C. §761[a]).

A partnership is a form of syndicate to which partners contribute money, land, or services as their capital contribution. If money is earned, the partners share in those profits; but if money is lost, the partners also share in those losses. In a general partnership, the partners are also responsible for the debts of the partnership. This means that if the partnership does not pay its debts, then the individual partners are required to pay. Thus, since the partners' personal assets may be drawn upon to pay debts, one of the risks of a partnership is the unlimited liability of the partners. For example, if A and B form the AB partnership, and the partnership has $75,000 in debt but no means of payment, the creditors may turn to A and B to pay the debts personally.

Limited partnership is a form frequently used in syndication. In limited partnership, there is at least one general partner who has personal liability and the responsibility of managing the partnership. The limited partners contribute capital and enjoy profits, but their liability for losses and debts is limited to the amount of their capital contribution—their personal assets are not subject to the partnership debts and losses.

Partnership syndication has advantages and disadvantages in formation, operation, securities, and taxation. In the following sections, these areas are discussed.

Formation of a Partnership—The Partnership Agreement

A partnership begins with a partnership agreement or articles of partnership. The purpose of a partnership agreement is to provide documentation that a partnership exists and to establish the rights and liabilities of the partners.

Name of Partnership The partnership agreement must set forth the name of the partnership. In some states there are restrictions on the types of names that may be used. For example, use of the word *company* is prohibited in some states because it might mislead others into interpreting it to mean *corporation*. In some states, the name must indicate whether the partnership is limited. The use of *Ltd* after the partnership name is typical, or simply *a limited partnership* written after the name. The name of the partnership is sometimes a combination of the partners' names, such as Smith, Jones, and Young forming the Smith, Jones, and Young Partnership. However, limited partners must not allow their names to be used in the partnership name because of the limited liability of these partners. The reason for this is to avoid confusing third parties, particularly creditors.

Names of Partners The agreement must include the partners' names. In the case of a limited partnership, the agreement must specify which partners are general and which are limited. In many states, addresses of general and limited partners are required.

Capital Contributions Each partner's initial contribution to the firm should be specified in the agreement. As already mentioned, the contribution may be services, money, or land. In many limited partnerships, the general partner contributes an undeveloped piece of property, and the limited partners furnish the money for its development. In limited partnerships, the limited partners are not permitted to contribute services as capital. Limited partners are silent or unknown partners and must not give the appearance of involvement in firm management.

Profits and Losses The allocation of profits and losses is a critical element of the partnership agreement. Under the UPA, profits are split equally and losses are split according to profits unless the agreement specifies otherwise. In most cases, the partners specify that their share of profits is proportionate to their capital contribution.

Management The management of the partnership may be handled by all partners, or it may be placed in the hands of one partner. In real estate partnerships, the management situation varies. In smaller partnerships, all partners may want to share the burden, whereas in larger partnerships, one or two experienced partners may handle the management.

In a limited partnership, only general partners are permitted to participate in management. A limited partner acting as a manager loses status as a limited partner. Limited partners should check the qualifications of the general partner to be certain that the partnership will be well-managed. In *blind pool partnerships* (partnerships in which the general partner is selling units in the partnership to raise money, but no specific real estate is as yet involved), the qualifications of the general partner are even more critical because the general partner will be entrusted with the investment decision.

Transfer of Partnership Interest Under the UPA, partners are permitted to transfer their rights in the partnership (the right to receive profits) but not their obligations (liability for partnership obligations). In the case of real estate partnerships, this lack of transferability may not be desirable. However, the agreement may permit transfers and then specify procedures and liabilities upon transfer. In the case of limited partnerships, the problems of liability do not exist and the agreement may make limited partners' interests freely transferable. One provision that may be included in the transfer portion is an agreement that before an interest is transferred to a third party, the partnership or other partners must first be given the option to purchase the interest.

Ownership of Partnership Property In real estate partnerships it is particularly important for the agreement to specify how title to the real estate is to be held. Many states permit the partnership to hold title to the property, but others require the property to be held in the name (or names) of one or more of the partners. Also, the partnership agreement should specify that improvements made on the property with partnership funds belong to the partnership. In real estate, the entire purpose of the partnership is generally to pool funds to develop a piece of raw land. The increased value of the land after such development is something in which each partner has an interest. In the following case, the issue of land improvements is discussed.

GAULDIN v. CORN
595 S.W.2d 329 (Mo. 1980)

Gauldin (plaintiff/appellant) and Corn (defendant/appellee) entered into an oral partnership agreement for the operation of piece of land as a ranch for the raising of cattle and hogs. Their agreement was a fifty–fifty partnership, with Corn allowing 25 of his 83 acres of land to be used for the partnership operation. The partnership did not pay rent or taxes on the land, and neither party considered this to be a contribution to the partnership by Corn.

With partnership funds, the 25 acres were bulldozed, seeded, and fertilized. A pond, fences, machine shed, barn, and hog-raising building were constructed on the land.

Corn became ill and upon his doctor's advice, notified Gauldin that the partnership would have to be terminated. Gauldin removed the animals and demanded half the value of the building improvements placed on the land. When Corn refused, Gauldin filed suit. The trial court held for Corn, and Gauldin appealed.

GREENE, Judge

. . . [T]he rule is "well-established" that improvements made upon lands owned by one partner, if made with partnership funds for purpose of partnership business, are the personal property of the partnership, and the nonlandowning partner is entitled to his proportionate share of their value. . . . [T]his is a fair and equitable rule which is consistent with the language contained in Missouri's Uniform Partnership Law. Section 8 states in part:

1. *All property originally brought into the partnership stock or subsequently acquired by purchase or otherwise, on account of the partnership is partnership property.*
2. *Unless the contrary intention appears,*

property acquired with partnership funds is partnership property.

It is clear from the cases that the general rule, governing the disposition of improvements upon dissolution of a partnership, is activated only where, as here, there is no agreement between the partners which controls such disposition. It matters not that the landowning partner contributed the use of his land to the partnership, that the nonlandowning partner knew that the improvements, when made, could not be removed from the land, or that a joint owner with the landowning partner was not joined in the suit for dissolution and accounting of the partnership.

Reversed and remanded for a determination of the value of the buildings at the time of the partnership dissolution.

Discussion Questions

1. What was the business of the partnership?
2. Whose land was used?
3. Was rent paid for the land use?
4. Who paid taxes on the land?
5. What improvements were made on the land?
6. What buildings were erected?
7. Why was the partnership dissolved?
8. What does Gauldin want?
9. Who wins and why?

Dissolution and Termination of the Partnership The agreement should specify when a partnership is dissolved and when it may be terminated and how. A *dissolution* occurs when one partner is no longer associated with the partnership (death or transfer of interest). Upon dissolution, the partnership may continue to do business or may terminate by paying debts and returning capital contributions. This dissolution aspect is one of the drawbacks to partnership because it makes the business relationship nonpermanent. The agreement should provide for the right to continue the business relationship upon the death of one of the partners, and should include methods for paying for the partner's interest (partnership pays for a life insurance policy on all the partners and is the beneficiary. When a partner dies, proceeds are used to pay the estate the value of the partner's interest).

In the case of a limited partnership, the death of a limited partner does not have the effect of dissolution and the only problem is paying for the limited partner's interest. In larger real estate partnerships, limited partners' interests are held by many investors and death does not affect the continuation of the business.

Recording For limited partners to have limited liability, their partnership agreement must be recorded. Without the recording of the agreement, the limited partners are general partners for purposes of their unlimited liability to third parties who deal with the partnership. In most states the place of recording real estate limited partnerships is in land records. Some states require recording or filing in the same place as for corporations. Some states require filings in two places.

(24.1) Consider:

A, B, and C are forming the ABC partnership. The partnership will acquire several duplex houses and will rent them with the idea of selling them at a profit in the next few years. A and B are contributing the $20,000 needed for the down payment on the duplex houses. C is negotiating the deal and will serve as landlord for the rentals. A and B claim they are entitled to a greater share of the profits since C is not contributing cash. C protests. Under the UPA, who is correct?

Operation of a Partnership—Rights and Liabilities of Partners

Fiduciary Duties In a partnership, each partner is a principal and agent to the other partners. Because of this agency relationship among the partners, each partner owes a duty of loyalty to the others. This means that the partners act in the partnership's best interests and do not make a profit at the expense of the partnership or withhold information or opportunities for the partnership from the other partners. For example, suppose A and B have formed the AB partnership for the purpose of developing a tract of land. An adjoining tract of land is undeveloped, and the AB partnership would like to acquire it, but the owner has been unwilling to sell. B learns that the owner of the adjoining tract is about to list it for sale. B approaches the owner and buys the property, with the idea that he will sell it secretly to the AB partnership for a profit. B's actions are a breach of a partner's fiduciary responsibilities.

Right to an Accounting Directly tied to the fiduciary duties is a partner's right to an *accounting*. An accounting is a procedure whereby the books and records of the partnership are examined to determine where partnership funds have been used and whether all partners have been treated equally or according to the terms of their partnership agreement. The term is derived from the procedure that requires an account of all partnership activities and funds.

In a real estate partnership where one partner is managing the firm's property or properties, an accounting serves to inform the other partners of the managing partner's activities, and whether partnership funds are being properly expended and profits correctly computed and distributed.

Authority of Partners Because an agency relationship exists among partners, the partners have express and implied authority for conducting partnership business. In real estate partnerships, one of the critical issues is whether one partner has the authority to convey title to land to third parties. If the partnership is in the business of buying and selling property, then one partner would have that authority because land transactions would be routine. If the partnership is formed for the purpose of developing one tract of land, then one partner would not have authority to sell that one tract of land. As noted in Chapter 11, buyers should check on the authority of partners when buying property from a partnership.

Also because of the agency relationship, partners are responsible for the contracts entered into by other partners authorized to do so. For example, if the partnership is developing a piece of property, a partner's contract for a survey of that property or another's contract for the grading of the property would be made with authority; and the partnership and individual partners would be liable for payment on the contract. If the partnership cannot pay for the services, individual partners and their personal assets are liable.

(24.2) Consider:

The AB partnership was formed for the purpose of developing a 6-acre tract of land as an office complex. B, unable to pass up a good offer, has sold 2 of the 6 acres to a third party. The architectural plans for the office complex will now have to be changed and the construction contracts rebid. A objects to the sale on grounds that B had no authority. What will be the result? Will the result vary according to who holds title to the property?

Tax Aspects of a Partnership

One of the reasons for forming a real estate partnership is to obtain tax benefits. In this section, some of the tax benefits and problems of partnership syndication are discussed.

Liability for Taxes

1. Income Tax The basic principle of taxation of partnerships is that the partnership does not pay taxes, the partners do (Internal Revenue Code; 26 U.S.C. §701). Each partner is responsible for reporting his or her proportionate share of loss or income on his or her individual tax returns. The loss or income of the partnership is determined by subtracting deductions from income, which includes rental income, sales (capital gains), interest, and any other sources of partnership income.

2. Property Tax In real estate partnerships, issues of taxation arise regarding the property contributed to, sold by, or developed by the partnership. If property is contributed to a partnership by a partner, there is no gain or loss. Thus, if a partnership is formed to develop property and one partner's contribution is a piece of property, there is no taxable event to the partnership or partner upon that initial contribution.

Another issue of property taxation is the partnership's basis in property contributed to the partnership by partners as their initial capital contribution. There are two categories of tax concerns that arise from this type of property contribution: The first comprises the tax consequences for the partnership and the partnership basis in the property. The second comprises the tax consequences for the contributing partner, the type of interest that partner holds, and that partner's basis in the property.

As just discussed, there are no tax consequences to the partnership upon the contribution. However there still remains the basis issue for the partnership. The basis of the property is, very simply, what has been put into the property. For purposes of a real estate partnership, the basis of contributed property is the partner's basis. Thus, if A, B, and C form the ABC partnership and A contributes a piece of property with a basis of $30,000, the partnership's basis is $30,000 (26 U.S.C. §723).

The contributing partner has no tax consequences upon contribution of the property to the partnership, but will have tax consequences if the partnership interest is transferred or if the partnership terminates and the partner is paid the value of his or her interest. At that time, the partner may have to recognize income.

Sale of Partnership Interests One of the reasons for formation of many real estate partnerships, and in many cases one of the reasons for success of the partnerships, is the ability of the partners to transfer their partnership interests. When a partner transfers a partnership interest, the individual partner will have tax liability.

Two-Tier Operation of Partnerships

Although the *two-tier partnership* may have arisen originally to enjoy maximum tax benefits, it continues to be a popular method of syndicate operation. Under this system, the partners or investors obtain interests in an *investment partnership*, which then obtains an interest in the *operating partnership*. The developer runs the operating partnership while the syndicator handles the investors. Under this structure, the syndicator works directly with the investors and can maximize influence with the developer. In addition, the syndicator then has the responsibility of collecting partners' payments while the developer's time is free for the project work. The two-tier operation began as a tax shelter but has continued as an effective management tool. For a complete discussion of the tax issues of two-tier operations, see Chapter 17.

Aspects of Securities in Partnerships

Today there is no question that the sale of limited partnership interests in real estate partnerships constitutes a sale of securities. Unless exempted, all sales of securities must be registered with both state and federal governments. When registration is required for the sale of partnership interests, the expenses of organization increase tremendously because of the complicated paperwork involved in the registration process.

Securities Act of 1933 The federal statute that governs the registration of the sale of securities is the *Securities Act of 1933* (15 U.S.C. §§77 et seq.). The 1933 act makes it unlawful to offer or to sell any security by use of the mails or other interstate commerce unless the security has been registered with the act's enforcement agency, the *Securities Exchange Commission (SEC)*, or unless an application for exemption has been filed with the SEC. Because of the time and expense involved in obtaining registration, most real estate partnerships are structured to avoid having to register.

If registration is required, the partnership must file a registration statement with the SEC. The registration statement includes financial information, background information on the general partners, information on the assets of the firm, and a history of the firm's operations. The partnership is also required to develop and submit for approval by the SEC a prospectus, which is a pamphlet to be given to investors. Included in the prospectus is much of the same information as in the registration statement but presented in a more attractive and readable fashion. Once all of the documents and the filing fee have been submitted, the SEC reviews the registration for completeness. (The SEC makes no findings on the accuracy of the information or the merits of the securities being offered.) The time it takes to obtain SEC approval on first-time securities offerings is an average of 6 months. Once approved, the partnership must still carry the burden of more paperwork by making sure all investors are given a copy of the prospectus. To avoid this complicated, costly, and time-consuming process, many firms structure their offering to fit the *exemptions* under the Securities Act of 1933.

Exemptions from Registration under the Securities Act of 1933

1. The Intrastate Offering Exemption The *intrastate offering exemption* exists because the Commerce Clause prohibits the federal government from regulating purely intrastate matters. To qualify for the intrastate exemption, the investors (offerees) and issuer must all be residents of the same state. (If there is one out-of-state offeree, the exemption will not apply.) Further, the issuer must meet the following requirements:

1. Eighty percent of its assets must be located in the state.
2. Eighty percent of its income must be earned from operations within the state.
3. Eighty percent of the proceeds from the sale must be used on operations within the state.

2. Small Offering Exemption—Regulation A Although the *small offering exemption (Regulation A)* is not a true exemption, it is a short-cut method of registration. The lengthy, complicated processes of full registration are simplified in that only a short form (S-1) registration statement is filed. Regulation A applies to issues of $1.5 million or less during any twelve-month period.

3. Small Offering Exemption—Regulation D Regulation D is the product of the SEC's evaluation of the impact of its rules on the ability of small businesses to raise capital. It was designed to simplify and clarify existing exemptions, expand the availability of exemptions, and achieve uniformity between state and federal exemptions.

Regulation D creates a three-tiered exemption structure that permits sales without registration. Sellers are, however, required to file a Form D informational statement about the sale. Rule 501 of Regulation D lists the definitions of various terms used in the three exemptions. For example, the term *accredited investor* includes any investor who at the time of the sale falls into any of the following categories:

1. Any bank.
2. Any private business development company.
3. Any director, executive officer, or general partner of the issuer.
4. Any person who purchases at least $150,000 of the securities being offered.
5. Natural persons whose net worth is greater than $1 million.
6. Any person whose individual income exceeded $200,000 in the last two years and who expects income greater than $200,000 in the current year.

Rule 502 places a number of limitations on the means an issuer can use in offering securities. The securities cannot be sold through general advertising or through seminars initiated through advertising. Further, all of the securities sold must be subject to restrictions to prevent the immediate rollover of the securities involved in these exempt transactions.

The three tiers of Regulation D exemptions are as follows:

The *Rule 504 exemption* applies to offerings of $500,000 or less (within any twelve-month period). The issuer cannot use advertising or make the offer to the public. Sales of stock to directors, officers, and employees are not counted in the $500,000 limitation.

The *Rule 505 exemption* covers sales of up to $5 million provided there are no more than thirty-five nonaccredited investors. Again, issuers qualifying under this exemption cannot engage in public advertising. Also, if the issue is sold to both accredited and nonaccredited investors, the issuer must give all buyers a prospectus.

The *Rule 506 exemption* has no dollar limitation but the number and type of investors is limited. There can be any number of accredited investors but the number of nonaccredited investors is limited to thirty-five. There cannot be advertising under a 506 exemption and there must be restrictions on the resale of the shares.

4. Problems with Integration Although many real estate partnerships qualify for one or more of these exemptions, the exemption issue can become a problem when a partnership issues two or more types of interests simultaneously. In other words, there is the possibility that two or more separate and exempt offerings may be considered part of one offering. This combining of separate, exempt offerings is called *integration*.

For example, two limited partnerships may be organized for the purpose of developing two different projects. One may be an intrastate exemption and one may be a private offering exemption. If the partnerships and their projects are deemed to be integrated, one or both exemptions may be lost because the private offering could be sold out of state and the intrastate offering could be sold to an unknowledgeable investor.

For those forming two or more partnership syndicates within relatively short periods of time, the projects undertaken should be geographically separate or of a different nature, and the offerings should be made in different ways or should be structured differently. For example, four different partnership offerings in each of four buildings in a complex are likely to be integrated as one offering. Four different partnership offerings in four geographically separate buildings would be considered separate offerings.

Figure 24.1 is a summary of the complex security issues in real estate syndication.

State Laws on Securities All states have some form of law governing the sale of securities. The types of registrations required and the available exemptions vary from state to state. In some states, copies of the federal registration information may be filed with the state for purposes of state registration; and when SEC approval is obtained, the state will give its approval. In merit review states, the securities and the partnership are actually reviewed to determine the quality of the offering. For partnership interests to be offered in more than one state, a uniform state registration application (developed by the National Association of

Figure 24.1 *Security Exemption Issues in Real Estate Syndication*

NAME	SIZE LIMITATION	OFFEREE/BUYER LIMITATION	RESALE LIMITATION	PUBLIC OFFERING
Intrastate exemption, 15 U.C.C. §77(c)(a)(11)	No	Buyers must be residents of state of incorporation; triple 80 percent requirements	Yes, stock transfer restrictions	Yes, in state
Regulation A Small Offering exemption, 15 U.C.C. §77D,	$1,500,000	Short form registration required	No	
Regulation D Rule 504—small offering,	$500,000 or less (in twelve-month period)	None, unlimited accredited and non-accredited alike	Some	No
Rule 505	Up to $5,000,000	No more than thirty-five excluding accredited investors.	Some	No
Rule 506	No	Unlimited accredited and thirty-five non-accredited investors.	Yes, stock restrictions	No

Securities Dealers) may be filed in all states to insure compliance with the information requirements of each state.

(24.3) Consider:

A, a promoter, has put together a real estate limited partnership for the purpose of constructing a shopping center. A has a great deal of experience in commercial development but no financing for the project. His plan is to raise money by selling $10 million of limited partnership interests at a cost of $10,000 each. A does not want to be limited to in-state investors for the sale of the interests. Will A have to register the sale with the SEC?

CORPORATIONS

A second method for creating a syndicate is the formation of a *corporation*. The corporate form of syndication has the advantage of limited liability for investors—losses are limited to the amount of the investment. The corporation has the advantage of perpetual existence because it is not terminated by the death or withdrawal of a shareholder. One additional advantage is that the corporate shares are freely transferable. The most obvious disadvantage of the corporate form of syndication is the loss of many direct tax write-offs. The corporation is a taxed entity; the shareholders do not share tax benefits directly, and their tax write-offs in owning shares are limited.

Formation of a Corporation

Forming a corporation requires more paperwork and more compliance with state-imposed procedures than is required for partnerships. The basic steps in corporate organization are summarized below, although each state has its own variations in procedure.

Articles of Incorporation The promoters are required to draft the articles of incorporation, which will generally include the following information:

1. *The name of the corporation.* Many states require the corporate name to include *Inc.* or *Co.* after the name to indicate corporate status.
2. *The proposed business of the corporation.* In real estate corporations, this statement of purpose has usually already been formulated, since the syndicate is set up for the purpose of accomplishing a project or development.

3. *The capital structure of the corporation.* The number of shares, their par value, their voting rights, and so on are all covered. Dividend rights are also covered.

4. *The structure of the corporate management.* The setup of the board and the officers are established. Initial members of the board of directors and initial officers are named.

5. *Administrative information about the corporation.* The address of the principal place of business and the name and address of a statutory agent are examples of details required.

The articles of incorporation are filed with a state agency, and all states require a filing fee.

Publication Most states require that new corporations publish their articles of incorporation in a newspaper of general circulation. The purpose of publication is to provide notice that a corporation exists and that liability of those involved will be limited.

Corporate Formalities Once a corporation is properly formed, the state issues a certificate of incorporation. The corporation may now act as a legal entity, entering into contracts and holding title to property. However, to ensure continued treatment as a corporation, the corporate management must be certain to comply with corporate formalities. Such formalities include holding meetings of the board of directors and annual meetings of shareholders, and keeping corporate accounts and business separate from personal accounts and business. If a corporation is used as a mere conduit for an individual's business, it is possible that corporate status will be set aside and individual liability imposed. With regard to smaller real estate corporations formed for tax purposes, it is possible for incorporators to have formed many corporations and to tend to become casual in the operation of the corporations. Such casualness may result in the loss of the corporate veil of liability protection, and the incorporators and shareholders may be held individually liable for the corporate debts.

Operation of a Corporation—Rights of Shareholders

Voting Rights Another distinction between partnerships and corporations is that usually a shareholder has voting rights and, hence, some say in the operation of the corporation. Even if the management of the corporation and the real estate project are left to someone else, the shareholders will have a say in who that someone else will be.

Dividends Payment of dividends is the corporate method of profit distribution. However, the declaration of a dividend is discretionary, and there is no right to a dividend unless the shares are set up with a guaranteed annual dividend.

Transferability of Shares One feature of a corporate syndicate that may make the investment better for shareholders is the ability to transfer the acquired corporate shares. The only restrictions that apply are the ones placed on the shares for purposes of qualifying for an SEC exemption from registration.

Tax Aspects of a Corporation

Organization In most cases the creation of a corporation is not a taxable event. As with partnerships, the contribution of property to a corporation by a shareholder is not a taxable event to either the corporation or the shareholder so long as the shareholder receives only stock in exchange for the property contributed (Internal Revenue Code; 26 U.S.C. §351).

The corporate basis in property contributed to the corporation in exchange for shares is the basis of the contributing shareholder. For the shareholder, the basis of the stock received is the stock's fair market value.

If a corporation is organized by an individual to shield the individual's income from tax, the organized corporation may be subject to a *personal holding company tax* (26 U.S.C. §541). The personal holding company tax was created to prevent corporations organized as "incorporated pocketbooks" for those attempting to shield personal income. A personal holding company tax is imposed on corporations meeting the following Section 541 criteria:

1. At least 60 percent of the corporate income is "personal holding company income," which is defined as some passive type of income such as rent, interest, royalties, or dividends. Generally real estate corporations qualify for this passive type of income production.
2. More than 50 percent of the corporate stock is owned by five individuals or fewer.

In forming a corporation, the issue of whether the personal holding company tax will be imposed is critical because of the additional cost and the loss of the corporate tax benefits.

Subchapter S Corporations One benefit of partnership structure that is usually lost in incorporation is the ability of the investors to directly deduct losses from their income. However, the Internal Revenue Code does provide for a form of corporate organization that permits the direct deduction of losses by shareholders: the *Subchapter S* corporation. With a Subchapter S structure, the shareholders have the protection of limited liability and the benefit of direct deduction of losses. This direct deduction of losses is critical in real estate corporations because of the depreciation deductions for real property.

Subchapter S structure is limited to certain types of corporations, and the decision to be treated as Subchapter S must be made before the taxable year ends and requires an election to be filed with the Internal Revenue Service. In order to qualify for Subchapter S treatment, a corporation must meet the following criteria:

1. The corporation must be a small business corporation, which is defined as a domestic corporation with not more than ten shareholders.
2. All shareholders in the corporation must be individuals as opposed to corporations or estates.
3. There must be only one class of stock.
4. All shareholders must consent to Subchapter S treatment.
5. The election to be treated as Subchapter S must be made by the end of the first month of the taxable year.
6. Income from passive sources must not make up more than 20 percent of the corporate income.

A corporation that qualifies for Subchapter S treatment does not pay tax, but the profits and losses of the corporation are recognized by the shareholders on their individual returns. The one difficulty for real estate corporations in qualifying for Subchapter S status is meeting the passive income requirement. (See Chapter 17.) In addition, the Tax Reform Act of 1986 placed strict controls on Subchapter S conversions to eliminate its use as a loophole for the TRA reforms.

Aspects of Securities in Corporations

The discussion of the sales, registration, and exemption of securities included under partnerships is also applicable to the sales of corporate shares. Corporate shares qualify as securities; thus, the same exemptions are applicable and the problems with integration also exist. The formation of several different corporations to sell interests in the same development may defeat the exemption status of all of the corporate offerings of securities.

INVESTMENT TRUSTS

Real estate investment trusts (REITs) and *mortgage investment trusts (MITs)* are tax legislation creatures. The purpose of these trusts is to permit the small investor to invest in a diversified portfolio of real estate. Instead of being a limited partner or a shareholder, the investor owns a beneficial interest in a trust. The idea for this form of real estate syndication originated in Massachusetts over a century ago, and investment trusts still exist because of the tax benefits afforded this form of investment.

The *Massachusetts business trust* originated because of the Massachusetts laws, which prohibited the ownership of any real estate by a corporate entity that was in excess of the real estate necessary for corporate operations. The Massachusetts trust allowed a trustee to hold title to property and then issue interest in the trust to investors. This form of syndication became very popular with large public sales of trust interests. But the popularity of the trusts declined when court decisions taxed the trusts as corporations.

In 1960 Congress passed provisions that allowed certain tax benefits for real estate trusts (Internal Revenue Code; 26 U.S.C. §§856 to 858), and REITs and MITs have since increased in popularity as a form of syndication. These vehicles, however, are used now for the income reporting mechanisms because the passive loss rules of TRA have greatly reduced their use as a tax shelter. (See Chapter 17.)

Formation of Investment Trusts

An REIT is set up in the same manner as any other trust. A trust agreement or declaration of trust is drawn up, and the properties involved are transferred to the trustee who will hold title and be responsible for the management of the properties or the portfolio of real estate investments. The following list is typical of the format and topics for a declaration of trust:

1. Name of the trust
2. Purpose of the trust
3. Description of beneficiary interests: their transferability, their sale, and the right of the trustee to buy shares
4. Voting rights of beneficiaries, meetings, and distributions to beneficiaries
5. Number of trustees, terms of office, compensation, and powers
6. Duration of trust and termination

Each investor is given a *trust certificate*, which evidences ownership of a portion of the trust and the amount of that ownership. Investors are beneficiaries of the trust arrangement and are not involved in the management of the properties or the portfolio; they allow the trustee to handle the real estate investments.

The portfolio of trusts can vary significantly. *Equity trusts* own real estate and have rental income as their primary source of income. The depreciation benefits for investors (discussed in the tax section following) are greatest with the equity trust. *Mortgage trusts* are trusts with investments in mortgages or other types of liens on real property. Many commercial banks and insurance companies have created mortgage trusts. The primary source of income in mortgage trusts is the interest earned on the owned mortgages. Some trusts are *mixed trusts;* they own both property and mortgages and have rental and interest income. In recent years, trusts have been used as methods for financing individual projects, as when a corporation creates a *specialty trust* for the purpose of expanding its operations. For example, a national restaurant chain could create a trust for the purpose of constructing new restaurants.

Operation of an Investment Trust— Rights and Liabilities of Beneficiaries

The beneficiaries are not personally liable for the obligations of the trust; their liability is limited to the trust assets. The beneficiaries, in most trusts, have a vote for the management of the trust in that they elect the trustees. In this aspect, the REIT is similar to the corporate syndicate.

The trustee owes a fiduciary duty to the beneficiaries and the trust, and must act with the best interests of the trust and its beneficiaries as a priority. Dealing with the trust without authority or beneficiary approval would be a breach of this fiduciary duty.

Tax Aspects of Investment Trusts

If a trust qualifies for REIT treatment, then certain tax benefits are applicable to the trust and the beneficiaries. The REIT is taxed only on undistributed income and gains. If the income or gains are distributed to the beneficiaries, there are no taxes to the trust. A REIT thus avoids the double taxation of corporations. The beneficiaries are taxed as individuals on the current or accumulated income; however, they are not entitled to the benefit of individual deduction of trust losses.

To qualify as a REIT for purposes of these tax benefits, the following criteria must be met:

1. At least 90 percent of the gross income must be derived from passive investments such as rent, interest, or dividends.
2. At least 75 percent of the gross income must be derived from interest or obligations secured by mortgages on real property or interest in real property, rents from real property, gains on sale of real property, or dividends or distributions from other REITs.

3. The trust interests must be held by 100 persons or more during at least 335 days of the taxable year.

4. The trustee may not be involved in the direct management or operation of the real estate. Management firms must be used to deal with tenants.

5. The trust must distribute at least 90 percent of its ordinary income.

6. There must also be compliance with other restrictions on income produced from assets held for less than a 4-year period.

If all of these qualifications are met, then the trust qualifies for REIT treatment under the Internal Revenue Code. If any of the requirements are not met within a given tax year, the trust is taxed as a corporation. Again, the passive loss restrictions of TRA have made these vehicles less attractive. (See Chapter 17.)

Aspects of Securities in Investment Trusts

Since a REIT requires at least 100 beneficiaries for favorable tax treatment, the issue of registration of securities is critical. A sale of a trust interest is considered to be a sale of a security, and few of the exemptions can be met with so many investors. Thus, a REIT may involve the expense of full registration with the Securities Exchange Commission (SEC).

In addition to the probable requirement of SEC registration, many states examine REITs very carefully in their registration process. Many states require REITs to have no more than 5 percent of their holdings in unimproved property before the sale of interests will be approved in that state. Other states prohibit REITs from issuing more than one type of interest and also restrict them to certain types of investment activities.

These federal and state registration processes make the REIT more costly and time-consuming to form than either the partnership or corporation.

RECOMMENDATIONS

Syndication enables the small investor to enjoy the investment returns and tax benefits of real estate without bearing all of the risk; and it enables the large investor to diversify greatly the types of holdings and the location of real estate holdings. Figure 24.2 is a comparison of the various methods of real estate syndication. Before becoming involved in any of the forms of syndication, the following information should be obtained and reviewed. An analysis of the benefits and disadvantages of the syndication should also be done.

1. What form of organization is being offered?

2. What parties are and will be in charge, and what are their backgrounds?

Figure 24.2 *Comparison of Methods of Real Estate Syndication*

CHARAC-TERISTICS	METHOD OF SYNDICATION				
	Partnership	*Limited Partnership*	*Corporation*	*Subchapter S Corporation*	*REIT*
Formation document	Articles of partnership or partnership agreement	Articles of partnership or partnership agreement	Articles of incorporation	Articles of incorporation	Declaration of trust
Filing	No	Yes	Yes	Yes	In some states
Investor's interest	Partner	Limited partner	Shareholder	Shareholder	Trust beneficiary
Personal liability	Yes	Yes: general partners; No: limited partners	No	No	No
Investor's losses and profits	Yes	Yes	No	Yes	Yes: distribution; No: losses
Regulation of securities	Yes (unless exempt)	Yes (unless exempt)	Yes (unless exempt)	Probably private	Yes (generally)
Investor's voting rights	Yes	Yes	Yes	Yes	Yes
Transferability	Difficult	Yes	Yes	Difficult	Yes
Taxation	TRA loss limitations if passive	TRA loss limitations if passive	Losses limited to value of shares	TRA loss limitations if passive	TRA loss limitations if passive

3. Are the interests registered with the SEC and the state, or are they exempt?

4. Are the qualifications for tax benefits met?

5. What is the nature of the syndicate's investment, development, or portfolio?

6. What voting rights, if any, exist for the investors?

7. Are the interests transferable? Are there restrictions on transfer?

KEY TERMS

real estate syndication

partnership

Uniform Partnership Act (UPA)

limited partnership

blind pool partnerships

dissolution

accounting

two-tier partnership

investment partnership

operating partnership

Securities Act of 1933

Securities Exchange Commission
   (SEC)

exemptions

intrastate offering exemption

small offering exemption

Regulation A

Regulation D

accredited investor

Rule 504 exemption

Rule 505 exemption

Rule 506 exemption

integration

corporation

personal holding company tax

Subchapter S

Real estate investment trusts
   (REITs)

mortgage investment trusts (MITs)

Massachusetts business trust

trust certificate

equity trusts

mortgage trusts

mixed trusts

specialty trust

CHAPTER PROBLEMS

1. A wishes to put together a syndicate for the purpose of purchasing and operating two apartment complexes. A feels she can best sell the syndicate interests if the investors are able to directly deduct the depreciation losses that will result from the first 3 years of operation. What form of syndication will allow A's investors to take such deductions?

2. A will sell twenty-five interests in her syndicate to both in-state and out-of-state investors. A wishes to know if she must register the sale of the interests with the SEC or the state.

3. A wishes to know which method of syndication will be the least costly and the least time-consuming. Advise A.

4. A believes she can sell the interests more easily if the interests are readily transferable. What form of syndication would be best?

5. A is curious about the liability of the investors. What forms of syndication will give them limited liability, and what forms will expose them to personal liability?

6. What are the requirements for a Subchapter S corporation?

7. What are the requirements for a REIT under the Internal Revenue Code?

8. Explain the difference between an equity trust and a mortgage trust.
9. What information is required (in most states) in the articles of incorporation?
10. What distinctions exist between a limited partnership and a general partnership in formation, liability, and operation?

25

SUBDIVIDING REAL ESTATE FOR RESIDENTIAL DEVELOPMENT

Plans get you into things, but you got to work your way out.

—Will Rogers

This chapter appears last because much of the information in the rest of the book is necessary to understand the *subdivision* process. Subdivision starts with the finding of a piece of property for development and continues through its purchase, development, and eventual resale to home purchasers. As the flow-chart in Figure 25.1 indicates, subdivision is not a one-step process. This chapter answers the question, What steps are required for the proper development of a subdivision? In answering that question, the process will be traced from beginning to end.

MARKET ANALYSIS

Because real estate investments have been so profitable in the past few years, the idea of doing a market analysis on buying and developing land seems redundant. However, many subdivisions have experienced bankruptcy because the units constructed were too expensive or were inappropriate for the needs of people in the area. Before acquiring land or deciding on the type of subdivision, a developer should determine the economic and physical needs of people

Figure 25.1 Steps in the Subdivision Process

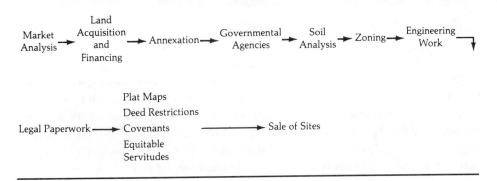

living in or moving to the area. The purpose for this is to determine the location and type of housing that can sell readily. For example, some areas of cities have the greatest concentration of families residing in them, and a subdivision with larger, single-family homes would most likely be profitable. In that same area, townhouses and condominiums might not sell. In college towns, on the other hand, smaller housing units would sell very well because investors and students tend to purchase smaller homes for rental properties or temporary residences.

This initial step of understanding the market may determine the subdivision's ultimate success, and it should not be cast aside because of the thinking that all real estate sells. Other factors that can be determined in the study include the economic status of residents and how much they can afford to pay for housing. With these factors in mind, construction costs can be appropriately budgeted.

LAND ACQUISITION AND FINANCING

A market analysis can be done on a large area or on several different parcels of property. Once the market analysis is complete, the developer faces the task of finding a parcel of land in the area or determining which parcel of land studied is the best for subdividing. The assistance of brokers and agents can be employed in both the market analysis and in finding an appropriate piece of property.

The method of financing the property will depend on the developer's position but could be a mortgage loan or a subdivision trust arrangement with the property owner. (See Chapter 12 for a complete discussion of financing methods.)

In addition to obtaining financing for the purchase of property, the developer will need to obtain construction loans for the housing units to be built. (See Chapter 20 for details on construction financing.)

ANNEXATION

In some cases, there are no land parcels located within city limits that are large enough for subdivision. However, the developer will have a difficult time selling properties in the subdivision if the city emergency services and utility services are not available to the buyers of the units. One alternative is to have a private corporation furnish these services, but a better and more frequently used alternative is to have the subdivision parcel annexed by the city.

The process of *annexation* is similar to a change in zoning and will require application, notice of a hearing, and a public hearing. The public hearing affords for all interested parties an opportunity to object.

COOPERATION WITH GOVERNMENTAL AGENCIES

At this stage in the development, the commitment to a particular piece of property has been made and the type of housing or lots to be sold has been determined. It is at this point that the developer should begin preparing (or have prepared) all documents necessary for compliance with any governmental agencies that might have jurisdiction over the sales. For example, if unimproved lots are being sold, the Interstate Land Sales Full Disclosure Act (ILSFDA; 15 U.S.C. §1701 et seq.) will apply and the developer must file statements of record and property reports with the Department of Housing and Urban Development (HUD). Approval of these documents can take time, so the developer should anticipate the possible delay.

If improved lots with dwellings or multiunit housing units are to be sold, the developer may wish to have Federal Housing Administration (FHA) and Veterans Administration (VA) financing available for buyers. To do so, the developer must obtain FHA and VA approval for the subdivision. Again, obtaining approval in advance will alleviate the problem of having to wait while buyers are ready to buy.

In recent years, governmental agencies have required developers to bear some of the costs of adding subdivisions. Subdivisions bring families in at rapid rates, and the cost of new schools is a burden local governments often cannot carry at accelerated paces. Many states have passed laws requiring developers to pay *impact fees* to provide local governments with needed funds to provide for expansion of services such as schools, police, and fire departments that is needed as a result of the development. As the following case indicates, these fees have been challenged but are generally upheld.

CANDID ENTERPRISES, INC. v. GROSSMONT UNION HIGH SCHOOL DISTRICT
705 P.2d 876 (Calif. 1985)

In 1974, the Board of Supervisors of San Diego County adopted a land-use policy called I-43 to help ensure orderly growth in the face of rapid and widespread development in the area. Among other things, the developers would be required to present a "school-availability" letter from the appropriate school district to the Planning Commission and Board of Supervisors to obtain approval to proceed with their proposed development. After Grossmont Union High School District (respondent) indicated in several proposals that proposed developments would cause overcrowding, the Board permitted few additional developments.

In the fall of 1977, Candid Enterprises, Inc. (plaintiff/petitioner) entered into an agreement with Grossmont to pay for additional school facilities, and the District would then issue an availability letter.

In the interim, the School Facilities Act was passed by the California Legislature, which authorized cities and counties to require developers to pay fees for temporary school facilities. The San Diego Board adopted ordinance 5120, which permitted it to enter into agreements with developers for payments of the fees authorized by the state legislation.

Some fees were collected and some commitments were made, but in 1980 enrollments declined and the Board monitored development but was not requiring availability letters nor fees. Candid then asked to be released from its $23,500 commitment to Grossmont because the funds were no longer needed. The request was refused by the Board. The trial court ordered a refund and Grossmont appealed.

MOSK, Justice

Respondents first contend that the imposition of Policy I-43 school-impact fees is not preempted by the School Facilities Act and is accordingly valid. Petitioner concedes as it must that the imposition of school-impact fees is generally valid.

Respondents proceed to argue successfully that the local legislation is not preempted by the Act on the ground that there is no conflict.

Under the police power granted by

the Constitution, counties and cities have plenary authority to govern, subject only to the limitation that they exercise this power within their territorial limits and subordinate to state law (Cal. Const., art. XI, §7.). Apart from this limitation, the "police power [of a county or city] under this provision . . . is as broad as the police power exercisable by the Legislature itself."

If otherwise valid local legislation conflicts with state law, it is preempted by such law and is void. A conflict exists if the local legislation "duplicates, contradicts, or enters an area fully occupied by general law, either expressly or by legislative implication."

Respondents argue and petitioner concedes that Policy I-43 school-impact fees do not contradict or duplicate the provisions of the School Facilities Act. Respondents further assert that such fees have not entered an area fully occupied by state law. They are persuasive.

First, the area of financing of school facilities needed by new development has not been expressly occupied by state law. The Legislature has not voiced such an intent in any of its enactments, and petitioner admits as much.

Second, the area has not been impliedly occupied by state law.

In determining whether the Legislature has preempted by implication to the exclusion of local regulation we must look to the whole purpose and scope of the legislative scheme. There are three tests: (1) the subject matter has been so fully and completely covered by general law as to clearly indicate that it has become exclusively a matter of state concern; (2) the subject matter has been partially covered by general law couched in such terms as to indicate clearly that a paramount state concern will not tolerate further or additional local action; or (3) the subject matter has been partially covered by general law, and the subject is of such a nature that the adverse effect of a local ordinance on the transient citizens of the state outweighs the possible benefit to the municipality.

First, the subject matter of the local measure—the financing of the construction of both temporary and permanent school facilities to meet the demands imposed by new development—has not been

so fully and completely covered by general law as to clearly indicate that it has become exclusively a matter of state concern.

Taken by itself, the School Facilities Act does not even purport to deal with the construction of permanent facilities (see §65970, subd. [e], 65974), and does not fully and completely cover the construction of temporary facilities.

The Act goes on to define "reasonable methods for mitigating conditions of overcrowding": they "shall include, but are not limited to, agreements between a subdivider and the affected school district whereby temporary-use buildings will be leased to the school district or temporary-use buildings owned by the school district will be used."

The evident absence of implied preemptive intent in the terms of the School Facilities Act—whether we consider it by itself or with other related legislation—is confirmed by the failure of the Legislature to fully cover the financing of school facilities. First, not all school districts in need of funds for permanent facilities can qualify to receive them under the Greene Act (see Ed.Code, §17740). Second, for a variety of reasons the Legislature has failed to provide adequate funding for even such "stop-gap, patchwork" programs as currently exist. In such circumstances, to construe alternative, local arrangements such as that before us to be preempted would severely impede local governments and school districts in carrying out their responsibilities. It would also frustrate the intent of the Legislature in enacting the School Facilities Act: "Adequate school facilities should be available for children residing in new residential developments." Developers who are expected to cause or aggravate overcrowding are required to mitigate it.

Reversed.

Discussion Questions

1. What was the development climate at the time Candid entered into the agreement to pay fees?
2. When was the state statute passed?
3. What happened to the development climate after the time the statute was passed?
4. Why did Candid want out of its commitment to pay fees?
5. Did the state law preempt the agreement with Grossmont?
6. Are the San Diego ordinances and agreements valid?

ZONING

If a change in zoning is planned, application should be made at this point. Although a zoning check is part of the property purchase checklist, the purchase may have been made knowing that a zoning change could be obtained. For example, the type of residential zoning may need to be changed for its density. Some cities limit the number of housing units per acre, and if the developer is planning a condominium development or single-family dwellings on minuscule lots, the density restrictions may need to be waived. (See Chapter 16 for a discussion of obtaining zoning variances.)

SOIL ANALYSIS

Although a soil analysis should also be done before the property is purchased, the purpose of the analysis at this point is to assure that proper construction procedures are followed not only for the housing units but also for the streets, sidewalks, and grading.

ENGINEERING WORK

This step in the subdivision process is the first step in which the land is entered and improvements are begun. It is important that financing be obtained before engineering work begins, so that the construction lender will have first priority in the event of default. (See Chapters 7 and 20 for discussions of lien priorities and construction lenders.)

In this step, the following tasks are accomplished. All of the tasks are required before construction of dwellings can begin.

1. Overlot grading
2. Sewer and water hookups
3. Gas, electrical, and telephone line hookups and installation
4. Curbs, gutters, and sidewalks

5. Storm sewer drainage
6. Street paving

LEGAL PAPERWORK

The developer must provide a subdivision or plat map with easements, roads, and lots clearly indicated and must record the map in the land records. The plat map will be used as a reference point for descriptions of all lots to be sold in the subdivision. (See Chapter 8 for more detail on plat maps and their importance in legal descriptions.)

In addition to the plat map, the developer will have drafted and recorded the *deed restrictions* or *protective covenants* for the subdivision. The purpose of these covenants is to control the type of structures and the conduct of persons residing in the subdivision. Typical provisions included in deed restrictions are:

1. Minimum square footage requirements for all dwelling units constructed within the subdivision
2. Restrictions on in-home business operations
3. Restrictions on the types of animals that may be kept on the lots
4. Restrictions on dividing lots and selling smaller portions of them
5. Restrictions on the types of structures that may be erected in addition to the dwelling units
6. Prohibitions on nuisances

The validity of the deed restrictions is based on the common law concept of covenants. At common law covenants were restrictions placed in the deed from the grantor to the grantee. In addition to the requirement that the covenant be in the deed, the following elements were required for a covenant to be enforceable:

1. The covenant had to *touch and concern* the land.
2. The grantor and grantee had to intend the covenant to operate as a permanent restriction on the land.
3. The covenant could be enforceable only as against those parties in privity of contract; that is, the grantor and the grantee.

The problem with the common law requirements is that privity exists in the initial sale between the developer and the first buyer but is absent once the first buyer transfers the property. To alleviate this problem, most deed restrictions contain a clause specifying the time period for which they are valid, and the deeds transferring title to the subdivision lots contain clauses saying the title is subject to all of the restrictions that have been recorded for the subdivision.

In some cases, the deed restrictions recorded for a subdivision are very general. Many developers use the same set of restrictions regardless of the type of homes being built in the subdivision. These restrictions provide little protection in the event the developer pulls out of the subdivision before all lots have homes constructed on them or before all land has been developed. To protect those who already own homes in the subdivision, the common law doctrine of *equitable servitudes* exists. An equitable servitude is a restriction on land use that exists because of the nature of the subdivision or area. In other words, if only certain types of construction standards have been permitted in an area, those standards remain in effect even after the developer leaves. Under this doctrine, buyers of land within a partially developed subdivision are required to use the land purchased in a manner consistent with the plan of development in existence at the time of their purchase. The basis for the doctrine of equitable servitude is notice; a party who purchases land in an area where a common scheme of development is obvious is bound to abide by the development scheme.

In addition, a developer who pulls out of a subdivision prior to its completion may face the issue of misrepresentation because the existing property owners purchased under the assumption that the subdivision would be completed with certain forms of construction. Both the doctrine of equitable servitudes and the remedy of misrepresentation serve to protect home owners from declines in property values in the event a developer decides not to complete a subdivision and sells the lots to others. In the following case, both of these issues are discussed.

BURGESS v. PUTNAM
464 S.W.2d 698 (Tex. 1971)

Ralph Burgess (defendant/appellant) had developed a subdivision in which Jack Putnam and others (plaintiffs/appellees) had purchased lots for the purpose of constructing homes. Burgess sought to sell the remaining lots to several purchasers who intended to use them as sites for their mobile homes. Putnam brought suit to enjoin the sales or require Burgess to include conveyance restrictions prohibiting the use of the lots as mobile-home sites.

Putnam claimed, although no restrictions had been recorded, that Burgess represented the subdivision as one in which no mobile homes would be located.

The trial court found for Putnam, and Burgess appealed.

MASSEY, Chief Justice

The question, therefore, is whether the representations made to plaintiffs [Putnam] relative to their plan of development of the entire subdivision, inducing plaintiffs to pay an enhanced price for their own conveyances which imposed restrictions upon them—including the prohibition of any use of the property purchased by them as sites for trailer houses—brought into existence their equitable right to compel the defendants to similarly restrict the use of any remaining subdivision property as a protection of plaintiffs' investment and of the lots they had purchased.

There was nothing fraudulent on the part of the defendants in their representations inducing plaintiffs' prior purchases. Their change of plan was occasioned by a diminished real estate market. Change in the market was such that permitted the defendants a ready profit if they were free to sell additional land within the subdivision as sites for trailer houses. If they adhered to their original plan for development there was a diminished likelihood of profit.

Finally we reach the "merger clause" or "merger clauses" common to all the contracts containing restrictions on the basis of which plaintiffs assert their right to injunction compelling defendants to similarly bind all others purchasing within the subdivision. We copy therefrom, as follows:

5. All representations, covenants and warranties and agreements between the parties are expressed in this written agreement and no other shall be recognized between the parties unless reduced to writing and attached hereto and approved by sellers.

THIS CONTRACT IS MADE SUBJECT TO THE FOLLOWING RESTRICTIONS:

These covenants are to run with the land and shall be binding upon the purchaser, his heirs, executors, administrators and assigns and may be enforced by the sellers at their option either by injunction or by action for damages.

Upon failure to comply with any of the above restrictions or any of the other covenants herein, at the option of sellers, the title to said property shall revert back to sellers or their assigns and all rights of purchaser or his assigns shall be forfeited. This clause, however, shall not affect pres-

ent or subsequent mortgage holders, and may be waived at the option of the sellers.

As a matter of principle it is necessary to weight the advantages of certainty in contractual relations against the harm and injustice that result from fraud. In obedience to the demands of a larger public policy the law long ago abandoned the position that a contract must be held sacred regardless of the fraud of one of the parties in procuring it. No one advocates a return to outworn conceptions. The same public policy that in general sanctions the avoidance of a promise obtained by deceit strikes down all attempts to circumvent that policy by means of contractual devices. In the realm of fact it is entirely possible for a party knowingly to agree that no representations have been made to him, while at the same time believing and relying upon representations which in fact have been made and in fact are false but for which he would not have made the agreement. To deny this possibility is to ignore the frequent instances in everyday experience where parties accept, often without critical examination, and act upon agreements containing somewhere within their four corners exculpatory clauses of one form or another, but where they do so, nevertheless, in reliance upon the honesty of supposed friends, the plausible and disarming statements of salesmen, or the customary course of business. To refuse relief would result in opening the door to a multitude of frauds and in thwarting the general policy of the law.

The same rules applicable in cases of fraud would likewise be applicable to a case such as the one before us where there was a nonfraudulent "misrepresentation" concerning future development, etc., of the remainder of the subdivision, inducing the plaintiffs to enter into contracts with the defendants.

Affirmed.

Discussion Questions

1. Why is the developer pulling out of the subdivision?
2. What use do the new purchasers wish to make of the property?
3. What representations do the plaintiffs use as the basis for their suit?
4. What provision in the contract makes the claim of misrepresentation difficult for the plaintiffs?
5. What relief do the plaintiffs want?
6. Will the plaintiffs be given their requested relief?

(25.1) Consider:

Shalimar Estates is a residential land development consisting of 134 acres in Tempe, Arizona. The development consists of a golf course and adjacent residential lots. The golf course is an integral part of the development, and the lots were sold to buyers with the sales representations that there would always be a golf course and that their homes would always overlook a golf course. There were, however, no deed restrictions on the use of the golf course property. The original developer sold the property, and the developers planned to eliminate the golf course to maximize the property value. The homeowners have brought suit on the basis of the representations made to them. Can they win? *Shalimar Association v. D.O.C. Enterprises, Ltd.*, 688 P.2d 682 (Ariz. 1984)

SALE OF SITES

The final step for the developer of a subdivision is the sale of the lots or housing units in the development. Contracts for sale should be drafted and eventually signed by purchasers. (See Chapter 11 for details on purchase contracts.)

SUBDIVISIONS AFTER THE DEVELOPER LEAVES

Once the developer has gone, it becomes the responsibility of the homeowners in the area to maintain the quality and integrity of the subdivision. The homeowners are responsible for enforcement of deed restrictions and may have to bring suit to see that those restrictions are honored. The following case involves the crossover in responsibility of the parties when the developer leaves and the property owners remain.

ARMSTRONG v. ROBERTS
325 S.E.2d 769 (Ga. 1985)

In October 1979, Sturgis Development, the developer of Ashton Woods Subdivision, recorded protective covenants pertaining to the subdivision.

Among other things, the covenants provided that "no building shall be located on any lot nearer than fifty (50) feet to the front line, unless approved in writing by the Sturgis Development Company, Inc."

In May 1983, Sturgis sold a lot to Audrey and Howard Oldmixon. This was the last lot Sturgis owned in the subdivision. In September 1983, the Oldmixon's builder, Roberts (defendant) obtained a written waiver from Sturgis for the placement of the Oldmixon home only 35 feet from the set-back line. The Armstrongs (plaintiffs) filed suit after construction began for violation of the deed restrictions and asked for an injunction to halt construction. The trial court denied the injunction and the Armstrongs appealed.

GREGORY, Justice

While the law is certain that a developer may retain the right to waive restrictions contained in protective covenants, the parties concede there is no Georgia authority clearly controlling a situation in which a developer waives such restrictions after he has divested himself of ownership in the subdivision. We acknowledge the New York and Illinois cases cited by plaintiffs. The rule announced in those authorities is a reasonable one. So long as the developer owns an interest in the subdivision being developed his own economic interest will tend to cause him to exercise a right to waive restrictions in a manner which takes into account harm done to other lots in the subdivision. There is some economic restraint against arbitrary waiver. After the developer has divested himself of all interest in the subdivision this economic restraint is lacking. We adopt the New York and Illinois rule. A developer of a subdivision who reserved the authority to waive restrictions in covenants running with the land no longer possesses that authority after divesting himself of his interest in the subdivision.

While the foregoing is the rule of law to be applied in this case, other considerations come to bear on the matter of injunctive relief.

In considering "an application for an interlocutory injunction there should be a balancing of the conveniences and a consideration of whether greater harm might be done by refusing than by granting the injunction." An "injunction should be refused where its grant would operate oppressively on the defendant's right."

Balancing the equities in this case, we take into consideration the following circumstances. Construction of the residence in question began April 9, 1984. By April 12, the layout of the residence was completed and on April 26 the foundation was poured. On May 15, plaintiffs, by letter, notified defendant that they considered him in violation of the protective covenants and on June 6, they filed suit for an injunction and damages. During this period the defendant continued construction of the residence.

Plaintiffs' complaint is that the placement of defendant's house blocks their view and diminishes the value of their property. The record is unclear as to whether it would have been feasible to construct the house within the set-back requirements prescribed by the protective covenants. Nonetheless, defendant's position is that he acted reasonably in seeking the waiver from Sturgis. Nothing in the record indicates the contrary.

There is every indication in the record that, had the request for waiver been made at the proper time, Sturgis would have complied. Nothing in the record suggests that Sturgis's decision to waive the set-back restriction four months after the sale of the lot was arbitrary or capricious, nor that the restriction was waived for any reason other than to accommodate the construction of this dwelling on an "awkward lot layout." Additionally, we note that plaintiffs were aware of the developer's authority to waive the set-back restrictions when they purchased their lot in the subdivision. Balancing the circumstances of this case, we conclude they are in favor of denying the injunction. Therefore, we affirm the denial of injunctive relief and remand for further action consistent herewith.

Affirmed.

Discussion Questions

1. What covenant was violated?
2. Who violated it?
3. When did Sturgis sell its interest in the subdivision?
4. Did Sturgis have the authority to issue the waiver?
5. Did the Armstrongs wait too long?
6. What was the problem with the waiver?
7. Are the Oldmixons allowed to continue the proposed building?

CONCLUSION

A successful subdivision results when experts from many fields work with a developer to bring together ideas and experience. The flowchart approach is necessary for a developer to keep track of project status as well as individual tasks that must be completed at certain times. The flowchart can be detailed to suit the particular subdivision project. Internal memos should also be kept as reminders and verifications of tasks. To achieve a problem-free subdivision, the developer must prepare and follow through.

KEY TERMS

subdivision
annexation
impact fees

deed restrictions
protective covenants
equitable servitudes

CHAPTER PROBLEMS

1. What is the purpose of a market analysis prior to subdivision?
2. Why is annexation important?
3. At what point in a subdivision development are statements of record and property reports required?
4. What are school-impact fees and who pays them?

5. What relation does the plat map have to the individual deeds of purchasers?

6. Why do common law covenants present enforcement problems?

7. How can the problems of common law covenants be eliminated?

8. What topics are covered in deed restrictions?

9. What is an equitable servitude?

10. Century Homes has been involved in a subdivision development of luxury homes for 3 years. The market for these large, expensive homes is no longer active, and Century is selling the remaining lots to builders who will be building small, inexpensive homes. Prior to Century's sales of the lots, the smallest home in the subdivision was 2,500 square feet. One builder is planning a 1,500-square-foot home. The existing home owners wish to know if they have any protections. What is the result?

GLOSSARY

Abstract   A concise statement of the substance of documents or facts appearing on the public land records that affect the title to a particular tract.

Accelerated Cost Recovery System (ACRS)   Method of depreciation giving property owners large depreciation deductions during the first years of ownership.

Acceleration clause   Provision in note, mortgage, or deed of trust that provides for the acceleration of the due date of the loan; generally results in the full amount of the loan being due for default such as nonpayment.

Acceptance   Action of offeree in agreeing to terms of an offer that results in a binding contract.

Accounting   In probate, process of providing report on the collection and distribution of the estate; in partnerships, an equitable proceeding in which the use and distribution of partnership funds are examined to determine whether each partner has received his or her appropriate share.

Accredited investor   Under federal securities law, an investor who meets certain financial standards and can qualify for purchases of certain types of securities exempt from registration.

Acid rain   An environmental hazard that results from sulfur dioxide pollution from factories and coal-fired utility plants; the pollution is carried long distances and appears in rain and snow in areas far removed from the pollution sources.

Acknowledgement   Notary signature and seal; appears on deeds and some contracts as well as on wills.

ACRS   See Accelerated Cost Recovery System (ACRS).

Action for dispossession   Court proceeding by landlord to have tenant removed from property; generally brought for nonpayment of rent or destruction of landlord's premises.

Adjustable rate mortgage (ARM)   A type of mortgage with a rate that changes according to some interest-rate index.

Adjustments   In zoning, variances or changes in the application of zoning; generally handled by a board of adjustments and is an approved exception to zoning regulations.

Administrator   Male party responsible for the probate of an intestate estate.

Administratrix   Female party responsible for the probate of an intestate estate.

Ad valorem tax   Tax based on value that increases as value increases. Property taxes are ad valorem taxes.

Advancement   Common law doctrine that subtracts amounts of inter vivos gifts from an heir's share of decedent's estate (still followed in some states).

Adverse possession   Method of acquiring title to land by openly taking possession of and using another's property for a certain period of time.

Aesthetic zoning Zoning that regulates the appearance of property and exists for beautification purposes or architectural uniformity.

Affirmative easement An easement that involves the use of another's property; e.g., a right of access.

After-acquired property clause Mortgage, note, or security interest provision that provides that the security for the loan includes the existing property and any property added after the note; mortgage security interest is attached to newly acquired property.

Agent One who acts on another's behalf. In real estate, the agent is the party who works to bring the buyers and sellers of real estate together in exchange for payment (generally a commission).

Air lots That portion of the air space from 23 feet above the earth's surface to the heavens.

Air Pollution Control Act The original federal act relating to air pollution; provided for studies but did little to control air pollution (1955).

Air Quality Act 1967 federal act that provided HEW with the authority to oversee state air pollution control plans and implementation.

All-adult covenants Deed restrictions that limit residency in particular areas to certain ages and prohibit residency of children less than a certain age.

Anaconda mortgage Mortgage covering all debt owed by the mortgagor to the mortgagee.

Anchor tenant The tenant in a shopping center that has the largest store and will draw the greatest amount of traffic; e.g., grocery store in a plaza or a major department store in a mall.

Annexation Taking in an area of land as part of a governmental unit (city, town, or county). Many subdivisions are annexed before they are developed.

Antenuptial agreements Premarital contracts in which the spouses-to-be waive their interests in each other's properties that will be accumulated during the course of the marriage.

Appraisal Process of valuing property; what a willing buyer would pay a willing seller when neither is forced to contract.

Architect Participant in the construction process; may oversee quality of subcontractors' work and issue lien waivers.

ARM See Adjustable rate mortgage (ARM).

Article IX Section of the Uniform Commercial Code that governs the taking of security interests in personal property and fixtures.

As is Clause in contract which waives any warranty protection.

Assessment Process whereby a tax amount is assigned to a parcel of real estate on the basis of the value of the parcel.

Assessor Public official responsible for the valuation and assessment of real property and the subsequent collection of taxes.

Assignment Process of transferring contract rights to another; e.g., assignment of a mortgage or lease.

Assumption Process whereby a buyer of real property agrees to assume responsibility for payments on an existing mortgage on the property.

At-risk rules Under the Internal Revenue Code, a restriction on taking losses that requires those taking the loss to have funds at the risk of the operation of the business.

Attached home A form of multiunit housing; it generally has common walls with other homes.

Attachment Process of creating a lien, security interest, or other creditor's interest in property; results when the creditor has complied with all requirements.

Balloon payment Provision in mortgage or mortgage note that calls for the payment of a large lump sum at the end of the mortgage period.

Bargain and sale deed Deed that transfers title but carries no warranties.

Baseline In the United States Government Survey, the major east-west guide lines.

Basis Property owner's cost of property; used for computing gain or loss on the sale of property.

BAT See Best available treatment (BAT).

BCT See Best conventional treatment (BCT).

Bequest A gift of personal property by will.

Best available treatment (BAT) The highest standard the EPA can impose for the control of water pollution.

Best conventional treatment (BCT) A standard for water pollution control that requires a firm to follow the best of the commonly used treatment methods; a standard that is lower than best available treatment.

Bid notice Call for bids on a project by a contractor.

Bill of sale Document used to transfer title to personal property.

Blind pool partnership A partnership in which the general partner is selling units in the partnership to raise money, but no specific real estate is as yet involved.

Blockbusting Illegal racial discrimination practice wherein real estate brokers attempt (by encouraging listings and sales in a neighborhood) to change the racial composition of the neighborhood.

Board of adjustment Governmental entity (usually at city or county level) that is responsible for approving variances and adjustments.

Bona fide purchaser (BFP) Good faith purchaser.

Broker Party who is licensed to handle property listings.

Brundage clause Provision in a mortgage that calls for the mortgagor to pay all taxes on the property.

Bubble concept EPA concept of examining all air pollutants in an area as if they came from a single source; this concept is used in making a decision regarding the possibility of a new plant in the area.

Building codes Statutes or ordinances requiring certain construction features in buildings and homes; e.g., the number of exits, sprinklers.

Bylaws In multiunit housing, the document governing the details of operation; voting rights of members, meetings, notices, etc.

Capacity Mental and age requirements for entering into contracts and executing a will.

Capital gains The amount of net gain made on the sale of property; before the Tax Reform Act it carried a special lower tax rate.

Cash-to-mortgage sale Sale of real property in which the buyer pays the difference between the sales price and the mortgage balance and then takes over the mortgage (assumption).

CCR See Declaration of covenants, conditions, and restrictions (CCRs).

CFR See Code of Federal Regulations (CFR).

Citation Legal shorthand for referring to cases, statutes, regulations, and ordinances.

Cite See Citation.

Clean Air Act One of the original air pollution statutes that gave HEW authority to monitor interstate pollution problems.

Cleaning deposit The amount set forth in a lease required of the tenant to be paid prior to commencement of the lease to cover the cleaning of the premises when the tenant has gone; under URLTA the lease must state if it is nonrefundable.

Clean Water Act Major federal statute on water pollution that gave the federal government authority and control.

Code of Federal Regulations (CFR) Compilation of regulations of federal agencies.

Column lots Portion of air rights from the surface of the earth to 23 feet above the surface.

Commission Percentage of the obtained sales price on real property that is used to compensate agents and brokers for finding a buyer for the property.

Commitment In a real property loan, an agreement in advance to loan a certain sum of money.

Common law Uncodified law found in cases or in the history of real property.

Community property Method of married persons' co-ownership of property; limited to certain states.

Comprehensive Environmental Response, Compensation and Liability Act (CERLA) The Superfund; program for private payment by polluting industries for clean-up of toxic waste.

Condition precedent In a contract, a requirement before the contract can be performed; e.g., delivering marketable title or qualifying for financing.

Condominium Form of multiunit housing in which the owner owns the area between the walls and ceiling.

Consent statutes Statutes that permit the attachment of a lien if the property owner consented to the work done by the lienor even though there was no direct contract with the owner.

Consideration The detriment given by each party to the contract; e.g., the land by the seller and the money by the buyer.

Consideration clause Portion of deed which includes payment terms.

Construction lender Party serving as financier for a project during construction.

Construction mortgage Mortgage that covers the loan for construction costs during the period of construction.

Constructive delivery Delivery other than direct delivery to the person; delivering by precluding access by all others.

Constructive eviction Process whereby a tenant is forced to leave leased premises because the premises are in a state of disrepair and uninhabitable.

Constructive notice Notice by public recording; something other than actual notice.

Consumer Credit Protection Act Federal law passed to ensure full disclosure of credit terms and costs; often called "Truth-in-Lending."

Contingent remainder Future interest that follows a life estate and that is not certain to follow or has unknown takers.

Contract for deed Another name for an installment contract; financing transaction in which seller carries the buyer and holds onto title until the buyer has paid in full.

Contract statutes With references to liens, statutes that require lienors to have a direct contractual relationship with property owner to be able to place lien on property on which work was performed.

Contractual liens Liens that arise because of a contractual agreement between the lienor and the owner of the liened property.

Conventional pollutants One of the categories of water pollutants of the EPA; subject to the least amount of restriction and regulation.

Conversion restrictions Laws that regulate the conversion of leased premises into multiunit houses to afford protection for the existing tenants.

Cooperative Form of multiunit housing in which a corporation owns the property and owners of the shares in the corporation live in each of the units.

Co-ownership Label given to ownership of property by more than one person.

Corporation Form of doing business that provides limited liability to the owners, continuity of operation, and centralized management.

Cost-plus formula In construction, a method of pricing in which the contractor charges all costs plus a profit margin.

Council on Environmental Quality (CEQ) Established in 1966 by the National Environment Protection Act as part of the executive branch of government and given the responsibility of formulating national policies on the quality of the environment and making recommendations to lawmakers based on its policies.

Counterclaim Claim made by the defendant against the plaintiff in a lawsuit.

Counteroffer Offer made in response to offeror by the offeree; can occur by a change in the offeror's terms.

Covenant Promise in a deed that affects or limits the use of the conveyed property.

Cumulative zoning Zoning system that permits higher uses in lower-use areas; e.g., residential uses in commercially zoned areas.

Curtesy Right of husband to a life estate in all real property owned by his wife during their marriage provided they had children.

Declaration of condominium Master deed for condominium project; the document recorded to reflect the units involved on the real property. See also Declaration of horizontal property regime and covenants.

Declaration of covenants, conditions and restrictions (CCRs) The restrictions and limitations on the use and construction of land.

Declaration of horizontal property regime and covenants Another name for the declaration of condominium; multiunit housing is often referred to as horizontal housing regimes; the master deed recorded to reflect the existence of the multiunit housing and the location and number of units on the property.

Deed Instrument used to convey title to real property.

Deed in lieu of foreclosure Process of borrower-property owner surrendering title to property to prevent lender's foreclosure.

Deed of trust Security interest in real property in which title is held by a trustee until the borrower and occupant of the land repays the beneficiary (lender) the amount of the loan.

Deed restrictions Provisions usually recorded for subdivisions; the CCRs; restrictions on the use, development, and construction of the premises.

Default Failure to comply with mortgage or promissory note requirements; generally a failure to pay or obtain insurance.

Deficiency judgment Judgment against the mortgagor or borrower after foreclosure sale, requiring payment of the amount due on the loan that was not obtained through sale of the mortgaged property.

Department of Housing and Urban Development (HUD) Federal agency responsible for regulation of interstate land sales and other federal acts affecting real property.

Depreciation Wear and tear on property; can be deducted each year and used to offset income earned on income-producing property; greatly limited under TRA.

Devise Gift of real property by will.

Disinheritance Process of leaving an heir out of a will; not giving anything to someone who would ordinarily receive a share of the estate if there were an intestate distribution.

Dissolution In marriage, another term for divorce; in a partnership or corporation, the ending of a business.

Doctrine of Ancient Lights Theory that originated in England that provides right to light if so used for 20 years or more; this prescriptive form of rights is no longer followed in the United States.

Doctrine of Worthier Title Theory that gives a grantee the full fee simple title when the grant is made "to grantee with remainder to the heirs of the grantee"; the two estates are merged into a fee simple estate for the grantee.

Dominant estate A property owner who holds an appurtenant easement in another's property; the land enjoying the benefit of an easement through another's property.

Dominant tenement See Dominant estate.

Donee Recipient of a gift.

Donor One who makes a gift.

Dower Right of a wife to a one-third interest in all real property owned by her husband during the course of the marriage; wife must survive husband to be entitled to dower rights.

Dower rights Rights of widow in husband's estate; not applicable in all states.

Dragnet mortgage Anaconda mortgage or mortgage that secures all debts owed by the mortgagor to the mortgagee.

Due-on-sale clause Clause in mortgage or mortgage note that requires full payment of the loan when the property is sold; in effect, a prohibition on assumptions.

Due process Constitutional protection requiring full adjudication of issues and rights before property may be taken.

Earnest money Deposit given by buyer on signing a contract for the purchase of property.

Easement Right to use another's property for access, light, and so on.

Easement appurtenant Easement that benefits a particular tract of land; generally an access easement or right of way.

Easement in gross An easement that does not benefit a particular tract of land; e.g., utility easements that run through all parcels of land in an area.

Effluent guidelines EPA standards for release of materials into waterways.

EIS See Environmental Impact Statement (EIS).

Emblements With regard to leases, the right of the tenant to harvest growing crops even after the lease has terminated if the tenant was responsible for growing the crops.

Eminent domain Process of governmental entity taking title to private property for public purposes.

Emissions Offset Policy EPA policy of requiring a reduction of other pollution sources in the area to allow the operation of a new plant and source of emissions.

Environmental Impact Statement (EIS) Report required to be filed when a governmental agency is taking action that will have an effect on the environment; e.g., construction of a dam by the Army Corps of Engineers.

Environmental Protection Agency (EPA) Governmental agency responsible for the enforcement of environmental laws.

EPA See Environmental Protection Agency (EPA).

Equitable liens Liens created as a result of a mortgage arrangement; also referred to as contractual liens.

Equitable relief Court remedies that require parties to perform certain acts or specifically perform a contract.

Equitable servitude Restriction on land use arising because an area has a common scheme or development that puts buyers on notice that particular uses and construction are required or prohibited.

Equity participating mortgage Creative financing technique in which the lender will share in the appreciation of the property and will be entitled to a portion of the equity on sale of the mortgaged property.

Escheat Process whereby property of a decedent is given to the state because of no available heirs.

Escrow Process whereby details of property transfer, payments, and deed conveyance are handled by a third party.

Escrow instructions Contract between buyer, seller, and escrow agent for the closing of escrow on a property transfer.

Exclusionary zoning Zoning that prohibits certain types of businesses, activities, or housing in certain areas.

Exclusive agency listing Listing agreement that requires the seller to pay the commission to the broker only if the listing broker sells the property; the seller may sell the property independently and not be required to pay a commission.

Exclusive right to sell Listing that requires the seller to pay the broker-agent a commission regardless of who obtains a buyer for the property.

Exculpatory clause Provision in contract that attempts to hold one of the parties faultless for his or her negligence.

Executor Male party responsible for the probate of a decedent's estate pursuant to the decedent's will.

Executory interest Future interest that is not a remainder and not an interest in the grantor.

Executrix Female party responsible for the probate of a decedent's estate pursuant to the decedent's will.

Exemptions Under the 1933 Securities Act, types of sales of securities not requiring full registration.

Federal Environmental Pesticide Control Act Federal law regulating the manufacture, containment, labeling, transportation, and use of pesticides.

Federal Water Pollution Control Act 1972 federal law that was the first anti–water pollution law with enforcement and details.

Federal Water Pollution Control Administration (FWPCA) Originally the agency responsible for developing and enforcing water pollution control; merged into EPA in 1975.

Fee Term to refer to an inheritable interest in land.

Fee simple Highest land interest; full title; right to convey or transfer by will or mortgage without restriction.

Fee simple absolute Another term for a fee simple.

Fee simple defeasible A fee simple estate that can be lost by violation of a condition or use restriction placed in the transfer by the grantor.

Fee simple determinable Full title to land so long as certain conduct is avoided; e.g., "To A so long as the premises are never used for a bar."

Fee simple subject to a condition subsequent Full title provided that there is compliance with a condition; e.g., "To A upon the condition that the property is used for school purposes."

Fee tail Full title restricted in its passage to direct descendants of the owner.

Fee tail general A fee tail.

Fee tail special Full title restricted in its passage to a limited group of descendents of the owner; e.g., "To A and his female heirs."

Fiduciary Party in a position of trust and confidence with another; agent or trustee.

Fifth Amendment Provision in United States Constitution that provides guarantee of due process.

Financing statement Document filed to protect a security interest; must contain information about the parties and a description of the collateral.

Fixtures Personal property that becomes attached to and is so closely associated with real property that it becomes a part of the real property.

Flow-down clause Clause in a construction contract that does not require the general contractor to pay subcontractors and suppliers until the owner has paid the general contractor.

Forcible detainer Action by landlord for rent; requires tenant to pay or be evicted by court order.

Foreclosure Process of selling mortgaged property to satisfy the debt owed by the defaulting mortgagor.

Forfeiture Loss of rights; in a contract for deed, the loss of all interest in the property for nonpayment.

Fourteenth Amendment Application of due process rights to the states (also known as the Equal Protection Clause), which requires uniform application of laws and non-discrimination; applied in cases in which land conveyances attempt to include racial restrictions.

Freehold Estates uncertain or unlimited in their duration.

Fructus industriales Vegetation that grows on property as result of work of owner or tenant; i.e., crops.

Fructus naturales Vegetation that grows naturally on property; not the result of efforts of the owner or tenant.

FWPCA See Federal Water Pollution Control Administration (FWPCA).

Garden home Form of multiunit housing; usually a townhome that includes a small enclosed yard or patio.

General contractor In a construction project, the party responsible for the construction; can hire subcontractors and suppliers but bears ultimate responsibility; has direct contractual relationship with owner, construction lender, or both.

General plan Development plan and zoning areas as developed by city or county; provides zoning designations for all areas within the municipality or county.

Geothermal energy Form of energy that is the result of naturally formed pockets of hot steam; can be a mineral right.

Gift Transfer of property without consideration with donative intent and by actual or constructive delivery.

Government survey Means of land description using the United States government's survey of the country; involves the use of a grid created by baselines, parallels, and meridians.

Grantee Person to whom title to land is conveyed.

Grantor Person conveying title to land.

Grantor/grantee index Method of recordkeeping for land transactions; all transactions are recorded under the name of both the grantor and grantee to permit title to be traced according to the transfers among parties.

Grid The 24-mile square created between each guide meridian and parallel in the United States Government survey.

Guide meridians Vertical lines placed every 24 miles on the United States Government Survey; intersect with parallels to create 24-mile squares used for describing land parcels.

Habendum Clause in deed indicating the type of land interest being conveyed; in mineral lease, a clause that establishes the length of the lease, the grounds for termination, and drilling delay penalties.

Hazardous Substance Response Trust Fund Fund created under federal environmental laws; known as the Superfund for use in clean-up of toxic waste.

Heirs Persons entitled to a portion of a decedent's estate.

HEW Department of Health, Education and Welfare.

Hold zoning Interim zoning adopted prior to the time of the finalized general plan.

Holographic will Will entirely in the handwriting of the testator and signed by the testator (valid in some states).

Homestead Debtor protection that entitles the debtor to a certain amount in real property that is exempt from attachment by creditors.

Horizontal property regimes Multiunit housing such as condominiums, cooperatives, and townhouses.

ILSFDA See Interstate Land Sales Full Disclosure Act (ILSFDA).

Implied warranty of habitability One-year implied warranty given by contractors of new homes to buyers; between landlord and tenant, the landlord's guaranty that the premises are fit for habitation and if not, will be put into that condition.

Inchoate Used with reference to dower; right that exists only if wife survives husband.

Incorporeal hereditaments Rights to remove something (water, minerals, top soil) from the land of another; also called a *profit a prendre.*

Injunction Equitable remedy; court order requiring a party to perform an act or cease certain conduct; e.g., to stop trespassing.

Installment land contract A contract for deed; method of selling property in which the seller serves as the financier for the buyer and the purchase; seller holds onto title until there has been payment in full under an installment payment plan.

Intensity zoning Zoning that regulates the number of structures, offices or other items in the area.

Interim zoning Hold zoning; temporary zoning before general plan is developed.

Internal Revenue Code (IRC) Federal law governing income taxation.

Interstate Land Sales Full Disclosure Act (ILSFDA) Federal law regulating the sale of property across state lines; requires advance filing of sales materials, mandatory disclosure of certain information, and prohibitions on promises about the land's future development.

Inter vivos   During the life of; while alive; e.g., an *inter vivos* gift.

Intestate   Death without a will.

Intestate succession   Statutory method for distributing the property of those who die without a will (intestate).

Intrastate offering exemption   Under the 1933 Securities Act, an exemption from SEC registration requirements for certain securities offered in one state by a corporation primarily operating in that state.

Investment partnership   In a two-tier structure, the partnership that has the investors and handles the collection of partner payments and the return of profits.

Invitee   Party who has a specific invitation to enter another's property or is a member of the public in a public place.

Involuntary lien   Lien that does not result from a contractual arrangement; e.g., a tax lien or a judicial lien.

IRC   See Internal Revenue Code (IRC).

Joint tenancy   Method of co-ownership that gives title to the property to the last survivor.

Joint will   Will made in conjunction with another's will; requires distribution of property in a certain way regardless of who dies first.

Judicial deed   Deed given by court after litigation of rights in the subject property.

Judicial foreclosure   Foreclosure accomplished by filing a petition with the proper court; not a power of sale.

Judicial lien   Lien on property that is the result of a judgment; lien to collect a court judgment.

Just compensation   In eminent domain, the requirement that landowners whose property is taken for public purposes be adequately paid for the loss of that property.

Land contract   Contract for deed; installment contract; a purchase contract in which the seller is serving as the financier for the buyer's purchase and will turn over title when the buyer has completed all payments.

Laughing heir statute   Statute that limits the degree of relationship of relatives who can inherit property from an intestate; causes property to escheat to the state before a remote relative would inherit an intestate's estate.

Lease   Agreement between the owner of land and another for the use and occupation of the land.

Lease-purchase   Financing method that permits potential buyers to lease property for a period with an option to buy.

Legacy   Gift of money by will.

License   Revocable right to enter another's property.

Licensee   Party who enters another's land with express or implied permission; i.e., a social guest.

Lien   Interest in real property that serves as security for repayment of a debt.

Lienor   Party who places a lien on real property.

Lien theory   One theory of mortgages that gives the mortgagor title to the property and the mortgagee a lien on the property as security for debt repayment.

Life estate   Interest in land that lasts for the life of the grantee.

Life estate *pur autre vie*   Life estate that lasts for the length of some measuring life other than that of the grantee.

Life tenants   Those who hold a life estate in property.

Limited partnership   A partnership with at least one general partner in which limited partners can purchase interest and be liable only to the extent of their interest and not risk personal liability.

Liquidated damages   Damages that are specified in formula or in amount in the written and signed agreement of the parties; must be reasonable.

Lis pendens   "Suit or action pending"; document recorded with the land records to indicate a suit involving the land is pending; filed in mortgage foreclosures and quiet title actions.

Listing agreement   Contract between a broker and landowner for the broker's services in helping to sell the owner's property.

Livery of seisin   English ceremony for passage of title; involved a physical transfer of a clod of earth between grantor and grantee.

Living will   Term for authorization to take testator off life-support equipment; authorized in many states but must use appropriate or required language and be formally executed.

Marketable title   Form of title generally required to be delivered in the sale of property; property is free from liens and no defects in title other than those noted or agreed to.

Massachusetts Business Trust   A trust originated by Massachusetts as a business form for dealing in real estate because state statutes prohibited corporations from doing so; the initial form of real estate syndication.

Master deed   In a condominium development, the document recorded to reflect the location of the project and the individual units.

Master plan   General plan for zoning.

Materials lien   Lien on property for the amount due for materials furnished to the owner or to others performing work on the land.

Mechanic's liens   Liens placed on real property to secure amount due to those who performed work or supplied materials for improvements or other projects on the land.

Meridians   Vertical guidelines in the United States Government Survey; placed every 24 miles.

Metes and bounds   Method of land description that begins with a permanent object and then through distances and directions describes the parcel of land.

Mineral rights   Subsurface rights in property; the rights to mine minerals.

Misrepresentation   Giving incorrect or misleading information to a party in contract negotiations or failure to disclose relevant information; inaccurate information that would affect the buying or selling decision.

Mixed trust   Real estate investment trust that owns both property and mortgages.

MLS   See multiple listing service (MLS).

Mortgage   Lien on real property used to secure a debt.

Mortgagee   Lender or party who holds the mortgage lien.

Mortgage trust   Real estate syndication trust that invests in real estate mortgages.

Mortgagor   Borrower or party occupying land that is mortgaged.

Multiple listing   A listing that appears in more than one broker's inventory of homes.

Multiple listing service (MLS)   A specific multiple listing service that is nationwide and to which most brokers subscribe.

Mutual will   Wills of parties that are reciprocal in their distribution; usually based on a contract to make a will; generally enforceable.

NAR   National Association of Realtors.

National Association of Realtors   Professional organization of brokers and agents; has standards for admission and maintenance of membership.

National Environmental Policy Act (NEPA)   Act that requires federal agencies to do an EIS before they approve a project.

National Pollution Discharge Elimination System   Permit system that requires EPA approval for water discharges.

Negative easement   An easement that prohibits a property owner from doing something that affects the property of another; e.g., a solar easement is a negative easement.

NEPA   See National Environmental Policy Act (NEPA).

Net listing   Type of listing that allows the broker to collect as a commission any amount received that is above the figure set as the seller's net take on the sale of the property.

Noise Control Act   Federal environmental regulation that requires labeling of products for noise levels.

Nonattainment areas   In environmental regulation, those areas that have not reached acceptable levels of pollution; highly regulated.

Nonconforming use   In zoned areas, a use that does not comply with the area's zoning but that existed prior to the time the zoning was effective.

Nonconventional pollutants   Second in line in terms of water pollution dangers; EPA can require higher pretreatment standards for nonconventional pollutants.

Noncumulative classifications   Method of zoning in which use in a particular area is limited to the zoned use; e.g., industrial zones cannot include residential buildings and apartment areas cannot include single-family dwellings.

Nonfreehold estates   Land interests that are limited and certain in their duration.

Notice statute   Form of recording statute that gives later bona fide purchasers priority in the case of multiple purchases for the previous purchasers' failures to give notice by recording their transactions.

NPDES permit   See National Pollution Discharge Elimination System.

Nuisance   Use of property in such a way so as to interfere with another's use and enjoyment of property; e.g., bad smells and loud noises.

Occupational Health and Safety Administration (OSHA)   Federal agency responsible for assuring safety in the workplace.

Offer   Initial communication in contract formation that, if accepted, results in the formation of a contract.

Open listing   Listing that pays commission to whichever broker or salesperson sells the property; permits the owner to list with more than one broker and be liable for only one commission.

Operating partnership   In a two-level partnership syndication, the partnership that is responsible for the operation of the firm, the handling of the assets, and the day-to-day real property management issues.

Option   Right (which has been paid for) to purchase property during a certain period of time.

Ordinances   Laws passed on a local level of county, state, or city governments.

OSHA   See Occupational Health and Safety Administration (OSHA).

Parallels   Horizontal guidelines in the United States Government Survey.

Partnership   Voluntary association of two or more persons as co-owners in a business for profit.

Passive activity   Under the TRA, type of business investment in which the investor does not participate or rely on for income; a limited partnership interest is an example of passive activity.

Passive losses   Losses resulting from passive activity; under the TRA there are limitations on taking passive losses, i.e., can only take passive losses from passive income and not from wages and other income as many taxpayers had done in the past to maximize the benefits of real estate ownership.

Patio home   Form of multiunit housing that generally includes a closed-in yard or patio area.

Payment bond   In construction, a bond on the general contractor to ensure payment to subcontractors and suppliers; i.e., if the general contractor does not pay, the surety will pay.

Per capita   Method of allocation of intestate property among heirs; basic principle is that each heir gets an equal share.

Perfection   Process of gaining priority on an Article IX security interest; requires a filing of a financing statement to give public notice of the creditor's interest.

Performance bond   Bond on general contractor that guarantees performance; or if the general contractor does not perform, the surety will provide performance or payment for damages resulting from noncompletion of the work.

Periodic tenancy   Temporary possessory interest in land that runs on a period-to-period basis such as a month-to-month lease.

Permanent lender   Once construction is complete, the lender who will carry the permanent financing on the project; pays the construction lender and assumes priority.

Personal holding company   Under the IRC, a doctrine that permits taxation of certain corporations as though they were not formed and the individuals are personally liable for the tax.

Personal representative   Party responsible for the probate of a will under the Uniform Probate Code; formerly referred to as an executor.

Per stirpes   Method of distributing property to heirs whereby those closer in relation to the decedent get greater shares.

Plat map   Method of land description that relies on a recorded map of a subdivision, with each deed making reference to the map and the particular lot being transferred.

Point sources   Discharge points where water leaves land and runs into streams, rivers, etc.

Possibility of reverter   Future interest in the grantor that follows a fee simple determinable.

Posthumous heirs   Heirs born after the death of the decedent.

Power of sale   In a deed of trust financing arrangement, the right of the trustee to sell the property on default by the trustor-borrower.

Power of termination   Future interest in the grantor that follows a fee simple subject to a condition subsequent.

Premises   The words of conveyance in a deed; e.g., "do hereby grant and convey."

Prepayment penalty   Clause in mortgage or promissory note that requires the mortgagor to pay an additional charge for paying off the loan early.

Prescription   Process of acquiring an easement through adverse use of the easement over a required period of time.

Price fixing   Antitrust violation of an agreement among competitors to control pricing; with regard to brokers an agreement to charge the same commission rate.

Prime contractor   General contractor on a project.

Prime meridian   The key vertical lines in the United States Government survey.

Principal meridian   See Prime meridian.

Prior appropriation   Water allocation theory that follows a policy of first to use the water gets the rights to that water.

Priority   Term used to describe relationship of creditors who have security in the same real property.

Private law   Laws between individual parties; e.g., landlord's rules and regulations or the terms of a contract.

Privity   Direct contractual relationship or direct blood relationship.

Probate   Process of collecting the assets of a decedent; paying the decedent's debts, determining the decedent's heirs, and distributing property to the heirs.

Profit a prendre   Right to enter another's land for the purpose of removing soil, water, minerals, or another resource.

Profits   Rights of removal in another's property; shorthand for *profit a prendre.*

Promissory note   Two-party debt instrument that, in real estate, is generally secured by a mortgage or deed of trust or some other interest in real estate.

Property report   Summary of facts about undeveloped land required to be given to purchasers (part of ILSFDA).

Property tax role   Assessor's formal records of parcels of land; the valuation and assessment.

Proprietary lease   Interest of cooperative owner in a dwelling unit.

Prorate   Allocation of prepaid insurance, taxes, and rent; generally done at close of escrow between buyer and seller.

PSD areas   See Point sources.

Puffing   Exaggerated statements of opinion made to induce someone to enter into a contract; not actionable statements.

Pur autre vie   For the life of another; life estates are sometimes created with a measuring life other than that of the grantee.

Purchase money mortgage   A mortgage used to secure a debt for the funds used to buy the mortgaged property.

Purchase money security interest (PMSI)   Under Article IX of the UCC, a security interest given to a lender who financed the purchase of the property that is the collateral.

Quasi-easement   A right-of-way as it existed when there was unity of ownership in a parcel of land.

Quiet title action   Court action brought to determine the true owner of a piece of land.

Quitclaim deed   Deed that serves to transfer title if the grantor has any such title; there are no guarantees that the grantor has any title or good title.

Race/notice statutes   State recording statutes that award title to the first bona fide purchaser to record his or her title when there are conflicting claims of ownership in the property.

Race statutes   State recording statutes that award title to the first party to record his or her title when there are conflicting claims of ownership in the property.

Range   In the United States Government Survey, the lines placed vertically every 6 miles between the guide meridians.

Real estate investment trust (REIT)   Form of real estate syndication in which investors hold trust interests and enjoy profits of trust's real estate holdings.

Real Estate Settlement Procedures Act (RESPA) Federal statute regulating disclosure of closing costs in advance and prohibiting kickbacks for referring customers to title companies.

Real estate syndication Group investment in real estate in the forms of trusts, partnerships and corporations.

Realtor Term used by the National Association of Realtors (NAR) to refer to one of its members.

Recording Process of placing a deed or other document on the public records to give notice of a transaction or interest in the land.

Recreational lease In multiunit housing, a lease that runs for a short period of time during each year; sometimes called timesharing.

Redlining Practice of targeting certain areas or neighborhoods as high-risk areas for loans or insurance or requiring lower valuation.

Refinancing Negotiating a new loan for real estate; generally done to obtain a lower rate or in the case of a sale to allow a buyer to be able to purchase a property.

Regulation A Under the 1933 Securities Act, an SEC regulation that permits a shorter form of registration for offerings amounting to less than $1.5 million.

Regulation D Under the 1933 Securities Act, an SEC regulation that provides three different small offering exemptions from registration according to limitations on size of the offering or the number of investors.

Regulation Z (Truth-In-Lending) The Federal Reserve Board's regulations on disclosures in all types of credit transactions.

REIT See Real estate investment trust (REIT).

Remainders Future interests in someone other than the grantor; a remainder follows a life estate.

Repair and deduct A tenant's right to repair leased premises when the landlord fails to do so and deduct the costs of the repairs from his rent.

Rescission Right to treat a contract as if it never existed; rescind contract rights; generally appropriate in cases of fraud and misrepresentation.

Resource Conservation and Recovery Act Federal law regulating hazardous waste and garbage that requires recordkeeping and controls amounts of garbage.

RESPA See Real Estate Settlement Procedures Act (RESPA).

Reversion Future interest in grantor that results after life estate terminates and no remainder interest was given.

Revocation With respect to offers, the offeror's cancellation of the outstanding offer.

Right of entry Future interest in grantor that results when the grantee fails to honor the condition placed on the grant of a fee simple subject to a condition subsequent.

Right of redemption In mortgage foreclosures, the right of the mortgagor to redeem his or her property for 6 months after the foreclosure sale by paying off the debts and the costs of foreclosure.

Riparian In water rights, the landowner who adjoins water; a theory that entitles all riparians to use of their water; does not allow one riparian to use all of the water.

Rivers and Harbors Act An 1896 federal statute that attempted to regulate dumping in rivers and harbors; a predecessor to today's environmental statutes.

Royalty clause In a mineral lease, the provision that specifies the consideration; whether the lessor gets a percentage of the profits and how much.

Rule against perpetuities Rule that prohibits the control of estates from the grave; provides a cap on use restrictions on contingent remainders and executory interests.

Rule in Dumpor's Case English rule that provides that if a landlord consents to one assignment of the lease by the tenant, the landlord consents to all subsequent assignments; most states have abolished by statute the effects of this rule.

Rule of capture In mineral rights, a first in time is first in right philosophy in which the first to take subsurface minerals has title regardless of property boundary lines.

Rules 504–506 Regulation D; the rules of the SEC on small offering exemptions in securities sales.

School impact fees A requirement by a city or county that developers pay the costs of building schools at the rapid pace necessary to accommodate the rapid development of subdivisions.

SEC See Securities Exchange Commission (SEC).

Secured party Under Article IX, the creditor with the security interest in the fixture or personal property.

Securities Act of 1933 Federal law governing the initial sale of securities on the public markets.

Securities Exchange Commission (SEC) The federal agency responsible for overseeing and policing the sales of securities on the primary and secondary markets.

Securities registration Process of obtaining SEC approval for the sale of securities; a process of providing information about the company and the proposed securities to the SEC.

Security agreement Under Article IX, the contract that gives the creditor a lien in the personal property or fixture; makes it the collateral for the loan.

Security deposit In a lease, the amount of money prepaid by the tenant to secure performance of the lease and often provide the amount of liquidated damages if the tenant does not perform.

Security interest Creditor's right in collateral under Article IX; the lien on the personal property or fixture.

Self-help Remedy for tenants with premises in disrepair; the right to repair defects on the property and then seek reimbursement.

Self-proving will A will that is acknowledged or notarized and thereby enjoys presumption of validity.

Servient estate Land through which an easement runs or which is subject to the easement.

Servient tenement Land though which an easement runs or which is subject to the easement.

Shared-appreciation mortgages Method of creative financing in which the lender charges a lower interest rate in exchange for the right to a return of a portion of the equity, including the increased value, of the home.

Shelley's Case Rule that merges the present and future interest when the grant is made to the grantor and the heirs of the grantor.

Sheriff's deed Form of title given to a buyer at a mortgage foreclosure sale; carries no warranties.

SIP See State implementation plans (SIP).

Small offering exemption Exception to SEC registration requirements based on limited amount of the offering or limited numbers of purchasers.

Social issue zoning Use of zoning to control influences in the community; e.g., the prohibition of adult theaters near residential districts.

Solar easements A negative easement that prevents the servient estate from doing anything that would block the sunlight access of the dominant estate.

Soldier's and Sailor's Relief Act   Federal law that provides time limitations on foreclosures involving those in active military service.

Solid Waste Disposal Act   Initial federal act on waste disposal that provided states with money for research on solid waste disposal.

Special permits   Exceptions to zoning uses provided by a board of adjustment.

Speciality trust   A trust created for a specific purpose such as a corporate trust created to expand the firm's real estate holdings.

Special warranty deed   Deed that provides warranty of title only for the period during which the grantor owned the property.

Specific performance   Equitable remedy that requires a party to a contract to perform the contract promise or promises.

Squatter's rights   A lay term for adverse possession or prescription.

Standard State Zoning Enabling Act   Standard act adopted by most jurisdictions to govern the development and enforcement of a zoning plan.

State implementation plans (SIP)   All state and local laws and ordinances that make up the state's air pollution control plan.

Statement of record   Under ILSFDA, the disclosure document filed with HUD before any sales of undeveloped land can occur.

Statute of Frauds   Statute dictating what types of contracts must be in writing to be enforceable.

Steering   Form of racial discrimination in which brokers or salespersons direct interested purchasers away from and toward certain neighborhoods to control racial composition.

Subchapter S corporation   A special form of corporation under the IRC that allows the protection of limited liability but direct flow-through of profits and losses.

Subcontractor   A worker hired by the general contractor on a project to complete certain portions of the project.

Subdivision   Parcel of land developed with streets, homes, parks, and so forth.

Subdivision trust   Form of financing in which seller and buyer are trust beneficiaries, and a third party acts as trustee. Seller and buyer will share in the profits of land development after the seller has paid for the property.

Subject-to-sale   A transfer of real property in which the buyer takes the property subject to an existing mortgage but does not agree to assume responsibility for the mortgage payments.

Sublease   Arrangement in which a tenant leases rental property to another, and the tenant becomes landlord to the subtenant.

Subordinate mortgage   Mortgage with a lesser priority than a preexisting mortgage.

Substantial performance   Construction doctrine that requires good faith completion of a project but not necessarily perfection.

Superfund   The fund created by the federal government to sponsor clean-up of toxic waste disposal sites.

Surety   One who stands as a guarantor for an obligation; as in a payment or performance bond.

Surface Mining and Reclamation Act   Federal law that regulates surface mining and the required clean-up afterwards.

Syndicate   Pool of investors in a real estate development or portfolio; a partnership, corporation, or REIT.

Taking   Term used to describe the government action of using private property for public purposes.

Tax deed   Form of title given in the event property is sold to satisfy taxes; carries no warranties.

Tax lien   Lien placed on property for amount of unpaid taxes.

Tax Reform Act (TRA) of 1986   Major revision of IRC that eliminated many of the tax benefits associated with real estate ownership and syndication.

Tax sale   Foreclosure sale on property for nonpayment of taxes.

Technology forcing   Statute that requires the development of new air pollution control devices; requires use of something better than current practice.

Tenancy at sufferance   Tenancy wherein the tenant is on the property of the landlord but has no right to be and may be evicted at any time.

Tenancy at will   Tenancy wherein the tenant remains as long as both parties agree; either party may terminate at any time and without notice.

Tenancy by the entirety   Method of co-ownership that is a joint tenancy between husband and wife.

Tenancy for a term   Tenancy for years; a tenancy for a specified period of time.

Tenancy for years   Tenancy for a stated period of time.

Tenancy in common   Simplest form of co-ownership; unless otherwise stated, the presumed method of ownership for multiple landowners.

Tenancy in partnership   Form of co-ownership in which the parties are partners; similar to joint tenancy in that the partners have a right of survivorship.

Testamentary   Disposition by will.

Testamentary capacity   The requisite mental capacity needed to make a valid will; a person's need to understand who his or her relatives are and how the property will be distributed by his or her will.

Time-sharing properties   Form of multiunit housing in which owners own the unit for a limited period of time during each year.

Title abstract   Summary of the history of title to a parcel of land.

Title insurance   Insurance that pays the buyer of property in the event certain title defects arise.

Title theory   Theory of mortgage law that puts title in the mortgagee and possession in the mortgagor.

Torrens system   System for recording land titles designed to prevent the selling of the same parcel of land to more than one person.

Townhouse   Form of multiunit housing in which the owner owns the area in the unit and also owns the land on which the unit is located.

Townships   Term in the United States Government Survey for the 6-mile squares formed between the guide meridians and the parallels.

Toxic pollutants   EPA classification for the worst form of water pollutants.

Toxic Substances Control Act   Federal law regulating the manufacture, labeling, and distribution of toxic substances.

TRA   See Tax Reform Act (TRA) of 1986.

Tract index   Form of land record that keeps history of title through identification of transactions with the particular tract.

Trade fixture   Personal property that is attached to real property but is used in the operation of a business; remains the tenant's property.

Trespass   Invasion of the property of another by a person or object.

Trust certificate   In a real estate trust, the evidence of ownership given to each trust holder.

Trustee Third party responsible for handling the property of another; as in deed of trust or real estate investment trust.

Truth-in-Lending Name given to federal statutes and regulations concerning credit terms and their disclosure.

Two-tier partnership In syndications, the use of an investment partnership and operating partnership to separate the investors from the day-to-day operations of the firm.

UCC See Uniform Commercial Code (UCC).

Unconscionability Conduct that is unfair, unreasonable, or oppressive in the contractual situation.

Undue influence The use of a confidential relationship to gain benefits under a will or contract.

Uniform Commercial Code (UCC) Uniform statute adopted in most states that governs commercial transactions; Article IX deals with security interests in fixtures.

Uniform Land Transactions Act Uniform act with provisions governing land contracts.

Uniform Partnership Act (UPA) Uniform statute adopted in most states governing the creation, operation, and dissolution of partnerships.

Uniform Probate Code (UPC) Uniform law adopted in about one-third of the states governing the distribution of intestate property, the making of wills and probate, and administration of estates.

Uniform Residential Landlord Tenant Act (URLTA) Uniform law governing residential leases.

Uniform Settlement Statement Under RESPA, the required form for showing how money was paid and distributed at close of escrow.

Uniform Simultaneous Death Act Uniform law designed to allow direct distribution to heirs next in line when husband and wife die simultaneously (or within 5 days of each other).

United States Code (USC) Compilation of all federal laws.

Unities In co-ownership, the presence of requirements on creation; i.e., whether the interests must have been created at the same time as in a joint tenancy.

UPA See Uniform Partnership Act (UPA).

UPC See Uniform Probate Code (UPC).

URLTA See Uniform Residential Landlord Tenant Act (URLTA).

USC See United States Code (USC).

Use restrictions Zoning that controls property by prohibiting certain uses in certain areas.

Usury Charging interest rates in excess of the statutorily allowed maximums.

Variances Approved uses of land outside the scope of an area's zoning.

Vested remainder A remainder that will automatically take effect when the life estate ends.

Vested subject to complete divestment A remainder that can be completely lost if the terms of vesting are not met; not automatic on termination of the life estate.

Vested subject to partial divestment A remainder that can be partially lost as other remaindermen develop; i.e., more children are born during the life estate.

Voluntary lien A lien created because of a contract as opposed to a tax lien, which is involuntary.

Warranty deed   Deed that conveys title and carries warranties that the title is good, the transfer is proper, and there are no liens and encumbrances other than the ones noted.

Warranty of habitability   Warranty given by landlords in residential leases that the premises are in good living condition, and by builder of new homes that the homes are free of major defects.

Water Pollution Control Act   Federal statute passed to control release of pollutants into rivers, streams, and other bodies of water.

Water Quality Act   One of the predecessors to today's federal water pollution control statutory scheme.

Water rights   System of priority for water use.

Will   Document used to specify the transfer of property after the testator's death.

Wrap-around mortgage   Mortgage given to a seller wherein the buyer will make the amount of existing payments on property to the seller along with payments on the amount of the selling price that is in excess of the mortgage amount.

Zoning   Process of regulating land-use by designating areas of a community for certain uses.

Zoning commission   Governmental agency responsible for developing the zoning plan.

APPENDIX

CASES

Allan v. Martin, 574 P.2d 457 (Ariz. 1978), **399**

Amos v. Coffey, 320 S.E.2d 335 (Va. 1984), **159**

Anderson v. Jackson County Board of Education, 333 S.E.2d 533 (N.C. 1985), **45**

Andrus v. Sierra Club, 442 U.S. 347 (1978), **652**

Armstrong v. Cione, 736 P.2d 440 (Hawaii 1987), **522**

Armstrong v. Roberts, 325 S.E.2d 769 (Ga. 1985), **699**

Baltimore Gas & Electric Co. v. Natural Resources Defense Council, 462 U.S. 87 (1984), **635**

Bandlow v. Thieme, 53 Wis. 57 (1881), **32**

Barrows v. Jackson, 346 U.S. 249 (1953), **565**

Bath Club, Inc. v. Dade County, 394 So.2d 110 (Fla. 1981), **504**

Beard v. Gress, 413 N.E.2d 448 (Ill. 1980), **253**

Block v. Tobin, 119 Cal. Rptr. 288 (1975), **370**

Board of Control of Eastern Michigan University v. Burgess,
        206 N.W.2d 256 (Mich. 1973), **278**

Bob Parrott, Inc. v. First Palmetto Bank, 211 S.E.2d 401 (Ga. 1974), **374**

Borchert Enterprises, Inc. v. Webb, 584 S.W.2d 208 (Tenn. 1979), **656**

Borland v. Sanders Lead Co., Inc., 369 So.2d 523 (Ala. 1979), **651**

Brady v. Skinner, 646 P.2d 310 (Ariz. 1982), **541**

Buckeye Power, Inc. v. EPA, 481 F.2d 162 (C.A. 6 1973), **625**

Buffington v. Haas, 601 P.2d 1320 (Ariz. 1979), **240**

Bunn v. Offutt, 222 S.E.2d 522 (Va. 1976), **100**

Burgess v. Putnam, 464 S.W.2d 698 (Tex. 1971), **697**

Burke v. Southern Pacific R.R., 234 U.S. 669 (1914), **320**

Burland, Reiss, Murphy & Mosher v. Schmidt, 261 N.W.2d 540 (Mich. 1977), **232**

Candid Enterprises, Inc. v. Grossmont Union High School, 705 P.2d 876 (Calif. 1985), **693**

Capitol Federal Savings and Loan Association v. Smith, 316 P.2d 252 (Colo. 1951), **564**

Carver v. Gilbert, 387 P.2d 928 (Alaska 1963), **460**

Casita de Castilian, Inc. v. Kamrath, 629 P.2d 562 (Ariz. 1981), **615**

CED's, Inc. v. EPA, 745 F.2d 1092 (7th Cir. 1984), **651**

Child World, Inc. v. South Towne Center, Ltd., 634 F.Supp. 1121 (S.D. Oh. 1986), **660**

City of Chicago v. Scandia Books, Inc., 430 N.E.2d 14 (Ill. 1981), **562**

City of Renton v. Playtime Theatres, Inc., 475 U.S. 41 (1986), **490**

City of Witchita v. Clapp, 263 P. 12 (Kan. 1928), **24**

Cleburne v. Cleburne, 473 U.S. 432 (1985), **483, 560**

Columbia Western Corp. v. Vela, 592 P.2d 1294 (Ariz. 1979), **309, 313**

Consiglio v. Carey, 421 N.E.2d 1256 (Mass. 1981), **111**

Curtis v. Board of Education, 23 P. 98 (Kans. 1890), **23**

Daniels v. Berry, 513 So.2d 250 (Fla. 1987), **188**

DeLorean v. DeLorean, 511 A.2d 1257 (N.J. 1986), **469**

Delson L. Co. v. Washington Escrow Co., 558 P.2d 832 (Wash. 1976), **414**

Dequindre Dev. Co. v. Charter Twp. of Warren, 103 N.W.2d 600 (Mich. 1960), **479**

Cases in italic are printed in text.

STATUTES, REGULATIONS, AND OTHER LAWS

INDEX